A Biographical Dictionary of
JERSEY

Herein may be seen noble chivalry, courtesy, humility, friendliness, hardiness, love, friendship, cowardice, murder, virtue, hate, and sin.

CAXTON.

A Biographical Dictionary of

JERSEY

G. R. BALLEINE

Hon. Librarian of the Société Jersiaise

STAPLES PRESS

STAPLES PRESS LIMITED
Mandeville Place, London, W 1

STAPLES PRESS INCORPORATED
70 East 45th Street, New York

Made and Printed in the Netherlands by N.V. Batteljee & Terpstra, Leyden,
for Staples Press Limited

FOREWORD

"BIOGRAPHY", wrote Carlyle, "is the most universally pleasant of all reading". And Dr. Johnson agreed. "The biographical part of literature", he said, "is what I love the best". If "the proper study of mankind is man", much can be said for their choice. This book contains biographies of about three hundred men and women from the island of Jersey. They fall into two groups. Some left home and gained distinction in the outside world, a poet like Wace, an archbishop like Walden, a prior like Weston, a statesman like Carteret, sailors like De Carteret the circumnavigator, and Joyce the mutineer, admirals like Durell and Le Hardy, colonists like the Cabots, who founded famous families beyond the seas, to say nothing of William Mesny, who became a Chinese General. Here are scholars like Lempriere of the *Classical Dictionary* and Durell, Vice-Chancellor of Oxford, educationists like Valpy of Reading and Dumaresq, whom Catherine the Great sent for to reorganize the schools of Russia, a university reformer like Jeune, painters like Monamy and Millais, judges like Lord St. Helier, merchants like Martel of Cognac, golfers like Vardon, a peerless impostor like La Cloche, a beauty like Lillie Langtry, and Philippe Dauvergne, hero of an almost incredible adventure story. When we remember how remote Jersey was from the main current of events and how small its population, it is remarkable that so many of its children should have won a niche in the Temple of Fame.

The other group remained at home as leaders of their own people, and their lives combine like a jig-saw puzzle to form a graphic picture of a small, self-governing community, cut off by sea and language from much intercourse with England, absorbed in its own politics and feuds, which were often fierce as those of Padua or Ravenna. We shall read of assassinations and riots and revolts, of stubborn defence of island privileges against encroachments by the British Government, of fortunes amassed

by privateers, who only differed from pirates by carrying let-
ters-of-marque, of sudden retaliatory raids by the French, of
bitter struggles between Charlots and Magots and between Rose
and Laurel, of duels and horse-whippings and interminable
lawsuits. Life in Jersey was seldom uneventful. Anyone who
will read the biographies in the order suggested by the Chronological Index will get a fairly complete idea of the island's
history from the fifteenth century. For earlier days there are
gaps in our knowledge, for in 1502 the Bailiff's house was burnt,
and with it perished all the old records, rolls, and registers.
But a certain amount of information has survived in French and
English archives, and we have tried to glean together every
available fragment.

Three points had to be settled, when this Dictionary was
planned. First, Who is a Jerseyman? Nine-tenths of the
articles deal with persons actually born in the island. But a
man's birth-place is not always decisive. Sir Philippe De
Carteret of the Civil War was a typical islander, Seigneur of
St. Ouen's, Bailiff, and Lieut.-Governor; but he was born in
Sark. Sir John Millais always claimed to be a Jerseyman, though
he was born in Southampton. "Being born in a stable", he
used to say, "would not make me a horse". So sons of Jersey
families are included, and in some cases grandsons also. Though
not *natifs*, they are *originaires*. Brief notes have been added
to show the connexion with the island of a few specially famous
men like Thoreau and Thomas Hardy. Appendix I adds the
lives of eleven non-Jerseymen, who could not be omitted from
any survey of the island's history.

Next came the question, Should the Dictionary be confined
to the really eminent? We decided, No. Leslie Stephen in
his *Studies of a Biographer* declares the most valuable part of
the great English *Dictionary of National Biography* to be "the
immense number of second-rate people, whose lives are full of
suggestion to any intelligent reader". So we have tried to include
every Jerseyman, whose life was in any way remarkable.
Readers will find particulars about minor characters whom they
may have met elsewhere. Students of Foxe's *Book of Martyrs*
will remember the Guernsey baby, born while its mother was
burning at the stake. We tell the lives of the two Jerseymen
responsible for that tragedy. Lovers of Pepys will learn a little
more of the bashful Philippe Carteret, who allowed the Diarist

to do his courting for him. Admirers of Swift will meet the
fat Mrs. Manley, who infuriated the Dean by her spelling.
Students of Napoleon's later years will find fresh facts about
Col. de Gorrequer, Military Secretary at St. Helena. Americans
will find names of interest in their country's history, for example,
Philippe de Carteret, first Governor of New Jersey, James
Carteret, the New Jersey rebel, and Philip English of Salem,
who narrowly escaped being burnt for witchcraft. Even with
fairly well-known personages local knowledge has helped us to
insert hitherto unrecorded details, e.g. how Lempriere of the
Classical Dictionary was pelted with clods, when he preached
in the Town Church, how Philippe Dauvergne supported the
Chouans, when in charge of the Secret Service, how Sir Hilgrove
Turner married an unknown girl, who was flung from a convent
window, how the local press hounded Bishop Jeune from the
island. Short notes are added on names about which local
inquiry is probable. We have an islet called Janvrin's Tomb,
a charity called the Don Gruchy, a park called the Howard
Davis Memorial Park, a Barreau Art Gallery. The explanation
of these names is given.

A third problem remained, the maxim *De mortuis nil nisi
bonum* (Say nothing but good of the dead). This we have
disregarded. The Strip-Jack-Naked School of Biography is
detestable, but tombstone eulogy is not biography at all. A
true portrait cannot be painted either in tar or whitewash.
Havelock Ellis in *Views and Reviews* protests against biographies in which the hero is "bleached, starched, and ironed into
a tailor's dummy". "If you refuse to note a man's weaknesses,
you are false to any intelligible conception of a biographer's
function, and have produced a lie". "The conscientious editor",
writes Professor Oman, "must not suppress evidence, even when
he thinks it a pity that it should have come to light" (*On the
Writing of History*). It is impossible to write a Life of Coleridge
and ignore the opium, of Bacon and suppress the bribes, of
Parnell and say nothing about Mrs. O'Shea. Jerseymen were
not plaster saints, and some blotted their copy-books badly ; but
we have tried to sketch them, as Cromwell wished to be painted,
"wart and all". One maxim we have adhered to — "Judge not
the play, until the play is done". Jerseymen still alive have
been left for some future edition.

The articles in this Dictionary are not compilations from older books. We have tried to avoid all second-hand authorities, and to get back, wherever possible, to contemporary records. Where our statements differ from those of previous writers, it may generally be assumed that we were acquainted with the earlier account, but have unearthed evidence that has enabled us to correct it. This is true even of our great exemplar, the *Dictionary of National Biography*, which, for example, confuses Jean Herault, the Bailiff, with Jean Herault, the Greffier, and Edouard Dauvergne with his nephew. This does not mean that we claim omniscience or infallibility. "Do not think", says Professor Oman, "that you can possibly produce a book without mistakes. However hard the writer of history may strive to obtain accuracy, it is certain that there will be errors of detail somewhere, perhaps errors of more than detail. Only the most purblind critic condemns the pioneer in any line of research for not having achieved absolute accuracy". This is specially true in a book like this, in which every page bristles with facts and dates. We shall be grateful to any reader who can correct a slip.

The present writer owes much to his predecessors, to old-time Jerseymen like Thomas Le Maistre (q.v.), R. R. Lempriere (q.v.) and John Le Bas, who made a rich collection of manuscripts, to the editors of the *Cartulaire*, who dug out every document referring to Jersey from the Archives of the Department of La Manche, to two Secretaries of the Société Jersiaise, H. M. Godfray (q.v.), and E. T. Nicolle (q.v.), who left notebooks bulging with extracts from documents in the Record Office and the British Museum, to J. A. Messervy (q.v.), whose notebooks form an almost complete digest of the Records of the Royal Court, to Ralph Mollet for his index of the unpublished Acts of the States. Other men laboured, and we have entered into their labours.

And now emerges this portrait-gallery of Jersey men and women. Can we form from it any conception of the typical Jerseyman of the Past? He was never afraid of work. Whether tilling the family farm or exploiting the Newfoundland fisheries or prowling the seas as a privateer in search of enemy shipping, he had learned "to scorn delights and live laborious days". And what he had gained by his toil he did not part with lightly. Aberdeen itself never bred a thriftier population. A Jerseyman has always been a shrewd man at a bargain. Whether it was

Sir George Carteret (q.v.) bargaining with victorious Roundheads, or Charles Robin (q.v.) establishing truck shops in
Canada, or James La Cloche (q.v.) swindling the Jesuit headquarters, the Jerseyman generally managed to get the best of
the deal. And his love for his property made him extraordinarily
litigious. When one has toiled for years for a plot of ground,
one does not lightly suffer encroachments. *Qui terre a, guerre a.*
Floquet, the French antiquary, writes in *Les Normands*: "In the
seventeenth century no true Norman ever died without having
had his little lawsuit before the Parliament. It was like the
Mecca pilgrimage, which every true Moslem must make at least
once in his lifetime". The Jerseyman shared to the full this
family characteristic. If he lost a case before the Royal Court,
he did not hesitate to spend a small fortune in appealing to the
Privy Council. Lawsuits were his one extravagance. As early
as 1572 the Council had in self-defence to refuse to hear any
appeal that concerned less than £7. But in spite of his peasant-
bred thrift the Jerseyman was at heart an adventurer. The sea
was always calling. From Elizabethan to Victorian days he
sailed his tiny boat every Spring to the Newfoundland fisheries.
From Drake to Nelson Jersey privateers made the Channel and
the Bay of Biscay dangerous for enemy shipping. No place
of its size can ever have produced half as many Admirals (In
this Dictionary we have only found room for the most distinguished), or sent more men of every rank into the Royal Navy.
Of the 590 men who formed the crew of the *Orion* under Sir
James Saumarez almost every one came from the Channel Islands
(and all were volunteers, for no press-gang was allowed to
land). Even studious clergymen like Bulkeley Bandinel (q.v.),
Librarian of the Bodleian, liked to spend a few years afloat as
naval chaplains. From Le Vesconte Point in the Arctic to
Dumaresq River in Australia, from Cape Carteret in the South
Pacific and Dauvergne Bay in the South Atlantic to Robinstown
on Cape Le Breton, Jerseymen have left their names dotted on
all the maps of the world. If this book proves dull, the fault
will lie with the writer, not with his subject.

ALEXANDRE, MATHIEU (1754—1808), First Jersey Printer. Third son of Jean Alexandre and Jeanne, daughter of George Marett. Born in St. Brelade's in 1754 in the house now called Les Ormes, and baptized in St. Brelade's Church 2 Feb. In 1774 he married Anne Alexandre of Franc Fief. He conceived the idea of becoming a printer, for there had never yet been a printing-press in the island. Philippe Dumaresq (q.v.), the Magot leader, who lived at St Aubin's, offered financial help; Alexandre's father sold a house to pay his son's share in the business; and Mathieu went to England, and thoroughly mastered the craft. (That he was no amateur the typography of the *Gazette* and *Liturgie* makes clear). In 1784 he returned with his press, which he set up at St. Aubin's. His first venture, a sixpenny monthly, *Le Magasin de l'île de Jersey*, appeared in October with a frontispiece by Philippe Jean (q.v.), an allegorical maiden with a case of type scattering the clouds and bringing to Jersey all the arts and sciences. The *Magasin* was vehemently Magot. "A Neutral", wrote Alexandre, "is a vile creature who dare not look you in the face. Begone, irresolute folk, who watch the tempest from afar, when a thousand arms are doing their utmost to save the ship of State". In 1785 he published the first Jersey Almanac. In July he rashly admitted to the *Magasin* A Letter from Mirza to Zadig, a skit about an island called Yeseri and its wicked rulers. Yeseri was manifestly Jersey, and each of its tyrants could be easily identified. Thomas Pipon the Storekeeper recognized himself in the man who had charge of the munitions, who in spite of his wealth was miserable because he was not of the blood royal, and who wanted to squash like beetles everyone whom he met. "He has grown rich on the labours of the poor. If the King knew his deeds, he would be sternly punished as a warning to others". The Cadi was obviously William Charles Lempriere (q.v.), the Lieutenant-Bailiff, "a young man without experience. His face is enough to show his character. He uses his power to oppress the people under the guidance of his father, who is the wickedest man in the island. So long as he lives Yeseri will be enslaved". Pipon promptly had Alexandre arrested for criminal libel, and then

Lempriere did the same, charging him with "black and infamous calumny on the public character of the magistrate who represents the sacred person of His Majesty, tending to stir up discontent with the government and to incite the people to sedition". The circulation of the *Magasin* had been dwindling from 300 to 200, and this prosecution killed it. The Mirza number was the last. Meanwhile to keep out of prison Alexandre had to find the enormous bail of £500 sterling, and Lempriere had his revenge by dragging out the trial for more than two years. But the St. Aubin's Press was not idle. After a year's silence Alexandre made a new plunge into journalism. On 5 Aug. 1786 he started a three sous weekly, *Gazette de l'île de Jersey*. Its local news had still a strong Magot flavour. A woman stole sugar. Her husband was a Charlot. Two boys broke a window. Their father was a Charlot. Some rowdies created a disturbance. They were of course Charlots. This proved more succesful than its predecessor, and lived for almost fifty years. Alexandre's next venture in 1787 was a new edition of the French Prayer Book. Previous editions had been printed in Genoa, the Hague, Amsterdam and London. In the same year he was elected by a large majority Constable's Officer for St Brelade's (G), a post which he held till 1792, when he was succeeded by his son Mathieu. In October 1787 he grew tired of the farce of appearing again and again before the Court, while two witnesses were asked whom they thought the Cadi personated, and then the case was adjourned. He refused to find bail any longer, and challenged Lempriere to send him to gaol. This Lempriere hesitated to do, and the question of bail was dropped. At the next sitting on 16 Nov. Alexandre demanded to be tried by a jury. The Attorney-General replied that there was no precedent. Alexandre retorted that there could not be, as there had never before been a printing-press in the island; but the Court refused the application. Alexandre then appealed to the Privy Council; but, before the appeal was heard, Lempriere, who was then a dying man, dropped the case. In March 1788 the Printing Works were moved to Hill Street, St Helier's; and in May Alexandre's name no longer appeared at the end of the *Gazette* as Printer. It is not clear whether his retirement was due to financial reasons, or to a quarrel with his party, or to weariness with the struggle. In Jan. 1794 his father died, and, as his four brothers were dead, he inherited the whole family estate, which was considerable. He then seems to have become the local money-lender. The Court records are full of cases of neighbours whom he sued for not repaying loans on the date they were due. He died in 1808, and was buried at St. Brelade's on 23 Aug. He had six children, Anne, Mathieu, who became Vingtenier of the Quennevais, Jean, George François, Marie, and Elizabeth. [*Magasin de Jersey*, and *Gazette de Jersey, passim*.]

AMY, JACQUES (c. 1500—c. 1586), Dean of Guernsey: second son of Jean Amy of la Rue de Grouville. His eldest brother, Philippe, was Centenier and his younger brother, Thomas, Fouageur of Grouville. Jacques was born about 1500, and was ordained Priest at Coutances on 17 Sept. 1525. In 1546 he is described as "Chaplain of the Mass founded by Collyn Le Guenetier". On 9 Oct. 1547 he became Rector of St. Saviour's, Guernsey, and on 11 Oct. Dean of Guernsey. He seems to have passively acquiesced in the Reformation changes under Edward VI; but, when Mary became Queen, he was eager to show his orthodoxy. Three women, Catherine Massey and her daughters, Guillemine, Guilbert, and Perrotine Massey, were accused of having stolen some pewter pots. The jury acquitted them, (1 July 1556) declaring that "they had always lived as honest women, saving only that they had not been obedient to the commands of Holy Church". On this new issue they were handed over by the Bailiff to the Ecclesiastical Court, which condemned them as heretics without even seeing them. The Bailiff refused to accept this verdict, and insisted that they should be examined. So on 13 July the Dean questioned them individually in the north-east aisle of the Town Church "concerning the Catholic Faith and the Seven Sacraments, the veneration of the Blessed Mary and the Saints, the efficacy of the Mass, and the ceremonies of the Church", and reported that their answers were "inane, dishonest, idle, empty, and contrary to the Catholic Faith". The Ecclesiastical Court then handed them over to the Secular Arm ; which condemned them to be burnt. (For the horrible scene at the stake see *Gosselin, H.*). When Elizabeth came to the throne, Amy was arrested for his part in this tragedy, deprived of his Deanery, and sent to England to be tried. In

1562 he humbly craved the Queen's pardon for his "erroneous
judgement". On 12 Jan. 1565 he was pardoned, and allowed
to return to his parish, but not reinstated as Dean. He was still
Rector of St. Saviour's in 1572. He died about 1586. [Foxe's
Book of Martyrs. Edith Carey's *Essays in Guernsey History.*
Bull. 1938, article, La Famille Amy].

ANLEY, THOMAS (1757–1827), Democrat. Son of Jean
Anley and Magdelaine Dumaresq; grandson of David Anley,
Constable of St. John's. Born in St. Helier's 1757, and baptized
in the Town Church, 29 Nov. His appearance was peculiar.
He was unusually tall and thin, and "his long legs were made
to appear even thinner by his habit of wearing very short, tight
trousers". (*Le Patrie*). His nickname was Baron de Latte
(lath). He was proud of a pigtail of his own hair, which he
tied with a red rosette. In later life he wore an old-fashioned
coat reaching to his heels with immense pockets, which were
always bulging with books and documents. Few knew more
than he did about charters and precedents ; yet he was no bookworm, but a man of action.

At the time of Rullecourt's raid in 1781 he was a Lieutenant
in the Town regiment of Militia. He was in bed, when the
French seized the Town, but he dressed quickly, and with the
curiosity that always characterized him hurried to the Market
Square, and questioned the French officers. They told him
that they had landed 10,000 strong, and that all the Regulars
had surrendered. He made his way into the Royal Court, and
listened to Rullecourt bullying Corbet into signing the capitulation. He then went home to breakfast. Later, hearing that
the Militia were gathering on Gallows Hill, he made his way
there by a devious route, and offered his services to Peirson
(*Trial of Major Corbet*). As most of his own men were trapped
in the Town, Peirson sent him to find a Company of the North
Regiment, which had halted at the Town Mill, and to guide
it by back lanes to Gallows Hill. This he did, "and by his
words greatly encouraged the men". (*G.* June 23, 1792). At
Corbet's Court Martial he was a witness for the defence, and
the Judge-Advocate remarked that "his distinct and accurate

manner of giving evidence must have struck everyone in Court".

In 1784 he was a Vingtenier of St. Helier's, and in 1785 was unanimously elected Centenier. In the same year he stood for Constable, his opponent being Jacques Lempriere Hammond, father of the future Bailiff. The result was disputed, and led to a series of lawsuits, which lasted nine years, during which the Town was without a Constable. Anley's popularity with his brother-officers is shown by the fact that one ground on which the result was contested was that the Colonel, Major, and one of the Captains of the Town Regiment had canvassed for him, thus intimidating their men. At last in 1794 both candidates dropped their appeals, and a new Constable was elected. During part of the interregnum Anley continued to act as Centenier. In Jan. 1787 he had a tussle with the hangman. The latter was accustomed on the Saturday after an execution to collect three sous from everyone who brought goods to market. He had no legal right to this, and Anley advised the market women not to pay. The Deputy-Vicomte was sent for, who threatened to open the women's purses, that the hangman might help himself. Anley replied that, if he did, he would arrest him for theft. The custom died. (G. August 11, 1787.)

Anley earned his living as book-keeper in a butcher's shop. His political opponents tried to use this fact to humiliate him. He was now a Captain in the Town Regiment. In Nov. 1787 he summoned one of his Sergeants before the Court for persistent absence from drill. The Attorney-General demanded the prisoner's discharge on the ground that the prosecutor was said to be Thomas Anley *Esquire*, whereas the only person who had appeared in the witness-box was a butcher's assistant. But it was not easy to catch Anley tripping on a point like this. He produced authorities to prove that every Captain in the King's Forces is an Esquire, and his claim was allowed. In 1792 he criticized at a Parish Assembly the amount claimed by the Attorney-General for expenses on a voyage to England. James Pipon, the Attorney-General's son, horsewhipped him on the steps of the Court. Anley challenged him to a duel; but Pipon would not fight on the ground that "Mr. Anley is no gentleman" (G. June 23, 1792).

In 1803 Anley was unanimously elected Constable of St. Helier's. He was now constantly in conflict with Sir Jean Dumaresq (q.v.), the Lieutenant-Bailiff. In 1804 and again in

1806 he was fined by the Court for "indecent reflections on the first authorities in the country". In 1807 he stood for election as Jurat, and nearly succeeded in defeating Philip Marett, Seigneur of Avranches. A few months later in December another vacancy occurred. This time he was elected by a majority of 1,269, the largest ever known. The Crown Officers opposed his swearing in, alleging among other reasons that "for many years he had acted as clerk at a slaughter-house, that he had repeatedly been brought before the Court, and had under- gone humiliating sentences, that on many occasions he had used words tending to vilify the constituted authorities, that his con- duct had been violent and tumultuous, and that he had rendered his loyalty suspect by speeches highly culpable". The case was tried in July 1808, and the Court refused to admit him. He appealed to the Privy Council, and 1942 electors petitioned in his favour. The Council reported (July 26, 1809) that "some of these charges ought not to have been made, some are wholly unsupported by evidence, and most of them have been abandoned by the Counsel of the Royal Court," but decided that there was ground for the last charge, "that he had rendered his loyalty suspect", and so rejected the appeal. St. Helier's at once made him Procureur du Bien Public. His election so alarmed General Don (q.v.), the Lieutenant-Governor, and Sir Jean Dumaresq, that they tried to get the method of appointing Jurats altered. They asked for a Royal Commission on the subject. This reported in favour of abolishing the system of election and having all future Jurats selected by the States and the Crown Officers ; but the Privy Council declined to make this change.

In 1816 Anley was again elected Jurat. The Court again refused to administer the oath, and Anley again appealed to the Council. Sir Hilgrove Turner (q.v.) was now Lieutenant- Governor, and he strongly backed up the appeal ; and this time the Council ordered Anley to be sworn in. He became one of the chief speakers in the States, and from his profound know- ledge of Jersey law was always listened to with respect. Age did not quench his fighting spirit. He fought the new Lieuten- ant-Bailiff, Thomas Le Breton (q.v.), with unremitting pugna- city. He was one of the eight Jurats who in 1818 informed the Privy Council that they refused to attend any Court over which Le Breton presided, because of his "dissolute and profligate conduct". In 1822 he challenged before the Privy Council the right of the Bailiff to try two forgers on the ground that he was uncle of one their accusers and brother-in-law of another.

His tendency to eccentricity seems to have increased as he grew older. Once he returned from London, where he had gone as Deputy of the States, with a marvellous two-wheeled tilbury with *"Devoué à ma patrie"* painted on the panels. He climbed to his high perch by the help of a ladder, and was sheltered from sun and rain by an immense umbrella. He died on 3 Sept. 1827.

Sir John Le Couteur (q.v.) noted in his Diary:— "Judge Anley, like many other great patriots, has died with scarcely anything left to bury his worn-out remains". Anley Street is named after him. He married Judith Du Parq on 3 April 1803, and at the same time acknowledged her daughter, Caroline, who had been born in 1797, as his daughter, thus by Jersey Law legitimizing her. After her father's death the States authorized a lottery for her benefit with a thousand £1 tickets, the first prize to be the Jurat's house in La Chasse Street, the second his pew in the Town Church. [*Gazette de Jersey,* passim; *Proceedings on the Trial of Moses Corbet; Jersey Magazine,* 1809; *Ordres du Conseil; Report of Royal Commissioners,* 1811 ; E. Allen's *Argument addressed to the Royal Commissioners,* 1811 ; articles in *La Patrie,* 1850.]

ANQUETIL, THOMAS JOHN (1784–1842), Brigadier General. Son of Thomas Anquetil and Marie Poingdestre. Born in St. Helier's 1784, and baptized 17 December. In 1804 his name appears in the list of Cadets for the Bengal Infantry. He reached India in 1805, became Ensign in the 22nd Native Infantry, and in the same year was promoted Lieutenant. He served in the operations in Hariana 1809, in the reduction of Kalinjar 1812, and in the Third Mahratta War 1817—18. In 1818 he was promoted Captain, and in 1824 was transferred to the 44th Native Infantry, and took part in the First Burma War. He commanded the Pioneers 1825—29, and then joined the 57th N.I. In 1833 he returned to the 44th as Lieutenant-Colonel. He was Deputy Adjutant General of General Stevenson's force in the Shekhawat Expedition 1834—35, and in 1837 he became Brigadier of the Oudh Auxiliary Force.

By 1838 the Indian Government had become alarmed at intrigues between Russia and Afghanistan, and decided to depose the reigning Shah, and replace him by Shah Shuja, who had been dethroned twenty years before. Anquetil was sent with the British expedition, which occupied Kabul and Kandahar. When Shuja was restored, all but 8000 of the troops were withdrawn, and Anquetil was left as Brigadier to create and train for the new Shah an army of native levies. For ten months the towns were held, but the wild tribesmen of the mountains were never subdued, and by the end of 1841 the position had become untenable. A treaty was signed between the Indian Government and the Afghan chiefs by which we agreed to evacuate the country in return for a safe-conduct. The difficult retreat through snow-bound mountain passes began on 6 January 1842. General Elphinstone commanded the British troops, and Anquetil had charge of the rear-guard. Their movements were hampered by 12,000 native camp-followers and a large number of women and children. On the first day it became obvious that the safe-conduct was worthless. Snipers lined every pass, and Afghan horsemen in the rear cut off all stragglers. On 7 January the rear was heavily attacked. "The panic-stricken camp-followers", wrote Eyre, "resembled a herd of stricken deer, and fluctuated outward and forward *en masse* at every shot, blocking the entire road, and fatally retarding the progress of the soldiers". Again and again the tribesmen came charging down the hills. On the 11th Elphinstone was invited by the Afghan Sirdar to a conference, from which he was not permitted to return. Anquetil then assumed command. On the 12th what was left of the little force reached the narrow two-miles-long Jagdalak Pass, which the Afghans had blocked with strong barricades of prickly oak. Here a withering fire was poured in from all sides, and Anquetil was killed. Only one wounded man escaped to tell the tale. There is a monument to Anquetil's memory in St. John's Church, Calcutta, and in the Town Church, Jersey. [Hodson's *Officers of the Bengal Army*, Eyre's *Military Operations at Cabul*.]

AVERTY, RICHARD (d. 1555), Priest. The Avertys were a St. Clement's family that gave many sons to the priesthood. Richard, though he lived in St. Brelade's Bay, probably belonged to this family, for the *Extente* of 1607 shows that he had held property in St. Clement's, which had been forfeited to the Crown. Though a Priest, he was not one of the parochial clergy, but Proctor of the Ecclesiastical Court, and in that capacity had been active in the restoration of Catholicism under Mary. He "grievously troubled the poor folk who were faithful to the Reformation, and especially wrought much harm to the unfortunate Priests who had married, forcing them not to consort in any way soever with their wives, and causing them to be punished bitterly, if they disobeyed" *(Chroniques)*. In 1555 he was arrested for infanticide. The Act of the Court (printed in Le Quesne's *Constitutional History)* states:— "On 27 June 1555 Richard Averty, who claimed to be a Priest, prisoner on a capital charge, who had tried to escape, but had been arrested by prompt pursuit, and detained in prison on demand of the King's Attorney and Solicitor, confessed freely for a second time before the Full Court, that on the Wednesday before Pentecost Marie Bellée, domestic servant, who had been long in his employ, was brought to bed, and without the aid of any woman was by his help delivered of a live boy, he alone being present, and that, when the child was born, he baptized it (so he said), and then straightway took it by the throat, and deliberately strangled it, and the same evening buried it beneath the hearth in his dwelling, where it was found, and disinterred by order of the Court. Therefore on account of the enormity of his deed he was sentenced to be dragged to the gallows, and hanged till he was dead, his body to be left on the gibbet till it should rot away. Whereupon Sire John Poulet (q.v.), Dean of the isle, appeared before the Court, and demanded that, inasmuch as Averty was a Cleric, he should be handed over for trial to the Bishop's Court, which the Dean held in the Island. To which the Jurats made answer, that the crime was so heinous that they could not allow Averty to pass outside the Royal Jurisdiction, but that the sentence must be carried out (which was done), and his goods confiscated into the hands of the King and Queen". One of the Le Maistre MSS. gives details of the execution. " 'Alas', said Richard to the Dean, 'you promised to save my life'; to which the Dean replied,

'Hush, I will bring them to repentance'. 'That', said Richard. 'will be too late for me'. Whereupon it became a proverb in Jersey for an over-late repentance, "Tis a Richard Averty repentance." The Dean had vested him in a surplice, when he was brought up for trial ; and he did so again, as he was being chained to the hurdle to be drawn to Gallows Hill, "that he might go to the foot of the gibbet wearing the ornaments of the Church. When the hurdle passed through a brook called the Douet d'Aulneville, (which then ran across the road now called Charing Cross,) he folded his surplice on either side, that it should not get wet. Whence sprang another proverb. When a sick man twines his sheet round him, they say, 'He's doing what Richard Averty did. He will not live long'. When he reached the gallows, his surplice was dragged off, before he mounted the scaffold. Thus died this wretched Priest to the great annoyance of his friend Dean Poulet". On 23 July Marie Bellée, the baby's mother, and another woman, Thomasse Clement, were tried as accomplices, and acquitted, but handed over to the Ecclesiastical Court to be punished for immorality. This case was important for its influence on the progress of the Reformation. At a time when Catholicism was beginning to recover ground under Mary, this crime, and specially the cold-blooded baptism of the baby, sent such a thrill of horror through the island, that anti-catholic feeling was immensely stimulated. [Authorities quoted above.]

BALLEINE, GEORGE ORANGE (1842–1906), Dean. Eldest son of George Balleine, merchant, and Marie, daughter of Jean Orange. Born in St. Helier's 31 Oct. 1842. Educated at Victoria College (1853—61) under Dr. Henderson, the future Dean of Carlisle. His father had worked in younger days for the famous Jersey firm of Charles Robin & Co. in Gaspé at the mouth of the St. Lawrence in Canada, and all arrangements had been made for the boy to follow in his steps. His sea-chest was actually packed, when Dr. Henderson called, and pleaded that he might be allowed to sit for an Oxford scholarship. He won an open scholarship at Queen's College, and added to that in 1863 the Taylorian University Scholarship. He gained a

Double First in Moderations in Classics and Mathematics and again another Double First in the Final Schools, a feat that has been accomplished very rarely in the history of the University. He was at once elected in 1865 Fellow and Lecturer of his College. In 1867 he was ordained, and in 1868 he married Florence, daughter of Austen Gardner of Ash-next-Sandwich, and was presented by his College to the Rectory of Bletchington near Oxford. Here he restored the Church, built new schools, and still kept in touch with the University, almost always having pupils in his house, whom he was coaching for examinations, and in 1884 being Master of the Examination Schools at Oxford. For many years he was one of the examiners for the Oxford Local Examinations. After seventeen years he moved to the Rectory of Weyhill in Hampshire. In 1888 the Deanery of Jersey became vacant through the death of William Corbet Le Breton (q.v.). Lord Salisbury appointed the Rev. P. R. Pipon Braithwaite, who was Vicar of St. Luke's, one of the modern daughter-churches in the Town ; but the States protested that he was inadmissible, because he was not a Jerseyman. This raised intricate legal and constitutional questions. The Jersey Canons of 1623 prescribed that in appointing Rectors to the twelve ancient parishes natives or *originaires* must be preferred (préférés). What did 'preferred' mean? Did it mean 'given the preference', or did it mean 'appointed' (as in the word 'preferment')? And what was the meaning of *originaire*? Did it include all members of Jersey families, wherever they might have been born, or did it mean persons brought up in the island? Could Braithwaite, who was born and bred in England, and whose father was a Yorkshireman, rank as an *originaire*, because his mother was a Pipon? Again, if he could not hold one of the Rectories, need the Dean be a Rector? Could he not become Dean, while remaining Vicar of St. Luke's? The Crown Officers in Jersey agreed that Braithwaite was not an *originaire*, but on the second point they were divided. So the problem was referred to Sir Edward Clarke and Richard Webster, the Crown Officers in England. They ruled on both points that Braithwaite's appointment was illegal; and therefore it was rescinded. The vacant posts of Dean and Rector of St. Helier's were then offered to Balleine, and in July 1888 he was sworn in and instituted. For eighteen years he remained leader of the Church in the island. G. S. Farnell, Headmaster of the College, wrote, "a truly wise chief, whose work was remarkable both for its quiet unobtrusiveness and efficiency". Durell described him as "quiet, dignified, a great scholar, a just man, tenacious of his position ; neither the frowns of the great nor the uproar of the multitude could disturb him. His unswerving sense of duty, his unchanging principles would have left him unmoved amid the crash of a world in ruins" (Men I have known). He had difficult and painful cases to decide as Judge of the Ecclesiastical Court, two of which involved the suspension of popular local clergymen. The States' Education Committee very largely accepted his guidance in all matters of education. More than once he tried to persuade the States to adopt the Gothenburg system of licensing, but here he had against him the teetotallers, who wanted total prohibition, and the liquor-sellers who were prospering under the existing laws. In Church matters one of his aims was to bring the local Church out of its insularity, and to make it an active part of the Diocese of Winchester. He established a Decanal Conference, which he hoped would become a local Church Parliament, discussing and initiating plans for Church work in the island. This was followed a few years later by an Interdecanal Conference, when clergy and laymen from Guernsey and Jersey took counsel together. And he saw to it that ten members, five clerical and five lay, were sent regularly to the Winchester Diocesan Conference. In 1891 he was appointed Honorary Canon of Winchester. On 29 March 1906 he died, and was buried in St. Saviour's churchyard. He had four sons, George Reginald, Robert Wilfred, and Austen Humphrey, who all became clergymen in England, and Cuthbert Francis, Fellow and Sub-Rector of Exeter, Captain in the Rifle Brigade, killed in the First World War, and two daughters, Estelle Marguerite and Hilda Catherine Mary (q.v.).

BALLEINE, HILDA CATHERINE MARY (1878—1921) Novelist. Younger daughter of the Very Rev. George Orange Balleine, Dean, and Florence Gardner, his wife. Born at Bletchington, Oxfordshire 24 March 1878. Educated at the Jersey High School for Girls. Died in Birmingham 25 Sept. 1921. She trained her pen by writing short magazine articles, and as a member of the Quill Club became Conductor of one of their groups. *The Quill*, their magazine, said at her death: — "Those who knew her are missing her discerning and helpful criticism. During her conductorship she helped struggling beginners and the more talented, if desponding, writers alike". At her death she left two full-length novels of Jersey life ready for the press. Both were published by Methuen, *Fig Blossom* in 1922 and *Rose and Laurel* in 1923. The first was given in the *Times* a long and eulogistic review, while the *Yorkshire Post* said of it:— "Like a breath of spring wind, heavily laden with the scent of gorse and violets, comes Miss Balleine's book to convince us that out of the winter of sordid realism, of poverty-stricken plot, of weariness of repetition, life and vigour can be renewed". The second is a study of the bitter political feuds in Jersey in the early nineteenth century.

BANDINEL FAMILY. Toward the end of the reign of Elizabeth, David Bandinel, an Italian (the surname Bandinelli is common in North Italy) settled in Jersey, became Dean, and died while escaping from Mont Orgueil (See Appendix I). Though, because of the Dean's antiroyalist zeal, his descendants were banned for ever from holding public office, five of them became Constables of St. Martin's and one Constable of St. Saviour's, three became Vicomtes, and one a Jurat. The Dean's great-grandson Georges bought from Lord Carteret in 1695 the Fief of Mélèches, and from him all the later Bandinels are descended. One of his grandsons, Philippe, gave the ground on which the General Hospital was erected ; another, James (q.v.) became Public Orator at Oxford, and was the father of Bulkeley (q.v.), Librarian of the Bodleian, and James (q.v.), head of the Foreign Office Department for the suppression of the slave trade.

BANDINEL, BULKELEY (1781—1861), Bodley's Librarian. Eldest son of James Bandinel (q.v.), Bampton Lecturer, and

Margaret Dumaresq. A direct descendant of Dean Bandinel (See Appendix I). Born in Oxford 21 Feb. 1781. Educated under Dr. Valpy (q.v.) at Reading, at Winchester, and at New College, Oxford, B.A. 1805, Fellow 1807, M.A. 1807, D.D. 1823. Like most Jerseymen of his generation his first thoughts turned seaward. In March 1808 the famous Guernseyman, Vice-Admiral Sir James Saumarez, was ordered to the Baltic to blockade the Russian fleet and protect Sweden. He hoisted his flag on the *Victory* (100 guns), of which Philippe Dumaresq (q.v.) was Captain. The crew consisted largely of Channel-Islanders, and Bandinel was appointed Chaplain. He remained in the Baltic two years ; but then his godfather John Price, Librarian of the Bodleian Library at Oxford, secured his appointment as Sub-librarian. In 1813 he succeeded Price as Librarian. The Bodleian was even then one of the largest libraries in Europe, and had the privilege of receiving a free copy of every book printed in England. He entered on his new duties with zest, and persuaded the University to treble its grant for the purchase of foreign books. When the allied sovereigns visited Oxford in 1814, Bandinel was Proctor of the University, and played a prominent part in their reception. He remained Librarian for nearly half a century, and enriched the Library by an enormous number of rare manuscripts, books, and prints, most of which were secured as gifts by his tact and courtesy. His great work was the compilation and printing of the Catalogue, of which the first volume appeared in 1843 and the fourth and last in 1851. Madan *(The Bodleian Library)* calls him "the last of the old type of librarian, the gentlemanly old-fashioned scholar, to whom the Library was a pleasant preserve, to which students were moderately welcome, if they knew what they wanted, and did not give too much trouble". He also edited in 1826 Clarendon's *History of the Rebellion,* and was one of the three editors of the new edition of Dugdale's *Monasticon* in eight large folio volumes, issued at intervals between 1817 and 1832. In 1822 he became Rector of Haughton, Durham. In 1850 he sold his family estates in St. Martin's, Jersey. In 1860 he resigned his librarianship, and retired on full salary ; but he only lived a few months, dying on 6 Feb. 1861. He married Mary, daughter of John Phillips of Culham. [*D.N.B.* ; Macray's *Annals of the Bodleian* ; Payne's *Armorial.*]

BANDINEL, DAVID.   See Appendix I.

BANDINEL, JACQUES (1602–45), Rector of St. Mary's.
Eldest son of David Bandinel, Rector of St Brelade's, who later
became Dean (q.v. App. I), and Elizabeth Stallenge.   Born in
St Brelade's Rectory 1602.   Educated at Oxford.   His father
wrote to Sir Edward Conway (14 Dec. 1618) during negotiations
about the Deanery, "For other affairs I refer you to my wife,
who has to go to Oxford to see her son placed there" (S. P.D.).
Jacques matriculated from Broadgates Hall (later Pembroke
College) in 1619, took his B. A. from Christ Church in 1622
and his M. A. in 1625.   On 26 Aug. 1626 he was inducted
Rector of St. Mary's.   The position there was difficult.   Samuel
de La Place (q.v.), a Puritan stalwart, had been ejected from
the Rectory, because he refused to acknowledge David Bandinel
as Dean; and the parishioners did not welcome the Dean's son
in his place.   Hugh Hue, the Constable, locked the Church,
and refused to allow Services to be held, on the pretext that the
Rector's mother had visited him from a plague-stricken parish
(there was plague in St. Aubin's), and that he might be a
carrier of infection.   The miller was also forbidden to grind the
Rector's corn (S. P. D.).   Another Sunday, when his mother
came to Church, the Constable "thrust her out with a halberd
in the face of her son" (ibid).   A third complaint was:— "Hue
presumes that all is lawful to him, because he is Constable, as
lately the profaning of the Church or Communion Table with
the blood of a dog, which he stabbed with a knife, while the
Minister was preaching" (ibid).   Next Sunday the Dean intervened, and sternly censured the parochial officials from the
pulpit.   The Constable and another prominent parishioner were
excommunicated by the Ecclesiastical Court for "railing against
their Minister".   Hue then denounced the Dean to the Royal
Court for treason, declaring that he had said, "This reign is
worse than Mary's".   He had really said, "Your behaviour is
worse than anything that happened under Mary".   But the Privy
Council took alarm, and he had to cross to England to clear
himself.

On 15 July 1628 Jacques was betrothed to Marguerite

Dumaresq, whose father, Richard Dumaresq, had been Constable of St Heliers's. Betrothal was then a religious ceremony. The *Discipline Ecclésiastique* ordered:— "It shall be done in the presence of the parents, friends, and guardians of the parties, and also in the presence of the Minister, before whom the contract shall be made with invocation of the Name of God, without which it is no contract. And from a promise thus made there is no departing". The La Cloche papers say:— "Mr David Bandinel, father of Jacques, promised to give to Marguerite and her children forty pounds sterling, payable within two years" *(Bull* II).

We hear little of Jacques during the next fourteen years. In 1634 he was appointed Vice-Dean by his father. In 1640 he had a lawsuit with the Constable about a communion-cup bequeathed to the parish. In the troubles that preceded the Civil War he evidently supported his father. On 17 Sept. Sir Philippe De Carteret (q.v.) complained to the Royal Court of a libel published against him by the two Bandinels. When hostilities broke out, Jacques became a member of the Parliamentary Committee, and was one of the five persons excluded from the King's offer of pardon. At his trial many papers were produced that he had written against Sir Philippe, and witnesses declared that he had actively assisted Lydcot to arm the men of St Mary's to attack the King's Castles. When Etienne La Cloche (q.v.) landed in St. Ouen's to rouse his parish for the King, Bandinel rode post-haste to Town to warn the Parliamentary leaders. When George Carteret (q.v.) recovered Jersey for the Royalists (21 Nov. 1643), the Bandinels did not escape to England with their colleagues. They were discovered in hiding on 5 Dec., and lodged in Elizabeth Castle.

On 2 July 1644 they were transferred to closer imprisonment at Mont Orgueil. As the Royal Court had always been debarred from trying cases of treason, their trial had to wait for the arrival of Royal Commissioners. They were allowed to walk on the ramparts by day, and in the evenings they played draughts. Their wives were permitted to bring them food. But, when Archbishop Laud was beheaded, they feared that they would be executed in reprisal. So they attempted to escape. By boring gimlet-holes close together they broke a plank in their door, and gained access to a room with a window on the outer wall. On 10 Feb. 1645 they lowered a rope lengthened with knotted napkins. "They waited for a night", writes Chevalier, "when it was blowing great guns, and trees were torn up by the roots, and one could scarce keep on one's feet inside the Castle. The son climbed down first, but the cord was too short, and he fell on the rock, and every limb was injured. His father would fain have followed, and squeezed through the window sideways, but, when he essayed to descend, grasping the rope with his hands, it broke at the top, ere he was half way down, and he crashed on the rock head over heels, and lay unconscious with bones and body broken. His son marvelled much to see his father in so sore a strait. At first he deemed him dead, but, perceiving that he was still breathing, he turned him on his back, covered him with a cloak, and fled. Though badly injured he made his way into the country to seek a hiding-place among friends. His mother, his brother, and his brother-in-law durst not receive him, foreseeing that their houses would be searched, but they passed him on elsewhere. The same day a warrant was issued for his arrest at sight; orders were sent to all the Constables to make a house to house search, and to close the harbours, so that no boat could depart. The Governor offered a reward of 200 francs for his detection. Whereupon there was great hue and cry night and day for him, and after two days he was found and arrested in the house of a widow in St. Lawrence, where he lay abed suffering from his fall. The Lieut-Governor himself came to arrest him. He was taken back to the Castle, and, finding himself very weak, asked that prayers should be offered for him in some of the Churches. He was not treated ill in the Castle, and partly recovered his health". On 9 July 1645 he was brought before the Commissioners for trial. On the following Saturday, when his case was resumed, he was too ill to appear. Two doctors sent to discover whether he was malingering reported that he was in a high fever. Had he been tried that day he would have been hanged that evening, for Carteret had ropes and scaffold ready; but he lingered on. Toward the end of his illness his wife was allowed to nurse him, and to bring his little son David. He died in the Castle on 20 March 1646, and was buried in St. Martin's churchyard near his father. The Commissioners declared his property confiscated to the Crown and his descendants banned from admission to any public office. He left two children, David, who in spite of the ban became Constable of St. Martin's in 1666, Greffier in 1670

and Jurat in 1676, and Elizabeth, who in 1653 married Clement
Lempriere. [*Calendar of State Papers, Domestic;* Chevalier's
Journal.]

BANDINEL, JAMES (1733—1805), Public Orator at Oxford,
First Bampton Lecturer. Fourth son of George Bandinel, Constable of St. Martin's, and Elizabeth Lempriere. Born in 1733,
and baptized in St. Saviour's Church 29 April. He entered
Winchester 1745, passed on to Jesus College, Oxford, 1752, and
was elected Fellow of his college 1754. He took his B.A. 1755,
M. A. 1758, B. D. 1767, D. D. 1777. For the first half of the
18th century Oxford had been passionately anti-Hanoverian.
Almost everyone drank the health of the King over the water,
and hundreds were eager to draw swords for the restoration of
the Stuarts. When Bandinel went up however, this feeling
was fast waning. Unlike his ancestor the Dean, he was an
ardent Legitimist. He became Secretary of the last surviving
Jacobite Club in Oxford, and travelled to Spa to assure the
Young Pretender of the loyalty of its members. In 1781 he
named his eldest son Bulkeley, after Philip Bulkeley, the famous
Jacobite agent and conspirator. There was still sufficient latent
Jacobitism in Oxford to make his devotion to the House of
Stuart no bar to his promotion. He was appointed Professor
of Moral Philosophy, 1767, and Public Orator in 1776, and held
this post till 1784. In 1780 the Heads of Houses had to select
a lecturer for the eight divinity lectures which John Bampton,
Canon of Salisbury, had just endowed. These Bampton lectures
became the most famous series delivered annually at Oxford ;
and Bandinel was the first lecturer. He chose no fancy title,
but published them simply as *Eight Sermons preached before
the University of Oxford.* He did not flaunt his Divine Right
of Kings views, but his High Church opinions could not be concealed, and he was accused of Popery. His first living was the
Rectory of Wigginton near Banbury. He was Rector of Furtho,
Northants, 1775—89 ; and in that year his relative Dr. Dumaresq
(q.v.), Prebendary of Salisbury, presented him to the living of
Netherbury with Beaminster, Dorset, which he held till his
death. He died at Winchester 20 Nov. 1804. He married

Marguerite Dumaresq, Dame de Hérupe, St. John's, and had two sons, Bulkeley (q.v.) and James (q.v.) and three daughters. "He was", says Payne, "a man of deep learning, sincere piety, refined manners, and great kindness of heart". [*Armorial*].

BANDINEL, JAMES (1783–1849), Clerk in the Foreign Office. Second son of James Bandinel (q.v.), Bampton Lecturer, and Marguerite Dumaresq ; brother of Bulkeley Bandinel (q.v.). For fifty years he was clerk in the Foreign Office, and for much of that time head of the department for the suppression of the slave trade. In 1843 at the suggestion of Lord Aberdeen, the Foreign Secretary, he published *Some Account of the Trade in Slaves from Africa*. It described (1) the rise and progress of the slave trade among European nations, (2) the abandonment of the trade by England, (3) the efforts of the British Government to effect its entire extinction. This book was issued as a Foreign Office publication, and was made the text of a long and eulogistic article in the *Edinburgh Review*. He retired on full pension in 1848, and died on 29 July 1849 at his house in Berkeley Square. He married in 1813 Marian Eliza, daughter of Dr Robert Hunter, Rector of Okeford Fitz-paine, Dorset, and had one son James, the author of novels popular in their day, *Luffra or the Convent of Algarve*, etc. [*D.N.B.* ; Payne's *Armorial*.]

BARREAU, ARTHUR HAMPTONNE (1879–1922), Artist. Son of Francis Hamptonne Barreau, M. R. C. S., and Eleanor Darley. Born in London 8 Oct. 1879. Educated at Parlett's Collegiate School and Victoria College. Studied Art under T. Larbalestier and then in the Royal Academy Schools. In May 1917 he joined the 3rd. Hants Regiment, and was sent to India. Most of his time there was spent in Hospital, for he contracted lung-trouble. From this he never recovered, and died in Jersey on 7 Feb. 1922. Many of his drawings appear in

Bulletins of the S. J., and examples of his work hang in the Barreau Art Gallery. This Gallery was presented to the Société in his memory by his aunt, Miss Emmeline Augusta Barreau, together with an endowment of £5000 for the purchase of additional pictures and £2000 to found a Barreau Art Scholarship to help local art students in their studies at any recognized Art School.

BARTLET, MRS MARIE, née MAUGER (1677—1741). Foundress of the General Hospital. Daughter of Captain Jean Mauger of St. Brelade's. Born 1677, and baptized in St. Brelade's Church 2 Jan. 1678. On 24 Sept. 1704 she married in the Town Church Francis Bartlet, a merchant of English origin settled in St. Aubin's. Among the merchants there was keen competition to secure the right to farm the import duties and anchorage fees, and Bartlet was successful in 1725, '26, '28, and '32. In 1733 he approached the Court as one of those who "proposed to continue the attempt previously made to build at St Aubin's a Chapel for the Services of the Anglican Church". He had no children, and at his death in Oct. 1734 he left all his property to his widow. She continued her husband's trade of importing foreign spirits, and at Michaelmas 1738 with Thomas Pipon as partner she again became farmer of the customs. In December she complained to the Court that Jean Le Hardy, whom she had outbidden, had caused the Constable of St. Brelade's to seal her cellars alleging that they contained undeclared brandy, and that "the said Le Hardy had pushed his violence so far as to raise his stick several times threatening to smash her head, and abusing her in most atrocious language". Le Hardy held up the case on the technical point that she had not described herself as "widow of the late Francis Bartlet" ; and she died before judgement was given. In 1741 she became involved in another lawsuit about a cargo of coal for New England, but on 24 Aug. she died, and was buried in St. Brelade's churchyard. At her death she was worth 91.567 *livres tournois* (O. C.).

After making certain personal legacies her Will ran: — "i bequathe to the Poore of Jersey on Honder livers Franche money to Iche Parihe to be distributed after my buriale: i give morear to the Poore of the Ilande Fifteay thousent livers turnois, taigne thousent to build them a house and forty thousent to beay a Reivenu to mantaigne the Poore that shall be Pouite in the House, wiche shall be Poore widows and Fatherlaise Childrane and Enchant Piple of the Ilande, and shale alwaise be quipe Foule ; and shale the saide House be built in St. tobins, and Everything be ordred as my Execrs hear after named and the Staites of the Iland shall judge Fiting". Her executors were her "good friends", Philippe Le Geyt, Lieut-Bailiff, and James Pipon, Seigneur of Noirmont. This will gave them endless trouble. First "by reason of the wrong spelling thereof and many disputes among her relations" (O. C.) the Court could not confirm it till 1744. Her cousin, Jean Mauger, to whom she had left only £10, tried to overthrow it. Then Philippe and Jean Shoosmith made a similar attempt. When at last the Will was registered, the States appointed a Committee to act with the Executors. In 1748 this Committee reported that it had failed to find any suitable site for sale in St Aubin's, but that Philippe Bandinel, Seigneur of Mélèches, had offered as a gift a piece of land on the sand-hills outside St Helier's. This they considered more convenient than any site in St. Aubin's, as the Hospital was intended for the whole island, and the doctors all lived in the Town. So the States appealed to the Privy Council, and in 1750 obtained leave to ignore the 'St tobins' clause in the will. But meanwhile the executors had recovered a field of Mrs Bartlet's which seemed to them fit for the Hospital ; and they appealed to the Privy Council to reconsider their decision. Again Advocates had to be briefed ; but the States won. More of the money was then wasted in a Chancery Suit in England, when Mrs Bartlet's London agent made difficulties about handing over her English investments. (The full story of this litigation is given in O. C.) In July 1765 the builders at last began work.

But envious military eyes were turning toward this new building. There were no barracks in the island, and troops who could not be accommodated in the Castles had to be billeted on householders. In 1775 the Lieut.-Governor asked permission to quarter soldiers in the Hospital, but was refused. In Sept. 1779 however Gen. Conway definitely requisitioned the building for this purpose. In July 1783 some gunpowder exploded, and wrecked two thirds of the structure. After much pressure the

British Government agreed to make good the damage ; but it
was not till 1788 that the promised £2,000 arrived, and not till
1793 did Mrs Bartlet's beneficiaries re-enter their rebuilt home.
It had taken more than fifty years to get the Hospital established.

The States erected an obelisk over her grave, and granted a
pension of £166—13—4 (order-money) to her niece Elizabeth
Bartlet, her only surviving relative. Portraits of Mrs Bartlet
and her husband hang in the Hospital Committee Room. [*Actes
des Etats ; Ordres du Conseil ; De La Croix' Ville de St.
Hélier.*]

BASIRE, ISAAC. See Appendix II.

BAUDAINS, LAURENS (c. 1546—1611), Founder of the Don
Baudains. Son of Edouard Baudains, *Fouageur* of St. Martin's,
and Susanne Hicques. His father, described as 'farmer and
merchant', was apparently of some erudition, for in 1566 he
was fined for ridiculing the Jurats in Court by addressing them
in English, French, and Latin. Laurens, born about 1546,
became his father's partner in trade. In 1587 and 1596 he is
mentioned as Constable's Officer. On the death of his only
son, Laurens, in 1595 he resolved to make the island his heir.
His first scheme was to found a College "for the instruction of
youth in Grammar, Latin, the Liberal Arts, and Religion". On
7 Oct. 1596 he presented to the States 18 quarters of wheat
rente and the Mill of Dannemarche for this purpose. In 1597
he obtained Letters Patent from the Queen allowing other
persons to add to this gift up to 200 quarters. In 1598 the
States appointed as Master, Edmund Snape, the Puritan who
for six years had been Chaplain to the troops at Mont Orgueil ;
but a few months later he left the island. In 1599 the States
added to the endowment 20 quarters from the revenues of St.
Mannelier and St. Anastase. In 1600 they authorized the two
senior boys to carry on the college as 'sub-regents'. It was then
in the Town. In 1602 the States discussed its temporary union

with St. Mannelier, but came to no decision. In 1603 William
Steward, 'a Scottish gentleman', was appointed Master, but left
the island within a year. Meanwhile covetous eyes were cast
on this endowment, and several attempts were made to divert it
to other purposes. In Jan. 1606 Sir Philippe De Carteret
proposed in the States that it should be used to pay the expenses
of the coming Royal Commission ; but in November in view of
the Commissioners' visit the States resolved that "some tutors
be appointed for the College in Town for the scholars' instruction, as is directed by his Majesty". Still however nothing
was done. So in 1608 Baudains presented a Remonstrance to
the States (printed in *Actes des Etats*), complaining that his
gift had been neglected, but offering to add to it 15 quarters
and also 200 crowns for the building of the College on condition, (I) that within a year a Graduate of an English University, capable of teaching Latin and Greek, should be appointed
Master: failing this his gift would pass to the Constables for
the relief of the poor ; (II) that, whenever the Master was absent,
the Rectors should carry on the teaching in turns ; (III) that a
suitable house should at once be built in the Town or its
neighbourhood. The States accepted these conditions, and
appointed as Master Pierre Guille, a young Jerseyman whom
they had supported at Oxford. But in 1610 he resigned, and
no successor was chosen.

Baudains then gave up all hope of seeing his College established ; and in 1611 applied for Letters Patent to create a Body
Corporate of "thirteen of the most substanciall and sufficientest
persons of the isle, to be called 'Governors of the Posessions,
Goods, and Chattells given by Laurens Baudains and others
for the maintenance of Poore Schollers for the service of the
Isle of Jersey' ". Their duty would be to support "in any Col-
ledge or Hall of either of the Universities of Oxford or Cambridge" "such Schollers as they think meetest to be chosen";
"and whereas the intention of Laurens Bawdein is for the
advancement of the poorest sort, we command that none be
elected but such whose friends are not able to keepe them at
either of the Universities". These scholars were to be pledged,
"soe soon as they shall become sufficientlie instructed in learn-
inge, to devote their services in and about the business of the
Isle", and "shall not dispose themselves from the service of the
Isle or of the Isle of Sercke without special licence of the

Governors". These Letters Patent were granted and sealed on 13 Sept. 1611 (The top membrane is now framed in the Bailiff's Chambers.); but Baudains did not live to receive them. He died 26 June 1611, and was buried at St. Martin's. By his will (printed in Syvret's edition of the *Chroniques*) he left to the church his silver cup for use at Communion, 100 crowns to repair the ruined Chapel, 50 crowns to each parish "to support the little children at school", 20 crowns to each parish for the aged poor, and other legacies to godchildren and relations and to the school-mistress of St. Martin's. He married (I) Collette Mallet, (II) Thomasse Esnouf. His only child, Laurens, died before him.

Up to the date of the German Occupation 120 young Jerseymen had been helped through their University course at Oxford or Cambridge by the Don Baudains. Among these were Elie Messervy (q.v.), the first Jersey Rector to receive Anglican orders, Jean Poindexter (q.v.), author of *Caesarea*, Marius D'Assigny (q.v.), Headmaster of Basingstoke and a prolific writer, Philippe Falle (q.v.), author of *An Account of Jersey* and founder of the Public Library, Martin De Gruchy (q.v.), the first Jersey Notary, Thomas Le Breton (q.v.), Dean, Philippe Morant (q.v.), Antiquary, Edouard Dupré (q.v.), Dean, John Dupré (q.v.), Headmaster of Berkhampstead, Richard Valpy (q.v.), the famous Headmaster of Reading, Henry Jean Knapp (q.v.), Chaplain to George IV, William IV, and Victoria, and Edouard Le Vavasseur dit Durell (q.v.), local Historian. But, apart altogether from conspicuous men, the Don has accomplished very successfully one of its founder's aims. It has provided Jersey with a steady stream of university-trained clergy. In 1670 five of the twelve Rectors had been Don Baudains scholars, in 1720 five, in 1770 four, in 1820 six, and in 1870 seven Rectors and the Incumbents of St. Luke's, St. Simon's, and St. Matthew's [*Bull* V ; *Actes des Etats* ; Minute book of the Don Baudains.]

BAUDAINS, PHILIPPE (1836–1908), Constable of St. Helier's. Son of Jean Baudains and Marguerite Valpy. Born at Les Mouriers, St. John's, 21 April 1836. Educated at the

Central School, St. John's. At fifteen he entered the Solicitor's office of Moses Gibaut as clerk. One of the French *proscrits* who came to Jersey with Victor Hugo coached the lad in Law. He then moved to the Vicomte's office, and in 1858 was admitted by the Bailiff as Ecrivain. Much of 1858—61 was spent in Paris studying at the Ecole de Droit, and those years left their stamp on him for life. Nearly thirty years later an American journalist who attended a meeting of the States wrote of him:— "His French is as rushing as Niagara, his accent perfect, his swing entirely continental. This Constable is *bon bourgeois*. Even his raiment is not English. Thousands who might be the Constable's brothers trot the dusty streets of provincial France" (*New York Independent* 18 Aug. 1896). On his return to Jersey he practised for seven years as a Solicitor.

He was a keen Freemason. In 1860 and 1861 he was Master of the Loge La Césarée, the only Jersey Lodge to conduct its ritual in French. But his impetuous spirit got him into trouble. His friendship with the French *proscrits* led him to found a new Lodge for their benefit, called *Les Amis de l'Avenir*; but as many of them were atheists, and so excluded from any Lodge under the English Constitution, he affiliated his new Lodge to a French group. English Freemasonry regarded this as an encroachment on its territorial rights, and excommunicated Baudains, his Lodge, and all its members. He went to London to appeal against this, and published a pamphlet to justify his action, but in vain. He persisted however, and remained Master of his schismatical Lodge from 1863 to 1868. But one by one his fellow-founders made their peace with the main movement. The Lodge died about 1873, but Baudains remained in the wilderness till he returned in 1888 to La Césarée Lodge, and in 1893 was re-elected to the Chair.

When the Jersey Bar was thrown open, he was the second to pass the qualifying examination. He was sworn in as Advocate 14 March 1868. His tempestuous eloquence and profound knowledge of Jersey law quickly made him the leading figure in the Court. And his magnificent presence helped him. Durell tells in his Reminiscences how Lord Haldane remarked during the Westaway case, "I have rarely seen such a splendid head" (*Men I Have known*). In 1892 he was elected Bâtonnier of the local Bar.

In 1869 he received the silver medal of the Royal Humane

Society for a rescue from drowning. In 1873 he was one of the
founders of the Société Jersiaise. For nearly twenty years he
was an officer in the Town Regiment of the Militia : Ensign
1859, Lieutenant 1860, Captain 1872. W.L. De Gruchy mentions how on one occasion an inspecting officer commented on
the unmilitary length of Baudains' leonine mane *(Reminiscences)*.

In May 1879 he made his first attempt to enter the States.
He stood as Deputy for St Helier's, but received only 86 votes.
In 1881 however he was elected Constable without a contest,
and was unanimously re-elected in 1884, 1887, 1890, and 1893.
In 1896 ill-health compelled him to retire, and in 1897 the island
paid him the unusual honour of erecting in his life-time a bronze
bust to his memory in the Parade. In the following year his
health improved, and in March 1899 he was elected without
opposition Deputy of St. Helier's, and in June regained his old
position as Constable, and was re-elected again in 1902. Thus
for twenty one years he was head of the municipality. He was
an able administrator, as he needed to be, for he was responsible
for the parish finance, the poor relief, and all street improvements,
while as head of the police he interviewed every year about 2,000
arrested persons to decide whether they should be released with
a caution or sent before the Court. During all this period he
was also the most active member of the States. He introduced
more than a hundred bills dealing with such varied subjects as
potato-diggers, pilotage, pawnbroking, sale of meat, storage of
gunpowder, eau-de-cologne duties, lotteries, electric light, limited liability companies, swimming-pools, cab fares, and cruelty
to animals. With many he was successful, his most important
triumphs being the introduction of voting by ballot and the lim-
itation of the power of imprisonment for debt. With others he
failed, notably in his persistent attempts to abolish seigneurial
rights.

He died of cancer in his home, Parade House, St Helier's, 4
June 1908. He married Jenny Rose Adèle Bianchi, widow of
Mons. Alavoine, French Vice-Consul, and left two daughters,
Marguerite Gabrielle (b. 1878) and Madeleine Jenny (b. 1880).
[Local newspapers, esp. *Jersey Express*, July 1896 ; Knocker's
Freemasonry in Jersey.]

BERTRAM CHARLES (1777—1854), Rear-Admiral. Son of
Charles Bertram, and Elizabeth Le Vavasseur dit Durell. Born
in St. Helier's 20 April 1777. He entered the Navy, Aug. 1794,
as 1st.class able seaman on the Nonsuch under Philippe
Dauvergne, Prince de Bouillon (q.v.). He was transferred to the
frigate Anson (44 guns), and after two years became a midshipman. In 1795 he took part in the ghastly fiasco of the Quiberon
expedition, and was wounded, while trying to rescue the defeated
French Royalists. In 1796 he was present at his ship's great
fight with the Etoile. He was moved to the Porcupine, and,
while taking a prize to England, was captured by the French,
and remained a prisoner-of-war till 1799. He was then exchanged, and, after a short time ashore in attendance on the
Court at Weymouth, was appointed to the Endymion (40), and
in April 1802 was promoted Lieutenant of the Dryad. After
four months on the Diligence, a boat on press-gang service, during which he added many hundreds of men to the Navy, he
passed to the Loire (46), in which he saw constant fighting,
which included the capture of two large French frigates, the
Libre and the Rhin. In 1807 he was First Lieutenant on the
Emerald, which in 1808 entered the port of Vivero to seize the
Apropos, a large French schooner, lying under the protection of
the forts. Bertram landed with a force of marines, stormed one
of the forts, and spiked the guns. His party then boarded the
Apropos, and, as they could not get her out, burned her. In this
fighting he received two severe wounds. Jersey was very proud
of him. When he returned home on furlough, the Gazette (23
July 1808) printed a poem of welcome:—

> As a fond mother with impatient joy
> Clasps to her bosom her long-absent boy,
> With like emotions, waked by glorious feats,
> Caesarea now her gallant Bertram greets.

He was promoted Commander, and given command of the
Persian (18). In this (13 June 1813) he was wrecked off the
Leeward Islands, and the crew eventually reached San Domingo
in an exhausted state. Bertram never fully recovered from the
effects of this exposure. He was court-martialled for losing his
ship, but honourably acquitted, as it was proved that the Admiralty chart was inaccurate, and he was given command of

the *Ariadne*. In 1846 he retired from the Navy with the rank of Captain, and in 1849 he was granted the rank of Rear-Admiral. He died in Jersey at the Crescent 10 Aug. 1854. He had married (2 March 1815) Susan, eldest daughter of Jacques Remon of St. Aubin's. His portrait, painted when he was in his seventies, in full dress uniform, is in the Barreau Art Gallery. His cutlass is in the Museum, and four of his commissions are among the MSS in the S. J. Library, also a long dispatch describing the capture of the *Apropos*, and the official report of his Court Martial and its verdict.

BERTRAM, SIR GEORGE CLEMENT (1841—1915), Bailiff. Son of Jurat George Bertram and Anne Delavel. Born in St. Helier's, Jan. 27, 1841. Educated at Victoria College (1853—6), then at Sherborne. Entered Trinity College, Cambridge, 1860, took his B.A., 1863, M.A. 1872 ; and was called to the Jersey Bar, Sept. 1863. He had in 1861 entered as a student of the Inner Temple, and was called to the English Bar in June 1865. He practised at the Jersey Bar till 1877, then at the Chancery Bar, London, till 1879, when he was appointed Solicitor-General in Jersey. In 1880 he became Attorney-General, and in Dec. 1884, Bailiff. On 1 Aug. 1885 he was knighted by Queen Victoria at Osborne.

Before long it became clear that there was friction between the higher officials in the island. In Nov. 1889 Sir George reported to the Court that the Vicomte, Gervase Le Gros, had twice left the island without informing him, and without showing the Court the letter, which by the terms of his patent he was bound to secure from the Home Secretary defining a Deputy-Vicomte's duties. The Court then ordered the Vicomte to produce the letter, which he was unwilling to do, until he had consulted the Home Office. The Bailiff told him his refusal was gross contempt of court, and publicly censured him. He then handed over the letter ; but later secured a new patent releasing him from this necessity in future.

Meanwhile there was in prison a Frenchwoman, Marie Françoise Daniel, who had been found guilty but insane, and was detained till her Majesty's pleasure was known. On Jan. 26. 1890, the Vicomte visited the prison with an order sent by the Home Office to the Lieutenant-Governor for her release. The Jailer consulted the Bailiff, who refused to let her go, until the warrant had been registered by the Court, quoting an Order in Council of 1679, confirmed by the Code of 1771, "that all Orders, Warrants, or letters relating to the public Justice of the Island, either coming from your Majesty or this Board, be registered in the Royal Court of that Island, before they be put in Execution". On Jan. 31 the Lieutenant-Governor, Lieut.-General Ewart, arrived at the prison with the Crown Officers during the Jailer's absence, secured the keys from a junior turnkey, released the woman, and had her shipped to France. The dispute came before the Privy Council, which decided that "a pardon by the Sovereign is an exercise of Royal Prerogative which operates immediately, and requires no further act to make it effective". It suggested however that in future such warrants should be communicated to the Bailiff as well as to the Governor, not for registration, but merely to give notice of the Queen's pleasure.

Before this matter was settled, another dispute had begun. General Ewart had more than once questioned the Bailiff's right to take the chair at the Prison Board, as every Bailiff had done since its formation in 1837. In Feb. 1890, during Sir George's absence in London about the Daniels case, the Lieutenant-Bailiff took the chair. General Ewart challenged his claim to do so, and when Jurat Malet De Carteret (q.v.) refused to give way, the Crown Officers left the meeting, taking the minute-book with them. Two points were now at issue:— (1) Had the Bailiff *ex officio* the right to preside and give the casting vote? (2) Had a Lieutenant-Bailiff any right to replace him, when he was absent? The Privy Council then asked the Bailiff on what grounds he claimed the right to preside. He replied that on his appointment he had been granted all powers enjoyed by his predecessors, and that since the formation of the Board the Bailiff or Lieutenant-Bailiff had always presided. However in June 1891 an Order in Council arrived, appointing the Lieutenant-Governor President of the Prison Board (the Bailiff to preside in his absence). Against this the States appealed, and the appeal was sustained, the Council (July 1894) deciding that the Order of 1891 had materially altered the agreement made in 1837, when the States consented to make a financial contribution to the Prison. The Home Secretary then declared that he con-

sidered it expedient for the Lieutenant-Governor henceforth to
be a Visitor rather than an actual member of the Board.

Sir George resigned the post of Bailiff in 1898 owing to ill-
health. The *Jersey Times* said of him:— "In every office which
he held under the Crown he performed his public functions
with marked ability and independence of character". He died
in London, Oct. 1915. He had married in 1866 Anna Maria,
daughter of General E. Lawder. They had no children. [Local
newspapers. *Jersey Prison Board Case with Appendix*, 5
volumes.]

BERTRAM, JOHN (1796—1882), American Merchant-Adven-
turer and Philanthropist. Son of John Bertram and Mary Perchard. Born in St. Saviour's 11 Feb. 1796. From his earliest years
he had heard the question of emigration discussed in his home,
and, when a sixth baby was born in 1807, the whole family,
parents and children, embarked for Baltimore. John alone could
speak English, which he had learnt at school. They settled in
Salem, where the father opened a grocer's shop, and the eleven
year old John served behind the counter. But the shop failed,
and the sea called him, and when sixteen he made his first
voyage as cabin boy to Lisbon and Alexandria. He then served
on two American privateers, the *Monkey* and the *Herald*. The
latter was captured by the British, but Bertram escaped from
the prison-ship. His next ship however was also captured, and
he was sent as a prisoner-of-war to England.

When peace was proclaimed in 1815, he returned to Salem,
and at once went back to sea. By 1821 he had risen to be mate,
and made several voyages to Java. On his last return voyage
he touched at St. Helena, and noticed that the local shops were
entirely sold out of what he called nick-nacks. So on reaching
Salem he secured a schooner of his own, loaded it largely with
small goods, and sailed for the island. But his secret had
leaked out, and a group of merchants sent a faster boat with
a similar cargo. This overtook Bertram off the African coast,
and then they were both becalmed. He invited the rival
captain on board, and, as they sat drinking together, each
assured the other that he was bound for Pernambuco; but

Bertram was not hoodwinked. He knew that St. Helena could not absorb two ship-loads. So that night, when a breeze sprang up, he jettisoned his deck cargo of 10,000 feet of lumber in spite of his mate's protests, outsailed his rival, and had sold his goods at fancy prices before the other ship dropped anchor. His eyes were ever open for trading opportunities, and the foundation of his fortune was laid by three years successful trading on the coast of Patagonia. He spent those years ashore buying hides and horns from the Indians, while two ships that he owned went to and fro transporting them to Salem. His last voyage as Captain was to Zanzibar in the *Black Warrior* in 1830. He was the first American merchant to trade with that island. He found the Sultan shipping a cargo of gum copal to India, and he bought it on the spot, and sold it at a big profit to varnish-makers in America. A merchant's life in those days was a life of constant adventure.

In 1832 he settled ashore as ship-owner and merchant. His clippers sailed to the four corners of the earth, specially to the Pacific. In later life he concentrated mainly on his trade with Zanzibar, though the first ship to reach California in the gold rush of 1848 was his brig *Eliza*. He visited his old home in Jersey in 1841, returning in time to be elected member of the Massachusetts Legislature at the end of that year. He was re-elected in 1857 and 1863. In his old age he devoted the greater part of his large fortune to philanthropy. "I want", he said, "to live as long as I can do good, and no longer". His private benefactions were innumerable. "His house", we are told, "was always resonant with the voices of real or pretended need". And in addition he founded the Bertram Home for Aged Men; he established a Fuel Fund to be kept in trust by the city ; and he gave endowments to the Salem Hospital, and the Children's Friend Society. "He was", says the *Dictionary of American Biography*, "the last of the merchants of the old type". He had strong Puritan principles. He was a teetotaller and non-smoker. Once in a foreign port he was persuaded to buy a lottery ticket, but, on hearing that he had won the first prize, he refused to touch the money and tore the ticket up.

He married three times. His first wife Mary Smith died in 1837 ; his second was Clarissa Millett ; in 1848 he married Mary Ann Ropes, who survived him. He died 22 March 1882 ; and his family presented his beautiful home in Essex Street, Salem, to the City to become its Public Library. There is a good portrait of him in Paine's *Ships and Sailors of Old Salem.* [Authorities mentioned above ; *Essex Institute Historical Collections* XV and XXI ; Osgood and Batchelder's *Sketch of Salem ; Salem Register,* 23 March 1882.]

BISSON, BENJAMIN, (1601—47), Parliamentary Commissioner. Second son of Edouard Bisson, Constable of St. Lawrence, and Elisabeth, daughter of Jurat Nicolas Lempriere. Born in St. Lawrence 1601. Educated at Cambridge: matriculated from Trinity 1618 ; B.A. from Corpus 1622 ; M.A. 1625. On the death of his elder brother in 1621 he became Seigneur of the Fief of Luce de Carteret. In 1629 he was elected Constable of St. Lawrence, an office which had become almost hereditary in his family. His father and elder brother had been Constables before him, and two of his sons were Constables later. In 1630 he was one of the Deputies sent by the States to the King to petition that the duty of garrisoning St. Aubin's Fort should not fall on the Militia (*Actes des Etats*). In 1631 he was elected Jurat. In 1641, on the eve of the Civil War, he was in London (*Bull* XII). When the War reached Jersey in 1643, he, like his cousin Michel Lempriere (q.v.), sided with Parliament, and in February was one of five Jurats appointed Commissioners by Parliament to arrest Sir Philippe De Carteret (q.v.), who took refuge in Elizabeth Castle, leaving the Five and their Committee in control of the island. Bisson took a vigorous part in the early stages of the struggle, and in July was excepted by name from the King's offer of pardon. He was still in the island on 17 Aug.; but his health broke down, and he went to Bath for a cure. He had just returned a little better, when in Dec. George Carteret (q.v.) regained the island for the King. Bisson, still a very sick man, was unable to escape with his colleagues He was seized in his house, and interned, first in Elizabeth Castle, then in Mont Orgueil. He remained a prisoner for eighteen months, and on 23 Aug. 1645 was brought up with five other Parliamentarians for trial before the Royal Commissioners. The Attorney-General, Helier De Carteret, urged that they were guilty of treason of the gravest kind, and demanded that they should be hanged, drawn, and quartered, and their goods confiscated. The prisoners then knelt, while their *greffier* pleaded for pardon. The Presiding Commissioner replied that the King loved mercy, and would pardon them, if they would promise to be loyal in the future. But first they must pay a fine. Bisson's was 8,000 *livres tournois*, and he had to find security in 2,000 *livres* more for future good behaviour. On the following Sunday they received Communion in the Town Church, and took the oath of allegiance three times, on a Bible, on the Bread, and on the Wine. To pay his fine Bisson was forced to sell a house and land on the Fief of Noirmont. He died 18 Dec. 1647, and was buried in St. Lawrence Church. He had married Rachel, daughter of Elie Dumaresq, Seigneur of Vinchelez de Bas. Nine years after his death, when the Roundheads again ruled the island, she petitioned Parliament:— "He died of diseases got by their cruelty, and left me and five small children (the eldest only nine) to the tyranny of a cruel enemy, and merciless creditors". *(S. P. Dom.).* She stated that her husband's losses "in fines, expenses, and plundering amounted to £916". The Council granted her £300 from delinquents' fines and £200 from her own discoveries of concealed lands and moneys not pardoned by the Act of Oblivion. Later she was granted another £500 "out of any discoveries she shall make and bring to effect before the Commissioners" *(S. P. Dom.).* Bisson left three sons, Edouard (later a Jurat), Abraham, and Benjamin, and two daughters, Sara (who married Jean De La Place, Rector of St. Mary's) and Rachel (who married Matthieu Le Geyt). [Chevalier's *Journal ; Bull.* XI ; and Authorities mentioned above.]

BLAMPIED, CHARLES (1769–1849), Methodist. Son of Thomas Blampied and Magdelaine Morrison. Born in Trinity Parish, 1769, and baptized in Trinity Church, March 31. By trade he was a stone-cutter. In 1787, when only eighteen, he married Marie Le Mesurier. The Methodist movement was just beginning in Jersey ; his wife persuaded him to attend one of the meetings at St. Mary's, and he became a zealous convert. In 1793 she died, and in 1794 he married Jeanne Le Quesne of

St. John's. His conscience had for some time been troubled about the Sunday Militia Drills. He absented himself, and took the consequences, which at first were only a fine and an extra drill on a week-day. But a few days after his second wedding he was arrested, and lodged in the Town Jail. Here his father-in-law visited him, and said that he would not allow his daughter to live with a jail-bird, and that she would leave him, unless he made his peace with the authorities. So he promised to parade on the following Sunday, and was released. But he found that his wife was proud of the stand he was making. On the Sunday he appeared on parade, but without uniform, and told the officers that his conscience forbad him to drill on the Lord's Day. He was rearrested, and on June 3 1794 sentenced to eight days' imprisonment. On May 7 1795 he again received the same sentence. On June 8 he was condemned to eight days' solitary confinement, and on June 18 1796 to a month's solitary confinement. Meanwhile other Methodists were stirred by his example. On June 21 1794 28 militiamen petitioned the States for permission to do their drill on weekdays, and Dean Le Breton (q.v.) presented their petition ; but it was rejected. They then refused to pay their fines ; so their goods were sold. The military authorities then resolved to suppress Methodism. Several of the protesters were sent to prison. The English Methodist ministers were expelled from the island. The Methodist Meeting House in St. Helier's was closed. And in Oct. 1798, in spite of protests from Dean Le Breton, the States passed an Act banishing from the island all militiamen who absented themselves from drill. As most of the men were farmers owning their own land this was very severe. They appealed to the Privy Council ; English Methodists and influential sympathizers like William Wilberforce used their influence; and on 28 Jan. 1799 the Council advised the King to refuse to sanction the Act (O. C. IV 582). Henceforth Methodists were allowed to do their drill on week-days. For more than fifty years Blampied remained a devoted Lay Preacher. He died in his house at La Ville à l'Evêque 23 Aug. 1849. [*Magasin Méthodiste*, Jan. 1850. *Histoire du Méthodisme.*]

BOSDET, HENRY THOMAS (1857–1934), Artist. Son of Captain Thomas Bosdet (Merchant Service) and Sophia Mary Le Roy, his wife. Born at St. Helier's, 7 Jan. 1857. Educated at Boyer's School, Beaumont, University College School. London, and the Royal Academy. On leaving the Royal Academy he became Director of an Art School in Islington. In 1890 he returned to the Royal Academy as Curator of the Life School. He painted a number of portraits and French landscapes, but abandoned this form of Art on becoming interested in stained glass through his friendship with Philip Westlake. Among his numerous stained glass windows in England are those at Hexham Abbey, Northumberland. His windows outside England include one in the English Church at Dinan and nine in the English Church at Utrecht. Examples of his work in Jersey are seven windows in St. Brelade's Church, five in the Fishermen's Chapel illustrating the life of St. Brendon, the Last Supper in St. Lawrence's Church, the Annunciation in St. Helier's, the Marriage at Cana in St. Aubin's, and the reredos in St. Saviour's. His windows at St. Ouen's Manor illustrate heraldically the history of the De Carteret family. He returned to the island in 1920, went to live in the south of France in 1927, but came back again in 1931. He married (1) Mrs. Julia Marion Reece Edwards of London (2) Mary Catherine, daughter of William Brereton, M.D. of Queen's College, Galway. By his second marriage he had one son, Harry Westropp Bosdet. He died at La Patrimoine, St. Lawrence, 23 May 1934, and was buried at St. Saviour's.

BOUILLON, HENRI FRANKLIN (1870–1937), French Journalist, Orator, and Politician. Son of Henri Bouillon, one of the French *Proscrits*, who in 1851 fled to Jersey after the *coup d'état* of Louis Napoleon. The father married Henriette, sister of Philippe Baudains (q.v.), later Constable of St. Helier's, and eventually returned to Caen; but, when in 1870 the Germans were overrunning the country, he sent his wife for safety to her brother's home in Jersey, and there in Parade House, St. Helier's, on 5 Sept. 1870 Henri Franklin was born. After a brilliant career at the Caen Lycée and Paris University he went to Cambridge, and then settled for a time as a teacher in London. But he went back to his own land, and in 1896 became a journalist. His first assignment was to be war-correspondent for the Sudan campaign. He then accompanied the Greek army in the Greco-Turkish War.

In 1899, when the Dreyfus retrial was convulsing France, he founded *La Volonté*, a pro-Dreyfus paper. This however was crippled by lack of capital, and after a few years died. Bouillon was now a member of the Radical-Socialist Party, and from 1905 to 1909 was editor-in-chief of their organ, *Le Radical*. He had been beaten, when he stood for election to the Chamber of Deputies at Caen in 1903, but in 1910 he secured a seat for the second electoral district of Corbeil (Seine et Oise). He was at once put on the Commission for Foreign Affairs. He had struck a bad patch in French politics. Between 1910 and 1914 eight ministries succeeded one another, paralyzed rather than supported by brittle coalitions. Bouillon kept aloof from inter-party squabbles, and throughout his parliamentary career concentrated almost wholly on international problems. This independence caused him to be mistrusted as no good party man ; but he retained his seat in 1914.

When war came, though as Deputy he was exempt from military service, he insisted on joining the colours, was promoted Sub-lieutenant, and made liaison officer between the French and British forces, and had an arduous time during the retreat from Mons. In 1915 Briand offered him a portfolio in his Ministry. This he refused, but put an immense amount of work into the Interallied Parliament which he founded and the Parliamentary Committee for Action Abroad. He was constantly sent on missions to England. He was in London in March 1916 and again in July, when Lord Riddell described him in his *War Diary* as "very able and energetic". In March 1917 Painlevé sent him to the United States to arrange for the enlistment of Polish and Czechoslovak troops. While still in America he was offered a seat in the Ministry as *Ministre pour les Missions à l'étranger*. In this capacity he visited England in June 1917, and again with Foch in October. In November he and Painlevé represented France at the Conference of Rapallo, which established a Supreme Council for the war in Italy. Shortly after, Painlevé's Ministry fell and Clemenceau became Premier. Bouillon, though now no longer a Minister, held the important position of President of the Commission for Foreign Affairs. Between him and the Premier there was war to the knife, and he became known as 'the Gadfly'. Week after week he thundered from the tribune with tempestuous ridicule against almost every aspect of the Premier's policy. He bitterly opposed the Treaty of Versailles, thinking it too lenient to Germany. "To surrender the Rhineland", he cried, "is to lose the war". And he voted against the ratification of the Treaty.

Nevertheless he retained his seat in the great *débâcle* of his party at the election of 1919 ; and no Government could do without his adroitness in foreign affairs. In 1920 he represented France at the Conference which fixed the frontier between Yugoslavia and Italy. In 1921 he nearly caused a rupture between France and Britain. He travelled to Angora, the seat of the Turkish Nationalist Government, ostensibly as a commercial traveller. When his presence was detected, it was said that he was there to arrange the evacuation of the French troops from Cilicia. He was really negotiating a secret Peace Treaty between France and Turkey. When the terms of this Franklin Bouillon Agreement were published, Lord Curzon, the British Foreign Minister, denounced it as the basest treachery, declaring that France had made peace with the enemy behind the back of her allies, and had given away territory that had been bought with British blood.

He held his seat at the elections of 1924, 1928, and 1932, and in 1924 he again became President of the Commission for Foreign Affairs. But he was becoming less and less a Party man. He pleaded passionately, but in vain, with the various groups in the Chamber to agree to a five years' political truce. In 1928 he resigned from the Radical-Socialist Party, and formed a new group of his own, *La Gauche sociale et radicale.* A considerable number of Deputies followed his lead, and his Group played a conspicuous part in the politics of the next few years. More than one Premier offered Bouillon a portfolio, but he always refused. He was now the determined foe of all that Briand stood for. Week after week he passionately denounced the folly of allowing Germany to rearm, the Young Plan, the Hoover moratorium, the Anschluss, the Disarmament Conference, and called on all Parties to unite against the dangers from abroad. To support this policy he founded the Union for the Nation, and addressed crowded meetings for it

in all the provinces. But he overtaxed his strength, and his
health failed. His last great speech in the Chamber in Dec.
1932 against the payment of debts to the United States led to
fall of the Herriot Cabinet. At the election of 1936 he was
defeated by a Communist by 62 votes. He died in a Paris
nursing-home 12 Nov. 1937. He married in 1902 Victorine
Lemarignier. Winston Churchill, who disliked him, summed
up his character as a diplomatist in the four words, "voluble,
plausible, ardent, ambitious" *(The Great War)*. [The fullest
account of his career is an article in *Le Temps* 14.11.37. His
portrait appears in Churchill's *Great War*.]

BREVINT, DANIEL (1617—1695), Dean of Lincoln. The
Dean's grandfather, Cosme Brevint, a Huguenot refugee, was
chosen by Helier De Carteret (q.v.) to be first Protestant Rector
of the newly-colonized Sark. Here he remained for 35 years
(1570—1605), "a true servant of God, as excellent in life as in
doctrine, who spared no man great or small in his rebukes"
(Chroniques). His eldest son, Daniel, the Dean's father, was
Rector of St. John's, Jersey, for 46 years (1604—1651). He was
the last of the Presbyterian stalwarts. "He had been", wrote
Chevalier, "the firmest adherent of the Religion of Geneva,
having accepted the Prayer Book greatly against his will.
Even when the Dean had made him use the book, he read the
prayers without any responses, rejecting all the ceremonies and
vain repetitions". *(Journal)*. He married Elisabeth Le Sebirel,
widow of Guillaume Le Goupil. His son, Daniel, the future
Dean, was born in 1617, and baptized in St. John's Church on
May 11. He was educated in the Protestant University of
Saumur, taking his M.A., when only 17, in 1634. He then
spent some time in teaching. Elie Brevint's *Notebook* says in
1635. "My nephew, Daniel, is in Poitou as tutor to some young
gentlemen". In 1636 the Channel Island Fellowships were
founded by Charles I at Oxford. Brevint and Jean Poindexter
(q.v.) were the first chosen. Brevint became Fellow of Jesus
College. He had some difficulty in getting his Saumur degree
recognized by Oxford, owing to Laud's opposition ; but he
succeeded. He remained here nine years. In the Civil War he

suffered "a long imprisonment in England on account of his
loyalty". (Clarendon Papers). He then returned to Jersey, and
in 1647 became Rector of Grouville, though still in Presbyterian
orders. When the Parliamentary Visitors purged Oxford he
was deprived (January 1649) of his Fellowship. In February
1649 Josué De Carteret (q.v.) charged him before the Royal
Court with disaffection and sedition. A Report on the case,
sent to the King, is among the Clarendon Papers: — "Mr. Daniel
Brevint gave a warning to Mr. Joshua De Carteret to abstain
from presenting himself for Holy Communion, unless first reconciled to a person against whom he had uttered publicly in Court
passionate expressions of revenge. Carteret in consequence
prosecuted Brevint before the Justices. The Commissioners
report that they find no ground whatsoever for the charges.
They have received good evidence of the integrity and ability of
Brevint, and are satisfied that Carteret's carriage was scandalous
and offensive". In November 1649 he preached before the King
in French in the Town Church.

In the following year he went to Paris, and received Anglican
Orders. Evelyn notes in his Diary:— "1650 June 12. Being
Trinity Sunday the Dean of Peterborough (Cosin) preached ;
after which there was an ordination of two Divines, Durell
(q.v.) and Brevint. The Bishop of Galloway officiated with great
gravity. They were presented by the Dean in their surplices
before the altar, the Bishop sitting in a chaire at one side ; and
so were made both Deacons and Priests at the same time in
regard to the necessity of the times. This was all performed in
Sir Rich. Browne's Chapell at Paris". Brevint then returned
to Jersey, and resumed his work as Rector of Grouville. When
the Parliamentary forces reoccupied the island in 1651, he did
not at once leave ; but in the following year he went to France,
and became Minister of the Huguenot Temple at Compiègne,
and later Chaplain to the famous Marshal Turenne, and tutor
to his children. At the Restoration in 1660 he returned to
England. For a short time he preached in the French Chapel
in the Savoy. On 17 December 1660 he was appointed
Prebendary of Durham and Rector of Brancepeth in that county.
In February 1663 Oxford conferred on him the degree of D.D.
On 7 January 1682 he was appointed Dean of Lincoln. He
died in the Deanery on 5 May 1695, and was buried in the
Choir of the Cathedral. He married Anne De Carteret.

daughter of Sir Philippe De Carteret, Bailiff and Lieutenant
Governor (q.v.) and had one daughter Charlotte, baptized in
the Protestant Temple at Charenton, outside Paris, in 1663,
who married Sir Edward Hussey.

His best known book was *The Christian Sacrament and
Sacrifice by way of Discourse, Meditation, and Prayer upon
the Nature, Parts, and Blessing of the Holy Communion.*
(Oxford 1673). This passed through many editions, and was
so valued by the Wesleys that they printed an abridgement of
it as an introduction to their *Hymns for the Lord's Supper* 1745.
Indeed many of the hymns are only a versification of Brevint.
His other books were rather virulent attacks on Roman Catholic
doctrine, e.g. *Missale Romanum or the Depth and Mystery of
the Roman Mass laid open ; Saul and Samuel at Endor, or
the New Waies of Salvation which tempt men to Rome refuted ;
Ecclesiae Primitivae Sacramentum ; Eucharistiae Christianae
Praesentia Realis et Pontificia Ficta ; Ducentae plus minus
Praelectiones in S. Matthaei XXV capita.* He also translated
into French the Judgement of the University of Oxford concern-
ing the Solemn League and Covenant. [Notice sur la Famille
Brevint in *Bull* VII 35. Wood's *Athenae Oxoniensis* ; Haag's
La France Protestante ; Walker's *Sufferings of the Clergy* ;
Hunt's *Religious Thought in England* ; Dic. Nat. Biog.]

BURRARD, SIR HARRY, BART, (1755–1813), Lieutenant-
General. For centuries the Burrards were the leading family
in the little town of Lymington, Hampshire. A Burrard was
Mayor of Lymington in the days of Elizabeth, and for 150 years
a Burrard sat in Parliament either for Lymington or for the
neighbouring constituency of Yarmouth.   In 1750 George
Burrard, a younger son, came to Jersey, and married Magdelaine
Anne Durell, daughter of Jean Durell, Attorney-General. She
through her mother, Anne La Cloche, was heiress of Longueville.
Their eldest son, Harry, was born at Vinchelez de Haut, and
baptized in St. Ouen's church on 1 June 1755 *(Church Register).*
He joined the Coldstream Guards as Ensign in 1772, was
promoted Lieutenant and Captain in 1773, and in 1777 exchanged into the 60th Regiment to see service in the American

War. He served under Sir Wm. Howe till 1780, when he returned to England on being elected M. P. for Lymington, which he represented till 1806. He was back in America in 1781, serving under Lord Cornwallis, and returned to the Guards in 1786 as Captain in the Grenadiers. In 1789 he was promoted Lieutenant-Colonel. In 1793 he went with the Guards to Flanders, in 1795 was promoted Colonel, and in 1798 Major General. In that year he landed with a thousand men, and blew up the gates of the Bruges Canal, which ran rapidly dry. General Cooke wrote in his dispatch, "To that excellent officer Major General Burrard I shall feel an everlasting obligation. To his counsel, exertions, and ability I in great measure attribute the success of the enterprise" (Annual Register). A gale however made re-embarkation impossible, and he had to surrender. He was soon exchanged, and in 1799 commanded the 2nd Brigade in Holland. In 1805 he was promoted Lieutenant General. In the raid on Copenhagen in 1807 to prevent Napoleon from gaining possession of the Danish fleet he was second in command, and received a vote of thanks for his services from the House of Lords, and on his return was created a Baronet, and made Governor of Calshot Castle.

In the following year the campaign in Portugal, which began the Peninsular War, was first entrusted by Lord Castlereagh to Sir Arthur Wellesley, the future Duke of Wellington. But the King and War Office disliked assigning so critical a task to a young General, whose reputation had only been won against native levies in India ; so two senior officers were sent to supersede him, Sir Hew Dalrymple with Burrard as second in command. Burrard arrived first, and reached the firing line in the middle of the Battle of Vimeiro. He did not interfere with Wellesley's plans till the victory was won ; but, when the French were in full retreat, he made what most historians consider the great mistake of his life. "The leaden hand of Sir Harry Burrard", says Oman, "was laid upon the army. Wellesley rode up to him crying, 'Sir Harry, now is your time to advance. We shall be in Lisbon in three days' ; but he refused to listen. He intended to wait for the arrival of Sir John Moore and the division from the Baltic" (History of the Peninsular War). "If I had not been prevented", wrote Wellesley in his Dispatch, "I should have pursued the enemy to Torres Vedras that evening, and in all probability the whole would have been

destroyed" *(Annual Register).* "The incubus of Burrard",
writes Oman, "succeeded in changing a decisive victory, which
might have laid a kingdom at his feet, into an ordinary, successful, defensive action" (op. cit.) Yet something can be said
in his defence. He had only been a few hours in the country.
He had no cavalry and next to no transport, for the native
drivers had fled with their carts during the battle. For all he
knew the French might have had a strong force in reserve.
Moreover large reinforcements were on their way from England.
A Court of Inquiry later declared that it "could not pronounce
with confidence whether or not a pursuit could have been
efficacious", but that there were "fair military grounds" for his
decision. Lord Moira, the ablest officer on the Court, told the
House of Lords that he could not make up his mind whether
Burrard had been right or wrong, but on the whole thought
that he had been judicious. But the outcry against him was
so bitter that he had to be recalled, and he was ordered to
hand over his command to Sir John Moore. "If ever two men
had an excuse for hating each other", writes Fortescue, "it was
this pair of Generals" *(History of the British Army).* Three
months before, though both nation and army considered Moore
the ablest of English Generals, his troops had been placed under
Burrard; now Burrard was superseded by Moore. "But", says
Fortescue, "Moore was too great a man and Burrard too great
a gentleman to condescend to quarrel" (op. cit). "Happy shall
I be", wrote Burrard, "if in anything I can serve an officer for
whose character I have the highest respect". "Sir Harry Burrard", wrote Moore, "seems to put himself aside and to give
everything to me with as much liberality as if he were himself
personally concerned in the conduct of it". When they parted
at Lisbon, Moore took Burrard's eldest son, Paul Harry Durell,
as his aide-de-camp, an unfortunate appointment for the young
Ensign, for three months later he was killed with his General
at Corunna.

In 1810 Burrard was given the command of the Guards in
London. In 1812 his mother died and he inherited the Fief ès
Payns and the Fief Collette des Augrès in St. Helier's. General
Don (q.v.) was then road-making ; and Burrard presented him
with a strip of land running through the former fief. The
Gazette de Césarée (21 March 1812) announced :— "The public
will learn with pleasure that Lieut.-General Sir Harry Burrard

is about to give a new proof of the lively interest he takes in the welfare of his native land by opening a road which will lead from New Street to Don Street and thence to the New Markets. This road will be called Burrard Street after its generous donor". Burrard married (20 Feb. 1789) Hannah, daughter of Harry Darby, a London merchant, and had five sons, Paul Harry Durell, killed at Corunna, John Thomas, R.N., drowned at sea, William, killed at San Sebastian, Edward, Captain in the Grenadier Guards, and Charles, who alone survived his father, and succeeded to the Baronetcy. Burrard died in Calshot Castle, 18 Oct. 1813. [Burrard's *Family of Borard & Burrard*; *Dic. Nat. Biog*; and authorities quoted above.]

CABOT, FRANCIS (1668—17--), Mayor of Southampton. Born in St. Helier's 1668; eldest son of François Cabot and Suzanne Gruchy. Emigrated to America, 1700, with his two brothers, George and John. George became a joiner at Boston. His descendants went into the wild West, and established many farming families. John settled in Salem (see below). Francis returned to Europe in 1701, and became a successful and very wealthy merchant in Southampton. In 1716 he was Sheriff, and in 1725 Mayor. In 1741 he bought the Manor of Houghton near Dover. He was still alive in 1748. His son Francis became Sheriff of Southampton in 1733. [Brigg's *History and Genealogy of the Cabot Family*.]

CABOT, JOHN (1680—1742), Merchant of Salem. Founder of the Cabot Family of America, that highly exalted and exclusive family of whom it was said in Boston :—

"The Lowells speak only to Cabots,
But the Cabots speak only to God".

Born in St. Helier's, 1680, youngest son of François Cabot and

Suzanne Gruchy ; brother of Francis Cabot (see above). In 1700 he emigrated to America, and established himself as a merchant at Salem. He prospered greatly, and became one of the wealthiest men in the colony. He married Anna Orne of Salem, and had nine children. His descendants became one of the leading mercantile families of America, and many of them amassed great fortunes by privateering, slave-trading, and the opium traffic. John died in 1742. [Briggs' *History and Genealogy of the Cabot Family*.]

CABOT, SEBASTIAN. See Appendix II.

CARTERET. See also DE CARTERET and MALET DE CARTERET.

CARTERET, SIR GEORGE (d. 1680), Baronet, Bailiff and Lieutenant-Governor, Treasurer of the Navy. (Though a De Carteret, he dropped the De, and his descendants followed his example ; so this branch of the family will be entered as CARTERET.) Eldest son of Jurat Elie De Carteret, Lieut.-Bailiff, (who was brother of Sir Philippe 3, Bailiff and Lieut.-Governor), and of Elizabeth, daughter of Hugh Dumaresq. The year of his birth is unknown ; but his parents married in Sark in June 1608, and he was the eldest son. If he was born in 1609, this would make him 20, when he received his first commission, and 71 when he died. (The *London Gazette* said that he was then "near eighty", but that would have made him born eight years before his parents' marriage.)

According to Lady Fanshawe's *Memoirs* he was "bred a sea-boy". Hence his lack of culture in later life. Marvell sneered at his "ill English". Pepys was shocked, when he asked what S.P.Q.R. meant, "ignorance not to be borne in a Privy Councillor". But, whatever else he did not know, he understood seamanship. Hyde described him as "undoubtedly as good, if not the best seaman of England" (*Clarendon Papers*). The State Papers trace his steady rise in his profession. On 20 May 1629 he received his first commission as Lieutenant of the *Garland* (700 tons). In 1631 he was transferred to the *Bonaventure* (700 tons) under Pennington, Admiral of the Narrow Seas, who remained his friend for years. When Pennington moved to the *Convertine* in 1632, he took Carteret with him. In March 1633 he was given his first command, that of the *Eighth Lion's Whelp*, one of a group of little vessels of 180 tons designed for chasing pirates. In 1635 he became Captain of the *Mary Rose* (400 tons) and in 1636 of the *Happy Entrance* (600 tons) with six ships under him to guard the Straits of Dover. He complained to the Admiralty that the new cords and cables supplied to the *Entrance* snapped when used, that a third of the men had never been to sea, and that there were not twelve able to take their turn at the helm *(S.P.)*. In 1637 he was given the *Antelope* (600 tons), and made Vice-Admiral of the expedition against the North African Pirate stronghold of Sallee. The ships proved too large to enter the harbour, but they blockaded it for three months, sending in boats at night to burn the pirate vessels. In this work Carteret gained a great reputation ; almost every ship in the port was sunk ; and at last the King of Morocco made peace by the surrender of his European captives. Carteret returned in September with 270 Englishmen whom he had rescued and a number of Dutch and Spanish sailors. In 1638 he was given command of his old ship the *Convertine*, and ordered to take back to Sallee the Moorish ambassador, who had come to ratify the peace-treaty. He then presented two silver Communion cups to St. Ouen's Church as a thank-offering for his safe return. The Diary, which he kept on this voyage, has been printed in Philadelphia, *A Journall keepte by me George Carteret in His Matie's Shippe the Convertine being bound for the Coast of Barbary.* This shows that, though he might not know the meaning of S.P.Q.R., he was able to write good, plain, straightforward, narrative English. In 1639 he was Captain of the *Leopard*.

He was now in love with his cousin Elizabeth, daughter of Sir Philippe De Carteret, Bailiff and Lieutenant-Governor (q.v.), and was looking for a shore berth which would enable him to marry. By a strange chance some of their love-letters are preserved among the State Papers. In March 1639 Elizabeth wrote bemoaning a quarrel between George and her father, for which she blamed their grandmother, "who hates us all". In July Carteret wrote :— "This day I landed the Earl of Leicester at Dieppe, who has given me a chain of gold. How much it is worth I know not, but such as it is I give it to my dear Betty. If you think fit, I will sell it, and put the money in a collar of pearls". In December 1639 he was appointed Comptroller of the Navy with rooms in the Navy Office. On 6 May 1640 he married Elizabeth in Mont Orgueil.

In 1642, when tension between King and Parliament was near breaking-point, Parliament appointed him Vice-Admiral of the Fleet. He referred the matter to the King, who forbad him to accept. Clarendon considered this a mistake. "If Captain Carteret had been suffered to have taken that charge, his reputation in the Navy was so great, that it was generally believed he would have preserved a major part of the fleet to their duty to the King" (*History*.) Later in his book Clarendon continued the story :— "Captain Carteret, having, after he had refused command of their fleets, without noise withdrawn himself and his family to Jersey, and being there impatient of being quiet, while his Master was in the field, transported himself to Cornwall, purposing to raise a troop of horse. Here he was unanimously importuned by the Commanders, after they had acquainted him with their desperate need of powder, to assist them, so that the ports in their power might be of use to them in the supply of powder. Whereupon he returned to France, and, first upon his own credit, and then upon return of such commodities out of Cornwall as they could spare, he supplied them with all kinds of ammunition, so that they never found want after".

He now established himself as King's Faciendary at St. Malo, selling captured Parliamentary ships, and buying munitions for the Royalists. When his uncle, Sir Philippe, was besieged in Elizabeth Castle, he kept the Castle and Mont Orgueil supplied, and made it hopeless for the Island militia to try to starve either out. In Aug. 1643 Sir Philippe died. The King had promised in 1638 that George should succeed him as Bailiff. In Oct. 1643 a messenger from Oxford brought to St. Malo a confirmation of this, and also his appointment as Lieut.-Governor. On 19 Nov. with a small force he landed at Mont Orgueil, which his aunt, Lady De Carteret, had been defending for eight months. The Militia, weary of besieging apparently impregnable castles, laid down their arms. The Parliamentary leaders fled. Carteret gained possession of the island without fighting. He marched to St. Helier's, and dismantled its fortifications. On 24 Nov. he called a meeting of the States in Trinity Church, and was sworn in as Bailiff and Lieut.-Governor. He seldom presided over the Court or the States. His duties as Bailiff he left to his Lieutenant, Jean Dumaresq. His work as Lieut.-Governor occupied most of his time.

His first care was to secure himself against a Roundhead rising. Though the leaders had fled, more than half the islanders still sympathized with Parliament. One small incident shows the spirit with which he had to contend. A woman was put in the pillory for saying that Lady De Carteret ought to be burnt, and that she would like to be the first to set fire to the faggots. Her niece stood in front of the pillory declaring that her aunt was as true a martyr as Christ (Chevalier). Carteret imprisoned those most likely to give trouble, including Bandinel, the Dean (q.v.), and his son, the Rector of St. Mary's. A second group he banished to Normandy. From a third group he took heavy monetary security for their good behaviour. The rest of the inhabitants were collected by parishes, and made to swear allegiance to the King on a Bible lying on a drum. The castles were filled with English and Irish troops.

His next problem was to find funds to carry on his Government, for none could be expected from the King. He seized the income of the exiled Republicans, and raised a forced loan. But he did not solve his difficulty, till he turned back to the sea. He had a swift galley built at St. Malo, schooner-rigged with twelve pairs of oars : he put on board one cannon and 36 armed seamen, and sent it out to prey on ships in the Channel. In six weeks it captured four prizes, one a fine vessel just off the stocks. Each of these was armed and turned into a privateer. By repeating this process he was soon in command of a formidable squadron. But not without protest. Etienne La Cloche (q.v.), the Royalist Rector of St. Ouen's, expostulated from the pulpit against Jersey being made "a little Dunkirk". Carteret imprisoned him for eleven months, and then banished him from the island. In Dec. 1644 the King regularized Carteret's proceedings by creating him Vice-Admiral in Jersey. By this commission his privateers became part of the King's Navy. What a steadily increasing danger to shipping they were can be seen from entries seven years later in Whitelock's *Memorial*:— "1651 26 Feb. Two Dutchmen laden with salt anchored off Dartmouth, but two Jersey pirates cut their cables and carried them away. 1 March. Jersey pirates very bold off the Western coast. 6. Several ships taken by Jersey pirates. 17. Jersey pirates take several merchants' ships. 19. Letters of piracies committed by those of Jersey. 17 April. Jersey pirates take two boats laden with corn and timber in fight off Portland. 21. More prizes taken by Jersey pirates." In this way Carteret not only harassed his enemies, and provided funds for his Government, but also amassed a large personal fortune. Marvell later calls him "Carteret the rich". Dumaresq says that he made a personal profit of "about three score thousand pounds" *(Survey)*. Pepys says that Carteret told him that at the Restoration he was worth £50,000.

One task laid on him by the King was the victualling of Castle Cornet, Guernsey, where gallant old Sir Peter Osborne was still holding out, though the whole island was Parliamentarian. He rather naturally disliked buying supplies for Guernsey out of his own pocket on the doubtful promise that the King would repay some day. "It hath not been without much difficulty", he wrote to Osborne, "that I have sent so much provision as I have. More I cannot do, except you will oblige yourself to repay the sums I have disbursed — one half six months after the reduction of Guernsey to the King's obedience, the other half eighteen months after the same, with interest ; in case of failing payment upon the revenues of Guernsey, then your estate in England to be liable" *(Chronicles of Castle Cornet)*. Sir Peter's caustic comment was:— "For a Comptroller of the Navy to misdoubt the King's payment seems to me a presumption I should not dare be guilty of". A violent quarrel between the two Governors ensued ; but for the next three years Carteret grudgingly sent supplies to Guernsey, though protesting that "every tub should stand on its own bottom".

About this time he was made a Knight and Baronet. The date is uncertain. Hoskins on the authority of "a private genealogy" says that he had been knighted in 1641 ; but this is improbable. The King in the Patent appointing him Bailiff in

1643 calls him "Captain George Carteret". Collins in his *History of the Carteret Family* states that he was knighted on 21 Jan. 1644 ; but, if so, Lord Jermyn, the Governor, knew nothing about it twelve months later, for, when appointing him his Lieutenant on 30 Jan. 1645, he merely calls him "le Colonell George de Carteret Esqr." Collins may be right when he dates the Baronetcy 9 May 1645 ; for soon after this we find Carteret addressed as Sir George. On 18 June Osborne refers to him as "Sir G. Carteret" (*Chronicles of Castle Cornet.*) A deed of 5 March 1646, by which he presented a site for a House of Correction to the Island, gives him his full title, "Messire George De Carteret, Chevalier, Baronet" (*A.E.*), which disproves the frequently repeated assertion that he was knighted and (or) created Baronet by Prince Charles when he came to the island, for the Prince did not arrive till a month later.

The Prince of Wales, a boy of fifteen, had been driven to Scilly for safety. It was now decided to remove him for greater security to Jersey. This threw a new responsibility on Sir George. Charles landed at Elizabeth Castle on 17 April 1646 with a retinue of three hundred, most of whom, including the Prince, were almost penniless ; and Carteret had not only to maintain them, but to provide the Prince with pocket-money from which to distribute largesse. Fortunately for his exchequer this first royal visit lasted only ten weeks. The Queen was anxious to have her son under her thumb in Paris, and on 25 June he left to join his mother. Many of his Court went with him, but some remained, among whom was Sir Edward Hyde, Chancellor of the Exchequer. As the King's cause in England grew more desperate, others joined them, and Jersey became a refuge for distinguished and destitute Royalists.

In October alarming rumours reached the island from Paris, that Lord Jermyn, the Governor, and the Queen were planning to sell Jersey to the French. Loyal though he was, Carteret could not tolerate that. On 19 Oct. he and three of the leading Royalists, Lord Capel, Lord Hopton, and Hyde, signed Articles of Association (*Bull.* III) pledging themselves to appeal to Parliament for help, rather than allow the French to take possession. Nothing more however was heard of Jermyn's supposed plot.

Carteret was now preparing for the inevitable Parliamentary attack. He reorganized the Militia, raised a troop of Dragoons,

built breastworks at all possible landing-places, strengthened
St. Aubin's Tower, and protected the approach to Elizabeth
Castle by building Fort Charles. But Parliament had other
fish to fry, and the attack was postponed. In Dec. 1647 news
came that the King was imprisoned in Carisbrooke Castle.
Carteret planned a rather desperate stroke to liberate him.
"There appeared", writes Falle, "a zeal in many of our most
resolute islanders to rescue the King by surprising the Castle.
The thing though hazardous was not thought impossible, because
ships going to Southampton pass close to this Castle. It was
presumed that four or five vessels with a number of chosen
hands concealed under hatches might come so near as to give
opportunity to scale the walls". But Cromwell was not caught
napping. He wrote to the Governor of Carisbrooke:— "Sir
George Cartwright hath sent three boats from Jersey under the
name of Frenchmen to bring the King, if their plot take effect,
to Jersey" (*Cromwell's Letters*). Forewarned was forearmed,
and the scheme came to nothing.

In Feb. 1649 Jersey heard of Charles' execution. On the
17th Carteret ordered Laurens Hamptonne (q.v.) the Vicomte
to proclaim Charles II as King. (Proclamation printed in *Bull.
IX.*) In July Sir George was summoned to meet the King in
Paris. Here it was arranged that Charles should make Jersey
his headquarters. On 17 Sept. he arrived at Elizabeth Castle
with his brother, the Duke of York. On 25 Sept. Carteret's
daughter Carolina was baptized with the King as godfather.
This time he remained five months, most of which were spent
in angry debates as to whether the safest route to the throne
was via Ireland or Scotland. On 23 Feb. he left Jersey for
Holland.

Carteret now embarked on his first colonial venture. Che-
valier says that the King gave him an island off the coast of
Virginia called Semis Eslan, to which he gave the name of New
Jersey. This was not the later colony of New Jersey, which
lies many miles north of Virginia. Chevalier's spelling is in
a class by itself : but if, as seems likely, Semis Eslan means
Smith's Island, it was not a gift of great value. The Captain
Smith after whom it was named had written of it:— "Smith's
Isles are a many of barren rocks, the most overgrown with such
shrubs and sharp whins you can hardly pass, without either
grass or wood" (*Advertisement for Planters*). But Carteret

prepared to occupy it with the zeal his great-grandfather had shown in the colonization of Sark. He gathered a party of Jersey emigrants under the leadership of Philippe De Soulemont, Advocate of the Royal Court, on one of his boats, which also carried the poet Davenant, the new Governor of Virginia. But on their first day at sea they were captured by a Parliamentary privateer. Whitelock writes:— "1650. 14 May. A ship of 5 guns belonging to Sir George Carteret, bound for Virginia with many passengers, all sorts of goods and tools for husbandry for planting an island which the Prince had given him, was taken by Captain Green and brought to the Isle of Wight" *(Memorial)*. We hear no more of the Virginian New Jersey.

For some reason Carteret now became unpopular with his fellow Royalists. In April 1650 Richard Watson, one of the leading exiled Divines in Paris, wrote:— "There is a general ill opinion of Sir George Carteret". A few days later Hyde wrote to Secretary Nicholas, "Poor Sir George Carteret is regarded in Paris as a reprobate". Again in October he asked. "Why do people from all quarters write so bitterly of Sir George Carteret?" *(Clarendon Papers)*.

On 20 Oct. 1651 the long expected blow fell. The Seigneur of St. Ouen's sent word that eighty Parliamentary vessels were in St. Ouen's Bay. Admiral Blake himself directed the naval operations from Carteret's old ship, the *Happy Entrance*. The 2000 troops on the transports were under Colonel Heane, Commander-in-Chief of Dorset. News of the Battle of Worcester and the King's crushing defeat and flight had reached Jersey. Even fervent Royalists felt disinclined to fight further for a cause that seemed hopeless. Sir George knew, says a contemporary account of the landing *(Bull. II)*, "that most of his men desired nothing better than to surrender without fighting" ; but he would not give in. Rough weather enabled him to reach St. Ouen's before the troops could land ; but then Blake set to work to tire the defenders out. He sailed round to St. Brelade's, and they had to follow. Then he doubled back to St. Ouen's. He sent some of his ships to St. Clement's. He made a feint at landing at L'Etac. For two days and nights he kept the militiamen marching and countermarching. When the real attack came, they proved no match for the veterans of the New Model, who had come to Weymouth straight from their victory at

Worcester. Carteret lost most of his guns, and was forced to take refuge in Elizabeth Castle.

His position now was desperate. Blake's fleet cut off all hope of help by sea. The garrison consisted largely of foreign mercenaries, who cared for little but their pay. Carteret sent word to the King that he could hold out eight months, but he was too optimistic. A great bomb from a mortar on the Town Hill fell on the Abbey Church in which gunpowder was stored. The explosion not only destroyed the powder, but two thirds of the provisions, and the troops began to desert. On 1 Dec. Sir George received a letter from the King, saying that help was impossible, and that he must make the best terms he could. On 3 Dec. his officers insisted on surrender. He opened negotiations with Heane, and after eight days' haggling Articles of Capitulation were agreed on. He was always good at a bargain, and he managed to secure extraordinarily lenient terms for himself. He was indemnified for all preceding acts of war, and allowed to keep his property, provided he committed no further hostile acts against Parliament, and was given a safe-conduct either to France or America. Other persons of position in the Castle were to retain their property on paying 'compositions' of not more than two years' income. The soldiers were given free transport either to France or England. On 15 Dec. the troops marched out with the honours of war. On the 16th Sir George sailed for St. Malo.

He was far too good a seaman to remain long unemployed. He obtained a commission in the French Navy, apparently as Vice-Admiral, under the Duke of Vendôme. On 6 Sept. 1652 Hyde wrote, "Sir George Carteret hath gotten infinite reputation in the late sea-fight with the Spaniard" (*Clarendon Papers*). In July 1653 Cromwell's Council of State resolved:— "We permit ten ships to go to the relief of Bordeaux" (where Frondeurs were in revolt), but, adds the writer, "the Duke of Vendôme with Sir George Carteret has so straitly besieged them, that it is thought our assistance will come too late". In November Hyde wrote again:— "Carteret in command of some French ships has captured the Vice-Admiral of Spain. He is a gallant, honest man, though Prince Rupert and the Lord Keeper cannot endure him" (*ibid*). In 1657 Cromwell made an alliance with France, and began to press for Sir George's arrest, apparently on a charge of trying to seduce the English troops

in Flanders. Mazarin would not surrender him, but in Aug.
imprisoned him in the Bastille. On 11 Nov. Lockhart, Cromwell's ambassador, reported an interview with the Cardinal.
Carteret had petitioned to be brought to trial, and the Cardinal
had demanded details of the charges against him. A stiff
struggle now took place behind the scenes. On 15 Dec. Lockhart wrote:— I gave the Cardinal the substance against Carteret.
He hath promised me justice, but said he would have hard work,
for the Duke of Vendôme had brigued (i.e. beguiled) the
Council, and the little Queen (i.e. Henrietta Maria) had begged
the Queen's friendship in it. I brought him to consider how
much his Highness' (i.e. Cromwell's) interests lay at stake. At
last he promised his least punishment should be to be sent out
of France". On the following day he wrote:— "Carteret is
banished from France, and is going to Venice" (ibid). He went
however to join Charles in the Netherlands.

In 1649 Charles had written:— "Carteret, I can never forget
the good services you have done to my father and to me ; if
God bless me, you shall find I do remember them to the advantage of you and yours" (Letter in St. Ouen's Manor). At the
Restoration he received his reward. He became Vice-Chamberlain of the King's Household, a post promised in 1647, a
Privy Councillor, and Treasurer of the Navy with a house in
Deptford Dockyard, then so much in the country that he was
able to take a pride in his cows and Kentish cherries. He was
also given manors in Devon and Cornwall to wipe out a loan
made to Charles I (S.P.). On 1 Jan. 1661 he resigned the office
of Bailiff of Jersey in favour of his brother-in-law, Sir Philippe
De Carteret (q.v.). When the King rode in state into London
on the day before his coronation, Carteret had a prominent
place in the pageant. "There followed the Vice-Chamberlain",
wrote Pepys, "a company of men all like Turks ; I know not
yet what they are for". At the Coronation itself he acted as
Almoner, the Earl of Essex being absent. In the same year
he was elected M. P. for Portsmouth.

His main work for the next six years lay in the Navy Office,
where he had as Clerk (or, as he would now be called, Permanent Under Secretary) Samuel Pepys ; and the diarist gives
many intimate pictures of him. This appointment was for him
a misfortune. Charles was desperately short of money. The
seamen's pay was in arrears, and the ships were seething with

discontent. The war with Holland was going badly, and the Dutch sailed up the Medway. For all this the blame was laid on Carteret's shoulders. He was obviously a very rich man ; and the suspicion spread that he was appropriating money belonging to the Fleet. In 1666 Parliament called for the Navy Accounts, and appointed a Committee to examine them. Pepys unblushingly confesses that the Accounts had been cooked. "Strange how we plot to make the charge of this war appear greater than it is". But this was to squeeze more money out of Parliament, not to enrich the Treasurer. The real trouble was the extraordinarily intricate system of accountancy. The Committee could make neither head nor tail of it ; nor could two Commissions of Accounts appointed afterwards. But eventually a Report was presented to the House that more than a million pounds could not be accounted for. Carteret protested that, so far from pocketing a penny, he had borrowed large sums on his own credit to keep the Fleet at sea ; but in 1669 the Commons by 138 votes to 129 found him guilty, and deprived him of his seat in the House. The Lords on the other hand decided that "Sir G. Carteret has done nothing contrary to his duty as Treasurer". The recent publication of the *Calendar of Treasury Books* has at last settled this question. The Editor, with far more evidence before him than either Commission had, entirely acquits Sir George. "The lasting impression is of an active, capable, honest body of officials struggling vainly against absolutely insuperable financial difficulties. Carteret kept the Fleet at sea by raising yearly a quarter of a million on his own credit at a time when the Treasury Lords were unable to assist him, and when the Fleet would otherwise have had to be laid up". The King knew this, and would not give him up to the wrath of the Commons. In 1666, when the trouble began, he allowed him to exchange posts with the Earl of Anglesey, and he became Receiver General and Treasurer of War for Ireland with an office in Dublin, a post he held till 1670. In 1673 he returned to the Admiralty as Commissioner.

Part of his wealth came from his colonial ventures. In 1663 he was one of eight Lords Proprietors to whom the King granted all the land between Virginia and Florida, a district to which had been given the name Carolina. In the following year he succeeded in establishing a New Jersey. In 1664 he and Lord Berkeley presented a detailed Report to the King showing how easy it would be to seize the sparsely populated Dutch Colony of New Netherlands, which divided the two blocks of British colonies on the Atlantic coast. An expedition was sent, which occupied the district, and the two originators of the scheme were rewarded with the part which now forms the State of New Jersey. In 1665 the two Lords Proprietors appointed Philippe De Carteret (q.v.), a distant cousin of Sir George, as Governor, and sent out the first shipload of colonists. (For the subsequent history of this colony see the article *De Carteret, Philippe, First Governor of New Jersey*). In 1670 the King made a grant to six Lords Proprietors, of whom De Carteret was one, of "all those islands commonly called the Bahama Islands with power to appoint Governors, make laws, wage wars, and transport colonists from England". Nor did he confine his interests to America. In 1672 he became one of the Foundation Members of the Royal African Company, to which the King granted the whole West Coast of Africa from Sallee to the Cape in return for a payment of two elephants to be made whenever he visited those dominions.

Speculations nearer home also attracted him. In 1665 he obtained a licence to dig for coal in Windsor Forest. In the same year he secured permission to try to reclaim many thousands of acres of land in Connaught which were flooded every tide. On 1667 he became one of the farmers of the Chimney Tax ; in the following year one of the farmers of the Import Duties into Ireland. Wherever an investment looked promising, Carteret jumped at it, for acquisitiveness was one strongly marked feature in his character. He was a very shrewd business man. Hyde described him as "the most dexterous man in business I have ever known" ; and Pepys said of him. "He is diligent, but all for his own ends and profit". When other Royalists lost their all, he came out of the Civil War with a very large fortune. This more unpleasant side of his nature is seen in his reluctance to help Castle Cornet, unless his hard-pressed fellow-Governor would pledge his estates to repay. His privateering came so near to piracy that at last the King was forced to disown it. At the surrender of Elizabeth Castle he secured far better terms for himself than for his officers. He was allowed to retain his estates and to remove all his furniture and plate to France. They had to compound for their estates by paying two years' income. In his colonial ventures he was the worst type of absentee landlord, contributing nothing toward the colony, but merely drawing his rents. Yet according to his lights he was no rogue. Pepys, who knew him as well as anyone, said, "I do take him for a most honest man". He was a tremendous worker. Even his enemy Coventry confessed, "He is a man that do take most pains and gives himself the most to do business of any about the Court without any desire of pleasure or divertisement" (*Pepys*) ; and he retained even amid the revels of Whitehall much of his Jersey Puritanism:— "He hath taken the liberty to tell the King the necessity of having at least a show of Religion in the Government and sobriety" (*ibid*). He was proud of his influence over Charles. "I have almost brought things to such a pass", he told Pepys, "as I mean to do, that the King will not be able to whip a cat, but I will be at his tail". Hyde called him the kindest of friends ; but he was a bad man to cross. Pepys described him as "the most passionate man in the world", and he was utterly merciless toward conquered foes. But the fine point in his character was his simple, undeviating, almost dog-like devotion to the Crown even in its darkest days.

The King was about to raise him to the peerage, when he died on 13 Jan. 1680 at Hawnes, Bedfordshire, in the manor he had bought. His widow was granted by royal warrant the same precedence that she would have had, if the promised creation had taken place ; and his grandson and heir was creation Baron Carteret of Hawnes. Sir George had three sons, Philippe (q.v.), James (q.v.), and George ; and five daughters, Anne, who was married to Sir Nicholas Stanning by the Bishop of London in the Savoy Chapel in 1662, Rachel, Elizabeth, Carolina, who married when fifteen Sir Thomas Scott, and Louise Margaretta, who when fifteen married Sir Robert Atkyns. It is noteworthy that in the Marriage Licences his daughters are called *De* Carteret. In his will Carteret left to each parish in Jersey a legacy for its poor. Portraits of Sir George and his wife by Lely are in St. Ouen's Manor. [Chevalier's *Journal* ; Clarendon's *History of the Rebellion* ; Pepys' *Diary* ; *Clarendon State Papers* ; Hoskins' *Charles II in the Channel Islands* ; *Dic. Nat. Biog.* Other authorities quoted above.]

CARTERET, JAMES (d. 1682), New Jersey Rebel. Second son of Sir George Carteret, Treasurer of the Navy (q.v.), and Elizabeth De Carteret, his wife. Chalmers in his *Annals* calls James illegitimate, and other writers have repeated this, but it is incorrect. A Royal Warrant of 11 Febr. 1680 grants "to Elizabeth, widow of the late Sir George Carteret, and to his younger son James the same precedence as they would have had, had Sir George been actually created a Baron, he having died before the Patent could be sued out". An illegitimate son would have had no precedence. Since his elder brother was born in Oct. 1642, James cannot have been born till 1643, and so was still a child in 1651 when, before the surrender of Elizabeth Castle, Lady Carteret sent her children to St. Malo. The boy was brought up in France, and, when old enough, like his father he was sent to sea, probably in a privateer. In 1664 he was in command of one of the slave-boats of his father's Royal African Company, and a letter from Barbados reported small-pox among the negroes on his ship (C. P.). In 1665 he entered the Navy, and, no doubt through Sir George's influence, became Lieutenant of the *Royal Prince*, and is mentioned as convoying a ship from Gottenburg (S. P.), and in the same year was put in command of the *Oxford* (22 guns) (S. P.). In July 1667 he was acting as Vice-Admiral of the British Fleet operating against the French in the West Indies. He kept Christmas in New Jersey. In 1668 he was in command of the *Foresight*, and in 1669 of the *Jersey* (48 guns). Then he left the Navy. In May 1671 he was appointed by the Lords Proprietors, of whom his father was one, a Landgrave of Carolina with "a barony of 12,000 acres in a commodious place near the head of Cooper River" (Pipon Papers in S. J. Library). In September he was in New York, and in May 1672 in New Jersey, of which his father was also a Lord Proprietor.

He found revolt brewing against his father and Philippe De Carteret (q.v.), a distant cousin, who was Governor. The malcontents, who refused to pay the quit-rents which the Lords Proprietors demanded, called an Assembly at Elizabethtown, and James put himself at their head. In the Report which the duly constituted officials sent to London they said:— "He gives forth continual threatenings against those that do not obey his orders, and has persons adhering to him that probably will be ready to execute his will, so that they may have the plundering of our estates ; and all these proceedings he carries on with the pretence that he hath power sufficient, he being Sir George Carteret's son, and that he himself is Proprietor, and can put out the Governor as he pleases, and that his Father hath given him his part of the Province, though he doth not shew any grant or commission, but saith he scorneth to shew his power to such fellows as we, neither need he so do being on his own land" (Whitehead. *East Jersey under the Proprietors.*). The rebels then deposed Philippe, and made James "President of the Country". He ordered the arrest of all officials who refused to recognize his authority, and the confiscation of their estates. Philippe sailed to England to report to the Lords Proprietors. The latter entirely repudiated James, and stern letters were sent to New Jersey, not only by the Proprietors but by the King, threatening his "high displeasure" on all who dared to resist the Governor's authority. The revolt then fizzled out, and James disappeared from New Jersey.

In April 1673, before the King's letter arrived, he had married Frances, daughter of Thomas de la Val, Mayor of New York. On 1 July he and his bride set out for Carolina, but the ship in which he was travelling was captured by the Dutch, and they were set ashore in Virginia. By April 1676 they were back in New York. Carteret's character now seems to have gone to pieces. We get a glimpse of him in Oct. 1679 in Dankers' *Journal*. The writer spent a night in a house at Harlem, "filled with people drinking for the most part execrable rum. Among the crowd was a person of quality, an Englishman named Capn. Carteret, a very profligate person. He married a merchant's daughter here, and has so lived with his wife that her father has been compelled to take her home again. He runs about the farmers, and stays where he can find most drink, and sleeps in barns on the straw. If he conducted himself properly, he could be Governor, for he seems to have been of a good understanding ; but that is now all drowned. His father, who will not acknowledge him as his son as before, allows him yearly as much only as is necessary for him to live".

Sir George died in 1680 a very rich man, and, as his elder brother was dead, James would normally have inherited a large share of the fortune, but his father left him only £100 a year, and that on condition that he renounced all claims to lands in Jersey. He returned however to Jersey, and was buried in St. Peter's

Church on 12 Sept. 1682. The Register records, "He was laid in the earth by De Carterets, three of whom were Knights". (These must have been Sir Edward, his uncle, Sir Philippe, his cousin, the Bailiff, and Sir George, his nephew. Two of these however were Baronets). This shows that, in spite of his past, he was not disowned by his family. Three years later his wife came to Jersey with her two small children, George and Elizabeth. She died in 1688, and the children were put under a guardian. When George came of age in 1702 he went to New York to try to recover property which her father had settled on his mother at the time of her marriage, but on his return he was killed in an accident in London (Pipon Papers in S. J. Library). Elizabeth married (1) Philippe De Carteret, Seigneur of Rozel, (2) Philippe Pipon (q.v.), Seigneur of Noirmont.

CARTERET, JOHN, EARL GRANVILLE (1690—1763), Seigneur of St Ouen's, Bailiff of Jersey, Whig Statesman. Eldest surviving son of George, first Baron Carteret, and Lady Grace Granville. He was great-grandson of Sir George Carteret (q.v.) of the Restoration, and grandson of Sir Philip Carteret (q.v.), who fell in the Battle of Solebay. He was born at Hawnes, his father's seat in Bedfordshire, 22 April 1690, and educated at Westminster School under Knipe, and when ten years old contributed to the volume of Latin verses written by Westminster scholars on the death of the Duke of Gloucester. He matriculated from Christ Church Oxford in 1706. Though he took no degree, until he was made a D. C. L. in 1756, he became probably the most erudite of English statesmen. Macaulay wrote of him: "No public man had such profound and extensive learning. He was familiar with the ancient writers, and loved to sit up till midnight discussing philological and metrical questions with Bentley. His knowledge of modern languages was prodigious. The Privy Council, when he was present, needed no interpreter. He spoke and wrote French, Italian, Spanish, Portuguese, German, even Swedish. He had pushed his researches into the most obscure nooks of literature. He was as familiar with Canonists and Schoolmen as with Orators and Poets. He had read all that the universities of

Saxony and Holland had produced on the most intricate questions of public law" *(Essay on Walpole's Letters).* But he was no
bookworm:— "No public man of that age had greater courage,
greater ambition, greater activity, greater talents for debate or
declamation. In council, in debate, in society he was all life
and energy. His measures were strong, prompt, and daring,
his oratory animated and glowing, his spirits consistently high"
(ibid).

On his coming of age in 1711 he entered the House of Lords,
and to the horror of his family with their Stuart traditions
threw in his lot with the Whigs. The accession of George I
in 1714 brought the Whigs into power, and in 1715 he became
a Lord of the Bedchamber and Bailiff of Jersey, and in 1716
Lord Lieutenant of Devon. In their hour of victory however
the Whigs split into sections, and Carteret became identified
with the anti-Walpole group. In 1719 he was sent as Envoy
Extraordinary to Sweden, where he brilliantly negotiated peace
between Sweden, Hanover, Prussia, and Denmark, and brought
to an end the war in the North. He was rewarded by being
made a Privy Councillor and one of the Secretaries of State.
As George I knew no English, and Carteret was the only
Minister who could speak German, he now gained great influence with the King. There were then two Foreign Secretaries,
one for the North, the other for the South. To Carteret was
entrusted the Southern Department, which included France,
Italy, Spain, and the Colonies. In 1724 a trivial incident, the
failure of the ambassador whom Carteret had chosen to secure
a French Dukedom for a Frenchman who was to marry the niece
of one of the King's mistresses, was used by Walpole to drive
him out of the Ministry. He was however sent as Lord Lieutenant to Ireland, where Swift, that savage critic of English
rule, admitted that "he had a gentler manner of binding the
chains than most of his predecessors" *(Letter to Gay).* In
1730 Walpole felt strong enough in the favour of the new King,
George II, to dismiss him. "I had some difficulty in getting
him out", he said, "but he shall find more difficulty to get in".
(Hervey's Memoirs).

For the next twelve years Carteret was leader of the opposition
to Walpole in the Lords. In 1741 in the greatest speech of his
life he moved that the King be asked to banish Walpole from
his counsels for ever ; but he was heavily defeated. In the

following year however Walpole resigned. Carteret now came back into office, being appointed (Feb. 1742) Secretary of State for Northern Europe. He at once abandoned Walpole's policy of insular isolation, and plunged the country into the maelstrom of continental politics, and perhaps it was his Jersey blood that made him so determined to humble the rising power of France. His knowledge of German gave him the same influence over George II that he had had with his father. He accompanied him abroad, and was present in his coach at the Battle of Dettingen (1743). But the war became unpopular, and Carteret was made the scapegoat. Pitt thundered against him as "that execrable minister", "an English minister without an English heart", who was making "this powerful nation" a hewer of wood and drawer of water for "the despicable little electorate" of Hanover ; and in Nov. 1744 Carteret was forced to resign.

In the same year by his mother's death he succeeded to the title of Earl Granville. In 1746 the ministry resigned, and the King asked Granville and Lord Bath to form a new ministry. They accepted the seals of office, but failed to secure colleagues or Parliamentary support, and the Long Administration, as the wits called it, lasted only four days. But he still retained the King's favour. In 1749 he was given the Garter. He was offered again the Lord Lieutenancy of Ireland, but refused. In 1751 he was appointed Lord President of the Council, and he held this position for twelve years till his death. This work exactly suited him. He presided over meetings of the Privy Council as the King's representative. "I am the King's President", he said, "I know nothing of the Pelhams" (the Prime Minister and his brother). He was independent of party politics and not responsible for policy. But his ripe wisdom and profound knowledge of European diplomacy were there to inform and advise. He died in his house in Arlington Street, 2 Jan. 1763, and was buried in General Monk's vault in Henry VII's Chapel in Westminster Abbey.

Historians have wondered why with such brilliant talents he never became Prime Minister, and was outstripped by commonplace men like Newcastle and Pelham. Three reasons are obvious. His main handicap was a haughty aloofness, an unconscious arrogance, partly aristocratic, partly intellectual. He despised his opponents too much to oppose them. He was too proud to court popularity, and never attempted to build up a party of his own. He disdained to secure supporters by judicious distribution of patronage. "What is it to me", he exclaimed, "who is Judge or Bishop? My business is to make Kings, and maintain the balance of Europe". He hardly recognized the existence of the House of Commons. Like all his ancestors he was a King's man. "Give a man the Crown on his side," he said, "and he can defy anything". That may have been true under the Tudors, but it was emphatically not the case in the eighteenth century. Another cause of his comparative failure was his intemperance. "He degraded himself", wrote Lord Chesterfield, "by the vice of drinking, which together with a great stock of Greek and Latin he brought away from Oxford, and retained ever after" (Letters). Macaulay says that he drank half a gallon of burgundy daily ; and his colleagues often note in their letters that he had too obviously dined before arriving at Council meetings. The Ministry of 1742, of which he was a member, was called the Drunken Administration. This habit probably accounts for the strange inertia which overtook him at critical moments. He who in his early years had been so hard a worker, who still sometimes was so full of energy that pamphleteers nicknamed him Jack Headlong, at other times became utterly apathetic and could not be roused to any interest in public affairs. Small wonder that he gained a reputation for being erratic and unstable. Lord Rosebery says of him in his Chatham:— "To a person of commanding beauty and an open and engaging demeanour he united superb qualities of intellect developed by ardent study. He was a scholar of signal excellence, know the whole Greek Testament by heart, and spoke German fluently. His contempt for money amounted to recklessness. He was a single-minded, jovial, reckless patriot, but out of touch with politicians, unsuited to parliamentary government, and so almost ineffectual".

When only twenty he married Frances, daughter of Sir Robert Worsley, a beautiful hoyden of sixteen, who on one occasion tossed Dean Swift's decanal hat out of the window on to the top of the high railings of a house across the street. By her he had three sons, Robert (q.v.) and two others who died in infancy, and four lovely daughters, who all made brilliant marriages. Grace married the Earl of Dysart ; Louisa married Lord Weymouth ; Georgiana married first John Stanhope, brother of the Duke of Marlborough, and then Earl

Cowper ; Frances married Lord Tweeddale. Lady Carteret died suddenly in 1743 while playing the harp, and was buried in Westminster Abbey. In 1744 Carteret married again, his bride being Lady Sophia Fermor, daughter of the Earl of Pontefract, the reigning toast of the season, a girl considerably younger than his own daughters. She however died in the following year, after giving birth to a daughter, who later married Lord Shelburne.

As a reward for the loyalty of the Carterets during the Civil War the office of Bailiff of Jersey had become hereditary in the family. In 1715, on the death of his distant cousin Sir Charles De Carteret (q.v.), Lord Carteret had become Seigneur of St. Ouen's and Bailiff. He never visited the Island, but he by no means regarded his Bailiffship as a sinecure. He corresponded regularly about things in Jersey with his kinswoman Elisabeth De Carteret, who had married Philippe Pipon (q.v.). In spite of his many interests he insisted that his Lieut-Bailiffs should always consult him before taking any important step. He interfered in elections of Jurats, sending recommendations to the voters to support the candidate he favoured. He appeared before the Privy Council, when Jersey matters were discussed, and often managed to secure privileges for the island. He even interfered in personal quarrels. He took infinite pains for example to reconcile Josué and Philippe Pipon (q.v.) after a fourteen years' feud, persuading them to submit their differences to arbitration. Two of his letters to Elisabeth Pipon are in the S.J. Library. In one he tells her that he heard that his Lieut.-Bailiff "has not behaved as he ought" toward her, and that he has rebuked him, and sent him "positive directions" to call and show her the letter. In the other he says that he has ordered the Lieut.-Bailiff to inform the Jurats that he wishes her husband to be elected Jurat at the next vacancy. Carteret was often in financial difficulties. In 1720 he sold Sark to Colonel John Johnson, but got no benefit, as the agent sent to receive the money decamped with it. In 1722 he parted with some of his Jersey property, selling the Fief of Vingt Livres to Josué Pipon (q.v.) and the Fief of La Motte to Jean Dumaresq. [Pemberton's *Carteret* (with bibliography) ; Ballantyne's *Lord Carteret* ; Oman's *Unfortunate Colonel Despard* ; Lucas' *George II and his Ministers* ; *Dic. Nat. Biog.* ; *Encyc. Brit.* ; other works mentioned above.]

CARTERET, SIR PHILIPPE (1642—72) Lieutenant R.N.
Eldest son of Sir George Carteret (q.v.) and Elizabeth De
Carteret. Born in Jersey, and baptized in Mont Orgueil 3 Nov.
1642, Sir Philippe De Carteret (q.v.) being his godfather.

At the Restoration he entered the Navy, and in 1660 was
Lieutenant of the *Dover*, and then of the *Plymouth*. In 1661
he was Lieutenant of the *Foresight* and in 1665 of the *Royal
Oak*. In that year he married. The story of his courtship is
one of the best known passages in Pepys' Diary. Pepys was
intimate with the household of the Earl of Sandwich, and as
a child the Earl's daughter Jemimah, a quiet, shy, delicate girl,
regarded him as a kind of benevolent uncle, who used to take
her to see the lions in the Tower. Pepys was Clerk of the
Acts of the Navy under Sir George Carteret, Treasurer of the
Navy. In 1665 Jemimah was nineteen, and Pepys describes
how he played the part of match-maker. On 3 Feb. he visited
Lady Sandwich:— "She discoursed largely to me of a match,
if it could be thought fit by my Lord, for my Lady Jemimah
with Sir G. Carteret's eldest son. I doubt he hath yet no settled
estate in land ; but I will inform myself, and give her my
opinion". On 23 June Lord Sandwich after a Tangier committee took Pepys aside:— "He did tell me how much concerned
he was to dispose of his children, and would have my advice
and help. He propounded to match my Lady Jemimah to Sir
G. Carteret's eldest son, which I approved of, and did undertake
the speaking with him about it as from myself". On the
following day he wrote:— "To Sir G. Carteret, and in the best
manner I could I moved the business. He received it with
great content and thanks to me, and promised he would do what
he possibly could for his son to render him fit for my Lord's
daughter". Next day the Diary says:— "I again visited Sir
G. Carteret, and received his (and now his lady's) full consent
to my proposal. My Lord Sandwich did direct me to return
to Sir George, and give him thanks for his acceptance of the
offer, and that he would next day be willing to discourse with
him about the business". "My Lord, I perceive intends to give
£5,000 with her, and expects about £800 jointure". On 2 July
he wrote:— "Sir George did send me word that the business is
fully agreed on, and is mightily liked by the King and the Duke
of York". On the 4th Sandwich entered in his Diary:— "This
morning Sir George Carteret and I signed and sealed agreements

for the marriage between his eldest son and my eldest daughter".

Meanwhile the young people had never yet met. On 9 July Pepys wrote:— "I took occasion to have much discourse with Mr. Ph. Carteret, and find him a very modest man, and I think verily of mighty good nature and pretty understanding". On the 14th we read:— "Mr. Carteret is to go to visit her tomorrow. My proposal of waiting on him (he being to go alone to persons all strangers to him) was well accepted. So I go with him". The entries now become amusing:— "15 July. Mr. Carteret and I to the ferry at Greenwich. Lord! what silly discourse we had as to love-matters, he being the most awkward man I ever met in my life as to that business". They arrived at dark. "To supper, and after supper to talk again, he taking no notice of the lady. So they led him to his chamber, where I stayed a little to know how he liked the lady, which he told me he did mightily, but, Lord, in the dullest insipid manner ever lover did". Next day was Sunday, and he wrote:— "Having trimmed myself, down to Mr. Carteret. I taught him what to do, to take the lady always by the hand to lead her, and that he should make these and these compliments". After church they came home by coach, "Mr. Carteret not having had the confidence to take his lady once by the hand, which I told him of, when we come home". On Monday the visit ended. "Before we went, I took my Lady Jem apart, and would know how she liked this gentleman. She blushed, and answered that she could readily obey what her father and mother had done". They had no long engagement. On the 31st they were married in Deptford Church. Pepys was late for the wedding, being held up at the Isle of Dogs, but he met the bride and bridegroom returning from the church. That evening "I got into the bridegroom's chamber, while he undressed, till he was called to the bride's chamber, and into bed they went. I kissed the bride in bed, and so the curtains drawn with the greatest gravity".

On 13 April 1667 Philippe was knighted by the King at Whitehall; and in May the two families combined to buy from Sir Samuel Luke a fine house at Hawnes in Bedfordshire, part of which had been designed by Inigo Jones, to be the young couple's home. It cost £25,000, and from it Philippe's son George took later the title Baron Carteret of Hawnes. Philippe now apparently had no naval duties, and settled down to a country life, and became "very busy and industrious" in county affairs (Sandwich MSS.). He had many hobbies, such as painting, drawing, and watch-making, and he became a Fellow of the Royal Society. Hawnes however proved rather beyond their means, and Lady Sandwich grew worried, because Jemimah was running into debt, and borrowing money (Carte MSS.)

In 1672 the Third Dutch War broke out, and Carteret was recalled to the fleet. His father-in-law, who was Admiral, took him on to his flag-ship, the *Royal James* (100 guns). On 28 May the English and Dutch fleets met in Solebay. In that Battle Carteret's ship fought one of the most famous sea-fights in History. She was grappled by the *Groot Hollandia* for an hour and a half, during which she repelled in hand to hand fighting attempt after attempt to board her. "Cuff it out to the last man", was Sandwich's order, though six hundred of his men had fallen. But, while this was going on, her gunners on the further side had sunk four enemy ships. Then a party of English soldiers sprang on to the Dutchman's deck, swarmed up its masts, and cut the ropes that were holding the ships together. The *Royal James* broke loose, but, under cover of smoke from enemy broadsides, a Dutch fireship got alongside and grappled her again. In a moment she was on fire from stem to stern, and Carteret and his father-in-law died together. (A detailed account of the Battle is given in Harris' *Life of Edward Montagu*.)

He left three sons, George (b. 1667), who was created Baronet in 1681, Philip (b. 1669), who became a Captain in the Royal Marines, and Edward (b. 1671), who was made Postmaster-General. [Authorities quoted above.]

CARTERET, ROBERT, Earl Granville, (1721—76), Bailiff. Only surviving son of Lord John Carteret (q.v.) and Frances Worsley. Born 21 Sept. 1721. Matriculated at Oxford from St. John's College 1738. M.A. 1743. The *Complete English Peerage* of 1776 describes him as "in his youth what is styled a Buck. His dress, his address, his manners all united to proclaim him one. The allowance his father made him, which was very handsome, was not sufficient to support his follies". Another account says:— "He commonly wore a large coachman's hat with the flaps down, a jockey's striped waistcoat, and garters below his knees". Elizabeth Wyndham wrote in 1744:— "Young Carteret has been at Wooburn, where he has raised the Devil in a manner so indecent that I cannot give you details. The Duke has told his father that he ought to have him put under control, for his head appears to be turned, as it may well be, for he drinks brandy from morning till night". Horace Walpole wrote:— "A fortnight ago he was at the Duke of Bedford's. At five in the morning he waked the Duke and Duchess all bloody, with the lapel of his coat held up full of ears. He had been in the stables and cropped all the horses". Twenty years later Elizabeth Montagu wrote:— "It is grievous to see such a creature represent the late Earl, who had all the grace and dignity of manner added to great talents". The office of Bailiff had now become so hereditary in the house of Carteret, that, when Earl Granville died in 1763, this drunken nitwit automatically succeeded to the Bailiffship, though he was so notoriously a bad character that his father had disowned him. He remained Bailiff for thirteen years, and pocketed his fees, but never visited the island. A contemporary Memoir describes him in 1776 as "rather deficient in his intellects, fond of low company, profuse, fickle, and debauched. He appeared constantly in the mean garment of a groom or coachman, shunning his equals, and rioting in taverns with pimps and prostitutes. The conclusion of his inglorious amours was a Fleet marriage with one Molly Paddock, a woman of vile extraction, bold, loose, and vulgar, the superintendent of a bagnio". He died childless 13 Feb. 1776, and his title became extinct.

CHEVALIER, JEAN (1589—1675), Chronicler. Second son of Clement Chevalier of St. Helier's and Jeanne Malzard. Since the Burial Register states that he was eighty-six when he died, he must have been born in 1589, but the exact date is unknown, as the Baptism Register does not begin till 1596. His family took their full share of honorary municipal service. His step-brother, Thomas, was Fouageur of the Town ; his elder brother, Clement, was Vingtenier of the Town Vingtaine ; and Jean is mentioned in 1624 as Constable's Officer. On his

brother's death in 1638 he was elected to succeed him as
Vingtenier, a post which he held till the conquest of the island
by the Parliament in 1651. In 1646 he became a Deacon of
the Town Church, and retained this office till his death. During
the whole Civil War he lived in his house in the Market Place
(Royal Square), which stood on the site of the house, built by
his grandson, Clement Chevalier, which now faces the back of
the statue. When, at the beginning of the troubles, in 1643
the Parliamentary leaders came to him to demand the keys of
the part of the church in which the parish pikes and cannon
were stored, in order that they might arm a party to arrest Sir
Philippe De Carteret (q.v.), he refused to surrender them,
"knowing that this would lead to bloodshed, though Le Boutillier threatened to pink me with his sword" (*Journal*) ; and they
had to break down the door. On the last day of the bombardment of the Town from the Castle a cannon-ball struck the
ridge of Chevalier's roof, bringing down the thatch and clay
(*Journal*). All through the struggle he made notes daily of
everything that happened ; and, when the war was over, he
wrote his book, which he called *Recueil des Chosses le plus
remarcables que se sont passés en ceste Isle de Jersey*, in the
form of a Journal "with the sole intention of leaving my children
something to remember me by, and to warn them against undertaking anything contrary to the laws of God or the authority
of the King". The result was a document of first-class historic
importance, described by the Commission on Historical Manuscripts (1871) as "the production of an eye-witness and a shrewd
observer as well as an official actor in many of the scenes that
he describes, whose style of composition, though quaint and
somewhat diffuse, leads to the conclusion that the chronicler
was by no means an illiterate man". It not only contains the
notes of an extremely accurate recorder, but also copies of
official documents reproduced in full. Hoskins speaks of him
as "a subaltern parochial officer, whose most authoritative
source of information could have been little more than second-
hand backstairs gossip" (*Charles II in the Channel Islands.*) ;
but backstairs gossip would not provide verbatim copies of
official correspondence, nor exact and detailed information about
all that was happening in both camps in Guernsey. Chevalier's
marriage with Marie La Cloche had brought him into the
family circles of the Royalist leaders. She was sister of Etienne

La Cloche (q.v.), the Royalist Rector of St. Ouen's, and her cousin, Jurat La Cloche, Seigneur of Longueville, had married a sister of Sir Philippe De Carteret. Moreover the details that Chevalier gives about the life of that roystering old ex-pirate, Sir Henry Mainwaring, show that the two men must have become intimate, and suggest that here was another source of his information. A third was probably Lord Colepepper, one of the Prince's Council, who lodged with Chevalier's son, while he was in the island.

The book shows Chevalier to have been a man of simple piety, not untinged with superstition — a comet or the striking of a steeple by lightning are to him unmistakable omens of disaster — a staunch Calvinist, much misliking Dean Bandinel's Anglican innovations, a Royalist, who bases his politics on the Bible, and makes much of a text in which Jews were bidden to pray for even a heathen King like Nebuchadnezzar. But the book is no party plea, glorifying the Cavaliers, and exulting in their victory. He does not hesitate to criticize the Royalist Governors. His constantly recurring refrain is a cry of horror at the wickedness of civil war:— "All is agonizing in civil war. It is a two-edged sword destroying life and goods. It sets father against son, brother against brother. Friends become foes. Justice and the fear of God are wholly overthrown. Robbery, rapine, and murder spread throughout the land". When introducing the first men who took up arms he exclaims:— "I am still astounded that He Who punisheth the wicked can refrain from hurling his avenging thunderbolt against men such as these". He carried his book from the outbreak of war in 1643 almost to the conquest of the island by Parliament in 1651, and he hints that he meant to write a sequel, describing Jersey during the Commonwealth and after the Restoration. This unfortunately was never written. When the King was restored, Chevalier came back to public life, and, though well over seventy, was one of the officers who compiled the *Extente* published in 1668. He and his wife died within a few days of one another in 1675, she on 23 Nov., and he on the 30th. They had five children, Clement, who became a draper in the town, Jean and Thomas, who were Vingteniers, Jeanne, and Marie. The original manuscript of his book is in the S.J. Museum, and the Société printed it in 1906. [His own *Journal* ; article on La Famille Chevalier in *Bull.* V. ; Durell's edition of Falle's

Jersey ; Hoskins' *Charles II in the Channel Islands* ; Saunders' *Jean Chevalier and his Times* ; *Report of the Commission on Historical Manuscripts* 1871 ; *Dic. Nat. Biog.* ; Extracts from the Journal with a running commentary by Dr. Hoskins appeared monthly in *The Guernsey Magazine* 1876—8.]

CORBET, MOYSE (1728—1817), Lieutenant-Governor. Eldest son of Moyse Corbet (son of Moyse, son of Moyse, son of Moyse, son of Moyse, all of St. Helier's) and Françoise Corbet (daughter of Jurat James Corbet, ex-Vicomte). Born at St. Helier's, and baptized in the Town Church, Jan. 21, 1728. When his father died in 1747, Charles Lempriere, Lieutenant-Bailiff, (q.v.) who had married Corbet's first cousin Elizabeth, placed him in the office of John Sharpe, a famous London lawyer. But Moyse did not like Law ; so in April 1748 his family bought him a commission in the Royal Fusiliers (Messervy's *Journal*). Here he did well. Lord Robert Bertie said at the court martial:— "My first acquaintance with him was in 1754, when I was honoured with the command of the Royal Fusiliers. I found him Adjutant and Captain-Lieutenant. He soon afterwards got a company ; and, the regiment coming to England, from his very extraordinary merit as an Adjutant I was induced to solicit the Duke of Cumberland that he might continue in that post. In 1756 he went with me in the regiment on the squadron for the relief of Minorca. After the action the regiment landed at Gibraltar. In 1759 he was obliged to come to England on account of health. The year after I made him my aide-de-camp. In 1761 he was made Major, and returned to Gibraltar, and continued there till the regiment came to England. A year or two afterwards he was obliged to quit the service on account of health after having served more than ten years to my entire satisfaction."

He retired in July 1766 and settled in Jersey as a half-pay officer. Being hard pressed for money he had to sell his property ; so, when he began to intervene in local politics, it was thrown in his teeth that he was not even a rate-payer. But he persisted, and in spite of his debt to the Lieutenant-Bailiff became a leader of the anti-Lempriere party. At a Parish

Assembly in the Town Church a fortnight after the Revolt of 1769 he cried, "Now or never is the time to grasp your freedom, and to break the yoke of tyranny". Messervy, a loyal Lempriere supporter, disliked him intensely. He calls him "as eccentric as his father", and adds, "His only talent is one for bad manners". At the next Parish Assembly he produced a petition for signature. The Rector (Dupré) and the Constable (Durell) left the Church, but Corbet made his speech. Messervy calls the document "as contemptible as its author", and says, "The poor man's booby face excited general laughter". (Jean's portrait of him shows a face that no one could describe as intellectual.) But the Petition received hundreds of signatures. It was an able and moderate statement of the case for reform. Corbet published it as a pamphlet with explanatory notes, *Griefs de l'Isle de Jersey contenus dans une Requeste presentée à Sa Majesté par Moïse Corbet, Ecuyer. 1770.* On January 25, 1770, he took it to London.

The Government had begun to realize that the Lempriere autocracy must be curbed. When Corbet called on Lord Albemarle, the Governor, with the Petition, he made so favourable an impression, that Albemarle appointed him Receiver-General in place of Lempriere's son-in-law Ricard, and promised that, when Colonel Bentinck, who had been sent to restore order, was withdrawn, Corbet should be the next Lieutenant-Governor. He succeeded to the post on 4 April, 1771. For the next ten years his main anxiety was France. In his first speech to the States he urged the repair of the magazines and guard-houses. The position steadily worsened. In 1776 the French began to send help to the revolted American colonies. In 1778 the Government let loose the Jersey privateers upon the French shipping. Dumouriez, the commander at Cherbourg, wrote:— "During the winter of 1778 there were in St. Helier's roads more than 150 French prizes and in the island over 1,500 seamen, prisoners from these vessels" (*Bull* VI.). Nor did the Jerseymen confine this buccaneering to the sea. The *Gazette des Deux Ponts* (Sept. 1778) reported:— "Jersey pirates landed near Caen, and carried off oxen, cows, and sheep, all the Curé's linen, and even the two washerwomen". Such acts invited reprisals.

Many plans for the capture of Jersey were discussed by the French Court, and in Dec. 1778 permission was given to a roistering adventurer, the Prince of Nassau, to raise a legion for this purpose. Corbet had a good spy service. "Not a cat can arrive here by land or sea", wrote the Commandant of Lower Normandy, "without his knowing it". And Jersey prepared for attack. On 15 April, 1779, Corbet sent all the captured French prizes in St. Aubin's Bay to England for safety. At 7 a.m. on 1 May the enemy was sighted. Corbet with the 78th Highlanders and Militia hurried to St. Ouen's Bay. There he sat all day watching the absurdest of fiascos. He dated his dispatch to Lord Weymouth, "From the heights above St. Ouen's Bay, observing the movements of the Enemy. 3.p.m.". As the tide was falling, the French warships refused to come close enough in to cover the landing with their guns. As their boats were uninsured, the captains of the transports refused to take them within range of the Jersey artillery. After hours of frantic argument and threats the Prince was forced to withdraw. Corbet assumed he would return. He sat up all night in St. Lawrence' Guardhouse, receiving reports hourly by horsemen from every coast. But the French were back in St. Malo. Meanwhile a cutter which he had sent to Portsmouth met in mid-Channel Admiral Arbuthnot's fleet on its way to America. This altered its course, and on 2 May anchored off Jersey. A few days later British frigates sailed into Cancale Bay and destroyed five of the Prince's ships. For the moment the danger was over. Corbet was commended for the steps he had taken. Lord Weymouth wrote, "I have great pleasure in acquainting you that his Majesty has been graciously pleased to approve of the diligence you have shown".

But a new Adventurer, the Chevalier de Luxembourg, hoped that he might succeed where Nassau had failed. He chose as his Commander a dare-devil soldier of fortune, the Baron de Rullecourt (q.v. Appendix I). This time the secret was well kept. Not even the Governor of Lower Normandy knew what was intended. Rullecourt's men were supposed to be gathering to form the crew of a new privateer. Corbet was worried about spies. On 15 Feb., 1780 he informed the States that signal fires had often been noticed on the north-east coast, which had been answered by other fires from France ; and the States offered two thousand livres reward for the detection of the signallers, but in vain (A.E.). No one knew when or how the next blow would fall. Corbet had under his command five

companies of the 83rd Foot (the rest were in Guernsey), whom
he quartered in Grouville to protect the eastern parishes, five
companies of the 78th Highlanders (again the other wing was
in Guernsey), whom he kept in the Town in the Hospital, and
half the newly raised 95th Foot, which he stationed at St.
Peter's to secure the west, a corps of gunners and a corps of
Invalids in Gorey and Elizabeth Castles. He had also the five
Militia Regiments ; and a few months later W.C. Lempriere,
the new Lieutenant-Bailiff, himself a Militia Colonel, stated
that these numbered "almost 3,000" men (*Bull* V). There was
a good shore-outpost string of batteries and guardhouses, admirably devised, but useless unless the men were on the alert.
Corbet's weakest point was that he had no naval scouts ; but
this was not his fault. He had prayed the Admiralty to provide
them, but had been refused. And so, when Rullecourt had
actually sailed, though he was held up by weather for a week
off Chausey, Corbet had no warning.

About twenty to seven on the morning of 6 Jan. 1781,
Corbet was awakened by the simultaneous arrival of three
messengers with news that the Market Place (now the Royal
Square) was full of French troops. Rullecourt had landed at
La Rocque, and reached the Town undetected. Corbet came
down buttoning his uniform, told one of his visitors to take a
horse and warn the troops at Grouville, and sent another to
rouse those in the Hospital. Then he made his first mistake.
His house, the Manor of La Motte, at the corner of what are
now Grosvenor and St. James' Streets, was then the last house
in the Town. North, south, and east stretched open country.
He had still a horse in his stable. If he had acted promptly, he
could have escaped in the dim light of dawn, and by a detour
have joined his troops. Witnesses at his trial disagreed as to
how much time he had, but he admitted that he had "little more
than five minutes", and that he spent those precious minutes
"reflecting" how to make his escape. Before his reflections
were finished, the French were at his door.

They took him to the Market Place. His wife accompanied
him, but was escorted home. After some delay, while keys
were found to unlock the Court, and vain attempts made to
discover Jurat Pipon, who in Lempriere's absence was acting
as Lieutenant-Bailiff, a few officials were gathered, including
Durell, the Solicitor-General, and La Cloche, the Constable of

St. Helier's. Rullecourt then put up an audacious bluff. If it came to a fight, his 650 tired and seasick men hardly had a dog's chance against Corbet's forces. But he told Corbet that the troops in the Market were only his vanguard, that 4,000 others had already occupied all important points in the island, that 10,000 more were on the sea and would land before nightfall, that the troops at Grouville had surrendered, and that he would give up the Town to fire and pillage, unless Corbet signed an immediate capitulation. Corbet was a St. Helier's man. His forefathers for generations were buried in the Town church. He had known the townsfolk since he was a boy. Resistance seemed hopeless. For a time he refused to sign. "I heard", said one witness, "the Lieutenant-Governor tell the French General that being a prisoner he had no right to capitulate, upon which the General, lifting up his arm, said in a very peremptory voice, 'Monsieur, I shall insist, I shall insist', and added he would give up the town to be plundered and laid to ashes. The Lieutenant-Governor said what he signed would have no effect on those who succeeded him in command. The General still insisted." According to another witness, "He seemed to delay as long he could in asking to read and making difficulties about the wording", but Rullecourt "put a watch on the table, and said, by such a time, if the capitulation was not settled, hostilities should begin". At about 8.30 Corbet signed:— "The local Militia shall deposit their arms in the Court House, until it be settled whether the island shall be kept by France or England. The garrison of Elizabeth Castle shall march out with all the honours of war in order to return to England. While waiting for transports, they shall deposit their arms in the Court House, and live unarmed in the houses of the inhabitants. Their arms will be returned at their departure. The same applies to all other forts, castles, and troops in the island". Corbet then signed orders to all commanding officers to surrender. His defence was that he knew that his chit would be ignored, and that by signing he gained time for the troops to assemble:— "In signing to save the town I was acting a feigned part. My imprisonment absolutely abrogated my command. I considered that by signing, not only would the town be saved, but by tying down the French to inexertion it would defeat the advantage gained by surprise by giving the Regulars and Militia the opportunity of collecting unmolested".

But he was not allowed to remain passive. The guns of Elizabeth Castle were booming out the alarm. As Corbet's message was disregarded, Rullecourt insisted that he should ride out with him to order the Castle to surrender. "But before we reached the Bridge a cannon-shot broke the leg of an officer. The Baron returned in a violent rage to the Court, threatening the town with destruction". Meanwhile the Highlanders had withdrawn from the Hospital to Gallows Hill west of the town. Here Militia regiments joined them ; and a little later Major Peirson (q.v. Appendix I) arrived from St. Peter's with the 95th. As senior Regular Officer present he assumed the command. He did not feel quite happy about disobeying Corbet's orders ; so he sent two officers with a flag of truce to ask whether the Lieutenant-Governor was a prisoner or not. One of these said at the court-martial:—"We met Lieutenant-Governor Corbet with the French General. We asked him if he was a prisoner. He did not answer, saying everything was settled. Not having satisfied us respecting his being a prisoner, we asked him a second time. The French General answered he was not, pointing to the Lieutenant-Governor's sword, which he had by his side. A second message came from Major Peirson asking if the Lieutenant-Governor would let him know, if he was a prisoner. The French General, on being made acquainted with this, permitted him to go with us to the Major under the care of a French officer. On our return we perceived the King's troops advancing from the hill. The Lieutenant-Governor said to Major Peirson, 'This has been a very sudden surprise. I was made prisoner before I was out of bed'. The Major answered, 'Sir, give me leave to inform you that the 78th and 95th have not been the least surprised as yet'." Corbet then read the terms of capitulation, and quoted the figures about the French troops that Rullecourt had given him. "Major Peirson then told him the commanding officers were determined to die before they would surrender. He then pulled out his watch, and asked the Lieutenant-Governor how long he would require to go back and inform the French General. The Lieutenant-Governor asked for half an hour. The Major told him he should attack in ten minutes".

Corbet had hardly reached the Court, when the troops burst into the Market Place. Rullecourt took him by the arm, and led him out on to the steps overlooking the mêlée. As they appeared, two bullets passed through Corbet's hat, and Rulle-court fell mortally wounded. In a quarter of an hour the fight was over, and the French threw down their arms. Corbet at once resumed command. He confined the prisoners in the Town Church. He kept the troops under arms all night waiting for the non-existent 10,000 men from St. Malo. He even dressed some of the Militia in captured French uniforms to decoy the invaders ashore. Next day he said in his orders:— "The Governor cannot sufficiently express his thanks to the Regulars for their distinguished behaviour on Saturday, by which and the assistance of the Militia he was released, and the country saved". He appeared at the head of the troops at the funeral of Peirson who had fallen in the battle. Contemporary letters show that opinion in the island was divided on the question of his behaviour. "Many approve and others condemn the conduct of our Governor", wrote Poingdestre (*Bull* XIII). He himself seems to think that Corbet's action saved the Town ; but Tho-mas Pipon of La Moye, one of the Militia Colonels, wrote, "His conduct so sunk and depreciated him in the opinion of everybody" that the Militia officers had decided to resign, if he were not removed (*Bull* V).

On 25 Jan. orders arrived for his arrest. On 17 Feb. he left the island, and on 1 May his court-martial at the Horse Guards began. The charge was "that he did, contrary to his duty and the trust reposed in him, sign with the commander of the French troops articles of capitulation, although the enemy had become masters only of the town of St. Hillier, and Eliza-beth Castle as well as the other forts were still in custody of his Majesty's troops ; and further that he did endeavour to induce others shamefully to abandon and deliver to the French the several forts and posts committed to their charge". The trial lasted five days. Corbet conducted his defence in an able and dignified manner. The verdict was:— "The Court are of opinion that Moses Corbet be superseded in his commission of Lieutenant-Governor". He was granted a pension of £250, and lived in seclusion till he was almost ninety. He died in 1817. He had at least one son, Captain James Corbet of the 95th, who took command of the regiment when Peirson fell. Of him some French verses, published after the battle, say:— "The father handed Rullecourt a laurel wreath. The son sent it to him in Purgatory".

[Messervy's *Journal ; The Proceedings at Large on the Trial of Moses Corbet, taken in shorthand by* W. *Williamson ; Relation des Attaques faits sur Jersey en 1779 et 1781,* published in London, 1781 ; Pirouet's contemporary account in Appendix to Mourant's edition of the *Chroniques de Jersey ;* contemporary documents printed in *Bulls* I, V, XIII, and in Appendix to Ouless' *Death of Major Peirson ;* additional chapter added in 1798 to Jeune's French translation of Falle's *Césarée ;* Rochfort's *Invasion of the Island of Jersey:* Perrot's *Surprise de Jersey ;* Brachet's *La Dernière Expédition contre Jersey:* Dupont's *Histoire du Cotentin et de ses Iles.*]

D'ASSIGNY, MARIUS (1643—1717) S.T.B. (*Sacrae Theologiae Baccalaureus),* Author. Son of Pierre D'Assigny, Rector of St. Helier's (q.v. App. I), and Elizabeth, daughter of Nathanael Marie, Pastor of the French Huguenot Church in Threadneedle St. Born in the old Rectory, St. Helier's, 1643, and baptized in the Town Church 15 March. His Christian name was probably suggested by the maiden name of his mother. When only seven months old he had a narrow escape from death. Elizabeth Castle was bombarding the Town during the Civil War, and Chevalier says, "A cannon-ball passed through the gable of the Presbytery, and fell down the chimney into the fire", at which Marius and his little brother were warming themselves. The same week a second cannon-ball burst through the wall. When the Royalists captured the island, his father fled ; and in January 1644 his mother was banished as "the wife of a fugitive rebel". She took her children with her to Norwich, where her husband had become co-pastor of the Huguenot Church. When Parliament regained the island in 1652, Pierre D'Assigny returned with his family to Jersey as Rector of St. Martin's, and remained till he was again deprived at the Restoration. In 1653 Marius was voted a grant from the Don Baudains, but he does not seem to have matriculated either at Oxford or Cambridge. He apparently studied abroad, for in 1668 he obtained from Cambridge the degree of B.D. *per literas regias* "after long and painful study in foreign Universities". He was now in Anglican Orders, and had been acting as Chaplain at Tangier to the Forces. In 1667 he had been appointed Vicar of Penrith, Cumberland. In 1668 the Archbishop of Canterbury issued a licence for the marriage of the Rev. Marius D'Assigny to "Elizabeth Effard of St. Martin in the Fields, aged 23, daughter of Captain Effard now beyond the seas". In 1671 Bishop Morley of Winchester appointed him Headmaster of The Holy Ghost School, Basingstoke, a post which he held for less than two years. He became Vicar of Cutcombe, Somerset, 1672—99, Rector of Tidmarsh, Berks., 1702, Vicar of Aveley, Essex 1706—12, and Vicar of Blackmore 1712. But his main work was done with his pen. He was a prolific writer on very varied subjects. Among his books were:— *The Assurance of the Faithful or the Glorious Estate of the Saints in Heaven described* 1670 ; *The Poetical Histories, being a compleat collection of all the stories necessary for a perfect understanding of the Greek and Latin Poets* 1671 (This was based on Gautruche's *Histoire Poétique,* and proved very popular. It reached an 8th edition by 1701) ; *The Divine Art of Prayer* 1671 ; *The Curiosities of Old Rome and of the most Remarkable Hieroglyphics of Egypt* 1672. Then, after more than a quarter of a century's gap, *The Art of Memory, a treatise useful especially to such as are to speak in public* 1697 (New editions followed in 1699 and 1706) ; *Rhetorica Anglorum vel Exercitationes Oratoriae in Rhetoricam Sacram et Communem* 1699 ; a translation of Dretincourt's *Christian's Defence against the Fear of Death* 1701 (This reached a 27th edition) ; *A History of the Earls and Earldom of Flanders* 1701 ; *Seasonable Advice to the Protestant Nonjurors, showing the Absurdity of acknowledging the pretended Prince of Wales for King of England* 1702 ; *An Antidote against the Pernicious Errors of the Anabaptists* 1706 ; *The Mystery of Anabaptism Unmasked* 1709. D'Assigny died on 14 Nov. 1717, and was buried in Woodham Walter Church, Essex.

D'ASSIGNY, PIERRE.   See Appendix I.

DAUVERGNE, CORBET JAMES (1765–1828), Commander
R.N., first British Governor of Heligoland. Second son of
Charles Dauvergne of St. Helier's by his second wife, Elisabeth
Bandinel. He was therefore a half-brother of Philippe Dauvergne, Duc de Bouillon (q.v.). Born in St. Helier's 1765 and
baptized in the Town Church on 1 April. He joined the
Navy, and on 19 Feb. 1800 as Lieutenant in command of the
armed brig *Aristocrat* (18 guns), one of the small boats under
the orders of his half-brother, he captured a French gunboat
off Cape Fréhel. In 1801 he was appointed Maître des Chasses
in Jersey (His patent is in the *Jersey Magazine*, Aug. 1809.).
He was the last person to hold this office. In 1802 he was
living at Grouville, for he was elected a member of the Roads
Committee of the parish. In 1804 he was Lieutenant in command of the *Severn* (44 guns) on the Jersey station, when on
21 Dec. she was wrecked in Grouville Bay (*Naval Chronicle.*
Vol. XIII). In 1807 he was First Lieutenant on the *Majestic*
(74 guns), the flagship of Admiral Russell, when Heligoland
was seized from the Danes. In his dispatch the Admiral
wrote:— "The Governor sent out a flag of truce, desiring that
an officer might be sent to treat on articles of capitulation. I
accordingly dispatched Lord Viscount Falkland and Lieutenant
Dauvergne (the First on this ship). At 2 p.m. they returned
with articles of capitulation, which I immediately ratified. I
have appointed Lieutenant Dauvergne as Acting Governor,
until their Lordships' pleasure is known, and I beg leave to add
that from his perfect knowledge of both Services and his zeal
and loyalty and high sense of honour I know no seaman more
competent to the trust". (The official correspondence on the
seizure of Heligoland is in the *Naval Miscellany* Vol. I). His
appointment was confirmed, and he was promoted Commander.
His instructions were:— "The internal government of the island
should be continued as it exists as present without any alteration,
and the gains of the inhabitants either from fisheries or pilotage
should be given up to them without tax or defalcation. All the
militia-men, amounting to about five hundred, who will take the
oath of obedience, may retain their arms". Thanks to this
conciliatory policy he made himself very popular, and, when
he left in Feb. 1808, a magnificent silver teapot was "presented
by the Magistrates, Quartermasters, and Aldermen of Heligoland to Corbet James Dauvergne Esq., the first and dearly

loved Governor under the British protection, as a token of their regard, affection, and gratitude" (*Bull* VI). Later he commanded the sloop *Autumn,* and attained Post rank 1 Aug. 1811. In 1820 he settled in England, and appointed Philippe Journeaux Deputy Maître des Chasses in Jersey. He died at Havre without heirs on 2 Feb. 1828. His wife was Victoria Adelaide Roehan Stuart. [Marshall's *Royal Naval Biography* and authorities quoted.]

DAUVERGNE, EDOUARD (1665–1737), Military Historian, Domestic Chaplain to the King. Third son of Philippe Dauvergne, Constable of St. Ouen's, and Madeline Le Maistre. Born 1665, and baptized in St. Ouen's Church 17 Feb. He entered Pembroke College, Oxford, as one of the first Morley scholars Sept. 1678. B.A. 1683. M.A. 1686. In 1691 he went to Flanders as Chaplain, first to the Earl of Bath's Regiment (the Lincolns), then to the Scots Guards, and there apparently he remained till the Peace of 1697. For seven years in succession (1692–8) he published an annual volume giving a full and accurate *History of the Campaign in Flanders* for that year. These books are still the chief authority for this period of the war. In 1693 he had been appointed Rector of St. Brelade's ; but is seems doubtful whether he ever visited his parish. He certainly never attended any meeting of the States. In 1699 he became Domestic Chaplain to William III, and returned with the King to Holland. His position at Court sometimes enabled him to help the island. In 1700 he and his fellow-chaplain Philippe Falle (q.v.) wrote to the Governor that certain Jerseymen could be redeemed, who were slaves in Morocco. A special meeting of the States placed 415 *livres* at their disposal for this purpose (*A.E.*). In 1701 he was inducted Rector of Great Hallingbury, Essex, without resigning St. Brelade's ; but in 1706 the Jersey Ecclesiastical Court deprived him of the latter living on the ground that he had been more than ten years absent from the island. From 1713 to 1727 he was again Chaplain of the Scots' Guards. In 1728 he hoped to be made Dean. Lord Newcastle wrote to Lord Cobham:— "Mr. Dauvergne, who was Chaplain to ye late King William,

and has formerly obtained of his present Majesty before his
coming to ye Crown a promise of his Majesty's favour, when an
opportunity should offer, has been strongly recommended to his
Majesty for this Deanery" (*Bull.* V). But he was disappointed.
He died at Great Hallingbury 2 Dec. 1737. In 1704 he married
Suzanne Sabenone in Westminster Abbey. (The statement in
D.N.B. that he married Esther Le Geyt confuses him with his
nephew.) He had one son, Philip. [*Dic. Nat. Biog.* ;
Macleane's *History of Pembroke College* ; *Bull.* VI ; Woods'
Ath. Oxon.]

DAUVERGNE, JAMES (1726—99), Major General. Son of
Charles Dauvergne and Elizabeth Corbet. Born in 1726 and
baptized in the Town Church 10 Aug. His father died when
he was three. He was educated at the Military Academy,
Greenwich, and obtained a commission as Lieutenant in the
Royal Fusiliers in July 1747. He transferred to the Household
Cavalry, becoming Cornet in the 1st troop of Horse Guards
1748, Adjutant 1754, Captain 1761, Major 1769, Lieutenant-
Colonel 1770, Colonel 1779, Major-General 1782. He was
Equerry to Prince George (later George III), whom he taught
to ride in Hyde Park. During all this time he kept in close
touch with Jersey. He was many times chosen by the States
to be their Deputy before the Privy Council. In 1755 he secured
twelve cannon for the defence of the island. In 1756 he again
appeared before the Council to plead for further defences. In
1757 he procured a number of new six-pounders and howitzers
to replace old ones. In 1758 he urged that ships sailing to and
from Jersey should be convoyed. In June that year the States
voted him a piece of silver plate "in recognition of the many
services he had so freely rendered to the island". In 1761 he
was thanked again, and in 1762 as spokesman of the States
he vehemently called for the annexation of Chausey (*A.E.*).
In 1759 he bought the Hougue Bie from Jacques Filleul, and
in 1792 he transferred this property to his nephew Philippe,
Duc de Bouillon (q.v.). On his retirement from the Guards he
settled in Southampton, where he became a Burgess in 1788,
Sheriff in 1792, and Mayor in 1795. He died at Southampton

19 Dec. 1799, and was buried in the catacombs underneath All Saints' Church, where Philip Fall (q.v.) and Philippe De Carteret the circumnavigator (q.v.) were also buried.

DAUVERGNE, PHILIPPE, DUKE OF BOUILLON (1754– 1816). Youngest son of Charles Dauvergne, Captain in the Royal Artillery, who had been Aide-de-camp to Marlborough, and Elisabeth, daughter of Philippe Le Geyt, Lieutenant-Bailiff. Born in St. Helier's, 1754, and baptized in the Town Church, 13 Nov. His father knew Lord Howe, Treasurer of the Navy, and through his influence the boy was gazetted in 1770 to the Royal Yacht, and thus escaped the rough time most lads had to pass through in their first years at sea. He became in 1772 Midshipman on the *Flora* (32 guns), and on a Baltic cruise the officers were presented to the Empress Catherine, who, attracted by the Midshipman's good looks, offered him a post in her service, but he declined. In 1773 he was transferred to the *Racehorse*, one of two vessels sent by the Admiralty to find the North Pole. He already showed interest in the scientific side of his profession, and on this expedition kept the meteorological register, took the astronomical observations, drew the charts, and made the sketches, which were published in Captain Phipps' *Voyage towards the North Pole.*

In 1774 he was appointed to the *Asia* (64 guns), one of the ships sent to operate against the American colonists. Here he was made acting Lieutenant of the *Kingfisher* (16), and then of the *Preston* (50). He was wounded in 1775 at the bombardment of Falmouth, and commended for his work in bringing off the Marines under fire. After a term on the *Chatham* (50) he was given command of the *Alarm*, a boat built for service up the American rivers. But she was cut off from the fleet by a French squadron, and Dauvergne burnt her to prevent her capture by the enemy. For this he was court-martialled, but honourably acquitted. He and his men now served ashore as part of the Naval Brigade with Dauvergne as Brigade Major.

He returned to England, and became First Lieutenant of "the saucy *Arethusa*" (32), famous in song and legend, whose duel with the *Belle Poule* opened the war with France. During the first months of war the exploits of the *Arethusa* were in everyone's mouth ; but in March 1779 she was wrecked off Ushant. Dauvergne and his fellow-officers were taken prisoners. He now experienced the most fantastic freak of fate that ever befell a Jerseyman. In the Belgian Ardennes, just beyond the French frontier, lay the little independent Principality of Bouillon, 18 miles long by 15 broad, with a population of 10,000. Its reigning Prince, Godefroi Charles Henri de la Tour d'Auvergne, a wealthy old reprobate, divided his time between the chorus-girls of Paris and his Normandy castle of Navarre. His only legitimate son was legless, witless, and childless. To prevent the Principality from passing to cousins whom he detested, the old Duke had decided to adopt a son. He was on the point of adopting the famous soldier, La Tour d'Auvergne, to whom Napoleon later gave the title of First Grenadier of France, when the latter destroyed his chance by mentioning that among the *Arethusa* prisoners was one named Dauvergne. (Goffre's *La Tour d'Auvergne*.) The Duke was interested, obtained Philippe's release on parole, and invited him to Navarre. The handsome, French-speaking, young Lieutenant took the old man's fancy, and he ordered his Chaplain to trace the connexion between the Jersey Dauvergnes and his own family. If Philippe should prove a cousin, he would be a more acceptable heir than La Tour, who only claimed doubtful descent from a Dauvergne bastard. Meanwhile the Duke secured an exchange for Philippe, who returned to duty.

He was given command of the sloop, the *Lark* (16), which in 1781 formed part of a fleet sent to wrest the Cape of Good Hope from the Dutch. The attempt failed, but Dauvergne captured four valuable Dutch East Indiamen. On returning to St. Helena, he learnt that he had been promoted Commander.

His Commodore then hoped to atone for his failure at the Cape by founding a new British Colony elsewhere. Seven hundred miles off the coast of Brazil was a desert island Trinidada (not of course the West Indian Trinidad). Dauvergne was ordered to go there in the *Rattlesnake*, survey it, and, if possible, colonize it. Captain Pasley, who accompanied him in the *Jupiter*, wrote in his *Journal*:— "27 Sept. 1781. My *Jupiter* is a perfect Noah's Ark. Bulls, cows, rams, ewes, goats, pigs, turkeys, geese, ducks, fowls. Singing birds of different kinds to be let loose. All kinds of trees to plant, and grasses, water-

cresses, sorrel, wild mint, thyme, and the Lord knows what.
Dauvergne is to remain and establish a settlement. I do not
think him anyway calculated for it, as he is trifling indolence
itself with a good deal of genius". Trinidada proved to be a
barren rock four miles long, but Dauvergne duly surveyed it,
and his beautifully drawn map was published later — *A Topo-
graphical Plan of the Isle of Trinidada situated in the Ethiopic
Ocean drawn and surveyed by Captain P. Dauvergne of His
Majesty's Navy.* While he was surveying, the *Rattlesnake*
was driven ashore by a gale, and became a total wreck. Pasley
remained for three weeks at the island, but then wrote in his
Journal:— "23 Oct. I resolved to write to Captain Dauvergne
a public letter to acquaint him of the impossibility of my
remaining longer in expectation of the Commodore's arrival,
as time pressed me to put in execution the remaining part of my
orders, and to demand to know whether he would evacuate
the island or remain on the chance of Commodore Johnson's
arrival or our return. His answer was full and candid. He
chose to remain". So the *Jupiter* fired five guns in salute, and
"by 3 p.m. we had lost sight of Trinidada". Dauvergne was
left with thirty men and a few French prisoners from a ship
they had captured on their way. Two months later Commodore
Johnson arrived. He professed to see in Trinidada "a jewel fit
to adorn the British crown" (His dispatch to the Admiralty),
landed additional stores, and ordered Dauvergne to remain.
He then sailed home to get married, and Dauvergne and his
men were apparently forgotten. No relief ship came to bring
stores or take them off. Their food was exhausted, and they
had to live on sea-birds and land-crabs. At last in Dec. 1782
a passing convoy of India ships saw their signals and took them
off, and brought them to Madras. Here Dauvergne was again
court-martialled for the loss of the *Rattlesnake ;* but the report
was so favourable that he was promoted Post Captain (22 Jan.
1784).

On returning to England he found peace proclaimed, and
the old Prince of Bouillon anxiously awaiting him in London.
Obliging genealogists had produced a pedigree showing the
Jersey Dauvergnes to be a branch of the Duke's family which
had settled in the island in the thirteenth century, and he was
eager to adopt Philippe as his heir. He presented him with a

bust of Turenne, the hero of his house, "as a sign of his tender love for his adopted son".

For the first three years of peace, Dauvergne was without a ship, and was able to gratify his taste for study. He attended lectures in Dorpat University (in Livonia) and in 1785 obtained the degree of L.L.D. In 1786 he was elected Fellow of the Royal Society as "a gentleman distinguished for his knowledge of many branches of Science, particularly Mathematics". He paid long visits to the Duke at Navarre, and in Aug. 1786 the Duke formally recognized the Jersey Dauvergnes as cousins, and the King ordered this recognition to be registered in the College of Arms, which confirmed Philippe's father in the right to use "the family armorial designs of His Serene Highness". In 1787 Philippe was appointed Commander of the *Narcissus*, and ordered to test various types of compasses under all sea conditions ; but his health had never fully recovered from his privations on Trinidada, and in 1790 he had to resign this congenial scientific task, and went again to Normandy.

The little Principality of Bouillon was growing anxious about its future. In 1791 its Assemblée Générale petitioned the Duke "to determine to which branch of his house he intended to convey the sovereignty in case the Prince, his son, died without issue". On 25 June the Duke replied, formally declaring his adopted son, His Highness Monseigneur Philippe D'Auvergne, to be his heir, if his son Jacques Leopold should die childless, and the crippled Jacques Leopold ratified his father's decision. On 4 Aug. the Assemblée Générale at Bouillon took an oath of loyalty to Philippe as Prince Successor, and ordered a Te Deum to be sung and bonfires to blaze in every village. On the same day in the Great Hall of the Castle of Navarre the Duke presented Philippe as his heir to his tenants and retainers. He was girded with the jewelled sword of Marshal Turenne, and all the officials of the Duchy knelt and kissed his hand. Meanwhile he had taken care to secure his own Government's approval. On 27 Feb. 1792 the King granted permission to Philippe to accept "the Sovereignty of the Duchy of Bouillon". But the atmosphere of Navarre Castle grew less and less congenial. As the French Revolution gained impetus, the old Duke threw in his lot with the Sansculottes. He called himself the Citizen Prince. He invited the National Guard to dinner. When the village cobbler addressed him as Bouillon, he replied, "I am Bouillon no longer, but Citizen La Tour". Soon after the adoption ceremony Philippe returned to England. The Duke died on 3 Dec. 1792, and was succeeded by his son.

In Feb. 1793, France declared war on England, and Dauvergne returned to duty. Jersey was now an important outpost within sight of the French shore, and he was given command of a flotilla of gunboats for the defence of the islands, and in 1798 the importance of this work was recognized by giving him the right to fly a Broad Pendant, the mark of a Commodore. For the next eight years his headquarters were in the Keep of Mont Orgueil, "which", wrote a visitor in 1798, "he is refitting and decorating with much taste in their ancient style" (*Bull.* XII). In a Memorial to the War Office in 1802 he said that in 1794 the Earl of Chatham had entrusted him with four tasks:— (i) to command a division of armed vessels to cover the islands ; (ii) to maintain communications with the insurgents in Western France ; (iii) to obtain information of the movements of the enemy ; (iv) to distribute the relief raised by the British Government for Royalist refugees in the island (MS. in S.J. Library). Each of these duties was urgent and vexatious. In Jan. 1794 the French Committee of Public Safety ordered the capture of the Channel Islands, and sent an army of 20,000 to St. Malo for this purpose. Dauvergne's little squadron of eight armed vessels, of which several were commanded by Jerseymen (the *Atlantic* by Lieut. Poingdestre, the *Liberty* by George Lempriere, and another by Lieut. Abraham Gosset) kept ceaseless watch on the invasion ports, and effectually blocked all coastwise trade in this part of the Channel. But it was his success in his second task that secured the safety of the islands. By keeping the Chouan Rising blazing in Normandy he gave the Republican army at St. Malo so much to do in its rear that it had no time to attempt invasion.

From Mont Orgueil Dauvergne organized a Secret Service, known as La Correspondance, an invisible army, who wore no uniform, who marched alone on moonless nights, whose casualty list was heavier than that of any other regiment. It contained almost as many women as men. One Jersey girl, Marie Le Sueur, made many secret trips into the interior with money before she was arrested. They were an extraordinarily difficult team to handle, tetchy aristocrats, dogmatic priests, smugglers, scoundrels, heroes. His first job was to keep in touch with the Chouan guerilla bands. Every dark night a Gorey boat dropped a watertight box near a rock off Portbail. In the morning a boy dived, and took the box to Madame de Bougainville, the circumnavigator's widow, who distributed the letters. Arms and ammunition were more difficult to smuggle ashore on cliffs swarming with patrols, but it was done. Records in the Tower of London show that in Sept. 1794 Dauvergne received 1,000 double-barrelled guns and 40,000 cartridges, and a fortnight later a cargo of powder and sabres, all of which reached the insurgents safely. Then there was a form of economic warfare. Emigrés in England had established papermills, which produced forged assignats. It was Dauvergne's task to introduce bales of these into France to destroy confidence in Republican paper money. A letter in the Record Office, written in 1798, runs:— "Two parcels of assignats are with La Toute Belle. I will forward them to La Canne's by the help of little Jeannot to a spot in Chausey". (Agents of La Correspondance were all known by nicknames.) The French had a highly efficient Counter-espionage Service under La Crosse, their Admiral at Granville. In July 1796 General Gordon, Lieut.-Governor of Jersey, wrote:— "By the vigilance of the Prince of Bouillon two Priests, who had been nursed here in the bosom of hospitality since 1792, were last night taken at sea on their way to France. One of the scoundrels threw his pocket-book overboard, but it was recovered. There was in it a National Cockade, charts of the French coast including this island, and a recipe to make flame chimycally, which no doubt has been used for signals at night, which have often been seen in the part of the island where these fellows lived".

One illustration will show some of Dauvergne's difficulties. Destouches, a rich shipowner of Granville, was a secret Royalist. He communicated with Jersey through his seventeen-year-old son, who often stayed in Mont Orgueil. The father died, and the son continued his work. But Quintal, a boatman, who had been a tobacco-smuggler between Granville and Jersey, decided that a crafty man could earn money from both Secret Services. He wormed his way into Dauvergne's confidence, and was entrusted with a letter for young Destouches. This he took to La Crosse, who steamed it open, read it, and sent it on. Destouches wrote a compromising reply, and was arrested. Fellow-Chouans set fire to Avranches Jail, but failed to rescue him. He was transferred to Coutances, where he was condemned to death. But armed Chouans broke down the prison doors and saved him. He then became leader of a guerilla band known as Destouches' Army, which Dauvergne kept supplied with funds and ammunition. But his privations turned his brain. After the Peace of Amiens he came to Jersey, demanding fantastic sums for his services. He went to London, where he was confined in Bedlam. When discharged, he returned to Jersey to worry everyone with crazy schemes for the capture of Granville. He eventually died in a French madhouse. Meanwhile Quintal managed to regain Dauvergne's favour. In 1808 he was arrested near St. Malo while trying to smuggle Chateaubriand to Jersey. The Court refused to accept his defence that he belonged to the French Secret Service, and he was shot (Du Coudray's articles in the *Pays de Granville* 1931 supplement Dupont's *Le Véritable Chevalier Destouches*).

The Normandy Chouans were only part of Dauvergne's responsibilities. The independent Chouan movement in Brittany gave him even more trouble, for here the work was complicated by the insensate rivalry of the leaders. Puisaye, the most capable, was in favour of a constitutional monarchy ; so the Diehard Royalists refused to co-operate with him. But Dauvergne was not responsible for the ghastly fiasco of Quiberon. This expedition was planned from London, and he was only carrying out orders in whatever he did to prepare for it.

He had too to keep in touch with the La Vendée insurgents far to the South. Here his chief troubles were distance and the difficulty of getting information. His first letters were addressed to a non-existent General Gaston, who was supposed in England to be in command of the rebels. His messengers had to cross all Brittany on foot, travelling only at night, and to swim the Loire with their dispatches between their teeth. Immense sums of money passed through Dauvergne's hands. In June 1795 he sent £33,000 to the Breton Chouans, dividing it among three messengers. Frotté, the Chouan leader in Normandy, received regularly £1,000 a month. One of his couriers to La Vendée carried 22,000 dollars.

In addition to his support of the insurgents Dauvergne created an efficient spy service to watch the movements of the enemy. When Hoche was preparing his expedition against Ireland, Dauvergne sent monthly reports of all ships in Brest, their names,

number of guns, number of men, their captains, and whether
their sails were bent or not (Letter Book in S.J. Library). In
one letter he reported that Captain Le Feuvre, a Jerseyman,
had sailed his schooner, the *Boston*, under American colours
into most of the French ports collecting information, but could
do so no longer, as every Harbour Master had been warned
against him. He was willing however to continue this work
in Spanish and Dutch ports, if the Government wished.

And, as if all this were not enough, the Government laid on
Dauvergne the task of distributing relief to the Royalist refugees
in Jersey. Two figures give some idea of their number.
L'Estourbeillon in his *Familles Françaises à Jersey* prints the
names of 3,200 Priests who had fled to the island, and admits
that his list is incomplete. For the Quiberon Expedition 3,500
lay refugees of military age were enrolled. In addition there was
a multitude of old men, women, and children. All these had to be
kept from starvation, and every penny spent had to be accounted
for to London. This was a thankless task. Those who were
relieved wanted more. Those passed over accused Dauvergne
of embezzlement. Suspicions and insinuations multiplied. A
London newspaper accused him of enriching himself at the
public expense; but his balance-sheets, now in the Record
Office, accounting for about £100,000 a year, were certified
as correct by the Government Auditor.

The States were proud of him. When someone in 1796
circulated "malicious and atrocious rumours" about him, they
offered a reward of 1,000 livres for information that would
lead to the conviction of his slanderer. But he did not get on
so well with his first cousin, Philippe Fall (q.v.), the Lieutenant-
Governor. Bois-Berthelot, one of the Chouan leaders, wrote:—
"Our chief difficulty lies in obstacles which Monsieur Fall puts
in the way of the wise plans of the amiable Duke of Bouillon.
We cannot speak too highly of the latter, whose zeal, talents,
and activity are beyond all that can be expressed without an
adulation that would be in bad taste". Friction was perhaps
inevitable. Fall was in charge of the island, and Dauvergne
was nominally only a naval officer in command of a squadron
at Gorey; yet actually Dauvergne was in closer touch with
the Home Government than himself. But, when Gordon became
Lieutenant-Governor in 1797, these difficulties died away.

In March 1802 England made peace with Napoleon by the

Treaty of Amiens, and the way seemed open for Dauvergne to claim his inheritance. The old Duke's son had died on 2 March ; so, armed with the necessary papers, he went to Paris in August to press his claim. But his Secret Service work was known, and he was arrested as a spy. This arrest of a naval officer caused a sensation in England. Fox thundered in Parliament that it was sufficient ground for the renewal of war. When after seven days the British ambassador secured Dauvergne's release, he was ordered to leave France within twenty-four hours. In May 1803, before he could take further steps, war broke out again, and he had to resume his duties in Jersey. The *Severn* (44 guns) was sent to him to command, and he recruited 100 seamen for her in the island.

The struggle now became keener than before, for Dauvergne's opponent was Napoleon himself. The First Consul was worried by the influence of Mont Orgueil. Many of the instructions to the Secret Police are in his own handwriting. He was constantly warning his officials in Picardy, Normandy, and Brittany to be on the alert. (The best account of this period is in Forneron's *Le Dernier Prince de Bouillon*.) In the Department of La Manche alone 108 names are marked in the Register of the Secret Police as "devoted to the Prince of Bouillon". But, though there was much conspiracy and a few rather futile acts of violence such as Cadoudal's fatal visit to Paris to assassinate Napoleon, the kidnapping of the Bishop of Morbihan who had signed the Concordat, and the seizure of the Government coach carrying the taxes from Alençon, no large-scale Royalist rising was any longer possible. One of Dauvergne's minor worries is revealed in a letter to the War Office complaining that so many French officers had been sent to him "to pass mysteriously to their destination", whom he often had to entertain for a week while waiting for a dark night, that his wine bill amounted to two-thirds of his year's pay. In 1808 a heavy blow was struck at his organization. Prigent, one of his agents, was arrested. He had made 184 journeys between France and Jersey, and on some had travelled as far afield as Paris and La Vendée ; but, when captured, he tried to save his life by revealing all he knew, the secret landing-places, the distributors of the letters, the peasants who had given him shelter. He wrote ceaselessly, filling portfolios with confessions, and every page meant death for those who had trusted him.

But he did not save his skin. He was shot on 11 Oct.
During this period Dauvergne's naval promotion proceeded
regularly. In 1805 he became Rear-Admiral of the Blue ; in
1810 Vice-Admiral of the Blue, in 1813 Vice-Admiral of the
White, and in 1814 Vice-Admiral of the Red. Other honours
came to him. He was made a Knight of the Prussian Order of
St. John of Jerusalem, and in Nov. 1803 a Grand Commander
of the Equestrian Order of St. Joachim. In 1811 the merchants
of Guernsey presented him with a silver statue of Britannia
"to testify their gratitude for his zeal and activity in protecting
their trade and interests". As early as 1792 his uncle, General
James Dauvergne (q.v.), had presented him with the property
of La Hougue Bie. (The tower, later known as Prince's Tower,
now removed, was built by the uncle, not by Philippe. *Bull.*
X.) In 1802 he bought Bagatelle in St. Saviour's, which he
made his home.

But this did not compensate for the loss of his Principality.
He was a bitterly disappointed man. In 1807 he wrote to
Puisaye:— "You know what a punishment it is for the lawful
owner of Navarre to vegetate in a sordid way in an obscure
hermitage". But while the war lasted — and it lasted twelve
years — there was no hope of recovering his inheritance. Bouillon had been annexed to France, and Napoleon had given
Navarre Castle to his divorced Empress, Josephine.

But in March 1814 Napoleon was at last beaten and banished
to Elba. A Bourbon again sat on the French throne. Dauvergne hurried to Paris, where his right to the Duchy was
recognized by the King. At Bouillon he was welcomed by the
inhabitants. The Assemblée Générale accepted him as Sovereign. The Supreme Court was reopened with pomp. State
officials were appointed. The tiny army in its white uniforms
was reorganized. A conspiracy in favour of the Duke of Rohan,
a cousin of the old Duke, proved a fiasco. Dauvergne at last
seemed firmly seated on his throne.

Napoleon however returned from Elba, and everything was
thrown again into the melting-pot. After Waterloo the Congress of Vienna was given the task of redrawing the map of
Europe. Dauvergne employed Sir John Sewell to plead his
claim before the Congress. The legal questions were complex.
Could an adopted son inherit to the prejudice of blood-relations?
Had the old Duke any right to alter rules laid down in 1696

for the succession? There were four other claimants representing different branches of the d'Auvergne family. But the
Congress decided on grounds of international expediency. It
deprived the Duchy of its independence, and annexed it to the
Netherlands, but gave the Duke of Rohan the right to the title
of Duke of Bouillon.

On 18 September 1816, two months after this decision,
Dauvergne died suddenly in Holmes' Hotel, Westminster. There
was an unproved suspicion that he had committed suicide. He
had nothing to live for. The costly litigation had ruined him.
Creditors were threatening. In Jersey alone he left debts of
over £7,000, and his property was sold in lots. He was buried
in St. Margaret's, Westminster.

He had made an unfortunate marriage in India with a Frenchwoman named Damfrecourt, by whom he had a son, and, as
she outlived him, he was never able to remarry ; but he formed
an irregular connexion with a lady in St. Helier's by whom he
had three illegitimate children, to whom he gave his name.
He brought these up at Bagatelle, and they were accepted by
local Society. When the eleven-year-old Anne Elizabeth,
"daughter of Vice-Admiral Philip D'Auvergne, Duke of Bouillon, and of Mary Hepburn of St. Helier's, Spinster", was
baptized in the Town Church (1 October 1811), Lady Imhoff
was her godmother. She married later Admiral John Aplin.
Mary Anne Charlotte (born 1794) was married at Bagatelle in
1815 to Sir Henry Prescott, who later became an Admiral.
Philip, who became a midshipman, died on H.M.S. *Africaine*,
and was buried at Colombo, 19 March 1815. [Kirke's *From
Gun Room to Throne* ; Forneron's *Le Dernier Prince de
Bouillon* ; *Naval Chronicle*, Vol. XIII ; Pasley's *Private Sea
Journals* ; *Bulls*. VI, X, XII, and XIV ; Gabory's *L'Angleterre et
La Vendée* ; Burke's *Vicissitudes of Families*. In the British
Museum are two volumes of Puisaye's correspondence with
Dauvergne, and two volumes of correspondence with refugees in
Jersey. In the Record Office is a large collection of Bouillon
papers. One of his Letter-Books is in the S. J. Library. Gilbert
Parker's novel, *The Battle of the Strong*, was suggested by
Dauvergne's career, but the Philip d'Avranche of the story
bears small resemblance to the real Philippe Dauvergne.]

DAVIS, HOWARD LEOPOLD.   See next article.

DAVIS, THOMAS BENJAMIN FREDERICK (1867–1942)
Benefactor, Son of Thomas Leopold Davis, ship's carpenter,
and Jemima Vickers.   Born at Havre des Pas 25 April 1867.
As a boy he was in the choir of St. Luke's Church.   At fourteen
he went to sea as apprentice in a sailing ship.   The snapping
of a rope in rough weather cast him adrift in an open boat at
night in the North Sea.   The following day he was picked up
by a Norwegian vessel, which some days later put him ashore
at Cowes.   He reached Jersey on a Sunday morning and went
to his old Church, where he found a Memorial Service in
progress for the drowned choir-boy!   For many years he served
before the mast, became a captain, and eventually settled in
South Africa, where he gradually gained control of the wharf-
inger business in port after port, till finally he owned all the
stevedoring services from Port Elizabeth to Dar-es-Salaam.
   The great wealth he acquired was most generously used.
He founded and endowed a fine University College of Science
at Durban.   He presented a training ship, the *General Botha,*
to the Union Government, stipulating that cadets must be
British and Dutch boys in equal proportions.   At the outset of
the Second World War he established a fund of £100,000 to
help dependents of South Africans serving in the Forces.   He
spent much of his time in Jersey in his big racing yacht, the
Westward, and was a generous benefactor to the island.   Most
of his local gifts were given in memory of his younger son,
Howard Leopold Davis, who was killed during the Battle of
the Somme in the First World War.   They include the Howard
Davis Experimental Farm at Trinity (1928), the Howard Davis
Scholarship Trust (1929), whereby he presented to the States
£50,000 to provide free maintenance at school and university
for twenty-five boys from the elementary schools, until they
should gain (or fail to gain) appointments in one of the Imperial
Services, the Howard Hall (1934) in the grounds of Victoria
College, containing J. St. H. Lander's portrait of King George
V, the Howard Davis Park (1938) with a portrait of Howard
in the Lodge, and the Howard Davis Lifeboat.   At the beginning

of the Second World War he set apart £25,000 for War Relief in Jersey. He died at Durban in October 1942, aged 75. He left one son Glenham and two daughters. [The best account of him was given in the *Victoria College at Bedford News Letter.*]

DE BARENTIN FAMILY. This family probably sprang from the town of Barentin, 11 miles from Rouen. Members of it appear in subordinate positions in the household of the Angevin kings. Alexander De Barentin was Butler to Henry II, who granted him the manor of Stoke (*Rot. Chart.*). Hugo De Barentin, one of King John's carpenters, appears frequently in the *Close Rolls* from 1206 to 1226. He too was rewarded with a confiscated manor. It is impossible to say whether either of these was an ancestor of the Seigneurs of Rozel. In the four-teenth century however De Barentins held the Manors of Rozel, Samarès, Longueville, Diélament, La Hougue Boete, Houmet, La Fosse, and Paisnel.

DE BARENTIN, DROGO (DROUET, DRUI, DREW) (d.c. 1265), Seigneur of Rozel, thrice Warden of the Isles, thrice Seneschal of Gascony, founder of the family in Jersey. We first meet him in 1223 as a knight serving Henry III in the Welsh wars (*Rot. Lit. Claus*). In 1224 he was in attendance on the King. He carried money from the King to Porchester, and witnessed many Letters Patent at Westminster (*P.R.*). In 1226 he paid his first visit to Gascony, when sent with other knights to suppress a revolt (*Rot. Lit. Claus*). In 1228 he was back at Court, and in Dec. 1229 was granted by the King the manor of Chalgrove, Oxfordshire (*Ch.R.*) In 1232 he was serving in Brittany, having charge of the important Castle of St. Jacques de Beuvron (*P.R.*). When war was resumed in 1234, he was sent to Brittany again.

In April 1235 he was appointed Warden of the Channel Islands. There were at this time two officials in charge of the islands, a Lord (*Dominus*) of the Isles, generally non-resident, and under him a resident Warden (*Custos*). De Barentin was

Warden under Henry De Trubleville. He held this office four
years (1255—9), but few records of his rule remain apart from
routine orders, such as one to allow three persons who had been
banished to return and stand their trial (C.R.). In 1259 De
Trubleville died, and De Barentin lost his post. The King then
sent him as ambassador to Rome, where trouble was brewing
over the Pope's financial demands for his crusade against the
Emperor. A letter survives from the King ordering him not
to let English privileges prevent a case between Simon De
Montfort and the Duke of Brittany being tried abroad (*Royal
Letters*). He was still at Rome in 1240, for there is an order
for his land in Guernsey to be restored to him, "when he returns
from Rome, whither he has gone as the King's envoy" (C.R.).
By June he was back in Westminster (*Cal.Doc.Ireland*), and
in July for the second time became Warden of the Isles, having
agreed to pay a farm of 400 marks, which was later reduced
to 350 (P.R.). This time he held office for twelve years (1240—
52), and, as no new Lord of the Isles was appointed during this
period, he was in sole charge. In May 1242 the King sailed
on an inglorious attempt to make good his claim on Poitou, and
in June De Barentin was ordered "to furnish with men and arms
all the galleys and other ships of our isles, and send them speedily
to the coasts of Normandy to cause damage to the King of
France by fire and every other means you can. Do all possible
diligence to occupy Mont St. Michel" (C.R.). In July he was
told to seize all French wine that he could at sea, and sell it
for the King's benefit (R.G.). This he evidently did, for a
fortnight later came an order that, if Ralph Pigou, a Knight
Templar, could prove that some of the wine seized was his
property, it was to be restored to him (R.G.). But the King's
expedition was a failure. In 1243 De Barentin received orders
to "meet the King's ship from Bordeaux off the coast of Brittany,
and escort it with galleys and other good vessels, fully manned
and equipped, till it reach England safely" (C.R.). Many orders
are preserved in the Record office dealing with the business of
the islands under his rule, including the annual statement of
accounts which he presented to the Exchequer.

In 1246 he was granted by charter ten livrées of land at Rozel
(*Cal.Rot.Chart.*). A livrée was a measure of land that in those
days was worth a rent of £1. Whether this was the original
grant of the manor, or, since nothing is said of manorial rights,

only an addition to it, is not clear. When John lost Normandy in 1204, Norman barons who held land in Jersey had had to choose which King they would serve. Silvester De Furnet, Seigneur of Rozel, had chosen Philip of France ; so his manor had been forfeited. In 1208 however it was granted to his brother, Enguerrand, "so long as he remains faithful" (*Rot.Lit. Claus.*). In 1222 Enguerrand was still in the King's service (*Rot.Lit.Claus.*) ; but later he must have fallen under suspicion, for Rozel was confiscated, and eventually granted to Drogo De Barentin. Our only information comes from a lawsuit of 1309, when Enguerrand's grandson tried to recover the manor on the ground that his grandfather had died in the King's peace (*Chancery Warrants*) ; but Drogo's grandson replied that "the said tenements were escheated to the King, who gave those tenements to Drogo de Barentin, my grandfather" (*Assize Roll* See also *Abbrevatio Placitorum*).

In Nov. 1247 De Barentin was given a new task. Gascony, which the English Kings had acquired, when Henry II married Eleanor of Aquitaine, was drifting into anarchy. Barons pillaged the countryside, and factions fought in the towns. While still remaining Lord of the Isles, De Barentin was sent there as Seneschal to restore order. But the chaos proved worse than had been foreseen. A commander of the first rank was needed. In Sept. 1248 he was replaced by Simon de Montfort.

On returning to Jersey he found a complaint awaiting him, that an Inquiry he had made into the customs of the islands was inadequate, and he was ordered to make "further diligent and accurate investigation through those who know best and are willing to speak the truth into the customs and services which the men of the isles were wont to perform in the days of the Kings, our predecessors, and also what laws King John, our father, established in the islands" (Printed in full in *Cal. Inq.*). His reply in answer to this was used later as the basis from which were fabricated the bogus Constitutions of King John, which were so often quoted in later constitutional struggles. In 1250 he was sent back to Gascony. Here De Montfort had been ruthlessly suppressing disorder, razing the barons' castles to the ground and massacring town rioters ; but such a storm of protest poured in to the King, that he was forced to take action, and De Barentin was commissioned "to view the occasions of the dissensions lately arisen" (*P.R.*). His report was that Simon had shown in some cases too much inhumanity, but that generally speaking the rebels had deserved what they got (Mat. Paris). In April 1252 he was relieved of his post as Warden of the Isles, and rewarded with the gift of an estate in Alderney (*P.R.*), which he exchanged with Richard de Grey, who succeeded him as Warden (1252–4), for the Fief Paisnel at St. John's, Jersey (*Ancient Petitions*).

In September 1252 De Montfort was recalled from Gascony, and in July 1253 De Barentin was sent there again as Seneschal "to treat with the barons touching trespasses done by them against the King" (*P.R.*). In August the King followed him in person, and De Barentin remained with him for twelve months, till Henry handed over the province to his son, Prince Edward, who appointed his own Seneschal. De Barentin returned to England with the King in December. Meanwhile he had not neglected his estates in various parts of the country. He still held the manor of Chalgrove in Oxfordshire. In 1253 he obtained a market for his manor of Hernestede, Norfolk (*Ch.R.*), and in 1257 a similar market for his manor of Ickburgh, Norfolk (*Ch.R.*). In Jan. 1257 he went abroad again with a letter from the King to the Countess of Provence (*P.R.*).

In 1258, when Prince Edward, afterwards Edward I, became Lord of the Isles, De Barentin for the third time was appointed Warden. An awkward situation almost immediately arose. The King and his son quarrelled, and Henry suspected Edward of siding with the rebellious barons. On 5 July an order was sent to De Barentin to guard the islands, not permitting Edward, the King's son, Drogo's superior officer, or anyone on his behalf to put any constables in the castles (*P.R.*) He was however absent from the country during the early stages of the troubles that led to the Barons' War, for in March 1259 he was again sent as Seneschal to Gascony (Shirley's *Royal Letters*). By 1263 he was back in England, for, when the King in October left Westminster after a violent quarrel in Parliament with De Montfort, and went to Windsor with the Earls and Barons who adhered to him, in the list of knights in Windsor Castle we find De Barentin's name (*P.R.*). On 20 Nov. he was appointed Keeper of the Castle, Town, and Forest of Windsor (*P.R.*). In December both sides agreed to accept the King of France as arbitrator ; but, when in Jan. 1264 he gave his verdict wholly in Henry's favour, the Barons again took up arms. In April the younger Simon De Montfort was captured at Northampton, and committed to De Barentin's custody at Windsor ; but De Montfort's victory at Lewes in May made the King and Prince Edward his prisoners. All letters sent in the King's name were now dictated by De Montfort. De Barentin was commanded to release the younger Simon (P.R.). This order he ignored ; so on 2 June he was dismissed from his post (P.R.), and on the 4th was ordered to surrender the Castle, and hand over his prisoners (Foed). When he took no notice of these instructions, efforts were made to persuade him to come to London. On the 6th he was told that "the King has special business to communicate to him" ; on the 11th he was summoned to "come without delay to speak with the King" ; on the 16th a third letter bade him and his knights "come with all speed, as the King has important matters to communicate, and, if they do not come, he excludes them as rebels and contemners of his mandate" ; a fourth letter of the 28th said, "Whereas the King has frequently commanded them to come to London, and they have put off, as they say, for want of safe-conduct, the King is sending to them Walter of Montchesny" (P.R.).

By October however the tables had been turned. De Barentin was a prisoner in the keeping of the younger Simon, and the King, now at liberty, was in vain trying to secure his release. One royal letter runs:— "As the King hath many times heretofore commanded Simon to send to him Drew De Barentyn, who is in his keeping, and he to the King's amazement has failed to do so," he is ordered to bring Drew at once to the King at Westminster (P.R.). What was the old knight's end does not appear, but on 16 Nov. 1265 a Patent Roll mentions "Joan, late the wife of Drew De Barantyn", so by that date he was dead. He left a son Guillaume (q.v.). [Calendar of Patent Rolls (cited as P.R.), Calendar of Close Rolls (C.R.), Calendar of Charter Rolls (Ch.R.), Calendar of Inquisitions (Cal. Inq.), Rotuli Chartarum (Rot.Chart), Rotuli Litterarum Clausarum (Rot. Lit. Claus.), Shirley's Royal Letters illustrative of the Reign of Henry III, Rymer's Foedera (Foed), Assize Roll of 1309 (published by S.J.), Ancient Petitions (published by S.J.), Michel and Bémont's Rôles Gascons (R.G.), Dupont's Histoire du Cotentin et de ses Iles, Le Patourel's Medieval Administration of the Channel Islands.]

DE BARENTIN, SIR DROGO (DREU, DRUY) (d.c. 1329), knight, Seigneur of Rozel, Warden of the Isles. Son of Guillaume De Barentin (q.v.). He is first mentioned in 1289, when he pledged as security for a debt, which he owed to Hugh de St. Philibert, Warden of the Isles, lands at Paglesham and Tilbury and other places in Essex (C.R.), which had come to him as one of the heirs of William de Blauminster, his mother's father (Cal. Inq.). In 1291, after his father's death, there was a family dispute, and these Essex lands "were taken into the King's hands for the default of Drogo de Barentin and Petronilla his wife against Joan, late the wife of William De Barentin" (C.R.). Drogo now inherited the great estates accumulated by his grandfather, the elder Drogo. In 1299 he is mentioned as holding the Fee of Chalgrove, Oxon (Cal. Inq.). We also hear of his holding the manor of Middleton, Suffolk (Cal. Inq.) and Ashby, Lincolnshire (Testa de Nevil) ; but he made his home at Rozel.

Here he was evidently unpopular with his neighbours. When Itinerant Justices visited Jersey in 1299, they were overwhelmed with complaints against him. On some of the charges he was acquitted. Agatha Gernet failed to make good her accusation that he had stolen two of her cows, and Jacob de Vinchelez' statement that he had threatened him with a knife as he was leaving the market was ignored. One case brought no advantage to either party. Gilbert Beauvallet sued him for a messuage in St. Helier's ; but, when it transpired that the land had been bought from someone who had remained in France during the war, the King's Receiver stepped in and confiscated it. In the majority of cases however Drogo was found guilty. Nicolaa Baillecorde complained that he had seized her tenements at St. Martin's. He was fined and ordered to restore them. Thomas Le Petit prosecuted him for appropriating 5 vergées of his land, and Gilbert Le Petit for the unjust disseisin of 9 vergées. He was fined and ordered to restore them. He was fined for summoning two men before the Bishop's Court at Coutances. (To prosecute one of the King's subjects before a foreign Court was a serious offence.) He was fined for driving his neighbours' beasts off his land in the time of banon, when all cattle might be turned loose to graze. He was fined £20 for ordering his warrener to levy a toll on all animals passing Rozel on the King's highway. (A copy of this Assize Roll is

in the S.J. Library.)   In 1305 an attempt was made to oust him
from Rozel.   Guillaume, son of Radulf Payn, petitioned Parliament for "a certain tenement called Rozel, which Drogo De
Barentin holds" (printed in Havet.)   He was told to sue for
it in the King's Court, but does not seem to have done so.

At some date between 1303 and 1309 Drogo was appointed
Warden of the Isles under Otho De Grandison.   Here again
he made himself unpopular.   The Assize Roll of 1309 refers
to "the very enormous trespasses of Drogo De Barentin, of
which grave complaints were lately made by the islanders of
Guernsey before the Council of the King".   Nevertheless he was
appointed one of the four Justices Itinerant for that Assize
(P.R.).   His colleagues spent five days in hearing the charges
against him ; but the courage of his accusers failed, and they
disowned their spokesman.   "The islanders being challenged
by divers means and days say to each point that certain islanders
being dissatisfied with the officers brought these schedules
without the knowledge or consent of the commonalty, and they
pray that the prosecutors may be punished, and not the commonalty, which did not consent to that deed, except certain plaintiffs
in particular.   And, having had upon these matters a long
discourse, it is considered that the commonalty shall be amerced
for non-suit upon each of the schedules" (*Assize Roll*).   Drogo
then took his seat with the other Justices, and proceeded with
the business of the Assize.   Their findings however raised a
storm of protest from both islands.   Seven Guernseymen complained that the Justices had wrongfully confiscated their
property (*Bills in Eyre*).   A Jersey petition protested that "these
Justices have made by themselves grievous amercements without
calling the Jurats thereto, who from time immemorial have always
been accustomed to make the amercements with the Justices".
But in this matter Drogo had opposed his colleagues:— "which
amercements Sir Dreu has repudiated in Court before the
Bailiff" (*Ancient Petitions*).   The petition also complained that,
since all the Justices had been on the staff of Sir Otho Grandison, it was impossible to secure redress for wrongs done by
officials.   The Council's answer was, "Let them come to Chancery".   They did so ; and the result was that they obtained
a ruling from the King that henceforth no member of the local
administration should be an Itinerant Justice (*Rot. Parl.*).

Drogo had ceased to be Warden by 1313, when Peter De

Baumes held this post ; but he was in office again in 1315,
when a petition complained that "Sir John of Ditton and Sir
Druy De Barentyn, ministers of Sir Otis (i.e. Otho de Grandison) and Sir Peter de Petifes (his lieutenant), who are in the
island Lords Wardens without a writ patent of the King, have
appointed Masse De La Court to be Bailiff of Guernsey"
(*Ancient Petitions*). In 1316 Drogo was still in Jersey (*P.R.*),
but soon after this he made Chalgrove his home. In 1322 he
was appointed Sheriff of Oxfordshire and Berkshire and Keeper
of Oxford Castle (*F.R.*), posts which he held till 1327 (*C.R.*)
By May 1329 he was dead, for then his nephew, Guillaume,
claimed his estates as heir (*C.R.*). [*Calendar of Patent Rolls*
(*P.R.*), *Calendar of Close Rolls* (*C.R.*), *Calendar of Fine Rolls*
(*F.R.*), *Calendar of Inquests* (*Cal. Inq.*), *Rotuli Parliamentorum*
(*Rot. Parl.*), *Bills in Eyre*, Selden Sy, MS copy of Assize Roll
of 1299 in S.J. Library, *Assize Roll* of 1309, pubd. by S.J.,
Ancient Petitions, pubd. by S.J., Havet's *Cours Royales*.]

DE BARENTIN, DROGO (DREW) (d. 1415), twice Mayor
of London. Thomas De Barentin, brother of Philippe, Seigneur of Rozel (q.v.) settled in England on inheriting the manor
of Chalgrove, Oxfordshire, given to the first Drogo (q.v.) by
Henry III. His son, Reginald, had two sons, Thomas, who
inherited Chalgrove, and Drogo, who became a goldsmith in
London. Records of the time give glimpses of the latter as a
man of business. In 1391 he sued the parson of Lantaglos,
Cornwall, for a debt of 8 marks (*P.R.*). The parson was evidently a bad payer, for he was sued again for the same amount
in 1400 (*P.R.*). In 1393 Drogo was paid £26 for a cup for the
Queen of Sweden (*I.R.*). In 1396 he obtained a licence to
melt for the Countess of Norfolk coins to the amount of £100
of her money to make vessels for her household, notwithstanding
any laws to the contrary (*P.R.*). In 1407 he was paid £550
for "a collar of gold garnished with precious stones for the
King's use" (*I.R.*). In 1412 he joined with other merchants in
shipping goods worth £24,000 to Talamone (*Italy*). This cargo
was stolen by the Genoese. So the King granted letters of
marque to Drogo and his partners to seize any Genoese by land

or sea, and hold them, till this sum was recovered plus £10,000 damages (*P.R.*).

Drogo became a prominent figure in London municipal life. In 1392 he was made an Alderman, an unfortunate time to take office, for that year Richard II tried to borrow £1,000 from the City, and, when the loan was refused, made a Fleet Street riot about a loaf a pretext for cancelling the City's charter, and throwing the Mayor, Sheriffs, and Aldermen into prison. After two months in gaol they made their submission, and bound themselves to pay the King £100,000. Later, however, on the Queen's intercession, their "misprisions, defaults, and contempt" were pardoned (*Foed.: P.R.*). In 1393 Drogo became Sheriff, his colleague being Dick Whittington. In Nov. 1398 he succeeded Whittington as Mayor. Now he was able to have revenge for his imprisonment. During his year of office Henry of Lancaster landed in England to claim the crown. Froissart's story of how he landed at Portsmouth, and how Drogo rode to Guildford to welcome him in the name of the City, is pure fiction. He landed in Yorkshire, and did not come near London, till he had won the victory, and taken King Richard prisoner. But then he brought his captive to London, and two contemporary chroniclers, one of whom was actually present at the scene, describe what happened:— "About two leagues from London the Duke (i.e. Henry) was met by the Mayor and all the commons, a very grand procession, and they carried the sword before the Mayor, as though he were a Duke" (*Traison*). "Each trade was marshalled by itself, clad in different garments, drawn up in rows, and armed" (*Creton*). "As the Mayor and his company approached the Duke, they dismounted, and saluted him very respectfully, and cried 'Long live the noble Duke of Lancaster, who has conquered England in less than a month. Such a lord deserves to be King'. When the noise subsided, the Earl of Arundel brought the King as though he were a thief. The Duke said, 'My lord, alight. Here are your good friends of London come to see you'. King Richard accordingly alighted from the little horse he rode, and his face was so covered with tears that they scarcely knew him. The Duke then said to the Mayor and Londoners, "My lords and friends, here is King Richard. I deliver him into your custody. I beg you to do with him as you will" (*Traison*). "Thus did King Henry surrender his rightful lord to the London rabble, in order that, if they should put him to death, he might say, 'I am innocent of this deed'" (*Creton*). While the conqueror rode to St. Paul's to return thanks, Drogo took the fallen King to Westminster ; and on the following day he was lodged in the Tower.

In Nov. 1408 he again succeeded Whittington as Mayor, and in 1410 he lent Henry IV £1,500 "for the defence of the realm in the present necessity" (*P.R.*). Several benefactions of his are recorded. In 1393 he obtained permission to alienate in mortmain 26 London shops to the Wardens of the Mystery of Goldsmiths for the maintenance of blind and infirm members (*P.R.*). In 1400 he gave the quit-rent of the Griffin on the Hoop to the parson and wardens of St. Matthew's, Friday Street, to provide a Chaplain to celebrate Divine Service daily for the soul of Nicolas Twyford, goldsmith (*P.R.*). A Harleian MS. says, "He builded a parte of Gouldsmiths' Hall, and gave them landes. He was buried in St. John Zacharias at the end of Foster Lane over against the Gouldsmiths', from which he made a gallery over the lane to his owne house" (No. 1349). He died on 15 March 1415, a rich man, owning nine manors in Oxfordshire, three in Berkshire, one in Bedfordshire, and one in Northamtonshire, together with much house property in London, and a garden outside Cripplegate (*Cal. Inq. post Mort.*). He married twice. His first wife was named Margery (*C.R.*), his second Christina. After his death an Inquiry as to his heir reported:— "The Jurors state that Reginald Barantyn, son of Thomas Barantyn, brother of the aforesaid Drogo, is next of kin, and at present the apparent heir, but that an infant still in the womb of Christina, lately the wife of Drogo, if God grant it to be born, will be the heir". (*Cal. Inq. post Mort.*). In 1420 Christina married John Manning (*P.R.*) [*Calendar of Patent Rolls*, cited as *P.R.*: *Extracts from the Issue Rolls*, cited as *I.R.*: *Inquisitiones post Mortem*: Rymer's *Foedera*: Creton's *Histoire du Roi d'Angleterre Rickart*, printed in *Archaeologia*, Vol. XX: *Lystoire de la Traison et Mort du Roy Richart*, cited as *Traison*.]

DE BARENTIN, GUILLAUME (d. before 1291), Seigneur of Rozel, Warden or Bailiff of the Isles. Son and heir (see *Hundred Roll*, 1279) of the eldest Drogo De Barentin (q.v.).

Little is known of this member of the family. He first appears in 1264 as one of the knights holding Windsor Castle under his father for the King against the King's orders (*P.R.*). On his father's death, before November 1265, he inherited Rozel Manor, Jersey, and Chalgrove Manor, Oxfordshire. In 1266 a Protection was issued to him, as he was going to France on the King's business (*P.R.*). In 1267 and 1268 he was Bailiff or Warden of the Isles (the titles were then interchangeable) under Prince Edward, afterwards Edward I, who was then Lord of the Isles ; but he had ceased to hold this office by 1269 (*Cartulaire*). According to Blomfield's *Norfolk* he founded and endowed a Chapel and Hospital for Lepers at Cheveres in that county on an estate that he had inherited from his mother. By 1291 he was dead, for there was a family dispute about his property, and certain lands at Tilbury, Paglesham, Twinstead, and other places in Essex were taken into the King's hands, because of the default of the heirs against "Joan, late wife of William De Barentin" (*C.R.*). She was a daughter of William of Blauminster of Child Canefeld (*Cal. Genealogicum*). He left two sons, Drogo (q.v.) and Jean. [*Calendar of Patent Rolls* (P.R.), *Calendar of Close Rolls* (C.R.), *Cartulaire* (published by S.J.)]

DE BARENTIN, PHILIPPE (Sold Rozel 1367), Seigneur of Samarès and Rozel. Son of Guillaume De Barentin. Unlike some of his ancestors Philippe is a colourless figure, whose only interest lies in his connexion with a melodramatic murder, a sixty years' lawsuit, and the passing of Rozel to the Lemprieres. In 1354, when John Maltravers ceased to be Warden of the Isles, De Barentin bought from him Samarès Manor, and some years later on his father's death he inherited Rozel. A Latin manuscript of about 1540, probably written by Dean De Soulemont (q.v.) (printed in *Bull* V), tells of a scandal about Philippe's wife:— "One day the wife of Philippe De Barentin said to her sons, Jehannet De St. Martin has called me an adultress. Avenge this insult on your mother. I would such slanderers had their tongues torn out by the roots". (The De St. Martins were at this time one of the leading families in the island. A Richard De St. Martin was Bailiff 1367—8. A Jean De St.

Martin, Seigneur of Trinity, was Bailiff in 1370. But it is not clear who Jehannet was.) "The sons in fury laid an ambush, and set a boy to whistle a warning, when De St. Martin drew near. When he came, they seized him, and tore out his tongue where today stands the Cross called the Cross of Jehannet about 400 yards from St. Martin's church, as one goes toward Trinity. This Cross was placed there in memory of the crime. The sons fled to Normandy. One however was arrested and hanged. The other made his home near Rouen, and his descendants are there to this day".

It is not surprising that after this Philippe left Jersey. Of his two sons Gilbert had been hanged, and Philippe the other could never return to the island. So the father began to make arrangements to sell his estates, which included not only Samarès and Rozel, but the Manors of La Hougue Boëte, Longueville, and Diélament (*Bull* V). In Sept. 1362 he was in England, and appointed Raoul Lempriere (q.v.) and Guillaume Payn (q.v.) his attorneys in Jersey (*P.R.*). His relations however made strenuous efforts to prevent the sale. Their first move was to declare that he was a leper. In October Guillaume De St. Martin reported to the Assize that "Philippe De Barentin was suspected of leprosy, and his kinsmen wished to deprive him of his heritage" (MS. quoted above). In the Middle Ages a leper was regarded as dead. The funeral service was read over him in church, while he lay beneath a shroud. He was then taken to a lonely hut, in which he must henceforth live, and given clappers which he must sound, whenever he walked abroad. The law of Normandy and the Channel Islands was stricter in this respect than that of the rest of Europe ; for a leper could not alienate his property, but only draw the income from it. (See Guillourd's paper *Etude sur la condition des lépreux au moyen age* in *Mémoires de Soc. des Ant. de Normandie. Vol. XXIX.*). Whether Philippe was really a leper is unknown. More than one De Barentin showed an interest in lepers, which suggests that there was perhaps a taint of leprosy in the family. Alexander De Barentin in 1242 had given land in Hampstead to the leprous maidens of St. James without London (*Cal. Charter Rolls*). Guillaume De Barentin (q.v.) had endowed a Leper Hospital at Cheveres. But the question was never settled, as Philippe had escaped to England.

His two attorneys, Lempriere and Payn, then bought from

him all his Jersey property. The contract, passed by the Court
in 1367 (printed in *Bull* V), shows that they promised to pay
him £200 sterling a year as long as he lived. But his nephew,
Pierre Payn, Rector of St. Brelade's, a son of his sister Mabel,
challenged this sale, claiming the *retrait lignager*. By Norman
law, if a man sold his property, any of his heirs, beginning with
the next of kin, could buy it back for the price paid, if he
asserted this right within a year and a day. (See the *Summa
de Legibus*, compiled about 1255 ; Fallettis' *Le retrait lignager
en droit coutumier français*, and Genestal's paper in *Travaux
de la semaine d'histoire du droit normand tenue à Jersey*.) There
was also the *retrait féodal*, by which the Seigneur had the same
privilege, if the heirs did not act. Both these claims were now
filed against Payn and Lempriere ; and the matter was further
complicated by the fact that they were of Breton origin, and
had omitted to obtain permission as aliens to buy property.
Here were all the ingredients for a really complicated lawsuit ;
and it lasted sixty years. Pierre Payn, the original challenger,
and both the purchasers died long before it was over ; but
eventually the attack failed. On Lempriere's death the property
was divided (the contract is in Bull. V), his son taking Rozel,
and Payn Samarès and Diélament. Meanwhile the unhappy
De Barentin faded out of the picture. When and where he
died is not recorded. But he evidently left no son besides the
outlawed Philippe, for his English property passed to the family
of his brother, Thomas. A daughter married John Lord of
Herdington (*Bull*. V). [Article, Ancienne Généalogie, in *Bull*.
V ; *Calendar of Patent Rolls* *(P.R.)* ; *Calendar of Charter
Rolls* *(Ch.R.)* ; *Calendar of Fine Rolls* *(F.R.)* ; De La Croix,
Jersey, ses Antiquités, Vol. I.]

DE CARTERET FAMILY. The De Carterets were for centuries the leading family in the island. They have provided 9
Lieutenant-Governors, 15 Bailiffs, 9 Attorneys-General, and at
least 48 Jurats. When a De Carteret was Jurat, he claimed the
right to sit next to the Bailiff. When a Governor died, the
Seigneur of St. Ouen's took command of the troops, till a new
Governor was appointed. Elizabeth granted them Sark "in

reward of the many services received by herself and her royal ancestors from this family", and Charles II granted them Alderney. They came from Carteret, the little town on the Cotentin coast almost opposite Jersey, where they were Lords of the Manor. Their property at St. Ouen's was at first only an outlying corner of larger estates in Normandy. Wace in his list of those who fought at Hastings mentions Onfrai and Maugier De Cartrai, of whom Maugier was newly made a knight. Doomsday Book shows that the latter was rewarded with estates in Somerset. We then for a time chiefly hear of the family through their benefactions to the Abbey of Mont St. Michel. Onfrai's son Renaud, who followed Geoffroi de Bouillon on the First Crusade, and was present at the taking of Jerusalem in 1099, gave to the Abbey in 1125 the Church of St. Germain at Carteret and land belonging to that Church in Jersey (Cart.). This gift his son Philippe, "moved by the counsel of evil men", tried in 1135 to recall, but "at length by the inspiration of God he repented", and not only confirmed the gift, but added "two plots of ground in Jersey outside his house" (Cart). This shows that the family had now a house on the island. By another charter he gave the Abbey the tithes of St. Ouen's and an acre of land to build a barn to receive them (Cart). In 1156 Robert of Torigny, the famous Abbot of Mont St. Michel, visited Jersey, and Philippe De Carteret, his kinsman, gave to the Abbey the Church of St. Ouen and the Chapel of St. Mary of Lecq in the same parish. In return the Abbey promised that one of the family could always be received as a monk of St. Michel (Cart). When John lost Normandy in 1204, Renaud, Philippe's son, had to choose between the French and English allegiance. He adhered to John, though this meant the loss of all his Norman possessions ; but the suspicious King kept Renaud's son Philippe for many years as a hostage. The interests of the family now centred on Jersey. Articles follow on RENAUD, who held Mont Orgueil against the French in 1338—9, GEOFFROI, who was Dean, and died in 1368, RENAUD, who in 1356 helped to recapture Castle Cornet, PHILIPPE (1), who in 1468 helped to recover Mont Orgueil from Maulevrier, PHILIPPE (2), who in 1494 was saved from a vindictive Governor by his wife's dash to England, HELIER, the Bailiff, who in 1528 defied Wolsey in the Star Chamber, HELIER who in 1565 recolonized Sark, EDOUARD, who in

1542 was defendant in a famous murder case, SIR PHILIPPE (3), the Royalist leader in the Civil War, SIR PHILIPPE (4), Bailiff 1661—2, SIR PHILIPPE (5), Bailiff 1682—93, SIR EDOUARD, Bailiff 1694—8, SIR CHARLES, Bailiff 1702—15. With Sir Charles the direct male line of the De Carterets of St. Ouen's ended. But meanwhile younger sons of St. Ouen's had acquired Manors and established branches of the family elsewhere in the island. In 1488 the childless Catherine de Vinchelis gave Vinchelez de Haut Manor to her godson, Richard De Carteret. His grandson JEAN (q.v.) was the bitter opponent of the Paulets. Younger sons of this line acquired the Manors of La Hague (St. Peter's) and La Hougue (Grouville). From La Hague came FRANCOIS, Parliamentary Commissioner (q.v.), and PHILIPPE (6), Cromwell's Judge-Advocate (q.v.) ; from La Hougue PHILIPPE (7), Governor of New Jersey (q.v.). In 1601 AMICE (q.v.), a cadet of St. Ouen's, acquired by marriage Trinity Manor. From him descended JOSUE, a scapegrace (q.v.), SIR EDOUARD, Usher of the Black Rod (q.v.). PHILIPPE (9), the Circumnavigator (q.v.), and SIR PHILIP DE CARTERET SILVESTER (10), Captain R.N. (q.v.) The Carterets who dropped the De were descendants of Elie, another cadet of St. Ouen's. Articles will be found under the heading CARTERET on:—SIR GEORGE, Governor and Bailiff, SIR PHILIPPE, friend of Pepys, JAMES, New Jersey rebel, JOHN, LORD CARTERET and ROBERT, LORD CARTERET. Eight De Carterets are buried in Westminster Abbey, some in the North Aisle, some in Henry VII's Chapel. Other Fiefs which at various times were held by De Carterets are:— Mélèches (1306—1442 and again 1643—95), Longueville (1382—1480), La Houguette (1600—1705), St. Clair (1600—1713), Rozel (1601—1711), La Hougue Dirvaut (1609—1699), Avranches (1650—1745), Morville (1650—1781), La Hougue Boëte (1662—1750), Vinchelez de Bas (1664—1826). A Fief, partly in St. Peter's and St. Brelade's and partly in St. Ouen's, is called Luce De Carteret. Luce was a daughter of Geoffroi De Carteret, Seigneur of Mélèches, and her estate was confiscated by the Crown, because during the Hundred Years War she married a Frenchman. There is also a Fief de la Fille de Carteret at St. Saviour's, and a Court record of 1539 mentions a manor of La Fille de Carteret at St. Martin's. There were also important branches of this family at St. Brelade's (see *Bull.* IV), Grouville (see *Bull.* VI), and St. Helier's. For the MALET DE CARTE-RETS see separate articles.

DE CARTERET, AMICE (c. 1559—1631), Bailiff and Lieut.-Governor of Guernsey, Founder of the line of De Carterets of Trinity. Second son of Helier De Carteret (q.v.), Seigneur of St. Ouen's and colonizer of Sark, and Marguerite, daughter of Helier de Carteret (q.v.), Bailiff. The St. Ouen's Registers do not begin till 1634 ; so the exact date of Amice's birth is not recorded ; but, since Sir Amyas Poulet was his god-father, he cannot have been born before April 1559, when Poulet arrived in the island. Of his early life the Chronicler writes:— "When the Seigneur of St. Ouen's had completed his business in Sark he bethought him by the advice of his wife and friends to marry Amice, his second son, to some maiden of high degree. Having pondered much on the matter, he recalled that Guillaume Lempriere, Seigneur of Trinity, had one only daugh-ter, who was heir to all his estate, that the Seigneur and his forbears had ever been allies of the House of St. Ouen's, and that the Seigneur held the Fief right nobly by homage to the King. For these and divers other reasons he deemed it meet to sound the Seigneur on the matter. And, when they had conferred together, and taken counsel with their friends, specially with Sir Amyas Poulet, Captain of Jersey, who was then in Paris as Ambassador for the Queen (for he was Amice's god-father, from whom he had received his name) they came to cordial agreement. After the betrothal and the calling of the banns, on Sunday 10 Oct. 1578 Amice De Carteret and Catherine Lem-priere were married in Trinity Church by Laurens Machon, the Minister, and high festival was kept for eight days and more with triumphant rejoicings. About twelve months later they had a son, whom they named Philippe, and at his Baptism there was well-nigh as much rejoicing as at the wedding. The said Amice, before he married, had been at Winchester College, and after that at Cambridge University, where he gained such profit from his studies, that he became one of the Jurats of Jersey, the Bailiff's Lieutenant, and Keeper of the Dean's seal, a man of great repute and much beloved by the people" (*Chroniques*).

In 1582, when Jean De Monange, Rector of St. Helier's, died, Amice adopted his little motherless daughter Josabet, and brought her up till she married. He was sworn in as Jurat 29 Aug. 1583. In April 1584 George Poulet, the Bailiff, nominated him Lieut.-Bailiff "by the advice of the Court". In Sept. he was appointed Recorder of Wills, a civil office made necessary by the suspension of the Dean's powers. In the same year in a letter to Lord Burghley, the Treasurer, he says that the Queen has conferred on him the Manor of St. Germain for life, and he asks that it may be granted in fee simple "at a reasonable price" (S.P.). The Government had now decided to build Elizabeth Castle. In March 1586 De Carteret was one of a Commission of Six appointed by the Privy Council to consider what kind of fortifications should be erected (Acts P.C.). In 1593 the States sent him to London to press for more money for the Castle (A.E.). In 1594 the States appointed him to superintend the workmen and to see that each parish sent its share of carts and material (A.E.). He tried to raise the workmen's wages, which had been fixed at eight pence a day for skilled men and sixpence for unskilled. Among the Salisbury MSS. at Hatfield is a letter from Sir Anthony Poulet, the Governor, to Sir Robert Cecil (13 July 1594) complaining that De Carteret had led the men to expect that the Queen would grant an increase:—"Mr Ivy, the Surveyor, and myself have laboured to put this conceit out of the people's heads ; but the authority of him that encourageth them and the plausibleness of the argument hath made them almost forget the terms of modesty and duty in their carriages toward us. For my part I cannot so much condemn the people as him that keepeth them in this error, which is Mr Amys Carteret, the rather for that my Lord Treasurer did in my hearing let him know what was intended touching wages. This is the first complaint that ever I made against any in this Isle". All the records of the time reveal him as the most active and influential of the Jurats.

In Jan. 1601 however the States received a letter from the Privy Council requiring them to free him from his office of Jurat as he had been selected to be Bailiff of Guernsey. They bowed before this command "with great regret, though they would have had many reasons to excuse them, if they had remonstrated" (A.E.). He was sworn in as Bailiff 4 March 1601 (Jugements et Records). But in Jersey the States took no steps to fill his place. By the death of his father-in-law in 1601 he had inherited

Trinity Manor, which meant that he would pay frequent visits to the island ; so in Aug. 1602 the States urged him to remain a Jurat ; but he replied that his Guernsey duties would take all his time. In May 1603 however he was back in Jersey as representative of the Guernsey Colloquy at the Calvinist Synod called to discuss certain points of difference between the two Churches. Guernsey observed Christmas and held a Communion Service at Easter, practices which Jersey regarded as Popish. Jersey forbad burial in churches, which Guernsey allowed. De Carteret was a strict Puritan, regarding Romanism, Anglicanism, and Witchcraft as the three blackest enemies of God. Against these he fought relentlessly. For example. in 1611 the Guernsey Court under his presidency decreed that all idolaters (i.e. Romanists) who persisted in their obstinate ignorance and showed that they had not renounced the abominations of Antichrist were to be hunted down, and brought before the Court to receive condign punishment. In 1614 it was discovered that French Roman Catholic Bibles were being bought in the island, because they were cheaper than the Calvinist Geneva Version. He promptly organized a house to house search throughout every parish to confiscate them. When King James's Government tried to establish Anglicanism in the islands, they succeeded in Jersey ; but in Guernsey De Carteret resisted strenuously. "The Bailiff", wrote Hussey, the Royal Commissioner, "doth much mislike the manner of our Church Government" (*S.P.*). He travelled to London, and fought the matter out before the Privy Council with such success that Presbyterianism survived in his Bailiwick for another half century. He was also a ruthless witch-hunter. Seventy-seven witches were tried before him (his predecessor had only tried two), and of these thirty-four were burnt alive and twenty-four banished.

He maintained his link with Jersey, and, though no longer a Jurat, generally attended the meetings of the States, when he was in the island. In 1605 he reported to the States that the King was sending Commissioners to correct abuses in the islands. In 1606 Jersey sent him as its Deputy to London to hasten the coming of the Commission. As a result he found himself appointed one of the Six Commissioners ; but owing to the opposition of some of the Crown Officers this Commission never functioned, and was superseded by the Commission of Gardiner and Hussey in 1607. In 1610 his wife died, and was buried on

12 Dec. in St. Peter-Port Church, where her monument can still be seen. From the Burial Register we learn that at this time he was not only Bailiff but also Lieut.-Governor ; and he held this dual post till 1620. He remained Bailiff till his death in 1631, and was buried in St. Peter-Port Church on 19 April. His two eldest sons Philippe and Edouard had died young. He was succeeded as Seigneur of Trinity by his third son Josué, who had been elected a Jurat in Jersey in 1616 ; but he only survived his father by six months, and was succeeded by his son Amice. The elder Amice had two daughters, Elisabeth, who married Thomas Andros of Guernsey and Sara who married a Greek Prince. [Authorities quoted above ; *Actes des Etats de Guernesey* ; *Ordonnances de la Cour Royale de Guernesey.*]

DE CARTERET, SIR CHARLES (1679–1715), Bart., Seigneur of St. Ouen's, Bailiff. Only son of Sir Philippe De Carteret 8 (q.v.), Bailiff, and Elizabeth, daughter of Sir Edouard De Carteret of Trinity. Baptized in St. Margaret's Westminster, 4 June 1679, his sponsors being King Charles II and the Duke of Monmouth. He was knighted by the King at Whitehall (25 Oct. 1687) when only eight years old. His father died when he was fourteen, and his father's uncle, Sir Edouard De Carteret (q.v.), was appointed to fill the office of Bailiff, till he should come of age. (The office had become almost hereditary in the family.) On 28 Sept. 1699 he made *comparence* before the Cour d'Héritage for the Fiefs of St. Ouen's, Morville, and Robillard. In 1701 he was faced by a revolt of his tenantry. In Sept. the Chefs of his Cinquantaines sued him to show "by what right he claimed annually from each Cinquantaine a cartload of vraic, the digging of a vergée of land, the cartage of wood and stone for the repair of the manor buildings, and manual labour". The Court ordered a Commission of Twelve, six from each side, to draw up a Report on the services due. This was then argued point by point before the Court, and finally (4 Nov. 1703) passed and registered. It is interesting as showing what seigneurial services survived into the eighteenth century. It lays down that every tenant must do homage to the Seigneur once in his lifetime. Tenants must cut and carry the

Seigneur's hay. Each Cinquantaine must provide annually a
four-horse cartload of vraic and dig one vergée of land, and
furnish a man and cart for repairing the manor and its mills.
The Chefs are personally responsible for collecting all corn,
fowls, or eggs due to the Seigneur. All corn must be ground in
the manor mills. Tenants must provide an escort to conduct
prisoners from St. Ouen's to the Prison, from the Prison to
the Court, and from the Court to the seigneurial gallows. The
tenants appealed against this schedule to the Privy Council, and
failed. They appealed again in vain against having to pay the
cost of the Inquiry (O.C.). Meanwhile much bad blood had
been aroused. Jean Tourgis, Greffier of the Seigneurial Court,
was prosecuted for providing the tenants with a copy of a paper
belonging to the manor. Simon De Caen, the tenants' leader,
was found guilty of falsely insinuating that Sir Charles had
instigated Tourgis "to endeavour to recover the paper by subtlety or violence". Both men were fined, and ordered to sue for
pardon on their knees. Sir Charles then demanded that Tourgis
be deprived of his position as Lecteur of St. Ouen's Church, and
the Royal Court dismissed him. The Dean claimed that the
removal of Lecteurs was a matter for the Ecclesiastical Court,
and reinstated him. Sir Charles appealed to the Bishop, who
supported the Dean. The case then went before the Privy
Council, which did not settle the dispute between the two Courts,
but granted Tourgis the Queen's pardon, and restored him to
his post (O.C.). Meanwhile a barrel of Militia gunpowder had
gone astray, and Sir Charles, who had just been appointed
Colonel of the North-West Regiment, charged De Caen, who
was one of his sergeants, with having stolen it. His next move
was to claim that all his tenants had forfeited their lands by
refusing their services. On this point the Court reserved judgement, and the case was eventually withdrawn.

On 5 Sept. 1702 he received his patent as Bailiff, but he continued to spend most of his time in England, where already he
was Gentleman in Ordinary to the Privy Chamber of Queen
Anne. He did not come to Jersey to be sworn in till May 1703.
In Feb. 1704 he returned to London, and did not appear in
Jersey again till Aug. 1707. In 1703 he had tried to prevent
Martin De Gruchy (q.v.) from establishing himself as the first
notary in the island ; but the Privy Council had reversed his
judgement. On his next visit he had De Gruchy arrested for

"holding up his administration of justice to ridicule by gestures and shocking words and impudent innuendoes". Part of his offence was that he had addressed Sir Charles as "your Excellency", and "in discoursing of him with his friends he said he was rough as a veal pye". He was fined 150 *livres tournois* and condemned to ask pardon on his knees. De Gruchy appealed to the Privy Council, but never prosecuted his appeal, preferring to leave the island, and settle as a notary in London.

Meanwhile some of the Jurats, led by Josué Pipon (q.v.) were growing more and more dissatisfied with Sir Charles' administration. They complained to the Council later:—"Sir Charles came young into the office of Bailiff, is not well acquainted with the French tongue, and a stranger to the laws and customs of the island. Since his admission to office he hath generally resided in England, having appointed Mr Charles De Carteret, a relation of his, for his Lieutenant, a man of no learning, who was half the year laid up with the gout. So that it hath often caused a failure of Justice, sometimes for two or three months. And since the said Lieut.-Bailiff's death, Charles hath appointed in his stead Mr Charles Dumaresq, who soon after was struck with a Dead Palsie and Delirium, which occasioned again, as it doth even now, a great interruption of Justice".

In 1710 the Bailiff was again in the island. When, having a case in the Royal Court, he asked the opinions of the Jurats, Philippe Le Geyt (q.v.) the commentator, the first to be asked, begged permission to retire, as he had petitioned the Queen to allow him to resign. Sir Charles demurred ; but Jean Dumaresq, Le Geyt's advocate, rose and quoted precedents. The Bailiff fined him for interrupting, and threatened to suspend him, if he did not sit down. Against this the majority of the Jurats protested, and the Court broke up in confusion.

In 1711 permission arrived for Le Geyt to resign, and there was a fiercely contested election to replace him. Sir Charles did his utmost to secure the return of James Corbet, parading the North-West Regiment to instruct them to vote for him, and entertaining all his tenants to urge them to do the same ; but Philippe Dumaresq, Seigneur of Samarès, was elected, thus strengthening the opposition.

In April the Greffier had to leave the island ; so it was necessary to appoint a Deputy-Greffier. Sir Charles instructed the Lieut-Bailiff to nominate Thomas Pipon (q.v). The majority

of the Jurats refused to accept him, alleging that "being bred
to the sea" he had no knowledge of Court procedure, and that
he was awaiting trial on two charges of assault. Instead they
swore in Edouard La Cloche, the Registrar. De Carteret appealed to the Privy Council, declaring that the Jurats were
trying "to usurp the government of the island from Her Majesty
and Her officers to themselves" ; and the Council ordered "that
such person as the Bailiff shall appoint be sworn in" (O.C.).

Then Sir Charles' supporters devised an ingenious scheme to
get rid of all opposing Jurats by the law of recusation on the
ground that they were cousins. In case after case it was pleaded
that one of the Jurats was in some way connected with one of
the parties in the suit, and that therefore not only he but all his
cousins were incompetent to judge. The effect of this would
have been to leave the work of the Court entirely in the hands
of the Jurats who supported the Bailiff. The other Jurats indignantly protested ; and Sir Charles complained to the Council
that he had been obliged "several times by reason of the violent
heats of the contending Jurats to break up the Court without
proceeding to any further business". But this time the Council
decided against him, and ordered (May 1713) "that the complaint
be dismissed and the said Sir Chas. Carteret do pay the said
Defendants five pounds for costs of this suit" (O.C.).

If Philippe Pipon (q.v.) is to be believed, "this unfortunate
blow to see his enemies triumph gave him his mortal wound,
for afterward he lived but a lingering life, had several sicknesses
(no sooner out of one than he relapsed into another), till at last
he died". Before his death he contemplated getting rid of his
Jersey property. In Feb. 1714 he obtained Letters Patent permitting him to alienate his Fiefs ; but in 1715 he died, and was
buried on 8 June in the north aisle of Westminster Abbey. He
had married Mary, daughter of Amice De Carteret, but their only
child, James (baptized at Isleworth 1694), had died before him.
With him ended the direct male line of the De Carterets of St.
Ouen's, who had held that Fief from father to son for about
seven hundred years. Of the seven sons of Sir Philippe De
Carteret 3 (q.v.) of Civil War fame all but two, Philippe and
François, had died childless.

The last male descendant of François had died in 1711, and
now in 1715 the last descendant of Philippe (4) had passed away.
By Sir Charles' will, made two years before his death, he left

all his property to Lord John Carteret (q.v.). But by Jersey law
real estate could not be devised by will ; it must pass to the
nearest heirs ; and four daughters of François were still living.
They however agreed not to contest the will, on condition that,
if Lord Carteret's line should become extinct, the property should
revert to their descendants. This actually happened in 1775
(See *Carteret, John, Earl Granville*). [O.C. ; *Groans of the
Inhabitants of Jersey ;* Payne's *Armorial ; The Humble Representation of Sir Charles Carteret to the Committee for the affairs
of Jersey and Guernsey.*]

DE CARTERET, EDOUARD (1518—1601), Vicomte and
Attorney-General of Jersey, and Bailiff of Sark. Illegitimate son
of Helier De Carteret, Bailiff (q.v.). Brevint, writing in his
Note Book about 1626, says, "Edouard De Carteret was the son
of a young English lady with whom H. De Carteret, Bailiff, slept
on the night before he should have married her. Then he left
her, and mounting his horse very early in the morning went and
married another lady in another county. The former lady sent
him the said Edouard, after he was weaned, and died shortly
after". Brevint was a gossipy old person, whose stories cannot
always be relied on, but as Chaplain to the De Carterets he
was in a position to have learnt facts like these. Helier accepted
responsibility for the child and brought him up. He seems to
have been a turbulent youth. On one occasion he was brought
before the Court for striking Jurat Nicolas Journeaux in St.
John's Church, but his father secured his release. On another
occasion he was accused of beating a man named Levesque with
whips and a dagger.

As soon as he was of age in 1539 his father secured his appointment as Vicomte. But on April 5 1540 he was arrested
on a charge of murder. According to his complaint "abought XII
of the clocke by nyght they brake the dores of his howse and
with great violence tooke the sayd Edward out of his bed, and
bounde his handes behynd hym and his legges under a horse bel-
lye, and sho shamefully and cruellye broght hym to the cryminall
prison, in which he hath been cruellye kept by the space of three
quarters of a yere". He was deprived of his position as Vicomte.

The charge was an extraordinary one. Michel Sarre, son of Simon Sarre, Constable of St. John's, was one of the richest men in the island. At the time of his death he had an income of 105 quarters of wheat rente, much property, and 300 sheep. He lived in the Maison de St. Jean on the road from St. John's to St. Mary's. Since Edouard married Sarre's widow in a semi-surreptitious way in the ruined Chapel of Lecq (in 1531 the Commissioners had reported "the Priory is in ruins") within a fortnight of her husband's death, there is ground for suspecting that there had been an intrigue between them. She was Marguerite De Carteret, daughter of the Bailiff's brother, Edouard De Carteret, Seigneur of St. Ouen's, and therefore the young Vicomte's first cousin. She must have been at least ten years older than he was, and was the mother of seven children. Katherine Sarre, Michel's mother, accused De Carteret of having broken into Sarre's bedroom, where he and his wife were in bed, dragged him out of bed, savagely **beaten** him, thrown him wounded into another room on a snowy night with nothing on but his shirt, fastened the door by a cord, and spent the rest of the night with his wife. She alleged that Sarre had died as a result of this treatment. The chief witness against De Carteret was Sarre's fifteen year old son, Edouard, who swore that he had found his father shut up and bruised and covered with blood, and that his father had told him on his deathbed that Edouard De Carteret had caused his death by beating him. De Carteret replied that he could prove that the boy was at school at St. Mannelier's three miles away at the time this was said to have happened, and did not return home till after his father's death.

On July 5 De Carteret escaped from Mont Orgueil. The following day the Court issued an Order forbidding all the King's subjects to give him food or shelter, counsel or comfort, under heavy penalties. He took Sanctuary in St. Peter's church ; but in those Reformation days the old respect for Sanctuary rights was disappearing, and he was dragged back to the Castle. He escaped a second time, and was again recaptured. But after nine months his father secured his release on bail.

He then turned the tables on his enemies by summoning before the King's Council on a charge of illegal imprisonment the Jurats who had committed him. The case was heard in the Star Chamber in 1542 (the Depositions are printed in *Bull* IX), but we do not know the result. By a curious freak of fate all the pleadings in the Star Chamber have been preserved in the Record Office, but its decrees have disappeared. De Carteret however seems to have been exonerated, for he returned to Jersey a free man. In 1546 he fought and won another case before the Privy Council with regard to his wife's dowry. He now seems to have been accepted as a respectable member of the Community. In 1549 he was elected Constable of St. John's. In 1559 he was Procureur of the Trésor of St. John's Church. In 1551 he was appointed Solicitor-General, an office which he held till 1561, when he became Attorney-General. A few years later however, as Court records show, he got into serious financial difficulties. He resigned office in 1564, and probably left Jersey for Sark, which in 1565 his cousin, Helier De Carteret (q.v.), was colonizing. In 1566 his son William, acting as his Procureur, surrendered to his creditors all his goods and property.

In 1579 the colonists of Sark decided to adopt a constitution modelled on that of Jersey with a Bailiff, twelve Jurats, a Constable, a Centenier, and two Vingteniers. Edouard De Carteret was appointed the first Bailiff. But Sark had always been a dependency of Guernsey, and the Guernsey Court refused to recognize the new consitution. When Helier De Carteret ignored its summons to come and explain by what authority he had acted, the Bailiff and four Guernsey Jurats visited Sark, and, after holding an inquiry, ordered Edouard and two of his Jurats to cross at once to Guernsey to account for their conduct in setting up a rival jurisdiction. On 2 June 1582 they were tried. The two Jurats were dismissed to Sark, but De Carteret was committed to prison in Castle Cornet "as a usurper". Here he remained till 21 July, when he was released on bail. (The documents in this case are printed in the *Report of the Royal Commission ; Guernsey*, 1848). Having vindicated its authority the Court did not proceed any further against De Carteret ; and he seems to have passed the rest of his life in poverty and obscurity in Guernsey. He died there in February 1601, and was buried on the 10th in St. Peter-Port church. He left two sons, William, who became an Advocate of the Jersey Royal Court, and Jean, who settled in Sark. [In addition to the authorities mentioned above, the article, La Carrière d'Edouard De Carteret, in *Bull* IX.]

DE CARTERET, SIR EDOUARD, (1620—83), Knight, Gentleman Usher of the Black Rod, Bailiff. Younger son of Lieut.-Bailiff Josué De Carteret and Jeanne, daughter of Edouard Herault, Rector of St. Clement's. Born in Trinity Manor 17 Feb. 1620. During the Civil War in June 1649 he went with Sir George Carteret (q.v.) to Paris to arrange for the King's visit to Jersey (Chevalier). He was one of the defenders of Elizabeth Castle when it surrendered in 1651 (Bull. II). He then shared the King's exile. The Patent appointing him Bailiff states:—"He has constantly served and followed our person in foreign lands". This meant nine years' aimless drifting from Paris to Cologne, Bruges, Brussels, Brittany, the Spanish frontier, back again to Brussels. In Aug. 1654 he is mentioned as one of the forty members of the King's Household who were to receive board wages out of the 72,000 guilders allowed by the King of France. He was then still Mr. (S.P.) At the Restoration in 1660 he obtained a position at Court. In 1665 he is described as "Knight, one of our Gentlemen Ushers in Ordinary and Daily Waiter" (O.C.). On 25 Nov. 1665 he was sworn in as Bailiff, the first of six non-resident De Carteret Bailiffs, whose English engagements left little time for their Jersey duties. Under them the office of Lieut.-Bailiff assumed a new importance, for Lieut.-Bailiffs now performed all the Bailiff's functions. Sir Edouard's Lieutenants were Jean Pipon, then Jean Poingdestre (q.v.), then Philippe Le Geyt (q.v.). For eleven years (1668—79) Sir Edouard did not once preside over the States. In 1675 he is mentioned as Keeper of the Little Park, Windsor (S.P.). In 1676 he became Gentleman Usher of the Black Rod, a title derived from his ebony staff surmounted by a gold lion. His duty now was to attend the King, when he went to the House of Lords, to maintain order in the House, and arrest recalcitrant peers, and to summon the Commons to hear the King's speech and his assent to their Bills. Moreover as Usher to the Order of the Garter he had to keep the door at all meetings of the Chapter.

In 1679 a constitutional crisis brought him back to Jersey. When appointed Bailiff in 1665 one of his first acts had been to call the King's attention to the danger of a French invasion. In response Sir Thomas Morgan had been sent as Governor, a fine soldier, but a testy old martinet with no respect whatever for civil officials. He told the Attorney-General that he "had been like to lay him by the heels", and during a sitting of the

Court he threatened the Constable of St. Martin's with his cane, shouting, "By God, Sirrah, I shall rub your nose". After much friction the States at last petitioned the King against him (their Remonstrance is printed in *Bull.* IV.) and in July 1679 secured an Order in Council granting all that they asked for, and stating that "no Governor shall disturb the inhabitants in the peaceable possession of their privileges". But Morgan had died in April. The new Governor, Sir John Lanier, who owed his appointment largely to De Carteret's influence at Court, protested that this Order would "much impayre the authoritie of the Governor", and secured its suspension till the States should produce a list of their privileges for his consideration. De Carteret realized that this required his personal attention. He spent the next nine months in Jersey. A new deputation was sent to the Council, but it could not prevent a revision of the Order much in Lanier's favour. Sir Edouard was still Bailiff in March 1682, when he protested successfully before the Council against the stopping of work on St. Aubin's pier, but later in the year he resigned in favour of his son-in-law, Sir Philippe De Carteret of St. Ouen's (q.v.), the husband of his daughter Elizabeth. On 18 Feb. 1683 he died while on a visit to St. Ouen's Manor. The St. Lawrence Church Register declares:—"He was buried with the pomp and splendour that his dignity deserved". Tradition says that all arrangements had been made to bury him in St. Ouen's Church, but, as the procession was about to start, a terrific thunderstorm frightened the six horses that drew the hearse, and they could not be reined in, till they stopped of their own accord at the gate of Trinity Church. The mourners who had followed this mad stampede took this as a sign that he wished to be buried in his native parish. The coffin was taken to the Manor, while a new grave was dug beside his family pew, and the funeral was finished by torch-light. (*Bull.* II). We have found no contemporary evidence for the bolting horses ; but it is a fact that he was buried in Trinity Church, where the finest mural monument in the island proclaims in Latin that "no juster man ever lived on earth or one more loving to a friend" (Photograph in *Bull* IX). He married Elizabeth, daughter of Robert Johnson, Alderman of London, and had three children, Elizabeth, born 30 Dec. 1663, and baptized in St. Martin-in-the-fields, who married Sir Philippe De Carteret 8 (q.v.), Charles, and Edward, born 1665, who died

when seven years old, and was buried in Westminster Abbey.
[Authorities mentioned above.]

DE CARTERET, SIR EDOUARD (c. 1630—98), Knight.
Vicomte, Bailiff. Youngest of the seven sons of Sir Philippe
De Carteret 3 (q.v.) of Civil War fame and Anne Dowse. Born
in St. Ouen's Manor about 1630. In the first stage of the Civil
War he was with his mother in Mont Orgueil during its siege
by the Parliamentarians. In 1649, when Charles II was in
Jersey, he was appointed Cup-bearer to the Duke of York, the
King's brother, the future James II, then a lad of sixteen (Chevalier). In 1650 he left the island with the Duke, and for two
years formed part of the exiles' little Court, first at Paris, then
at Brussels, then again at Paris. When in 1652 the young
Duke joined the army of Turenne, De Carteret did not accompany him, and what he did during the next eight years is not
known. At the Restoration (1660) he rejoined the Duke in
London, and resumed his duties as Cup-bearer.

On 30 May 1663 he was granted by Letters Patent (printed in
O.C.) all the *perquages* in Jersey in acknowledgement of the
services that he and his father had rendered to the King and his
father. These were roads leading from the churches to the sea,
down which criminals who had taken sanctuary could reach a
boat unmolested. "He made conveyances of the parcels thereof",
wrote Poingdestre, "to those persons who had lands bordering
thereon, and by that means quite razed and extinguished them"
(*Caesarea*). This statement is too sweeping. He did not sell all.
He offered part of his St. Helier's *perquage* for the building of
a cornmarket (*A.E.*). He presented part of his St. Peter's *perquage*, which ran near St. Aubin's, to the parish of St. Brelade's
"as a sign of the great affection that he had for that parish".
After his death his widow was still selling "the *perquages* which
the King had given him" (Acte de Catel). A large batch of
these were bought by Sir Edouard's sister, Anne, widow of
Dean Brevint (q.v.), and from 1700 to 1706 her procureurs were
busy selling them. Another batch was sold in 1713 by her grandchildren, Charlotte and Sara Hussey.

Though not a member of the States, Sir Edouard was often

chosen to be their Deputy before the Privy Council. In Dec.
1665 he went to ask for more arms for the Militia ; he went again
in Sept. 1666 to seek sanction for a law to check the subdivision
of estates (A.E.).

On 30 May 1668 he was sworn in as Vicomte, an office which
occasionally had its exciting moments. Once, when "a lewd
woman" was rescued from the police by soldiers, "in that uproar
your Majesty's Sheriff himself was in danger of being slain"
(Bull. II). (The word 'Vicomte' was often translated 'Sheriff.')
He still paid frequent visits to Whitehall to perform his Cup-
bearer's duties. About this time he was knighted. In August
1668 he was still "Edouard De Carteret Esquire" (A.E.) ; but
in April 1671, when an Order in Council confirmed his right
to appoint a Deputy-Vicomte, when absent from the island, he
was "Sir Edward De Carteret, Knight" (O.C.). In 1673 he apparently accompanied the Duke of York to Dover, when he went
to meet his bride, Mary of Modena : for James gave him the
handsome suit which he wore, when the marriage was ratified
before the Bishop of Oxford, and the saddle and bridle of his
horse, "and he wore that suit", says an old Jersey chronicler,
quoted by Payne, "at general reviews and on ceremonial occasions". In 1675 he was still described as Cup-bearer to his
Royal Highness", and in 1679 as "servant to the Duke of
York" (S.P.).

In 1679 a battle was raging between the States and a new
Governor, Sir John Lanier. The King had issued an Order confirming the island's privileges ; but the Governor had persuaded
the Council to suspend this, until he had time to discover what
these privileges were. De Carteret had been partly responsible
for his appointment. "Sir Edward Carteret, Usher of the Black
Rod (q.v.), and I (the two Sir Edouards were distant cousins,
having had the same great-grandfather) went to all our friends,
and represented that there was nobody so interested as we, that
had our estates in the island, and that we thought him a very
fit man to be our Governor, being reported a good soldier and
one that understood French" (Bull IV). Now he went as Deputy
to the Privy Council to protest against Lanier's action. (His
statement of Grievances is printed in Bull. IV). This led to
angry scenes at the Council Meetings. "Sir John Lanier's Secretary told me that I was a pitiful fellow and a rascal. I complained to Sir John, but he did me no justice". This nearly led

to a duel. "Sir John told me in my ear, 'You and I will decide this presently', and took me by the hand, and so into the court, where he told me, 'We will take a coach and go to Hyde Park'." But the King heard what was afoot, and sent for Lanier, and the Lord Chamberlain ordered De Carteret in the King's name "to give no challenge nor to receive any" (*Bull* IV). But De Carteret failed to prevent the Council from revising several points in the Order in Lanier's favour.

On their return to Jersey the feud continued. Lanier vetoed the payment of De Carteret's expenses by the States, and an appeal to the Council was needed before he could secure them (*A.E.*). In 1678 a commission had been issued "to Sir Edward Carteret to be Lieutenant of a troop of horse to be raised in Jersey" (*S.P.*). This troop, of which Sir Edouard was now Captain, led the van in their sky-blue uniforms, whenever the Militia appeared on parade. Lanier now gave another troop this place of honour. In June 1682 he wrote:— "Some companies of the West Regiment were ready to mutiny for the youngest Captain, pretending only as having the name of Carteret to take place of an elder company, thinking themselves of a better family, contrary to discipline. Being set on by some of the chief officers of that name, they put themselves into a posture of disobedience, and, had I not been there myself, disorders might have followed" (*S.P.*).

In 1683 De Carteret resigned his office of Vicomte. He evidently hoped to become a Jurat, for in 1684 he obtained an Order in Council that, if elected, he should sit next to the Seigneur of St. Ouen's (*Bull* XI). This ambition was however never gratified. In 1687 the Order was expanded to include his male descendants, but he had none. In 1689, after the Revolution and the flight of James II, Jurat Jean De La Cloche, Colonel of the East Regiment, circulated a paper accusing De Carteret, no doubt because of his long connection with the late King, of being a Papist, and of having urged him not to resist the French, if they landed. De Carteret prosecuted him for libel ; and, as he refused to submit to the Court, he was degraded from his Juratship. De La Cloche's charges evidently gained no credence, for, when the Bailiff, Sir Philippe De Carteret 8 (q.v.), died in 1693, and his eldest son, Sir Charles (q.v.), a boy of fourteen, was too young to succeed him, William III appointed Sir Edouard to hold the office of Bailiff, till Sir

Charles should come of age. (The office had now become almost hereditary in the De Carteret family).

Though he had a house in the Town (an Order in Council speaks of him as "Sir Edward de Carteret of St. Helier's"), he spent more and more of his time in London. He presided twice over the States in 1694, and then not again till July 1697. In 1698 he died, and was buried on 15 Oct. in the Town Church. In 1673 he had married Jeanne Herault, Dame de la Godelière. She died in 1694. The same year he married Madeleine Durell, the twenty-year-old daughter of Jean Durell, his Lieut—Bailiff. In his will he speaks of her as "my beloved Madeleine, my very dear companion and spouse", and leaves her all his personal estate in Jersey, England, or elsewhere, "in recognition of the tenderness, love, and affection that she has for me and I for her". She survived her husband for forty-four years. Her death was followed by a famous trial in which Sara Messervy, her companion, was charged with destroying her employer's will (*Transactions of La Société Guernesiaise*. Vol. IX). Her monument with an amazing catalogue of her virtues can be seen in the Town Church. Sir Edouard had no children. [Authorities quoted above.]

DE CARTERET, FRANCOIS (1601—70), Jurat, Seigneur of La Hague. Eldest son of Jurat Helier De Carteret and Sara, daughter of Henri Dumaresq, Seigneur of Samarès. Born 1601. At his father's death in 1616, when he was only fifteen, he inherited the Fief de La Hague (for which he had to maintain a prison and be answerable for the prisoners at his peril), the Fief ès Ricards (for which he owed the King a pair of white spurs), the Fief des Nobretez, the Fief des Nièmes, and the Fief de la Hougue Dirvault, all in St. Peter's. But, when he came of age, and appeared before the Cour d'Héritage to make *comparence* for his Fiefs, he fell out with his powerful kinsman, Sir Philippe De Carteret of St. Ouen's (q.v.), Lieutenant-Governor and Bailiff. "Sir Philippe demanded from Mons.François homage on bended knee, but he refused saying he owed such submission to no man but the King, to God on two knees and to the King on one" (Brevint's *Diary*). On 20 Feb. 1627 he was sworn in as

Jurat, and next year was chosen by the States to superintend the building of the guard-room at St. Aubin's Fort. In 1629 he built at La Hague the dovecot to which the manor was entitled, and in 1634 he rebuilt the house (La Cloche Memoirs. *Bull.* II).

On the eve of Civil War Michel Lempriere (q.v.) and Henri Dumaresq (q.v.) were in London to protest against the De Carteret regime, and they seem to have mentioned François as an anti-Sir-Philippe Jurat, for, when in 1643 Parliament decided to arrest Sir Philippe, François was one of the five Commisioners appointed to do this. He was obviously taken by surprise. He did not refuse the commission, but kept rather aloof from his colleagues and signed none of their proclamations. He was absent from the meeting of the States at which Lempriere demanded Sir Philippe's arrest. A few days later Sir Philippe wrote to him from Elizabeth Castle:— "Aware of your influence with your fellow-commissioners, and never doubting your loyalty to the King and your love for your country, I adjure you, as I have often done before by word of mouth, by all that you hold most dear to help me to keep the people peaceful in obedience to the laws, and to convince them that neither they nor you are justified in joining with any political party that will disturb our peace, in bringing troops to our island, or in executing any commission inconsistent with your allegiance". But François did not reply. In July he was excluded by name from the King's offer of pardon. In September however, so Chevalier writes, "Mons. de la Hague, who had always lagged behind the other committee-men, and had tried to bring them into some agreement with Sir Philippe, seeing he could do nothing, severed himself from them. Therefore they called him traitor". In October some of his party challenged him to declare where he stood. He replied ambiguously that he stood for King and Parliament. In November Lydcot, the Parliamentary Lieutenant-Governor, realizing that the Castles were impregnable, sent him with two others to Mont Orgueil to try to make peace with Lady De Carteret. (Sir Philippe was now dead.) He returned with proposals to lay before the States, but on 19 Nov. George Carteret (q.v.) landed with Royalist reinforcements, and most of the Parliamentary leaders fled.

François however remained. The Royalists evidently did not regard him as a rebel. He was not mentioned in the warrant for the arrest of the Roundheads, nor was he degraded from his Juratship. For more than two years he attended meetings of the States. But in April 1646, when the Royal Commissioners got to work, he had an unpleasant interview with them (*quelque parole piquante*). Next day he slipped away secretly to France "for the sake of his health". "If the Commissioners had known of his hasty departure, they would not have let him go. It was thought he did this for fear of yet graver danger, for he had been mixed up with both sides, more through timidity than for any other cause. His own wish was to remain neutral" (Chevalier). But some weeks later he returned "holding his head high". In July he was back again in the States.

When Parliament recovered the island in Oct. 1651, he took refuge with Sir George Carteret in Elizabeth Castle ; but, when the Castle capitulated, he remained in Jersey, his life and liberty being secured by the terms of surrender. He was however blacklisted as one of the "chief Actors and notorious Delinquents against the Commonwealth", who were "for ever disenabled to bear any Office or Trust" (*Bull* V). In 1653 he was degraded from his Juratship. Meanwhile the question of his property hung fire. Royalists were allowed to compound for their estates, but the fixing of their fines took time. In March he asked leave to lease his land, till Parliament's pleasure was known, pleading rather disingenuously that he had been "compelled to comply with others, when the island was under the command of the King's forces" (*S.P.*). This request was granted. In November he petitioned again to be allowed to compound by paying one tenth of his personal estate and two years' value of the land. This offer was accepted and the fine fixed at £476. On 15 Dec. the fine was paid, and the estate discharged (*S.P.*).

At the Restoration in 1660 he resumed his position as Jurat, and in 1661 was appointed to administer the oath of allegiance to the men of St. Peter's (*A.E.*). In 1665 on the death of the Bailiff, François, as the oldest Jurat on the Bench, was appointed Judge Delegate. He died in 1670, and was buried at St. Peter's on Christmas Day. He left by will a field on the Quennevais and four cabots of rente to support the House that he had built for the poor of St. Peter's near the churchyard. He had married Judith, daughter of Germain Le Febvre, and had four children, Philippe (6) M.D. (q.v.), Cromwell's Judge Advocate, François, who became Seigneur of Dirvault, Helier,

and Sara, who married Michel Lempriere, Cromwell's Bailiff.
[Chevalier's *Journal* and authorities mentioned above.]

DE CARTERET, GEOFFROI (*Galfridus*), Dean of Jersey
(d.c. 1368), Son of Renaud De Carteret, Seigneur of St. Ouen's.
In return for many benefactions of the De Carterets to Mont
St. Michel the Abbey had promised always to receive one member of the family into its brotherhood (*Cart.* 52). Geoffroi had
claimed that privilege, and become a Benedictine monk. In
1295 he was appointed Rector of St. Martin's (*P.R.*). His father
had received the Fief of Mélèches from the King, and at the
partition of the estate this fell to Geoffroi's share, but, since a
Priest might not marry, it was to revert at his death to his elder
brother Philippe or his heirs. For this Fief he had to pay the
King 60 *livres tournois* annually and a pound of cummin. He
was evidently a man of impetuous temper. At the Assize of
1299 he was amerced for entering the house of Nicolas De La
Hague, and beating Thomasia, his wife, and dragging her from
her home, for breaking a window in the house of Lucie De
Carteret by night, and entering, and abstracting a green over-
coat (*supertunicam*) with cape, for beating Simon le Coveror in
his cart till blood flowed, and striking Pierre le Marchand, the
Vicomte's servant, though he raised the *Clameur de Haro*. He
had by this time ceased to be Rector of St. Martin's. At the
Assize of 1309 he was summoned to show by what warrant he
claimed wreckage on his Fief. The Viscomte failed to return
the Writ to the Justices, and "when it was urgently demanded,
at last brought it back vilely mutilated. As this seemed to the
Court a grave contempt, the Viscomte was heavily fined. Thereupon he complained of Maître Geoffroi, saying that as a favour
at his urgent request he had given him the writ whole to be
copied and returned, and afterward had great difficulty in recovering it ; but at length one of Geoffroi's brothers had returned
it thus marred. Geoffroi being present acknowledged this, but
solemnly swore that he did not know how the writ got damaged.
So the Viscomte's fine was remitted" (*Assize Roll*).
    But worse trouble lay ahead. The Justices had been ordered
to stop the practice of summoning Jerseymen before the Bishop's
Court at Coutances. Bishops at this time insisted on their right

to try all cases connected with marriage, divorce, or legitimacy, since marriage was a sacrament, all cases connected with wills and executors, since these were intimately linked with the dying man's last confession, all cases connected with oaths and perjury, since an oath pledged a man's hope of salvation, all cases of sexual immorality, of usury, or of defamation, and of course of blasphemy, heresy, and witchcraft. Moreover they claimed every case in which a cleric was concerned either as plaintiff or defendant, and they stretched the word 'cleric' to cover men in minor orders like acolytes, and even tonsured church-servants like bell-ringers and sextons. In Jersey this was specially objectionable, as it meant haling the King's subjects before a foreign Court. The King had written to the Bishop. "We expressly forbid you to cite any from the islands to appear before you or your commissaries" (*Foed*). He had ordered the Warden of the Isles to proclaim "that no one under pain of forfeiture of his lands and tenements shall cause anyone to be cited before the aforesaid Bishop" (*Foed*). But Pierre Faleyse, Dean of Jersey, ignored this proclamation, protesting that it was a breach of the Church's liberties ; so, when the Justices reached Jersey, they arrested and heavily fined many of his summoners and apparitors (See article *Faleyse, Pierre.*). De Carteret was present at the meeting in St. Helier's Rectory, when the clergy and their lay supporters decided to defy the Justices. Early next morning he was one of those who accompanied to the Court the Dean, who demanded the withdrawal of the proclamation, and, when the Justices refused, excommunicated them by name. The Justices ordered the Dean's arrest, but "the clergy who accompanied him violently rescued him from prison" (*Assize Roll*), and he escaped to Normandy. When "the Justices inquired concerning the names of the aforesaid clergy", De Carteret's stood first on the list. "Immediately after the said Maître Geoffroi had sworn fealty to the King" (i.e. for his Fief of Mélèches) "he abetted the Dean, inciting and encouraging him to stir up the islanders to ignore the Justices, and he together with his brother Robert was ringleader in taking the Dean out of the jurisdiction of the Court in the very presence of the Justices".

On the death of Faleyse in 1315 De Carteret succeeded him as Dean. He at once resumed the struggle for the rights of the Bishop's Court, arresting sinners and sending them to Coutances, as though nothing had happened, and even claiming prisoners from the Royal Court. And, so great was the prestige of the Church, he largely succeeded. Among presentments made by jurors of St. Saviour's at the Assize of 1324 was a complaint that "many persons are causing others to be cited to the Court of Christianity". Two cases may be taken as examples. The same jurors reported that "Guillaume Diervaunt, Lieutenant-Bailiff of our Lord the King, was slain with a knife on the King's highway while on his way home from St. Helier's after holding the Royal Court. Roger De Costillon, cleric, did this deed three years ago. Guillaume Diervaunt carried under his arm a large Gascony blade naked, which the said cleric slowly drew out, and by so doing caused Guillaume's death, for the veins of his arm were severed, and the blood gushed out. It is said that the cleric had no ill-will against Guillaume, nor did he mean to kill him ; and this we believe to be true. Pierre Ugon, cleric, and Guillaume Le Petit, cleric, were in Guillaume's company. Pierre was taken to the Bishop's prison at Coutances, and set free ; but Roger De Costillon remains in the said prison". From the Bishop's certificate presented later to the Justices Itinerant (printed in *Second Report of Commissioners on Criminal Law: Guernsey*) we learn that the two clerics were first "committed by the secular authorities to prison in the island, but afterward liberated by the Dean, who committed them to our prison at Coutances". After three years a strong effort was made to secure De Costillon's release. The Dean took ten other clergy to Coutances, "neighbours of Roger, whose word can be trusted", who "swore on the Holy Gospels, laying their hands upon them, that they believed Roger innocent". "Therefore," wrote the Bishop, "regarding this purgation as legally correct and canonical, we declared the said Roger not guilty, and have liberated him, and allowed him to depart". He arrived home while the Assize of 1329 was sitting, and was at once rearrested by the Vicomte who brought him before the Justices ; but the Dean compelled them to recognize the Bishop's acquittal as final. One other case shows how completely De Carteret had won recognition for the Church Court. "Ranulf Hamond, arrested for breaking open the chest of Oranga De Bovere of St. Lawrence and purloining a skein of wool, on being indicted, declared that he was a cleric, and could not be tried before any lay judge. On this point came Geoffroi De Carteret, Dean, and demanded that he should be set free ; and he was released to him".

In 1339 began the Hundred Years War with France, interspersed with brief intervals of truce. The first of these lasted from Sept. 1340 till Oct. 1342, the second from Jan. 1343 till 1345. In Jersey they seem to have been celebrated by a spate of charges and countercharges of treason. Many Jersey families had intermarried with families in Normandy, and had obtained in this way estates on the mainland. In Jan. 1342 an order had come to confiscate the land and chattels of traitors, "as the King is informed that divers landowners have absented themselves from the island during the war, tarrying among the King's enemies, and adhering to them, and returning afterward in time of truce to reoccupy their lands" (C.R.). In October the war was resumed, and De Carteret and others placed some of their property in Mont Orgueil for protection. In December however they complained to the King that "Henry de la More, who represents the Warden, is detaining divers sums of money, victuals, garniture, and goods, brought to the Castle for safety against the King's enemies". The King ordered their property to be restored (C.R.). By March 1343 however there was so much unrest that three Commissioners were sent "to inform themselves by such means as shall seem expedient touching the dissensions that have arisen between Thomas de Hampton, Warden, and the men of Jersey, whereby divers evils have happened in those parts, and greater loss will ensue, as is feared ; to hear complaints of any that will come forward, and find by inquisition by whom the dissensions were set in motion ; to inquire touching conspiracies among themselves and with the King's enemies ; touching those who have sent good money, victuals, and armour out of the island to the King's enemies, and brought back base money ; touching those who since the outbreak of war have left the island without licence from the Warden or sent their wives and children to Normandy, and why ; and touching who have arisen against the King in the islands, and by whom the houses called *loges*, erected on account of the war, have been burnt down" (P.R.). But, before the Commissioners arrived, De Carteret and his friends had fled. In May they sent a petition from Barneville in Normandy "in the name of the Jerseymen driven from the island by their enemies", asking for safe conducts to return, that they might lay before the Commission their complaints against de Hampton and de la More (Cart.). But meanwhile the King's Council had decided against them. In August an order

arrived that the Warden was to retain the animals and goods,
"as the King has learnt that they belong to enemies and rebels"
(C.R.).

The Dean was now branded as a traitor, and, as a monk of
a French monastery and an official of a French Bishop, he may
well have been suspect ; but the charge was not pressed home,
for Mélèches was not escheated. We hear no more of him till
1353, when he was appointed by his Abbey Prior of the Vale
in Guernsey. Unless he had been made Rector of St. Martin's
much below the canonical age, he must now have been over
eighty, but his fighting spirit had not abated. He began his
incumbency with a lawsuit as to whether he or his Abbot had
the right to appoint the Seneschal of the Priory. In 1364 he
had a lawsuit with the Warden, claiming a quarter of all wreckage washed ashore at Castle Cornet (Cart.). In 1368 he was
still alive, though now well over ninety, and contesting the
claim of the Treasurer of St. Michael in the Vale to receive a
contribution from the Priory toward the repair of the church
(Cart.).

[Authorities quoted above.]

DE CARTERET, GEORGE FREDERICK CECIL. (1866–
1932), Bishop of Jamaica. Son of Hubert Guille De Carteret
R.N. Born, 1866. Educated at Western College, Brighton, and
Wadham College, Oxford. B.A. 1889 M.A. 1892. D.D. 1913.
Ordained at Canterbury, 1889. After curacies at St. Dunstan's,
Canterbury, Tulse Hill, and Cheltenham, he became Vicar of
St. Paul's, Southwark, 1897–1901, and of Christ Church, East
Greenwich 1901–1913 ; Assistant Bishop of Jamaica, 1913–
1916 ; Bishop of Jamaica, 1916–1931, Assistant Bishop of
Leicester 1931. He died, 3 Jan. 1932.

DE CARTERET HELIER (1480–1561), Bailiff of Jersey :
fourth of the twenty sons of Philippe De Carteret (2), Seigneur
of St. Ouen's (q.v.) and Margaret Harliston. His elder brother,
Edouard, became Jurat in 1504, a younger brother, Pierre, in
1505. Nothing however is heard of Helier till he was 33 ; but,

since in 1518 the Chronicler says that he "had for a long time been familiarly acquainted" with the Duke of Norfolk and Sir William Compton, we may assume that some of his early years had been spent at Court. In 1502 Sir Hugh Vaughan became Governor of Jersey, a Welshman of low birth, originally a tailor, who had attracted the notice of Henry VII before he became King, and had risen to be Gentleman Usher. He was one of the worst Governors Jersey ever had. The Chronicler writes:— "He became so lecherous that he carried off young girls by force, so that they dared not walk the roads alone for fear of him. Moreover, if he claimed any man's land, he would summon him to produce his title-deeds, and, when he saw them, would break the seals, and tear the deeds in pieces. He beat and belaboured certain persons, so that they almost died". And these charges are confirmed by contemporary evidence. In 1513 Thomas Lempriere, the Bailiff, went to England to complain to the King. Vaughan then fortified his position by alliance with the De Carterets, taking two of the brothers, Richard and Jean, into his service, and offering Helier the post of Bailiff. He sent him to the all-powerful Cardinal Wolsey with a gift of Normandy cloth to make sheets for the Cardinal's servants, and a letter stating that the Governor had appointed him Bailiff (S.P.).

In May 1514 the deposition of Lempriere was confirmed by the King and the appointment of De Carteret as his successor. But in 1515 a Commission of Inquiry did come to Jersey, two English lawyers, who could not understand Jersey-French, and were easily hoodwinked by Vaughan and his officials. Their Report found Lempriere guilty of various irregularities and slurred over most of the Governor's misdoings. "Thus", says the Chronicler, "by the help of the Seigneur of St. Ouen's and his brothers, all was quieted for the moment".

But not for long. In 1515 Drouet Lempriere, who had married De Carteret's sister Mabel, inherited Trinity Manor on the death of his uncle. Vaughan suddenly claimed that the Manor was forfeit to the Crown for treason, because sixty years before, at the time of the French occupation, Lempriere's uncle, Thomas De St. Martin, had sided with the French. He ignored the fact that in 1480 De St. Martin had received the King's pardon. The case came before the Royal Court, which, because of the plague in St. Helier's, sat in Jurat Payne's house near Grouville Church. When the Bailiff was about to give judgement against the Governor's claim, in the words of the Chronicler, "Vaughan with his hand on his sword said, 'If you do not decide in my favour, I will plunge this into your belly'. The Bailiff sprang to his feet, and ordered the doors to be opened, and, drawing his own sword, grasped Sir Hugh's wrist firmly, and told him that, if he moved, he would be a dead man. Then the people rushed in, and the Bailiff gave judgement. The Captain, seeing himself frustrated, wanted to depose the Bailiff ; but the Bailiff told him firmly that he held his office of the King. The Captain said, 'Though it cost me my all, down to my shirt, 1 will turn you out' ".

The case now had to go before the Privy Council, and De Carteret hurried to Greenwich, where the Court was staying, and told his story to his friends, the Duke of Norfolk and Sir William Compton. By all accounts he was at this time a most attractive person. The Chronicler describes him as "very handsome, fascinating, and extremely eloquent," "good-natured and large-hearted, invariably cheerful and amusing". He made many friends, and before long attracted the notice of Henry VIII by his skill with cross-bow and arquebus. The king was enormously pleased with an arquebus that De Carteret invented which would fire five bullets without reloading. (The gun is probably the one now in the Armoury of the Tower of London marked "Early XVI Century"). Henry gave him a post in the Royal Household as Sewer of the Chamber (a Sewer's duty was to arrange the seating of guests.), and he secured good positions for three of his brothers, Guillaume in the service of the Princess Mary, Pierre in the service of Cardinal Wolsey, and Jean in the household of Sir Thomas Compton. Jean soon distinguished himself by his athletic skill. He could clear twenty-five feet at the long jump, and, when the Emperor visited Henry, and a contest was staged between his followers and those of the King, Jean secured the victory for England by winning the prize both for running and jumping.

Among other friends whom Helier made was William Sulyard, the distinguished lawyer, who was Master of the Court of Requests, and through him he secured Chambers in Lincoln's Inn. The entry runs:—"1519 Jan. 20. Helyer de Carteret alias Senton (i.e. St. Ouen) was admitted, and pardoned all vacations and offices: he may be at repasts: he shall not be charged with grand repasts nor with pensions, unless he have chambers within the Inn, and then he shall pay for the time and otherwise not: he gave a hogshead of wine." This means that he was a privileged person, who only paid for such meals as he ate, and for rooms when he actually occupied them.

To this early part of his life in London belongs the story in Brevint's Note Book:— "Edouard De Carteret was the son of a young English lady with whom H. De Carteret, Bailiff, slept on the night before he should have married her. Then he left her, and mounting his horse very early in the morning, went and married another lady in another county. The former lady sent him the said Edouard, after he was weaned, and broken-hearted by the insult, never wished to marry, and died shortly after." The name of neither lady seems to have been preserved, but Edouard (q.v.) appears later.

At Court De Carteret remained in favour. In Dec. 1521 the King confirmed his appointment as Bailiff ; and in March 1522 granted him for life the Manor of St. Germain in Jersey (S.P.). But what did not go well was the business which had brought him to London. Wolsey was now at the height of his power, and the wily Welshman, Vaughan, knew that Wolsey was bribable. This is not a libel on the part of the De Carteret Chronicler, for in the Record Office is a letter of 1522 from Vaughan about the case, in which he mentions that he is sending Wolsey five hundred gallons of Anjou wine and that there is more to follow (S.P.). Influenced partly by the bribes, and partly perhaps by the belief, that the longer De Carteret was out of the Island, the less trouble there would be in it, the Cardinal adopted the simple expedient of always adjourning De Carteret's case for consideration next term. In this way he dragged out the suit for nearly twelve years.

Meanwhile Vaughan was not idle. In July 1522 he started proceedings in Chancery to annul the grant of the Manor of St. Germain. It was a bold step to challenge a direct grant from the King, but he hoped by protracting the case to hold up a slice of De Carteret's income. The latter however slipped over to Jersey, and collected the arrears of rent, before Vaughan knew he was there. The Governor then cut off the Bailiff's official income by appointing a series af Acting Bailiffs (*Juges pour l'office de Bailli*) "thill the case shall be decided". He secured the support of Dean Mabon (q.v.). In July 1522 he sent Mabon to Wolsey with a letter stating that the Dean's views could be accepted as those of the island (*S.P.*). In June 1524 Vaughan forwarded a petition from eight Jurats, sealed with the Dean's seal, asking that De Carteret be dismissed from office (*Bull. VII.*). In August Mabon and Jean Lemprière of Rozel were appointed to act together as Bailiffs (*Prison Board Case*). From time to time De Carteret paid surprise visits to Jersey. On one of these, according to the Chronicler, Pen, the Acting Bailiff, tried to assassinate him in the Market Place. There was certainly a fight with drawn swords, and Pen only escaped by running into a house and barring the door.

At last De Carteret lost patience. On the closing day of Summer Term 1528, when his Counsel rose, and Wolsey as usual called the next case, he shouted, "I demand justice". "The Cardinal", says the Chronicler, "pretended to be deaf, and went on with the other case ; but the Bailiff cried at the top of his voice, 'I demand justice or at least some show of justice'. He made such a noise that the Cardinal could no longer pretend not to hear. So he said, 'Justice! If you had justice, you would be punished as a man who has wrought much harm to his country.' The Bailiff replied 'You do wrong to charge me with things you cannot prove'. The Cardinal rose in a rage, and said to the Lords of the Council, 'Did ever you see such insolence? We can guess how he lords it in his own land, if he is so malapert here'. And he called for the Keeper of the Fleet Prison. The Bailiff answered boldly, 'Before you send me there, I beg you tell me why. Is it for demanding justice? You have kept me waiting in this city by your command for three years and more, and I have not had a hearing. You have cut off my livelihood. My money is spent. I am a poor Gentleman with a wife and children, whom I cannot support as I should. Have I not good cause to protest?' Everyone marvelled that he spoke so stoutly ; but the Cardinal snapped back, 'You are a freak (*homme extraordinaire*) and quite unfit to rule'. The Bailiff replied, 'You cannot prove that'. The Cardinal said, 'I will show it you, sealed with the island seal', (referring evidently to the petition with Mabon's seal). The Bailiff retorted, 'That you cannot do, for I have the seal in my keeping'. (He had brought the seal with him to England, and in spite of much pressure had refused to part with it). The Cardinal knew not what to answer ; so he suspended the sitting in a rage".

But the outburst had done good. De Carteret's friends pulled

strings behind the scenes ; and on the first day of Michaelmas Term his case was heard, and he was restored to his position as Bailiff and his manor. In 1529 he returned to the island, and made his home at Handois, the manor-house on the
fief of St. Germain. He remained Bailiff for the next thirty
years. Wolsey fell in 1529, and Wolsey's protégé, Vaughan,
did not long survive him. A batch of fresh petitions against
him was sent to the Privy Council. A new Commission of
Inquiry was appointed, and he was recalled. With all subsequent Governors De Carteret seems to have worked well; but
in those hot-tempered days trouble was always simmering. On
Jan. 18, 1536 he wrote to Cromwell, "I hear complaints are made
against me, the causes whereof I do not know". In 1539 he put
himself seriously in the wrong in a quarrel with Nicolas Hue,
Constable of St. Mary. The Constable in the course of his
duty asked De Carteret how much he was contributing toward
the new cannon. De Carteret resented this, and summoned
Hue to St. Ouen's, where, according to evidence given in Court,
he "struck, beat, and maimed him in an inhuman manner". The
Privy Council ordered a Commission of Inquiry, which censured De Carteret in the strongest language. (The verdict is
printed in Le Quesne.) In the same year he secured the post
of Vicomte for his illegitimate son, Edouard (q.v.), but he a few
months later was arrested for murder. As five of the Jurats
were his accusers, the trial was eventually transferred to the
Star Chamber. The final Judgement has been lost, but, since
Edouard was not hanged, and in 1551 was appointed Solicitor
General, we may assume that he was acquitted. But the case
caused great scandal in the island ; and, as the Bailiff supported
his son, many of the Jurats, who had been friends of the murdered man, refused to work with him. In 1546 the Privy
Council sent a stern rebuke to the Jurats complaining that the
work of the Court had been thrown out of gear, "partly because
many of you refuse to be present, and partly because you refuse
to declare your minds". "His Grace's commandment is that
henceforth everyone of you shall on reasonable notice from the
Bailiff show yourselves diligent and attendant upon him. You
will answer for the contrary at your peril" (Acts of Privy
Council).

When the Reformation came, De Carteret early threw in his
lot with the Protestant side. In 1548 we find him subscribing

two quarters of wheat to support two Huguenot ministers who were brought over from France "to preach the Word of God purely to the people". On his shoulders as Bailiff fell the task of enforcing the religious changes ordered by the Government of Edward VI. In 1548 the Rectors were summoned to bring their books and rent-rolls for inspection. In 1549 the Royal Court ordered the arrest of "all maintainers of the superstitions of the Bishop of Rome". Injunctions then followed one another thick and fast. All endowments for Masses, Obits, Lights, or Fraternities were to be confiscated for the Crown. All church-yard and wayside crucifixes to be destroyed. All images to be removed from the Churches. All censers and other superstitious ornaments to be seized. All church bells, except one for each church, to be sold. Twice De Carteret received letters of thanks from the Council for his zeal. This made things awkward, when Mary came to the throne, and the Catholic ritual was restored. But with the support of Hugh Poulet, the Governor, De Carteret kept his post, and on one occasion firmly resisted the claims of the Church. In 1555 a Priest named Richard Averty (q.v.), not a Rector but an official of the Dean's Court, was arrested for murdering an illegitimate baby, of which he was the father. The Dean fought hard for his life, claimed Benefit of Clergy, and demanded that he should be tried and punished by the Bishop of Coutances ; but De Carteret and the Jurats stood firm, and he was hanged.

In Jersey in those days even the Bailiff was not safe from assault. On New Year's Day he had been dining with Sir Amias Poulet, the Lieutenant-Governor. As he left the Castle, he tossed a crown to the Master Porter for the garrison. Cook, the Castle caterer, grumbled, "That is not enough". That night with four soldiers he went to the Bailiff's house, and roused him from sleep, crying, "Urgent news from England! A letter from the Lieutenant". When the door was opened, they rushed into De Carteret's bedroom with the highwayman's threat, "Your money or your life". He took things coolly. "There is enough for us all", he said, "Take what I have. I shall not starve. I shall get more later from my rentes". They helped themselves to his gold chain, some silver cups, and five hundred crowns, and compelled a Bouley Bay boatman to take them to Portbail. Here however they were arrested, brought back to Jersey, and hanged.

As a Protestant he was a Bible-reader, and he came across the proclamation which Samuel made before he laid down his Judgeship. He determined to follow this example. In 1557, when he was 77, he ordered the Constables to proclaim in every parish in the island that, if he had wronged anyone during his long term of office, that person had only to call at his house, and he would compensate him (Le Quesne).

Of his first wife's children we hear only of Margaret, who married first Clement Dumaresq, Seigneur of Samarès, and later her cousin, Helier De Carteret (q.v.), Seigneur of St. Ouen's. In his old age the Bailiff married again, Jehanne Colles, a cousin of Sir Hugh Poulet. By her he had a son, who was christened Hugh after his godfather, the Governor. For the boy's sake the old man of eighty undertook another voyage to England to beg from the Queen that the grant of his manor might be extended to himself and his heirs, instead of only for life. He crossed with Sir Hugh Poulet to Lyme Regis in Oct. 1560, spent some time with Sir Hugh in his home at Hinton St. George, Somerset, then rode on to spend Christmas with his wife's brother, Humphrey Colles, then went to London, where again he was Sir Hugh's guest in his town house in Clerkenwell. He was apparently successful in his mission, for later Brevint tells us that Hugh, son of Helier De Carteret, the Bailiff, sold Handois to his cousin Helier of St. Ouen's, as he had been appointed one of the Keepers of the Queen's Forests, and no longer wished to live in Jersey. But the effort cost the old man his life. He caught fever, and died in Sir Hugh's house, and was buried in St. John's Clerkenwell, 19 Feb. 1561. [*Chroniques de Jersey.* Other authorities mentioned above.]

DE CARTERET, HELIER (1532—81), Seigneur of St. Ouen's and Colonizer of Sark ; son of Edouard De Carteret, Seigneur of St. Ouen's, and Marie Sarre ; grandson of Philippe De Carteret (2), (q.v.) and Margaret Harliston. His father died in 1533, when he was a year old, and for nineteen years his uncle, Helier De Carteret (q.v.), the Bailiff, was his guardian. When nineteen he married his cousin, Margaret De Carteret, his guardian's daughter, widow of Clement Dumaresq, Seigneur of Samarès. In 1552 he took control of his estates after doing homage to the Governor, and received the homage of his tenants at a banquet of over 200 guests. In 1553 be was elected Jurat. His chief work was the colonization of Sark. In the 14th. century Sark had been a prosperous little community with its own Bailiff and Jurats ; but French and Pirate raids had depopulated it, and for many years it had remained uninhabited. In 1549 the French had landed 400 men, and fortified the island, but bored by loneliness most of them had deserted, and in 1558 some Flemish adventurers surprised the remnant and presented Sark to Queen Mary. She however did nothing with it, and again it became uninhabited. Helier De Carteret realized the danger to Jersey, and specially to St. Ouen's, if Frenchmen or Pirates should reoccupy it, and conceived the idea of adding this desert island to his own estates. In 1563 he crossed to Guernsey, and secured the consent of the Governor and of Royal Commissioners then in the Island. In 1565 he received Letters Patent from Queen Elizabeth (Printed in Selosse's *Ile de Serk*). These state that Sark had long been uninhabited and uncultivated, whereby the Queen had lost her revenue and the creeks had become lairs for pirates ; that the best way to keep pirates out was to fill it with the Queen's subjects. She had therefore granted the island with all that it contained, including the right to hold a Court, to establish markets, and to tax bread, wine, and beer, to Helier De Carteret and his heirs in return for an annual payment at Michaelmas of 50/-, on condition that he keep at least forty men permanently living there. In 1565 he and his wife and a party of servants went to stay in Sark. "The island", says the Chronicler, "was so full of rabbit-holes and heather, briars, brambles, bracken, and undergrowth, that it looked impossible to cultivate. There were no tracks down which a cart could pass, nor harbour where a boat could unload safely". They camped at first in a ruined chapel, while they cleared space for a house, all materials for which had to be brought from Jersey, and carried up the face of the cliff on men's backs. They fought the rabbits and the bracken. They planted corn and vegetables. They sent to Jersey for horses, cattle, pigs, and farm implements. Before long they had forty houses, each in its own garden. The names show that these first colonists were all Jerseymen:— Alexandre, Balleine,

Chevalier, Dupré, Gaudin, Guille, Hamon, Hotton, Le Brocq, Le Cerf, Le Couteur, Le Gros, Masurier, Nicolle, Noel, Poindestre, Vaudin, and Vibert. Next De Carteret built a church, and brought over an excellent French Huguenot, Cosmo Brevint, to be minister. Bit by bit he improved his domain. He built a windmill and a watermill. He planted fruit and timber trees. He made a road. He pierced a tunnel through the cliff to a bay facing Jersey, so that carts could get down to the boats.

But he did not give himself wholly to Sark. He was still Seigneur of St. Ouen's and Senior Jurat of Jersey. We find him constantly present in the States, and he became leader of the Puritan Party. "The Seigneur of St. Ouen's", writes the Chronicler, "has been a strong supporter of the Reformed Churches, and has always done his utmost to promote the truth of the Gospel". Under Mary he had refused to go to Mass, and had crossed to Normandy to receive Communion in the Huguenot church at St. Lô. In Oct. 1565 he persuaded the Royal Commissioners to obtain from the Privy Council permission for the Huguenot Service Book to be used instead of the Prayer Book in the two Town Churches of St. Peter-port and St. Helier's. He was present in St. Helier's church for "the first Communion administered according to the purity of the Gospel". In 1576 he attended the Presbyterian Synod at Guernsey, and was one of the signatories of the new *Book of Ecclesiastical Discipline.*

In 1572 he went to England as Deputy of the States to protest against the plague of appeals to the Privy Council, and secured an Order forbidding appeals (a) on matters involving less than £7, or (b) on cases still undecided in Jersey, or (c) more than three months after judgement had been given (*A.E.*). On this occasion he showed Queen Elizabeth a map of Sark, and she presented him with six cannon from the Tower of London, which are still at the Seigneurie. In 1579 he handed over the government of Sark with all its revenues to his eldest son Philippe (born 1552), who proved, according to the Chronicler, "a wise, discreet, and very modest ruler". He made, however, one mistake. He called a meeting of tenants, which adopted a new constitution for the island, modelled on that of Jersey. This led to trouble with Guernsey (See *De Carteret, Edouard*). The Guernsey Court issued a summons: — "Helier De Carteret, farmer of the isle of Sark, is ordered to appear before the Court of this isle to explain by what authority Jurats and other officers have been established in that isle, and to account for other acts committed".

This dispute was not finally settled till after Helier's death. He was present in the States on 8 June 1581, but on 1 Feb. 1582, his son Philippe was sworn in as Jurat in his place. He had three sons, Philippe, Guillaume, and Amice (q.v.). [Authorities quoted above.]

DE CARTERET, JEAN (1552—1608), Seigneur of Vinchelez de Haut, son of Nicolas De Carteret, who was son of the Richard De Carteret who received the Manor of Vinchelez de Haut as a gift from his godmother, Catherine de Vinchelez (see De Carteret, Philippe 2, d. 1502). On 8 Dec. 1570 Jean De Carteret was sworn in as Solicitor-General, a post which he held till he became Jurat on 30 Jan. 1580. Sir Amias Poulet was the Governor and his son Anthony Lieutenant-Governor. This powerful family ruled the island for fifty years. Sir Hugh Poulet was Governor 1550—1571, his son Sir Amias 1571—1588, and his son Sir Anthony 1590—1600, and George Poulet, brother of Amias, was Bailiff 1583—1586, 1587—1591, and 1596—1614. Thanks to Jean De Carteret it is generally believed that the Poulets were tyrants, whereas they seem to have been remarkably honest and efficient rulers, who gave the island fifty years of peace and prosperity. The only trouble-maker was De Carteret. It began through a cod-fish case tried by Bailiff Poulet in Sept. 1587. The Jurats could not agree, and during the heated discussion Jurat Henri Dumaresq made a remark which the Bailiff resented, and he threatened to report him to the Privy Council. Two other Jurats, Jean De Carteret and Philippe Journeaux, took Dumaresq's part, and at last Anthony Poulet, the Lieutenant-Governor, who was present, removed the three obstreperous Jurats to the Castle.

Four days later they were released on bail, but De Carteret could not forgive the Poulets for this humiliation. He now began his career as agitator. He chose as his point of attack the Cour Extraordinaire. In spite of its name this was an old-established Court dealing with small debts, shipping disputes, and petty crimes. De Carteret suggested that the Bailiff was accumulating cases in this Court, because here he got fees, whereas in the other Courts he had to give justice freely. He began to collect signatures to a petition for the abolition of this Court, knowing that, if he succeeded, he would cut off a slice of Poulet's income. Circulating a petition sounds quite a constitutional act, but it provided wide scope for agitation. The Commissioners reported later, "A dangerous faction was bred in the isle, and many conventicles in great numbers were held day and night". The Lieut-Governor asked the advice of the States, who unanimously resolved "that it was necessary that the Cour Extraordinaire continue". The three Jurats were rearrested, fined, and suspended from office. They appealed to the Privy Council, but only De Carteret prosecuted the appeal.

In London he met no encouragement. On 25 March 1588 the Council Minutes record:—"This day John De Carteret being heard upon appeal from a sentence given in Jersey for procuring signatures to a petition for extirping an ancient Court in the isle, her Majesty's Attorney-General and Solicitor made report that the sentence was just and his appeal without cause. Whereupon their Lordships have committed Carteret to the prison of the Marshalsea, as well for soliciting to overthrow an ancient Court of Justice, as for appealing without cause from a sentence justly given". In September he was released, but, as he was embarking for Jersey, he heard that Sir Amias had died on Sept. 21st. De Carteret returned at once to London to present a petition against the appointment of his son, Anthony, the Lieutenant-Governor, as his successor. He then crossed to Jersey, where he began a vehement agitation against Anthony, adopting his old plan of collecting signatures to a petition. This asked for the appointment of Lord Seymour as Governor. The Commissioners reported later:— "Carteret and his confederates combined themselves into a new league and solicited from house to house. During the time of which unsettled estate, what insolent behaviour, riding, assembling, and practising to alienate the subjects from due obedience to her Majesty's Lieutenant! how they made themselves patrons of the lewd and unruly people within the isle, that her Majesty's Lieutenant was forced to keep his Guards about him! what affray all the best subjects were in, did appear most evidently to us by the

relation of all the Jurats and States, who especially remembered
the dangerous time they lived in". Helier Faultrart, Rector of
St. Martin's, gave evidence: — "I do certify that these two years
there have been very dangerous factions in this isle, whereby
the people have been greatly out of order, giving themselves
unto divers insolencies whereunto they were not wont".

On 4 May 1589 De Carteret was again before the Council:—
"John De Carteret being heard at length upon certain injurious
and slanderous articles framed against Anthony Poulet, her
Majesty's Lieutenant, and George Poulet, Bailiff, and not being
able to produce any proofs of any of his aforesaid articles,
which, it appears to their Lords, proceeded rather from former
spleen than upon just cause and reason, their Lordships have
committed him to prison of the Marshalsea, there to remain
during their Lordships' pleasure, until he submit himself unto
their Lordships and to the said Anthony Poulet". Within a
fortnight however he produced another long list of charges,
which he offered to prove by many witnesses. He was allowed
to return to Jersey to collect his evidence, and a local committee
of five was appointed to investigate the matter on the spot.
This apparently produced no result ; so on 15 Dec. it was
decided to send a Royal Commission to the island. Meanwhile
on 4 July 1590 Anthony Poulet was at last sworn in as Governor. De Carteret had succeeded in holding up his appointment for nearly two years.

About this time Jean Perrin, Seigneur of Rozel, joined De
Carteret. He too had a private grudge against Bailiff Poulet.
He had been imprisoned in the Castle for slandering his stepmother, and the Bailiff, who had married a Perrin, had taken
a prominent part in the family quarrel. He and De Carteret
now drew up a formidable-looking list of charges against the
new Governor:— He had sold cannon from the Castle as
scrap-iron and pocketed the proceeds. He had sold corn to
Spain, when Spain was at war with England. He had kept
innocent men in prison without bringing them to trial. He had
removed Jurats and other Officers from their posts contrary to
the Constitution. He had exacted forced labour from the people.
He had cut down trees on private property, etc., etc. In March
1591 the Royal Commissioners Dr. Tertullian Pyne and Robert
Napper, arrived in the island. Under their examination every
one of these accusations broke down. They reported wholly in

favour of Poulet, and recommended that De Carteret and Perrin should pay the whole cost of the Commission. In June we find De Carteret again before the Council protesting against this report, and for the third time he was sent to the Marshalsea, until he should acknowledge his fault, and pay his half of the expenses (£83-10-0). On 29 July he made his submission:— "I, John Carteret, do humbly confess my unadvised offence in neglecting that duty I owe the Governor as her Majesty's Lieutenant, and for going about to work his discredit by such informations as have not been proved true, promising that hereafter I will lay aside all malice and factions, and behave myself as becomes a good and dutiful subject toward the Magistrate set in Authority by her Majesty". On his return to Jersey however he again became awkward. He refused to appear before the Royal Court to make his submission in person to the Governor, and went into hiding. On 5 Jan. 1592 a warrant was issued for his arrest and removal to the Castle. On 15 Jan. he appeared, and made his submission. Soon after he was restored to his seat on the Bench, for on 6 Sept. 1593 we find him sitting as Jurat.

His next interest was a dispute between the two Vinchelez Manors. In 1595 the Procureur of John Dumarest of Vinchelez de Bas raised the Clameur de Haro against De Carteret for holding his Court on the Grand Becquet des Tenets, which was claimed as Dumarest property. In 1598 the case reached the Privy Council, who decided in De Carteret's favour, but the Dumarests still fought on ; and at last, to avoid the great cost of these lawsuits, De Carteret consented to arbitration. Three arbitrators carefully mapped out the boundaries of the two manors, certain fields being exchanged to make the boundaries simpler, one curious point being that each manor retained half the Chapel of St. George, and the two Seigneurs were to share its upkeep.

By 1598 the feud with the Poulets seemed to be dead, for in December George Poulet appointed De Carteret Lieutenant Bailiff. But in 1602 it flared up again, and Sir Walter Ralegh, who was then Governor, had to hurry back from England to settle it. After investigation on 10 July he committed De Carteret to the Castle. On 24 July he succeeded in reconciling the two men. "The Governor insisted that peace and concord must be restored. He pointed out to De Carteret how grave had been his fault in insulting the Bailiff on the seat of Justice, not considering that he represented there the authority of the Prince. The said De Carteret being touched by these remonstrances voluntarily recognized and confessed that he had made a grave mistake in using such words toward the Bailiff. Nevertheless the Bailiff did not feel satisfied with this apology ; but the Governor and the States after due consideration found the apology adequate, and prayed and exhorted the Bailiff to accept it for the sake of the peace of the island ; to which under these considerations he consented to agree" (A.E.).

Jean De Carteret married Jeanne, widow of Richard Le Brocq, and daughter of Clement Dumaresq, Seigneur of Samarès. He had three children. Philippe who became Attorney-General, Jean, and Esther. He died 1608. [Most of the documents on the Poulet feud, including the Commissioners' Report, will be found in the printed *Manuscrits de Philippe Le Geyt.* Vol. IV. Others are in the State Papers.]

DE CARTERET, JOSUE (d. 1664). Jurat. A black sheep in the De Carteret fold. Second son of Josué De Carteret, Seigneur of Trinity, and Jeanne Herault. We first hear of him in 1636, when he carried off Jeanne, the child heiress of the wealthy Jean Le Febvre, Seigneur of La Hougue, to Normandy. The Huguenot ministers there refused to marry them, as she was obviously under age ; but he took her to Sark, and married her there (La Cloche Memoirs. *Bull* II). At the beginning of the Civil War he was arrested as a Royalist and imprisoned for a time on the Parliament ships in Bouley Bay, but was later released on bail (Chevalier). When George De Carteret recovered the island, Josué "showed himself", says Chevalier, "bitterly opposed to the Parliament-men, and avenged himself for the wrongs he had suffered by laying complaints before the Commissioners who came to Jersey, and they granted him compensation from those against whom he complained. He was very friendly with Sir George, and went at all times to the Castle to bring charges against all and sundry, saying they were disaffected. He got some of these imprisoned, and so made himself feared. He ingratiated himself so successfully with Sir George that he made

him a Jurat". This was in 1644. But it is no use eloping with
an heiress, if your father-in-law lives on in possession of his
property. "So he brought an action against his father-in-law,
representing that he had held for the Parliament by every means
in his power", and, when his fellow-Jurats could not stomach
this, he "uttered publicly such passionate expressions of revenge"
that Daniel Brevint excommunicated him. He then accused
Brevint to the King of sedition, but the only result was that his
behaviour was declared to be "scandalous and offensive". But he
was irrepressible. He wrote to the King accusing his father-in-
law of treason, "and to strengthen his case induced several to
sign his appeal. Sir George heard of this, and demanded to
see the document, and, when he would not produce it, sent him
to the Castle" (May 1649). He was then "dismissed by His
Majesty from all public service", and, in the euphemistic language of the Court Rolls, "he withdrew to France for the benefit
of his health". He went to Paris and appealed to Charles II,
who promised to look into the matter, when he came to Jersey.
De Carteret then returned to the island. "On his arrival Sir
George sent him back to prison. Eight days later he was released
at the request of his brother, the Seigneur of Trinity. At the
Cour d'Héritage on 20 Dec. he took his seat on the Bench, but
the Presiding Jurat ignored him, and treated him as though he
were not there. He made a second attempt to resume his place
on 28 Sept., but again no notice was taken of him. Though
receiving slight after slight he still was not abashed, and a third
time took his seat among the other Jurats. This time Sir George
presided, and upbraided him for daring to be present and ordered
him to withdraw. When the King came to Jersey, he made
friends with some of the Court, but nothing came of it, nor
could he regain Sir George's favour" (Chevalier). So he returned
to Paris ; and later, when the King had left the island, approached Lord Jermyn, the Governor, alleging that he had been
sent by the people of Jersey to beg him to dismiss Sir George
and appoint a new Lieutenant. When Lord Jermyn visited
Jersey, De Carteret preceded him by a few days (May 1651) :
but Sir George arrested him, and kept him prisoner till the
Governor arrived, when he was brought to trial, and found guilty
of having carried off his wife by force, of having taken bribes to
let men escape militia service, of having beaten a man so severely that he died, and of having forced persons to bear false

witness against his father-in-law. He was condemned to imprisonment, but later through his brother's influence was released on bail, on condition that he did not go outside his own grounds.

Then came the conquest of Jersey by Parliament, and immediately Josué posed as a Parliamentary martyr. In a Petition to Parliament he said: — "I was oft indicted as a rebel and traitor to the late King, and was prisoner therefor, when the island was taken". But Jersey knew his record too well, and again he had to leave the island. He returned however, and for five years made himself a nuisance with interminable applications to the Court and petitions to the Council against his brothers-in-law about the division of the property of his wife's mother. At the Restoration he was not restored to his Juratship, and he died in 1664, and was buried on Good Friday, 8 April. He had one daughter Jeanne, who married Dean Clement Le Couteur.

(1) DE CARTERET, PHILIPPE (b.c. 1432), Seigneur of St. Ouen's. The Wars of the Roses had grave repercussions in Jersey. In 1460, when the Lancastrians were losing ground, Henry VI's French Queen, Marguerite of Anjou, was hatching some secret plot with her first cousin, Pierre de Brézé, Count of Maulevrier, the French Seneschal of Normandy. "If those around her knew her intentions", he wrote to the King of France, "they would put her to death". The scheme almost certainly was that de Brézé should raise troops to support the Red Rose in England, and be rewarded by the post of Lord of the Isles. The royal family would then have a harbour of refuge, if the Yorkists should triumph. John Nanfan, a Cornish veteran of Henry V's wars, devoted to the House of Lancaster, was Constable of Mont Orgueil. He possibly agreed to allow de Brézé to surprise the Castle, an act which would not seem to him treason, but a handing over of his charge by the Queen's orders to the new Lord of the Isles, who was the Queen's cousin. Whether he did this deliberately, or, as the *Chroniques* say, through "culpable carelessness and neglect of duty", cannot now be proved ; but one summer night in 1461 Jean de Carbonnel, de Brézé's cousin, seized the Castle without resistance.

158 A BIOGRAPHICAL DICTIONARY OF JERSEY

The Seigneur of St. Ouen's at this time was a Philippe De Carteret. Payne's *Armorial*, following Collins' *History of the Carteret Family*, identifies him with Philippe, son of Renaud, who was under the guardianship of Roger Walden (q.v.) in 1382. But this Philippe came of age in 1385 (*Ancient Petitions*), and would have been a centenarian at the time of his famous ride mentioned below. More than one generation must have intervened between the two Philippes. An Act of the Court (Le Maistre MSS, S.J. Library) shows that the later Philippe was the eldest son of Philippe De Carteret, Seigneur of St. Ouen's, and nephew of Renaud De Carteret, Seigneur of Vingt Livres, and that in 1441 he was still a minor. In 1452 his name appears on a contract as Jurat ; so he had then come of age. In 1453 he appealed to the Court against the judgement of 1441, which had left his uncle in possession of Vingt Livres, protesting that it had been given while he was a minor under the guardianship of the Prince. His mother (not his wife, as Payne states) was daughter and heiress of Sir William Newton, Kt., of Gloucestershire.

The *Chroniques* make him the hero of the French occupation:— "The French captured the Seigneur of Samarès and many other men of substance, who dwelt near the Castle, to whom they wrought no small hurt both in their goods and bodies ; but they could not subdue the six parishes in the West ; they durst not pass the town of St. Helier, for Philippe De Carteret with the men of those parishes raised a force and fought stoutly against them all the time they held the Castle, and oft-times skirmished with them even under the Castle walls". Poingdestre, followed by Falle, adds that Grosnez Castle is "famous for having been a retiring place to Philippe De Carteret and his party against Peter de Bressé" (*Caesarea*). For the last assertion there is no evidence. Grosnez Castle had probably long been in ruins. Nor will the legend of the defence of the six parishes bear investigation. For seven years, after the seizure of the Castle, de Brézé's officers controlled the whole island. Life seems to have gone on quite normally. There is no hint of war between the East and West. Nicolas Morin, the Bailiff, remained in office; signing himself during the occupation, "Bailiff under the high and puissant lord, the Count of Maulevrier, Lord of the Isles"; nor, after the island was liberated, was he regarded as a traitor. The Court met regularly. A contract, printed by De la Croix, shows that on one occasion the Bailiff was at St. Ouen's to pass an agreement to pay a priest to say Mass in St. George's Chapel. In December 1463 the French investigated an alleged pro-English plot in which the chief suspects were the Seigneur of Rozel (see *Lempriere, Renaud*) and the Rector of St. Martin's (see *Le Hardy, Thomas*). Much was said about surreptitious communication with Guernsey, but nothing of any pro-English force in arms in the western parishes. On the contrary we learn that, when John Hareford, an English soldier of fortune, landed in St. Ouen's Bay in 1462 with a party on plunder bent, De Carteret had arrested him, imprisoned him in the Manor, and then handed him over to the French authorities, who put him in irons in the Castle. Later he was released on parole, perhaps as a French spy. He then wandered freely about the island, which was certainly not rent by internal war, dining sometimes at Rozel Manor in the East, and sometimes at St. Ouen's Manor in the West. We learn too that the Lady of St. Ouen's and the Lady of Rozel dined in the Castle at Whitsuntide 1463 with the French Commander, whose wife had just returned from Normandy. Moreover on the Feast of the Assumption the French Marshal gave a dinner to the Fraternity of our Lady "in the De Carteret house" (*Bull* X). Clearly there was no open warfare between De Carteret and the Castle, though De La Croix' statement that De Carteret was Lieutenant-Bailiff under de Brézé is based on a careless mistake (See *Bull* IV. 28).

By 1467 however the position had materially altered. In England the White Rose seemed to have triumphed. Edward IV was on the throne. His rival, Henry VI, was a prisoner in the Tower. Marguerite was an exile. In France Pierre de Brézé was dead. Louis XI's policy of centralizing the French government and suppressing any autonomous rights that survived in Duchies like Normandy, had provoked the Norman barons to rebel. De Brézé had fallen in battle, and Carbonnel was so deeply involved in the revolt that he could hope for no help from Louis. In Jersey there was a real chance of throwing off the French yoke. Then it probably was that De Carteret began to show pro-English sentiments, and the French tried to kidnap him. "It befell one day that he went to catch fresh-water fish in his pond near St. Ouen's Bay, and the French came stealthily along the beach between the shingle and the sea, thinking to take him unawares, and bring him captive to the Castle. But the Seigneur ever kept a good horse, and he espied them, and sprang to the saddle, seeking to attain his Manor. But, ere he could reach the crest of the hill, another troop appeared, hoping to cut him off, and he was constrained to swerve toward the Val de la Charière. Thereupon, since he was so hard-pressed that he could not gain the end of the track, he made his horse leap the sunken road at its deepest place, where it is 18 feet deep and 22 feet wide, and, spurring toward the Landes of St. Ouen, so made his escape. But, ere he could arrive at the Manor, his horse fell dead beneath him ; whereat the Seigneur was greatly grieved, and he would not suffer it to be devoured by dogs or birds, but caused it to be buried in his garden for the good service it had done him" (*Chroniques*). A slight confirmation of this story was found in 1904, when a bone was dug up in the Manor grounds, which London experts identified as the shoulder-blade of a horse, which had been buried for several centuries.

In 1468 Edward IV informed Parliament of his intention to invade France "to subdue Louis, the usurped King, and recover his Duchy of Normandy", a project which came to nothing ; but he sent Vice-Admiral Sir Richard Harliston with part of the fleet to Guernsey. "Sir Richard was minded to visit Jersey privily by night ; so, leaving his ships in Guernsey, he landed at Plemont, and made his way through the darkness to St. Ouen's Manor. The Seigneur received him right gladly, and they commune together, and agreed that Harliston should go back to Guernsey, and set his ships in array, and return with all speed, while the Seigneur, who had now the most part of the island under his sway, would recruit all men available. Meanwhile he spared no pains to keep their plans secret, merely warning his folk to be alert and armed, whenever a call should come. When Harliston had set all things in trim, he again came ashore during the night at Plemont, and led his troops at once to the Manor". (From other sources we know that he brought a number of Guernseymen with him: see Nicolle's *Mont Orgueil Castle*.) "The Seigneur mustered his men forthwith, and they marched right stealthily all night along the north coast, and, so well did they do their duty, that—God be thanked—ere day dawned, they were encamped before the Castle. Thus they encircled it on every side, so that no one durst come out" (*Chroniques*). The siege began on 17 May 1468 ; and after nineteen

weeks lack of provisions forced the garrison to surrender.
    "After the fall of the Castle Sir Richard tarried in the island
awhile to gain full possession and to restore order, and then
committed the defence of the Castle to the Seigneur of St. Ouen's,
while he himself hasted to the King with all speed to acquaint
him with what had happened" (*Chroniques*). Meanwhile however Lancastrian risings were again breaking out, and Louis had
gathered a fleet at Harfleur for the invasion of England ; so it
was two years before Harliston could again spare time for Jersey,
and De Carteret remained in charge. Soon after Sir Richard's
return as Governor in 1470, De Carteret must have died, if the
family tradition is true (given by Collins from "an ancient manuscript"), that his eldest son Philippe 2 (q.v.) was so young when
he inherited the estate that, "when he performed his homage
alder-trees did grow in the hall and other places of his manor-
house by the covetousness of those that had custody thereof
during his nonage" ; for the son was old enough to become a
Jurat in 1476 ; so, if the father died in 1470, this would have
given the trees only six years to grow. The father married Penna, daughter of Perrine de Caux of Normandy, according to
Collins, who apparently obtained his information from a genealogy (said to have been drawn up by Sir Henry St. George,
who became Richmond Herald in 1660), which he found in a
notebook in the College of Arms. [*Chroniques de Jersey*: Collins' *History of the Noble Family of Carteret* 1756: Payne's
Armorial of Jersey.]

(2) DE CARTERET, PHILIPPE (d. 1502?), Seigneur of St.
Ouen's, opponent of Baker. Eldest son of Philippe De Carteret
1 (q.v.), and Penna de Caux of Normandy. He was a minor
when his father died, and, according to Collins, when he came
of age, "alder-trees did grow in the hall of his manor by the
covetousness of those that had custody thereof during his nonage". He married, when she was sixteen, Margaret Harliston,
daughter of the Yorkist Governor, and by her had twenty sons
and a daughter. Of these Philippe, the eldest, died young ;
Edouard became Seigneur of St. Ouen's and Jurat ; Helier (q.v.)
became Bailiff ; Pierre became Jurat and Lieut.-Bailiff ; Jean
became Rector of St. Ouen's ; Thomas became Rector of St.

Sampson's Guernsey ; Richard became Seigneur of Vinchelez ;
Mabel married Drouet Lempriere, Seigneur of Trinity.

In 1476 Philippe De Carteret was elected Jurat, an office
which he held for 23 years. On 28 Jan. 1484 his father-in-law
Harliston granted him in the King's name permission to crenel-
late his manor:— "Whereas our dear friend Philippe De Carteret, Seigneur of St. Ouen's, has made clear to us that his
manor, goods, servants, and tenants are in peril both night and
day from malefactors and the King's enemies through the propin-
quity of his house to the sea, we grant him leave to fortify his
manor, without and within, with towers, battlements, bulwarks,
moat, drawbridge, and artillery for the defence of himself and
his family" (Licence in De La Croix). From 1484 he was involved in one of those interminable property disputes so common
among Jersey families. Katherine of Vinchelez gave her manor
of Vinchelez to his youngest son Richard then a minor, who
was her godson. The Dumaresqs however claimed right of
succession. Philippe died before the case was settled.

Like many Jerseymen of the official class he is chiefly remembered for his quarrel with a Governor. The story is told in the
Chroniques. When the Yorkist Kings lost their throne, Harliston lost his Governorship, and was succeeded in 1486 by
Matthew Baker, Constable of Kenilworth Castle, one of the
Esquires of the King's Body, who had been Henry VII's companion in exile. The Chronicler describes him as "very peevish,
malicious, and vindictive". Between him and De Carteret a
bitter feud arose, aggravated by Baker's demand that all Seigneurs should produce their title-deeds to prove their right to their
estates. At last in 1494 Baker forged a letter from De Carteret
to some Norman nobles offering to betray Mont Orgueil to
them. He caused this to be dropped in a road near Longueville
along which he always rode on his way to Town. One of his
followers, Roger Le Boutillier, picked it up. Baker laid it before
the Royal Court, accusing De Carteret of treason. When De
Carteret repudiated the letter, Le Boutillier threw down his
glove, and challenged De Carteret to ordeal of battle. De
Carteret demurred on the ground that Le Boutillier was a notorious criminal, whom he had saved from the gallows ; but
Clement Le Hardy (q.v.), the Bailiff, ruled that the combat must
take place. (A wager of battle at this time was fought on foot
with staves and leather shields. The defeated party was judged

guilty and punished). Meanwhile he committed both men to the Castle. Here Le Boutillier was allowed fresh air and exercise and fed like a fighting cock ; while De Carteret was kept in close confinement. But Baker knew that De Carteret had friends at Court ; so he hurried to London to tell his side of the story first, leaving an order that no other boat was to leave the island.

Four days before this, Margaret De Carteret had given birth to the last of her 21 babies ; but she rose from her bed, crossed in a fishing boat from St. Ouen's to Guernsey, where she appealed for help to Guillaume Beauvoir, a Jurat, whose mother had been a neighbour of the De Carterets at St. Ouen's. He took her in his own boat to England. As they approached Poole, they saw Baker on the quay ; but a hail-storm drove him indoors, and they landed without being recognized, and rode via Salisbury to London. Here by the help of Bishop Fox of Winchester Margaret obtained an interview with Henry VII, who, after hearing her story, gave her an order, sealed with the Great Seal, for the release of her husband, until the case could be heard by the Privy Council. As she left the Presence Chamber, she met Baker just going in. She rode to Southampton, found a boat leaving for Jersey, and arrived home on the day before that fixed for the combat. She presented her order to the Royal Court, and secured her husband's release. It was found later that covered traps had been dug on the spot chosen for the fight to trip De Carteret up and make his defeat certain. A few days later he crossed to England loaded with testimonials to his loyalty, and was acquitted by the Privy Council.

Such is the dramatic story told by the Chronicler. No other documents directly confirm its details ; but among the State Papers is a Writ of Privy Seal (printed in *Prison Board Case*), dated 3 Nov. 1494, stating that divers doleances and complaints had been received from Jersey against Baker, and that the Writ was issued "to obliterate the said controversies and to nourish perfect amity". Seven months later, on 17 June 1495, came an Order in Council, (also in *Prison Board Case*) mentioning no Governor by name, and ordering that, when any variance arises between the Captain and a Jurat, neither is to use force against the other, but the matter is to be referred to the King. By this time Baker had been recalled from Jersey, but not in disgrace, as the Chronicler would have us believe, for twice later he was sent as the King's ambassador to France, and in 1502 was granted the custody of the Royal Palace of Westminster.

De Carteret ceased to be Jurat in 1499, and, according to the Genealogy in the *British Compendium* (1731), which is not always reliable, died in the 16th year of Henry VII, i.e. 1502. [Authorities quoted above.]

(3) DE CARTERET, SIR PHILIPPE (1584—1643), Knight, Seigneur of St. Ouen's and Sark, Lieutenant-Governor and Bailiff. Eldest son of Sir Philippe De Carteret, Seigneur of St. Ouen's, and Rachel, daughter of George Poulet, Bailiff ; grandson of Helier De Carteret (q.v.), colonizer of Sark. Born in Sark, 18 Feb. 1584 (Certificate presented to prove his age, when he claimed his estate). In 1594, at the age of ten, he matriculated at Oxford from St. Alban's Hall. His brother, Elie, aged nine, matriculated at the same time. On 20 May 1594 his father died. By feudal tenure Philippe now became a ward of the Crown, which meant in Jersey of Sir Anthony Poulet (q.v.), the Governor. The latter sold the wardship to his uncle, George Poulet (q.v.), the Bailiff, who was the boy's grandfather. He seems to have cared well for the nine children and their mother. But by 1602 he was too old to look after the estate properly ; so Philippe, who had taken his B.A. in 1601, "abandoned his studies which he loved more than anything else in the world" (his reply to the Crown Officers), left Oxford, and came to Jersey to take charge of his property, though still under age. He at once took a prominent place in local life. In 1602, when a Spanish invasion was feared, though only eighteen he was put in charge of the defence of St. Ouen's and St. Mary's (*A.E.*). While still under age, he married Anne, daughter of Sir Francis Dowse of Nether Wallop, Hampshire.

In March 1605, being now twenty-one, he claimed from the Court possession of his inheritance, and on 27 Sept. was sworn in as a Jurat. But the Crown Officers demanded the income of his estate for the last 4½ years, asserting that George Poulet had ceased to be Guardian when Sir Anthony died. The case was fought to the Privy Council, where Francis Bacon arranged a compromise, by which Philippe escaped by paying £30. The States quickly accepted him as a leader. In 1606, when they sent a deputation to the Privy Council "to accelerate the coming of the Commissioners", he and the Rector of St. Helier's were chosen, and for the next twenty years he formed part of every deputation sent to England. This was probably diplomatic : for, as a Poulet on his mother's side, he had influence at Court. Baron Poulet and the Marquis of Winchester were his cousins, and Sir Edward Conway, later Lord President of the Council, was a personal friend. On 23 Feb. 1617 he was knighted by the King at Whitehall ; and in 1619 James promised that he should be the next Bailiff. As became an Oxford scholar, his attitude toward island controversies was cool-headed and tolerant. In the struggle between Bailiff and Governor he remained on good terms with both ; and to work harmoniously with Bailiff Herault (q.v.) was something of a feat. "The Governor and Bailiff stand on ill terms", he wrote in 1620, "I have endeavoured to pacify them, but to no purpose". In the controversy between Anglicanism and Calvinism he personally leant toward Geneva, but, when he saw that the King had made up his mind, he yielded. "St. Ouen advised them" (i.e. the States), wrote Herault in 1619, "to accept a Dean according to the King's will. He declared that, if they persisted in demanding continuance of their discipline, they must choose another than he to present their requests" (S.P.). From Feb. 1624 to July 1625 he acted as Lieut.-Governor during Peyton's absence in England.

In 1625 he bought from Abraham Perrin the Manor of Rozel, but omitted to get the King's consent. For this his new estate was confiscated, and a fine inflicted ; but in 1627 he obtained the Royal pardon. His troubles however were not over. He was involved in a long series of lawsuits with Perrin's widow about her 'dot', and with others who claimed from the manor debts which Perrin owed them.

On the death of Herault, De Carteret became Judge-Delegate (March 1626), and on 18 Jan. 1627 he was appointed Bailiff. He took a wide view of a Bailiff's duties. For example, he worked hard to strengthen Elizabeth Castle, which one would have thought was definitely the Governor's job. By building the Lower Ward he more than doubled the Castle's size and strength. He supervised the works almost daily. "The slothfulness of the workmen and the backwardness of the labourers', he wrote, "doth impose on me intolerable trouble".

Governing Jersey in those days was no bed of roses. It was

almost impossible to squeeze money out of the Home Government. During his first short term as Lieut.-Governor he wrote in 1625 that he had advanced £2539 out of his own pocket to pay the garrison, and that his credit was exhausted (S.P.). Later as Bailiff in 1627 he secured a promise of £1200 for works at Elizabeth Castle, but in December he complained that he was "unable to procure payment of the same from the Lord Treasurer, who would willingly pay the money, if he knew out of what receipts to charge it". A year later he reported that 200 men had arrived to reinforce the garrison, but that 50 of them had neither pike nor musket (S.P.).

He was always badgering the naval authorities for better protection against pirates, and in 1628 he proved in person how much this was needed. He was returning from a successful visit to London with £400 to pay the troops, a supply of powder and munitions, an engineer, a master-gunner, and some additional soldiers, when on 10 March the *Diana* in which he was travelling was captured by Dunkirkers. (Dunkirk privateers were then the scourge of the Channel). By May most of the captives were free and back penniless in Dover, but De Carteret was kept as hostage for a Scots Priest, who was prisoner in the Gatehouse, and his ransom was not accepted, till the Priest arrived in Flanders. The raising of this ransom so impoverished him, that he seriously thought of entering the Dutch service.

In 1630 Sir John Peyton, the Governor, died. With him De Carteret had got on well. But shortly before his death, he had appointed as Lieut.-Governor Captain Francis Rainsford, and Sir Thomas Jermyn, the new Governor, continued him in office. Rainsford was a damn-you-do-as-you're-told hustler, who soon got on everyone's nerves. He ordered St. Lawrence parish to provide a garrison for St. Aubin's Fort. The Constable asked, "Why St. Lawrence?" "Upon this stubborn and mutinous reply", wrote Rainsford, "I committed him to the Castle as an example to others. But I was frustrated in my intentions, for upon his confinement most of his parish with all the Constables and some of the Jurats came to visit him as a martyr. If the people continue in this stubbornness, I will keep the leaders of the mutiny in prison, till I understand His Majesty's pleasure" (S.P.). He chose this awkward moment to quarrel also with De Carteret. A sailor was accused of having piloted a Spanish privateer. The evidence against him was weak, and the Court

released him on bail ; but Rainsford rearrested him. De
Carteret pointed out in a friendly way that this was a quite
irregular encroachment on the functions of the Civil Court ; but
Rainsford raged at him. The matter was then referred to the
Privy Council. In 1634 Rainsford was recalled.

Jermyn the Governor now thought that De Carteret would
be the best man to restore peace ; and in 1634 he was appointed
Lieut.-Governor. This solved some difficulties, but it created
others. As Bailiff and Lieut.-Governor he was head of both
the military and civil administrations. Moreover, according to
the authors of *Pseudo-Mastix*, who as Jurats under him should
have known, he was also "Receiver of the King's Revenues".
(There is some mystery about this. Court Records show that
Robert Foxhall was Receiver from 1638 to 1641 and Jean Dean
from 1641—1643. Perhaps one of these was a man of straw
working under Sir Philippe.) His brother Elie De Carteret was
Solicitor-General ; his cousin Helier Attorney-General ; among
the Jurats were his nephew and three cousins : of the twelve
Captains who commanded the Militia, one in each parish, seven
were De Carterets, two more were nephews, and another his
sister's husband. This concentration of offices in one family
was bound to cause jealousy. There were other families which
thought themselves every bit as good as the De Carterets, and
resented being shut out from all share in the Island's government. An Anti-Carteret Party began to form led by three
Jurats, Michel Lempriere, Seigneur of Maufant, Henry Dumaresq, Seigneur of Samarès, and Abraham Herault, Seigneur
of La Godelière ; but at first they could do little. De Carteret
was seated very firmly in the saddle. As King's representative
he took a high hand even with his own cousins. He sent Amice
De Carteret, Seigneur of Trinity, for trial before the Privy
Council, because he had twice left the island without Sir Philippe's permission. When François De Carteret, Seigneur of La
Hague, did homage for his fief, he ordered him to kneel, but
François replied that he knelt to no man but the King (Brevint's
Note Book) ; and this quarrel added him to the ranks of the
opposition.

Sir Philippe as Lieut.-Governor now lived in Mont Orgueil
with his wife and eleven children, leaving his Manor to his
mother, Rachel Poulet, a rather difficult old lady, who did
not get on well with the younger generation. "She hates us

all", wrote her grand-daugther Elizabeth. Here for nine years he maintained something of the splendour of a little Vice-regal Court. "Roast partridge", wrote Brevint, "is served at every meal in the Castle". Distinguished guests from France and England were frequently entertained. Once his visit to London was delayed by the unexpected arrival of five Portuguese Princesses, who had crossed France, and were waiting for a ship to take them to their uncle, the Prince of Orange, in Holland. On another occasion the Duc de Vendôme, the Queen's half-brother, claimed his hospitality. He had fled from France to escape a charge of bribing hermits to bewitch Richelieu.

Notable prisoners too were committed to his charge. In 1637 arrived Prynne, the acid little Puritan lawyer, sentenced by the Star Chamber to life-long imprisonment. De Carteret and his family with their Puritan sympathies showed him great kindness. Prynne, a merciless critic of all that did not conform to his narrow ideals, gives them a warm testimonial:— "His family was the most orderly, pious, religious, courteous of any in the island. He was the greatest favourer, advancer, incourager of godly Ministers, and more helpful to the poor and sick than all the island beside, there being scarce one day wherein his lady did not send physic and cordials to divers diseased persons. He was a man most cordial and helpful to distressed Protestants in France during the late persecutions, a noble harbourer of them and theirs upon all occasions. He was an enemy to the Bishop's tyranny and innovations" (*Lyar Confounded*). Prynne dedicated his poem *Mont Orgueil* "to his ever honoured worthy friend, Sir Philip Carteret", another poem "to his special kind friend, the truly virtuous and religious Lady Anne, wife to Sir Philip Carteret", a third to "his highly honoured friend, Mistress Elizabeth Carteret, daughter to Sir Philip", while in a fourth he apostrophized two other of the daughters as

> "Sweet Mistress Douce, fair Margaret,
> Flowers of the House of Carteret".

There was one man in the island with whom De Carteret had never been able to get on. He had disliked the change from Calvinism to Anglicanism. He had resented the revival of the Ecclesiastical Court. But above all he detested the man

chosen to be the new Dean, David Bandinel (q.v. App. I), an
Italian. Among the State Papers is one undated, docketed as:—
"Petition of Sir Philip De Carteret. Complaints against proceedings of David Bandinel, an alien made Dean, Prays that a
Commission be issued under the Great Seal to inquire into the
conduct of the said Bandinel, and of all canons and innovations
in Church government introduced by the Dean". Nothing
seems to have come of this. But in 1640 Sir Philippe made an obviously false move. When the Deanery was revived, the King
had specifically endowed it with the Great Tithes of St. Saviour's,
which, since the Reformation, had been paid to the Crown.
Sir Philippe suddenly claimed that these were still part of the
Governor's stipend. When Jermyn had been made Governor
he was granted all revenues conferred on his predecessor Peyton.
But Peyton in his early days had received the St. Saviour's
tithes. Therefore, argued De Carteret, Jermyn's Patent, which
was later than Bandinel's, cancelled the grant to the Dean.
He therefore demanded from Bandinel all that he had received
for the last twenty years. The claim was quite untenable.
The Royal Court, in spite of De Carteret's influence, decided
in the Dean's favour, and so did the Privy Council later (1642)
when De Carteret appealed. The only result of this move was
that the Dean now became leader of the Anti-Carteret Party.

Events in England were about to give this party its chance.
When news reached Jersey in 1640 that the King had been
forced to summon Parliament, and that grievances of all kinds
were being ventilated in London, they drew up *An Humble
Information of the State of the Isle of Jersey* (Printed in *Pseudo-
Mastix*). They made twenty-one definite charges against De
Carteret, of which the most important were:—that, though Jersey
was a frontier post, and in danger of invasion, he left it in
charge, sometimes of a son of 20, sometimes of a nephew of 23 :
he "bears offices incompatible in one person" ; as King's Receiver he prosecutes a man, judges him as Bailiff, and as
Lieut.-Governor pockets the fine ; he "doth intrust with all
the chiefest offices those of his own family" ; he "procureth
the nomination of his own kindred for the judicature" ; he "hath
presumed to raise imposts unheard upon goods imported into
the isle" ; "with arbitrary power he doth release out of prison
those committed by sentence and doth commit to prison without
order of the Court". Dumaresq brought this document to

London, and distributed it among Members of Parliament.

Sir Philippe also was in London as part of a deputation from the States. When he learnt of this personal attack on himself, he appealed to Prynne for help. One of the first acts of the Long Parliament (1640) had been to release Prynne. He had been welcomed back to London as a martyr, "the common people strewing flowers and herbs in his path". He was now able to repay Sir Philippe's kindness. "I should have manifested myself a Monster of ingratitude", he wrote, "had I not contributed my best assistance to support Sir Philip's reputation against the malicious aspersions of his inveterate, backbiting enemies" *(Lyar Confounded)*. He caused Dumaresq, and Bandinel who was also in London, to be summoned before a Committee of the House of Lords. They were asked (1) Whether, since the *Information* claimed to state "the Grievances of the Inhabitants of Jersey", they could show any commission from the inhabitants to speak in their name ; (2) What proofs they could produce that their charges were true. They had to admit that they had no commission and that all their evidence was in Jersey. The Committee then threatened to "commit them both for malicious, libellous articles, which they could not prove ; but by Sir Philip's importunity their commitment was taken off" *(id.)*. Prynne then skilfully used their first complaint to procure an order for De Carteret to return at once to Jersey to secure the island against invasion.

In England the struggle between King and Parliament moved on toward its inevitable end. In Jan. 1642 Charles tried to arrest the five members. A few days later he left London, and both sides began to arm. In Jersey some of the younger Seigneurs swaggered about with *Vive le Roy* on their hats ; but, as Chevalier says, "the great majority of the common people ranged themselves on the other side", and Dumaresq, Lempriere, and their friends formed a Committee to keep in touch with the Puritan leaders. De Carteret's first aim was to keep Jersey out of the struggle. By his advice the States "joined together in two petitions, the one to the King, the other to the Parliament, to this effect: That they were deeply affected with the dissensions between the King and Parliament ; that it was their cordial desire not to look on the King or Parliament as divided, but united, and would thus adhere to both without siding against either". In April 1642 a Public Fast was observed in

Jersey "to divert the wrath of God threatened for the divisions in England".

In October Edgehill was fought, and open war began. Sir Philippe was now a man of divided mind. Family traditions bound him firmly to loyalty to the King, but his Puritanism made him lean toward the other side. When both sides were determined to fight, he hoped to keep Jersey neutral. "If the King and his Parliament have disputes", he said, "why should we interfere"? No Jerseyman had any personal grievance against the King. He had imposed no new laws, exacted no taxes, nor had he in any way tampered with the constitution. The troubles of the English Parliament were no concern of Jersey. But, when war fever gets abroad, it is hard to keep heads cool.

The man who made neutrality impossible was Sir Philippe's nephew George (q.v.). He was now the King's 'faciendary' at St. Malo. In Jan. 1643 he called with one of his ships at Jersey and commandeered "divers hogsheads of ammunition out of the Castle stores", and took them to the beleaguered garrison at Pendennis. Sir Philippe might plead that he dared not disobey the orders of an officer holding the King's commission : but this was stretching neutrality to its breaking point. On 16 Feb. Parliament issued an order for his arrest. Five Jurats who were known to favour the Parliamentary side were commanded "to apprehend the person of Sir Philip Carteret and bring him to Parliament to answer to such crimes as shall be objected against him". This however was more easily said than done. De Carteret as Lieut.-Governor was Commander of the troops, and his Cornish and Irish mercenaries cared nothing for Jersey Jurats.

But, when the States met on 23 March, Michel Lempriere (q.v.) rose and read the order for De Carteret's arrest, and summoned him to go to London to answer the charges against him. Sir Philippe made the perfectly sound constitutional reply, "This island has nothing to do with the English Parliament, but only with the King in Council", and asked to see the warrant. Lempriere had only brought a copy ; so De Carteret adroitly ruled that the States could not discuss the matter, till the original document was before them. But a boy brought news that militiamen from three parishes were marching on the Town. So Sir Philippe hastily retired to Elizabeth Castle, never to return.

But he remained conciliatory. For nearly three months he made no attempt to use his troops against the islanders. He merely withdrew behind the Castle walls, where his enemies could not touch him, and wrote long letters to all and sundry, urging sobriety. "I conjure you by all that is most sacred", he wrote to his kinsman, François De Carteret (q.v.), "unite with me in seeking to convince the people that neither they nor you are justified in uniting with any political party outside the island". He wrote to London offering to answer any charges against him, if the King would appoint a substitute to rule the island in his place, and if his accusers would give pledge for his personal security, should he be found not guilty.

His next move, if his it was, increased his unpopularity. On 20 May the Queen Regent of France issued orders to all seaports forbidding the export of goods to Jersey, except to persons who could show a permit from Sir Philippe. This may have been obtained without his knowledge by his nephew George ; but he had to bear the blame for this attempt to starve the island into subjection.

On 11 June one of his peace-moves had the opposite effect. It was Market Day, and he ordered the Vicomte to proclaim in the Market Place the King's Pardon for all who would lay down their arms. The Vicomte "made some difficulty about this" ; so some young Cavaliers staying in the Castle offered to escort him. When the people ran up to hear the proclamation, these newcomers thought they were going to be attacked, drew their weapons, and fled to the Castle. Boiling with indignation these young hotheads demanded an attack on the Town. Weakly Sir Philippe gave way. "I could have wished it had not been", he wrote to his wife, "but they cryed upon me that delays did spoil all" (*Pseudo-Mastix*). "I was persuaded", he wrote to the Governor of Guernsey, "by those who had more experience in martial affairs than I" (*Chronicles of Castle Cornet*). He gave two hours warning to the Town that he was going to fire, bombarded it with forty cannon balls, and then allowed his young men to attack across the sands. The assault utterly failed. The streets were barricaded with faggots, the garden walls lined with musketeers, and the attackers had to retire to the Castle, carrying their wounded with them.

What had hitherto been a passive siege now became active war. "The next day", wrote De Carteret, "both Castles were beset, and so continue, surrounded by sentries, that not a dog can stir out of either, nor none have been suffered to venture in. My wife is in the other. I send to her sometimes by sea, but with much hazard" (*Chronicles of Castle Cornet*).

Then illness broke out in the Castle. On 24 July Gédeon, his son, died ; and the Committee gave permission for twelve of his tenants to carry the body to St. Ouen's for burial. On 10 Aug. Sir Philippe himself fell ill. On the 16th, he felt himself dying, and wrote to the Committee:— "I desire in your Christian charity that you will permit Mons. La Cloche (q.v.) to administer unto me such Christian comforts as are usual in such extremities, and that you will permit my poor wife to come to do me the last duty of closing my eyes. The Lord forgive you, as I forgive you all". The Committee at first suspected this to be a trick to get in touch with his friends ; but by the 21st they realized that he was dying. On that day they allowed his old mother to pay him a visit, and the Rector of St. Clement's was sent to minister to him. On the following day his wife was brought under safe conduct from Mont Orgueil, and a few hours after her arrival he died (23 Aug. 1643). "He gave orders on his death-bed that they should not bury his body, till the King had overcome all his enemies" (*Pseudo-Mastix*). Lady De Carteret sent for a surgeon from St. Malo to embalm the body. The heart and viscera were buried in the old Abbey Church on the Islet. The body was kept in a lead coffin till 20 June 1644, when, the island having been conquered by the Royalists, it was carried in state to St. Ouen's Church and buried. At the restoration of the Church in 1869 the coffin was found and opened. It contained the skeleton of a tall man over six feet high, whose reddish hair was still in good preservation. Sir Philippe had seven sons, Philippe 4 (q.v.) who succeeded him, François, who became a Jurat, Peyton, who was drowned with Prince Maurice off the West Indies in 1652, while harrying Parliamentary shipping, Zouch, who died in Rouen in 1648, Gédeon, who died during the siege, Thomas, a Captain in Ireland, Edouard, who became Vicomte, and four daughters, Dowse, Margaret, Anne, who married Dr. Brevint (q.v.), Dean of Lincoln, and Elizabeth, who married her cousin Sir George Carteret. [Chevalier's *Journal* ; *Calendar of State Papers, Domestic* ; Prynne's *Lyar Confounded* ; Hoskins' *Charles II in the Channel Islands* ; *Dic. Nat. Biog.*]

(4) DE CARTERET, SIR PHILIPPE (1620—1662), Seigneur of St. Ouen's, Sark, and Rozel, Lieut.-Governor and Bailiff. Eldest son of Sir Philippe de Carteret 3, Lieut.-Governor and Bailiff (q.v.), and Anne Dowse. If he was "scarce twenty-one years old" (*Pseudo-Mastix*), when appointed Lieut.-Governor in 1641, he was born in 1620. When his father was besieged in Elizabeth Castle in 1643, Philippe shared with his mother in the defence of Mont Orgueil, and on her death in 1644 assumed the command. In 1645, when the Prince of Wales was in Jersey, he was knighted by him at a Review of the Militia on St. Aubin's sands. In July 1647 he was sworn in as Jurat and Lieut.-Bailiff, and his cousin Sir George Carteret (q.v.) left all the Bailiff's work in his hands. In 1649 he was "privately married to the beautiful Mistress Anne Dumaresq" (*Clarendon Papers*), daughter of Abraham Dumaresq. In 1650 Parliament resolved that all his lands should be sold for the benefit of persons exiled from the island, but, as Jersey was still held for the King, this had no effect. But on 19 Oct. 1651 he saw from his Manor a fleet of eighty Parliamentary ships approaching St. Ouen's Bay. He sent word to Sir George in Elizabeth Castle, and called out the St. Ouen's Militia, and took command. When the enemy landed, the St. Ouen's company was the only section that stood firm, but it proved no match for the soldiers of the New Model, and Sir Philippe retired with Sir George into Elizabeth Castle. During the negotiations for surrender he was one of the hostages handed over to the Parliamentarians. By the Articles of Capitulation Royalists in the Castle were allowed to compound for their estates by paying not more than two years' income. In 1652 François Messervy (q.v.) and other Parliamentarians urged that Sir Philippe's estates were not protected by this clause, as they were forfeit before the capitulation ; but Heane, the Parliamentary Governor, stood firm. He wrote to Parliament, "I beg not to be forced to act in breach of my own Articles" (*S.P.*). During this dispute De Carteret visited London, and the Société Jersiaise has a letter dated from Jersey (1 Aug. 1652) in which he thanks an unnamed "Noble Sir" for the kindness shewn him during his stay there. At the Restoration (1660) he resumed his position as Jurat and Lieut.-Bailiff, and, on the resignation of Sir George, was sworn in as Bailiff on 26 Feb. 1661. He died in November 1662, and was buried in St. Ouen's Church on

the 16th. He had a son Philippe 8 (q.v.) who became a Baronet and Bailiff, and a daughter Ann (born 1666).

(5) DE CARTERET, PHILIPPE (d. 1665), of Grouville, Bailiff. Second son of Jurat Elie De Carteret, Lieutenant-Bailiff, and Elizabeth Dumaresq ; brother of Sir George Carteret (q.v.). On the death of his father he was elected to his seat as Jurat, and was sworn in on 17 Sept. 1640. In 1642 he was Colonel of the Castle (Mont Orgueil) and on 19 Oct. he married in St. George's Chapel Marie De La Place, daughter of Elie De La Place, who three years later succeeded Dean Bandinel as Rector of St. Martin's. He was Colonel of the Castle under Lady De Carteret during the first siege (1643), and retained this position when his brother became Lieut.-Governor (1644—1651). In 1647 he also became Colonel of the Militia of the four parishes of St. Helier's, St. Saviour's, St. Clement's, and Grouville. When the Parliamentary troops landed in 1651, at first he refused to surrender the Castle, but the garrison compelled him to capitulate. "The English Major, who had been placed there by order of the King, caused all to mutiny. The Master Gunner refused to act, and all threatened to hand him over to the enemy, if he did not surrender" (Contemporary account printed in *Bull.* II.). The terms were generous. He was allowed to retain his estate, and granted an Act of Oblivion for all past offences. At the Restoration (1660) he resumed his seat as Jurat ; and on the death of his nephew and namesake was sworn in as Bailiff on 5 March 1663. He died in September 1665, and was buried on the 18th. in Grouville Church. He had two sons, Elie (b. 1651) who became Fellow of Exeter, Oxford, and Rector of Coates, Gloucestershire, and Philippe (b. 1652), and four daughters, Elizabeth (b. 1647), Marie (b. 1649), another Marie (b. 1655), and Jeanne (b. 1659).

(6) DE CARTERET, PHILIPPE, M.D. (1620—72), Cromwellian Judge-Advocate. Eldest son of François De Carteret

(q.v.), Seigneur of La Hague, and Judith Le Febvre. Born
1626, and baptized at St. Peter's 4 March. Matriculated at
Oxford from Exeter College March 1637, when only eleven, and
took his B.A. in 1640, when he was fourteen. He took his
M.D. at Leyden 8 July 1645. In Feb. 1649 he petitioned Parliament for permission to compound for a small farm at Netley,
near Southampton, bought by his father to support him during
his studies in England, which had been sequestered, because
his father was in Jersey under enemy (i.e. Royalist) rule. His
petition was granted (C.C.). In Jan. 1650 a pass was issued
for him to proceed to Ireland with three horses (S.P.). There
he was appointed Advocate-General to the Army. The Judge-
Advocate was the officer who supervised the proceedings of all
courts-martial and reviewed their sentences. When Ireton
died in Ireland, and his body was sent to Westminster Abbey
for burial. De Carteret was responsible for arranging the Irish
ceremonies, and was paid £450 for his expenses (S.P.). In 1653
a letter from Ireland said, "I commend to you a petition which
concerns De Carteret, our Judge-Advocate, who is of great
service to the Lord General and his army, and is a most faithful
and ingenious man" (S.P.). In April 1654 a letter from James
Standish to Carteret at Army Headquarters, Dublin, ran:—
"Dear Brother, My wife hath seen your daughter, who is well.
The things you sent for will be suddenly reddy to send to
Chester. Be confident I shall not be wanting nor my wife in our
care of your child and goods" (Rawl. MSS). Army pay in
those days was always in arrears, and, when De Carteret protested, Cromwell pacified him by granting him estates in Limerick. In 1654 he visited Jersey, and in Jan. 1655 the Captain
of the Hopewell reported that he had "brought back Dr Carteret
and family from Jersey" (S.P.). In February he was nominated
by Cromwell as a Jurat, but he did not take the oath till June
1656. In Aug. 1657 we find him sending a Report to the
Council that the Cour de Billet was useful and necessary (S.P.).
In 1659 he returned to London as Judge-Advocate to the Army
in England (S.P.). After the Restoration he went to Ireland
to visit his Limerick estates, but was arrested (1662) on the
Lord-Lieutenant's warrant, and imprisoned for a time in the
Castle (S.P. Ireland). He took refuge however under the Act
of Oblivion, and returned to England, and in 1665 was elected
a Fellow of the Royal Society. On 1 May 1672 he died in

Southampton, leaving his Jersey estates to his son Henry, who later became a Jurat, and his Irish estates to his daughter Sarah. A third daughter, Judie, married Jean Ralins, Deacon of the French Church at Southampton. De Carteret's wife was Marie Hewson.

(7) DE CARTERET, PHILIPPE (1639—1682), Seigneur of La Hougue, first Governor of New Jersey. Eldest son of Helier De Carteret, Attorney-General, and Rachel La Cloche. Born Dec. 1639. In March 1664 Charles II granted to his brother, James, Duke of York, the district between Connecticut River and Delaware Bay, then occupied by the Dutch ; and a small force sent to capture it did so without difficulty. In June the Duke of York transferred the part west of the Hudson, henceforth to be known as New Jersey, to Sir George Carteret (q.v.) and Lord Berkeley, who had suggested the expedition. Sir George chose as first Governor his fourth cousin, young Philippe De Carteret. He sailed from England in the ship *Philip* in April 1665 with a party of settlers largely recruited from Jersey, and after visiting Virginia and New York, landed in New Jersey in August, marching to the nearest settlement with a hoe over his shoulder, to show that he came as a planter, not as a conqueror. He named this little group of four log cabins Elizabethtown in honour of Lady Carteret. Here he built a large white house with "orchards and grounds" and measured out the 2,000 acres of land granted him by Sir George. The first wedding in Elizabethtown was that of Daniel Perrin of the isle of Jersey and Marie Thoreau. The Service was conducted by J. Bolleine.

De Carteret's task was not easy. A number of New Englanders had settled in the district before he arrived, and they did not see why they should pay quit-rents to two absentee landlords who had done nothing for them. Nicolls, the Duke of York's Governor, had known nothing of the alienation of New Jersey from his territory, and had already confirmed many planters in the possession of their land. Some of the new settlers were of poor quality, sent out of their own country for their country's good. The States of Jersey for example, "moved by Christian compassion", resolved to use the colony called by its name as a dumping ground for all its paupers, if the King would give permission (A.E.). Trouble began in the first Assembly, which met in 1668. In 1672 the malcontents called an Assembly of their own, which deposed Philippe, and chose as "President of the Country", James Carteret (q.v.), a scapegrace son of Sir George. Philippe sailed to England to report to the Lords Proprietors. They fully confirmed his authority ; the Duke of York repudiated Nicolls' grants ; and the King sternly ordered the rebels to submit to the Proprietary Government. But, before Philippe could return, the Dutch recaptured New Jersey and New York, and occupied them for fifteen months. In 1674 peace was made, and the district restored to England.

Lord Berkeley now sold half New Jersey to the Quakers ; but Sir George retained his half, now known as East Jersey ; and Philippe returned as Governor. For six years all went well. Annual Assemblies were held. Useful legislation was passed. The number of settlers increased steadily. But Governors of New York had always resented the alienation of New Jersey. The Governor now was Sir Edmund Andros, Seigneur of Sausmarez, Guernsey. On Sir George Carteret's death in 1680 he challenged outright Philippe's authority. On 13 March he issued a proclamation ordering Philippe and his officials to cease from exercising jurisdiction. De Carteret replied that he and his province would defend themselves by force, if necessary. "It was by his Majesty's command that this Government was established, and without the same command it shall never be resigned". In April Andros came to Elizabethtown. As he arrived attended only by his Council, he was civilly received. He claimed that he had been commissioned by the King to receive the whole country from the Dutch. De Carteret produced his commission to be Governor of New Jersey. After a futile discussion Andros departed, and issued a warrant for De Carteret's arrest. Jaspar Dankers, who was in New York at the time, tells what followed in his *Journal:*— "Andros corrupted one of De Carteret's domestics, for Carteret had no soldiers or fortifications, but resided in a country house only. He then equipped some yachts and a ketch with soldiers, arms, and ammunition, and dispatched them to abduct Carteret in any manner it could be done. They entered his house at midnight, seized him naked, dragged him through the window, struck and kicked him terribly, and even injured him internally. They threw him, naked as he was, into a canoe, and carried him in that condition to New York, where they put him immediately in prison. While Carteret was in prison he was very sick. Meanwhile a Court of Assizes was convened. The Governor presented Carteret as guilty of usurping the government of New Jersey". Carteret faced his accusers with courage. At first he refused to plead or to recognize the power of the Court to try him ; but eventually he showed the jury his letters from the King. In spite of Andros' effort to browbeat them—he sent them back three times to reconsider their verdict—they declared "Prisoner at the Bar not guilty" ; and De Carteret was allowed to return home after giving security "not to assume any jurisdiction there, civil or military", till the matter had been settled in London. In March 1681 a letter was received from Lady Elizabeth, Sir George's widow, stating that the Duke of York wholly disowned the acts of Andros, and the Duke confirmed this in a letter to his Governor. So De Carteret was reinstated.

Andros was now summoned to England to answer charges against him, and De Carteret hit back by claiming Staten Island as within the jurisdiction of New Jersey. Brockholst, Andros' deputy, refused to hand it over, and a fierce struggle began. There was also internal dissension, and for the first time De Carteret dissolved the Assembly. But all these disputes were stopped by unexpected news. The Trustees under Sir George's will in Feb. 1682 had sold East Jersey by auction, and it had been bought by a group of Quakers. De Carteret resigned, and, in Dec. 1682 he died in Elizabethtown at the age of 42. He had married in April 1681 Elizabeth, daughter of Richard Smith of Long Island, and widow of William Lawrence. They had no children. By his will (published in *Bull.* III) he left his New Jersey estates to his widow and his property in Jersey to his mother, stipulating that two quarters of wheat rente should be paid yearly to the poor of St. Peter's parish. [Whitehead's *New Jersey under the Proprietors* ; Smith's *History of the Colony of Novo-Caesarea* ; Vol. I of *New Jersey Archives* ; Johnson's *Dictionary of American Biography*.]

(8) DE CARTERET, SIR PHILIPPE (1650—93), Bart, Seigneur of St. Ouen's, Bailiff. Only son of Sir Philippe De Carteret 4, (q.v.), Seigneur of St. Ouen's (d. 1662), and Anne Dumaresq. Born in St. Ouen's Manor, Christmas Day 1650. In 1671 he was created a Baronet. In 1676 he married at St. Mary's, Savoy, Elisabeth, daughter of Sir Edouard De Carteret of Trinity, Bailiff (q.v.). She was then a child of twelve. The marriage contract stipulated:— "On the day of the marriage Sir Edouard shall pay to Sir Philippe £1,000 sterling as part of the marriage settlement. The said Elisabeth shall immediately after the marriage return to her parents, and remain with them till she is fifteen years old. Then Sir Edouard shall pay to Sir Philippe for a marriage portion the sum of £1,500 sterling together with the £100 bequeathed to the said Elisabeth by Mrs Anne Skelton. If the said Elisabeth survive her husband, she shall receive one third of the revenue of the manor". In 1674 he obtained a promise from the King that he should be the next Bailiff. In 1676 he was elected Jurat. Pirouet (quoted by Payne) says of him:— "He became a man very wise and prudent and of a handsome countenance, who ever behaved honourably, courteously, and justly, and made himself loved by all. His wealth was so great and his fame so conspicuous that he kept a coach with six horses, which he used both in Jersey and England. Wherever he went, his coach followed him". He rebuilt the Manor, and obtained letters-patent permitting him to build a pier at Sark. On 3 Aug. 1682 he was sworn in as Bailiff. The accession of James II (1685) created grave anxiety. He confirmed the privileges of the island, but made no secret of his desire to lead his subjects back to the Roman Church. This the sturdy Protestantism of Jersey would never tolerate ; and its fear of Popery had been stimulated by the revocation of the Edict of Nantes and the arrival of a stream of Huguenot refugees. "The King", writes Philippe Falle (q.v.), who was a member of the States at this time, "had determined to bring in Popery in this island by a Popish garrison. He sent us early a Commander of that Religion with a Priest to prepare the way ; and Elizabeth Castle began to fill with soldiers of the same principles or of no principles at all, who would have served the purpose as well" (*Account of the Island of Jersey*). When the King fled to France, a new fear was felt. In 1687 De Carteret had warned Samuel

Pepys, Secretary of the Admiralty, that the new naval harbour
at Granville was a grave danger to Jersey (*Bull.* V). Now would
the King's Catholic troops hand over the island to France?
"Those men", wrote Falle, "had Elizabeth Castle wholly in their
keeping, and might think they could answer their Master's intentions no way better than by delivering it up to that Power
unto which he himself had fled for refuge. But it pleased God
to inspire our Magistrates with such wisdom and force of persuasion that in some conferences with the Commander they
prevailed with him to admit the inhabitants to mount guard in
the Castle in equal proportions with the garrison" (*op.cit.*).
Thus the crisis was tided over, till William and Mary were on
the throne. Then the States sent an Address of Congratulation
(printed in Falle), declaring that, though their language was
French, their hearts and swords were truly English, and entirely
their Majesties'. Jersey's old loyalty to the House of Stuart was
dead. De Carteret died, 23 Oct. 1693, and was buried in St.
Ouen's Church. His only son, Charles (q.v.) succeeded him as
Seigneur, and later became Bailiff.

(9) DE CARTERET, PHILIPPE (1733–96), Seigneur of Trinity, Circumnavigator, Rear-Admiral, stated by D.N.B. to "rank
among the greatest geographical discoverers of his time". (In
his first commission the De was accidentally omitted ; so in
all naval records he is known as Carteret.) Younger son of
Charles De Carteret, Seigneur of Trinity, and Françoise Marie
St. Paul. Born in Trinity Manor, 22 Jan. 1733. He entered
the Navy, and received his commission as Lieutenant in 1757.
In Sept. 1761 on the death of his elder brother François he inherited the Manor, but so encumbered with debt that he had
practically to buy it back. He put his sister Anne to live in it,
while he was at sea. The Government was now beginning
to use the Navy for exploration. In 1764 it planned an expedition to the South Pacific, and commissioned for this service the
Dolphin (24 guns, 150 men) under Captain John Byron, the
poet's grandfather, and the sloop *Tamar* (14 guns, 90 men). De
Carteret was First Lieutenant on the *Tamar*. They left the
Downs on 21 June, and on their way out annexed the Falkland

Islands, thereby nearly causing a war with Spain which claimed previous possession. After passing through the Strait of Magellan Byron moved De Carteret to the *Dolphin* as First Lieutenant. In June 1765 they sighted the northernmost fringe of the Paumotu Archipelago. But Byron was entirely devoid of the instinct of a born explorer. Here were hundreds of islands awaiting discovery, if he had spread his ships out, and zigzagged a little ; but he merely named the islets the Disappointment Islands, because he could not land, and sailed on. He then performed the almost incredible feat of sailing more than five thousand miles across the Pacific studded with innumerable archipelagos without sighting any further land. He must have kept an absolutely straight course, only anxious to get home. He reached the Dutch East Indies in November, rounded the Cape of Good Hope in Feb. 1766, and reached England in May. On his return De Carteret was promoted Commander.

Byron's voyage had been almost fruitless ; so the Admiralty ordered a new expedition. The *Dolphin* was given to Captain Samuel Wallis, and De Carteret was given command of the *Swallow*, a sloop of 278 tons with 16 guns and a crew of 125. "She was an old ship, having been in service thirty years, and was in my opinion by no means fit for a long voyage ; but I was told that the vessel and her equipment were very fit for the service she was to perform, and none of the requisites for which I applied were allowed me". The two boats left Plymouth on 22 Aug. 1766 with a storeship, the *Prince Frederick*, and in December reached the Strait of Magellan. Here on 11 Jan. 1767 De Carteret wrote a long account of the Patagonians, which was published in Vol. 60 of the *Transactions of the Royal Society*. The *Swallow* had now amply proved her unfitness for the task before her. She would not answer her helm, even when the rudder had been broadened. "We could seldom make her tack without the help of a boat to tow her round". De Carteret proposed that she should be sent home with the sick, while he continued the voyage as Lieutenant on the *Dolphin* ; but Wallis would not agree. Before they got out of the Strait however the other boats forged far ahead, and De Carteret never found them again.

He was now without any stores but those he had on board ; yet he sailed on into the unknown. On 2 July he discovered Pitcairn Island (later made famous by the mutineers of the

Bounty), and named it after the midshipman who first sighted it from the masthead. He next reached the southern edge of the Paumotu Archipelago. Here he stopped at the island of Maruroa, which he called Osnaburg after one of the King's sons, and then passed on to the Duke of Gloucester Group, which still keeps the name he gave it. By this time "the ship was become very crazy ; our sails also were much worn and were continually splitting". Most of the crew were down with scurvy ; the stock of log-lines was exhausted ; and to crown their troubles the ship sprang a leak, and the pumps had to be kept going night and day. On 12 Aug. he found the Santa Cruz Islands, which he named Queen Charlotte Islands. Here his landing party was attacked, the master and three seamen killed by the natives' flint-tipped arrows, and others wounded ; but he found a bay in which he was able partially to stop the leak. De Carteret himself was now ill, and forced to keep his bed. In this group Lord Howe Island retains the name he gave it, and Swallow Island preserves the name of his ship. Four of these islands he called Jersey, Guernsey, Alderney, and Sark, but these names have not survived. On 29 Aug. he reached the great island which the old buccaneer Dampier had discovered in 1710, and named New Britain. De Carteret found that this was not one island but two. He sailed through the channel that divided it, which he called St. George's Channel, and named the land to the north and east of it New Ireland. Here he gave his men a week on shore, where fresh water and green food restored most of them to health. "I took possession of this country with all its islands and harbours for his Majesty King George, and we nailed on a high tree a piece of board faced with lead on which was engraved the English Union (i.e. the Union Jack) and the name of the ship and her commander". Here Cape Carteret preserves his memory, and many places, Duke of York's Island, Mother and Daughters, Cape Stephens, etc., retain the names he gave them.

Sailing on he came to another island, which he called New Hanover, and the channel which separates it from New Ireland he called Byron's Strait after his old commander. His next discoveries were the Portland Islands on 13 Sept., the Admiralty Islands on the 15th., Durour's Island on the 19th., Maty's Island on the 20th., and Stephens' Island, named after the Secretary of the Admiralty, on the 24th. On the 25th. he reached a cluster of islands where the natives proved very friendly. One who came on board refused to leave ; so De Carteret added him to his crew, and called him Joseph Freewill, and his islands Freewill Islands. Then passing the dangerous reef still known as Carteret's Reef he reached the southernmost of the Philippines. Here the threatening attitude of the natives made it impossible to land. His crew were again down with scurvy ; but, when they were attacked at midnight by a pirate ship, which mistook them for a merchantman, they soon brought their guns into action, and sent it to the bottom. He then made for the Dutch East Indies, where he was allowed to revictual and make necessary repairs. He apologized to the Dutch officers who came on board, because he could offer them no refreshment but biscuit full of weevils. On 15 Sept. he left Batavia ; on 28 Nov. he reached the Cape ; and on 20 March 1769 he dropped anchor at Spithead. The *Cambridge History of the British Empire* says of this voyage:— "With a sick crew and a poorly equipped vessel he had made greater discoveries than any of his predecessors since Tasman".

On 12 Jan. 1770 he came home to Trinity Manor, and the colours of the *Swallow* were hoisted on the Manor flag-post (Messervy's *Journal*). The island was seething with excitement after the anti-Lempriere revolt (See *Lempriere, Charles*), in which Trinity Parish had played a leading part. De Carteret soon showed that his sympathies were with the rebels. On 13 Feb. he gave a dinner at the Manor to the leaders of the anti-Lempriere party, and invited Colonel Bentinck, who had been sent from England to investigate the trouble, to meet them. In November on rumours of war with Spain about the Falkland Islands he crossed to England hoping to get another ship ; but the scare passed, and in Dec. 1771 he came back to Jersey a Post-Captain. In March 1772 he returned to London, where on 5 May he married Marie Rachel, daughter of Sir Jean Silvestre, a French Protestant doctor, who had been medical officer to the British Troops in the Low Countries. (Her brother, who spelled his name Sir John Silvester, became Recorder of London). But the Jurats in Jersey suspected that his honeymoon did not absorb all his attention. Messervy noted in his Journal that De Carteret was supposed "to be helping Captain Le Geyt and Dr. Shebbeare against the Jersey Court in their effort to secure Royal Commissioners. It is said that the Seigneur of Trinity

was the first to sign the petition which Le Geyt is to present".
On 30 June 1772 he brought his bride back to Jersey, and the
Manor became their home for the next eight years. Here three
of his children were born, Silvester Samuel in 1775, Philippe
10 (q.v.) in 1776, and Caroline in 1780.

But the American War of Independence, followed by War
with France, brought him back to active service. In 1777 he
was in command of the frigate *Druid* in the West Indies. In
1779 he was appointed to the *Endymion* (44 guns) with which
he joined Rodney. In Jan. 1781 he wrote home from the West
Indies that he was doing very well out of his prizes. He then
brought back a convoy from Jamaica, and wrote in July that
he was at Leith with a very rich prize. Meanwhile in 1780
owing to the danger of invasion his wife with her children had
moved from Jersey to Southampton, and here he settled, when
in 1794 his health broke down, and he was retired from the
active list with the rank of Rear-Admiral. He died here on 21
July 1796, "having long been afflicted with loss of speech"
(*Gent. Mag.* XLVI.), and was buried in the catacombs of All
Saints' Church. In addition to the children mentioned above
he had a daughter Elizabeth Mary, born in England, who married Sir William Symonds R.N. De Carteret's portrait is in
the S.J. Museum, and was reproduced in *Bull* XI. [Hawkes-
worth's *Voyages* contains the Journal of his second voyage round
the world, together with Byron's and Wallis' Journals. See also
The History of Carteret and Wallis' Voyage round the World,
London, 1784. Gossip about his life in Jersey will be found in
Daniel Messervy's *Journal*: and details about his later life in the
Letter Book of Chas. Poingdestre in S.J. Library. *Dic. Nat.
Biog.*]

(10) DE CARTERET, PHILIP (In 1822 he added the surname
SILVESTER) C.B. (1776—1828), Seigneur of Trinity, Captain
R.N. Son of Philippe De Carteret (9), Seigneur of Trinity, cir-
cumnavigator (q.v.), and Marie Rachel Silvestre. Born in Trin-
ity Manor 2 Dec. 1776, and baptized in Trinity Church 22 Dec.
Educated first by François Le Couteur (q.v.), Rector of Grou-
ville ; then at Winchester College 1789—92. He entered the
Navy in 1792 under the care of Captain Erasmus Gower, who

had been his father's First Lieutenant on his voyage round the world in the *Swallow*. He went with Gower on the *Lion* (64 guns) to China, returning in 1794. He was with Gower on the *Triumph* (74 guns) in the Battle of the 17th of June 1795, and was wounded. In Oct. he became Lieutenant of the *Impérieuse*. In the following year on the death of his father he inherited Trinity Manor. He then served in the *Greyhound* (32), the *Britannia* (100), and the *Cambrian* (40) round the French coast. In 1802 he was promoted Commander, and appointed to the sloop *Bonne Citoyenne* (20) in the Mediterranean. From 1804 to 1809 he commanded the brig *Scorpion* (18 guns), in which he captured the Dutch schooner *L'Honneur* with a cargo of arms for the Dutch fleet and the famous French Captain Saint-Faust, who was on his way to take command of it. The *Scorpion* was then sent to the West Indies to watch the French fleet and report its movements. It did this so skilfully that for months the French could neither capture it nor shake it off. In 1806 he was promoted Post-Captain. He then escorted a French prize to England and joined the Plymouth squadron. In 1807 he captured a formidable French privateer the *Bougainville*, off Scilly.

In 1809 he volunteered for service on the *Superb* (74 guns) in the expedition to the Scheldt. Here he commanded a flotilla of gunboats and was frequently mentioned in dispatches, and won special praise for his work in covering the evacuation of Walcheren. In 1811 he was appointed to the frigate *Naiad* (46 guns). In this he performed his most sensational exploit. Napoleon was holding a naval review at Boulogne, when the *Naiad* appeared in the offing. By his orders seven 12-gun praams, ten brigs, and a sloop put out under Rear-Admiral Baste to capture her. De Carteret fought the whole flotilla for two and a half hours, till they retired into the shelter of their shore batteries, when he anchored in his original position. In the night he was reinforced by three brigs and a cutter. At sunrise the French renewed the attack with twenty-two vessels. Carteret led his tiny squadron into the midst of the enemy giving orders to reserve fire till within pistol-shot. He nearly captured the Admiral's praam ; but the *Ville de Lyons* separated them. So he lashed the *Naiad* to the side of the intruder. "The small-arms men soon cleared her deck, and the boarders sword in hand completed her subjugation". (De Carteret's Report). The French then retired again to the shelter of their forts, and De

Carteret brought his prize to England. In the same year he captured two large French privateers.

In April 1812 he nearly lost his life. His gig upset off Cowes, and he was brought ashore apparently drowned ; but he recovered. His next command was the frigate *Pomone* (46 guns). In 1813 in hazy weather he fell in with a French frigate in the Bay of Biscay. At the same time he sighted another large ship, which he took to be French. He ran down to engage this, only to discover that she was a Portuguese East-Indiaman ; and meanwhile the frigate escaped. De Carteret, hearing that he was accused of cowardice in running away from the frigate, demanded a court martial, and was acquitted. He remained in command of the *Pomone* till the end of the war. In 1814 he recaptured from the Americans H.M.S. *Linnet*, which they had taken and converted into a privateer. In 1815 he was made a Companion of the Bath. In the same year he was appointed to the frigate *Désirée* (36), from which he removed with officers and men to the *Active* (46). In her he served on the Jamaica station till he retired in 1817.

In 1822 he added his mother's surname, anglicized as Silvester, to his own, and, when his mother's brother, Sir John Silvester, Recorder of London, died in that year, he succeeded to the baronetcy. He died suddenly of apoplexy at Leamington, 24 Aug. 1828. He never married, and his sister, Elizabeth Mary, and her husband, Sir William Symonds, inherited the Manor. In all his wanderings he never forgot that he was Seigneur of Trinity, and after his retirement spent much of his time at the Manor. The *Chronique* said of him at his death:— "The poor feel that they have lost a friend and a protector, and the parishioners of Trinity do not tire of praising all the good he has done".

[Article in *Naval & Military Magazine* 1828 ; in *Guernsey & Jersey Mag.* 1838 ; *Dic. Nat. Biog.* ; Marshall's *Royal Biography* ; *Chronique* 6 Sept. 1828. The official Report of his exploit off Boulogne is in *Annual Register* 1811.]

DE CARTERET, RENAUD (REGINALD), Seigneur of St. Ouen's (d. 1349). Eldest son of Sir Philippe De Carteret, Seigneur of St. Ouen's, and nephew of Dean Geoffroi De Carteret (q.v.). We first hear of him in June 1328, when the King wrote:— "Whereas Renaud De Carteret, son and heir of the late Philippe De Carteret, cannot immediately present himself in person before us in England to do homage for the lands that belonged to his father, because he is responsible for guarding our Castle, we have granted him respite from doing homage for a full year" (C.R.). In the following June the King was at Amiens, and Renaud crossed to France, and took the required oath of fealty (Rot.Fin.). The *Extente* of 1331 records:— "Renaud De Carteret holds the Manor of St. Ouen's with all that appertains to it by homage, by suit of court (i.e. personal attendance at the King's Court, which in Jersey meant the Assise d'Héritage), by relief (i.e. a fee exacted from the heir before he could take possession of his inheritance), which, when it has to be paid, amounts to 10 *livres tournois*, and by service. This service he must render in time of war personally to our Lord the King at his own expense in Gorey Castle for two periods of forty days accompanied by two men horsed and harnessed. The King has also the custody of the aforesaid Manor, should the heir be under age, and this guardianship in an ordinary year is worth £50 sterling."

In 1337 the Hundred Years' War with France began, and Jersey found itself in the forefront of the battle. In March 1338 "on the day after the Annunciation Sir Nicolas Béhuchet, Admiral of France, invaded the island with a great host, and burnt every blade of corn and the houses and other property" (Compte de T. de Ferriers. *Bull* III). In a sortie from the Castle on 10 Sept. Jean De Barentin, the Constable, was slain, and Renaud assumed command, for it had become an established custom that, "if the Captain of the Isle died, the Seigneur of St. Ouen's took custody of the Castle, till the King appointed another Captain" (*Chroniques*). He at once increased the number of crossbowmen from 56 to 115 and of archers from 22 to 87 (*Bull* III), and held out so staunchly that the French withdrew. Béhuchet however conquered Guernsey, and in October the French King appointed Robert Bertran, wealthiest of the Cotentin barons, Lord of the Isles. In March 1339 he renewed the attack on Jersey. A petition sent to Edward III says:— "On St. Gregory's Day Sir Robert Bertran, Marshal of France, with a force numbering 8000, so far as we could estimate, in 17 Genoese galleys and about 35 other ships from Normandy,

landed, and summoned us to send notables of the island to
parley. Thereupon two of their great men and two of ours met
between the armies. They bade us surrender to the King of
France ; otherwise they would storm the Castle, and spare
neither great nor small, and devastate the country ; but, if we
would hand over the Castle, they would confirm in the name
of the King of France our possession of all our lands, liberties,
and charters. To which we made answer that, while ten men
were alive in the Castle, it would not be surrendered. Thereupon they retired to their ships, and sent to reconnoitre the
Castle by sea and land to discover the best place to make the
assault ; but, God be thanked, they found every point so strong
and well guarded that they again withdrew.. On the third day
they landed once more, and burnt no small number of houses,
manors, and mills, and carried off great spoil of cattle and
chattels. But certain of our men made a sortie from the Castle,
and slew about forty of them, and returned safe. On the mor-
row Sir Robert Bertran departed with all his men for Normandy, and the seventeen galleys set sail for Guernsey" (The French
original is printed in full in *Bull* III). For the second time De
Carteret saw the enemy retire thwarted, though he had not been
strong enough to protect the open country. Then news came of
a truce between France and England, which gave the island
two years' welcome peace ; but Renaud lost all the property
which his family had acquired, probably by marriage, in Normandy. This was so large that his father had employed a
Norman advocate permanently to look after it (*Assize Roll*).
But now in 1340, when Guillaume de St. Hilaire, Seigneur of
Samarès, joined the French, and had his lands in Jersey escheated, the Bailiff of the Cotentin compensated him by a grant
of 78 *livres* of rente from the confiscated lands of Renaud De
Carteret (*Bull* XI).

   In March 1341 Thomas of Hampton was appointed Warden
of the Isles, and he made Henry de la More his Lieutenant in
Jersey. With these two De Carteret quarrelled violently. In
October 1542 war was resumed, and De Carteret and his
friends placed some of their property in Mont Orgueil for
safety. In December however they complained to the King that
"Henry de la More is detaining divers sums of money, victuals,
garniture, and goods, brought to the Castle" (*C.R.*). A flood
of indignant petitions poured in to the King. A party of Jer-

seymen even boarded his ship in the Bay of Morbihan to deliver one:— "Many good people have been put to death in the island. Henry de la More has burnt many houses, and goods which the people had put in the King's Castle he caused to be taken before him, and broke open the chests and hutches ; and in the country he has robbed many, and imprisoned not a few. And since the truce Sir Thomas has come to the island with a large company of archers, and they have killed and robbed many of your lieges, and driven out of the country about three hundred of the best. Since the truce he keeps 300 serjeants, whereas he had only twenty" (*Ancient Petitions*). By March 1343 the trouble had grown so serious that three Commissioners were sent from England "to inform themselves touching the dissensions that have arisen between Thomas of Hampton and the men of Jersey, whereby divers evils have happened in those parts, and greater loss will ensue, as is feared" (*P.R.*). But, before they arrived, De Carteret and his friends had fled. A new truce had enabled them to escape to Normandy. In May they sent a petition from Barneville "in the name of the Jerseymen driven from the island by their enemies", asking for safe conducts to return, that they might lay before the Commission their complaints against Thomas of Hampton and Henry de la More (*Cart.*). But the King's Council had decided against them. In August an order arrived that the Warden was to retain the cattle and goods, "as the King has learnt that they belong to enemies and rebels" (*C.R.*). De Carteret was now branded as a traitor, but the charge was not pressed home, for his Manor was not escheated.

About the last six years of his life we know nothing ; for Payne's statement in the *Armorial*, for which he gives no authority, is almost certainly a mistake. He says:— "He joined the English fleet, and mainly contributed by his complement of men in the recovery of the island of Guernsey": but Payne is confusing him with his son Renaud (q.v.), who five years after his father's death did help to retake Castle Cornet. He may have been allowed to return to the island, when in July 1343 Thomas of Hampton was replaced by Thomas Ferrers. On the other hand he may have had to spend most of those years in exile, for his son Philippe, who had fled with him, was not pardoned till 1351 (*P.R.*). We only know that he died in the second week of Lent 1349 (*Cat.Inq*). At that time he was not only Seigneur of St. Ouen's, but also Seigneur of Longueville, and of the Fief of Homet, which had the curious custom, that, whenever the Seigneur was in residence, the Rector of St. Clement's was bound to convey the Lady of the Manor to church on a white horse. His son Guillaume also died in 1349 "in the first week of March" (*Cal.Inq.*). As this was the year in which the Black Death devastated Jersey, they may both have been its victims. Renaud was succeeded by his son Philippe, "aged 35 or thereabout" (*Cal.Inq.*). He had married Genette de Guerpil, and had three sons, Philippe, Renaud (q.v.), and Guillaume.. [Authorities quoted above.]

DE CARTERET, SIR RENAUD (REGINALD), Seigneur of St. Ouen's (d. 1382). A contract among the Le Maistre MSS in the S.J. Library records that in 1354 "Renaud De Carteret transferred to Guille De Carteret, his brother, as his share in the inheritance of Philippe De Carteret, their father, the manor of the Fief Estourmy and the Fief de Mélèches". This proves that he was the son of Philippe De Carteret, who died in 1352, and not the brother, as the *Armorial* states. Another contract, which he passed in 1351, shows that he was already a Jurat.

The Hundred Years War with France had been dragging on for nearly twenty years, when in 1356 the French made a raid on Guernsey, and recaptured Castle Cornet. When this news reached Jersey, De Carteret with Richard De St. Martin, Seigneur of Trinity, Jean de Garis, Seigneur of St. Germain's, Raoul Lempriere (q.v.), Jean De la Hougue, and other Jerseymen, "assembled their strength, and after a severe combat took the Captain of the Castle, who ransomed himself from them for 80,000 florins called *moutons*" (French coins stamped with a lamb and the text, 'Behold the Lamb of God'). "They might have taken those florins in aid of their expenses; yet they surrendered the Captain without ransom in return for the surrender of the Castle" (*C.R.*). After its recovery a prominent Guernseyman named William Le Feyvre "was slain as a traitor and adherent of the enemy by the common assent of the armed men and others there present" (*C.R.*). This execution caused deep resentment in Guernsey; and his wife Nicholaa, sister of Matthieu De Saumarez, one of the leading Seigneurs, moved heaven and earth to avenge him. She secured the arrest of all the killers, and prosecuted them before the Guernsey Court. Renaud had not been present either at the court-martial or execution, but "considering that the accused had nothing to be ashamed of, he said before the Bailiff and Jurats that he was as blameworthy as any of those impeached ; whereupon the Bailiff and Jurats recorded that he was guilty of the death, and adjudged him to the King's Prison to be detained till justice were done on him in respect of the said acknowledgement" (P.R.). In August 1357 Thomas of Langhurst, the Warden's Deputy, appeared before the Council to plead for the prisoners, and secured an order from the King "to supersede till further notice all processes against those indicted for the death of William Le Feyvre, because Thomas de Langhurst has testified before the Council that William was a traitor at the time of the death" (C.R.). The Warden was permitted to release the prisoners, "if they shall each find mainpernors, who undertake to have them before the King's Justices at the next Assize" (C.R.). But the inexorable Nicholaa would not tolerate this. In November she obtained a new order : — "Whereas the King ordered the Warden to supersede all processes against Renaud De Carteret, knight, and other men of Jersey, now Nicholaa, late wife of the said William, has shown the King that William, at the time he was slain, was under the King's special protection and his liege man, and that he neither adhered to the King's enemies nor abode with them, and that he was killed out of ancient enmity and malice, and not for treason". The Warden was ordered "to take diligent information on the matter, and, if he finds that William was the King's liege man, and did not deserve death, to cause justice to be done" (C.R.). Renaud was rearrested, and again imprisoned in Castle Cornet, and did not obtain his freedom till March 1359, when a Letter Patent arrived : — "The King, having regard to the good service often done by Renaud De Carteret, and specially to the assiduous labour which he performed in the recovery of the island and castle from the King's enemies, and because he was not at the killing or consenting to it, has pardoned him, whatever the Bailiff and Jurats have recorded against him" (P.R.).

In 1373 Du Guesclin, Constable of France, was besieging Brest. On July 6 the garrison agreed to surrender, if not relieved within a month. Du Guesclin used that month to raid Jersey. About this attack Payne in his *Armorial* has given publicity to a De Carteret legend, which had appeared in the *British Compendium* of 1731:— "To Sir Reginald belongs the signal distinction of having repulsed Du Guesclin, confessedly the greatest soldier of his age, who crossed from Brittany with 10,000 men, including the *élite* of the chivalry of France. Sir Reginald however, having secured the Castle, defended it with such distinguished skill and valour that the French General after many fruitless assaults withdrew his discomfited forces decimated by sword and disease. For this gallant achievement De Carteret and his seven sons were knighted in one day by Edward III". The truth was very different. De Carteret was not in command, but William de Asthorp. Du Guesclin won a lightning victory. The Black Mastiff of Brittany wasted no time on a siege. He stormed the walls with scaling ladders, and drove the garrison into the inner keep. There, like their comrades in Brest, they promised to capitulate, if relief did not reach them by Michaelmas. Within ten days of landing Du Guesclin was back in Rennes, having left a French force to guard the Castle. The surrender was apparently due to divided counsels within the walls. Jerseymen had long resented the fact that the Constable of the Castle was always an Englishman. As far back as 1358 Otto de Holand had warned the Chancellor that certain Jerseymen had promised Edmund de Cheny £300 sterling a year, if he would agree, when appointed Warden, to entrust the Castle to them (*Inq. post mort.*). Later in 1373, when the French had been ejected, Jean de St. Martin (q.v.), the Bailiff, was accused of having sold the Castle "to a certain enemy, Bertrand Claykin, knight". (This spelling of Du Guesclin's name appears in more than one contemporary English document.) He was imprisoned in the Tower of London, but eventually acquitted. The King however sent a stern rebuke on 1 Feb. 1374 to the Bailiff and Jurats for intermeddling with military matters : — "Inasmuch as we learn on sure authority that we have sustained and are sustaining intolerable injuries through your negligence and rebellion and frivolous answers and disobedience to ourselves and our order, we forbid you in the most peremptory manner possible at your own peril henceforth to interfere in any trials, inquests, or disputes with which you have no concern" (*Foed.*). In all this De Carteret must have been deeply involved. The terms on which he held his

Fief required him to take part personally in the defence of the Castle. As Senior Jurat he was implicated in the action of the Royal Court. But we hear nothing of any 'gallant achievement' that won knighthood for the whole family. As a matter of fact Renaud is described as a knight as early as 1357 *(C.R.)* ; and, since his eldest son was still a minor at the time of his father's death eight years after the recovery of the Castle *(Foed)*, there cannot have been seven sons all of knightable age.

On 18 August 1373 the King sent orders to his Admirals to proceed at once to Jersey "to liberate our Castle of Gurry" *(Foed.)*. They evidently succeeded, for on 20 November Edmund Rose was placed in command of the Castle *(Foed.)*. But the rest of the island remained at the mercy of the French. In 1374 and again in 1375 the Receiver reported that it was impossible to raise the King's revenue "owing to the frequent incursions of the enemy and the ravages they commit". In 1376, when the Pope was trying to make peace, Edward III complained to the Cardinal Commissioners at Bruges that "Bertrand Du Guesclin, with whom our subjects in Jersey arranged a ransom for one year only, and then arranged again a ransom for one year only, which ransoms were paid in full according to the terms agreed, has forced them by harsh imprisonments and burnings to agree to another ransom for a year without our knowledge, and contrary to the truce". What part Sir Renaud played in these troubles we are not told. We only know that he was dead by 15 March 1382, when the King made Roger Walden (q.v.) guardian of "all the lands belonging to Sir Renaud De Carteret, deceased, because his son, Philippe, is still a minor" *(Foed.)*. [The story of his imprisonment for the killing of Le Feyvre is in the *Calendar of Patent Rolls*, cited as *P.R.*, and in the *Calendar of Close Rolls*, cited as *C.R.* Documents dealing with Du Guesclin's raid are in the Appendix to Lemoine's article, 'Du Guesclin à Jersey', in *Revue Historique*, Mai, Juin, 1896. Others are in the Appendix to Nicolle's *Mont Orgueil*. But the best contemporary account is in *Les Chroniques du Bon Duc, Louis de Bourbon*.]

DE FAYE, EUGENE (1860—1929), Professor at the Sorbonne. His great-grandfather came to Jersey in 1750 as a Huguenot refugee from Poitou. His grandfather, François de Faye (born in Grouville), was the first Minister of the Independent Chapel at St. John's. His father, Clement de Faye, was Minister of the same Chapel, 1848—56. His mother, Catherine Leslie Henderson, was daughter of Dr. William Henderson, lecturer in Materia Medica at Marischal College, Aberdeen. Eugène was born at Lyons, 22 July 1860, educated at Aberdeen Grammar School, and in 1881 graduated M.A. at Aberdeen University with first-class honours in Classics. He became a Minister of the Eglise Réformée Libre in France, and worked for a time at Roubaix and then at Paris, where he studied at the University and became Doctor of Theology in 1898. In 1908 he was appointed to the Chair of Patristic Literature in the Faculty of Protestant Theology in the Sorbonne. He served as Chaplain during the first World War with the 32nd. Army Corps, and became a strong advocate of the League of Nations, on behalf of which he lectured later all over France. In 1921 Aberdeen conferred on him the honorary degree of D.D. On his own subject his reputation was world-wide. Oxford University invited him to lecture on Gnosticism in 1914, and Upsala University on Origen in 1924. After his death an invitation came from Oberlin College, Ohio, to give a course of lectures there. His books are recognized by scholars, Catholic as well as Protestant, as indispensable for the study of Church History in the Second and Third Centuries. The most important are : — *Idées religieuses d'Eschyle*, 1884 ; *Les Apocalypses juives*, 1892 ; *Clément d'Alexandrie*, 1898 ; *Introduction à l'étude du gnosticisme*, 1903 ; *Origines des églises apostoliques*, 1909 ; *Gnostiques et gnosticisme*, 1913 (couronné par l'Académie des Inscriptions et Belles Lettres.) ; *Idéalisme et réalisme*, 1920 (an application of the teaching of Plato and Aristotle to post-war problems) ; *Origen*, Vol.I, *Biographie et oeuvres*, 1923, Vol.II, *Ambiance philosophique*, 1927, Vol. III, *Sa doctrine*, 1928. He died in Paris, 12 February 1929. His only son, Alexandre, was killed in 1918, after being mentioned six times in dispatches, and winning three Palms and the Legion of Honour. His published Letters from the front revealed marked literary ability and a deeply religious outlook. [Family information.]

DE GRAMONT, FERDINAND LEOPOLD (1812–97),
French Poet. Son of Ferdinand Léopold De Gramont, native
of Montbéliard, near Belfort, a French Royalist officer, who
took refuge in Jersey after the Revolution. He settled at St.
Martin's, where on 14 Nov. 1803 he married a Jersey girl,
Susanne Gaudin. They had a large family. One son, Ferdinand Léopold, died in 1806, but a second Ferdinand Léopold
was baptized at St. Martin's on 5 Jan. 1812. He was admitted
to the famous French military school of St. Cyr in 1828, and
left in 1830 ; but he gave up the army for literature. He became known as a poet in 1840, when he published a volume of
Sonnets ; but before that he had been 'ghosting' for Balzac.
Most of Balzac's novel *Don Gigadas* was written by him, as
were the articles on the French Kings in the *Dictionnaire de
la conversation*, though they bear Balzac's signature. He also
supplied Balzac with verses for his novels. Under his own
name he published in 1841 a prose translation of Petrarch's
Poems, and in 1843 the Book of Job translated into French
verse. This was followed by *Chants du passé*, 1854 ; *Comment on se marie* 1858 ; *Gentilhommes riches, Gentilhommes
pauvres*, 1860 ; *Les bébés*, 1861 ; *Les bons petits enfants*, 1862 ;
L'arithmétique de Mlle. Lili, 1866 ; and other volumes of poetry.
But his special contribution to French literature was the revival
of that very intricate form of verse, the Sestina, invented in the
twelfth century by the Provençal troubadour, Arnaud Daniel.
It consists of six six-line stanzas with an envoi, in which the
line endings of the first stanza are repeated in all the other five
in a different order. He published in 1872 *Sextines, précédées
de l'histore de la sextine*, in 1875 *Vers français et leur prosodie*,
a work crowned by the Académie, and in 1882 *Olimes, sextines,
et sonnets*. He died in Paris 1897. His son, Louis, became
a well-known journalist, dramatist, and writer of realistic novels.

DE GRUCHY, ABRAHAM (1780–1864), Merchant. Son of
Philippe De Gruchy of St. Saviour's and Elizabeth Le Geyt.
Born 29 Sept. 1780. In 1810 he opened a small general store
near St. Peter's Church ; but soon built a new shop, which
forms part of the present Alexandra Hotel. The firm still pre-

serves the Day Book and Ledger for 1811, containing the accounts of General Don, Sir John Dumaresq, and other famous customers. In 1818 De Gruchy advertised that he had returned from London with a large stock of cloth and cotton goods (*Chronique*). In 1825 he opened a branch in Town in Broad Street, announcing that he had engaged one of the best master-tailors in London and five workmen to make men's clothes and riding habits for ladies (*Constitutionnel*). In the following year he moved his shop to its present site in King Street. In all this expansion he was financed by his wife's uncle, Jean Le Brocq. He was evidently a first-rate business man, for his trade increased and prospered. The shop was enlarged again and again by buying neighbouring houses. In 1854 Dumaresq's *Tourist's Handbook to Jersey* said:— "Among many improvements due to private enterprise none reflects so much credit on the town as the handsome shop of Mr Abraham De Gruchy. It will not be saying too much to compare it to the best in London. This immense block of buildings is accessible from three streets, King Street, Dumaresq Street, and New Street". Nine years later he made yet another extension, buying up a large property to the east of the old shop. But he made his mistakes. In 1833 a customer asked him to sign a petition 'to speed up the administration of justice, and without reading it he added his name. A few days later he was astounded to find himself hooted in the street and his shop boycotted. He had signed the Petition of the Fifty-Seven for the abolition of the Royal Court. In 1851 he was again in hot water. Much trade was still done in *livres*, *sols*, and *deniers*. With a few other tradesmen he advertised that henceforth he would "sell exclusively in British sterling". The *Jersey Times* vigorously denounced "the arrogance of a handful of persons presuming to mould a long-established currency to their own will". De Gruchy replied that his only aim was simpler bookkeeping ; but the storm was so great that the scheme had to be withdrawn. He died in Grosvenor St. 9 Oct. 1864, and was buried in Green Street Cemetery. He married Marie Le Brocq, and had six children, William Philippe, Marie Anne, Philippe, Jean, George, and Thomas. [Local Newspapers, specially *Jersey Express* 18 April 1894.]

DE GRUCHY, GUY FORTESCUE BURRELL (1867—1940),
Jurat. Only son of William Laurence De Gruchy (q.v.), Jurat,
and .Augusta Chambers Smith. Born in St. Helier's, 22 March
1867. In 1870 the family moved to Beau Coin, St. Brelade's,
and then to Rochebois, St. Aubin's. He was educated at J.E.
Vibert's School, St. Aubin's, 1877—81, and then at Wellington
College till 1884. He entered Gonville and Caius College,
Cambridge, 1885. He had already begun to take his lifelong
interest in birds. The Jersey bank failures of 1886 forced him
to earn his living, and he entered the Bank of Rio de Janeiro,
and in 1889 was sent from London to the Rio branch. In 1891
he moved to the office of Norton, Megaw and Co, English
merchants in Rio, where he remained till 1908, when he took
charge of their Head Office in London. In 1914 he became
a Director of his firm, and finally Chairman of the Board, retiring in 1931 after forty years' service. While in London he
was an active member of the Jersey Society there, writing two
of its publications, *The Normans in Sicily* (1909) and *The Settlement of Normandy with special reference to the Channel
Islands* (1911).

In 1909 he bought Noirmont Manor, and settled there in
1916. Its grounds afforded welcome opportunities for bird-study.
From 1915—40 he wrote annual reports on ornithology for the
Bulletins of the Société Jersiaise, and was President of the
Société 1932—4.

He was a keen student of the island's history, and his interest in this led him to revive the old Seigneurial Court for the
Noirmont tenants. He wrote erudite articles for the *Bulletins*
on 'Entries relating to Jersey in the Great Exchequer Roll of
Normandy', 'The Family of Walsh and the Seigneurie of St.
Germain's', 'The Perquages of Jersey', and similar historical
subjects. A few weeks before his death he finished a book on
Mediaeval Land Tenures in Jersey. He was one of the three
editors of the *Cartulaire des Iles Normandes.*

The palaeolithic cave-dwelling at La Cotte stood on his
property. He not only gave the Société permission to excavate,
but presented most of the finds to the Société's Museum.

He first became prominent in Jersey public life by fighting
an attempt to extend British Income Tax to residents born in the
United Kingdom. In 1927 he became Treasurer of St. Brelade's
Hospital, and in 1928 was elected Constable. In both capacities

he was brought up against the problem of pauperization, and he determined to find a remedy, while he was in the States. A heart-attack made him resign in Jan. 1931 ; but his health improved, and he was elected Jurat in August of that year. He then specially interested himself in Housing, Social Assurance, and Old Age Pensions. Bills on the first two were successfully piloted by him through the States ; and much work was done on the Pensions scheme, though he did not live to see this become law. As President of the Harbours Committee he took an active part in constructing the Airport. While President of the Defence Committee four important subjects were dealt with, Aliens, Militia, Police, and Air Raid Precautions. As President of the Committee for the Preservation of the Natural Beauties of the Island it gave him great satisfaction when the States took over a stretch of cliffs on the north coast.

In 1938 however his political work came to an abrupt conclusion. The States' auditor challenged the right of the Harbours Committee to provide on its own authority pensions for its employés and to grant an honorarium to the engineer, who had supervised the building of the Airport. In the first case the pensions had appeared for years in the pay-sheets approved by the Auditor. In the second the payment had appeared in the Treasurer's Accounts. In each case they had apparently escaped notice. The President of the Finance Committee now carried a resolution in the States that the Harbours Committee had acted *ultra vires*. As this was virtually a vote of censure, De Gruchy resigned his Juratship, feeling that no useful purpose could be served by continuing his work with a hostile majority against him.

In June that year he became very ill, and henceforth was subject to periods of severe illness. He died 27 Nov. 1940. In 1916 he married Catherine May, daughter of H. Campbell Miller, and left a son, Philip, and two daughters, Hope May and Elisabeth Noémi. [Private information. Local newspapers.]

DE GRUCHY, MARTIN (1666–1720), First Notary Public in Jersey. Only son of Martin De Gruchy, Centenier of St. Lawrence and Rachel, daughter of Helier De Carteret of La Hougue, Attorney-General. Born in 1666, and baptized in St.

Lawrence Church on 8 July, his grandfather, the Attorney-General, being his godfather. His father died, when he was two years old, and he was brought up by Jurat Philippe Payn of Grouville, his mother's second husband. In 1680 the latter obtained for him a grant from the Don Baudains, which enabled him to go to Gloucester Hall, Oxford. He returned to Jersey and became an Ecrivain. In 1685 he married Sara, daughter of Jean Le Gallais, in the Town Church, and they *firent leurs regards* in St. Lawrence Church, so the Register of that Church informs us, on the following Sunday. This refers to the custom of newly married couples making their first appearance in the Church of the parish in which they were going to live wearing their wedding clothes. He soon moved to St. Helier's and there he became the father of nine children, Rachel (b. 1687), Jeanne (b. 1690), Elisabeth (b. 1692), Martin (b. 1694), Jean (b. 1696), Philippe (b. 1699), who became Rector of St. Lawrence, Elie (b. 1702), Anne (b. 1704), Florence (b. 1705). In 1698 he was elected Procureur du Bien Public of St. Helier's. Notaries, though now appointed by the Lord Chancellor, were then licensed by the Archbishop of Canterbury. In May 1701 De Gruchy obtained from him a faculty creating him a Tabellion and Notary Public. This he duly registered in the Ecclesiastical Court. Jersey had hitherto known nothing of Notaries, and in May 1703 the Royal Court decided that such an office "tended to diminish the rights of the Bailiff and the authority of the Court", and forbad De Gruchy to practise. In *The Groans* it is alleged:— "Durell, the Lieut.-Bailiff, resenting a suit which De Gruchy had brought against his eldest son, stirred up the spirit of the Bailiff". De Gruchy appealed to the Privy Council, and, while waiting for his case to be heard, practised as a Notary in London. In May 1705 the Council ordered that the prohibition of the Court should be repealed, "and the said Martin De Gruchy permitted to execute his faculty with the same liberty that he might do in this Kingdom" (O.C.). He returned to Jersey, and got this registered both in the Ecclesiastical and the Royal Courts. In the same year he was appointed Greffier of the Ecclesiastical Court. In 1707 his quarrel with the Bailiff flared up once more. "Having offered to Sir Charles De Carteret, Bailiff, and to the Jurats in Court a cause about some appurtenances of his notarial practice, wherein the Bailiff thought himself concerned as being apprehensive it might be a diminishment of some of his perquisites, Sir Charles rejected the cause, and at the same time charged De Gruchy with an accusation about pretended defamatory words, gestures, and insinuations, which he alleged De Gruchy had spoken and acted against him. Sir Charles publicly declared that they consisted, (1) that in private conferences Gruchy had called him His Excellency, (2) that in discoursing of him with his friends he said he was rough as a veal pie" (*Groans*). The actual charge, as recorded in the Court Rolls, was that he had "maliciously uttered many insults and defamatory words, both during the session of the Court and elsewhere, against the honour of the said Charles De Carteret, holding up to ridicule his administration of justice by gestures and shocking words and perverse insinuations". *The Groans* continues the story:— "Gruchy having had occasion to go over to Guernsey, as soon as he was absent, they condemned him without jury or witnesses to beg upon his knees pardon of God, the Queen, the Bench, and De Carteret, and he was further condemned to an unlimited fine. The matter being brought to her Majesty in Council, it was transmitted to the said Magistrates ; yet five or six months after it had been served upon them they attempted to assess the fine to 150 *livres tournois*. By Her Majesty's Order in Council of 30 Dec. 1708 Gruchy was admitted to appeal" (Cf. *O.C.*). He seems now to have decided to leave Jersey, for he did not prosecute his appeal, but settled in London as a Notary, and there he died in 1720. He may have been the author of the anonymous attack on Sir Charles De Carteret, published in 1709, *Groans of the Inhabitants of the Island of Jersey by a Well-Wisher to his Country*. [Authorities quoted above, and his own pamphlet, *Manifeste de Martin De Gruchy tendant à prouver que des Contracts d'Aliénations d'héritage passez devant Notaire sont en touts esgards de mesme force que ceux qui passez devant Messieurs le Bailiff et Justiciers*.]

DE GRUCHY, MATTHIEU, (1761—1797) Roman Catholic Priest. Second son of Philippe De Gruchy, a small farmer at St. Saviour's. Born 31 Aug. 1761. When he was six, his father died, and his mother had a hard struggle to run the farm and support her six children. Matthieu was brought up in the Church of England. Two uncles, merchants in St. Helier's, seeing that he was studious, offered to pay for his education, and in time to send him to Oxford, hoping that one day he would become a Jersey Rector. But the boy's heart was set on the sea. In 1776 a cousin took him on board his ship, which was engaged in smuggling, and the lad became an expert in dodging excisemen and running contraband. In 1778 war broke out with France, and he joined the Jersey privateer, *General Conway*. On their first trip they captured a large French ship and brought her to Jersey. Setting out again, they captured the *Pucelle d'Orléans*, and De Gruchy was one of the prize crew put on board to take her to St. Helier's. But they were recaptured by a French squadron, taken prisoners to Brest, and interned in the Castle of Angers. Here De Gruchy was made hospital orderly, and, as he knew French and English, interpreter between the sick prisoners and the French nurses. These were Sisters of the Order of St. Vincent de Paul, and they set their heart on converting the young sailor. Eventually they succeeded, and in 1780 he was received into the Roman Church. This made him so unpopular with his fellow-prisoners, that the Governor transferred him to another prison at Saumur. Here he helped himself to a blank passport from the Governor's office, forged the Governor's signature, and escaped. He found work on a remote farm, first as vinedresser, then as shepherd. In 1783 peace was proclaimed, and an amnesty offered to escaped prisoners. De Gruchy gave himself up, and obtained his formal discharge. He then became apprentice to a cabinet-maker in Trémontine. While making a pulpit, he became friendly with the Curé, who interested a rich lady in him, who arranged for his training for the priesthood. In 1787 he was ordained Sub-deacon, and in 1788 Priest, in the Diocese of Luçon in La Vendée.

Then came the Revolution. In 1791 all Priests who refused to take an oath accepting the new Constitution were deprived of their parishes, and De Gruchy was one of them. For a time he wandered from château to château where hospitality was shown to ejected Priests. In one he showed his zeal for orthodoxy by looking through the library and burning 360 books that seemed to him tainted with Jansenism. In 1792 all nonjuring Priests were expelled from France, and he returned

to Jersey. He found the island full of French Royalist refugees
including three Bishops and 1,800 Priests. For the latter the
Royal Court had made the stipulation that, if they received
hospitality, they must not attempt to proselytize. This condition
most of them loyally observed; but De Gruchy did not consider
himself bound by it. He was no foreigner, staying in the island
on sufferance, but a Jerseyman and a landed proprietor, for his
elder brother had died, and the farm was now his. His ambition was to convert first his own family, and then his fellow-
countrymen. He took care to secure for this task full ecclesiastical authority. In the Library of the Société Jersiaise is his
commission, signed and sealed by the Bishop of Tréguier, as
Vicar General in Jersey for the Bishop of Coutances, giving him
authority *"abjurationes haereticorum et schismaticorum in hac
insula recipiendi"* (to receive the recantations of heretics and
schismatics in this island). Though he fitted out a room on his
farm as a private chapel, he took care never to hold a public
service, or do anything to provoke opposition. He trusted
entirely to private conversation. He dressed as a farmer, and
lived as a farmer, working in his fields, and making friends
with his neighbours and numerous cousins. At the end of
two years he had made eighteen converts. In the Society's
Library are two letters that he wrote to a young Jerseyman,
whom he had sent to be trained as a Priest in the English
College at Rome. But the conversion of Marie and Elizabeth
Grandin, daughters of a St. Martin's farmer, brought his work
to an end. Their father was furious, and asked why De Gruchy,
like other farmers, had not been called up for the Militia. He
was summoned to St. Saviour's arsenal for drill, and declined
to serve on the ground that the Roman Church at that time
forbad its Priests to bear arms. He was then arrested as a
deserter. The Royal Court refused to grant him exemption,
and in 1794 he left the island to lay his case before General
Conway, the Governor, and the Privy Council. During his
stay in London he wrote and printed a doctrinal Catechism in
French and English for distribution in Jersey.

At last he obtained from the Governor dispensation from
military service, and returned home. But the conversion of two
more young women, Elizabeth and Suzanne Pinel, roused a
new storm. Their father appealed to the Court for protection
against émigré priests who were sowing discord in families,

and the Court ordered the arrest of the Bishop of Tréguier as the person responsible for the behaviour of his clergy. The refugees were now (1795) alarmed, lest De Gruchy's zeal should cause them all to be expelled, and they hurried him away to England. Here he became Chaplain at Southampton to the Irish soldiers in hospital.

Meanwhile preparations were being made for the ill-fated Quiberon expedition. The refugees in England and Jersey were being formed into regiments, which, stiffened by English troops, were to be landed in Brittany, where the Chouans still kept the Royalist cause alive. Simultaneously another rising was to take place in La Vendée. De Gruchy was still a priest of a Vendéan diocese; so the Vicar General of Luçon ordered him to return there secretly, though detection meant certain death, to carry dispatches to Charette, the Vendéan leader, who after the suppression of a previous revolt still held out in the marshes. He embarked on the frigate *Indefatigable*, which tried to drop him on the coast; but the French fleet drove her away, and she was wrecked off Portugal, and De Gruchy found himself stranded at Lisbon. He eventually got back to England in another frigate in time to sail with the Quiberon expedition itself. On landing in the Bay of Quiberon he did not stay to share the fate of the main army, but with five companions made his way down the coast in a fishing boat to La Vendée. After many adventures, for the Republican guards were wide awake, they reached Charette's Camp, and delivered their dispatches. When this was done, the political side of De Gruchy's work ended. Priests were scarce in La Vendée after the great purge; and in the midst of a fervently Catholic population his time was fully occupied with his legitimate work.

Meanwhile Hoche, the ablest of the Republican generals, had defeated and destroyed the Royalist army at Quiberon, and then turned south to pacify La Vendée. Charette was hunted down and killed; and De Gruchy became an outlaw hiding in woods and standing corn. He tried to work his way north to the Channel ports, hoping to get to Jersey; but at Nantes he was arrested. On 28 Nov. 1797 he was led to execution. Twice the firing squad deliberately missed him. Then an officer stepped forward and blew out his brains. He was only 36.

DE GRUCHY, WILLIAM LAURENCE. (1838—1920). Jurat.
Born in St. Helier's, 9 Dec. 1838. Elder son of William Philippe De Gruchy, who was Constable of St. Saviour, 1872—78.
Educated first at St. Mannelier Grammar School, 1848—52.
Of this period he wrote:— "As an old St. Mannelier boy I have
most pleasant recollections of my school-time there, and intense
gratitude for the careful and thorough way in which the
boys were taught. Robert Philip Mallet, the Regent, an
Oxford graduate, had had a wide experience of life, including
a visit to New Zealand and a long tour in Italy. He was an
Italian scholar, and there was included in the school curriculum,
what must have been rare in 1848, a course of natural science.
There were two 'hostiarii', one a Scots University graduate and
one a very competent Jerseyman. There were 36 boys, 6 from
each of the eastern parishes, recommended by the Constables.
We were excellently lodged and fed, and free to roam about
the country". In 1853 he went to Rugby, then under Dr.
Goulburn, leaving in 1857. He returned to Jersey, and served as
an officer in the Militia from 1858 to 1878, rising to the rank of
Captain. He married in 1864 Augusta Chambers Smith,
authoress of two Novels, *Lalage* (1876) and *Octavia's Lovers*
(1880), and a volume of verse, *Under the Hawthorn* (1893). He
and Jurat Le Gros were founders of the Société Jersiaise.
They formed their plans, and then called a meeting of all who
might be interested, and in 1873 they got the Society started.
For the first ten years of its existence De Gruchy was its
Honorary Treasurer. In 1875 he was called to the Bar at
Gray's Inn, and in 1876 was elected Constable of St. Helier's.
In 1878 he became a Jurat. In 1881 he published a carefully
collated and annotated edition of the French and Latin texts
of *L'Ancienne Coutume de Normandie*, the thirteenth century
code which is the basis of Jersey Law. No edition of this had
been printed since the sixteenth century, and copies had become
very scarce. His reprint was adopted as text-book by the University of Caen. Other publications were:— a paper on *Les
Edifices Religieux de Jersey in* the Transactions of the Congrès
Archéologique de France, 1883 ; a paper on *The Land Measures in the Channel Islands* in the Transactions of the Cambridge Antiquarian Society, 1886 ; a delightful little book, *Jersey,
My Reminiscences*, published by the Jersey Society in London,
1915 ; and his privately printed *Reminiscences of Church Life*

in Jersey by *Caesariensis.* He was ruined by the crash of the Jersey Banking Company in 1886, resigned his Juratship, and went to live in London. Here he became Assistant Secretary of the Additional Curates Society, a Church institution for increasing the number of clergy in poor parishes, and he served this Society for twenty-seven years. He returned to Jersey in 1920, meaning to make his home in St. Aubin's, but died on June 13th., and was buried at St. Saviour's. C.T. Le Quesne has described him: — "Very gentle speech, breaking out now and again into a shy humour, always so modest and unassuming that he almost concealed the stores of his learning and observation. The mark of the scholar and the gentleman was on all he said or did. He abhorred slovenliness and inexactitude. Slapdash and hustle were qualities foreign and abhorrent to him. He had the scholar's passion for finding out the history of words and rites and institutions, and the scholar's relish for precise and beautiful language. He had the reverence of a noble mind for every worthy thing". [De Gruchy's *Jersey, My Reminiscences.* C.T. Le Quesne's Note in Durell's *Men I have known.*]

DE LA CLOCHE. See LA CLOCHE.

DE LA CROIX, JEAN NICOLAS RENE (1796—1869), Local Historian. Born in a house in the Royal Square, 25 Nov. 1796, of French parents, Claude Marie Lacroix, ironmonger, and Marie Marguerite Berthé, (The De was added by himself. His father and brother continued to sign their names Lacroix). He was baptized as an infant by the priest in charge of the French Roman Catholic Chapel (Certificate in *Constitutionnel,* 12.2. 46), and, surprisingly, again in the Town Church, 19 April 1805 (Church Register). He was educated at Plees' Academy, and later "at a College in England" (*Const.* 10.10.46). He then tried many ways of earning a living. "He has been in turn", said the *Impartial* (2.5.46), "tailor, farmer, school-master, editor, author, musician, sacristan, second-hand dealer, then once more editor". In 1832 he compiled for the States a catalogue of the

Public Library. In 1847 he was an unsuccessful candidate for the post of Librarian. But his large and rapidly increasing family kept him always out at elbows and poverty-stricken. His house was in Hilgrove Lane, then the worst slum in the Town : and once, when someone whom he had libelled went round to break his windows, he failed, because he could not find a whole pane of glass in them.

Journalism however was clearly the work in which he was most at home. He wrote French fluently and forcibly, and his mind was well-stored and nimble, but two things wrecked his influence, the violence of the personal abuse in which he habitually indulged—He described the editor of the *Chronique* as "a demoniac whose mind is quite unhinged" (Const. 9. 1. 36), the editor of the *Impartial* as "a beardless young imbecile" (23. 8. 45), the editor of the *Jersey News* as a "vile bankrupt, who, while boasting of the number of his subscribers, is trying to persuade his English creditors to accept a 50 per cent loss" (2. 7. 36), and the editor of the *Jersey Times* as a "venomous reptile, which drives its fangs into the hand that feeds it" (2. 10. 37)—and the fact that he was ready to write for whichever side paid best. "During the ten years we have known him", said the *Impartial* (16. 3. 31), "we have seen him serve both parties in turn ; we have seen him pass to the service of men he had previously insulted ; we have seen him sacked for trying to serve more than one master at a time". First he edited for some time the *Gazette de Césarée* ; then he moved to the *Chronique*, the leading Rose paper ; then to Mourant's Gazette ; then for ten years (1833—43) he edited the *Constitutionnel*, the organ of the Laurel Party. But in 1843 (1 Feb.) the *Chronique* declared that it held proofs that he had also been secretly editing the *Gazette*, and inserting articles in one paper, which he answered in the other. This was too much for the owners of the *Constitutionnel*, and they dismissed him ; but good journalists were scarce in Jersey, and three years later (1846) they took him back again.

He was constantly in hot water. In 1838 he was horsewhipped in the street in the presence of his schoolchildren for an article he had written. In 1840 he demanded an explanation from H.L. Manuel (q.v.), who had called him a "penny-a-liner", but retired with "two black eyes and a bloody nose". The fight is described with great gusto in the *Miroir* of 4 April. In 1842

Harriet Cleverly, his wife, complained to the police that he beat her, and he was bound over to keep the peace, and had his whip confiscated. In 1846 a stolen axe was discovered in his second-hand store, and he was arrested as a receiver of stolen property. A grubby, disreputable little man. Yet the island owes much to him. He had a genius for patient, painstaking research. For more than twenty years—so he tells us in the *Ville de St. Hélier*—he had been pertinaciously searching for material for his histories. It was not easy work. Country folk did not welcome this inquisitive little stranger, who asked permission to examine their family parchments. They suspected that he hoped to find something wrong in their title-deeds. But in spite of snubs he persisted. He discovered and printed many documents that have since disappeared. In one farm-house, for example, when a woman emptied out for him a sack full of contracts, he found among them the original ordination-certificate, dated 1497, of Jean Hue (q.v.), the founder of St. Mannelier *(St. Hélier)*. Previous books on the history of the island, like that of his old schoolmaster, Plees' *Account of Jersey*, had been mainly Falle and water. De La Croix' writings are based on original authorities. They are of course far from perfect. Pioneer work is almost bound to contain inaccuracies, and, as he pleads, they were "written in haste amid grave preoccupations", with the printer's devil always at his elbow demanding the next instalment. They are not well-planned or balanced. It was absurd to devote ten pages to Victoria's drive through the Town. Occasionally he lapses into the worst type of gutter-journalism, as when he interrupts his account of the Reformation by an attack on two contemporaries, "a rich and narrow-minded public functionary" (probably Charles Ahier, the Greffier), and "a metal-worker whose name is the opposite of a circle" (obviously George Square), whom he accuses of having plotted to burn the two Roman Catholic Chapels. But with all their faults De La Croix' books were the most valuable contribution yet made to Jersey history. And, however arrogant he might be as a journalist, as an author he was becomingly modest. He merely claimed that he had "collected for some future historian much scattered material, and laid foundations for an edifice yet to be built". *(Etats* 118).

First, in 1845, came *La Ville de St. Hélier,* published in six shilling parts of 40 pages each. This was followed by *Les*

Etats, also in shilling parts, in 1847. In 1851 he published a *Guide du Voyageur français à Jersey*. Then in 1860 appeared his great work, *Jersey, ses Antiquités, ses Institutions, son Histoire*, in three twelve shilling volumes. This carried the history of the island to the end of the reign of Mary. He began to prepare a fourth volume, which was never completed. One work of his fortunately never saw the light of day. In 1846 he announced that he was about to publish *The Black Book of Jersey*, in which he would reveal hideous scandals in the lives of all his enemies. He published the Preface in the *Constitutionnel*; but no one saw any more of it.

He died on 16 Aug. 1869 in the General Hospital, and, according to the Hospital records, was "buried by his relations", i.e. his was not a pauper's funeral. [Authorities quoted above.]

DELAGARDE PHILIP CHILWELL (1797—1871). Surgeon. Son of Philippe De la Garde, Rector of St. Martin's, and grandson of Charles De le Garde, for fifty years Rector of Grouville. Born 1797. Educated Exeter Grammar School. Apprenticed to Peppin and Barnes, surgeons, Exeter. House Surgeon, St. Bartholomew's, 1818. M.R.C.S. 1819. Hon. F.R.C.S. 1843. Surgeon at Eye Infirmary, Exeter, 1836. Surgeon, Devon and Exeter Hospital, 1841. After the retirement of Barnes he became the most popular operator in the West of England. Mayor of Exeter 1834—1836. Published *A Treatise on Cataract* and *A Commentary on the Construction of Hospitals*. Married Susan, daughter of Rev. John Lemprière. Died 1871. [*Medical Times*, 2 Dec. 1871 ; *Lancet*, 16 Dec. 1871.]

DE LA HAYE, HUGH (1835—1906). Originator of the Royal Jersey Fluke. Son of Jean De La Haye and Marie Voizin. Born 1835, and baptized in the Town Church, March 25. For many years he farmed Bushy Farm on Mont Cochon, St. Helier's. From 1858—63 he was Vingtenier of Mont Cochon. About 1880, at the dinner which he gave his neighbours after the Grande Charrue or Big Plough, he passed round two huge potatoes, which had been presented to him as curiosities at Le

Caudey's Stores on the Esplanade. One of these had sixteen eyes. After dinner these were cut into pieces ; of the largest, one eye was damaged, but this left fifteen pieces ; and all were planted on a côtil above Bellozanne Valley. Next Spring they produced a very large and very early crop ; but De La Haye was surprised to find that, though the parent potatoes had been round, all the produce of one of them was kidney-shaped. He nursed these new potatoes carefully, until he had enough to trade with; and then exhibited them in the window of the *Nouvelle Chronique,* and Charles Le Feuvre, owner of the paper, named them Royal Jersey Flukes. From this small beginning sprang all the later types of Royals and the early potato-trade which brought such financial prosperity to Jersey. In September 1892 his fellow-farmers presented him with an illuminated address and a purse of gold "as a feeble recognition of our appreciation of the service you have rendered to your native isle by the introduction of the Royal Jersey Fluke". In the previous year his neighbours had shown their respect for him by carting free all the stone needed to rebuild his stable after it had been destroyed by fire. De La Haye was a leader among the Plymouth Brethren, and their Services were held every Sunday in French in his farm-kitchen. He never made any effort to exploit for his own advantage his lucky discovery, and, when ill-health compelled him to give up his farm, his income was very small. In old age he spent most of his time on a seat in Victoria Avenue smoking and chatting with friends. He never married ; and he died in the General Hospital on 2 Sept. 1906. [Articles in *Les Chroniques* 15—29 Sept. 1943.]

DE LA PLACE, SAMUEL (1580—1637), Member of the Westminster Assembly of Divines. Son of Pierre De La Place, a Huguenot refugee from Angoulême, who became Rector of St. Ouen's, (1576—98), and Michelle Girard of Normandy. Born at St. Ouen's, 1580. Educated at Oxford. Matriculated from Merton College 1594. In 1596 the Calvinist Colloquy in Jersey accepted him as a candidate for the ministry, and in 1600 he was approved, and ordained as Rector of St. Mary's. There were then no medical men in the islands, so De La Place, who had gained some knowledge of doctoring, added

to his income in this way. A page from his ledger (printed in
Bull VI) shows that his patients included the families from the
Manors of St. Ouen's, Trinity, Diélament, and Longueville,
and that most of the payments were made in kind. A bottle of
senna, rhubarb, and jalap cost a quarter of mutton, and a plaster
for spleen a dozen eggs. In 1613, when the Government began
to feel its way toward the introduction of Anglicanism into the
islands, De La Place was one of the four ministers sent to defend
the Calvinist system before the Privy Council. In 1620, when
David Bandinel (q.v.) came to the Court to be sworn in as
Dean, De La Place and Daniel Brevint (q.v.), Rector of St.
John's, "rose and protested against the oath Mr Bandinel was
to take, and said they could not acknowledge him as Dean nor
their superior in anything, that the word Dean was not found
in Holy Scripture, and that they had signed and sworn another
Discipline" (S.P.). The Dean succeeded in conciliating Brevint,
but De La Place remained obdurate. Sir John Peyton wrote
to the Council:— "Notwithstanding the Dean's mild proceeding
and discreet delay he has been forced to suspend one of the
brethren for unreverent speeches against the Book of Common
Prayer. He pleaded pretence of conscience in refusing it, yet
would not accept the Dean's offer of rectifying his scruple by arguments" (S.P.). De La Place left Jersey for Guernsey, where
Presbyterianism survived for another forty years, and became
Rector of St. Martin's (1620). Here he continued doctoring and
preaching, and maintained his reputation as a Calvinist stalwart. "The Minister of St. Martin's", wrote Quick, "is a fiery
champion of the Geneva platform" (*Icones*). In 1640 the Guernsey Colloquy sent him to Jersey, where his brother Elie was
still Rector of Grouville, on the hopeless mission of trying to
reunite the two Churches and "to remedy the Jersey schism".
This or other business then took him to London, where the
Long Parliament had just met, full of Puritan reforming zeal.
He now got a chance of avenging himself on his old enemy
Dean Bandinel. The Dean came to London to defend his right
to the tithes of St. Saviour's, and in the *Journal of the House
of Commons* we read:— "Ordered that Mr. David Bandinel,
Dean of Jersey, be summoned to appear here tomorrow morning
to answer the petition put in against him by Mr. Samuel De
La Place of Jersey". And on the following day:— "The peti-
tion of Samuel De La Place was read, and it was ordered that

Mr. David Bandinel be sent for as a Delinquent by the Serjeant-at-Arms, and that petition be referred to the Committee that is to inquire after scandalous Ministers". The result, Prynne tells us, was that the Dean "was committed to the Commons' House for two or three months to the Serjeant's custody" (*Lyar Confounded*). In 1643 Parliament, which had abolished Episcopacy, summoned to Westminster an Assembly of Divines, two from each county, to devise a new form of Church Government. The Channel Islands were invited to send two, and De La Place was one of those chosen. He left his son Jean in charge of his parish ; but in 1645 the States refused to recognize him as his father's representative, "because of the erroneous doctrine he preached and his scandalous scorn of the Colloquy". (Jean had a varied career. On leaving Guernsey he became Minister of the Huguenot Church which met in the crypt of Canterbury Cathedral. Then he was for a time Pastor at Middleburg ; then for two years at Haarlem. In 1651, when the Parliament recovered Jersey, he became Rector of St. Mary's, his father's old parish. At the Restoration he refused to accept episcopal ordination, and became Pastor of the French Church in Southampton, where he died in 1664). Meanwhile his father remained in London for the next six years, for the Assembly sat till 1649. Its members took turns in opening with prayer every meeting of each House of Parliament, but De La Place was excused this duty, "English not being his native tongue". He became Assistant Minister of the French Church in Threadneedle Street, the leading Huguenot Church in London, and was evidently respected, for the Minute Book of the Colloquy, the Central Body of all the French Churches in England, records:— "16 June 1646. Because of important and difficult business which has arisen concerning Canterbury and Dover, it was thought good to strengthen the Colloquy by the addition of Mons. De La Place." But his vehement apocalyptic preaching, which approximated to that of the Fifth Monarchy Men, aroused strong controversy, and in Jan. 1646 the Lord Mayor had to hasten from the Mansion House to quell a riot in Threadneedle Street, when "some hundreds of the faithful tried to prevent him from entering the pulpit". Two of his daughters were married at Threadneedle St., Esther to Jean Du Quesne in 1647, and Angélique to Jacques Dambrin in 1648. In 1649 the Westminster Assembly ended its deliberations, and De La Place returned to his Guernsey parish. In 1650 Brevint notes in his Journal:— "Samuel De La Place is afflicted since the Spring with a pain which seizes him in the breast for hours and nearly suffocates him" ; but he lived till 21 Feb. 1658, and his tombstone can still be seen at the west door of his Church. He married Judith, daughter of Josué Bonhomme, Rector of St. Lawrence, and in addition to the three children, Jean, Esther, and Angélique, mentioned above, he had four sons, Samuel, who was agent for a London merchant at Malaga in Spain, Daniel who became Greffier of Jersey under the Commonwealth, Josué who became Rector of Trinity, Jersey, and Pierre, who became Rector of St. Ouen's, both during the Commonwealth period. [Schickler's *Eglises du Refuge ; Bulls.* VI and VIII.]

DE L'ESTOURBEILLON, JOSEPH LOUIS ARMAND
(1794—1864), French Royalist. Son of Joseph Jean, Marquis of L'Estourbeillon, Royalist refugee in Jersey, and Renée Gabrielle du Matz. Born in Jersey, 16 March, 1794. Became Sub-lieutenant in the 138th regiment, May 1813. Seriously wounded at the Battle of Arcis-sur-Aube. Rejoined army, May 1815. Became Major in the 2nd battalion of the 4th legion of the army of Morbihan. After the Peace became Captain in the Royal Guards, 1816, Major, 1819, Chevalier de St. Louis, 1825. Retired on pension, 1826, to his château of Penhoet, and was for many years Mayor of the Commune of Avessac. Died 4 April, 1864. He married in 1823 Zoé Julie Gabrielle de Penfentenys de Cheffontaines. One of his sons, Régis Marie Joseph de l'Estourbeillon, published in 1886 *Les Familles Françaises à Jersey pendant la Révolution.*

DENTON, THOMAS (1701—70), and JEANNE (1697—1770),
Founders of St. Aubin's Hospital. Thomas Denton (the Church Register spelt his name D'Enton at his baptism, marriage, and burial, and his wife signed her will thus ; but he as

Treasurer of the Hospital always signed his accounts Thos. Denton), was son of Thomas Denton, Harbourmaster at St. Aubin's, and Jeanne Hamelin. He was born in 1701, and baptized in St. Brelade's Church on 16 Feb. He became a well-to-do merchant and ship-owner at St. Aubin's. On 16 May 1732 he married in St. Brelade's Church Jeanne, daughter of Pierre Le Bailiff and Marie Le Brocq. (She had been baptized in St. Brelade's on 6 July 1697). Their children all died young. In 1733 he was one of the Founders of St. Aubin's Church, and his name appears in the first subscription list for £50. In 1750 he and his wife presented to the Church a handsome silver baptismal dish. (Fonts had not yet come back into use). On 7 Oct. 1757 he made an offer to the Parish Assembly. If they would provide a suitable Hospital (i.e. Poor House) for the Parish, he would give £1,006, invested in 5% consols, the income from which might be used for the support of the inmates. His offer was accepted. A house was taken (the old house two doors from the Church Hall), and Denton made first Treasurer. He died in 1770, and was buried in St. Brelade's Church on 5 Jan. On 4 May his widow made her will, by which she left to the Hospital an additional £1,500 sterling. The income was now sufficient to provide for more than the old house could accommodate ; so the present house was bought from Thomas Pipon, who took the old house in part exchange. This Charity was soon after further augmented by gifts of £600 from Jeanne Marett and £100 from Françoise Hue. Thomas Denton's portrait hangs in the Hospital.

DE QUETTEVILLE, JEAN (1761—1843), Methodist Pioneer and Hymn Writer. Eldest son of Elie De Quetteville and Marthe Perchard. Born at St. Martin's 22 May, 1761. Educated at a school in Winchester. While there he went out of curiosity to a Methodist meeting, and was impressed by the earnestness of those present. Later he was confirmed in the Church of England, and this stirred him deeply. But on his return to Jersey in 1777 these feelings faded away. At his Easter Communion in 1783 a deep depression seized him. He felt that as a backslider he had committed the unpardonable sin. Like Bunyan he passed through a time of intolerable mental agony. "By day I feared that the earth would open and swallow me up. By night I feared to go to sleep, lest I should wake in Hell". He went to the Rector of St. Martin's, who merely suggested sea-bathing and cheerful company. But after a year of nightmare he entered, he says, "into the glorious liberty of the children of God."

At this time Madame Perrot (See *Perrot, François)* was holding religious meetings in some of the farm kitchens, and at one of these in St. Mary's De Quetteville gave his first address, and showed his power as a preacher. He then began to preach regularly on Sunday mornings at St. Ouen's, in the afternoon at St. Mary's, and in the evening at St. John's. As his father disapproved, and would not lend a horse, he made the journey on foot. In 1784 the first Methodist Society was established in Jersey through the arrival of a new regiment which contained some Methodist soldiers, and De Quetteville joined this circle. Two years later Methodism reached Guernsey, and it became necessary to find a French-speaking leader. England could not provide one ; so an appeal was made to Jersey, and the local Methodists recommended De Quetteville. He arrived in Guernsey in Feb. 1786, and in July was recognized by the English Conference as a Lay Preacher.

His work roused strong opposition. When he paid his first visit to La Valle, a crowd entered the house where his meeting was held, dragged him to the parish boundary, and kicked him into St. Sampson's. He appealed to the Court for protection, but the Jurats passed an Act ordering the Constable to arrest any Methodist who attempted to preach in La Valle, and offering similar 'protection' to any other parish that asked for it *(Gaz. Guern.* 17 Nov: 1787). Elsewhere he was pelted with rotten eggs, smothered with dung, and drenched with buckets of water, on his way to his meetings. On one occasion the Court tried to banish him from the island on a charge of causing disunion in families, but the witnesses disagreed, and the case collapsed. He paid frequent visits to Alderney, and for years made it his rule to spend two months in Jersey three times a year, thus maintaining the Methodist ideal of itineration. Here too he was often assaulted and had his meetings broken up. Once his impetuous spirit brought him into conflict with Wesley himself. He tried to make a sinner confess before the congregation, a practice which Wesley disapproved, and for a time defied his leader's authority. (Wesley's *Works* XIII. Tyerman's *Life of Wesley*). He was more of a mystic than most Methodists, and rejoiced when his hearers saw visions. Of one young woman he wrote:— "During the sermon the Lord appeared to her several times, hanging on His Cross, and once or twice He showed her His pierced hands and side."

In 1791 De Quetteville volunteered for work among French Canadians, but Conference preferred an unmarried man, and another Jerseyman, Abraham Bishop, was chosen. His offer however, suggested that he might be used elsewhere. In France the Revolution had led to a proclamation of religious liberty, and Coke, who had charge of Methodist Foreign Missions, was planning to open a Methodist mission in Paris. French-speaking Methodists were few, so De Quetteville was chosen for the work. Coke ordained him (Sept. 1791) in the Chapel at St. Helier's (an act which got him into trouble with the Methodist Conference, as his authority to ordain had been confined to America), and the two men travelled to Paris. But Paris in the throes of the Revolution proved unpromising soil for evangelism, and after a few weeks they returned to Jersey ; and De Quetteville resumed his Channel Islands ministry.

By 1815 his health began to fail, and Conference Minutes record that he was given an assistant, "because of his infirmities." In 1816 he had to give up itinerating and confine himself to such work as his health allowed ; but for the rest of his life he was regarded as a kind of Bishop of the French congregations in all the islands. English Methodism had been immensely helped by its rich hymnody, but French-speaking Methodism had only the Huguenot Metrical Psalms. De Quetteville tried to remedy this. As early as 1795 he had published a *Nouveau Recueil de Cantiques Spirituels,* containing 467 hymns, mostly written by himself. In 1803 he brought out a revised and enlarged edition, and in 1818 at the request of Conference a third edition containing 761. He followed this in 1835 by a Sunday School Hymnal. He was no inspired poet. It might be said of him, as it was of Sternhold, "His piety was better than his poetry." But he provided his fellow-Methodists with a book of devotion, which satisfied their needs for more than seventy years. Moreover by this book he gave to Channel Islands Methodism that touch of mysticism and wistful melancholy which made its outlook definitely different from that of the English movement. In 1817 he started the *Magasin Méthodiste*, which with a short break he edited for twenty-four years. He also translated several English religious books into French, among others that queer old Puritan work, Janeway's *Tokens for Children*. He paid his last visit to Jersey in 1837, when he preached in all the sixteen chapels, which had been built during his ministry. He died in Guernsey on 1 Feb. 1843. He had married in 1788 Susanne, eldest daughter of Henri De Jersey of Mon Plaisir, Guernsey. Their only son died young ; but two daughters, Jeanne and Rachel, survived him. [H. De Jersey's *Vie du Rév. Jean De Quetteville*. M. Lelièvre's *Histoire du Méthodisme dans les Iles de la Manche*.]

DE ST. MARTIN FAMILY. The Jersey De St. Martins probably originated from the village of St. Martin le Gaillard in Upper Normandy. They held Trinity Manor, Jersey, for about two hundred years. A judgement of the Jersey Royal Court, given in 1315, (*Bull* III) in a lawsuit between the sons of a Drogo De St. Martin, shows that their father, then dead, had been Seigneur of Trinity. The *Extente* of 1274 mentions the same Drogo as holding 5 vergées in Trinity parish, wrongfully withdrawn from the Crown lands, when Drogo De Barentin was Bailiff (i.e. 1259—61). The family produced 4 Bailiffs of Jersey, 2 Bailiffs of Guernsey, a Dean of Guernsey, and at least 9 Jurats ; but it was often suspected for its pro-French sympathies. When Bailiff Richard De St. Martin (q.v.) was accused of murder in 1368, he fled to Normandy. Bailiff Jean De St. Martin (q.v.) was twice tried and acquitted on a charge of betraying Mont Orgueil to Du Guesclin in 1373. In 1452 Jurat Thomas De St. Martin went over to the French allegiance. In 1461, when Normans sent by Pierre de Brézé captured Mont Orgueil, Guillaume De St. Martin (q.v.) was accused by Renaud Lempriere of having "sold us like meat on a butcher's stall". He was Attorney-General throughout the French occupation, and other members of the family served in the French garrison. On the expulsion of the French in 1468 the brothers, Guillaume, Raulet, James, and Jean, and their cousins, Thomas and Guy, had their estates confiscated "by reason of treason of selling and delivering of the King's Castel in Jarsey" (*Extente* of 1528). They fled to Normandy, where the French King granted them the Manor of Breuil d'Anneville. [*Bull* IX.]

DE ST. MARTIN, GEOFFROI (*GALFRIDUS*), Bailiff 1373. Younger son of Richard De St. Martin, Seigneur of Trinity, and brother of Jean De St. Martin (q.v.). He is mentioned as a Jurat in March 1369. He was Sub-warden of the Isles under Walter Huwet, and handed over his duties to Edmund Rose in 1372 (Exchequer Accounts of Rose in *Revue Historique* 1896). In 1373, when his brother was arrested on the charge of betraying Mont Orgueil to Du Guesclin, he was appointed Bailiff (*ibid*). In 1374 his brother was acquitted, and resumed his office. In 1377 Thomas Trym accused Geoffroi of entering his house with Clement Hardy, Geoffroi Hugon, and Philippe Le Feyvre, while Trym and a friend, John Logge, were sitting at wine, and creating a disturbance during which Logge was killed and Trym left for dead. De St. Martin and his companions declared that Trym had murdered Logge, but after twenty-two weeks imprisonment he was acquitted. Trym then petitioned that De St. Martin's trial should take place before the Governor, and not before the Bailiff and Jurats, as Geoffroi was "a Jurat and so closely allied to the other Jurats and Bailiff that the said Thomas will not be able to have justice before them" (*Ancient Petitions*). This however was refused. The result of the trial is not recorded; but, as De St. Martin remained a Jurat, he must have been acquitted. During his brother's second imprisonment he apparently acted as Senior Jurat, for in 1380 the King ordered him to maintain in his cure a Rector of St. Martin's whom the Bishop of Coutances refused to institute (*Foed*). He is last mentioned as a Jurat in 1391. [*Bull* IX].

DE ST. MARTIN, GUILLAUME, Seigneur of Trinity, Attorney-General 1460, Traitor. Second son of Jannequin De St. Martin, Seigneur of Craqueville, and Collette De La Rocque.

A fierce family feud existed between Guillaume and his brothers, Jannequin, Raulet, James, and Guy, on one side and their first cousin, Thomas De St. Martin, Seigneur of Trinity. In 1447 Thomas obtained Letters of Protection from the King "for fear of Jannequin and Raulet De St. Martin", who were threatening him, his provost, and his tenants. In Jan. 1452 Thomas, who with his son Thomas had been taken prisoner by the French, in order to pay their ransom, sold Trinity Manor to his brother-in-law, Thomas De La Court of Guernsey, who had married his sister, Jenette. The family strenuously resisted the sale, and first his brother, John, and then Guillaume, his cousin, tried to annul it by claiming the *retrait lignager* (See App. III). These family dissensions reached such a pitch that in Feb. 1452 Thomas De La Court had to obtain Letters of Protection from the Earl of Warwick, Lord of the Isles. Within a year however Thomas De St. Martin went over to the French allegiance. This by an ordinance of Henry VI made the sale null and void ; but Thomas De La Court junior, son of the purchaser, obtained from the King a Letter Patent ratifying it, and on 16 Sept. 1456 the Jersey Royal Court adjudged him to be rightful possessor of the Fief. Meanwhile from Oct. 1452 to Jan. 1459 Guillaume and his brother James had held some official position in Jersey, for in the latter month a Commission was appointed to audit their accounts.

When the Wars of the Roses broke out in England, the dispute was embittered, for the De St. Martins became Lancastrians and the De La Courts Yorkists. The position was further complicated by a quarrel between the De St. Martins and Otis Colin, the Lieutenant of Mont Orgueil. In Jan. 1457 Jannequin appeared before the Royal Court, and showed wounds caused by soldiers from the Castle, and asked to be placed under the King's Protection for fear of the Lieutenant and his followers. The Court ordered the Vicomte to warn Colin not to interfere with him or arrest him without the Court's order. A month later the brothers' mother, now a widow, complained to the Court that Colin was holding three other of her sons, Guillaume, Raulet, and James, prisoners in the Castle, and asked that they might be presented for trial to answer the charges against them. Colin then removed them to Guernsey, out of the jurisdiction of the Jersey Court, and they remained for eighteen months in a dungeon in Castle Cornet.

In Sept. 1458 their mother appeared before the Guernsey Court, pleading that they were suffering grievous bodily injury for lack of food, and were detained in contempt of the King's Letter Patent. The Court ordered them to be sent back to Jersey for trial. Here our information ends ; but the order was apparently obeyed, for in 1460, after the defeat of the Yorkists at Ludford and the flight of Warwick to Calais and the forfeiture of all his estates including "our island of Jersey with all the other islands", on 5 June Guillaume De St. Martin was made Attorney-General of Jersey and his brother Raulet Comptroller-General of Jersey and Guernsey. In 1461 Mont Orgueil was 'surprised' by troops of Pierre De Brézé, Seneschal of Normandy. He was first cousin of Marguerite of Anjou, Henry VI's Queen, the moving spirit of the Lancastrian cause ; and this was possibly done with the connivance of Nanfan, the Lancastrian Warden. In this transaction Guillaume De St. Martin played a notorious but not clearly definable part. The *Extente* of 1528 records:— "Forfeiture of St. Martins, that is to say Guille, Raulet, Jamys, Guy, John, and Thomas De St. Martin, by reason of treason of selling the King's Castle in Jersey". In 1463 Renaud Lempriere, Seigneur of Rozel (q.v.), was accused of saying, "Cursed be the man who brought the French into the island", "that false traitor, Guillaume De St. Martin, who sold us like meat on a butcher's stall" (*Bull.* X). De Brézé continued Guillaume in office as Attorney-General, and in Dec. 1463 he was one of the tribunal of three, who tried Renaud Lempriere (q.v.) and Thomas Le Hardy (q.v.), for conspiring to expel the French. Other members of the family served in the French garrison (*Bull.* X). He also took possession of the disputed Manor of Trinity. Warwick the Kingmaker, as Lord of the Isles, declared all the De St. Martin estates forfeited, and gave them to the Guernsey cousin, Thomas De La Court ; but, as Jersey remained for seven years under Norman rule, the latter could not obtain them, till the French were expelled. When the English recaptured the Castle in 1468, the brothers fled to Normandy, where the French King gave them the Manor of Breuil d'Anneville, which had been granted to their father by Henry V, when the English conquered Normandy. Here one of their descendants was still living thirty years later. [Article, 'The Family of De St. Martin' in *Bull.* IX.]

DE ST. MARTIN, JEAN (Bailiff 1370—6), Seigneur of Trinity, Bailiff, and Comptroller-General of the Isles. Eldest son of Richard De St. Martin, Seigneur of Trinity, and Marguerite, daughter of Philippe De Carteret, Seigneur of St. Ouen's. He was Bailiff in 1370, and was reappointed 12 Aug. 1372 (Havet, *Cours Royales*). This was the most difficult period in the Hundred Years' War, when the French were constantly raiding Jersey. In 1372 Evan of Wales, a Welsh adventurer in the pay of the French, overran Guernsey, "and then", says Froissart, "they entered Jersey, and burnt and wasted there also". In the following year Bertrand Du Guesclin, the famous Constable of France, having obtained from Brest a promise to surrender, if not relieved within a month, filled in the time by invading Jersey. "On landing they ravaged and plundered the isle, setting everything afire, and took captive all who did not escape to a Castle called Gorey" (d'Argentré). De St. Martin and the Jurats took refuge in the Castle, and, when the outer walls had been stormed and the garrison driven to the Keep, they urged that a pact should be made to surrender, if they were not relieved by Mychaelmas, and William of Asthorp, the Constable, a new man, who had only just arrived, agreed. De Guesclin then returned to France, leaving only a small force behind. Before the time was up however the English fleet arrived, and the situation was saved. The garrison was then blamed for its surrender, and De St. Martin was accused of having sold the Castle. He was imprisoned, first within its walls, then in the Tower of London. "On being interrogated later in the presence of the Council, when every point had been considered, the Council pronounced him wholly guiltless (*penitus immunem*) of this treason" (Final Judgement). On 1 Feb. 1374 he was restored to his post as Bailiff, and in addition "in compensation for his unjust imprisonment" he was made Comptroller of the Crown Revenues for all the islands. This was a new office. He had to supervise the expenditure of the two Wardens and to pass the Receiver's accounts. He received as Bailiff £30 a year sterling and as Comptroller £40. But on the same day he and the Jurats were given a sharp rebuke:— "Inasmuch as we learn on sure authority that we have sustained and are sustaining intolerable injuries through your negligence and rebellion and frivolous answers and disobedience to ourselves and our orders, we forbid you in the most peremp-

tory manner possible at your own peril henceforth to interfere
in any matters with which you have no concern" (Foed).

Through his work as Comptroller De St. Martin became
involved in a dispute between De Appelby, the Receiver, and
Edmund Rose, the Warden of Jersey. The Council instructed
De Appelby to give no more money to Rose until further orders.
Rose was thus unable to pay the garrison. The Council evidently suspected him of drawing money for more men than he
had in his pay. Appelby, who lived in Guernsey, was ordered
to go to Jersey to check the number of soldiers. He says that
he "hesitated greatly about approaching Edmund owing to the
great number of his men and their threats" (Petition). Nevertheless he went to the Castle accompanied by De St. Martin
and the Jersey Jurats. He asked Rose whether he would obey
the Council's order, and call a muster of the men for whom he
was claiming pay. Rose replied that he would take a few days
to consider the matter. "Thereupon the Receiver, Bailiff, and
Jurats departed out of the Castle, but, when they had gone
half a bowshot, Nicholas Lowier, a personal servant of the
aforesaid Edmund, came and struck Thomas on the shoulder
and stabbed him through the neck with a javelin in presence
of the Bailiff and Jurats, and in full view of the men in the
Castle, who hallooed for joy, when they saw him wounded"
(Petition). This happened before June 1375, for De Appelby's
Accounts sent to the Exchequer that month contain the item:—
"For hire of a boat, when Thomelyn Appelby, Receiver of the
Isles, was wounded, 3 francs". Apparently Rose then seized
Appelby, and imprisoned him in the Castle, for another item
runs:— "For hire of a boat, when Thomelyn Appelby was in
prison, 2 francs". Thomas De Beauchamp, Warden of Guernsey, then came to Jersey to arbitrate, for we read:— "For the
expenses of Mons. Thomas Beauchamp, when he came to
negotiate with the English in the Castle by the consent of the
King's Officers, 9 fr.". Meanwhile the unpaid soldiers carried
their protest a step further by preventing De St. Martin from
holding his Courts, for a later entry is:— "For the hire of a
boat by Jehan De St. Martyn to send news to Guernsey how
those to whom wages were due in the Castle would not suffer
him to hold his Courts, 2 francs;" and the next is, "Paid for
the aforesaid Johan to send queries, answers, and news, when

Mons. Thomas Beauchamp came to negotiate with the men at the Castle to whom wages were due, 2 francs".

This violent quarrel was abruptly stopped by a return to the old practice of having only one Warden for the group of islands, and the appointment (12 Dec. 1376) of the distinguished soldier, Sir Hugh De Calveley, as Warden of the Isles. One of his first steps was to rearrest De St. Martin on the old charge of having sold the Castle to Du Guesclin. He was then kept "in close confinement", apparently for ten years. His Pardon states:— "He sent his wife to us and our Council to procure his deliverance, and, when he could get no tidings of what progress she was making, to save his life he escaped from the Castle by the help of God, and made his way direct to the Council, and surrendered himself, declaring the cause of his coming, and humbly imploring the Council not to judge his escape harshly, but to act graciously toward him". This was in August 1386, and the Council accepted his "recognizances for 2,000 marks that he would be ready day by day before the King and Council upon warning received, and would pass not the sea without licence of the King, and would behave himself henceforth as a true Englishman before the King and people" (C.R.). His case was heard on 16 Jan. 1387. "Whereupon it seemed to the Council after full consideration that the said Jean was entirely innocent of the alleged treason, and that his imprisonment had been contrary to justice. Wherefore we have pardoned Jean his escape, and receive him fully into the King's peace, and will that henceforth he be not impeached or disturbed on this charge by ourselves, our officers, or anyone". He was not however restored to his post of Bailiff. It is not possible to discover from the Court Rolls how much longer he lived, as he cannot be disentangled from a namesake, a cousin, who was also a Jurat. He had four sons, Guillaume, who succeeded him as Seigneur of Trinity, Drouet, Richard, and Jannequin, Seigneur of Craqueville.

[The final judgement of the Council on the case and extracts from De Appelby's Exchequer Accounts are in *Revue Historique*, May 1896. Four bundles of his accounts are preserved at the Record Office. De Appelby's petition is in *Transactions of the Guernsey Sy*, Vol. VII. See also article on the Family of De St. Martin in *Bull* IX.]

DE ST. MARTIN, RICHARD, Bailiff 1367—8. We have
not sufficient information to be able to fit him into the De
St. Martin family tree, for, since we are told later that he had
neither land nor chattels in Jersey, he cannot have been the
Richard who was Seigneur of Trinity. We first meet him in
1363, when as Seneschal of the Prior of St. Clement's he gave
judgement in a dispute concerning certain seigneurial rights
(*Cart.*). In 1364 he is mentioned as a Jurat, and was still a
Jurat in 1367 (*Cart.*). By 2 May he had been appointed
Bailiff, for on that date, according to a petition presented to
the Court of Chancery by Nicolas des Augrès (a long Latin
Report on this case is printed in Havet's *Gardiens et Seigneurs
des Iles Normandes*), "Richard De St. Martin, Bailiff of Jersey,
and John Coke, Lieutenant of Walter Huwet, Warden of the
Isles, seized André, des Augrès, his brother, in his house by
night, and took him to Gorey Castle, and imprisoned him there,
and ill-treated him, and afterwards foully slew him, where he
still lay unburied whole and without decay, and they carried
off goods belonging to the aforesaid André to the value of 500
florins". The King summoned Richard to appear before the
Council ; but he refused to come. His arrest was then ordered ;
whereupon he fled into Normandy. The Warden was then
instructed to seize his property ; but replied that he had none.
John Coke however did appear, and stated that André was a
man of bad reputation, accused of felony and treason, who
had been arrested by the Bailiff and examined in the presence
of the Jurats, when it was found that both in time of peace and
war he had imprisoned men of the King's allegiance, and taken
ransoms from them. He had therefore been handed over to the
Constable of the Castle for safe-keeping pending his trial. The
500 florins worth of goods had only been put under arrest until
his conviction or acquittal. The Court (16 Nov. 1368) appointed five commissioners to inquire into the case. The result is not
known. [*Bull.* IX.]

DE ST. MARTIN, THOMAS (d. 1515), Seigneur of Trinity,
Gentleman Usher to Henry VII. Eldest son of Jean De St.
Martin, who was buried at St. Saviour's 1462, and Jenette Le

Hardy. When the Norman troops of Pierre De Brézé surprized Mont Orgueil in 1461, Thomas was involved with his cousins (See *De St. Martin, Guillaume*) in the rather mysterious treason of "selling and delivering the King's Castell". On the expulsion of the French in 1468, he fled to Normandy, and his estates were confiscated. On 16 Oct. 1480 however he received a Pardon from Edward IV, "that he may freely enter into certain lands, lordships, and fees of his ancestors, to whom he is heir, in the islands of Gersey and Guernsey, as of the fee called the *Fee de la Trinité*" (*P.R.*). Then followed a long lawsuit with Thomas De La Court, whose grandfather had bought Trinity Manor in 1452. De St. Martin claimed that this sale had been invalidated by a challenge under the *Retrait Lignager* (See App. III) ; but the Court decided against him. De St. Martin then petitioned the King. In 1485, when Thomas Hutton arrived as Commissioner to inquire into the administration of the Channel Islands, an agreement was made in his presence, by which De La Court gave up the Manor for a payment of 140 crowns (*P.R.*).

Meanwhile Henry VII by the Battle of Bosworth (22 Aug. 1485) had seized the throne. On 28 Nov., within a month of the coronation, a grant was made to Edmund Weston (q.v.) and Thomas De St. Martin, "in consideration of good and gratuitous services performed by them with great labour and great personal cost to themselves", of the office of Captain, Keeper, and Governor of the island of Guernsey "to hold the same in survivorship without rendering any accompt thereof" (*P.R.* : cf *M.R.H.*). What those services were is not known, but they must have been connected with the expedition that gave Henry the crown. De St. Martin went to Guernsey, for the collectors of customs at Poole received £8 for their expenses in sending him there (*M.R.H.*) ; but four months later he dropped out of the Governorship, and Edmund was made sole Governor for life. De St. Martin then received a post at Court. On 31 Oct. 1486 he is mentioned as "one of the Gentlemen Ushers of the King's Chamber", for which he received an annuity of £12 (*P.R.*). On 1 June 1488 he is described as "Gentleman Usher with our dearest son, the Prince" (i.e. Prince Arthur), and received £5 "for the costs in going upon our message into our Isle of Guernsey" (*M.R.H.*). In 1493 and 1497 we find him styled Premier Usher to the Prince of Wales. But he did not lose touch with Jersey. On 24 May 1499 he appeared before the Royal Court in St. Helier's, acting for the executors of "that venerable and discreet person Jean Neel (q.v.), deceased, for the accomplishment of his promise to found and endow schools" (Le Maistre MSS.). His will was drawn up in Jersey in 1514 (a copy is in the S.J. Library), and signed in the presence of Richard Mabon, the Dean (q.v.). He left a silver chalice to Trinity Church, and money for masses to be said in that Church for his own soul, and that of his wife, and those of his brother and sister and his friend, the venerable Jean Neel, and for bread to be distributed to the poor who assisted at these services. He married Anne Brocas. He died at Easter 1515, leaving no children, and was succeeded by his nephew Drouet Lempriere, son of his sister Thomase. [Article, Account of the Family of De St. Martin *Bull.* IX; *Calendar of Patent Rolls* (cited as *P.R.*) ; *Material illustrative of the Reign of Henry VII* (cited as *M.R.H.*).]

DE SOULEMONT, THOMAS (d. 1541), Dean of Jersey, French Secretary to Henry VIII. Eldest son of Pierre De Soulemont, Jurat, of St. Helier's and Marguerite, daughter of Guillaume Messervy, Jurat. Thomas' three brothers, John, Nicolas, and Thomas junior all became Jurats. He was educated at Oxford (Woods' *Athenae*). In 1533 he is mentioned as Rector of Grouville (*Bull.* VII.), and in 1534 he became Dean of Jersey. (*Bull* IX.). On 25 April, 1537 he was collated to a Prebend in York Cathedral, and on 23 July in the same year to a Prebend in Hereford (*S.P.*). But, like many ecclesiastics in the days immediately before the Reformation, he seems to have regarded Church appointments merely as sources of income with no corresponding duties. He can hardly ever have lived in Jersey after he left Oxford. Louis Hamptonne, Rector of St. Lawrence, acted as Vice-Dean. De Soulemont devoted himself entirely to secular work. His only act as Dean seems to have been a stiff letter to the States, demanding that they should respect the ancient rights of his Court, and specially that every case in which a cleric was concerned, either as plaintiff or defendant, should be left to the Ecclesiastical Court,

unless it was a case of treason (*Bull.* IX). Before October
1532 he became French Secretary to Henry VIII, a position
which he secured, no doubt, because as a Jerseyman he could
speak French fluently. In that month we learn from a letter
preserved in the Record Office that he wanted to go with the
English Ambassador to the Court of Charles V, but that the
King could not spare him on account of Henry's approaching
interview with Francis at Calais. In 1537 he became Secretary to Thomas Cromwell (S.P.). On 21 Sept. 1540 he was
appointed 'Clerk of the Parliaments' with fees of £40 per an-
num (S.P.). He was evidently a busy Civil Servant. A large
number of the State Papers of the Period are in his neat handwriting, and others are inscribed, 'Translated by Mr. Soulemont
out of French'. He also knew Italian, for in 1539 he was
ordered to be present at the Tower to interpret for a Florentine
merchant who was to be examined. Apart from his official
duties he was a scholar and historian. Brevint wrote in his
Journal, "In the time of Henry VIII Thomas de Souslemont of
Jersey wrote divers notes of History". Wood mentions two of
his books, *Select Antiquities relating to Britain*, and *The Acts
and Ghests of St. Thomas of Canterbury*, neither of which
seems to have survived. In the Library of Rozel Manor is one
of his note books, containing documents relating to the history
of Jersey, which he had copied in the King's Library. Toward
the end of his life he began to accumulate property. On 5
Jan. 1539 he received the Manors of Forwood and Fowey
in Cornwall. On 13 July he was granted a lease of buildings
on the site of Greyfriars, London. On 13 Dec. he acquired
the suppressed nunnery of Canonleigh (S.P.). Apart from his
neglect of his clerical duties he seems to have been an estimable
character. He is several times spoken of as "good Mr.
Thomas"; and such different persons as Bishop Bonner and
Anthony Roke both wrote of him as "gentle Mr. Soulemont".
He was a friend of Leland, the King's Librarian, who wrote a
poem about him, included in his *Praise of Illustrious Men*. In
Leland's Map of the Channel Islands, drawn about 1540, he
scribbled against Jersey, "*Hic natus fuit T Sulmo*" (Here was
born T Sulmo), which probably means Soulement, for the spel-
ling of his name puzzled Englishmen. We find it spelled in the
State Papers Solimont, Sentemount, Colemount, Sowlemount,
Sulemount, Solyman, Soleman, Soloman, Soilyman, Suleman,

Soulemo and Solme. He died on 12 July 1541 ; and, according to Wood, was buried in the Carmelite Monastery in London. His heir was his brother John. [*Dic. Nat. Biog.* and authorities mentioned above.]

DE VEULLE, SIR JEAN (1799—1848), Bailiff. Son of Jean De Veulle, Greffier, and Elisabeth, daughter of Lieut-Bailiff Nicolas Messervy. Born in St. Helier's, 25 April 1799. Admitted Advocate, 1819. He seldom practised, but on the death of Thomas Anley (q.v.) he was unanimously elected Jurat. He married in 1829 Anne Eliza, daughter of Thomas Tindal, Treasurer of the County of Buckingham, and niece of Lord Chief Justice Tindal. When Sir Thomas Le Breton, senior, resigned the post of Bailiff in 1831, Tindal secured the appointment for De Veulle, and also the honour of knighthood. This was no real kindness. Sir Jean was an honest, well-meaning man, but he had been epileptic from youth, and had little strength of character. In his Court there were turbulent Advocates, like François Godfray (q.v.), whom he could not control, and it often became a bear-garden. In March 1852 Charles De La Garde, Colonel of the East Regiment, when the Bailiff described a petition he had signed as "the work of a few restless agitators", challenged him to a duel. De Veulle, fearing to be called a coward, accepted the challenge, though duelling was forbidden by law, and shots were exchanged at Jardin d'Olivet. A few months later there was an angry scene in the States, when Godfray questioned the accuracy of the Bailiff's report on a deputation to London. Each accused the other of inviting him to fight, and Godfray was suspended from his position as Advocate, till he appealed to the Privy Council, whose decision was:— "Their Lordships are sorry to see much to regret in the conduct of both parties ; but they consider that the order of suspension cannot be supported, and they reverse the same with costs". In July 1852 De Veulle had the extraordinary experience of being committed to prison for contempt of court by his own Jurats. He was called as a witness in a case between the Lieut.-Governor and Godfray, and absented himself. This matter too was taken before the Privy Council. All the news-

papers of the time agree in their estimate of his character. The
Chronique, the one most friendly to him, wrote after his death:—
"His disposition was upright, and his integrity beyond suspicion, but he had not enough energy or courage to punish or
even to reprimand subordinates less scrupulous than himself".
In 1848 he went to England, prepared to resign his position,
if arrangements could be made for a pension ; but he died suddenly in a fit on 1 June in his father-in-law's house at Ayles-
bury, and was buried in that town. He left five sons and four
daughters. [Local newspapers.]

DON, SIR GEORGE, Lieut.-Governor. See Appendix I.

'DUMARESQ', ANNE, (fl. 1782—4), Claimant. Jean Dumaresq, son of Jean, son of Jean, son of Abraham, was a
wealthy merchant in St. Helier's. He was Constable 1732—45
and Jurat 1745—67. He married Anne Marie Madeleine La
Fosse Chastry, and had many children, among them a daughter
named Anne, who was sent to a convent in Caen to be educated. In 1762 news arrived from the convent that she had
died. Her parents received her death certificate "duly and
legally attested" and a copy of the entry in the Burial Register
of the parish of St. Jean in Caen. They paid the funeral expenses. Twenty years later in 1782 the following paragraph
appeared in the *Annual Register*:— "Jersey. 26 Jan. A flag
of truce arrived here last week from some ransomers and a
young lady who about twenty years since was sent to France
for her education, and was shut up in a convent. Her mother
had frequent assurances of her death and certificates from the
holy fathers and went into mourning for her ; but about two
years since was surprised to receive a letter from her child informing her of her long-meditated escape, which she had never
been able to effect. At length she found a method of getting
away, hired a vessel, and came over. Her name is Du Merich.
She has a brother a lieutenant in our service, and a cousin who
commands His Majesty's ship, *Repulse*".
As England and France were then at war, there was no

possibility of testing her story. Madame Dumaresq (her husband had died in 1767) welcomed her as her long-lost daughter, but Jean, the eldest son, was convinced that she was an impostor. In the *Magasin de l'île* (Nov. 1784) he described her as "a shameless and audacious woman, whose manners and speech show unmistakably her base-born origin. Her hideous and disfigured face discloses clearly the disgusting spectacle of vice exhausted by its own excess, and her ghastly complexion makes it impossible for her to blush". But to please his mother he agreed to submit the question to Jean Thomas Durell, the Solicitor-General, a close friend of the family, and Charles Poingdestre, the leading Ecrivain in the Town. These came to opposite conclusions. Durell felt sure that the woman was a liar, but Poingdestre accepted her story.

Meanwhile in 1785 she had married Josué Pallot, a landowner in St. Saviour's. In May he sued Jean Dumaresq, the principal heir, for his wife's share in her father's estate. The case caused as much excitement in Jersey as the Tichborne trial did in England, and opinion was sharply divided. The first day's hearing was stormy, and Dumaresq was fined 50 *livres d'ordre* (about £1—18—6) for making remarks derogatory to the Court, and had to apologize. At later hearings Anne produced many witnesses, including Madame Dumaresq, who all claimed to recognize her as the dead Jurat's daughter. The case dragged on till Oct. 1784, when, as the Treaty of Paris had now made communication with France possible, Dumaresq demanded that a rogatory commission should be sent to Caen to take depositions on the spot. By Dec. this evidence had arrived, and the Court met to decide the case. But, as neither Pallot nor his wife were present, the matter was postponed, and the Vicomte ordered to warn them that, if they did not appear on the first day of the following term, their case would be dismissed. No further reference to the matter appears in the Court Books ; but in Jan. and Feb. 1785 Pallot sold his property ; and it seems probable that he and his wife left the island. [Actes of the Cour d'Héritage ; authorities mentioned above.]

DUMARESQ, DANIEL (1712–1805), Scholar. Fifth of the eleven children of Jurat Elie Dumaresq, Seigneur of Augrès, and Elizabeth, daughter of Jean de Carteret of Vinchelez de Haut. Born at Les Augrès, Trinity, and baptized in Trinity Church, June 22, 1712. He was educated at St. Mannelier Grammar School and Abingdon Grammar School, and, when seventeen, matriculated at Oxford from Pembroke College (March 1730). He held a Morley Scholarship there from 1732 to 1736, took his B.A. in 1733, and his M.A. in 1736. In 1740 he was elected to a Jersey Fellowship at Exeter College. While at Oxford he planned and superintended the making of the walk up Headington Hill. In 1744 he became Curate of Merton near Oxford, and in 1745 took his B.D. After that we might have expected him to remain in Oxford for the rest of his life. He had comfortable quarters in College, an income sufficient to live on, supplemented by pupils' fees and his curacy. It would have seemed a pretty safe prophecy that forty years later he would be found, a dim, stooping, cap-and-gowned figure, still poring over tomes in the Bodleian and swopping syllogisms at night over the port in the Senior Common Room, peradventure correcting proofs of a ponderous commentary on the works of Dionysius the Areopagite or an exhaustive refutation of the heresy of the Supralapsarians.

But Dumaresq was a Jerseyman, and the *wanderlust* was stirring in his blood. In 1746 he abandoned Oxford for the Chaplaincy of the English Factory at Petersburg. About forty years before, on a swampy islet inhabited only by wild-fowl, Peter the Great had cut the first sod of what was to be his new capital. The city was still little more than a cluster of wooden shanties built on piles in the mud round the gloomy fortress of St. Peter and St. Paul. To most Englishmen Russia was still as unknown a land as Bokhara ; but shrewd London merchants had seen that the great River Neva, at the mouth of which Petersburg stood, would become one of the main trade-routes of Europe. They had formed the Russia Company ; and, when Dumaresq was there, "greatly above a half of the commerce of Petersburg" passed through the Company's hands. Above an enormous wooden warehouse lived about a hundred Englishmen, factors, apprentices, clerks, porters, and Dumaresq was given rooms among them as their Chaplain.

He remained in Petersburg seventeen years, and learnt to speak

Russian fluently, and translated at least one Russian book into English, *An Account of that part of America which is nearest to Kamtchatka, extracted from the Description by Professor Krasheninncoff, printed at Petersburg in 1759, and translated by the Rev. D. Dumaresq.* Nor did he neglect his studies ; for in 1752 he wrote a thesis for which Oxford granted him his D.D. by diploma. But in 1755 that erratic Welshman, Sir Charles Hanbury Williams, came to Russia as British ambassador, and made Dumaresq his Chaplain. It was a big change from his trading factory to the household of this wealthy exquisite. He had as Secretary a handsome young Pole, Stanislaus Poniatowski, who soon became the lover of the Grand Duchess Catherine, the young wife of the Grand Duke Peter, the heir to the throne.

Dumaresq now had the entrée to the Palace, and made friends with most of the leading men of Russia. It was not easy to walk unspotted through the corruptest Court in Christendom ; but he seems to have managed to retain the respect of everyone. Poniatowsky and Catherine, of whose guilty secret he probably remained ignorant, showed great affection for him. Poniatowsky wrote:— "I well remember the many days we spent together exchanging ideas", and later, "For ten years I have proved from personal knowledge the goodness and sweetness of his character".

After two years Williams was recalled, and Dumaresq returned to his Factory, but he still remained a welcome visitor at Court. He saw Poniatowski banished, and Peter become Czar ; but after the *coup d'état* of 1762, which made Catherine autocrat of Russia in place of her murdered husband, he returned to England, and became Rector of the little Somerset village of Yeovilton, a living which he held till his death forty-two years later. This was a Manorial Rectory, and the Court Roll mentions him as Court Baron in 1768, 1778, 1786, 1791, 1798, and 1803. But, when Catherine became Empress of Russia, one of the many spectacular reforms that she planned was to establish primary and secondary schools throughout her vast dominions, and she sent for Dumaresq to help her. "Mistaking my zeal and industry", he wrote, "for marks of uncommon abilities, she was pleased to call me from this quiet village, and repeatedly invited me to return to Russia to be consulted in matters that related to schools which she purposed to establish"

(*A.E.*). He stipulated that he should have as colleague the learned Dr. John Brown, whose *Estimate of the Manners of the Times* was running through many editions. Brown had just published a pamphlet on Education, and was writing an eight-volume work on the *Principles of Christian Legislation.* Moreover he spoke Russian fluently. (The correspondence between Dumaresq and Brown is printed in *Biographia Britannica.*) Brown agreed, and the Empress sent him £1,000 for his journey ; but gout and rheumatism prevented him from starting, and in a fit of melancholia he committed suicide. So Dumaresq had to carry out his task alone with the help of "a plan very judicious, extensive, and *détaillé*", which Brown had drawn up. When his work in Russia was ended, Stanislaus invited him to Poland to reorganize education there:— "I am doing what I can for the schools of my country, but I shall do far better, when you are willing to help". He spent part of 1766 in Poland advising the King, and the watch which Stanislaus gave him is in the Museum of the Société Jersiaise.

By the end of the year he was again in his Somerset rectory (built about 1530). Here Pitt often stayed with him, and "in his humble snug parlour the Premier would resuscitate his earlier days by discussing with his learned friend some disputed classical passage" (*Arm*). Pitt introduced him to George III, and the King was attracted by his erudition and modesty. Payne tells a story how once, when the King was at Weymouth, "a tall, ungainly, travel-stained ecclesiastic" stepped off the Jersey packet. George clapped him on the back, took his arm, and walked up and down with him for an hour, saying afterwards to his courtiers, "That was Dr. Dumaresq, one of the most worthy and disinterested men in my dominions" (*Arm*). Pitt tried in vain to persuade him to accept a bishopric ; but in 1766 he became Prebendary of Salisbury and in 1770 of Wells. In 1790 he was made Rector of the little neighbouring parish of Limington ; and in 1798, being then 86, he retired to Bath. In 1800 he presented his library to the Jersey Bibliothèque Publique, thus almost doubling Falle's original bequest (*A.E.*). He resigned the Rectory of Limington in 1802, and died at Bath, 28 October 1805 at the age of 93. The *Annual Register* wrote of him (1805):— "Perhaps the uniform conduct of no man in this or any other country came nearer to that of the Primitive Christians in the Apostolic Age than that of this venerable divine in his very long life". He never married. There is an engraving of him, aged 86, by W. Nutter from a miniature by T. Le Hardy. [Authorities quoted above.]

DUMARESQ, HENRI (c. 1614—1654), Seigneur of Samarès, Parliamentary Commissioner. Samarès was one of the four chief Manors of the island, and the Dumaresqs had been Seigneurs of it since about 1500. Henri was the eldest son of Daniel Dumaresq, Seigneur, and Elizabeth De Carteret, his wife. He was born about 1614, for, when appearing before the Court on 22 Jan. 1635 to make 'comparence' for the manor on the death of his father, he stated that he had recently come of age. In Dec. 1635 he was elected Jurat in place of his father. On 24 Feb. 1636 in St. Helier's Church he married Margaret, only daughter of Abraham Herault (q.v.). His quarrel with Sir Philippe De Carteret, Bailiff and Lieutenant-Governor (q.v.), began with a dispute about the appointment of a lieutenant to the Militia Regiment which Dumaresq commanded. "He was justly questioned by Sir Philippe for an affront against him as Deputy-Governor in laying down his Captain's staff and command in the open field, because he could not have his will in disposing of the Lieutenant's place in his band to a person altogether unfit" (*Lyar Confounded*). A definite anti-De-Carteret party was now forming in the island, exasperated by the way Sir Philippe and his relations were monopolizing all important posts. Dumaresq joined these malcontents, and helped to draw up twenty-two *Articles exhibited against Philippe Carteret, Governour of the Isle of Jersey* (See article *De Carteret, Sir Philippe*). These he and Michel Lempriere (q.v.) took to London ; but then they made a mistake. They entrusted their petition to Prynne, the popular Puritan lawyer, whom they knew because he had been a prisoner in Mont Orgueil. But he was grateful to Sir Philippe for kindness shown him, when he was his Jailer, and he suppressed the document, and, though the two Jurats "used their utmost endeavours and solicited him every day", they could not persuade him to do anything with it. So they had their accusations printed as *A Word left by the Way touching Sir Philip Carteret of Jersey*, and put packets of them on the stocks in Cheapside and other public places, "desiring any well-affected who shall find them to present them to the Houses of Parliament". Dean Bandinel (q.v.), who had come to London to defend his right to the tithes of St. Saviour's which De Carteret was trying to appropriate, now threw in his lot with them, and between them they persuaded the Earl of Stamford to bring their complaints before the House of Lords. It was referred to a Committee. Prynne attended with De Carteret and took charge of his defence. Dumaresq and the Dean were asked by what right they spoke in the name of the island. Could they show any document giving them authority to do so? Could they produce any witnesses to support their charges? They had to admit that they were acting on their own initiative, and that their witnesses were in Jersey. The defence, thanks to what Dumaresq called "Sir Philippe's deceitful and politic carriage and Mr. Prynne's lying commendations", was so successful that the Committee reported (26 March 1642) that the charges "seemed rather to be exhibited through malice than upon just grounds and that Sir Philippe hath carried himself with great discretion and with much loyalty and fidelity" (*Lords' Journal*). The Lords then threatened to commit the petitioners for circulating "malicious libellous Articles which they could not prove" : but De Carteret pleaded for them, and they were dismissed.

A month later (21 April) Dumaresq and De Carteret met again in the States, which passed, though not unanimously, a resolution repudiating the accusations brought against Sir Philippe "in a certain petition presented to Parliament". But Dumaresq and his friends then printed a French edition of their pamphlet, and spread it through the island. So Sir Philippe prosecuted them for libel ; but Dumaresq escaped through the rule that all disputes between Jurats and Governor must be tried by the Privy Council.

In August the Civil War began, and Dumaresq was one of the five Jurats to whom in Feb. 1645 Parliament issued a commission "to apprehend the person of Sir Philip Carteret, to suppress all tumults which may be raised in aid of him, and to suspend from their charges all persons confederated with him". Sir Philippe withdrew to Elizabeth Castle, and Dumaresq was active in pressing forward the siege of the two castles. When George Carteret (q.v.) landed at Mont Orgueil in November,

Dumaresq, like most of the Parliamentary leaders, fled, first to Guernsey, then to England. In Feb. 1644 his seat on the bench of Jurats was declared vacant, and in Oct. 1645 he was tried in his absence by the Royal Commissioners and sentenced to be hanged for high treason as soon as he could be arrested, and meanwhile to be hanged in effigy in the market-square, and his goods and property confiscated. His wife for the time was allowed to go on living in Samarès ; but the Manor was a suspected spot. When Jacques Bandinel, the Dean's son, escaped from Mont Orgueil, the Manor was the first place searched, but nothing was found except Dumaresq's horse, which Carteret took for his own use. In 1646 Carteret cut down all the timber on the Samarès estate. In April 1651 Madame Dumaresq was found to be secretly corresponding with her father in Guernsey, and was banished to France.

Meanwhile Dumaresq was in London. In 1646 with Michel Lempriere (q.v.) and Abraham Herault (q.v.) he wrote and published *Pseudo-Mastix, the Lyar's Whipp*, an answer to the charges brought by Prynne against the Jersey Parliamentarians in *The Lyar Confounded*. In their pamphlet they speak of "our incredible wants, necessity, and distress in this City of London these years without any relief". Dumaresq eventually found work as Teller at the Mint in the Tower of London at a salary of £55.6.8 (*S.P.*). In May 1651 Parliament granted him a pension of forty shillings a week to be paid out of the Earl of Chesterfield's estate, till Jersey should be reduced (*S.P.*). Like other Jersey exiles he drifted away from orthodox Presbyterianism into the camp of the Anabaptists (De La Rocque's Statement among MSS in S.J. Library).

When Parliament reconquered the island in Oct. 1651, Dumaresq returned home and resumed his position as Jurat. In Aug. 1652 he was appointed one of the County Committee for Jersey and a few days later one of the four Commissioners for Compounding in the island ; but he still spent most of his time in England, for he had not resigned his post as Teller at the Mint. In Dec. 1654 he died, and was buried on the 12th in St. Clement's Church, leaving four children, Philippe (b 1637), Henry (b. 1639), Marguerite, and Esther.

DUMARESQ, JEAN (d. 1603), Bailiff. Eldest son of Jurat Richard Dumaresq, Seigneur of Vinchelez de Bas, and Collette, daughter of Antoine Larbalestier. Richard lived all his later life in his wife's house at Trinity. Here Jean was born, and resided till his death. In Jan. 1557 his father died, and he became Seigneur. In the same year he was appoointed Vicomte. In 1564 he was elected Jurat, and on the death of Hostes Nicolle (q.v.) in 1566 Sir Hugh Poulet (q.v.) appointed him Bailiff (The Governor's letter to the States is printed in *P.B.C.*). He was sworn in 18 Dec. In 1580 he became involved in a quarrel with his brother-in-law, Hugh Perrin, Seigneur of Rozel. The Rozel Seigneurial Court had declared the land of a tenant named Richardson forfeit, until he paid some arrears. He appealed to the Royal Court. Litigants had the right to 'recuse' any Jurat whose impartiality was doubtful. Perrin 'recused' not only Dumaresq, whom he called his 'mortal enemy', but the whole bench of Jurats. Apparently this had never happened before, and no one knew what should be done. Perrin claimed that by the old Coutumier of Normandy no judgement could be given, till the reasons for each recusation had been debated before the King. Dumaresq ruled that any appeal to the laws of Normandy was repugnant to the privileges of the island, and proceeded to try the case. He decided that the land should remain in Richardson's possession, provided he paid the arrears. Perrin however refused to accept payment ; so Dumaresq imprisoned him in the Castle for contempt of court. Here he fell ill, and the Lieut.-Governor secured his release for a fortnight to recover his health. He used this respite to escape to England and to lay his case before the Council, who appointed a Commission of three Jerseymen and three Guernseymen "to examine all the said matters, and certify their Lordships what they shall find, and, if they be able by their mediation to bring about an agreement, to do their best to compound all matters, so that their Lordships be no further troubled" (*A.P.C.*). The Commission met in 1582 and again in 1583, but eventually reported:— "We have laboured to bring them to some good composition, and begged Sir Amias Poulet, the Governor, to take pains in the matter. He exhorted all the parties to give over contentions, and acquit each other without claiming recompense ; but this Perrin refused. The mediation has therefore been frustrated" (*S.P.D.*). But then the matter seems to have been allowed to drop.

In Aug. 1583 gout caused Dumaresq "such distress that it was impossible for him to sit for any length of time on the Seat of Justice and to pay due attention to the proceedings"; so he asked permission to resign; George Poulet (q.v.) took his place. By May 1586 his health had improved, and Poulet relinquished the post, that he might be reinstated. In Oct. however "crippled with infirmity" he again retired, and Poulet once more succeeded him. In May 1591 Poulet became Lieut.-Governor of Guernsey, and for a third time Dumaresq was appointed Bailiff. One of his first acts was to sign the Ordinances drawn up by the Royal Commissioners Napper and Pyne. It was debated later whether these Commissioners had any authority to issue Ordinances, but for the moment Dumaresq and the States accepted them. One of them abolished 'recusation'. In Jan. 1596 ill-health again compelled him to resign.

In May he raised the Clameur de Haro against his neighbour Jean De Carteret, Seigneur of Vinchelez de Haut, to stop him from holding his Seigneurial Court at the Jonetz or the Grand Becquet des Tenets. Did this spot belong to Vinchelez de Haut or to Vinchelez de Bas? Many witnesses were produced on either side, but in 1597 it seemed to be proved that thirteen years before the matter had been settled by mutual consent, and Jonetz included in the De Carteret domain. But Dumaresq went on raising difficulties. At last in 1598 a letter from the Privy Council ordered judgement to be given, and it was decided that the Clameur de Haro had been wrongly raised. Dumaresq appealed to the Privy Council, but, as he did not appear to plead within the three months' limit, in 1599 his appeal was quashed, and his son Jean, who had stood guarantor, had to pay the costs (*Bull.* XI). This however did not end the litigation between the two Seigneurs, for in Aug. 1599 De Carteret petitioned the Council "concerning other matters depending between us". "As my adverse party is of great authority in the isle, I crave that the controversy be heard before you at the Council Chamber" (*S.P.D.*).

Dumaresq married in Sark in 1568 his cousin, Collette Dumaresq of Samarès. By her he had a son Jean, who became Seigneur of Samarès by his marriage with Esther Dumaresq, the Dame, and later a Jurat. He had also a daughter Judith, who married Jurat Pierre De Carteret of St. Peter's. When his first wife died, he married Isabel, daughter of Edmund Perrin, Seigneur of Rozel. By her he had three sons, Elie, who bought from his brother the Fief of Vinchelez de Bas, and became a Jurat, and Lieut.-Bailiff, Abraham, who bought from Jean the family home at Trinity, and Josué, and two daughters, Susanne and Esther.

His will, dated 13 Oct. 1601, throws light on his character. In a very long theological preamble he commended his "poor, sinful soul to its Creator, trusting that He will pardon all my faults, innumerable though they be, for the sake of the merits of Jesus Christ, who shed His Precious Blood for their purgation". He left 500 *livres tournois* to the poor of the island, to be distributed "not at the door of the deceased, a reprehensible custom", but by the deacons of each parish. He appointed as sole executor and *tutrice* of his children his wife, "who has always lived in the fear of God with a sound knowledge of His Word, has solaced and succoured me in my household affairs and in all other duties entrusted to her, and has well and truly instructed our children in all things necessary to their salvation". To his eldest son Jean he left his best arquebus, a steel-lined chest, his black velvet robe, and ten crowns to make a silver goblet, and remitted a debt of 100 crowns which Jean owed him, "and I charge him by all the authority that God has given to a father to be content with this, and not to worry his stepmother or his brothers and sisters for more, remembering how much I and his stepmother have spent for his advancement, and how his stepmother has done more for him than a mother could be expected to do, both before and during and after his marriage". To his three sons by his second marriage he left 100 crowns each with instructions that Josué was to be kept at a good school as long as his mother thought fit. To his two little daughters he left dowries on condition that their mother approved of their marriage. "But if, which God forbid, they act against her counsel, I revoke and recall all gifts made to them". Everything else he left to his wife. His witnesses declared that the will was signed in their presence by his own hand "so far as his infirmity would permit". The will was proved on 23 May 1603 ; so he must have died shortly before then. [Authorities quoted above.]

DUMARESQ, SIR JEAN (1749—1819), Magot Leader, Lieut.-
Bailiff. Eldest son of Jurat Jean Dumaresq (son of Elie) and
Marie Robin, who inherited from her father the Fiefs of Hérupe,
d'Orville, du Prieur, and Sauvalle. Born in 1749, and baptized
in St. Peter's Church, Nov. 22. His father died in 1761, when
he was 13, and Philippe Robin of St. Aubin's became his
Guardian. He was sent to Winchester (1764—7), where he rose
to be Captain of the School. "After that", wrote his grandson,
John Le Couteur, in his Diary, "he received high polish at the
French Court". When a lad it was assumed by the two families that he would marry Sophie, the high-spirited daughter
of Charles Lempriere, Lieut.-Bailiff (q.v.) ; and her father had
promised to nominate him as an Advocate, when he came of
age. But the young people drifted apart (Sophie eventually
eloped with a Guernsey brewer) ; and, when Dumaresq asked
for his nomination, Lempriere refused. Dumaresq knew however that the ultimate choice of Advocates lay, not with the
Lieut.-Bailiff, but with the Bailiff. He crossed to England,
and returned with a nomination from Lord Carteret, and Lempriere had to swear him in (10 July 1773). This began a life-
long quarrel between the two men. But its roots lay deeper
than personal ill-feeling. Lempriere was a conservative and an
autocrat, whose policy for years had been to rule the island
through the little group of Seigneurs who formed the Royal
Court, many of whom were his relations, and all of whom were
under his thumb. Young Dumaresq on the other hand was an
enthusiast for the new ideas of Liberty and Democracy that
were fermenting in France, and was eager to make the States,
purged of Rectors and Jurats and transformed into a Chamber
of Deputies, the real ruler of the island.

Between such ideals there could be no compromise, and two
bitterly hostile parties arose. Charles Lempriere's followers
were known as Charlots and Jean Dumaresq's as Jeannots,
though the latter soon adopted the nickname of Magots (cheese-
mites) given them by their opponents. Dumaresq is called on
his tomb "the Intrepid Defender of the Liberties of his Country
and of the Rights of the Unfortunate". In his early years he
was a born demagogue, a brilliant speaker, an untiring organizer,
quick to exploit to the uttermost every popular grievance. In
1776 he became Constable of St. Peter's, a post which he held
for twenty-five years. Every election in the island was now

fiercely contested, neither side shrinking from outrageously illegal acts. In the Eastern parishes it was not unknown for voters to be kidnapped and marooned on the Ecréhous, till the election was over. By 1782 most of the Constables were Magots and even some of the Jurats. As eight of the Rectors always voted with this party, in 1784 Dumaresq secured a majority in the States. The conflict now became a fight between the States and the Royal Court.

In 1781 Charles Lempriere grew weary of the struggle and resigned in favour of his son, William Charles (q.v.). But the tussle went on. Dumaresq decided that the first reform to work for was the establishment of Trial by Jury. As this had been the rule in England for centuries, it seemed reasonable to assume that the Privy Council could be easily persuaded to permit this in Jersey. And, once granted, it would clip the claws of his old enemies, the Jurats. But this proved an unfortunate choice. More than ten years' strenuous work led to nothing.

Dumaresq was now an extremely busy man. As the leading Advocate in the island he appeared in every important case. He was Colonel of the North-West Regiment of Militia. He was Constable of St. Peter's, and a Constable's post was no sinecure. He was Leader of the States ; and in 1786 he was appointed Receiver-General. He was constantly in touch with his party in every parish, frequently addressing meetings, and always busy with his pen (see List of his publications at the end of this article). In 1784 his brother Philippe (q.v.) financed the establishment of the first Printing Press in Jersey (see *Alexandre, Mathieu*), and published the monthly *Magasin de Jersey*, and, when this failed, began (Aug. 1786) the weekly *Gazette de l'Ile de Jersey*. The possession of the only Printing Press and the only newspaper in the island gave Dumaresq a great advantage over the Lemprieres. Moreover the States had discovered that he was the best man to negotiate with the Privy Council. Twenty-one times they sent him to London to plead their cause ; and crossing the Channel was a dangerous adventure in war-time. In 1795 his cutter had a narrow escape from being captured by a French privateer. On most of these visits he secured what he asked for. He persuaded the Government to pay for the rebuilding of the Hospital, which had been blown up, when troops were billeted in it ; to remove the duty that had been imposed on the importation of Jersey cider into England ; to provide convoys to protect the Jersey food-ships ; to withdraw the proposal to establish an English custom-house in the island ; to exempt Jersey from the order to ship-owners to draft a proportion of their men into the Navy, which would have crippled the local privateers. His greatest triumph was when he appeared in 1788, not before the Privy Council, but before the House of Commons. A report had gained circulation that most of the wool sent from England to Jersey was being smuggled into France, and a clause was inserted in a Bill drastically curtailing the amount of wool allowed to the island. As more than a thousand Jersey folk still gained their living by knitting stockings, this would have killed an important industry. By pertinacious lobbying Dumaresq gained permission to be examined at the bar of the House. He carefully provided friendly members with questions that he wanted them to ask him, and he made so good an impression that the clause was withdrawn.

His chief failure was in the matter of Trial by Jury. In 1785 he had begun to stir up the Parish Assemblies to bombard the States with petitions for this reform. In July 1786 the States appointed a Committee to examine the proposal. In August Dumaresq lodged au Greffe a Bill to establish juries, which was passed by the States with amendments in October, and sent to the Privy Council for approval. The Royal Court followed this with a strong protest stating that impartial juries could not be secured in Jersey. In 1789 after hearing both sides the Council decided that it must learn more about the procedure of the Jersey Courts before coming to a decision, and asked Dumaresq and Jurat Hemery who represented the States, and the Attorney-General and Solicitor-General who represented the Court to draw up Statements on the subject. These were printed and presented to the Council in 1790, and Pitt gave up two days to listen to the pleadings. In 1791 two Royal Commissioners were sent to the island to investigate the question on the spot. On their return to England Dumaresq followed them, and spent two periods of three months in almost daily attendance on them as they drew up their Report. But this report was then shelved, and nothing more was heard of it. In 1795 an entry in Dumaresq's Diary runs:— "Wrote to the Lord President on the matter of Juries requesting his Lordship to fix a day when the Report of the Commissioners will be taken into consideration". In 1797 he printed the proposals which the

Commissioners had agreed to recommend to the Council. But nothing further was ever done in the matter.

Meanwhile from his point of view the question had become less urgent, for he had captured the Royal Court. Jurats in Jersey were elected for life. As early as 1782 the Magots had secured two seats on the Bench, and one of the older Jurats had begun to work with them. From 1782 to 1790 seven vacancies occurred, and in each election the Magot candidate was victorious. With ten out of the twelve Jurats on the Magot side, Court and States now worked in harmony. Dumaresq was the idol of his party. The *Gazette* describes a dinner given him in 1787 on his return from one of his visits to England:— "A tent was erected on the Town Hill, and magnificently decorated to receive this patriotic guest. Flags floated everywhere, and everything testified to the joy which the presence of Mr. Dumaresq instilled in every heart. The interior was decked with branches of oak, emblems of that perseverance with which he upholds the People's cause. Above his chair hung a triumphal wreath composed of laurel and the finest flowers of the season. Two hundred persons sat down, all devoted to the public weal" (G. 16.6.87). After this Dumaresq was chaired through the Town. What the other Party thought about the matter can be seen in the complaint which William Charles Lempriere sent to the Privy Council:— "A mob to the number of some thousands was assembled by the firing of guns, and exhibited a scene of the greatest riot and disorder. In the evening the party attended by the populace paraded in the most tumultuous manner the streets of St. Helier, wearing in their hats blue cockades with an inscription 'Dumaresq and Liberty', the said Dumaresq being seated in a chair and carried upon their shoulders with colours flying and music playing ; and we are sorry to observe that two Jurats and several of the Clergy and Constables were among the most active in the crowd" (*Collection of Petitions*).

When William Charles Lempriere died in 1790, Dumaresq hoped that he might become Lieut.-Bailiff, but Charles Lempriere, the father, who still led the Charlots, had sufficient influence with Lord Carteret to secure the post for his nephew, Thomas Pipon, the Storekeeper, and he was followed in 1801 by another Thomas Pipon (q.v.), the Attorney-General. Dumaresq succeeded him as Attorney-General ; but, on his death, at last in Jan. 1802 he became Lieut.-Bailiff. On 30 May 1803 he was knighted. Meanwhile his views had been changing. The Reign of Terror in Paris had made him less keen about Democracy and Liberty. Moreover the Magots had developed a left wing which was causing serious alarm to their leaders. In 1795 the States offered £100 reward for the discovery of the author of a paper that was being circulated calling on Jerseymen to rise like their brothers in France and cut the throats of the Jurats. In 1797 the States passed a series of Acts against secret and illegal meetings "tending to stir up the hate of the inhabitants against the constituted authorities". As Lieut.-Bailiff, Dumaresq became as masterful an autocrat as Lempriere. In 1804 and again in 1806 Thomas Anley (q.v.), by no means an extremist, was prosecuted for showing disrespect to him ; and, when in 1807 Anley was elected Jurat by an immense majority, Dumaresq refused to swear him in, giving as one of his reasons that he "had acted many times without respect for the constituted authorities". As Dumaresq in his younger days through the columns of the *Gazette* had harried Lempriere, so now he himself was mercilessly baited by a new generation of scribblers with squibs and lampoons printed in Guernsey and smuggled into the island. Typical of these was *Dr. Scurvy's Last Shift* (a copy of which is in the S.J. Library), which pilloried him as "the Great Dum":— "Knighted by his Sovereign he became regenerate. He associated with the swinish multitude no more. He had inhaled the delicious odour of courtly favour. Verily he shall obtain the reward adjudged to martyrs for the sake of apostacy".

We get a more pleasing picture of him in his later years in the Diary of his grandson, John Le Couteur (q.v.):— "I look back to the happy Christmas Days our family have enjoyed at St. Peter's, where my grandfather, Sir Jean Dumaresq, a pattern of the fine old English gentleman, used to receive his children, grandchildren, nephews, and nieces with most joyous hospitality. As a college boy I used to look forward to that day for months. I carry my recollections back to when I was six years old. Then my grandfather was in the beauty of elderly manhood. He was rather above five feet six, of admirable form for any feat of strength, with inexpressible grace of manner. He used to whip me up on his shoulder, and march round the room to the tune of the British Grenadiers. He was without a peer the first Jerseyman of his age". Not every old gentleman inspires such feelings in his grandchildren.

He resigned office in 1816, and died on 20 March 1819, and was buried in St. Peter's Churchyard. His tombstone says, "After retiring from public life he devoted his closing years to providing for the needs and watching over the education of the poor". He lived in the house now called St. Peter's House, which he inherited from his mother in 1784, and enlarged. From her he also inherited the Fiefs of Orville, Le Prieur, and Sauvalle. He married Marie Le Mesurier, daughter of John Le Mesurier, hereditary Governor of Alderney, and had ten children, Marie (b. 1774 ; md. Lieut.-Gen Jean Le Couteur of Belle Vue), Jean (b. 1775 : later Attorney-General), Harriet (b. 1776: md. François Valpy dit Janvrin), Marthe (b. 1777: md. Charles Pipon), Elizabeth (b. 1779: md. Capt. Philip Pipon), Philippe who became Captain of the *Victory* after Trafalgar, Sophie (b. 1783: died young), Thomas, George (b. 1786: died young), and Louise (b. 1787: md. Philippe Bouton). Among his publications were:— *Memorial to the Lords Commissioners of the Treasury by J. Dumaresq and H. Le Mesurier, joint Deputies from the Merchants of Jersey and Guernsey. 1785. Proposition touchant le Rétablissement des Enquêtes. 1786. A Collection of Petitions, Representations, and Answers of the States and Royal Court relative to Political Differences with explanatory notes (252 pages) 1788. Statement of Mode of Proceeding and Going to Trial in the Royal Court of Jersey by. J. Hemery and J. Dumaresq (60 pages) 1789. Règlements proposés aux Etats pour le Rétablissement du Jugement par Enquête. 1791. Règlements proposés pour l'établissement du Jugement par Enquêtes dressés par MM les Commissionaires Royaux assistés de Thomas Pipon et Jean Dumaresq 1797.* [*Magasin de Jersey ; Gazette de Jersey ; Actes des Etats ; Ordres du Conseil* ; his own writings. Two of his Diaries are preserved at Belle Vue, St. Aubin's.]

DUMARESQ, PHILIPPE (1657–90), Seigneur of Samarès, author of *A Survey of Jersey.* Eldest son of Henry Dumaresq (q.v.), Seigneur of Samarès, and Marguerite, daughter of

Abraham Herault (q.v.) He was born in Samarès Manor on
2 May 1637, and baptized in St. Clement's Church, Sir Philippe (q.v.) and Lady De Carteret being his godparents, for the
Civil War had not yet separated the families. But, when the
War began, Henry Dumaresq became a leader on the Parliamentary side, and, when the Royalists recovered the island, had
to fly to England, leaving his wife and six-year-old son at
Samarès. In 1651 Madame Dumaresq and her children were
banished to France. Baker's *Caesarea* (pubd. 1840) says that
Philippe "entered the Navy and rose to the rank of Post-Captain", a statement repeated in the *Armorial* and *D.N.B.* If so,
it must have been the Commonwealth Navy, for the King's
Navy had ceased to exist, before he was old enough to join :
and the Order in Council restoring his estates under the Act
of Indemnity grants him pardon for his political misdemeanours
during the Civil War. He does not appear in Pepys' *Register
of Sea Officers*, which records all who held naval commissions
between 1660 and 1688. Any naval service however seems
doubtful, since he describes himself in his *Survey* as "a stranger
to the profession of the sea".

At the Restoration in 1660 he petitioned the King:— "As
God hath not only restored you in so wonderful a manner, but
touched your heart with mercy toward your enemies, I beg pardon for myself and my late father, and the taking off of the confiscation of the manor and seignory of Samarès". His petition was
granted, and he did homage in Dec. 1660. His hobby was
gardening. A letter to his friend John Evelyn, the diarist, in
1666 thanks him for the help he has gained from *Silva*, Evelyn's
book on tree-culture, "the subject being so suitable to my inclination and kind of life, that no fear of invasion from our ill
neighbours can hinder me from putting daily in practice the
directions there prescribed". He wrote again in 1670 that he
has "planted about a score of cypresses from France and some
borders of phillyrea (i.e. mock-privet), whereof most parts were
of slips. I have this year began a little plantation of vineyard,
encouraged by *The French Gardener*" (another of Evelyn's
books). But, though he grumbled that "the ambition of others"
dragged him away from his "rustic employment" to London, he
seems to have revelled in lawsuits before the Privy Council.
A dispute with the Seigneur of Trinity about precedence lasted
from 1668 till 1685. Everyone agreed that among the Manors

St. Ouen's, Mélèches, and Rozel ranked first ; but did the fourth place belong to Samarès or Trinity? In 1662 it had been granted to Trinity. Against this Dumaresq protested, and in 1669 won his case. In 1670 however Trinity got this decision reversed. The question was carried before the Council again and again ; and at last in 1685 Samarès was granted the precedence. In 1674 he claimed "free warren" (i.e. exclusive shooting rights) on the Town Hill, a claim that no Seigneur of Samarès had made for four hundred years. This was indignantly resisted by the Procureurs du Bien Publique, and, though he appealed from the Royal Court to the Council, he was unsuccessful. In 1678 he became involved in another "long and tedious suit concerning some rents relating to the tenements of one Helier Messervy" (O.C.). It took Dumaresq twelve years to recover his 7 quarters of wheat. In 1682 Sir Edouard De Carteret, the Vicomte, accused him to the King of misleading Sir John Lanier, the Governor: "Sir John became acquainted with one Philip Dumaresq—your Majesty doth know that his father was hanged in effigy is a traitor—which said Dumaresq gave him such counsel that has caused all our differences, he being a man of the same temper as his father" (Bull IV).

But in the midst of these controversies he was busy making a Survey of the island, and drawing the most accurate map that had yet been produced, one, says Falle, "equally calculated for a Sea Chart or a Land Map" (Caesarea). It marks the frontiers not only of the parishes but the vingtaines, giving the number of houses in each. It names not only the bays, but the rocks and shoals round the coast. He presented this to James II at his accession in 1685 together with a manuscript Survey of ye Island of Jersey, Being an account of the Situation, Soyle, Inhabitants, Fortification, Landing-places, Rocks, and Tides about the same. He estimates the population at 15,000, of whom "half at least depend upon the manufacture of stockings", a "lazy manufacture that robbs the island of half its inhabitants, none adicting themselves to husbandry", so that Jersey, which used to export corn, has to import £3,000 worth annually. He describes the Militia, and discusses the value of Mont Orgueil, deciding that its only use is "to lodge a company of foot". He makes suggestions for strengthening Elizabeth Castle, one of which fortunately was not adopted, the blowing up of the Hermitage. But the main part of his work is a detailed description

of the tides, currents, rocks, and shoals round the coast, pointing
out the landmarks to be looked for, when entering the various
bays, and giving warning as to likely places where an enemy
might try to land. By this time he had shed the Parliamentary
sympathies of his family, and spoke of Cromwell as "the
Usurper" and the Civil Wars as "the unnatural rebellion".
This manuscript remained in the archives of the Admiralty till
the Napoleonic War, when it was sent to Philippe Dauvergne
(q.v.), Duc de Bouillon, naval commander in Jersey, who allowed some copies to be made. Extracts from it had been seen
previously by Philippe Falle (q.v.), who in his *Account of the
Isle of Jersey* in 1694 acknowledged the help he had received
from "a set of curious observations which that very ingenious
gentleman, Mr. Dumaresq, was pleased to impart to me a little
before his death". The *Survey* was published in 1935 by the
Société Jersiaise with an Introduction by Miss Julia Marett.

In 1682 Dumaresq was elected a Jurat. In 1689 he was
appointed Admiralty agent in Jersey for the Commissioners for
Prizes. At the time of his death he was Farmer of the Import
Duties on Wines and Spirits. He died in London in 1690,
and was buried there on 3 June. He had married in the Savoy
Chapel, the French Church in London, in June 1672 Deborah,
sister of Sir William Trumbull, who later became Secretary of
State. He left one daughter, Deborah, who married Philippe
Dumaresq of Les Augrès, and died childless. [Introduction to
his *Survey* ; *Ordres du Conseil* ; *Correspondence of John
Evelyn* ; *Dic. Nat. Biog.*]

DUMARESQ, PHILIPPE (d. 1741), American Privateer. Second son of Jurat Elie Dumaresq, Seigneur of Augrès, and
Françoise De Carteret of St. Ouen's. He emigrated to Boston,
and on 12 June 1716 married Susanne Ferry in the French
Church there. He became one of the first Vestrymen of Trinity Church. In 1739 the War of the Austrian Succession broke
out, and the King by proclamation offered Letters of Marque to
all who would fight the Spaniard. John Jones, a Boston merchant, fitted out a two-masted bilander, the *Young Eagle*, with
thirty guns as a privateer, and gave the command to Dumaresq.

On 21 and 22 August he beat up for volunteers in Boston, and secured 120. Michael Dumaresq was his Second Lieutenant, and a William Dumaresq was one of the crew. But men who enlisted on privateers were not an easy crowd to handle. On the eve of sailing he learnt of a plot to seize the ship and launch out as pirates. He summoned all hands on deck by the beating of the drum, made his clerk read aloud the Articles which every man had signed, with special emphasis on the Mutiny Article, and then ordered the three ringleaders to be stripped and fastened to the guns to receive 39 lashes. Jones however interceded for them ; so he merely sent them ashore, "the company hissing them all the time they were getting into the boat in token of their satisfaction of being rid of such villains". Then Dumaresq made a speech:— "Brother sailors, we are going against our enemies the Spaniards. Therefore I will have no quarrelling or fighting but against them. If any man will not comply with my commands, or thinks he shall be afraid when he comes to action, here is a boat to put him on shore".

He crossed the Atlantic, and between Madeira and Teneriffe attacked a large Spanish vessel. Just as she was about to strike her colours, a Spanish man-of-war appeared, and the *Young Eagle* had to fly. But she captured a Swedish ship laden with wheat, heading for Teneriffe, which was an enemy port, and took her to Madeira. Here Dumaresq had a violent quarrel with Rous, his Lieutenant. During the Captain's absence from the ship, Rous took her out of the harbour to chase a passing vessel, though Dumaresq from a rowing boat shouted to him to stop. On his return there was a scene. Rous threw his sword on the round-house, leaped to the main deck, "using many vile expressions, and then drawing his pistols went forward and fired them off, saying he would carry no further command on that ship". This caused a division in the crew, and Rous was imprisoned at Madeira for nine days, but then allowed to enlist on H.M.S. *Ruby* as Master's Mate. At Gibraltar there was more trouble, and Dumaresq's Mate became so mutinous, that he too was transferred to one of His Majesty's ships.

The Spanish Government now fitted out a special cruiser with 280 men to capture the *Young Eagle*, but it failed to find her. Meanwhile Dumaresq captured the *Amsterdam Post*, a sloop laden with beef, butter, pilchards, and hats, and Michael Dumaresq was put in command of the prize crew. This capture

led to a long complicated law-suit, for the *Amsterdam Post*
carried two sets of papers, one Spanish, to be used if she was
overhauled by a Spanish war-ship, and one Dutch, to be used
if she fell into British hands. (The Dutch were neutral.) But
the Boston Admiralty Court eventually adjudged her to Dumaresq. (The papers in the case are printed in full in Jameson's
Privateering and Piracy.) The two boats next met a heavily
armed Dutch fly-boat with a cargo of wheat, which surrendered
without firing a shot, thinking that the *Amsterdam Post* was a
second privateer. Before returning to Madeira they also seized
a Spanish sloop. These three prizes were valued at £20,000 :
and up to this point the Surgeon was the only one of the crew
who had died.

On 7 August 1740 Dumaresq captured a Spanish barque with
a cargo of charcoal, and on the 12th a French polacca laden
with Malaga wine. On 1 September he took a French tartan
carrying gold lace, rings, jewellery, tapestry, books, and clothes
(this was valued at £5,000), and on the 13th a settee flying
the colours of the Pope. This put up an hour's fight, but, when
captured, was found to contain nothing but four barrels of wine.

In October a Captain Willis wrote from Gibraltar:— "Off
St. Paare two Spanish privateers engaged Captain Dumaresq,
but after a smart engagement the Don thought proper to make
the best of his way to Cadiz". But he was not only taking
prizes. He was doing a lot of voluntary work in escorting British merchantmen. In December he wrote to his owner:—
"Your sloop has done as much service to King and Country as
any fitted out in a warlike manner. Many vessels have escaped
falling into the hands of the Spaniards by our means". In
January 1741 the Spanish Government sent out another ship
specially to hunt down Dumaresq. They met, and fought, and
in the battle 52 Spaniards were killed, and 40, including the
Captain, wounded ; and then the Spaniard, the faster vessel,
fled. Dumaresq himself was wounded, and his ship so damaged,
that he had to put in to Lisbon for repairs. In the Spring he
captured his last prize, a French ship, off Seville. In January
1744 his wife was described as a widow, and the Court granted
her the guardianship of their youngest son. By her he had five
children, Edward, Philip, who later was a Loyalist in the War
of Independence and Aide-de-camp to Lord Dunmore, and three
daughters who all married Channel-Islanders. Susan married

Matthew Saumarez, the father of the Admiral ; Douce married George Bandinel ; and Anne married Nicolas Mallet. [Chaplin's *Privateering in King George's War* ; Kendall's *Private Men of War* ; Jameson's *Privateering and Piracy* ; Perkin's *Sketch of the Family of Dumaresq.*]

DUMARESQ, PHILIPPE (1751–?1822), Founder of the *Gazette* and Constable of St. John's. Youngest son of Jean Dumaresq and Marie Robin. Born in St. Peter's 1751, and baptized in St. Peter's church, 13 Nov. As Lieutenant of Grenadiers of the St. Peter's Battalion of the North-West Regiment of Militia he distinguished himself at the Battle of Jersey in 1781. When Peirson fell in the Market Place (now the Royal Square), the Regulars retreated down what is now King Street, and took cover in the courtyard of Thomas Durell, the Vicomte, at the corner of Don Street. Seeing this, the Militia too began to give ground. It was a critical moment in the fight. Dumaresq ran into the courtyard, rallied the troops, led them out, and recovered the ground lost. (The story is told in the additional chapter added to Falle's *Jersey* in the French translation published by Jeune in 1798. As this appereared only seventeen years after the battle, and was never contradicted, it may be accepted as correct.)

He bought Belle Vue, St. Aubin's, from Pierre Le Vesconte, and for some years was an active and aggressive member of the St. Brelade's Parish Assemblies, often demanding special meetings to send protests to the States, for his elder brother Jean (q.v.) was founder and leader of the Magot Party, and Philippe was his enthusiastic Lieutenant. On one occasion he contemplated standing as candidate for election as Constable, (his printed election address, undated, is in the S.J. Library), but apparently he did not go to the poll. In February 17, when Nicolas Fiott (q.v.) died, he was the Magot candidate for the vacant Juratship. The Charlots made desperate efforts to recover the seat. Dumaresq complained that they brought many to the poll who had no right to vote, that the Jurats who acted as returning officers intimidated the voters, and made many alter their votes, and that a number of his supporters had been made too drunk to record their votes at all. The Charlot can-

didate, Jacques Hammond (q.v.), Seigneur of Samarès, defeated
him by 959 votes to 939. Dumaresq demanded a scrutiny, but
the Court refused, and swore Hammond in. Dumaresq then
appealed to the Privy Council, which decided that the Court
had acted "in a most arbitrary and unwarrantable manner", and
ordered the Court to take down the evidence on both sides
in writing. This it proceeded to do in such a leisurely way,
only occasionally appointing a day for the purpose, that by
December 1795 only half the evidence was completed, and Dumaresq withdrew his appeal, and Hammond was allowed to take
his seat.

In 1784 Dumaresq introduced the first printing-press into the
island, and in October began to publish the monthly *Magasin
de l'Ile de Jersey*. Mathieu Alexandre (q.v.) was printer and
editor, but Dumaresq seems to have provided most of the money.
This was not a success. In the following July Alexandre was
arrested for criminal libel, but in any case the magazine could
not have continued. A circulation of 500 would have made it
self-supporting ; but it never sold more than 300. Dumaresq
complained, "Our subscribers are dropping us day by day.
Many, having satisfied their first curiosity, no longer care to
pay twelve sous". He specially bewailed the stinginess of those
who clubbed together to buy a single copy, and pass it round
a group. The *Magasin* died in July 1785 ; but in Aug. 1786
he started a new venture, a weekly newspaper, the *Gazette de
l'Ile de Jersey*. This was more successful, and had a long life ;
and the possession of the only newspaper and the only printing-
press in the island gave the Magots a great advantage over
their opponents.

The bitter party-spirit of the time is shown by an incident
reported in the *Gazette* of 5 July 1788. Thomas Lempriere, one
of the Charlot Leaders, called at the office to demand the name
of the writer of an article that had appeared. When it was
refused, he distributed a paper calling Dumaresq a coward.
Some days later they met in the Market Place, and "walking
sticks came into play. Mr. Lempriere began to retreat beneath
the weight of his adversary's blows. Then a vigorous stroke on
his arm caused him to drop his stick. Mr. Dumaresq immediately seized his opponent's ear with one hand, while with the
other he thrashed him soundly. During this correction Mr.
Lempriere tore Mr. Dumaresq's shirt from top to bottom, and

smothered it with his own blood. Mr. Dumaresq then dropped his stick, and got home some heavy blows with his fists, and ended by gripping his antagonist by both ears, and rubbing his nose again and again in the mud. Mr. Lempriere was helped to the house of Dr. Lerrier to have his wounds dressed". Thus did gentlemen of Jersey conduct political arguments in the eighteenth century.

In Nov. 1787 Dumaresq was still living at Belle Vue, but by April 1790 he had moved to St. John's, for in that month there was a hot dispute in the Parish Assembly about his pew in the church. He had bought the property that made him Seigneur of Boutevillon and Lulague. In his new parish he devoted much time and money to a curious enterprise. From time immemorial crowds from all parts of the island had gathered at Bonne Nuit on St. John the Baptist's Day. No one knew why. It may have been a survival from the Church Dedication Festival or from some older Pagan Midsummer rite. Dumaresq determined to give the people something to do, when they got there. He established an annual Fair. He gave free use of a piece of his ground, and erected fifty stalls from which clothes, cakes, cutlery, butter, and vegetables could be sold. He arranged horse-races and a cattle market, a troupe of comedians, a tightrope dancer, and a firework display. An ox was roasted whole and distributed to the poor. His first attempt in 1792 was washed out by rain ; but he persevered, and in 1795 over 6,000 people visited the Fair. But then difficulties arose. The tenants of the Fief Chesnel objected to the Fair being held at Froidment, and it had to be moved to the Clos de Douaire. Finally in 1797 the States suppressed it as "contrary to good morals", and forbad any private person to start a new fair or market.

In Dec. 1798 Dumaresq was elected Constable of St. John's. At the end of his three years term of office he was re-elected with a majority of three votes. His Charlot opponent challenged this result, alleging irregularities, but the Court in July 1802 decided in Dumaresq's favour. In Jan. 1803 it was reported that he had sold his property and was leaving the island. In Dec. 1803 the Court ordered a new election, as he was a prisoner of war in France. He never seems to have returned to Jersey. In Oct. 1821 he is mentioned in the Court records as alive, but acting through an administrateur. In 1825 however he is spoken of as dead.

DUPRE, EDOUARD (1755—1823), Dean of Jersey. Younger
son of Jean Dupré, Rector of St. Helier's and Marie Millais.
Born at St. Clement's where his father was then Rector, and
baptized 31 March 1755. He entered Pembroke College, Oxford, as a Morley scholar, 1772, and obtained a grant from the
Don Baudains 1773 : B.A. 1776. In that year he was elected
Fellow of his college. M.A. 1778, D.C.L. 1780. In 1782 he
published a *Sermon preached before the University of Oxford.*
In 1784 he succeeded his father as Rector of St. Helier's. Here
he had to face two problems, the spread of Methodism to Jersey
and the arrival of 2,500 French priests as Royalist refugees.
Toward the Methodists he was more sympathetic than most of
his fellow-Rectors ; when Coke, Wesley's 'Minister for Foreign
Affairs', visited Jersey, Dupré invited him to preach in the
Town Church. With regard to the priests he had often to call
on the Bishop of Tréguier to remind him that the condition on
which his clergy were allowed to stay in the island was that
they should refrain from proselytizing. In 1788 he lodged au
Greffe a bill to stop the Shrove-Tuesday cockshying at live
cocks ; but nothing came of this, for twenty years later we find
protests against the cruelty of this 'sport'. From 1797 to 1802
he added to his other duties that of Minister of the French
Episcopal Huguenot Church at Southampton, but his congregation there did not see much of him, for he put in his brother
Michel (q.v.) as Curate.

In local politics he first supported Jean Dumaresq (q.v.) and
the Magots. His name appears on most of the Magot petitions
to the Privy Council between 1784 and 1787. In 1784, when
a conference was held between the rival parties, he was one of
the five chosen to represent the Magots, and he declared that he
would gladly resign his right to sit in the States as Rector, if
the reform of the constitution made this desirable (*Mag.* April
1785). In the following year, when a Magot was elected Jurat,
he wrote, "The cause of liberty has triumphed gloriously today"
(*Mag.* March 1785). But he was thoroughly frightened by the
French Revolution, and his views changed. He became strongly
antidemocratic. Before the Royal Commission of 1811 he
pleaded for the abolition of the election of Jurats, and gave as
an example of the evils of popular election the fact that "the
son of a soldier, a tailor by trade", had been elected Almoner
of his own church, "an office which gentlemen of the highest

distinction have not disdained to hold" (*Report of Commissioners*). When he died, the *Constitutionnel*, the ultra-Conservative paper, wrote, "He sustained with all his power the sacred cause of Order, and he was the most redoubtable foe of licence".

In 1802 he was appointed Dean. In the following year he made himself intensely unpopular by advocating the placing of the island under military law. A halter and a whip were fixed to his front gate. In the pulpit he was always impressive. "No orator in this island", said the *Constitutionnel*, "has ever before spoken in such noble and persuasive tones". But his political views caused dissension in the parish, where the Rose Party, the successor of the Magots, became predominant. In 1812 trouble arose over the communion wine. The custom had been for the Churchwardens to deliver at the Rectory, which then stood next to the Church, four dozen bottles of wine before each quarterly communion. Any wine left unused was the Rector's perquisite. When Jurat Aaron De Ste. Croix, a Rose leader, was elected Churchwarden, he brought the wine direct to the Church, and removed what was not consecrated for use on the next occasion. Dupré protested ; whereupon De Ste. Croix's son, Aaron junior, published in the *Gazette de Césarée* some insulting verses, suggesting that the Dean's girth was due to the turkeys he bought by the sale of the surplus wine. Dupré appealed to the Royal Court, but General Don, the Lieutenant Governor, stepped in as peacemaker. The younger Aaron published an apology, and the 'remonstrance' was withdrawn. But this did not end the dissension. Jurat De Ste. Croix got so annoyed with his Rector's politics that he suggested building a second Church, in which Rose Churchmen could worship without irritation. A good case could be made out for this. The parishioners now numbered over 10,000, and only a small proportion of them could find seats in the Town Church. In English towns this difficulty had been eased by building Proprietary Chapels, akin to those attached to colleges and hospitals. These were not Parish Churches, but remained the property of their founders. Such a Chapel already existed in Jersey at St. Aubin's. In 1812 a group of townsmen petitioned the Privy Council for permission to "build a private Chapel for the performance of Divine Worship according to the Rites and Ceremonies of the Church of England". The Council authorized this in 1815, and gave the Founders, their heirs and successors, "the perpetual right of nominating and appointing the Minister to officiate therein" (O.C.). No clergyman welcomes the secession of part of his congregation. Dupré opposed the registration of this Order, but failed. The foundation-stone of the new Chapel, which was to be dedicated to St. Paul, was laid in 1815, and the opening services held on 14 Dec. 1817 by François Ricard, Rector of St. Ouen's. The Dean then formally inhibited all local clergy from officiating in this building, and it had to be closed. The Founders next got in touch with a young Frenchman, Paulus Emilius Frossard, a minister of the French Eglise Réformée, who was willing to receive Anglican Orders. (The Services in those days were in French.) He passed the Bishop's examination, and was promised ordination, and meanwhile in November 1818 began to minister in the Chapel. The Dean however protested to the Bishop, and stopped Frossard's ordination, and then in July 1819 summoned him before the Ecclesiastical Court to show that he had been ordained, and, when he did not appear, excommunicated him. Frossard appealed to the Royal Court, pleading that St. Paul's as a private Chapel was outside the Dean's jurisdiction. The founders then advanced a new plea. The Act of Uniformity which enforced episcopal ordination on all Church of England clergy had speccifically excepted "foreigners of the foreign Reformed Churches" ; so they claimed that Frossard's ordination in the Eglise Réformée fulfilled all legal requirements. This was too abstruse a point for Jersey Jurats ; they referred the matter to the Privy Council, meanwhile forbidding Dupré to take further action, till the Council's decision was known. On 21 March 1821 the Council declared that its previous Order "did not in any way exempt the Chapel from the jurisdiction of the Ecclesiastical Court". This ended the struggle. Frossard preached his farewell sermon on 13 May 1821, and returned to France, where he became Pastor of the Eglise Réformée at Caen ; and St. Paul's remained closed till Dupré's death. (For this case see O.C., and *Chronique*, 20 Nov. 1819).

In 1818 Dupré gave his enemies another chance to attack him. He invited subscriptions toward a cenotaph to be erected in England in memory of Princess Charlotte. Three Banks opened subscription lists, and in March sent £ 56 to the Dean. Four months later it was discovered that the English Committee had not received this money. It was only slackness on Dupré's part, but the *Chronique*, the leading Rose paper, asked, mentioning no name : "What is the right word to apply to a person, who, after receiving holy orders and a good benefice, turns swindler (se fait escroc), and invites subscriptions for a monument, and then sticks to the money, until his rascality is exposed ?" Dupré sued the Editor, Pierre Perrot (q.v.), for libel, and was awarded £ 2,000 damages, and Perrot was ordered to make a public apology. This he refused to do, and appealed to the Privy Council (See *Chronique*, 24 April 1819).

Dupré died on 27 March 1823, before the case was heard. He was buried in the Town churchyard. He had married in 1784 Marie Patriarche, granddaughter of Lieut.-Bailiff Philippe Le Geyt, and had seven children, Edouard Falle, who became a Captain in the Army, John William (q.v.), later Attorney-General, Marie, Jeanne, Eliza, and two daughters named Eleanor. The *Annual Biography and Obituary* said of him : — "At an early date he displayed great taste for the belles lettres, which he never afterward abandoned". In 1799 he published *Nelson : a poem on the Battle of the Nile.* His translation into French of Pope's *Dying Christian to his soul* found its way into many French hymn-books. [Article, La Famille Du Pré, with pedigree, *Bull.* IX 358. Local Newspapers.]

DUPRE, JOHN (1752—1854), Master of Berkhamsted Grammar School. Eldest son of Jean Dupré, Rector of St. Helier's, and Marie Millais ; brother of Dean Edouard Dupré (q.v.) and Michel Dupré (q.v.). Born at St. Clement's, where his father was then Rector, May 1752. He obtained a grant from the Don Baudains, and matriculated from Pembroke College, Oxford, 1769. Jersey Fellow of Exeter 1772. B.A. Feb. 1776. D.D. 1790. He resigned his fellowship on his marriage in 1783 to Eleanor Bayley of Tring. He became Headmaster of the Grammar School at Tring in Hertfordshire ; and in 1788 he was appointed Headmaster of Berkhamsted, one of the Edward VI Grammar Schools. He used his annual visits to Jersey to collect pupils for his school. The *Gazette* announced in 1789 his arrival in the island "with Masters Le Couteur,

Marett, Nicolle, Le Feuvre, Janvrin, and the two sons of Mr. Hemery, his pupils". In 1794 he published some samples of his boys' work in *Musae Berkhamstedienses or Poetical Prolusions in the English and Latin languages by some young gentlemen of Berkhamsted School*. A second edition was printed in 1799. Though his schools absorbed almost all his time, he accumulated livings in the way that was then a common Church scandal. He was Vicar of Mentmore, Buckinghamshire, for fifty years 1784 to 1834, Rector of Bow Brickhill, Buckinghamshire, 1795—1825, and Rector of Toynton, Lincolnshire, 1824—34. He was also Almoner to the Earl of Marchmont. He published *Sermons on Various Subjects* (2 vols) 1782—87 ; and *Discourses from the Pulpit*, 1815, dedicated to the Rector, Tutors, and Fellows of Exeter College "in remembrance of the many happy years passed in this learned Society". He died in Wyke Cottage, near Weymouth, 12 Dec. 1834. He had one son, Thomas, who succeeded his father as Master of Berkhamsted, and three daughters, Mary Ann, Margaret, and Maria Purvis.

DUPRE, JOHN WILLIAM (1790—1866), Attorney-General. (He was christened Jean Guillaume, but always signed himself John William.) Second son of Dean Edouard Dupré (q.v.) and Marie Patriarche. Born in St. Helier's, where his father was Rector, 16 Nov. 1790. When thirteen he entered the Navy as midshipman on the *Kite* under Commander Philippe Pipon, and was present at the bombardment of Granville in 1803. He was captured by the French in 1809, and remained a prisoner of war at Verdun till the Peace of 1814. His letters, which his father read to the States, led them to start a relief fund for Jersey prisoners. When Napoleon was crushed, many naval officers were unable to obtain ships, and Dupré's uncle, Thomas Le Breton (q.v.), Attorney-General, advised him to take up Law. By paying an elderly Advocate to retire he obtained a place at the Jersey Bar, where the number of Advocates was then limited to six. He was sworn in 18 March 1815. Here he soon came to the front. In his first term he earned £15, in his second £75. In 1816 his father appointed him Greffier of the Ecclesiastical Court, and in 1822 he acted for a time as Deputy Greffier of the Royal Court. He plunged strenuously into local politics, and

soon became one of the foremost champions of the Laurel Party.
This led him into journalism. From 1817 to 1819 he edited the
Gazette de Césarée, and in 1820 with five friends he started the
Constitutionnel as a counterblast to the Rose Party's *Chronique*.
For fifty-six years this remained one of the leading papers in
the island. He edited it till 1826, and afterwards often wrote
its leading articles. Many of his verses appeared in its *Almanach*. In Dec. 1820 he had to fly from the island to escape
arrest. In a duel between Thomas Le Breton and Aaron De
Ste. Croix the latter was killed, and Dupré had been Le Breton's
second. He was back however by 1 Feb. 1821, when he married Jeanne Hemery of Plaisance. The wedding was followed
by an unpleasant Breach of Promise case, when a Janey Messervy sued him for damages. This was eventually settled out
of Court. On 10 Jan. 1824 he was sworn in as Solicitor-General.
He then resigned his commission as Captain in the Town Regiment, which he had entered as 2nd-Lieutenant in 1815. In
1826 he published anonymously with a Rev. J. Haynes *A Brief
Description and Historical Notices of the Island of Jersey*, a
good little guide-book which passed through many editions. It
gave the best short account of the history of the island yet
written, and its chapter on Law is interesting as the work of the
leading lawyer of the day. On several occasions he was sent
by the States to plead various questions before the Privy Council. In 1835 he drafted a Law on Judicial Procedure in Criminal
Cases. This was debated clause by clause in the States, and each
separate clause accepted ; yet, when the final vote was taken on
the Bill as a whole, it was rejected. He had it reintroduced however in 1863, and it was them adopted. It immensely sim-
plified and entirely altered the procedure at criminal trials. H.
E. Le V. dit Durell (q.v.), a later Attorney-General, said, "It is
a law of which any country might be proud. I had the privilege of applying it for many years as an Advocate and as a
Crown Officer, and everything has been provided for ; no fun-
damental principle has been altered, and it remains today a
model of simplicity, of accuracy, protecting on the one hand the
rights of society and on the other those of the accused" (*Men
I have known*). At the time of his death Dupré was drafting a
similar Law on Procedure in Civil Cases. In 1848 he was appointed Attorney-General, and in 1858 it was expected that he
would become Bailiff ; but he was passed over. The *Voix des*

Iles asserted that the French ambassador had represented to the British Government that Dupré's friendship with the *Proscrits* who came over with Victor Hugo made him undesirable. Le Cras called him in 1859 "the best read man in the island" (*Laws and Customs of Jersey*). A. Mourant described him as "a scholarly man, a deep thinker, quick in repartee, and full of caustic flashes of wit" (*Life of Le Sueur*). The *Nouvelle Chronique* said at his death, "He was fond of irony in his pleadings and sarcastic banter, but he never stooped to personalities. He had remarkable charm of character. His affability was proverbial, and he was accessible to everyone. He was friend, counsellor, and guide to all beginners at the Bar. They flocked to him for advice, and he always received them with the greatest kindness". Toward the end of his life he was handicapped by deafness. He died on 23 June 1866, and was buried at St. Saviour's. His portrait by W. W. Ouless hangs in the Royal Court. [Local Newspapers.]

DUPRE, MICHEL (1767—1818), Rector of St. John's. Youngest son of Jean Dupré, Rector of St. Helier's, and Marie Millais ; brother of Dean Edouard Dupré (q.v.). Born at St. Helier's 1767. Entered Pembroke College, Oxford, 1780, as a Morley scholar, at the age of thirteen ; B. A. 1784 ; M. A. 1791 ; B.D. 1803. In 1792 he was elected Fellow of Exeter. The *Gentleman's Magazine* described this election as "the strongest contest ever remembered". There were fourteen candidates for five fellowships, and the examination lasted three days. "The Rev. Michael Dupré, afternoon preacher of Tring, was unanimously elected. The other four were elected by a small majority". From 1797 to 1802 he took charge of the French Episcopal Huguenot Church at Southampton, as Curate to his brother, Edouard, who was non-resident Minister. In 1806 he became second master of Berkhamsted Grammar School, under his nephew Thomas. From 1809 till his death he was Rector of St. John's Jersey, but he hardly ever visited his parish, as he was also Chaplain to a Foot Regiment. His absence caused many troubles in his parish, where his curate. Michel Lusignan, and the Constable were at loggerheads. He died of apoplexy at Southampton, 18 Oct. 1818. He never married.

DURELL FAMILY. The Durells are not, as the *Armorial* states, part of the old Jersey family of Le Vavasseur dit Durell (q.v.). In 1531 a French slater, named Juin Durel was working on repairs to Mont Orgueil (*Bull* VI.). He settled in St. Saviour's. His eldest son Juin carried on his father's trade as a slater, but his second son Nicolas rapidly came to the front. Difficulties were raised, when he was elected Centenier of St. Helier's, because he was son of an alien ; but testimony was produced to his character and loyalty, and he was allowed to take the oath. In 1597 he became Constable of St. Helier's, and in 1602 Treasurer of the States. His son Jean bought the Fief Collette des Augrès (the land round the present Upper Halkett Place) in 1617, and the Fief ès Payn (which included the present Halkett Place, King Street and Hilgrove Street) in 1622. He became an Advocate in 1616, Greffier in 1625, and a Jurat in 1631. Jean's son Thomas was Greffier under Lydcot, and was imprisoned by Sir George Carteret, and only regained freedom by paying a fine of 8,000 *livres tournois*. He had three sons, Thomas, who became Constable of St. Helier's (1667–9), Jean, who became Jurat in 1682, and Lieut.-Bailiff (1694–1708), and Nicolas who was Secretary to Lord Lansdowne, British Ambassador in Spain, and became Solicitor-General in 1684. This latter office remained in the family for four generations. In 1701 the Lieut.-Bailiff's son Jean succeeded his uncle. His son Jean, who became by marriage Seigneur of Longueville, succeeded his father in 1726, and his son John Thomas was Solicitor-General 1771–1800. He was the author with Thomas Pipon (q.v.) of the much quoted *Statement of the Mode of Proceeding in the Royal Court of Jersey* 1789. His sister Magdelaine Anne became the mother of Sir Harry Burrard (q.v.). Other members of the family chose the Navy as a career. The first Jean to become Solicitor-General had three brothers who all rose to the rank of Captain, and of his sons Philip (q.v.) became Vice-Admiral, Thomas (q.v.) became Captain of the *Kent* (70 guns), and George commanded the frigate *Liverpool*.

DURELL. See also LE VAVASSEUR DIT DURELL.

DURELL, PHILIP (1707—66), Vice-Admiral. Second son of
Jean Durell, who was Solicitor-General 1701—26, and Elizabeth Corbet. Born in St. Helier's 1707, and baptized in the
Town Church 25 May. He received his early education from
his aunt, Madelaine Durell, his father's sister, widow of Sir
Edouard De Carteret (q.v.), Bailiff, and many years later in his
will he left £500 for "a handsome monument to be erected in
the church where she is interred with a due epitaph enumerating
her exemplary virtues and life". In 1720 when thirteen he entered the Navy as midshipman on the frigate *Sea-horse* commanded by his uncle, Thomas Durell, and on his first voyage
carried the newly appointed Governor to New York. In 1739
he was evidently on one of the ships with which Admiral Vernon
captured from Spain Puerto Bello on the isthmus of Darien, for
a plan of Puerto Bello "drawn by Lieut. Durell" is reproduced
in Traill's *Social England*. In 1741 he beame Captain of the
fireship *Success*, and in 1742 of the fireship *Strombolo*. In 1742
he was promoted Post-Captain, and commanded the frigate
Gibraltar (50) in the second battle of Finisterre. In 1743 he
had just been transferred to the *Eltham* (44 guns), when he was
ordered to join in the disastrous attack on Puerto Cabello in
Venezuela. He fought till all his ammunition was expended,
and then escaped badly mauled. In 1745 the *Eltham* took part in
the expedition against Louisbourg, the famous fortress on Cape
Breton, which the French had just spent a million pounds in
strengthening. Its great, land-locked harbour sheltered scores of
privateers which preyed on the North Atlantic shipping. Thanks
to the help of another Jerseyman (See *Messervy Nathaniel*)
the attack was entirely successful, and Durell published
*A Particular Account of the Taking of Cape Breton from the
French* 1745. In Sausmarez Manor, Guernsey, is a portrait of
him holding a roll inscribed, *Plan of Louisbourg* 1745. In June
1747, when he was in command of the *Chester* (50 guns), his
squadron made a haul of fifty French West-Indiamen. In October, in command of the *Gloucester* (50) he took part in Hawke's
victory over the French off Finisterre. In 1749 he was given command of the newly launched *Rochester*. In 1755 he was in command of the *Terrible* (74) ; and in 1756 in the *Trident* (64) he
fought in the drawn battle off Minorca, for which Admiral Byng
was shot. Durell was one of the witnesses at his trial. His next
ship was the *Prince George*, and in 1758 he was again off the

coast of Nova Scotia as Commodore in the *Diana*. Louisbourg had been given back to the French at the Peace of Aix La Chapelle, and they had made it the strongest fortress in America. It had now to be retaken. Durell was given the task of reconnoitring the rock-bound coast to find suitable spots for the troops to land. After the victory was won, his work was rewarded (Sept. 1758) by promotion to the rank of Rear-Admiral of the Blue. He was left in command of the part of the fleet that was to winter in America. In Feb. 1759 he became Rear-Admiral of the Red. The next step in the campaign was to capture Quebec, the French capital of the Canadas. Durell began badly. His orders were to intercept a convoy that was on its way from France to Quebec with stores and reinforcements ; but, thinking that the river was still ice-bound, he lingered too long at Halifax, while the convoy slipped up the river three days before he arrived, and he only captured three stragglers that had lagged behind. When he did move however, he acted with vigour. Quebec stands nearly a thousand miles up the St. Lawrence, and the strong and complicated tides of that river, its shoals, and reefs, and currents, and almost perpetual fogs made it a terror to seamen. Even today it needs skilful navigation, and in those days there were no charts, and the only pilots were French. Durell on the *Princess Amelia* (80 guns) led seven ships up the river. Off Bic, the pilot station, by flying the French colours (an unpleasing but legitimate ruse) he enticed several French pilots on board, and compelled them to show the way. Four days later he anchored off the Ile aux Coudres, 60 miles below Quebec. He then sent the *Princess Amelia* back to pilot the transports and the rest of the fleet up the river, while he took soundings in the channels that yet lay ahead. "The enemy", wrote Vaudreuil, the French Governor-General, "have passed 60 ships of war, where we hardly dared risk a vessel of 100 tons". The actual taking of the city was the work of Wolfe and the Army. On his return from America in 1761 he was appointed Port Admiral at Plymouth. In 1762 he was promoted Vice-Admiral of the Blue. At the conclusion of peace he was appointed Commander-in-chief on the American station, and hoisted his flag on the *Launceston*. He died at sea on 23 Aug. 1766 through eating dolphin, and was buried in St. Paul's Church, Halifax, Nova Scotia, where his portrait "after a painting by Sir Joshua Reynolds" (reproduced in *Bull* XIII) hangs in the vestry. He married three times (1) his first cousin, Madeline de Sausmarez of Guernsey, (2) a lady named Skey, (3) the widow of Capt. Wittewronge Taylor. His only daughter Anne married Rev. Thomas Warwick. [Clowe's *Royal Navy* ; Charnock's *Naval Biography* ; Waugh's *James Wolfe* ; Parkman's *Montcalm and Wolfe*.]

DURELL, THOMAS (1685—1741), Captain R.N. Son of Jurat Jean Durell and Anne, daughter of Elie Dumaresq, Seigneur of Augrès. Born in St. Helier's 1685, and baptized in the Town Church 27 September. He joined the Navy, and from 1716 to 1718 was in command of the sloop *Swift*, (14 guns), then of the *Seahorse* (20) from 1719 to 1724. In May 1724 he is mentioned as Commissioner appointed by His Majesty at a trial of captured pirates in Boston, Massachusetts. In 1726 he was promoted to post rank, and given the command of the *Solebay* (24). In 1727 he was transferred to the *Kent* (70), and in 1731 to the *Exeter* (60). In this, as peace had now been made between England and Spain, he helped to convoy Spanish troops to Leghorn to place Don Carlos in possession of Parma and Piacenza. His next ship was the *Scarborough* (24). In this in 1733 he was convoying thirty-six merchant ships, which were loading salt from an island off Barbados, when two large Spanish ships of war, one of 60 guns, the other of 70, attacked them. The little *Scarborough* kept the great Spaniards in action for several hours, and thus enabled all but four of the merchant ships to escape. From 1738 to 1739 he was in command of the *Strafford* (60), and then was put back on the *Kent*. In this he took part in Admiral Vernon's capture of Puerto Bello (1739), and then returned to European waters, where he fought on 8 April 1740 his historic duel with the *Princesa*, the monster of the Spanish navy, one of the largest ships afloat, with walls so thick that few cannon-balls could pierce them. Of the *Kent's* two consorts the *Lennox* was dismasted by the first broadside, and had to draw away ; the *Oxford* had her rigging so disabled, that she too had to drop astern to knot and splice. So the brunt of the battle fell upon the *Kent*. A contemporary ballad gives a spirited picture of the struggle (reprinted in *Naval Songs and Ballads*):—

"Then up ran the *Kent* with Captain Durell bold ;
We gave them a good broadside like jolly hearts of gold.
Yard-arm to yard-arm for hours there we lay ;
With great guns, small arms, cutlasses, we made a bloody fray.
Dead men in numbers lay about ; our scuppers filled with
blood,
Which made the seas around us seem like a purple flood.
Broadside for broadside nine hours did we fight."

One handicap was the towering height of the *Princesa,* which
enabled her to rake the *Kent's* deck with her lowest tier of guns.
But at last the Spaniard struck her colours, and was towed
triumphantly into Plymouth. (Monamy (q.v.) has painted a picture of this fight.) The ballad records one detail of the battle:—

"Three fingers from one hand brave Captain Durell lost,
But yet he was not daunted."

While the *Kent* was being repaired, Durell was transferred to
the *Elizabeth* (64), in command of which he died off Spithead
in 1741. He married Sophia Weld, and had three children,
Thomas Philip, Sophia, and Anne.

FALEYSE, PIERRE (d. 1515), Rector of Grouville and Dean
of Jersey. Our only information about him comes from the
Assize Roll of 1309. A long struggle against 'Benefit of Clergy'
was raging throughout Western Europe. In the Middle Ages
the Clergy had managed to make their persons sacrosanct. No
lay Court could touch them. They were responsible to their
Bishop alone. In the rough days, which followed the Barbarian
Invasions, this was a valuable protection, and Bishops' Courts,
which based their procedure on Roman and Canon Law, were
undoubtedly more even-handed than those of local chieftains.
But this privilege had become an anachronism. The Civil Courts
had established a fine tradition of justice, and the so-called
Courts Christian were arousing caustic criticism. They claimed
exclusive authority to deal with cases in which Clergy were
concerned either as plaintiffs or defendants, and by 'Clergy'

they meant, not only Priests, but Monks and men in Minor Orders like Acolytes and Subdeacons. Even married Church-servants, such as Vergers, Bell-ringers, and Grave-diggers, were tonsured and regarded as 'Clerics', whom secular Courts could not touch. At the Assize of 1309 a Guernsey soldier claimed to be a 'Cleric', because he had taken the Crusader's vow. More-over Church Courts were accused of gross partiality. It was said that a 'Cleric' could commit almost any crime with im-punity, for, however strong the evidence against him, he was always able to escape by producing compurgators, to swear they believed him innocent, whereas in the Bishop's Prison at Cou-tances laymen were serving life-sentences for comparatively tri-vial offences against the Church. In the 12th century Henry II had tried to restrict this immunity, proposing the compromise that clerical criminals should first be degraded from Orders by the Bishop, and then surrendered to a secular Court for punish-ment ; but Becket had taken a rigid 'Touch-not-mine-Anointed' attitude, and the King had been beaten.

At the beginning of the 14th century the struggle flared up in Jersey with Faleyse as protagonist on the side of the Church, backed up by Robert d'Harcourt, the masterful Bishop of Cou-tances. Laurence of Sevenoaks, the Greffier, was a rogue. Later the Justices Itinerant declared him "unfaithful both to King and People, and wont to take gifts from both sides ; he fined men without knowledge of the Bailiff and Jurats, and caused such money to be levied for his own advantage" (*As-size Roll.*). In 1306 he was arrested for stealing two silver cups (*ciphi*), and lodged in the King's Manor at St. Clement's. It is not clear whether he was a 'Cleric', or whether he had robbed them from a church (*Ciphi* in mediaeval Latin is often used of chalices, and d'Harcourt's Statutes show that in his diocese Communion was still administered in both kinds) ; but Faleyse obviously considered this a matter for the Church Court. "He brake into the King's Manor, and took Laurence therefrom to-gether with the two cups and many other goods, and put him in irons, and sent him under strong guard out of the realm" (*id.*).

When Justices-Itinerant visited the Islands in 1309 an effort was made to check this Benefit of Clergy. In April, before they arrived, the King sent a personal letter to the Bishop of Cou-tances:— "We emphatically forbid you to cite anyone from the Islands to appear before you or your Commissaries. If you do so, we shall regard it as a grave assault on our royal dignity" (*Foed.*). In May he wrote to the Warden of the Isles:— "Whereas we are informed that certain men ignoring our royal rights have maliciously summoned officers of yours to appear before the Bishop of Coutances to answer concerning inheritances and fiefs, the cognizance whereof belongs exclusively to us, we command you publicly to proclaim in full Court and in such other places as seem to you expedient that no one under pain of forfeiture of lands and tenements shall cause anyone to be cited before the aforenamed Bishop for matters of which the cognizance belongs to ourselves" (*Foed.*). When the Bailiff of Jersey published this proclamation, Faleyse retaliated by sending one of his Summoners to cite him to appear before the Bishop's Court at Coutances for attacking the rights of the Church. The Justices began work in Guernsey in June, where they arrested several 'Clerics'. When they reached Jersey, they sent a summons to the Bishop of Coutances to answer two charges:— (1) that he had usurped cognizance of matters belonging to the Crown alone, (2) that, whereas in the past clerical wrongdoers had been surrendered to the Bishop on the understanding that, if guilty, they would receive appropriate punishment, he now compelled the Bailiff by threats of excommunication to deliver arrested 'Clerics' to the Dean, who sent them out of the realm, even though the crime had been committed against the King's conies, and he favoured the 'Clerics', and sent them back to the Island without punishment, and such 'Clerics' were living in the island as though they were law-abiding citizens, nor dared any for fear of excommunication lay hands upon them. The Bishop made Faleyse his Proctor to answer these imputations.

The Justices next struck hard at Faleyse's staff of Summoners and Apparitors, who for years had been haling Jerseymen to Coutances. The Roll is full of entries such as these:— "Ranulf du Bolloun is wont to compel the King's lieges to appear out of the realm at the Court Christian. Therefore let him be heavily fined"; "Richard Poubele caused Peter Le Telier to be cited to Coutances contrary to the prohibition. Therefore let him be arrested, and let the Vicomte take into the King's hands his lands and tenements"; "William Lenginour complained of Simon Le Curreur that, whereas the said William was Constable of the King's Castle, the said Simon caused him to be sum-

moned to Coutances. Simon cannot deny this. Therefore he
is committed to gaol" ; "Jordan Le Serf caused Ranulf De
Quetteville to be summoned to Coutances and excommunicated.
The said Jordan cannot deny this, but says that he did it be-
fore the proclamation, and throws himself on the mercy of the
Court, and offers pledges that he will not repeat the offence".
The resentment aroused can be judged from the fact that the
Prior of Bonne Nuit threatened that "the Bishop would send
eighty men-at-arms to seize the Justices and take them to prison
at Coutances", for which he was fined twenty livres. The
Clergy and their leading lay supporters held a meeting in St.
Helier's Rectory, and decided to defy the Justices. "Early next
morning, while the Justices were sitting, the Dean arrived with
a great crowd of Clergy, and demanded on behalf of the Bishop
of Coutances the surrender of the Clerics arrested in Guernsey,
no matter what charge lay against them, and declared that the
Bailiff's proclamation was a breach of the Church's liberties.
Though the Justices told him that the proclamation was made
by the King's mandate, the Dean refused to accept this answer,
and said that a Papal Decretal laid down that all pleas (i.e.
in which Clerics were involved), save those concerning hereditary fiefs, belonged wholly to the Church Courts, and that any
who denied this would incur the greater excommunication. The
Justices pointed out that the King and his ancestors had ever
had cognizance of all trespasses by whomsoever committed, which
did not concern wills or marriages ; but the Dean four times
admonished them to have the proclamation withdrawn. Though
the Justices repeatedly informed him that the proclamation was
made by the King, he first gave notice in general terms that all
responsible for it were excommunicate, and then proceeded to
excommunicate the Justices by name ; and this he did in their
presence in open Court, and charged the whole population of
the island not to obey them under pain of excommunication.
The Justices at once passed sentence of imprisonment on the
Dean, and arrested him ; but the Clergy who accompanied him
violently rescued him from prison" (*Assize Roll*). Among his
rescuers were Geoffroi De Carteret (q.v.), his successor, and the
Rectors of St. Helier's, St. Lawrence, St. Brelade's, St. Peter's,
St. John's, and St. Clement's. Faleyse then escaped from the
island, and, "though often and solemnly summoned, refused to
submit to the King's jurisdiction, unless his Diocesan gave per-

mission". He was therefore outlawed, and his chattels confiscated, which included a horse worth 60 solidi and small goods
worth 40. But it was added:— "If the Dean chooses to return
to the King's Peace, let him find sound security for 50 livres in
addition to his confiscated chattels". This apparently he did,
for he was still Rector of Grouville, when he died in 1315. In
that year we read:— "On St. Paul's Day Thomas was appointed
to the church of St. Martin de Grouville vacant by the death
of Pierre Faleise" (*Archives de la Manche*). [*Assize Roll
of 1309.*]

FALL, PHILIPPE (1736—1811), Lieut.-Governor. (His father
and brother spelt their name Falle, but he dropped the final letter). Son of Clement Falle, Captain in the South Regiment of
Militia, and Jeanne, daughter of Philippe Le Geyt junior, Lieut.-
Bailiff. Born in St. Helier's, 1736, and baptized in the Town
Church, 3 Nov. In 1767 he was living in Jersey as a Captain on
half pay of the 67th Foot. He became prominent in local politics
on the anti-Lempriere side. Messervy notes in his *Journal:* —
"Monsieur Falle, a Captain on half pay, is one of the grumblers
and petitioners". In 1770 he became Adjutant-General of the
Militia, and in 1772 one of the Receivers-General. On 5 Oct.
1781, a few months after Moyse Corbet (q.v.), had been removed
by court-martial, Fall was appointed Lieut.-Governor. In 1783
he was promoted Lieut.-Colonel. The problems of his thirteen
years of office might have baffled a stronger man. The island
was fiercely divided into factions by the Charlot versus Magot
feud. (See *Lempriere, William Charles*, and *Dumaresq, Jean*).
The French Revolution flooded it with Royalist refugees, causing
a serious food and coal shortage. The ever-increasing threat of
war with France made it imperative to strengthen the fortifications, but the States could not raise the money. The Militia
was inefficient and undisciplined. In 1792 there were ugly
clashes between the farmers and the English troops, who were
helping themselves to fruit and poultry. The States declared:—
"The most inveterate animosities prevail ; fatal encounters have
already taken place ; every breast beats with apprehensions of
the most direful events" (*A.E.*).

In Jan. 1793, when war was inevitable, the Government did not trust Fall's military capacity ; so James Henry Craig, Colonel of the 16th. was made Commander-in-Chief. Fall was promoted Colonel, and received a tactful letter from Dundas:— "From the variety of matters connected with the civil government every moment of your time must be occupied. His Majesty has therefore thought right that an officer who might appropriate all his time to military objects should take Chief Command of the troops. His Majesty has no doubt from the zeal you have always manifested for his service that you will readily co-operate with him in every measure judged necessary by him for resisting any hostile attempts. The training of the Militia is an object which Col. Craig will be instructed particularly to attend to". But this division of authority raised difficult problems. Who would now represent the King in the States? Craig suggested that he should only be summoned when military matters were discussed, and that on other occasions Fall should retain his seat. But the States replied that the separation of the civil and military powers of the Governor was "unknown to the Constitution, and would involve serious inconveniences", and that, "though convinced by experience of the zeal which the Lieut.-Governor has always shown for the well-being of the country", they "could not in conformity with the Constitution receive him to sit in the States".

The demarcation of powers evidently proved difficult to adjust. Letters in the Record Office reveal Fall dealing with matters that would seem to be clearly within the province of the Commander-in-Chief. In Jan. 1795 he reports that he has handed over Mont Orgueil to Philippe Dauvergne (q.v.), and transferred the Company of Invalids from the Castle to Fort Henry. In February he complains that the plans for the new barracks show no provision for heating. In March he writes, "I shall soon resume the drill of the Militia". There must have been much overlapping. With Dauvergne too, his first cousin, who was in command of the flotilla at Gorey, there was friction. A French Royalist writes:— "Our chief embarrassment is the obstacles which Monsieur Fall puts in the way of the wise ideas of the Duke of Bouillon". Fall specially resented the fact that the relief of the refugees had been placed in Dauvergne's hands.

Toward the end of 1795 his health broke down. In December there were complaints about his prolonged absence from the island. In the S.J. Library is a letter from Lyme, Dorset, dated 14 June 1796, in which he asks for extension of sick-leave:— "I am apprehensive that in the course of my long illness I have through want of recollection, of which indeed I have been totally deprived, been guilty of neglect of duty. As yet 1 have found but little alteration for the better". When Lord Townsend became Governor, he did not renew Fall's appointment, but in Oct. 1797 gave the Lieut.-Governorship to General Gordon, the Commander-in-Chief, thus once more uniting the two sets of duties. Later Fall settled in Southampton, where he died childless in 1811. He is buried in the catacombs of All Saints' Church, which also contain the bodies of General James Dauvergne (q.v.) and Philippe De Carteret, the circumnavigator (q.v.). [*Bull.* V.]

FALLE, JOSUE GEORGE (1820–1903), Jurat. Son of Josué Falle of Hambie, St. Saviour's, and Esther, daughter of Jurat George Bertram. Born 1820, and baptized in St. Saviour's 12 Dec. The Falles had been engaged in the Newfoundland cod-fisheries from 1795, and the firm of Richard Falle & Co., Newfoundland shipowners and merchants, was founded at Point George, Little Burin, about 1830 by Josué's two uncles, Richard and Elie Falle. In 1838 they took their nephew into the firm, and, when both were lost at sea while crossing with cod to Oporto, he remained in control of the business. In 1848 he became Member for Burin in the Newfoundland House of Assembly. Some years later he returned to Jersey, leaving two nephews in charge of the firm, and married Marie Elizabeth Godfray, daughter of Advocate François Godfray (q.v.). He was now a handsome and wealthy man of great personal dignity, who was generally seen astride a powerful horse. In 1864 he became Deputy of St. Helier's, and, though later so staunch a Conservative, he won his seat on a Reform programme. Nine months afterwards he was elected Constable. "He was", wrote Durell, "one of the most distinguished Constables the Town has ever had. Social prestige is not everything ; but it forms a splendid background for an intelligent, hardworking, and painstaking administrator" (*Men I have known*). He held this post for nine years, and during his tenure of office the Town Hall was built, the Lower People's Park laid out, and the Town Church restored. In 1873 the prestige of the Bench of Jurats was badly shaken by the sentencing of Jurat Josué Le Bailly to five years' penal servitude for embezzling the funds of the Mercantile Union Bank of which he was chairman. It was necessary to choose someone to take his place who would in-spire confidence. Falle was the man chosen, and his election was almost unanimous, only two votes in the whole island being cast against him. For the next thirty years he was leader of the Conservative party in the States, strenuously resisting any tampering with the ancient constitution of the island, either on the part of the British Government or of local reformers. He crushingly defeated proposals to allow the use of English in debates, to exclude the Rectors from the Assembly, and every suggestion of this kind, and he was largely the instigator of the long and expensive fight with the Home authorities over the presidency of the Prison Board. But he was not averse to every form of change. The island owes to him the Law on the Will-ing of Realty, which enables an owner to will as he likes property he himself has bought. The *Jersey Times* said at his death : — "He was a keen debater, always watching for weak points in his adversary's armour. Sarcastic, he could make his opponents wince under shafts from a never empty quiver ; and he interspersed his oratory with apt quotations which always told, and his intimate knowledge of Shakespeare enabled him to draw from a never-failing source". Some of his work was done as President of the Harbours Committee. "I was told", wrote Durell, "by Mr. Knipple, the Engineer, who was in the habit of appearing before Committees and Harbour Boards all over the Empire, that he had never seen a Chairman manage a Committee with more tact and judgement, with more knowledge of detail, with more dignity and general aptitude" (*Men I have known*). At the outbreak of the South African War he per-suaded the States to vote £ 5,000 for the purchase of a field battery of artillery, and he himself added £ 500 to this gift. In 1887 he had advocated the building of a Museum and Art Gallery in the Royal Square to commemorate the Queen's Jubi-lee, and, when this proposal came to nothing, he presented in 1893 to the Société Jersiaise the usufruct of the magnificently built granite house in Pier Road to contain its treasures. He died in Plaisance, his home, 15 Feb. 1903, aged 82. He left two daughters, Rozel and Lily, and a son Bertram Godfray, who later (1910) became M.P. for Portsmouth, and in 1934 was created Baron Portsea of Portsmouth. [Local newspapers.]

FALLE, PHILIPPE (1656—1742), Author of *An Account of Jersey*, Founder of the Public Library. Eldest son of Thomas Falle, Centenier of St. Saviour's, (whose farm-house, pulled down in 1902, stood on the road from St. Mannelier to La Chasse) and Marie, daughter of Advocate Richard Dumaresq. In a Memorial presented to the Archbishop of Canterbury in 1696 (printed in *Bull.* II) he said :— "I was born in Jersey in 1656, the eldest of four brothers, who have all done service to His Majesty in the present War. Being by my father destined for the Ministry I was sent very young into England ; and after some years spent in two of the best schools in the Kingdom, viz. that of the famous Paul Faarrberenny, a Transylvanian, who taught in Great Queen Street, and that of Mr. Dalgarno at Oxford, I was, anno 1670, admitted into Exeter College, and put under the tuition of the learned Mr. Marsh, now Archbishop of Dublin. I removed with him to Alban Hall, when he was made Principal of that House, and there I took my M.A., anno 1676, being then but nineteen". When his father died in 1673, David Bandinel, his guardian, obtained for him a grant from the Don Baudains, which enabled him to complete his University course. In 1676 he was incorporated at Cambridge, and in his *Sermon sur l'Hymne Angélique* he describes himself as *"Maître aux Arts ès Universités d'Oxford et de Cambridge"*. He continued his account of his life : — "I received Deacon's Orders from Bishop Brideoake of Chichester anno 1677, and of Priest from his successor, Bishop Carleton anno 1679".

In 1681 Sir John Lanier, Governor of Jersey, appointed him Rector of Trinity. "I then applied myself", he said, "to serve my parish. I read Divine Service and preached constantly twice every Lord's Day. I also preached to the English garrison, which was then destitute of a Chaplain". In 1684 the

Governor promised him the Rectory of St. Saviour's, his home parish, when it became vacant. At Trinity he had disputes with his parishioners. In Jan. 1685 on complaint of the Seigneur of Augrès he was fined by the Court "for wishing to regulate points of honour and precedence which he was not competent to deal with". In June he brought a libel action against Renaut Coutanche. So perhaps he was glad to leave. "In 1687", he wrote, "Lord Jermyn, who succeeded Sir John Lanier as Governor, invited me to England to take charge of his only son. I was two years in this family". He lived at Rushbrook, near Bury St. Edmund's, Lord Jermyn's country seat, and in 1689 was appointed Prebendary of Brecon. But in August the Jersey Ecclesiastical Court intervened. It severely censured him for "non-residence in his parish for more than two years without permission of his Ordinary", and for "making himself suspect of leaning toward Romanism by his friendship and travels with a Roman Priest". This was the famous Jesuit, Father Petre, the King's Confessor. He was first cousin to Lady Jermyn, and spent much of his time at Rushbrook. He offered to get Falle a Crown living, but the tutor had sufficient worldly wisdom to refuse preferment obtained through Jesuit channels. He made his submission to the Jersey Court, and promised to conform to Protestant and Anglican doctrine (*Acts of Eccles. Court.*).

In Sept. 1690, according to promise, he was transferred from Trinity to St. Saviour's. St. Mannelier's, one of the free Grammar Schools, was in his parish. By Letters Patent of Henry VII the appointment of Regents lay with the Dean and Rectors, but in recent years the Seigneurs of Trinity had assumed this right. Their appointments were not a success. In 1691 St. Mannelier's had not a single pupil. Falle began to agitate for reform. "Anno 1680", he wrote to the Privy Council, "ye late Seigneur of Trinity thrust into ye School a young man, a cousin german of his, Edward De La Cloche, who from 1680 to 1691 by his insufficiency, his negligence, and his many other avocations so dissipated ye School, yt it was in a manner quite shut up". (De La Cloche was Registrar of Contracts, Registrar of Wills, and a Captain in the Militia). Falle blamed Dean Le Couteur. "Complaint was made against the Dean for ye little care he took of those Schools, not having visited them in above fifteen years, though by the Rules of his Court he ought to visit them twice every year. But ye Dean was cousin to De La Cloche, and resolved to wink at his faults". In Dec. 1691 Falle roused the Ecclesiastical Court to visit St. Mannelier's, and De La Cloche was deposed. At the next session (Feb. 1692) De La Cloche presented a letter from the Seigneur of Trinity reappointing him Regent. But Falle had supplied the Rectors with copies of the Letters Patent, and the case went before the Royal Court to decide who had the right to nominate. The Court by a majority of one decided in favour of the Seigneur. Most of the Rectors submitted : but Falle and Jean Dumaresq of St. Clement's appealed to the Privy Council.

Meanwhile the States had grown nervous about the naval power of France, and in Sept. 1692 they sent Falle and Jean Durell, the Solicitor-General, to appeal to the King for protection. They were received by William III at Kensington on 6 Feb. 1693. "The King had too discerning a judgement not to see what a fatal error it would be to suffer the French to make themselves masters of the islands. The Lords and Great Men of the Court happily concurred with His Majesty (*Account*). "For about eighteen months I constantly attended the Council Board, sometimes the Ordnance, Admiralty, and Victualling Office, never ceasing to represent how much it would be for the interest of the Kingdom to provide for the safety of the islands, until I obtained almost everything I askt : the repair of the barraques, all manner of warlike stores and provisions, cannon to be placed round the island, arms for the Militia, light frigates to cruise about the islands" (*Memorial*). While he was in England the St. Mannelier's case was decided. On 13 Nov. 1693 the Privy Council gave judgement that "the sentence of the Royal Court be reversed, and the election of Masters be according to the tenor of the Letters Patent" (*O.C.*).

During his negotiations in London Falle discovered how little most Englishmen knew about Jersey. "We were as great strangers as if these islands had been some degrees beyond the line. Then it was that honest zeal for my country suggested the thought of doing something that might remove prejudice and rectify misapprehensions. For, though we stood secure in His Majesty's favour, it seemed desirable to have the Body of the Nation come to the same sentiments" (*Account*). So he wrote and published in London in 1694 the first edition of his *Account of the Isle of Jersey*. On the strength of this he has often been called the Historian of Jersey; but he never claimed this title. True, one chapter gives a sketch of the island's history; but this does little more than recapitulate facts known to every Jerseyman of his class. The *Chroniques de Jersey* had been written more than a century before. Most Members of the States possessed copies of the so-called "Constitutions of King John", the Ordinances of Henry VII, and the Charter of Elizabeth. Every merchant knew all about the Bull of Neutrality. Falle's book was not a History, but, as its name proclaims, an *Account of Jersey* as it was in his own day, written in the hope of making England take some interest in the island and its difficulties. The descriptive part was based on a book, which one of his parishioners, Jean Poindextre (q.v.), had written, but never published, *Caesarea or a Discourse of the Island of Jersey*. (It was published by the Société Jersiaise in 1889.) "I was favoured", he said, "with a transcript of it in his life-time, and I frankly acknowledge that in the present undertaking I do but write after that excellent man's copy". Falle dedicated his book to William III, and was rewarded by being appointed one of the King's Chaplains.

He returned to Jersey in July 1694 to report the success of his mission, but went back to London in December to preach before the Court. He seems never to have paid another visit to the island, though he retained the Rectory of St. Saviour's, where the new Regent of St. Mannelier's took his Services. "Here (i.e. in London) I have remained ever since", he wrote in 1696, when he approached the Archbishop, asking for preferment. He had at this time fallen under suspicion of disloyalty. While tutor to Lord Jermyn's son, he had become friendly with Bishop Watson of St. David's, who had tried to secure promotion for him. But Watson was a Jacobite, and he had just been deposed, and Falle feared that he might be involved in his patron's ruin. 'I will not conceal", he wrote, "that many discouragements have sometimes tempted me to quit the service of the Church, in which I never found but loss and trouble". But the cloud passed. In 1699 it was reported in the Cour d'Héritage:— "M. Falle is at present in Holland or Germany with the King, as one of his Chaplains". In 1700 the Acts of the States record that he was still in Holland. In the same year he became a Prebendary of Durham. We also gather from his sermon preached at the Bishop's Visitation that he held a living in the diocese of Lincoln.

On 28 Jan. 1706 the Jersey Ecclesiastical Court again took action. It declared that, since the Rector of St. Saviour's had notoriously and incontestably been absent from his parish for many years, the benefice must be considered vacant. In 1709 he became Rector of Shenley near Barnet. Here he spent the last thirty-three years of his life. He still kept his interest in his native land. In 1722 he contributed an account of the Channel Islands to Bishop Gibson's translation of Camden's *Britannia*. In 1734 he published a much enlarged edition of his *Account of Jersey*. And his deprivation evidently left no ill-feeling. As early as 1696 he had written, "Considering the want of good and useful books among the Clergy of the island, which, straitened as they are, they are not well able to purchase, I greatly augmented a collection, which I had begun some years before, designing to give it toward the erecting of a Library in the Island, and I have already laid out about £300" (*Memorial*). The selection of additional books for this Library was the hobby of his old age. In the second edition of his *Account of Jersey*, he wrote:— "Nothing is more wanted in this island than a Public Library. There is already some advance toward this by the promise of more than Two Thousand Volumes in most kinds of good literature, the execution of which Promise is only suspended till a convenient Place can be provided for the reception of the Books". The offer had been made in 1729, and warmly accepted by the States (*A.E.*) ; but Jean Seale's promise to erect a building had somehow fallen through. So Falle wrote again offering £300 for this purpose. But difficulties arose. The old gentleman had set his heart on a site in the Rectory garden, north of the churchyard ; but Tapin, the Rector, was unwilling to give this up, making the queer alternative suggestion that the Library should be built on the Church roof:— "There is an aisle in ye Church whereon a superstruction may be raised at a moderate charge with a fine north light and an eastern one open to ye Market-place". When this was turned down, he demanded that the Rector of St. Helier's should always be Librarian, and that he should have two rooms in the new building. Falle grew so annoyed that he dropped the whole scheme:— "My age requires peace and quietness, which I will not interrupt by disputing with so much perverseness".

Tapin however wrote a conciliatory letter, and the building was begun. The foundation stone was laid on 4 July 1737. In Jan. 1742 Falle wrote:— "The building being finished except the shelving, my thoughts have turned toward settling a Fund for the maintenance of the fabric, to answer all repairs which time may make necessary. Though the building has been expensive beyond all expectation, I am disposed to find £200 for the purchase of rentes to complete the work". He died at Shenley on 7 May 1742, before the rentes were bought, but his heirs, his nephew Jean Aubin, the Denunciator, and his niece, Judith Aubin, his housekeeper, carried out his wishes. On 16 April 1743 it was reported that the books were on their shelves, and the Library ready for use. Two portraits of Falle hang in the present Library, one over the fire-place, the other in the office. He never married. Durell wrote:— "There is a tradition that, while he resided at Trinity, he paid his addresses to one of the daughters of Clement Le Couteur, the Dean. The match was broken off by the interference of her friends".

His publications were:— *Sermon sur l'Hymne Angélique et Eucharistique, prononcé dans l'Eglise de St. Sauveur en Jersey, 3 Avril 1687, jour de Cène* ; pubd. 1688. *A sermon preached at St. Hilary's in Jersey before the Garrison, 10 April 1692 ; An Account of the Isle of Jersey, the Greatest of those Islands that are now the only remainder of the English Dominions in France ; printed for John Newton at the Three Pigeons over against the Inner Temple Gate, 1694.* In 1734 he issued a "revised and much augmented edition" with the title *Caesarea or an Account of Jersey, the greatest of the Islands remaining to the Crown of England of the ancient Duchy of Normandy. Printed for T. Wotton at the Three Daggers and Queen's Head over against St. Dunstan's Church.* In 1757 "Mr. Le Rouge, Ingénieur Géographe du Roi", published in Paris "chez la Veuve Delaguette, rue S. Jacques," a slightly condensed translation of Falle's first edition under the title *Histoire détaillée des Iles de Jersey et Guernesey, traduite de l'anglois.* In 1797 a reprint of Falle's second edition was published by Eglin and Pepys, Chriswell Street, "improved and considerably enlarged with a map of the island, views of churches, castles, druidical remains, etc." This is stated on the title-page to be "began by Philip Falle, continued by Philip Morant", but Morant's only contribution was his Letter on Selden's Mare Clausum, which

Falle had already printed in his second edition. In the following year, 1798, Herbert and Harding of Pall Mall printed yet another edition. In the same year François Jeune published in Jersey a French translation. *Césarée ou l'Histoire Générale et Description de l'Ile de Jersey, traduit de l'anglais de l'histoire de M. Falle par Mr. H., corrigée et augmentée jusqu'à cette présente année.* In 1837 Edouard Durell (q.v.) published a new edition, *An Account of the Island of Jersey by the Rev. Philip Falle, to which are added Notes and Illustrations by the Rev. Edward Durell,* in which the Notes, which fill more than two hundred pages, are often of more value than the original work. Falle's other publications were:— *Of the Impunity of Bad Men in the World, a Sermon preached at White-Hall December 30 1694 ; On the Descent of the Paraclet, a Sermon preached before the Right Honourable the Lord Mayor and Court of Aldermen at the Guildhall Chappel, April 21 1695 ; A Sermon preached at the Triennial Visitation of the Right Reverend Father in God, James, Lord Bishop of Lincoln, held at Hartford, June 12 1700 ; Against Rudeness and Ill-Manners upon Account of Differences in Religion: a Sermon preached at the Abbey Church in St. Alban's, February 13 1715, on occasion of the Charity School set up in that Town.* He also edited his friend Edouard Dauvergne's *History of the Last Campagne. 1695.* [Holograph document in Lambeth Library, *Bull II* ; Life by Durell, prefixed to 4th edition of *Account of the Isle of Jersey* ; *Dic. Nat. Biog* ; Notice sur la Famille Falle. *Bull V* ; The Story of the Public Library, *Bull. XIII* ; Letters from Falle among MSS in Library of Société Jersiaise.]

FALLE, SAMUEL (1854—1937), Dean of Jersey. Son of Edouard Falle, for more than fifty years Rector of St. Brelade's, and Carterette Le Couteur Balleine, daughter of George Balleine, Rector of St. Martin's. Born at St. Brelade's, 15 July 1854. Educated at Thompson's School, Jersey, and Balliol College, Oxford. B.A. 1877, M.A. 1881. Ordained 1877. He became Curate of St. George's, Hulme 1877—1880 ; of Holy Trinity, Hulme, 1880—1884 ; and Vicar of Brampton, Cumberland 1884—1899. Here his sturdy independence of character soon asserted itself. The country town was on the Haworth Castle estate, then ruled by that redoubtable lady, Rosalind, Countess of Carlisle. With many of her views, political and temperance, Falle was in full sympathy, but he was not prepared to accept orders from the Castle, or to support every crusade which the patroness of his living sponsored. So she used her powers as landlord of his house, and gave him notice to quit. Before the time expired, the Bishop of Carlisle offered him the living of St. James', Barrow-in-Furness, 1889—1906. He was Honorary Canon of Carlisle, 1904—1906 ; Rural Dean of Dalton in Furness, 1899—1906 ; Chaplain to the Bishop of Carlisle and Proctor in Convocation 1905—1906. A Broad Churchman of the School of Maurice and Charles Kingsley, he always took the keenest interest in social questions. For four years he was Chairman of the Carlisle Diocesan C.E. Temperance Society. He was member of the Barrow School Board 1899—1906, and of the Barrow Education Authority 1903—1906. On 5 May 1906 he was appointed Rector of St. Helier's and Dean of Jersey. His tireless energy soon began to get things done. As Rector he completely restored the Town Church without asking for any help from the Parish Rate. As Dean he found a solution for three thorny problems. The first was the private ownership of pews in the Parish Churches, which had been for centuries a fruitful source of disputes. By the Law on Pews passed by the States in 1908 this difficulty was overcome. Another was the Enabling Bill, passed in 1919 by the British Parliament, which gave the Church of England a new constitution. This Bill did not include the Channel Islands, and Jersey with its own Laws and Canons was difficult to fit into the new system of Church Councils and Church Assembly. For ten years conferences on this subject were held in Winchester and London. At one time the English Authorities suggested taking the islands out of the Diocese of Winchester, and transferring them to the Bishop of Northern Europe. Falle strenuously resisted this. At last in 1931 a solution was found, which brought the Jersey Church into the new system, while safeguarding the island's independence, the rights of the States, and of the local Parish Assemblies ; and the Channel Islands' Church Legislation Measure and the Channel Islands' Church Representation Measure were passed with the consent of the States. A third knotty point was the future of the Church Schools. The earliest schools in the island had been charitable institutions, founded by the Anglican, Roman, and Methodist Churches, and supported by voluntary subscriptions. But, as education grew more expensive, the Churches were unable to keep their schools up to the required standard. They had to be absorbed into a national system. But on what terms? Churchmen attacked Falle for surrendering the Church's property. Secularists attacked him for demanding too much in return for the buildings. But eventually it was agreed, that the denominations should retain the use of the buildings out of school hours and the right to give half an hour's religious teaching every morning, if ten parents asked for it ; but that all secular education should be controlled and financed by the States. As a citizen he made his influence felt in innumerable directions. At Barrow he had been one of the founders of the Barrow Eisteddfod and its Chairman for seven years. In 1908 the Jersey Eisteddfod was started at his instigation, and he became its President. He founded the successful St. Helier's Church Literary Society, the Jersey District Nursing Association, and the Jersey Maternity and Infant Welfare Centre. He was Chairman of the Jersey Dispensary. Indeed there were few good causes in the island that did not owe part of their success to the Dean's enthusiasm and drive. He married in 1880 Elizabeth Minna, daughter of Austen Gardner of Ash next Sandwich, by whom he had three children, Amabel De Carteret, Harold De Carteret, Theodore De Carteret. He married again in 1922 Mildred Amy, daughter of Walter Vibert. He died at St. Brelade's 23 July 1937, and was buried in Mont-à-l'Abbé Cemetery.

FILLEUL, PHILIPPE (1792—1875), Rector of St. Helier's. Son of Philippe Filleul, a St. Clement's farmer, and Elizabeth Nicolle. Baptized in St. Clement's Church, 10 June 1792. By the help of the Don Baudains he went to Pembroke College, Oxford. Matriculated 1813, B.A. 1817, M.A. 1820. For six months he was a Curate in Guernsey, and then came as Curate to Dean Dupré (q.v.), Rector of St. Helier's and in 1817 went as Curate to St. John's. In 1818 he became Rector of St. Brelade's. In 1823 he married Catherine Elizabeth Blanche, daughter of Dr. Valpy (q.v.), Headmaster of Reading. In 1829 he was appointed Rector of St. Peter's. The abolition of Sunday elections in 1830 was largely due to his strenuous advocacy. In 1842 a Methodist Revival swept the island, and Filleul disapproved of its methods. He wrote a long article in the *Magasin de l'Eglise Anglicane* on 'Religious Excitement is not Religious Awakening', and roused much controversy by public debates with Daniel Robin, one of the leading Methodist preachers. On the death of Dean Hue (q.v.) and again on the death of Dean Hemery (q.v.) he was nominated by the Governor for the Deanery, but on each occasion the Crown appointed someone else. In 1848 on the death of Edouard Durell (q.v.) he was transferred to St. Saviour's, and in 1850 to St. Helier's, where he remained for twenty-five years. His boundless energy transformed his parish, but his lack of tact made his incumbency a very stormy one. He saw the need for new churches and for dividing the parish. St. Paul's, St. James', All Saints', and St. Mark's had already been built, but had no districts assigned to them. St. Luke's was being built. As soon as it was consecrated in 1852, he allotted to it an independent Ecclesiastical District. For one of his Curates he hired in 1850 a carpenter's shop in Castle Street, which he fitted up as a Mission Church. From this sprang the original church of St. Andrew's on the Esplanade, intended to be the church of the sea-going population, consecrated and given a separate District in 1869. Another Curate was sent to begin services in the Cannon Street Ragged School, and from these sprang the church of St. Simon's, opened in 1866, consecrated and granted a District in 1870. But this division of the parish was not accomplished without friction. Civil and ecclesiastical parochial affairs were closely intermingled in Jersey, and many parishioners intensely resented being cut off from their parish church.

One of his ventures in this direction led to a scandalous quarrel. In 1853 he bought for £1,000 a Dissenting Chapel in Union Street known as the Chapelle Sion, which he renamed St. Jude's, and put in charge of another of his Curates, Thomas Le Neveu, who later became Rector of St. Martin's. Le Neveu was a popular preacher, who rapidly filled his church, and attracted many members of the Rector's congregation. He also was friendly with Nonconformists, and sometimes took part in their Prayer Meetings, which gave offence to Filleul's stiff

Churchmanship. At last after much heart-burning the Rector
in 1860 withdrew Le Neveu to the Parish Church, and sent
another of his Curates to take the Services at St. Jude's ; but
the Churchwardens there refused to allow him to officiate. Filleul then declared that he would take the St. Jude's services
himself ; but, when he entered, the congregation used to rise in
a body and walk out. As he persisted, some of the younger and
more hot-headed St. Judites used to follow him home hooting,
and there was some stone-throwing, and he had to appeal for
police protection. Bishop Sumner of Winchester was appealed
to ; but his sympathy lay with Le Neveu. "I have no hesitation
in saying", he wrote, "that you have a moral claim to be permitted to officiate. The fact of your having taken the services
at St. Jude's since Jan. 1854, and the printed appeal circulated
by the Rector in 1856, in which you are designated 'the first in-
cumbent', constitute a species of right so nearly equivalent to an
incontrovertible title that it would be unquestionably admitted
by a Court of Equity, if not of Law" (British Press. 11 Dec.
1860). But the Rector was adamant. The building belonged
to him. Officially Le Neveu was his curate. So St. Jude's remained closed, only to be reopened two years later to accommodate the Town Church congregation, while their own church
was restored.

This restoration was the next task the Rector tackled. The
old church was in a deplorable condition. The tracery of the
windows had vanished. The beams supporting the galleries
were so rotten that at any moment a gallery might have collapsed on the heads of the people below. There was neither
font nor altar, but an ingenious combination of the two, rather
like a carpenter's bench, was carried in and set in front of the
pulpit, when needed. The whole interior of the building was
choked with high, square, deal pews, all facing the pulpit, those
in the chancel stretching back to the east wall, and facing those
in the nave. In 1863 the church was closed for repair. The
Parish Assembly voted £2,500 toward the cost.
William Laurence De Gruchy (q.v.) and two friends promised
another £2,000. The Rector guaranteed £600. But then came
hitch after hitch. The Committee engaged Bodley, a well-
known ecclesiastical architect, who prepared three alternative
plans ; but the Parish Assembly turned them all down   Local
amateur architects then submitted proposals, but eventually the

work was entrusted to John Elliot of Southampton. The big struggle however was over the pew problem. The pews were private property, which could be let or sold, and the owners claimed the right to keep them locked, when they were not using them. Filleul wanted to abolish the pew system altogether. But the vociferous François Godfray (q.v.) made himself the spokesman of the pew-holders, and by his tempestuous rhetoric swayed every Parish Assembly against the Rector's plans. The work of restoration was not actually begun till 1865, and the church was not reopened till 1868. Even then the trouble was not over. More than one of the papers stormed against the font inside the door, declaring that it was a Popish device, which the Rector meant to use to hold holy water, and one ingenious writer discovered that the surplice-cupboards in the vestry were so constructed that they could be used as confessionals! The main features of the restoration were, in addition to the introduction of font and altar, the removal of the north and south galleries and three private galleries, the prolongation of the nave toward the west, the building of the south transept and gallery, the substitution of open oak seats for the locked square pews, the provision of choir seats in the chancel, and the insertion of tracery and stained glass in the windows.

All this church-building and restoration cost money. So in 1858 Filleul launched a scheme which caused him endless embarrassment. Ten years before, his two youngest sons had emigrated to New Zealand, and bought a sheep-run in Otago. They sent home glowing accounts of the profits to be made, and their father published a sixty page pamphlet, *An Earnest Appeal to Stewards of the Lord's Goods, inviting their aid in the Subdivision of the Parish of St. Helier's into Smaller Incumbencies, each with a Separate Endowment and Free Church for the People, by means of a Safe and Profitable Investment of Capital for a limited period as Lent to the Lord and Increased by His Blessing.* Broadly speaking the plan was that investors should buy sheep in New Zealand and entrust them to his sons, being content with a return of 5 per cent on their money, all additional profits being devoted to Church purposes. Filleul persuaded many Jersey Churchmen to invest, and at first all went well. One year's dividend was 18 per cent, the next 22 per cent. But then came a slump. Profits disappeared, and investors turned furiously on the Rector declaring that he had swindled them. In vain he urged them to be patient. He passed through a painful period, and "nowhere", said the *Chronique*, "did he receive the smallest sympathy". But eventually the industry recovered. Before his death he was able to repay every investor and to add a handsome bonus.

Another scheme for which he worked hard was the establishment of a Bishopric of the Channel Islands, which should also have the supervision of the Continental Chaplaincies. Between 1858 and 1865 he paid frequent visits to England interviewing Bishops and Politicians to expound his plans, but, though he obtained some support, this came to nothing.

He died in St. Helier's Rectory 13 Oct. 1875, and was buried in the New Cemetery, St. John's Road. His published pamphlets were numerous, and largely controversial. Among them was a sermon on Dissent, *Christ, est il divisé?* (1825), a course of thirteen sermons, *Sur le Schisme* (1842), and his sermon at the reopening of the Town Church. He had six children, Philippe Valpy Mourant, who became Warden of Christ's College, Tasmania, and later Vicar of Biddisham, Somerset, Mary Jane Valpy, Anne Penelope, William Valpy, who died young, and William Gabriel and Richard Anthony, the sheep-farmers.

After his death it was found that his will made no provision for the disposal of St. Jude's. The Chapel remained for years derelict, till the fall of its roof called attention to it. His eldest son then sold it, and presented the money to Dean Balleine to form the nucleus of a Filleul Church Endowment Fund (1892) "for increasing the endowments of the poorer benefices of the Church of England in Jersey". [Local Newspapers.]

FIOTT, NICOLAS (1704—1786). Merchant. Youngest son of Jean Fiott of St. Saviour's and Catherine Ahier. Born in St. Saviour's, 1704. He was brought up to the sea ; but in 1740 he married Anne Dumaresq (daughter of Edouard Dumaresq and Anne de Carteret) and settled on shore as a merchant. In 1743 he was trading with Newfoundland as Fiott and Co. (O.C.), and later established a large trading station on the Ile Percée Bay on the Canadian coast. In 1764 a petition of the Principaux of St. Helier's declared:— "Mr. Nicolas Fiott is one of the principal merchants of this island, who employs as many, or more, people in his services by land and sea as any other person in the island". (Sheb.). In 1755 he became a Centenier of St. Helier's. The chief interest in his life lies in his long struggle with the two Lemprieres, Charles, the Lieut.-Bailiff (q.v.) and Philippe, the Attorney-General (q.v.). It began with an action which Fiott brought in 1759 against Philippe Mattingley, Regent of St. Mannelier, for caning his small son, Edouard. Lempriere dismissed the case, and in 1764 the Privy Council confirmed his decision. Meanwhile Fiott had visited the camp of the French prisoners of war, and protested against conditions there. As Philippe Lempriere was Agent for Prisoners of War this amounted to a charge of starving the prisoners to swell his own profits. A third quarrel arose from the fact that Fiott had bought an estate from Charles Lempriere's wife, and accepted an old measurement. Later, when he resold two of his fields, they were found to be smaller than stated. He then had the whole remeasured, and it was found to be 4½ vergées short. And Lempriere refused to rectify this. Fiott declared that, as all Advocates were appointed by the Lieut.-Bailiff, he could not get one who would whole-heartedly fight a case against him. A fourth dispute began in 1761 about a privateer, the *Charming Nancy*, in which Fiott had a sixth share. The Lemprieres also were shareholders. Fiott had just returned from Southampton, where he had been superintending repairs to this boat, when the brothers decided to get rid of him by selling her. In 1762 they passed in Court an Act for her sale in Fiott's absence, and she was sold to their brother-in-law, Thomas Pipon. In all these cases Fiott appealed to the Privy Council.

Pierre Mauger had been Fiott's Advocate, but had deserted him for the Lemprieres. In Feb. 1764 he was appointed Deputy-Attorney-General. Fiott protested in Court that he would not "think himself secure either in his public or private concerns, if Mauger were permitted to become the only King's Officer in the Court". Lempriere promptly ordered his arrest for slandering Mauger's character. Fiott challenged, as he had a right to do, the presence on the bench of the Lieut.-Bailiff and three Jurats with whom he had recent lawsuits. He was told to put his objections in writing. These were judged to be "frivolous, false, and malicious, thereby setting His Majesty's subjects a most pernicious example of disrespect to the Royal

Jurisdiction". He was sentenced to pay a fine of 300 livres tournois, to be deprived of his office of Centenier, and to make the amende qualifiée, which meant asking pardon on his knees of God, the King, the Court, and the person injured. Anyone who did this was regarded as so infamous that he was debarred for ever from giving evidence on oath or holding any public office. Fiott refused to submit and was committed to prison. He appealed by doléance to the Privy Council and a monster petition was sent to the Council asking for his release. The Council on 16 April ordered him to be granted bail. As he was a Captain in the Militia, his men turned out to welcome him with a feu de joie ; and this was reported to England as a threat of armed insurrection. Feeling that his enemies would soon find an excuse for getting him back to jail, and wishing to keep an eye on his cases before the Council, he decided to forfeit his bail, and cross the Channel. On 26 July the Council heard his appeal against his sentence, decided to back up the authority of the Court, and ordered him to return and make his submission. For the next six years however he remained in London. The Royal Court now treated him as a fugitive from justice. If he was sued for money, it declined to hear his defence. If his debtors refused to pay, he could not sue them. In 1765 he made up his mind to settle in England, and sold his Jersey property to Philip De Gruchy ; but the Court would not register the Deed of Sale ; so the transfer could not take place.

In 1769 came the revolt against Lempriere rule (see *Lempriere, Charles*). One of the demands of the rioters was permission for Fiott to return. He was accused quite unjustifiably of having organized the rising. Daniel Messervy (q.v.) declared in his *Diary* that "Captain Fiott, fugitive, was leader of this rebellion, who, though ordered to return and perform his sentence, preferred to remain in London and foment disturbances". But the insurrection opened the eyes of the English authorities to the fact that all was not well with the government of Jersey. Col. Bentinck's Report on the situation strengthened this conviction. And one result was that in 1771 Fiott received the King's free pardon for "all manner of trespasses, contempts, and misdemeanours committed against us or our Royal Court". His return to Jersey was a triumph. "He was chaired ashore", wrote his grandson (Letter in S. J. Library), "and went to the

Court, where all his company of Militia were waiting to receive him ; but the Lieut-Bailiff refused to proceed, till they were dismissed. They departed at Mr. F's request ; upon which the Lieut.-Bailiff was obliged to reinstate him in all his rights and possessions".

In the same year he struck his hardest and most effective blow. John Shebbeare was an utterly unscrupulous political pamphleteer. He had first served the Tories, and in the sixth of his *Letters to the People of England* had held up the reigning dynasty to scorn. For this he had been put in the pillory and imprisoned. The Court Party had then bought him with a pension, and he had vilified as vigorously his former employers. His daughter married Charles Le Geyt (q.v.), and he came to visit her in Jersey ; and Fiott hired him to hold up the Lemprieres to execration. In quick succession there appeared anonymously, *An Authentic Narrative of the Oppressions of the Islanders of Jersey* (2 vols. of nearly 1,000 pages), 1771 ; *Six Letters to Philip Le Hardy*, 1772 ; *An Effectual Remedy to the Complaints of the Islanders of Jersey*, 1772 ; *Tyranny of the Magistrates of Jersey demonstrated from Records of their Courts*, 1772. In all these the misdeeds of the Lemprieres were painted in the blackest colours. They were read not only in Jersey, but in England. Philippe Lempriere gave up the struggle, and went to live in Devon. But Charles stood his ground.

In 1772 Fiott enjoyed a short triumph. The Seigneur of Mélèches went bankrupt, and made over his estate to his creditors. Of these Fiott was one. He paid off his fellow-victims, and took possession of the property. He then appeared at the Cour d'Héritage as Seigneur of Mélèches, and produced an Order in Council of 1715 declaring Mélèches to be the second Fief in the Island, ranking next to St. Ouen's. He thus claimed precedence over Charles Lempriere, who was Seigneur of Rozel. Lempriere promptly appealed to the Privy Council, which in 1781 restored the precedence to Rozel. Fiott then claimed a higher dignity. Lempriere was only a Seigneur by marriage ; but Fiott claimed descent from the Fiots d'Arbois of Burgundy, one of the most distinguished families of the old French nobility. If so, the connexion was remote, for Fiotts had been in Jersey for at least two centuries ; but he satisfied the Earl Marshal's department, and the illuminated grant from the Garter King-of-Arms, which permitted him to use the arms of the Burgundian Fiots, differenced with an anchor on the chevron, is in the Library of the Société Jersiaise.

The Battle of Jersey in 1781 was fought under his windows, for his house stood in the Market Place (now the Royal Square) ; and his wife was slightly wounded by a bullet, which passed through the shutter. In 1782 the old man was elected Jurat. He could now meet his enemies on equal terms in Court and States ; and he did not neglect his opportunities. He died on 9 Feb. 1786. By his first wife, Anne Dumaresq, who died in 1763, he had six children:— Anne (b. 1747 ; married Capt. John Ireland, and then Thomas Axford), Nicolas (b. 1748 : d. 1785), Thomas (d. young), Edouard, Marie (b. 1751 : married Jean Le Geyt), and John. In 1772 he married his partner's sister, Jeanne Remon of St. Lawrence. [Shebbeare's *Narrative of the Oppressions*, *Vol.* II ; Fiott MSS. in S.J. Library ; Article, Some Old Fiott Papers, in *Bull* XIII ; *Ordres du Conseil*.]

GALLICHAN, WALTER MATTHEW, (1861—1946), Author. Born above the silversmith's shop in the Royal Square, Jersey, 26th October 1861. Son of John Gallichan and Elizabeth White. Educated at a private school in Reading. Assistant Editor of the *Free Review*. Special Commissioner for the *Daily Mail* in Spain. He regarded himself as a pioneer in Sex Education, and published *The Blight of Respectability* 1901, *The New Morality* 1902, *Woman under Polygamy* 1914, *The Great Unmarried* 1916, *The Psychology of Marriage* 1917, *A Text Book of Sex Education* 1919, *Modern Woman and How to Manage Her* 1919, *The Critical Age of Woman* 1920, *Youth and Maidenhood, or Sex Knowledge for Young People* 1920, *Youth's Secret Conflict* 1921, *Pitfalls of Marriage* 1926, *Sexual Apathy* 1927, *The Sterilization of the Unfit* 1929, *The Poison of Prudery* 1929. He also wrote books on Angling, *Fishing in Wales*, *The Happy Fisherman*, *The Trout Waters of England*, *Where Trout Abound* and *Practical Hints on Angling* ; and Guide Books including *The Story of Seville* in Dent's *Mediaeval Towns* Series, and *Old Continental Towns* ; and Novels including *The Conflict of Owen Prytherch*, *A Soul from the Pit*, and *The Veil and the Vision* ; and many miscellaneous books, *Our Invisible Selves: an Intro-*

duction to Psycho-analysis, The Religion of Kindness, Youthful Old Age, and with Gladys Davidson *A Book of Nature Stories*. In 1934 he was granted a Civil List Pension. He married (i) Ada White, (ii) Norah Kathleen Mutch. He died 27 Nov. 1946.

GAVEY, SIR JOHN (1842—1923), Electrical Engineer. Only son of Captain John Gavey of the merchant service and Elizabeth Jeanne Falle. Born in St. Helier's 11 Aug. 1842. Educated at Victoria College. He received his professional training under Sir W. H. Preece in the service of the Electric International Company. When the Telegraph System was transferred to the State, he was appointed Superintendent of the South Eastern Division (1870) and of the Great Western Division (1872). He became Superintending Engineer of the South Wales District (1878), Chief Technical Officer of the General Post Office (1892), Assistant Engineer in Chief (1897), Engineer in Chief (1902), Consulting Engineer (1908). He was closely associated with all the telegraphic and telephonic developments of the Post Office for over forty years. He was made a Companion of the Bath (1903), and was knighted (1907). He was President of the Institution of Electrical Engineers. He printed several papers read before Engineering Institutions, and made many contributions to the technical press. On his retirement he lived at Hampton Court, and died there 1 Jan. 1923. He married Mary De Gruchy in 1870, and had two sons and three daughters.

GODFRAY, FRANCOIS (1807—68), Leader of the Laurel Party, Advocate, and Constable. Born in St. Helier's, 8 Jan. 1807, youngest son of Hugh Godfray, Dénonciateur. Educated at St. Servan, where his special school-friend was the future Dean Jeune (q.v.), and later at Wandsworth. At eighteen he entered as clerk the office of Thomas Le Breton (q.v.), then Attorney-General. At twenty he went to Paris to study Law under Beaufils, later the tutor of Pierre Le Sueur (q.v.). When twenty-two he returned to Jersey, and was sworn in as Advocate (1829). In Court and Parish Assembly he quickly revealed a wonderful gift of vehement and dramatic rhetoric. With whirling arms and voice of thunder he beat down all opposition. No such oratory had been heard in Jersey for generations. Auguste Luchet, the famous French journalist, who knew all his own politicians, described him as "a splendid man, an orator full of fire and passion, whose burning words set debates ablaze, a man who would have attained front rank in any Parliament" (*Chron.* 24.4.61). The Laurel Party, then a minority, looked to this eloquent young man as their hope for the future. When only twenty-three they ran him (1830) for the Constableship of St. Helier's, and to everyone's surprise he beat Pierre Perrot (q.v.), the Rose candidate, by 33 votes.

He had now three spheres of action, as Constable, as Advocate, and as Member of the States. As Constable, he retained his position in the Town only for one term of office. At the next triennial election he was defeated by Perrot: In the following year a vacancy occured at St. Martin's, and he was elected Constable of that parish. He was challenged, because he was not a parishioner, but the Court confirmed his election. He was re-elected in 1838 ; but that year he had to face the revolt of the oyster-fishermen. The Gorey oyster-fisheries, once so prosperous, were threatened with ruin. The best beds lay just inside French territorial waters, and the French had begun rigorously to arrest poachers. In 1837 the States had laid down new beds in Grouville Bay, but had protected them with strict regulations, only allowing them to be dredged at certain seasons. But the fishermen would not wait till the close season was over. On 9 April 1838 120 boats set out for the forbidden beds. Godfray did not lack courage. He followed in a rowing-boat, and as Constable he ordered them to stop. When they jeered, he took the name of every boat present. Next morning he went to the harbour, though the fishermen threatened to throw him in, and arrested the three ringleaders. Four days later the men raided the beds again. Godfray appealed for help to the Lieut.-Governor, who came with the Garrison, the Town Militia, and Artillery. Two cannon-balls among the smacks brought them back to port, and Godfray arrested 96 captains, each of whom was fined £1-6-2. But this undermined his popularity in the parish. At the 1841 election he was defeated. He had however bought Bagatelle, and was now living in St. Saviour's. In 1842 he was elected Constable of that parish, and was re-elected in 1845, 1848, 1851, 1854, 1857. In 1860 he resigned the Constableship, and became Deputy, a post which he held till 1866.

As Advocate, he was for nearly forty years the leading man at the Bar. He and Pierre Le Sueur appeared on opposite sides in every big case, but always on party lines. Laurel litigants engaged Godfray, Rose litigants Le Sueur. There were tremendous verbal fights between these two men, and Godfray's temper often got him into serious trouble. His own paper, the *Constitutionnel*, which he controlled for thirty years, confessed after his death:— "He could not endure any opposition or submit to any restraint". He was responsible for 'scenes' in Court of amazing violence. In 1855 his eyes began to trouble him, and in 1858 he went completely blind ; but he did not give up his work at the Bar. Some of his most difficult cases were won during his last ten years of blindness.

For thirty-three years he was in the States. At first he was full of reforming zeal. He had seen the Bourbons overthrown in Paris. He had watched the efficiency of the French legal and parliamentary system. And he found much in Jersey that he wanted to set right. He secured the admission of the public to meetings of the States. He raised the age for joining the Militia from fourteen to eighteen. He shortened the time during which prisoners had to wait for trial. Then he produced an ambitious plan for reorganizing the Court and the States. Jurats were to be abolished, and their place taken by two paid judges. The States were gradually to be transformed into a Chamber of Deputies. But even the spell of his eloquence could not persuade his fellow members to consent to this. Soon he lost his ardour for reform. The traditions of the Laurel Party were conservative. When A.J. Le Cras (q.v.) and his Jersey Reform Committee began to agitate for the wholesale adoption of the English system, Godfray recoiled in indignation, and became the passionate defender of old institutions.

In the States as elsewhere he was constantly in hot water. In 1852 he had a terrific row with Sir Jean De Veulle, the Bailiff. As he was criticizing a Report, the Bailiff said, "This is false". Godfray protested with such violence that the States had to adjourn. At the next meeting he persisted in his demand for an apology, and followed the Bailiff into his private room, where a stormy interview took place. The Bailiff complained to the Court that Godfray had challenged him to a duel, and, though he denied it, he was bound over to keep the peace. In the Court he spoke, as he confessed, "under feelings of considerable excitement and just indignation". His opponents' report was:—"He broke out into a violent and most indecent harangue and inveighed against the Bailiff in language most acrimonious and offensive". For this speech the Bailiff suspended him from being an Advocate. The case went before the Privy Council, who saw "much to regret in the conduct of both parties", but cancelled Godfray's suspension. (The story occupies many pages in *Ordres de Conseil* Vol. V). This case was hardly over, before he was involved in an equally furious conflict with the Lieut.-Governor. As one obituary notice said:— "His savage energy made his life tempestuous and tormented". Yet in spite of this he was trusted and respected. He was Treasurer of the States from 1853 till he went blind. He was not all thunder and lightning. W.L. De Gruchy wrote of him:— "He had a singularly constructive mind, ready at a moment's notice to suggest expedients to meet difficulties, and cutting often the Gordian knots of political pedantry in an effective and common-sense way" (*Reminiscences*).

He fell dead in his office from apoplexy on 11 Feb. 1868, as he returned from Court after winning two cases. His closing years were clouded with financial troubles. He bought La Moye quarries and made other land speculations which proved unsuccessful, and at the time of his death creditors had seized his property. He married Mary Le Vesconte. One son, Charles Le Vesconte Godfray, was for twenty-six years Surgeon of the Hospital. A daughter, Marie Elizabeth, married Jurat Josué George Falle (q.v.). His portrait by W.M. Hay hangs in the Royal Court. [Sullivan's *Biographie de François Godfray* ; Local Newspapers ; *Relation du Procès intenté par le Major-Général Thornton contre Frs. Godfray.*]

GODFRAY, HUGH, (1821—1877). Mathematican and Astronomer. Born in St. Helier's, 1821, son of Hugh Godfray, master of a vessel in the Labrador trade. Educated at Denziloe's

Academy, St. Helier's, then at St. Servan College, then at Paris University, where he studied mathematics. After a year as tutor to a nobleman's son in the south of France, he returned to Jersey, and in 1842 he opened a School of Navigation and Mathematics, which became very successful. In 1843 he married Jane, daughter of Charles Gruchy of Trinity and sister of Jurat Gruchy, by whom he had four sons and one daughter. During 1846 and 1847 he surveyed the island for his *Map of Jersey*, published 1849. He frequently contributed articles to the *Mathematician* and other scientific periodicals, and so became known to scientists in England. One of these, Professor Davis of Woolwich, persuaded him to go to Cambridge, where he entered St. John's College in 1848. He was Third Wrangler in 1852, the year in which another Jerseyman James Lemprière Hammond, (q.v.) was Senior Classic. Being a married man he was ineligible for a Fellowship, but in 1852 he was elected Esquire Bedell of the University, a post which he held till his death. He was Lecturer at Corpus Christi and Pembroke Colleges and at Trinity Hall, and was famous as a most successful private coach in mathematics. He took a leading part in starting the Cambridge Local Examinations, and for many years was responsible for all the French papers. In 1852 he published his *Elementary Treatise on the Lunar Theory*, which became a text book at Oxford and Cambridge (Fourth Edition 1885). He followed this in 1867 by his book on *Plane Astronomy*. In 1858 he made maps and diagrams for facilitating Great Circle Sailing and a diagram for determining the sun's true azimuth. These were engraved and published by the Admiralty for use in the Navy. His last work was the long and elaborate article on Dialling in the *Encyclopaedia Britannica*, which he dictated to his youngest son from his deathbed. He died at Cambridge in 1877.

GODFRAY, HUMPHREY MARETT (1865—92), Greffier. Eldest son of Walter Bertram Godfray, Greffier, and Frances Sophia, daughter of Major Peter Daniel Marett. Born in St. Lawrence Parish, 2 Oct. 1865. Educated at Victoria College, where he won the gold medal for mathematics, the gold medal for French, and the Queen's history prize. In 1882 he gained a Channel Inlands' exhibition for mathematics at Exeter College. While at Oxford he became Treasurer and President of the Union, 1886—7, and took second class honours in Law. He entered as a student of the Middle Temple, but decided to join the Jersey Bar, and was admitted Advocate in 1887. In 1889 he succeeded his father as Greffier. Brought up, as it were, in the archives of the Greffe, he had a profound and accurate knowledge of Jersey history, which he was constantly extending by fresh researches. The library of the Société Jersiaise is enriched by many notebooks containing transcripts of documents about the Channel Islands which he had copied at the British Museum, the Record Office, the Bodleian Library, and the Archives of La Manche. While still an undergraduate, he was elected a member of the executive of the Société, and in 1888 became its Secretary. For several years he edited its *Bulletins*, and contributed many valuable articles, e.g. Notes and additions to Havet's *List of Guardians and Lords of the Isles* ; *Documents relatifs aux attaques sur les Iles de la Manche, 1328—43* ; *L'Origine des Jurés Justiciers dans les Iles de la Manche* ; *Early Protestant Refugees in the Channel Islands.* In 1890 he edited for the Huguenot Society in London the *Registre de l'Eglise Wallonne de Southampton*, and was editing for the States the printed edition of the *Ordres du Conseil*, and had reached the year 1678, when he died. Col. Le Cornu, the President, described him as "one of the most brilliant minds that has ever adorned our Société".

But his interests were not all antiquarian. He was an ardent reformer, and an enthusiastic worker for the Reform Association. He felt that, if Jersey was to retain its home-rule institutions, it must make them conform to modern ideas. He was an eloquent speaker and powerful debater, and was mainly instrumental in arousing the demand for voting by ballot, and himself drafted much of the Bill that eventually became law. As Greffier his zeal for his work won him the good opinion of the States. He was a popular Captain in the East Regiment of the Militia, the energetic Secretary of the Rifle Club, and a Freemason. Everything pointed to a brilliant future, when he fell a victim to influenza, followed by typhoid and pneumonia, and died, 17 Jan. 1892, aged only 28. The *Jersey Express* published a sonnet in his memory, and the *Chronique* wrote of him:—

"Peu de vies furent mieux remplies et peu de morts plus regrettés".

GODFRAY, JOHN WILLIAM (1850—1921), Brigadier-General. Son of John William Godfray, Dénonciateur, and Matilda Le Gallais. Born 20 Oct. 1850. Educated at Victoria College, Cheltenham College, and Sandhurst. He entered the army 1871, and became Captain 1879. When the Royal Jersey Militia was reorganized in 1881, Godfray, who had graduated at the Staff College, was detailed to assist. From 1882 to 1888 he was Quartermaster-General in Jersey. He was promoted Major in 1888. After serving as Deputy Judge-Advocate in India, and Deputy Assistant Adjutant-General in Cyprus, he rejoined his regiment, the King's Own Scottish Borderers, as second in command, for the Chitral Relief Expedition in 1895. For his work at the storming of the Malakend Pass he was mentioned in dispatches, received medal and clasp, and the brevet of Lieutenant-Colonel. He served in the Tirah Campaign 1897—8, gaining two more clasps. In Jan. 1898 he succeeded to the command of the 1st Battalion King's Own Scottish Borderers, and went with them to South Africa. He took part in Lord Roberts' march to Bloemfontein, and in 1900 was appointed Chief Staff Officer of the Seventh Division with headquarters at Pretoria. In 1901 he became Chief Staff Officer for the Orange River Colony. His work here was rewarded with a Companionship of the Order of the Bath. He returned home in 1902, and commanded the 25th Regimental District with headquarters at Berwick-on-Tweed 1902—5. In 1905 he was created a Commander of the Royal Victorian Order. He was Brigadier-General in charge of Administration, Scottish Command 1905—7. In 1908 he returned to Jersey as Assistant-Adjutant-General of the Militia, a post which he held till 1914. In 1911 he was appointed Aide-de- camp to the King. During the Great War he was Assistant-Adjutant-General and Quartermaster-General, Jersey Defences, 1914—19. He died in Jersey 10 Jan. 1921. He married Annie Julia Muntz, and had one son, John C. Lerrier Godfray.

GOSSELIN, HELLIER (d. 1579), Bailiff of Guernsey ; second
son of Thomas Gosselin of St. Helier's, and Catherine Le
Bastard ; the eldest son Guillaume Gosselin, who became Lieut.-
Bailiff of Jersey, 1551. The Gosselins were one of the earliest
Jersey families to become Protestant. Hellier was born in Jersey,
in *"la grande maison de Gosselin en ville"*. In 1539 he received
permission to build a house in Guernsey. In 1546 he was appointed King's Procureur in that island ; and on 4 Oct. 1549
he was sworn in as Bailiff. Under Edward VI it fell to him
to enforce the Reformation changes. When Mary became
Queen, his position was critical. Hence perhaps his severity
toward three Protestant women, Catherine Massey and her
daughters, burnt in 1556 (See *Amy, Jacques*). It was Gosselin
who sent them before the Ecclesiastical Court, and, when the
Dean had pronounced them to be heretics, it was Gosselin who
condemned them to be strangled and then burnt. Foxe tells the
story of their death:— "Then were three stakes set up. At the
middle post was the mother, the eldest daughter on the right
hand, the youngest on the other. They were first strangled, but
the rope broke, before they were dead, and so the poor women
fell in the fire. Perotine, who was great with child, did fall on
her side, where happened a ruefull sight ; for, as her belly burst
asunder by the vehemence of the flames, the infant, being a fair
man-child, fell into the fire, and efstoons, being taken out of the
fire by one W. House, was laid upon the grass. Then was the
child had to the Provost, and from thence to the Bailiff, who
gave censure that it should be carried back and cast into the
fire". The accuracy of Foxe's account has been challenged ; but
every detail is confirmed in the appeal made by Catherine Massey's brother to Elizabeth that those guilty of his sister's death
should be punished ; and the facts are recited again in Elizabeth's pardon eventually granted to the Rectors and Jurats. For
this execution Gosselin was deprived of his post by Elizabeth
and imprisoned (Dec. 1562). He remained in prison till Jan.
1565, when he was pardoned. On his return to the island he
was elected Jurat by the Catholic Party (March 1565). He married four times:— (1) a daughter of Thomas Dumaresq of La
Haule : (2) Perotine, daughter of François Henry of Guernsey,
1543 : (3) Emet, daughter of James Blondel : (4) Thomasse,
daughter of Collas Effard. His eldest son, Nicholas Gosselin,
became Greffier of Jersey in 1560. Hellier died in Dec. 1579.

[Foxe's *Book of Martyrs*. *Transactions of Société Guern.* VIII and X].

GOSSET, ISAAC (1713—1799), Modeller of Portraits in Wax. Sixth and posthumous son of Jean Gosset, a Huguenot refugee from Normandy, who had settled in Jersey, and married Susanne D'Allain. As the father was buried in the Town Churchyard six weeks before Isaac was born, his birth on 2 May 1713 probably took place in St. Helier's, though later his mother lived at Grouville, where the boy was brought up. His uncle, Matthew Gosset, had acquired some fame in London by modelling portraits in wax. Isaac joined him, and learnt this art, and soon excelled his uncle. The Royal Family and many famous men of the time sat for him. Among surviving specimens of his work are portraits of George II, George III, Queen Charlotte, Frederick, Prince of Wales, Lord Chesterfield, David Garrick, General Wolfe, Henry Pelham, George Grenville, Mrs. Delany, Bishop Hoadly of London, Bishop Trevor of Durham, and Francis Hutcheson, the philosopher. The National Portrait Gallery contains medallions by him of General Conway, Governor of Jersey, and Charles Townshend, Chancellor of the Exchequer. Eight of his portraits hang in the library at Windsor Castle, and others are in the South Kensington Museum. Part of his success was due to his discovery of a secret process, by which he tinted his wax to look like old ivory. In 1760 he was elected a member of the Incorporated Society of Artists. He died at Kensington 28 Nov. 1799, and was buried in the old Marylebone Cemetery. His portrait was painted by Gainsborough. The *Gentleman's Magazine* in its obituary rather quaintly described him as "one of those ingenious men rarely to be met with, who are at the same time equally amiable and inoffensive". He married in 1737 Françoise Buisset and had five children, Jeanne Madelain (b. 1743), Elizabeth Ann (b. 1744), Isaac (q.v.), Abraham (b. 1749) and Françoise (b. 1749). [A Family of Modellers in Wax in *Proceedings of the Huguenot Society of London* III ; *Dic. Nat. Biog.* ; *Gent. Mag.* 1799 ; Redgrave's *Dic. of Artists*.]

GOSSET, ISAAC (1745—1812), D.D., F.R.S., Bibliophil. Son
of the above. Born in 1745 in Berwick Street, Soho, and baptized in St. Martin's in the Fields on October 20. Educated
at Walker's Academy, Mile End, and Exeter College, Oxford.
B.A. 1767. M.A. 1770. D.D. 1782. He was elected F.R.S. in
1772. He was ordained, but delicate health prevented his taking
regular clerical work. He was however much in demand as a
preacher of charity sermons. As a boy he developed an intense
love for collecting books, and later became a well-known figure
at book-auctions. Indeed he was one of the minor 'characters'
of London, referred to in many memoirs of the time as "the
celebrated bibliomaniac". Many tales are told of him ; how
he infuriated his opponents at auctions by refusing to advance
his bids more than three pence at a time ; how once he was
completely cured of severe illness by an offer to take him to
see a volume of the first Complutensian Polyglot Bible in its
original binding. He died suddenly on 16 December 1812,
and was buried in the same grave as his father. The sale
of his library by Sotheby, which lasted for three weeks in June
1813, is still referred to as one of the great events of the
bibliographic world. He married in 1782 Catherine, daughter
of Haydock Hill. Several portraits of him have been engraved,
some in his wig, gown, and bands, one sitting at a table in
Lochee's auction room. His eldest son, Isaac, became Vicar of
Windsor and Chaplain to four sovereigns. His younger son,
Thomas Stephen, was Senior Fellow of Trinity College, Cambridge, and Vicar of Old Windsor. [Dic. Nat. Biog. and
literature there quoted.]

GOSSET, SIR RALPH ALLEN (1809—85), Serjeant-at-Arms.
Only son of Sir William Gosset (q.v.), and nephew of Matthew
Gosset, the Vicomte. Born 1809. His early years were spent
in the Navy, but on 1 July 1836 he was appointed by his
father, who was Serjeant-at-Arms, Assistant Serjeant-at-Arms
to the Speaker of the House of Commons. In 1854 he was
promoted to be Deputy-Serjeant. In 1875 "in response to the
unanimous feeling of the House" he was appointed by the Queen
to his father's old post of Serjeant-at-Arms. The Serjeant-at-

Arms is the disciplinary officer of the House, whose duty it is to expel unruly members and to keep in custody in the Clock Tower persons condemned to imprisonment by the authority of the House. He sits sword at side in a special seat at the Bar of the House. For many years his work was peaceful, but in his last Parliament he became a central figure in many stormy scenes.

In 1880 Bradlaugh was elected M.P. for Northampton, and as a militant atheist declined to take the oath, and claimed the right to affirm. The Law Officers of the Crown reported this to be illegal. Bradlaugh then agreed to take the oath ; but the House decided that, as he had asserted that no oath was binding on his conscience, this could not be allowed. The Speaker then ordered him to retire, and, when he refused to do so, called on Gosset to remove him. Bradlaugh was a burly six-footer, and Gosset a little old man of over seventy, but he took Bradlaugh by the shoulder and marched him out of the House. A few weeks later Bradlaugh again claimed his right to take the oath. He was allowed to speak from the Bar, but the House by a large majority adhered to its previous decision. "Mr. Bradlaugh declining to withdraw", wrote Gladstone to the Queen, "was removed by the Serjeant-at-Arms. Having suffered this removal, he came again before the Bar, and entered into what was almost a corporal struggle with the Serjeant". The House then ordered Gosset to arrest him, and keep him a prisoner in the Clock-Tower. Gosset did all he could to make his prisoner comfortable, providing him with a pleasant room, and allowing his daughters to wait on him. "Never", said the *Illustrated London News,* "can there have been a courtlier gaoler, never a more comfortable prisoner. To watch them suggested that the tall, large-framed man was the favoured guest of the white-haired Serjeant in knee-breeches, silk stockings covering Malvolio limbs, sword at belt, and tail coat". Bradlaugh then appealed to the Law Courts, which decided against him ; so in April 1881 he again entered the House, and demanded permission to take the oath. Once more Gosset was ordered to exclude him from the precincts. In August he made a fresh attempt to force his way into the House, and Gosset had to call in the help of ten policemen to remove him.

Meanwhile the intransigeance of the Irish members provided

Gosset with another problem. In February 1881 he was called upon to expel thirty-seven of them from the House. Some like Parnell went quietly on being tapped on the shoulder ; others made a fight of it, and to remove one Gosset had to call in four attendants. But, as he got £5 a head for every member ejected, this was a profitable night to him financially.

The 'Silent Member', who contributed weekly a Review of Parliament to the *Illustrated London News*, wrote of him on his retirement:— "The urbanity and ever-ready courtesy, that distinguished his conduct during the smooth-water times of the premierships of Lord Palmerston, Earl Russell, Mr. Disraeli, and Mr. Gladstone's first term of office, never failed him in the stormy scenes of the last Parliament. No member who witnessed the rare combination of firmness and coolness he showed, when called on to conduct Mr. Bradlaugh to the Bar and to pilot Mr. Parnell and his colleagues out of the House, could help admiring the unfailing tact and good temper of the venerable Serjeant-at-Arms. It may be that the personal geniality and creature comforts said to have been forthcoming to privileged visitors in his sanctum had something to do with the readiness with which his every mandate was obeyed. None the less is warm praise his due for doing his ministering so gently". Harry Furniss, the caricaturist, in his *My Bohemian Days* also refers to the influence of Gosset's private room : — "The Serjeant-at-Arms was a jolly old sort, a little, round man, rather bent, with a merry face, and somewhat bowed, short legs. In his official black Court dress, cutaway coat, knee-breeches, and black silk stockings his back view strongly resembled a black beetle, and as such I always depicted him in *Punch*. His private room leading out of the Lobby he made into a club, to which he invited members, who were good fellows, irrespective of politics. They became 'members of Gosset's room'. Tremendous decanters of whisky and boxes of cigars were provided by members for the benefit of all".

In August 1885 ill-health compelled him to retire, and he was created a Knight Commander of the Bath. The House passed a resolution, moved by Sir Michael Hicks Beach and supported by Sir William Harcourt and Parnell, recording its "sense of the exemplary manner in which he uniformly discharged his duties for nearly fifty years". He died in November that year at Richmond, aged 76. In 1835 he married Arabella

Sarah, daughter of Sir Thomas Butler. He had four sons, Thomas William Butler, who became Colonel in the Royal Engineers, Henry Allen, who became Paymaster in the Army, Matthew John Alfred, who became Chief Clerk in the Inland Revenue Office, and Francis Russell, who became Assistant Serjeant-at-Arms. Gosset constantly figured in pictures in the *Illustrated London News* during the stormy years 1881—5, and a striking portrait of him appeared in that paper on 5 December 1885. [*Hansard* ; newspapers of the period.]

GOSSET, SIR WILLIAM (1782—1848), Major-General, Under-Secretary of State for Ireland, Serjeant-at-Arms. Fourth son of Matthieu Gosset and Marguerite, daughter of Thomas Le Vavasseur dit Durell. He was thus step-brother of the Vicomte, Matthew Gosset, Seigneur of Bagot, of Elizabeth, wife of William Charles Lempriere, Lieut.-Bailiff (q.v.), and of Magdalen, wife of Jurat Philip De Carteret. He was born in 1782, and baptized in St. Saviour's 26 Jan. When fifteen, he obtained a commission in the Royal Engineers, and shortly after saw active service in the expedition to Holland (1799), and then in the jungle fighting of the Kandyan War in Ceylon. In 1815 he was Secretary to the Legation sent to try to arrange terms with the Barbary States, and, while in Algiers, secretly surveyed the fortifications ; so, when it was decided in 1816 to smash this pirate stronghold, he was sent with Lord Exmouth's expedition. During the bombardment of the City, an Algerine frigate under shelter of the forts was doing considerable damage to the British fleet. "At length", says the *Annual Register*, "the Admiral yielded to the request of Major Gosset, and permitted him to attack in the *Queen Charlotte*'s barge. The frigate was instantly boarded, and within ten minutes was in a perfect blaze". For this Gosset was made a Companion of the Order of the Bath and a Commander of the Neapolitan Order of St. Ferdinand.

At the General Election of 1820 he was returned as Member of Parliament for Truro. His first speech in the House was a defence of the Government against the charge of having hurried the body of the notorious Queen Caroline out of the country with indecent haste for its burial in Brunswick. He explained that he had been in charge of the troops at Harwich, when the coffin was embarked ; that, finding the Church in no state to receive it, if it should miss the tide, he had prepared his own dining-room as a mortuary ; but that the hearse had arrived just in time to lower it into the boat. He was entirely exonerated from blame. His next speech was a defence of the Jersey Militia against Hume's accusation of inefficiency (*Hansard*).

In 1828 he became Secretary to Lord Beresford, Master-General of the Ordnance ; and in the following year Lord Anglesey, Lord-Lieutenant of Ireland, invited him to become his private Secretary. Here he did so well, that in 1830 Lord Anglesey knighted him, and secured his appointment as Under Secretary of State for Ireland. In 1831 he was created Knight Commander of the Royal Guelphic Order. His five years as Under-Secretary were the most trying of his life. Ireland was seething with revolt. Daniel O'Connell was far more powerful than the British authorities. Every attempt to enforce the law was met by fierce outbreaks of crime and bloodshed. The Home Government kept on changing its policy, sometimes trying to conciliate, sometimes to coerce. In 1835 Gosset was glad to resign his thankless task, and accept the quieter post of Serjeant-at-Arms to the Speaker of the House of Commons.

Here he became involved in the four years' struggle on the question of privilege between the Commons and the Court of Queen's Bench. In 1836 a Parliamentary Report on Prisons described as obscene a book found in a prisoner's possession. Stockdale, the publisher of the book, sued Hansard, the Parliamentary printer, for libel. The Commons maintained that its official publications were privileged ; but this the Lord Chief Justice emphatically denied. In the course of this conflict Gosset arrested by order of the House and held as prisoners in the Clock Tower, not only Stockdale and his son, his lawyer and his lawyer's clerk, but also the two Sheriffs of the County of Middlesex, who had distrained upon Hansard. Gosset himself had to fight more than one case in the Courts, for Stockdale's lawyer sued him for illegal arrest, and the Queen's Bench condemned him to pay £200 damages. Hume then moved in the Commons, "that this House will deem it a high breach of its privileges on the part of any person who shall dare to levy damages upon one of their servants for having obeyed the Speaker's warrant". But the Government shrank from action, which might involve the imprisonment of the Lord Chief Justice in the Clock Tower, and chose the less sensational course of suing for a writ of error, which the Court of Exchequer unanimously granted (*Hansard* ; May's *Constitutional History*).

Gosset died in his home at Charlton Grove near Woolwich on 27 March 1848, and Lord Russell expressed in the Commons his "admiration for the manner in which he had discharged for twelve years with firmness and courtesy duties which were always difficult and sometimes painful". He married in 1808 Gertrude Martha, daughter of Ralph Allen Daniell, M.P. for West Cornwall, and had one son Ralph Allen (q.v.) and three daughters, Elizabeth Louisa, Gertrude Mary, and Janette Anne. An article in the Huguenot Society's *Publications*, Vol. III, suggests that Gosset Street, Spitalfields, was named after him. [*Annual Register* 1848 ; *Illustrated London News* 1848 ; and authorities quoted.]

GRANDIN, LILIAN MARY (1876—1924). Missionary Doctor. Daughter of Francis Philip Grandin and Anne Benest. Born in St. Helier 25 Nov. 1876. Educated at the Jersey Ladies' College. When twenty she offered herself for medical work in the West China Mission of the United Methodist Church, and went to Edinburgh for training. She was the first Jerseywoman to obtain a medical degree, L.R.C.P., and L.R.C.S. Edin., and added a special course in dentistry. She then studied Midwifery in Dublin, Eyes at Moorfields, and Tropical Diseases in London. In Jan. 1806 she sailed for Shanghai. During the long journey up the Yangtse, then the only way of reaching the province of Yunnan, her boat was wrecked in the rapids, and her medical stores damaged. Then followed a fortnight's journey to Ch'ao Tong. In this old walled city, 6,000 feet above sea level, she worked for many years, part of the time with a male colleague, and then with an English nurse. In addition to her duties as hospital doctor she trained Chinese women to be midwives and nurses, and made difficult journeys through the mountains on her pony to hold clinics at spots where aboriginal tribes could gather. She was the only qualified doctor in a district as large as France. Later she started a leper colony. During a furlough in 1912 she married Mr. Edwin J. Dingle, author of *Across China on foot* and *The Chinese Revolution*, whom she had first met when he was making an adventurous tramp across China.

Though now not connected with any Mission, the need for doctors was so great, that she undertook temporary medical work at Hankow, Wenchow, and Shanghai. She also helped her husband to compile his enormous *Chinese Atlas and Gazeteer*. During the War (1914—18) she returned to England, and after a refresher course at the London Hospital was able to set free a male doctor. After the War she returned to far Yunnan, and took charge of the Mission's medical work in the whole province, which was then in a very disturbed state with the roads infested with brigands. The strain brought her life to an unexpected end on 5 Dec. 1924. On her grave are the words, "A Beloved Physician".

GRUCHY, JEANNE (1763—1848), Donor of the Don Gruchy. Daughter of Jean Gruchy of St. John's and Jeanne Baudains. Born 1763. In her will she calls herself "a native and resident of St. John's". In this will, which was signed on 3 Feb. 1843, she says, "I bequeath to the most necessitous Poor of this isle the sum of 1,728 silver *livres*, according to the ancient currency of France, that is to say 144 *livres* in one payment for the poor of each of the twelve parishes, to be distributed at the discretion of my executors". Then comes a list of personal legacies to relations and friends ; and the will ends. "As to the rest of my property I leave it for the benefit of the Poor of the twelve parishes to be divided equally between the parishes, on condition that the sum received by each parish be used by the Parochial Committee for the purchase of land, and that the produce or rent of that land be employed every year to succour the necessitous Poor, my wish being that the distribution be made extraordinairement (i.e. not as ordinary parish relief) to the native poor of this isle who are not in receipt of relief". (The will is printed in full in *Le Constitutionnel* 7 April 1849.) She died on 6 Jan. 1848, aged 84. Each parish received £725, according to the Commissioners' Report of 1860, and in that year the land produced an annual income of £338.

GUERDAIN, AARON (d. 1676), M.D., Master of the Mint. Eldest son of Michel Guerdain, Constable of Trinity, and Marie, daughter of Aaron Stocall, Constable of St. Saviour's. In 1627, being then a B.A., he was admitted to Jesus College, Cambridge, and as a member of that college took his M.A. He became Fellow of Queens' in 1631, but had vacated that post by October 1633. He graduated Doctor of Medicine at Rheims in April 1634. On 7 November 1640 he was cited before the College of Physicians and admonished, because he had been practising in London without a licence for four and a half years. When the Civil War began, it became known in Jersey that he had joined the Parliament's side ; so Sir George Carteret seized the large house at Trinity, known as La Guerdainerie, which Guerdain had inherited from his father, and gave it to a rascal named Col. Smyth to establish a Mint in it, where silver plate of the Royalists could be transformed into half-crowns for the King's use (Chevalier). Furnaces and crucibles were installed : but then it was discovered that Smyth was using them to flood the island with base coins for his own profit, and he had to fly to escape the hangman's rope. In 1649 Sir George Carteret cut down all the trees on Guerdain's estate to build a store in Elizabeth Castle.

By this time Guerdain was sufficiently well-known in England as a Parliamentarian for his name to be borrowed by the author of an anti-Cromwellian satire:— *A most learned, conscientious, and devout Exercise or Sermon held forth the last Lord's Day of April at Sir P.T.'s house in Lincoln's Inn Fields by Lieutenant General O. Cromwell, as it was faithfully taken in Characters by Aaron Guerdain.* In the same year by a strange coincidence he, whose own house had been transformed into a Royalist Mint, was appointed Master of the Mint in the Tower of London at a salary of £400 in place of Sir Robert Harley, who had refused to take the King's head off the coins. He held this post till 1660, and was responsible as 'Master-worker of the

Monies' for the coining of all the new Commonwealth money (Ruding. *Coinage of Great Britain*). In 1652 a State Paper asserts that his post "should be worth £1500, now that he is Melter also" (*S.P.D.*). He was put on the Commission of Peace "that he may better prevent disorders in the Mint" (*S.P.D.*) ; and in 1653 it is mentioned that part of his duty was to hunt down and prosecute all false coiners (*S.P.D.*). But he still practised as a physician. In 1653 Parliament ordered "the two Dr. Guerdains" (the other was his brother Denis. q.v.) "to examine 220 sick soldiers to select those who should be sent to Bath" (*S.P.D.*). In 1655, when Cromwell nominated eleven new Jurats for Jersey, he was one of those selected, but he declined to serve. At the Restoration he lost his post as Master of the Mint, but he seems to have made his peace with the authorities, for in December 1664 he and his brother were both elected Honorary Fellows of the College of Physicians. He died in 1676. [Munk's *College of Physicians*, and authorities quoted above.]

GUERDAIN, DENIS (d. 1668), Physician. Second son of Michel Guerdain, Constable of Trinity, and Marie Stocall. Brother of Aaron Guerdain (q.v.). Where he took his degree we have not discovered, probably in some foreign university, but his M.D. was recognized by the College of Physicians. In the Civil War the Guerdains and Stocalls were zealous Parliamentarian families, and in 1643 Denis had tried to negotiate the surrender of Mont Orgueil to Parliament. When George Carteret (q.v.) recaptured Jersey for the King, he and his brother had to fly to England. He established himself as a Doctor in London, and in 1653 was Physician in charge of Ely House, the town house of the Bishops of Ely, which Parliament had converted into a great Hospital for Wounded Soldiers. Everything did not run smoothly there, and in May the Council of State received a petition "from Dr. Guerdain's patients at Ely House". A Committee was appointed "to consider the abuses of Ely House and report the remedies thereunto". This Committee exonerated Guerdain from blame, and declared that what was needed was stricter discipline ; and the Council decided that "all patients in Ely House shall be liable to court-martial as though still in the army and be judged according to the articles of war" (S.P.). On 17 May the Council ordered "the two Dr. Guerdains" to examine 220 sick soldiers and decide which were suitable for treatment at Bath (S.P.).

By 1655 Denis was practising in Jersey, and on 28 Feb., when Cromwell nominated eleven new Jurats, he was one of those selected. But he declined to take the oath, perhaps because he had imbibed Quaker views about the sinfulness of oaths, perhaps because he was too good a Republican to recognize Cromwell as Protector. In Jan. 1659 we read in the Acts of the Court:— "The Lieutenant-Governor and the Attorney-General pointed out that some Jurats were in England and others infirm, and so to the great prejudice of the community there were not enough to carry on the business of the Court. They urged that it was desirable that Dr. Denis Guerdain, who had lately taken up his residence in the island and had been nominated by His Highness as a Jurat, should undertake this duty. The Court finding this suggestion reasonable appointed Mons. Lempriere of St. John's and Mons. Le Sebirel to wait on Dr. Guerdain and prevail on him to accept the charge". But the Deputation failed to persuade him. After the Restoration he made his peace with the authorities, and with his brother was elected an Hon. Fellow of the College of Physicians in Dec. 1664. He died in May 1668, and on the 27th was buried in Trinity churchyard. In 1656 he married at St. Lawrence Marie Herault, daughter of the Constable of St. Helier's, and the Register states that they were married "in the New Style", i.e. by the Bailiff not the Rector, according to the decree of the Barebones Parliament that all marriages must be solemnized before a Magistrate. Like other of the Jersey Republican exiles in London, he had evidently adopted Anabaptist views, for none of his children were baptized till after his death. Four of them, Martha, aged 12, Denis, aged 9, Marie, aged 7, and Jean, aged 5, were baptized together in Trinity Church in 1672, and Aaron, aged 12, was baptized at St. Lawrence in 1677. His eldest son Michel became Fellow of Exeter in 1680. In 1651 Chevalier, who is generally accurate, speaks of "Dr. Guerdain, one of the members of this new Parliament". The records of the Rump Parliament are incomplete, and it is not clear whether this refers to Denis or Aaron. Nor do we know what constituency he represented.

HAMMOND, JAMES LEMPRIERE (1829—1880.). Fellow of
Trinity, Cambridge. Born in Jersey 1829, second son of John
Hammond, Bailiff. Educated at Christ's Hospital, where he
early became a "Grecian". Gained a sizarship at Trinity College, Cambridge 1848, Scholar 1850. In 1852 he was bracketed
Senior Classic and was also 16th Wrangler. B.A. 1852. M.A.
1855. He became Fellow of his College 1853. Assistant Tutor
1854—62, and Senior Bursar 1863—70. He examined in the
Classical Tripos in 1858, 1864, 1865, and in the Moral Science
Tripos in 1862 and 1863. As executor of Dr. Whewell's will
he carried out additions to Trinity at a cost of £100,000. He
was a fluent composer of Greek, Latin, and English verse, and
famous in the Common Rooms as a brilliant conversationalist.
He resigned his Fellowship after a lawsuit with the College
on the issue whether a layman could be Senior Fellow. This
action he lost. He was then called to the Bar. He became a
Charity Commissioner, and did a great work in reorganizing
the old Public Schools. He was on the governing bodies of
Christ's Hospital and Westminster School. As a politician
he frequently appeared on Liberal platforms. He died unmarried, 23 July 1880, and was buried in Highgate Cemetery.

HAMMOND, JOHN (1801—80), Bailiff. Third son of Jacques
Lempriere Hammond of Petit Ménage and Rachel, daughter of Thomas Durell, Vicomte. Born 9 March 1801. Educated at Caen, where he took the Law Course. Admitted to
the Jersey Bar 1821. In 1836 he stood for election as Constable
of St. Saviour's as candidate of the Rose Party, and obtained
a majority of two. His Laurel opponent, Abraham Aubin, appealed. The case dragged on for nearly three years, and then
both withdrew. As an officer in the East Battery of the Militia
he served in all grades, becoming Colonel in 1843. He was
appointed Solicitor-General in 1848. When Sir Thomas Le
Breton died, the obvious person to succeed him as Bailiff was
J.W. Dupré (q.v.), the Attorney-General, but through over-
friendliness with Victor Hugo and the French proscrits he was
out of favour with the English authorities, and Hammond was
appointed instead. He was sworn in on 27 Feb. 1858. At

once he had to face a constitutional crisis. There were now more than 15,000 English residents in Jersey, most of whom cared nothing for the history of the island. They were merely annoyed at finding laws different from those of England. Abraham Jones Le Cras (q.v.) made himself their spokesman. He contended that the local home rule was "founded on fraud and usurpation" (*Letter to Lord Palmerston*), that the States had "no more right to make laws than the Corporation of Southampton" (*Evidence before Royal Commission*), and that Jersey was subject to the British Parliament. This agitation had begun before Hammond became Bailiff. The first objective of the attack had been the Jurat system, and a Royal Commission in 1846 had reported in favour of the abolition of the Royal Court and the appointment of three paid Judges ; but no results had followed. Now Le Cras began to stir up Members of Parliament to assert their alleged powers. In Feb. and March 1859 George Hadfield, M.P. for Sheffield, made two long speeches in the House of Commons calling attention to "the unsatisfactory state of the laws of Jersey", and presented a petition, organized by Le Cras, praying "that the recommendations of the Commissioners may forthwith be carried into effect". The result was the appointment of a new Royal Commission, which spent two months in the island. Hammond's evidence fills twenty-five closely printed pages of its Report. These Commissioners repeated their predecessors' recommendation, that three paid professional Judges, of whom the Bailiff should be one, should be substituted for the twelve Jurats. The States referred this proposal to the twelve Parish Assemblies, but not one voted in its favour. The Commissioners' printed Report, a volume of over 800 pages, did not reach Jersey till Feb. 1861 ; but on 1 May Serjeant Pigott, M.P. for Reading, introduced into the House of Commons a Bill embodying their recommendations. On its second reading however he withdrew it, when the Home Secretary urged that the States should be given time to consider the Report. The States however adopted a policy of passive resistance ; so in 1864 John Locke, M.P. for Southwark, reintroduced Pigott's Bill. This passed its second reading. The States then petitioned to be heard at the Bar by counsel ; but the Government's lawyers advised that Le Cras' constitutional theories were unsound, and the Bill was withdrawn. The States then resolved to take a

plebiscite of the island on the question:— "Are you in favour
of substituting two Paid Judges for the twelve Jurats?". In
spite of strenuous efforts by Le Cras' committee only 180 votes
were recorded in favour of the change. On 23 March 1875
Locke returned to the attack, and introduced a new Bill into
the House of Commons. By this the office of Bailiff was to
be abolished, and Hammond to receive a pension, the Jurats
to be deprived of judicial functions, but to remain members
of the States, and three paid Judges to be appointed by the
Crown. But again the Government brought pressure to bear,
and the Bill was withdrawn.

Hammond by his probity, his industry, his personal character
won universal respect. "He set himself pertinaciously", wrote
W.L. De Gruchy, who was a Jurat under him, "to reduce the
long list of cases in arrear, and at the end of his tenure of
office a comparatively clean sheet was passed on to his successor" (*My Reminiscences*). When he took office he had found
one case (Gabeldu v Le Quesne) which had been waiting nine
years for the Court's judgement on a preliminary point. H.E.
Durell wrote of him as "a kindly man, stern and unbending
when any moral principle was involved, but forgiving and
large-hearted" (*Men I have known*). He not only gave fatherly
advice from the bench to the prisoners he sentenced, but visited
each in prison to talk over plans to help them to reform. He
was a strong supporter of the Jersey Industrial School, and the
Jersey Female Orphans' Home, and took a leading part in
founding the Jersey General Dispensary. "He had", wrote
Durell, "one weakness. He took snuff, and, if he had not got
his snuff-box, he was absolutely lost. I have seen him in the
course of an address take his snuff-box, open it, and finding nothing in, stop, call the usher, and wait for his return" (*id*). He was
a keen horticulturist, and gave his name to the apple known as
Hammond's Seedling. For most of his time he was very popular ; but in 1873 he had to face a terrific storm of abuse. The
failure of the Mercantile Bank roused great sympathy for the
victims, and George Vickery, Deputy of St. Helier's, proposed a
lottery with a prize of £25,000, which he hoped would raise
£100,000 for the Relief Fund. This proposal passed the States
by a large majority, but Hammond for the first and only time
during his tenure of office exercised his right of veto. Vickery
exclaimed dramatically, "Would to God I had the power of

Oliver Cromwell to say to you, Make room for a better man".
Vickery's idea that he could sell half a million tickets in England and France had been a wild chimera ; but all who had
been ruined by the crash now held Hammond responsible for
their beggary. The Privy Council however supported his action.

He died suddenly on 14 Feb. 1880. Jurat W.L. De Gruchy,
who was present in Court, wrote:— "He was presiding over a contentious case, and the Court had retired to consider its judgement. He took his seat in his accustomed chair ; but before
he could use his invariable formula, 'Well, gentlemen, what do
you say?' he fell back dead" (*My Reminiscences*). He was
buried in Green Street Cemetery. His portrait by W.M. Hay
hangs in the Royal Court. He married Jane Penrose Le Breton,
sister of Dean Le Breton, and had four sons:— John William,
Fellow of St. John's College, Oxford, James Lempriere (q.v.),
Tutor of Trinity College, Cambridge, Lawrence Nicholas Dyer,
Major, and Vavasor Fitz Hammond, Vicar of Drighlington,
Yorkshire, and four daughters, Penrose Durell, Emily Jane,
Louisa Anne Charlotte, and Eleanor Gertrude. [*Bull*. VI:
Hansard's Parliamentary Debates: Report of Commissioners,
1860: Local Newspapers.]

HAMPTONNE, LAURENS (1600—65), Vicomte. Son of Edouard Hamptonne, Constable of St. Lawrence, and Elizabeth,
daughter of Jean Dumaresq, Bailiff. The Hamptonnes had
become the leading family in St. Lawrence. Between 1539 and
1604 six were Constables, and Louis Hamptonne (Rector
1502—58) had built at his own expense the North Chapel of
the Church and made slips to the shore for the vraicers (seaweed
gatherers). Laurens was born in 1600. His father died next
year, and he was brought up by his mother's second husband,
Jean Le Hardy, Solicitor-General. In 1621, when only twenty-
one, he was appointed Vicomte. In 1639 he bought the house
at St. Lawrence still known as Hamptonne. His property in the
parish then covered 100 vergées.

It was part of the Vicomte's duties to read aloud all public
announcements at the Market Cross. A few weeks after the
outbreak of Civil War, when Sir Philippe De Carteret (q.v.)

had withdrawn to Elizabeth Castle, and the Town was ruled by the Parliamentary Committee, he sent Hamptonne a proclamation to publish "enjoining the people not to take up arms with the factious", and declaring "the authors of the disorders rebels and disloyal, naming a few of the chief of them" (De Carteret's letter to his wife, printed in Hoskins). It is not surprising that the Vicomte, though a Royalist, "made some difficulty" about proclaiming this (ibid.). So on 11 June 1643 De Carteret provided him with a mounted escort. "It was Market-day", writes Chevalier, "and the English gentlemen who accompained him were newcomers, unfamiliar with our ways. When they saw the people running up from all sides to hear the proclamation, they took fright, and cocked their carbines, and retreated to the Castle. The Vicomte escaped in another direction". Shortly afterwards he was arrested, and imprisoned on one of the Parliamentary vessels then watching Mont Orgueil : but a few days later the Committee to the disgust of their extremer supporters ordered his release. "When Laurens Hampton was committed", complained De La Rocque, "after reading ye Commission of Array, the Committee at the intercession of Lempriere released him, and replaced him in his office. They were also continually drinking, eating, and keeping company with ye said Viscount". He continued to live at St. Lawrence, perhaps protected by his brother-in-law, Benjamin Bisson (q.v.), one of the Parliamentary Commissioners ; Chevalier tells of two letters from Sir Philippe that failed to reach him, and fell into the hands of the Committee.

In April 1644, when George Carteret (q.v.) regained Jersey for the King, Hamptonne was ordered to seize the property of the Parliamentarians, an awkward job, for this consisted largely in rentes, and those who owed them were loth to disclose the fact. In 1645 he had to hang thirteen of the Committee, including his brother-in-law, in effigy in the Market. When news came in 1649 of the King's execution, he proclaimed Charles II as King in the Market on Saturday 17 Feb., at Elizabeth Castle on the Sunday, and at Mont Orgueil on the Monday, though Parliament had declared that anyone so doing would be hanged as a traitor. He then nailed the parchment to the door of the Court. (It is now in the S. J. Museum. Text in Bull. IX.) One of the Vicomte's duties was to superintend executions. On one occasion a criminal flung the hangman from the scaffold, and climbed to the top of the gallows, and defied anyone to fetch him. The executioner, shaken by his fall, was helpless ; so Hamptonne prodded the man down with the ladder. Le Geyt (IV) discusses at length whether his action was legally justifiable, and decides against him, as no one but the executioner can execute.

In June his son Edouard accompanied Carteret to France to arrange for the King's visit to Jersey, and, knowing that his father would soon be a Jurat, obtained from Charles Letters Patent promising him the Vicomteship, when his father should resign. In September the King arrived, and remained for nearly five months. The Hamptonne family believed later that the King had stayed in their house, and showed two trunks that he was said to have left behind, containing an embroidered fawn-coloured doublet and a blue satin vest, but this tradition is doubtful. Chevalier, who kept a day by day record of all the King's movements, says : — "If any of the island Gentry invited the Duke (i.e. the King's brother) to their house, neither he nor the King ever accepted the invitation ; but the Lords of the Court used to accept, and the King counted this as a compliment paid to himself". The Hamptonnes also showed gifts received from the King, a pair of silver spurs, a brace of pistols, and a silver dolphin-shaped seal. When the King sold part of the Crown revenues in Jan. 1650, Hamptonne bought rentes in St. Brelade's and St. Lawrence for 2,040 *livres tournois*, and obtained the coveted right to rebuild the dovecot in his garden. The estate was also made "impartible and descendible to the eldest heir, and it shall not be lawful to dismember the same, any law or usage in the island to the contrary notwithstanding" (*Bull.* XII).

In April 1651 Laurens was elected Jurat. When he took the oath he claimed that his long service of the King entitled him to a higher place on the Bench than that of a new member, "whereupon Mr. Le Geyt, Mr. Jean Pipon, and Mr. Thomas Pipon voluntarily agreed to yield precedence to him" (*Chevalier*). His son succeeded him as Vicomte. Neither however enjoyed his honours long. In October a Parliamentary force landed in St. Ouen's Bay, and Hamptonne with other Royalists took refuge in Elizabeth Castle. In December the Castle surrendered, and he was one of the three defenders whom the Parliamentary commander demanded, partly as hostages, partly as delegates to arrange terms. These were very moderate. The besieged were promised life and liberty and permission to remain in the island, but they had to compound for their estates by a fine not exceeding two years' revenue. Hamptonne decided to remain. In Oct. 1652 Parliament referred to the Council of State a list of Proposals for Jersey, one of which was "that Laurens Hamptonne and his son Edouard, being notorious delinquents, be for ever disinabled to bear any office of trust" (*Bull.* V). In Aug. 1653 he was deprived of his Juratship ; but otherwise he was not molested. By selling some of his other property he was able to retain Hamptonne ; and for eight years he lived in retirement. In Nov. 1654 he stood as godfather to the baby daughter of the Rector of St. Lawrence ; and in Sept. 1659 he and the wife of Michel Lempriere (q.v.), Cromwell's Bailiff, stood together as godparents to a son of Philippe Dumaresq.

In May 1660 news arrived of the Restoration, and on 2 June Hamptonne heard his son again proclaim Charles II as King. Laurens at once resumed his place as Jurat, and in 1663 became Lieut.-Bailiff. On 2 Feb. 1665 he died. A monument to him and his son is on the outer wall of St. Lawrence Church. He married three times : — (1) his cousin Sara Hamptonne, (2) Marthe (d. 1636), daughter of Edouard Bisson, Constable of St. Brelade's and widow of Jean Herault, (3) Philippine Sealle, (d. 1639), widow of Jean Botterel of St. Ouen's. Besides his son Edouard (b. 1628. d. 1651) he had four daughters, Elisabeth, who married Josué Ahier. Rector of St. Lawrence, Anne, who married Lieut.-Bailiff Jean Poingdestre (q.v.), author of *Caesarea*, Rachel, who married David Patriarche, and Sara, who married Philippe Payn, Deputy-Vicomte. The St. Martin's Register describes this last wedding : — "On 3 Feb. 1663 Philippe Payn married Sara Hamptonne. As he left his manor in Grouville on his wedding morning, musketeers fired a volley. As he passed through Trinity with a fine array of the island *noblesse*, the parish cannons fired. Near Sieur Hamptonne's house two musket volleys greeted them. The discourse in which Philippe Le Couteur, Dean and Rector of St. Martin's, put the question to the damsel lasted half an hour, and was much admired. Sieur Hamptonne responded admirably, and gave the damsel's hand to the Dean, who placed it in that of Sieur Payn. They then went to St. Lawrence Church where the ceremony was celebrated. The parish cannons fired, and there were three musket-volleys. As they passed Elizabeth Castle on their way to Grouville, the Governor awaited them in his carriage at the end of the bridge, and two cannons fired from the Castle. St. Helier's also fired its cannons as they passed ; and so did St. Saviour's and St. Clement's. On reaching Grouville the cannons fired, and the tocsin was beaten at their house". [Chevalier's *Journal* ; Hoskins' *Charles II in the Channel Islands* ; *Guernsey Magazine*, Aug. 1878 ; Payne's *Armorial* ; and authorities quoted above.]

HARDY, THOMAS (1840—1928), Novelist,
HARDY, SIR THOMAS DUFFUS (1804—78), Archivist, and
HARDY, SIR THOMAS MASTERMAN (1769—1839), Vice-Admiral, 'Nelson's Hardy', were all of Jersey descent. Jean Le Hardy, younger son of Clement Le Hardy, Bailiff of Jersey under Henry VII, settled in Dorset. The Admiral and the Novelist were descended from him. The Archivist was the great-great-grandson of Jean Le Hardy, Attorney-General under George II.

HELIER, SAINT. See Appendix I.

HEMERY, JAMES (1814—49), Dean. Third son of Clement Hemery of Colomberie. Born 30 April 1814. Admitted to Westminster School 1827. King's Scholar 1828. Rowed number 6 in race against Eton 1831. Elected to Trinity College, Cambridge 1833. Scholar 1834. B.A. 1837, bracketed 7th Wrangler. Fellow and Assistant Tutor 1839—44, M.A. 1840. Appointed Dean of Jersey and Rector of St. Helier's 1844. For three years he was very active and popular, but then con-

tracted tuberculosis. He went to Madeira and Torquay in hope
of recovery, but in vain. He returned to Jersey, where he died,
22 Novermber 1849. In 1845 he had married Ellen Charlotte,
daughter of Thomas Newcourt.

HERAULT, JEAN (1569—1626), Bailiff. Eldest son of Thomas Herault, Vingtenier of St. Saviour's, and Mabel, sister of
Bailiff Hostes Nicolle (q.v.). Born in St. Saviour's 1569. Of
his early life little is known. (*The Dictionary of National
Biography* confuses him with his cousin, Jean Herault the
Greffier, a much older man, who had been appointed in 1573,
and in 1615 resigned on the ground that he was "enfeebled
through age in limbs and sight.") In 1595 he bought half the
manor of Longueville from his cousin Hugh, son of Hostes
Nicolle, but soon resold it (*Bull.* XI). In 1597 he matriculated
at Oxford from All Souls at the unusually late age of twenty-
eight, but did not take a degree. He held some Crown appointment under Elizabeth, for he wrote later, "The Bailiff has
devoted a great part of his life to the service of the King and
of the late Queen" (*P.B.C.*), and again "Your servant hath for
a long time served the State, both in time of war and peace". In
1604 he was in Jersey, for he was fined for having affronted
the Court by the way he worded a remonstrance (*Bull. IV*).

In some way he attracted the notice of the Privy Council,
for in 1607, when Sir Robert Gardiner and Dr James Hussey
were sent as Royal Commissioners to the islands, they were
told:— "For your assistance we have made choice of our trusty
and well-beloved John Herault of St. Saviour's in regard of his
experience in the language and customs of those isles, to attend
you, whose service we require you to use, as occasion shall
serve" (*A.E.*). In 1611, "in consideration of the good and willing service he has rendered and is rendering" to the King, he
secured "on the recommendation of the Duke of Lennox" Letters Patent promising him the Bailiffship, when it became vacant (*O.C.*).

His next step was to persuade George Poulet (q.v.) to resign,
"which cost him much money". But then, when the way
seemed clear, Sir John Peyton, the Governor, produced a clause

in his own Letters Patent giving him the right to nominate
the Bailiff. It was a case of Letters Patent contradicting Letters Patent, and the matter was referred to the Council. Here
Herault pleaded his cause in person, and evidently made a
good impression, and the King's high doctrine of Kingship gave
him an easy victory. "To constitute a Magistrate", wrote the
King, "is one of the essential marks of our supreme power, an
act regal, inseparable from our Royal Person" ; and he added,
"Forasmuch as we always intended that a competent pension
should be allowed to the Bailiff, we command that 100 marks
be paid yearly out of the revenues of the island to Herault
for life over and above all other emoluments" (*P.B.C.*). This
meant that Peyton, a testy, gouty, old Elizabethan veteran,
lost, not only the right of nomination, but 100 marks a year out
of his own pocket. And he and Herault became enemies for
life, a feud which had important results on the island constitution.

Herault was sworn in on 16 Sept. 1615. He came of a good
Jersey family, mentioned as landholders in the Extente of 1274.
His mother's father had been Seigneur of Longueville. But all
his life he was hampered by poverty, and this handicap seems
to have developed in him an inferiority complex, which manifested itself in the usual symptom of swelled-headedness. On
securing the Bailiffship he began quite absurdly to magnify
his position. He assumed the magniloquent title Monsieur de
St. Sauveur from a small property that he owned near Bagot
in that parish, a form of address hitherto strictly limited to Seigneurs. He loved to call himself High Bailiff. He was the first
Bailiff to wear red robes like an English Judge. According to
Peyton, he ordered the Clergy in their public prayers to put his
name before the Governor's. He even claimed the title of
Governor, asserting that Peyton was only "Muster-master and
Captain of the troops". He sent a long Memorandum to the
Council "to show that the Bailiff is of greater authority than
the Captain". Here are some of his points: — The Bailiff keeps
the King's seal. The Bailiff is the King's Representative. The
Bailiff is required by his oath to see that the Captain keeps
the Castles in repair. The Bailiff administers the oath to the
Captain, and it is always the greater who administers an oath
to the less. The Bailiff alone has the right to use the plural
"we". "Therefore it seems evident that the name of Governor

may be more properly attributed to the Bailiff than to the Captain" (*P.B.C.*).

This audacious claim seems to have sprung from his study of the Old Coutumiers of Normandy, where it was said of the Bailiffs, "There is no one above them except the Duke in the district committed to their care"; and partly perhaps from his experience in Guernsey as Assistant to the Commissioners, for there he had seen the Governor's powers rather drastically curtailed. But his contention was entirely unhistorical. Island Bailiffs had never had such power as Bailiffs of the Bessin or the Cotentin. Early Wardens had treated them as servants, whom they appointed, paid, and dismissed at will. Even under the Tudors, when the Bailiff in theory was appointed by the King, it was absurd to imagine the Duke of Somerset taking orders from a local Seigneur, or Ralegh regarding old George Poulet as his superior officer. This must have been as obvious to Herault as it is to us; but he began a resolute and ingenious campaign for making the Bailiff, not the Governor, the real ruler of the island.

He posed before the Council as the highly efficient official in charge of Jersey. He constantly reported Peyton for neglect of duty:— "The Captain is sending his butler to be Master-Porter of Castle Elizabeth, an office hitherto filled by gentlemen brought up to war. To put there his butler, who only understands serving pots of wine at table, is as bad as to send him pilot to Muscovy" (*S.P.D.*); or again, "There are only four poor men, and they feeble in mind and body, in residence in each of your Castles" (*P.B.C.*); or again "Castle Elizabeth has been abandoned of all its guard save one, who sent on market-day to all the taverns to seek his companions" (*P.B.C.*). In those years of peace Peyton had evidently cut the Castle garrisons almost to vanishing point. Herault suggested that Peyton, instead of receiving all the Crown revenues, defraying all expenses, and keeping what was left, should be paid a fixed salary, and the King's assets be received by an independent official, who "should be bound once a year to render his accounts before your Bailiff"; and he enclosed a balance sheet to show that the King would then draw from the island an income of £1,459 (*P.B.C.*).

Peyton's officers took up the cudgels on his behalf. Philippe Maret (q.v.), the Receiver, who had to pay Herault, took a malicious delight in wounding him on his tenderest spot. His poverty made his smallest perquisites of importance to him ; so Maret kept raising ingenious reasons for witholding, first the 20 sous paid for a taverner's licence, then the fee paid for testing shopkeepers' scales. He challenged also Herault's right to call himself Monsieur de St. Sauveur, asserting that his small estate was on the King's Fief. Aaron Messervy too, whom Peyton left as Lieut.-Governor, when he went to take the cure at Bath, got on Herault's nerves. He resented having one of his Jurats raised to equality with himself. He tried to compel him to live in the Castle, "as Captains use to do". But Messervy was as proud as himself. When summoned to Court, he refused to attend, saying that he was responsible to the King alone.

Peyton then laid a charge against Herault of "usurping the office of Governor", and he was summoned before the Council in Nov. 1616 ; but, when the case was called, Peyton's witnesses had not arrived, "whereat", wrote the Council, "we not a little marvel". It was not till Feb. 1617 that the verdict was given. This was almost a complete vindication:— "We acquit the Bailiff of any undutifulness to the King's Majesty or any injustice in the civil government, but not from heat of words, which have unfittingly fallen from him, for which we thought fit to give a sharp reprehension" (P.B.C.). Peyton was ordered to pay £60 for Herault's expenses in London, and then the rule was laid down, which became a turning point in Jersey Constitutional History:— "We hold it convenient that the charge of the Military Forces be wholly in the Governor and the care of Justice and Civil Affairs in the Bailiff" (A.P.C.).

Three times in the course of his career Herault's conduct was investigated by impartial experts, and on each occasion the verdict was the same. He was irritable (once he threatened to crop the Dénonciateur's ears for a mistake), cantankerous, preposterously self-assertive, but in an age of universal corruption, when even the great Lord Chancellor Bacon was convicted of taking bribes, Herault remained scrupulously honest, upright, and incorruptible.

But there was still far too much friction between local officials. "Things here", he wrote, "are in disorder". So he appealed for a Royal Commission. The Commissioners, Sir Edward Conway, who later became Secretary of State, and Sir William Bird, Master in Chancery, arrived in April 1617. They dealt with an immense number of questions. The Church question was a burning one,—Could the Anglican system be grafted on to the Huguenot Church?—but in this Herault took no decisive part. His sympathies were with the Calvinists ; but, as he wished to keep in with the Council, he lay low and said nothing. His own conduct was again vindicated:— "We find good cause to clear the Bailiff of all personal imputations. His violence is rather in words to keep up his authority, than in act. We believe him, even by the testimony of his enemies, to be very sincere. His place is painful, and he diligent in the execution of it". Maret, the Attorney-General, had brought a long list of charges against him (see article, *Maret, Philippe*), but they were all disproved:— "Whereas Maret laid foul imputations upon the Bailiff of bribery and unlawful proceedings, which upon examination were found by the Commissioners to be false and slanderous, it is ordered that Maret do acknowledge his offence, and make public satisfaction" (*S.P.D.*). But Herault's claim to be supreme in the island was more than the Commissioners could swallow. Following their advice the Council defined the position of Bailiff and Governor:— "Forasmuch as the Governor is trusted by His Majesty with the charge and government of the island, it is ordered that he be known by the title of Governor" (*S.P.D.*). The States must obtain his permission before they hold a meeting, and he was granted "a negative voice", i.e. a power of veto, over any decisions that seemed "prejudicial to His Majesty's service" (*P.B.C.*). But in Court and States the Bailiff was given precedence over the Governor.

Up to this point Herault had been surprisingly successful ; but now he overstepped the mark. In 1620 the King appointed a Dean, and restored the Anglican system. (See *Bandinel, David*). Herault acquiesced with reluctance, and looked askance at the new Ecclesiastical Court, which might be a rival of his own. When Bandinel ordered the election of Churchwardens, and it became clear that these would be sworn in by the Dean's Court, Herault protested vehemently. This robbed him of another small perquisite. "The temporal power", he wrote, "has always administered their oath, authorized their commission, and received their accounts. To take from the

Bailiff the profit of the seal, given him for life, and retrench his jurisdiction without his being heard, is very extraordinary" (S.P.D.). Protest was permissible ; but he went further. He forbad the elections, till the question was settled.

Peyton saw his chance. This was open defiance of the King's Instructions to the Dean. He reported Herault to the Council, who ordered the elections to be held, "notwithstanding any edict of the Bailiff to the contrary (P.B.C.), and summoned Herault to Westminster to explain his conduct. Here his temper tripped him up. "I was too vehement", he said, "in my answers to the Lord Chancellor". He was committed to the Marshalsea, suspended from office, and his duties entrusted to Sir William Parkhurst, (O.C.), a place-hunter, who spent only a few days in Jersey, appointed a Lieut.-Bailiff, and departed to draw for the next few years the Bailiff's salary.

Herault was released the same evening, but forced to sign a bond not to leave London, and was kept kicking his heels about Westminster till Aug. 1624. The death of Sir Ralph Winwood, Secretary of State, had deprived him of a friend at Court, and the Council had grown tired of Jersey squabbles, and hoped that Herault's absence might calm the troubled waters. But he had been appointed for life, and could not be got rid of, unless some serious charge warranted his dismissal. So they tried to persuade him to resign. He was offered a pension of £100 a year, and the pill was gilded with the phrase, "The King having need of his services near his person" (S.P.D.). But Herault demanded a public hearing of the charges against him. At last in 1624 his pertinacity was rewarded. His case was tried, and the Council wrote:— "His Majesty, finding no charge against the Bailiff, and holding it not suitable to remove an officer without sufficient cause, is graciously pleased that John Herault be redintegrated in his office with all perquisites, and that arrears grown due since his sequestration be forthwith paid to him" (S.P.D.). He was nervous about his reception after so long an absence. "I am afraid", he wrote, "of returning to a place of judicature among rich and potent enemies unprovided with means to keep up its dignity (S.P.D.). But he need not have been worried. An Act of the States runs:— "Bailiff Herault having obtained from the King his entire reinstatement, the States assembled to receive him, and three of their body, a Jurat, a Minister, and a Constable, were deputed to escort him to his seat, as a sign of the joy felt at seeing him return happily" (A.E.).

He did not however remain long in the island. The Receiver declared that he could not refund his arrears of salary, as the full amount had already been paid to Parkhurst. Herault sued him, and the Royal Court decided in his favour ; but the Receiver appealed to the Council, and Herault had again to go to Westminster. His case was heard in May 1625 and he was unsuccessful:— "We conceive the sentence against the Receiver is erroneous, neither do we see any cause that Sir J. Peyton should be constrained to a double payment" (S.P.D.). He returned toward the end of the year, and died in St. Helier's on 10 March 1626, and was buried in St. Saviour's Church. He never married.

Olivier, Rector of St. Helier's, said in his funeral sermon: "Though he had faults, as the wisest have, those faults never tarnished his virtues. We know how sincere he was in his Christian profession, God-fearing, constant in prayer, regular in public worship. He was a friend to everyone of good repute, and a scorner of the idle and profane. In private life he was studious, staid, sober, chaste, and generous, specially to poor students, whom he helped in their education, never sparing himself in the service of his country, striving to maintain its rights and liberties, even at his own expense without help or support from anyone" (Bull IV). His very foibles, his obstinacy, his tantrums, his absurd exaggeration of his dignity, helped to accomplish the work for which he is remembered. There was real danger that successive Governors might establish a military dictatorship, in which every department of the island's life, civil as well as military, would be controlled by retired Generals sent over from England. Herault won for Jersey the right to govern itself.

Though dead, the Council had not heard the last of him. His younger brother, who was also named Jean, disputed his will as "contrary to law and custom" (O.C.: S.P.D.). The dispute was carried from the Royal Court to the Council, where it dragged on for years, and was not concluded, owing to "many intricate questions concerning the custom of that island and other cross passages", till Feb. 1652, when, as might have been expected, the will was found to be "duly made" (O.C.). What was left of the "small estate" after the lawyers had done with it, History does not relate. [Authorities quoted above.]

HERIOT, FREDERICK GEORGE, C.B. (1786–1843), Major-General. Born in Jersey 11 January 1786, third son of Roger Heriot, Surgeon of the 13th Foot, then stationed in the island, and Anne, daughter of Major Walter Nugent, a resident in St. Helier's. At the age of fifteen he obtained a commission as Ensign in the 49th. In 1802 his regiment was sent to Canada. When war broke out in 1812 between Britain and the United States, the young officer, now a Captain of 26, was released from regimental duties to be second in command of a volunteer force of French-speaking irregulars, known as the Canadian Voltigeurs. With these he fought all through the war, and for gallant conduct at the Battle of Chrystler's Farm was rewarded by a gold medal and a C.B. When peace was made, he was granted a large tract of land in the Eastern Townships, and there he founded in 1816 the town of Drummondville, named after his old chief, General Sir Gordon Drummond. This is now the capital of Drummond County, Quebec. He laid out the plan himself, and gave the streets the names they still bear. From 1829 to 1833 he represented Drummondville in the Legislative Assembly of Lower Canada, and in 1840 was appointed member of the Executive Council. In 1841 he was promoted Major-General, and died in his home, Comfort Hall, Drummondville, 29 December 1843. He never married.
[Canadian Antiq. and Numism. Journal, 1911. Dic. Can. Biog.]

HUE, CLEMENT (1779–1861), Physician. Brother of Dean Corbet Hue (q.v.). Son of Jean Hue of St. Helier's, merchant. Born at St. Helier's, 1779. Educated at Abingdon Grammar School and Pembroke College, Oxford. B.A. 1801. M.A. 1803. M.D. 1807. Fellow of Royal College of Physicians, 1808. Harveian Orator, 1829. Physician to the Foundling Hospital, 1815–1857. Physician and Lecturer at St. Bartholomew's, 1823—1861. Registrar of National Vaccine Establishment, 1824—1861. He was offered the President's chair of the College of Physicians, but declined it. Died 23 June 1861.

HUE, CORBET (1769—1838), Dean. One of the ten sons of Jean Hue, Vingtenier of St. Helier's, and Anne Dolbert. Brother of Clement Hue (q.v.). Born in St. Helier's 3 July 1769. Matriculated at Oxford from Exeter 1786. B.A. 1790. He was Fellow of Jesus College 1790—1820. He took his M.A. in 1792, his B.D. in 1800, his D.D. in 1818. He became Rector of Braunston, Northants., in 1819, and held this living till his death. His elder brother Nicholas lived with him at Braunston, and a marble memorial in the church records his virtues and his death in 1822. A board on the Church wall records that he gave £50 toward the building of the village school, that Corbet gave £260, and that a male heir of Dr. Clement Hue (q.v.) was to be trustee of the school for ever. In 1823 Corbet was appointed Rector of St. Helier's and Dean ; but he did not resign Braunston. He put in a Curate ; the Registers show that he only paid it three short visits after his appointment to Jersey. At his first appearance in the States he caused a sensation by making a speech in English. Few details of his work as Dean survive, though he had to deal with the difficult and unpleasant case of Edward Le Vavasseur dit Durell (q.v.). He died in St. Helier's 12 Jan. 1838 and there is a monument to his memory in the Town Church. He never married.

HUE, JEHAN (d. 1508), Rector of St. Saviour's and Founder of St. Mannelier's Grammar School. The Hues were a St. Mary's family, mentioned as holding land in that parish in the Extente of 1331. Early in the 15th century Jean Hue of St. Mary's married a wife from St. Saviour's, who brought him a field in that parish. This field in time descended to his second son, Jehan who, after training in the Diocesan Clergy School at Coutances, was ordained in St. Lawrence Church in 1460, by the Bishop of Porphyris in partibus, acting for the Bishop of Coutances, and in 1461 was put in charge of St. Saviour's parish. His actual title seems to have been rather indefinite. The Vicar-General of the Diocese describes him as 'Rector and Curé or rather Perpetual Curate' (*Rector et Curatus seu Vicarius Perpetuus*). He was evidently a man of business-like habits. In his first year he compiled a Register, which remains the most detailed picture we possess of Church life of the period. It gives full particulars of the Rector's income, which lands paid tithes and which owed one or two cabots of corn a year ; full details of all benefactions left to the poor, and of the Chuch's income. Five houses in the parish were responsible for supplying wax for the church candles, eight for supplying corn to make the *pain béni*, eleven for supplying wine for the Mass. It gives the income and rules of the four Fraternities, the Clerks of St. Saviour, the Clerks of St. Katherine, the Clerks of St. Nicholas' Feast in Winter and those of his Feast in Summer. Every member absent from the Fraternity Mass was fined two *pots* of good wine. Every sister had to provide a capon for the community supper. It gives the names of everyone buried in the Church and what benefactions they had left for the privilege. Later on he added the benefactions made in his own time. Richard le Viellard gave the Church an image of St. Sebastian. Madame Philippe De Carteret left two cabots of wheat rente to maintain the candle before the Crucifix. The mother of Alinor Poingdestre left one cabot of rente to maintain the candle before our Lady of Pity. Hue made benefactions of his own. In 1480 he gave one cabotel of rente to provide *pain béni* for the Feast of the Transfiguration. In 1493 he gave nine cabots of rente to provide an Obit every 27th. of November for the souls of his parents. For this he left detailed instructions. On the previous day, the Curé, a Chaplain, and the Cousteur were to recite the Commendation. On the day itself three masses were to be sung, a Mass of the Virgin, a Mass of the Holy Spirit, and a Mass for the Dead by five Priests and a choir of young children. By his will he left to his own Church a pair of black damask vestments and a silver chalice worth forty crowns of gold. To each of the other Churches in the island he left a silver groat, to the Chapels in his own parish and to the Chapels of St. Maur, Ste. Marie de Grouville, Notre Dame des Pas, St. Brelade, and Ste. Marie de Rozel two sterlings, and to St. Katherine's Chapel a silver groat. He left his books to a fellow priest, Nicolas Dolbel, and he directed his executors to divide the rest of his property among the poor.

But the benefaction by which he is best remembered is his foundation of St. Mannelier's Grammar School in 1477. Near the field he had inherited from his mother stood an old chapel dedicated to St. Magloire, locally known as St. Mannelier. All the documents connected with this gift have been preserved. First, a letter (7 Sept. 1477) from Sir Richard Harliston, the Governor, to the Dean, Bailiff, and Jurats, stating that Hue had called his attention to the fact that the island schools were of little value for lack of good masters and suitable premises, and that he had offered to build a house in a field near the chapel of St. Manely, which had a fine situation, good water, was approached by good roads, and was central for the six eastern parishes, in which a Master could live rent free and have the field as his endowment. If the island would accept this offer, and petition the King to free it from the Law of Mortmain, the Governor would support their request. Next came a letter from Guille Hamptonne, the Lieut.-Bailiff, saying that the Royal Court had accepted the gift. By this time Hue had expanded it, offering to build an additional room for the Master to live in, and to set aside a sum to free the property from all seigneurial dues. The school was to be entirely free, even for boarders, and the Master, if a Priest, must say a weekly Mass in the Chapel for the King, the Governor, Hue's parents, and all future benefactors. In February 1478, at a Synod at St. John's, the Dean gave his written approval to the scheme, adding that the Master and scholars must sing Mass in the Chapel on all Festivals, and that the Master must help the Curé of St. Saviour's on Sundays. Two years later (Oct. 1480) came a formal ratification of the gift from the Vicar-General of Coutances, and in June 1481 the Bishop of Coutances sent a Pastoral exhorting all the faithful in the island to see that the buildings were kept in good repair, and granting twenty days remission of penance to all who would help in this work. In 1496 Hue saw his school receive further endowments. (See *Neel, Jean* and *Tehy, Vincent*).

We get one or two other glimpses of Hue at work. In 1481 he was appointed by the Parishioners one of the Trustees of the Hotel Dieu, an almshouse for the poor which stood to the north of the Church. The Parish Priest in those days was also the

Parish Lawyer. A contract of 1481 describes him as 'Curé of St. Saviour's and Procureur and Attorney-General of the said parish'. In 1502 we find him drawing up a marriage contract between Philippe Le Fayvre and Tomasse Pirouet. But, whenever we see him, he is always engaged in his parish work. He lived in exciting times. In the year of his appointment the French conquered the island, and ruled it for seven years. When they were expelled, Harliston the Governor supported the Yorkists, and was besieged in Mont Orgueil. Baker, the next Governor, was in constant conflict with the people. But no trace of these troubles appears in any of the good Curé's writings. His sole interest seems to have been the care of his Church and Parish. He died probably in 1508, for in Feb. 1509 his successor was appointed to St. Saviour's 'vacant through the death of Sire Hue'. [There is an account of the Hue family in *Bull.* V. Copies of his Register, the ducuments connected with St. Mannelier, and of many contracts which refer to him are among the MSS in the Société's Library.]

JACOB, HENRY, Sectary. See Appendix II.

JANVRIN, PHILIPPE VALPY DIT (1677—1721), of "Janvrin's Tomb", Captain of the *Esther*. Third son of Jacques Valpy dit Janvrin of St. Brelade's and Marie Le Couteur. Born in St. Brelade's 1677. Married Elizabeth, daughter of Philippe Orange, in St. Brelade's Church on 27 Sept. 1710. The following extracts give the story of his death and burial. Jean Dauvergne's contemporary Diary says:— "While an order was in force that every vessel that came from certain ports must go into quarantine, because of the plague at Marseilles and in other parts of France, there arrived from Bordeaux and other places a vessel named the *Esther* of which Mr. Philippe Janvrin was master, meaning to spend its period of quarantine beneath the house of the Seigneur of Noirmont. As the said Janvrin died on board, and no one, not even his relations, wife, or children, dared to go to him, permission was given by the Court with the consent of the Lieut.-Governor to bury him on a little islet, called the Ile ès Guerdains, only three persons to carry him in the boat, the Minister and people to remain on the hill. When the signal was given, the Minister read the usual Service for the Burial of the Dead". The entry in the Burial Register at St. Brelade's runs:— "Mons. Philippe Janvrin, returning from Nantes, and being forced to undergo quarantine in the harbour of Belle Croute, died at the end of two days on board his ship. The Court ordered that he should be buried on an islet called the Ile au Guerdoin, and he was buried thus on 27 Sept. 1721". The inscription on his tombstone ran:— "Here awaiting a happy resurrection lies the body of Philippe Janvrin of St. Brelade's, who having been attacked by an ordinary fever, while returning from Nantes to Jersey, died in his vessel on 25 Sept. 1721 aged 44 on the 2nd day of quarantine, which he was obliged to undergo, because of the plague which desolated part of the Kingdom of France. The Magistrates of the isle having ordered that he should be buried in this spot, Elizabeth Orange, deeply touched by the death of her dear and faithful husband, has caused this tomb to be erected as a sad and pious monument of her love and to preserve his memory". He had five children, Philippe (b. 1713), Jacques (b. 1715), Jean, Elizabeth, who died young, and another Elizabeth (b. 1718). Guide books state that his body was later removed to St. Brelade's churchyard, but there is no entry of this reburial in the Register nor is there any trace of his tombstone in the churchyard. If left on the islet, the stone was probably destroyed, when ninety years later the tower was built during the Napoleonic wars.

JEAN, PHILIPPE (1755—1802), Portrait-painter and Miniaturist. Son of Nicolas Jean junior and Marie Grandin. Born 1755, and baptized in St. Ouen's Church 30 Nov. Money's Diary (written 1798) speaks of him as "a self-taught genius, originally a barber here", i.e. in Jersey (Bull XII). Edward's Anecdotes of Painters (1808) says:— "He was brought up in the Navy; during the peace which succeeded the American War he applied himself to the study of miniature painting, in which he acquired much skill". By 1784 he was established as a well-known artist in London. In that year he drew an allegorical frontispiece for the new *Magasin de l'Ile de Jersey* representing the Spirit of Printing laying at the feet of Jersey a compositor's case of type and a couple of inking-pads, and introducing a swarm of cherubs personifying music, painting, architecture, and all the other arts and sciences, while light from the printing-press shines on the farmer at the plough and the sailor on the sea.

His earliest dated miniature seems to be that of the Hon. Miss Berkeley, painted in 1785. From 1786 onward the *Gazette de Jersey* contains frequent paragraphs recording his success in London. Between 1787 and 1802 he exhibited 118 pictures in the Royal Academy, which still retains one striking example of his skill, a portrait of Mrs. Malin, the first Academy sweeper (i.e. charwoman), painted in 1788. But he did not neglect his island clients. An advertisement in the *Gazette* in 1788 thanked his friends in Jersey for their patronage, and assured them that he would spare no pains to make himself still more worthy of their favour.

He had three distinct styles. One was large, almost lifesize, oil paintings, such as the portrait of George III in the Royal Court. In 1795 the States, "having long desired to possess a portrait of His Majesty", petitioned the King to grant a sitting to Jean, and he consented. When this picture was exhibited in the Royal Academy of 1796, it was severely criticized. Pasquin's *Critical Guide* praises two of Jean's miniatures, but of the King's portrait it says:— "This is a complicated copy, the body being after Sir Joshua Reynolds, the head after Gainsborough, the whole so imperfectly managed, that it were a sort of petit treason to offer any adoration to objects so equivocal". Edwards (loc. cit.) bluntly charged him with having copied the portrait by Sir Joshua Reynolds in the Council Room of the Royal Academy. But the unveiling of the picture in Jersey was made an imposing ceremony. It was placed on the Court steps for everyone to see. The Lieutenant-Governor stood on one side, the Bailiff on the other. Admiral Dauvergne and the officers of the fleet were present. The portrait was unveiled. The Militia marched past and saluted. Then amid the thundering of cannon it was hung on the Court House wall. A banquet followed in the evening, at which Jean was presented with a silver-gilt tea-urn (now in the S.J. Museum). The portrait of Lieut.-Bailiff Thomas Pipon (q.v.) in the Court is also probably his work; and he painted another large-scale portrait of Queen Caroline.

More pleasing is his work on smaller canvases. Good examples of this are his portraits of Mrs. Kemble as Urania and of Sir John Dick. The S.J. Art Gallery contains a portrait of an unknown man in this style. Occasionally he worked in water-colours, and his portrait of Admiral Rodney in the same Gallery shows that he got good results in this medium. It is however as a miniaturist that he excelled. In this delicate art he varied his style constantly, imitating sometimes Cosway, sometimes Shelley, sometimes Meyer. His best miniatures are very good indeed. The S.J. Museum has a group of them, including a charming one of his second wife and his children, one of the lady alone, and one of Major Peirson. In the National Portrait Gallery is one of Dominic Serres, the artist. Three in the Victoria and Albert Museum are merely catalogued, 'A Child', 'A Gentleman', 'A Gentleman'.

Jean was frequently patronized by Royalty. He painted miniatures of Queen Caroline, the Duke of Clarence, the Duke of Gloucester, the Duchess of Gloucester, their daughter Princess Sophia Matilda, and their son Prince William. Other well-known persons, whose miniatures he exhibited in the Academy, were fellow-artists like Paul Sandby R.A., John Richards R.A., Francis Newton R.A., Benjamin West R.A., singers like Madame Mara, Signora Storace, and the boy Martin Walsh, Society leaders like Lady Fauconberg, Lady Balcarres, Lady Mansfield, Lady Waldegrave, sailors like Admiral Mount-Edgecumbe, Admiral Saumarez, Admiral Barrington (the S.J. has a coloured print of this), play-wrights like Miles Andrews and Edward Topham, Benevolent Birch the banker, and Cyril Jackson, Dean of Christ Church, Oxford. Some of his miniatures are character-sketches, e.g. 'Mary Owen, a Welsh Pedlar', or 'A Jewish Top-seller'. But the majority can be no longer identified, and are labelled in the Galleries 'Portrait of a Naval Officer', 'Portrait of a Nobleman', 'Portrait of a Lady of Quality'.

Jean's first wife was Anne Noel, who died in June 1787. By her he had one son, Roger, who died young. He then married Sara, daughter of Aaron De Ste. Croix. By her he had

three daughters, Hariot a pianist, and Mary and Henriette
Elizabeth, who kept a School for Young Ladies in Don Street.
He lived first at 50 Margaret Street, Cavendish Square, and then
in George Street, Hanover Square, but frequently visited Jersey.
He travelled much about the country to paint his clients in their
homes, and died on 12 Sept. 1802 in Captain Hodges' house
at Hempstead, Kent, where he was painting a portrait. His
own portrait, painted by himself, is in the S.J. Art Gallery.
He left his family badly off, and in 1810 the States granted
"permission to Sara De Ste. Croix, widow of the distinguished
artist, Philippe Jean, to dispose of her husband's pictures by
lottery". In 1850 the Hospital Committee commissioned Demoi-
selle Henriette Elizabeth Jean to copy the portraits of François
Bartlett and Marie Mauger (q.v.) for their Committee Room".
[Long's *British Miniaturists* ; *Bull.* VI.]

JEUNE, FRANCIS HENRY, BARON ST. HELIER (1843—
1905), Judge. Eldest son of François Jeune, Dean of Jersey
(q.v.), and Margaret Dyne Symons. Born in the Deanery, St.
Helier's, 17 March 1843. Educated at Exmouth, then at Har-
row (1856—61). He won a Balliol scholarship at Oxford, gained
a first-class in Moderations 1863 and in the Final Classical
School 1865. In 1864 he was President of the Union. In 1863
he won the Stanhope prize for an essay on 'The Influence of
the Feudal System on Character', and in 1867 the Arnold
prize for one on 'The Mohammedan Power in India'. In 1874
he became Fellow of Hertford.

He was called to the Bar by the Inner Temple, 17 Nov. 1868.
Before that, he had worked in the office of Baxter, Rose, and
Norton, Solicitors : and in 1869 had been sent by them to
Australia to investigate the claim of Arthur Orton to be Sir
Roger Tichborne. He was Junior Counsel for the Plaintiff in
the famous action which followed. A large part of his practice
was in ecclesiastical cases, generally on the Evangelical side.
He appeared against the Ritualists in the Mackonochie, Green,
Dale, Enraght, and Bell-Cox cases, but in the trial of the Bishop
of Lincoln he was counsel for the Bishop. He served on the
Royal Commission on Ecclesiastical Patronage in 1874, on that

on Ecclesiastical Courts in 1881, and on that on Ecclesiastical Discipline in 1904. Before his appointment to the Bench he was Chancellor of eight dioceses. A case of a different character was his pleading before the Privy Council for the life of Louis Riel, the Canadian rebel.

In 1880 he stood as Conservative candidate for Colchester, but lost by two votes. He then sat as one of three commissioners to inquire into charges of corruption at the Sandwich election, and their report led to the disfranchisement of the borough. In 1888 he became a Queen's Counsel, and in 1890 declined the Solicitor-Generalship. In 1891 he was made Judge in the Probate, Divorce, and Admiralty division, and in 1892 President of this division. Of his new work he remarked, "It is hard to do justice between man and man, harder still between ship and ship, but hardest of all between man and woman". The Admiralty work at first gave him most trouble, for of shipping he had no special knowledge, but by hard reading he speedily mastered the necessary technical information. The legal world soon came to regard him as a great Judge, painstaking, courteous, and considerate, a sound lawyer and a strong man. Once he vindicated the decorum of his Court by committing to prison the Duchess of Sutherland. He made his division a model of efficiency and dispatch, and arrears were practically unknown. "He continued the line", said the *Times*, "of Judges at once scholars and men of the world, bringing to law the culture and large amenities, which redeem its administration from pedantry and self-sufficiency".

In 1891 he was knighted, and in 1892 became a Privy Councillor. In the same year he added to his duties that of Judge-Advocate-General, the official who has to confirm or quash the finding of every general court-martial, a post which during the South African War gave him much extra work. His services were rewarded by his creation as K.C.B. in 1897 and G.C.B. in 1902. His health, which had for some time been failing, was gravely affected by the death of his only son in India in 1904, and in Jan. 1905 he resigned the Presidency of his division. He was then created a peer, and chose the title Baron St. Hélier. (He insisted on the acute accent). "He was", wrote his wife, "most devoted to his native town, and more proud of taking the name of St. Hélier than of anything else". He died in his house in Harley Street, 9 April 1905, and was buried in the churchyard of Chieveley, Berks., of which he was Vicar's Warden. In appearance he was tall and distinguished. His peaked beard and eyeglass suggested, according to one London daily, a dashing courtier of King Charles II's time. He married in 1881 Susan Mary Elizabeth Stewart-Mackenzie, widow of Lieut.-Colonel the Hon. John Constantine Stanley. He had one son, Christian Francis Seaforth (b. 1882) of the Grenadier Guards. [*Dic. Nat. Biog.* ; *Memorials of Lord St. Hélier* by a Jerseyman ; Lady St. Hélier's *Memories of Fifty Years* ; *Diary of an Oxford Lady*, i.e. his mother.]

JEUNE FRANCOIS (1806—1868), Dean of Jersey, Bishop of Peterborough. The Jeunes, a French Huguenot family, had settled in Jersey in the reign of Elizabeth. When the Methodist movement reached the island, they were some of its earliest supporters. In 1787 François Jeune of Les Vaux, St. Aubin's, the Dean's grandfather, furnished a shed in his yard as a Methodist Meeting-Place, a shed often wrecked by the local roughs. He and his wife went later as Methodist missionaries to the French-speaking slaves of Grenada, Windward Islands. His son, François, the Dean's father, remained a miller at St. Aubin's, and in 1800 was sentenced to eight days' solitary confinement on bread and water for refusing to do Militia drill on Sunday. He married Elisabeth Le Capelain. François, their eldest son, was born at Peterborough House, St. Aubin's, 22 May 1806. He was educated at Le Maistre's School, St. Aubin's, at St. Servan's College, Rennes, and at Saumur University. Sir Jean de Veulle, the Bailiff, then advised him to go to Oxford. He matriculated from Pembroke, 1822, was elected to a Morley scholarship, passed first class in the final school, and graduated B.A. 1827, M.A. 1830, D.C.L. 1854. From 1828 to 1832 he was Tutor of his College, and from 1830 to 1837 Fellow. In 1832 he went to Canada as Secretary to the Governor-General, Sir John Colburn. In 1834 he returned to England, and became Head Master of King Edward's Grammar School, Birmingham, which he resuscitated and remodelled. In 1836 he married Margaret Dyne, only child of Henry Symons of Axbridge.

In 1838 he became Dean of Jersey and Rector of St. Helier's.
He tackled his new work with energy. He persuaded the parish
to sell the dilapidated old Rectory, next door to the Church,
and build the present one. He obtained a grant from the States
for rebuilding St. Anastase Grammar School. He raised money
to build St. Matthew's Church (consecrated 1843) and St. Mark's
Church (opened 1844). But his six years in Jersey were not
happy ones. He inherited from Dean Hue the unsavoury Durell
Case (See *Le Vavasseur dit Durell, Edouard*). Hue had suspended Durell, but the Royal Court had decided that the Ecclesiastical Court had exceeded its powers, and Durell went on conducting Services in an empty church. Jeune felt that this scandal
must be stopped, and appealed to the Privy Council, which
reversed the judgement of the Royal Court ; and Durell was
forced to retire into private life.

Meanwhile the powerful Rose Party, of which Durell had
been a leader, had rallied round the accused Rector. The Rose
papers reviled the Dean with incredible scurrility, and made
him publicly declare that he bitterly regretted having returned
to Jersey. Many portraits survive (There is one in Victoria
College) that show that the Dean was a singularly handsome
man, yet the *Miroir* wrote of him:— "His fat face is almost
square, his appearance vulgar, his expression coarse. His enormous nose is triangular like the pointer of a sun-dial, but he
can hold it all in his loose, lubberly, mouth, when he draws
his lower lip over it. His eyes protrude like those of a fat ox.
His look is stupid and crafty".

The *Impartial* never ceased to sneer at "our very reverend,
very holy, very winsome Father in God" and his "sumptuous
palace", which it nicknamed "the Val Plaisant Folly". Week
after week it had a column headed *A monsieur le Doyen*,
holding him up to ridicule. One week they accused the Parish
Clerk of a gross act of cruelty. A poor man had suffered from
insomnia. He had tried every known remedy. At last he was
advised to hear the Dean preach. The effect was miraculous.
He sank into health-giving slumber. But the cure was spoiled
by the Clerk shaking him, because his snores were disturbing
the preacher. The worst offender was the *Jersey Gazette*. In
1840 a crazy pot-boy tried to shoot the Queen. The special
Form of Thanksgiving for her escape did not reach the island
in time for use on the following Sunday. The *Gazette* accused

Jeune of suppressing it, and of preaching, in "a spirit that might have done honour to a McNeil, a Roby, or a Bradshaw", that Sovereigns who forget their Maker should be put to death. (He had preached a quite unobjectionable sermon on Samuel's rebuke to Saul). He sued the publisher for libel, but failed through a legal quibble. The culprit claimed that the summons was addressed to François Romeril, whereas he was François Amice Romeril (q.v.).

In 1843 Jeune was offered the Bishopric of New Brunswick in Canada, which he declined. A few months' later the London *Morning Herald* and other papers announced that the Archbishop was pressing the Government to separate the Channel Islands from Winchester and make them a separate Diocese, and that Jeune would be the first Bishop. But this came to nothing. In 1843 he became a Canon of Gloucester and Vicar of Taynton, Gloucestershire, posts which he retained for twenty-one years. In 1844 he was elected Master of his old College. Here he was in his element. He initiated sweeping reforms, which ranged from sacking the famous French cook to abolishing compulsory Communion. "Henceforth, no one will be compelled to eat to his own damnation". The historian of Pembroke says : — "During the twenty years of his Mastership he lifted a small and poor college into a leading position. As a reformer he went on his way like a Roman road, regardless of obstacles and scenery". Cordy Jeaffreson in his *Annals of Oxford* writes : — "He effected wonders for the Society of which he was ruler. He gave it honorable status in the Class-lists, procured the enlargement of its buildings, reformed its economy for the benefit of students of narrow means, and was indefatigable in his endeavours to inspire its members with manliness of purpose and contempt of frivolity. A finer Master of a College never lived".

He reformed not only his College, but his University. When in 1850 the Government appointed a University Commission, Jeune was one of the Seven, and undoubtedly the leading spirit. He never missed a meeting, and himself drafted the greater part of their Report. The result was that the Colleges were freed from mediaeval statutes and invested with new constitutions. Fellowships were thrown open to merit. Scholarships were increased ; vexatious oaths swept away. To Jeune is also ascribed the establishment of the Schools of Natural Science and of Law and Modern History.

He was the ablest man of business in Oxford. Gladstone said that he would have made an admirable Chancellor of the Exchequer. From 1858 to 1862 he was Vice-Chancellor of the University. The domestic side of his Oxford life is pictured in his wife's diary, which has been published as *The Diary of an Oxford Lady*. He did not lose interest in Jersey. When Victoria College was planned, the committee constantly consulted him, and on every knotty point accepted his advice.

In 1856 Palmerston offered him the Bishopric of Gloucester. He mentioned this to friends in Oxford, and someone sent the news to the *Times*. The Queen knew nothing of this, until she read the paper, and so she refused to sanction the appointment. In 1861 Palmerston nominated him again for the Bishopric of Durham, but the Queen had not forgiven him. In Jan. 1864 however he became Dean of Lincoln, and a few months later Bishop of Peterborough. In 1865 he revisited Jersey and laid the foundation stones of St. Simon's Church and St. James' Schools. He died at Whitby, 21 Aug. 1868, after a brief episcopate which was described as of "dragoon-like vigour", and was buried in his cathedral yard. He had three sons, one of whom became Lord St. Hélier (see above), and two daughters. In the lane off Mont les Vaux, St. Aubin's, is a ruined house bearing the inscription F.I.: M.C. 1776, the initials of the Bishop's grandparents, François Jeune and Marie Carcaud. [*Dic. Nat. Biog.* ; Macleane's *History of Pembroke College* ; Le Lièvre's *Histoire du Méthodisme dans les Iles de la Manche* ; Local Newspapers ; Jeune's detailed plan for Victoria College is printed in *Actes des Administrateurs des Impots sur l'établissement d'un College dans cette Ile. 1847.*]

JOSLIN, FRANCIS JOHN (1874—1915), Major. Son of John James Joslin and Mary Ann Sarah Cabot. Born in Almorah Crescent 2 Sept. 1874. Educated at Victoria College 1886—92. Entered the Army throught the Militia, and obtained a commission in the Royal West Kent Regt. 1895. He served through the South African War, being present at the actions of Biddulphsberg and Wittenbergen. He was mentioned in despatches, and obtained the Queen's Medal with three clasps and the King's with two. He was Adjutant of his Battalion 1904—7. He travelled on Secret Service in the interior of China, and received the thanks of the War Office for his work. He then passed through the Staff College, Quetta, joined the Headquarters' Staff, and was Brigade-Major to General Braithwaite, another Old Victorian, at the great Durbar at Delhi. He had travelled extensively, and was well-known as a writer on military subjects. In the First World War he was Commandant on Lines of Communication at Rouen ; but in Feb. 1915 he rejoined his regiment, which had suffered severely, and was Second in Command of his Battalion. On 17 April he led the assault which captured Hill 60 near Ypres, but on the following morning he was killed during a German counter-attack.

JOYCE, VALENTINE (1769—   ?), Leader of the Mutiny at Spithead. Son of Valentine Joyce, one of the Corps of Invalids stationed in Jersey, and Elizabeth Lamb. Born in Elizabeth Castle, 1769, and baptized there, Aug. 13. For a time he was a tobacconist in Belfast, but then joined the Navy. By 1797 he had risen to be Quartermaster's Mate in the *Royal George* (100 guns), which shows that he was a sound seaman. The Fleet alone at this time stood between the country and invasion, but it was seething with discontent. Parliament had raised the pay of the Army, but the pay of the Navy still remained what it had been under Cromwell. The food was disgusting. The men were prisoners on the ships, for leave was hardly ever granted. There was no system by which complaints against brutal officers could be investgated. Joyce was not the original instigator of the mutiny. It began in the *Queen Charlotte*, which suggested that every ship at Spithead should petition the Admiralty to redress grievances. No notice was taken of these petitions ; so on Easter Sunday 1797, when the order was given to the Fleet to put to sea, the men in all the sixteen line-of-battle-ships refused to weigh anchor. The *Queen Charlotte* invited the other ships each to send two delegates to form a "General Assembly". Joyce was chosen as one of those from the *Royal George*.

From the first meeting Joyce took the lead, and in all future correspondence with the Admiralty always signed first. The policy of the Delegates was by no means extreme. Strict discipline was to be maintained, watches kept, respect shown to officers. Only the big ships were to remain anchored. Frigates and sloops required for convoys were to obey orders. Trade must not be hampered. On the other hand the Delegates took over the command of the Fleet. When visiting ships they were received with the ritual reserved for Captains. Earl Spencer, First Lord of the Admiralty, hurried to Portsmouth, and offered certain concessions. During Joyce's absence on shore Admiral Gardner visited the Delegates, and persuaded them to accept these. Joyce returned just in time to prevent them from signing the letter, and induced them to insist that the increase in pay must be made firm by an Act of Parliament, and the mutineers' safety secured by the King's Pardon. Spencer went to London, and returned with the Pardon, and everyone regarded the mutiny as ended.

But the ways of Parliament are leisurely. The promised Act could not be produced with the same promptness as the Pardon. The sailors waited three weeks, and then suspected that they were being bamboozled. The mutiny flared up again with increased violence. On the *London* there was bloodshed. The First Lieutenant shot a gunner, and was about to be hanged by the men, when Joyce arrived, and flung his arms around him crying, 'If you hang this young man, you must hang me'. He calmed the crew, and there was no more talk of summary executions ; but all unpopular officers were put ashore, and the ships moved across to St. Helen's. The Government, now thoroughly alarmed, hurried the Bill through Parliament, and sent the most popular living Admiral, the aged Lord Howe, Black Dick as the sailors called him, to Portsmouth as peacemaker. Burke bitterly denounced the disgrace of "sending the first name in the Navy to take the law from Joyce". But Howe was successful, even though just before his arrival the position had worsened through an attempt to entrap Joyce. A Government agent discovered that his parents were living in Portsmouth. A message was sent to him that his mother was dying ; but he arrived with such a bodyguard of sailors that the plot came to nothing.

Howe did not hesitate to deal directly with Joyce and the Delegates. He visited every ship and addressed the men. He produced the Act of Parliament and a new King's Amnesty. He dismissed 59 officers, including an Admiral and four Captains. When Joyce called at the Governor's House to arrange the final scene, Howe invited him in to drink a glass of wine. Next day the Delegates escorted Howe around the Fleet. He visited almost every ship, beginning with Joyce's *Royal George*. On returning to Portsmouth he entertained the Delegates to dinner. Next morning every mutineer reported for duty. No one was victimized. Joyce retained his position as Quartermaster's Mate. Great reforms had been won, not only for the Channel Fleet, but for the whole Navy. Very different was the later Mutiny at the Nore, which under wilder leadership blockaded London, plundered the Isles of Grain and Sheppey, and ended in ghastly hangings, floggings, and imprisonments. [Manwaring and Dobrée's *Floating Republic ;* Gill's *Naval Mutinies of 1797 ;* Neale's *History of the Mutiny at Spithead and the Nore.*]

KEMPENFELT, RICHARD, Admiral.   See Appendix II.

KNAPP, HENRY JOHN (1779—1850), Priest in Ordinary to George IV, William IV, and Victoria. The Knapps had been settled in Guernsey for many generations. Henry John's grandfather, Henry Knapp, was a famous Guernsey privateer, Captain of the *Hope* (100 tons, 14 guns, 70 men). His father, Gabriel Knapp, moved to Jersey about 1777, and married Anne, daughter of Philip Taylor. He became a Lieutenant in the Town Battery. Henry John was born in 1779, and baptized in the Town Church on 29 January. He matriculated at Oxford from Pembroke College in 1795, and the following year received a grant from the Don Baudains. He took his B.A.

in 1800, his M.A. in 1804, his B.D. and D.D. in 1840. In 1816 he joined the staff of St. Paul's Cathedral, and rose steadily through the ranks of the Minor Canons, becoming Librarian 1821—4, Senior Cardinal 1824—33, and Sub-dean 1833—50. In 1821 he was appointed Priest of the Chapel Royal and Vicar of Kingsbury, Middlesex ; and in 1833 the Dean and Chapter presented him to the rich Vicarage of Willesden. He was a prominent Freemason, and in 1813 was sent as Deputation from the Grand Lodge to open a new Lodge in Jersey. From 1814 to 1817 he was Grand Chaplain of the United Grand Lodge. When Dean Hue (q.v.) died in 1838, the island expected Knapp to succeed him, but the Crown chose Hemery (q.v.). Knapp's *Abridgement of Universal History*, published in 1810, reached a sixth edition in 1830. He also published a large number of sermons, including some preached in French in the French Church in Westminster, and an *Appeal to the Bishop of London as Visitor of St. Paul's Cathedral* 1848. He married Elizabeth Jenkyns ; and died without children on 18 July 1850. [Knapp's *History of the Knapp Families*.]

LA CLOCHE, ETIENNE (d. 1653), Rector of St. Ouen's. Son of Edouard La Cloche, Centenier of St. Helier's, and Elisabeth Le Gallais. He was one of the island noblesse, his first cousin being Seigneur of Longueville, and he himself connected by marriage with the Seigneurs of Trinity and St Ouen's. He was regarded as a very rich man. He owned much property in Jersey including the Malassis Mill and other mills. Brevint says that he bought more than a hundred vergées of land near Southampton, and his wife had a dowry in Brittany. He was probably the "rich preacher" mentioned in a letter of the bogus J. La Cloche (q.v.). In 1612 the Minutes of the Calvinist Colloquy show that the parish of St. Peter's asked that he might be appointed Rector, and the Colloquy supported this request ; but the Governor had other plans (See *Messervy, Elie*). In 1625 he was appointed Rector of St. Ouen's. He was evidently a self-willed man, impatient of control, and he soon got into trouble with the Ecclesiastical Court. He had a house on Mont au Prêtre, St. Helier's, and refused to leave it to live in his parish. Here at least three of his children were born, and baptized in the Town Church. In 1624 the Vice-Dean charged him with absenting himself from his parish, and going to England in spite of a written prohibition from the Dean. La Cloche complained of "the tyranny of the Vice-Dean, who issued prohibitions like a Pope"; but he was ordered to apologize for his conduct. In May 1630 he was again prosecuted. At the Dean's Visitation he refused "to explain the cause of his non-residence or his neglect to officiate at funerals, to visit the sick, or to catechize the young, hoping by his obstruction to make himself independent of all authority". The Court decided: — "In view of his contemptuous insubordination toward his superior, notwithstanding the friendly offers made to overlook his contumacy, if he would agree to live in his parish and perform his neglected duties, in view too of his scornful disregard of the salutary reproofs of the Lieut.-Governor and of the Attorney-General, in view too of his absence from Court on three occasions, though duly summoned, he is suspended from his ministry". This sentence he apparently ignored, for in July 1631 "in virtue of an order from the Bishop of Winchester" he was given six weeks to take up his residence or be suspended. Some compromise must then have been arranged, for there were no further complaints, though thirteen years later his home was still on Mont au Prêtre. In 1627 he quarrelled with Jacques Dauvergne, Constable of St. Ouen's, and was fined for "maltreating him by word and deed".

When the Civil War reached Jersey, he was an outspoken Royalist; but for a time the Parliamentarians left the clergy undisturbed. In July 1643, when Gédeon De Carteret died in Elizabeth Castle, and the besiegers allowed the coffin to be taken to St. Ouen's for burial, La Cloche officiated at the funeral. In August the dying Sir Philippe De Carteret (q.v.) asked that he might be allowed to come to minister to him, but this was refused. When however Lydcot, the Parliamentary Lieut.-Governor, arrived in September, La Cloche, fearing imprisonment in England, escaped to St. Malo. His goods, sheep, and horses were seized, and even the new flooring in his house ripped up, and three waggon-loads of the timber taken to build shelters on the Mont de la Ville for the gunners bombarding the Castle. The *Journal* of his brother-in-law,

Jean Chevalier (q.v.), who had married his sister Marie, now often mentions him. In October he was waiting for a favourable wind to carry to the King a petition from the Royalist exiles in St. Malo urging that steps should be taken to recover Jersey, when he learnt that George Carteret (q.v.) had been ordered to do what they asked. He then volunteered to carry to the island the King's Proclamation. With Jean Dumaresq, Constable of St. Ouen's on 28 Oct. he landed after dark in an unguarded creek near Plemont, and sent a letter by Jacques Guillaume, husband of his daughter Douce, to be delivered to Lydcot. When Lydcot read it, he broke Guillaume's head with his stick, and tore the letter and burnt it, for it bade him prepare for the coming of the King's men and a Governor appointed by the King. The following day was Sunday. La Cloche went to his church, where another Minister was taking the service, and, after baptizing a baby, read the Proclamation from the pulpit, and "harangued his parishioners, telling them that the King had pledged his word to maintain Religion as it was in the days of Elizabeth (i.e. Presbyterianism), and to pardon all who had rebelled against him, provided they laid down their arms". He had hoped to get his parish to rise, before the authorities heard what was happening, and then to call a meeting of the States; but Lydcot was too quick for him. At dawn next morning he arrived with troops at Vinchelez de Bas Manor, where La Cloche was hiding; and the Rector fled by a back door, and eventually took refuge in Mont Orgueil. His attempted *coup* had failed. His house was again sacked, though most of the valuables had been hidden; a reward of 20 crowns was offered for his capture; and his tenants were forbidden to pay him rent. Three weeks later George Carteret arrived, and the Parliamentary regime collapsed.

La Cloche then fell out with his own party. Carteret financed his government by privateering, which was so like piracy that the King eventually had to forbid it. In July 1645 La Cloche denounced this from the pulpit, declaring that Carteret was making Jersey a second Dunkirk (a notorious haunt of pirates). He was promptly arrested, and imprisoned for eleven months in Mont Orgueil without ink or paper. Here various officials visited him, offering him freedom, if he would recant and pay a fine; but he stubbornly refused. He was then deprived of fire and candle, and in May 1646 banished to Brittany, whence he made his way to London. The MS. of Chevalier's *Journal* gives a long letter that he wrote to his parishioners, but this is omitted in the printed edition. In Jan. 1648 his wife Esther De La Planche of Brittany (in some documents her name is anglicized as Planson) was banished to St. Malo for writing a letter to the Countess of Ducé complaining of Carteret's tyranny in preventing her tenants and millers from paying their rent. Six months later her eldest son Louis was drunk, and, when someone said, 'Can I do you service?' replied, 'Take my sword and run it through Sir George'. He too was exiled. In June, when her younger son Jean returned to Jersey from school, he was deported also. In 1651 however, when Jersey was threatened with a Parliamentary invasion, Louis made his peace with Carteret, and arrived with two fine horses ; "but", says Chevalier, "when the Parliament men came, he behaved like the rest and turned tail, and Col. Heane secured those horses". When Carteret had been driven out, La Cloche came back to Jersey. He was not allowed to return to his parish, but he settled in the Town, where he died in 1653, and was buried on 6 Feb. Six of his children were Louis, "a soldier who spent his youth at the wars in the service of the King of France, and later in the Low Countries" (Chevalier), Esther (b. 1620), Douce, who married in 1641 Jacques Guillaume of Mont au Prêtre, who became Constable of St. Helier's, Jeanne, who married Philippe Le Geyt, Rachel (b. 1628) who married Helier De Carteret of St. Saviour's, and Jean (b. 1625) who married Marguerite De Carteret of Trinity, and became a Jurat. [Chevalier's *Journal* ; *Bull.* VIII ; Minutes of the Ecclesiastical Court.]

LA CLOCHE, JAMES DE (1644?—1699?), alleged son of Charles II. Attention was first drawn to this young man by the discovery in 1861 of eight letters in the archives of the Jesuits at Rome. The only known facts about him are these. In the Register of Admissions to the Jesuits' Novice House on the Quirinal the arrival is recorded on 11 April, 1668 of 'Jacobus de la Cloche of the island of Jersey, aged 24', and a list is added of the scanty wardrobe that he brought with him. He handed in three Certificates of Identity. The first "given at Whitehall, 27 Sept. 1665, written and signed with our own hand, and sealed with our accustomed seal", bore the signature of Charles II, and declared: — "We acknowledge as our natural son Jacques Stuart, who in obedience to our command has lived in France and other lands up to the year 1665... We have again commanded him to live under yet another name, that of De la Cloche du Bourg of Jersey, and for important reasons which affect the peace of the realm we forbid him to speak of his relationship to us, until after our death, when he may present this our declaration to Parliament". The second, dated eighteen months later, ran: — "Jacques Stuart, now known by the name De la Cloche, whom we have already acknowledged as our natural son, has pointed out that, if he should survive us, he might have nothing to live on. We therefore assign him out of our estate, if our successor and Parliament agree, £500 yearly, which however he shall not enjoy, unless he lives in England, and follows the religion of his fathers and the Anglican liturgy".

The third certificate was signed with the name of Christina, the ex-queen of Sweden, and declared: — "James Stuart, born in the isle of Jersey, who now passes under the name of De la Cloche du Bourg, is a natural son of Charles II, King of England, as his Majesty has privately acknowledged to us. Having quitted the sect of Calvin in which he was brought up, he joined the Holy Roman Church at Hamburg on 29 July 1667." These papers must have suggested to the Jesuits that their recruit would prove useful in negotiations with England, specially as he had proved his sincerity by making a financial sacrifice for the sake of his religion.

Four months later it was learnt that Christina was coming to Rome. De la Cloche then handed in two more letters, which, he said, had arrived from London. The first, signed "Charles, King of England", was addressed to Oliva, General of the Jesuits. It stated that the King had long been praying that he might find someone to whom he dared speak freely of his desire to become a Catholic. Now he had learnt with joy that he had a Catholic son, "the young Cavalier whom you have received under the name of De la Cloche of Jersey, for whom we have always felt a singular affection, because he was born to us, more through the frailty of early youth than from deliberate wickedness, when we were not more than sixteen or seventeen years old, of a young lady belonging to one of the most important (*qualifiées*) families in our Kingdom. Weighty reasons which concern the peace of our Kingdoms have hitherto prevented us from publicly recognizing him as our son, but this will shortly be altered". He asked that De la Cloche might be sent to him at once. "We know that you could easily find some other secure channel of communication, but it will cause us great displeasure, if you confide your letter to anyone else". Above all nothing must be said to the Queen of Sweden about him, for "being a woman, she cannot keep a secret". If there are difficulties in getting him ordained at once in Rome, he must be sent to Paris, where the King's sister, the Duchess of Orleans, can arrange for his secret ordination. "We believe that your Paternity has too high a respect for crowned heads to refuse so reasonable a request...... If you will let us know by our dear son, if there is any way in which we can help your Society we will gladly do so". The other letter was adressed to "our most honoured son, the Prince Stuart, residing at Rome with the Reverend Fathers, the Jesuits, under the name of Monsieur De la Cloche". It urged him to consider carefully before he took the Jesuit vows. "Remember you could claim from us titles as great, if not greater, than those of the Duke of Monmouth. Moreover we are without children by the Queen, and those of the Duke of York are sickly. Should the Catholic Religion be restored in this Kingdom, you might hope for the Crown. If we and our honoured brother should die childless, the Kingdom would belong to you. Parliament could not lawfully exclude you on any ground, except that the law, as it is at present, prevents it from electing a king who is not a Protestant. Because of your mother's rank you could claim to be preferred to the Duke of Monmouth. Such is what the Queens (i.e. the Queen Mother and the Queen Consort) counsel me to write to you". Elsewhere the letter says "The Queens are most impatient to see you".

A month later came an urgent letter for Oliva demanding that James should leave Rome, before Queen Christina arrived. The General is to pretend that he knows nothing of the secret of James' birth, and, if she should ask about him, is to say that he has gone to Jersey to receive his mother into the Catholic Church, and to claim the inheritance of his father, a rich preacher, who had died some time before. Meanwhile James is to travel by Jersey to Southampton, where he will find 50,000 crowns waiting for him to form a fund which he can put in a bank. On reaching London he is to wait on the Queen Consort, *when she goes to visit our dear and honoured mother*, (The sentence in italics is omitted in Monsignor Barnes' reprint of the letters, but appears in the earlier copy made by Father Boero). Four times in other parts of this letter the writer asserts that he has talked matters over with the Queens. With this arrived another letter dated a week later — "We had scarcely sealed our former letter, when the Queens advised us not to send it immediately, because they wished to consider further how our dear son's arrival might be made more secret. Their Majesties have learnt that in your Society novices are not allowed to travel alone, but are always accompanied by someone to report on their conduct. This prudent rule we admire. Nevertheless we pray your Paternity to grant a dispensation to our dear son in this matter, because we absolutely command him, by virtue of the authority given us over him by God, to come to us alone. We wish him to find an English ship at Genoa, and travel as Henri de Rohan, a French Calvinist Prince. We who make this plan are precisely three, Ourself, my beloved Mother, and the Queen Regent". Oliva apparently agreed to all that was asked, for a draft of his reply is written on the back of this letter: — "From the bearer of this, who is a French gentleman, your Majesty will learn that I have carried out his instructions given in your three letters".

De la Cloche returned to Rome with one more letter, dated 18 Nov. This says that the King's dear son will tell the General what the King desires. Charles will send "a notable sum in expiation for our sins" toward the repair of the Jesuit buildings, as soon as Oliva tells him how he would like to receive it. Meanwhile he asks that James may be sent back at once to London, and provided with all that he needs for the journey, the amount to be charged to the King's Account. At this point De la Cloche disappears. The most careful search through Jesuit records has failed to find any Father James Stuart or Father De la Cloche. He does not die. He is not expelled. He is not sent on a mission. He simply vanishes.

Monsignor Barnes has written a book suggesting that he was the Man in the Iron Mask.

The authenticity of these letters has been keenly debated. Were they genuine or were they forgeries? Was James really a son of the king or was he an impostor? A close investigation leaves little doubt as to the answer. (I) The first certificate is dated "Whitehall, 27 Sept. 1665"; but at that time plague was raging in London, and the Court had fled to Oxford. (II) The King constantly writes that he has talked things over with his dear mother; but Queen Henrietta had gone to live in Paris three years before, and never returned to England. (III) Not even in his drunkenest moment could the King have written that one of his bastards would be heir to the throne, and that Parliament could not legally object except on grounds of religion. (IV) Charles always refused to allow his illegitimate children, even his favourite, Monmouth, to use the surname Stuart. His heralds invented surnames for them: — Fitzroy, Fitzcharles, etc. He would never have adressed a letter to De la Cloche, *"Notre très honoré fils le Prince Stuart"*, or written of him as *"le Sieur Jacques Stuart"*. (V). Whitehall was littered with the King's acknowledged bastards, many of whom he ennobled. Lucy Walter's son was Duke of Monmouth, Nell Gwynne's Duke of St. Albans, Barbara Villiers' Duke of Southampton, Catherine Pegge's Earl of Plymouth, and so on. It is nonsense to say, as he does again and again in these letters, that he is longing to recognize De la Cloche as his son, but dare not do so, because "it would imperil the peace of the kingdom." (VI). Moreover, if De la Cloche forged the letters himself, this would explain two points emphatically urged in them. (a) No letter must be sent to the King, unless James himself is the bearer. If a query had really reached Charles, he would probably have replied that he had never heard of any such person. (b) Not a word must be said to Queen Christina about him. It would have been awkward, if he had been mentioned to her as her protégé, and she had disclaimed all knowledge of him. (VII) One final point may be added: — De la Cloche's own statement, when he joined the Jesuits, proved his story a lie. He gave his age as 24 in 1668. This would have made him born in 1644; and Prince Charles did not come to Jersey till 1646.

There is little doubt that James was an exceedingly clever

rogue, who for eight months was smart enough to get the Jesuits to support him and to provide him with considerable sums for travelling expenses ; and then, when he had stretched the hoax to the very limit of safety disappeared into space. But there is a sequel to this story. In the year De la Cloche disappeared there arrived in Naples a man who called himself James Henry de Bovere Roano Stuardo. Notice the James and the Stuardo, and Roano is reminiscent of De Rohan. He claimed to be an Englishman, but could only speak French. He married an innkeeper's daughter, and made such a show of his money, that he was arrested on suspicion of being a coiner. He then claimed to be a natural son of the King of England, and to have been born in Jersey. The British consul reported this to the King, who declared he knew nothing about him. But the coins proved genuine, and he was released from prison. In the following year he died of fever, making a most devout end, and leaving a preposterous will, in which he asserts that he is a son of King Charles by the Lady Mary Henrietta Stuart of the Barons of St. Marzo (a person whom no one can trace). He appoints his "cousin", the King of France, his executor. He commends his unborn child to the King of England, and, if it should be a boy, he asks that he may be created Prince of Wales or Monmouth. He leaves enormous sums to all his wife's relations, to be paid by the King of England, and transfers to them his dominions including the Marquisate of Juvigny, which can be found on no map. There was obviously some connection between James Stuardo and James De la Cloche. Lord Acton thought that he was a servant, who had stolen De la Cloche's papers ; but it seems more probable that he was De la Cloche himself. The megalomaniac will is closely akin to the letters which offered to De la Cloche titles greater than those of the Duke of Monmouth and eventually the English Crown.

One point has still to be considered, De la Cloche's connection with Jersey. This was probably genuine. A British subject, who knew no English, and whose native language was French, certainly suggests a Jerseyman. The constant references to Jersey in the letters would be natural to a Jerseyman and to no one else. He asserts that he was born in Jersey, his mother still lives in Jersey ; he has an inheritance in Jersey. Christina is to be told that he has gone to Jersey.

He is to travel to England via Jersey and Southampton. He knows that King Charles has been in Jersey, and that Jersey is Calvinist. La Cloche or De La Cloche was a well known Jersey name (The 'De' need not bother us, for in those days the family wrote its name in both ways. The famous Royalist Rector of St. Ouen's called himself Etienne La Cloche, but his son called himself Jean De la Cloche. It was not till 1711 that the Royal Court decided, "The name of this family is La Cloche, not De la Cloche".) And the Rector of St. Ouen's may well be the "rich preacher" mentioned in one letter.

In quite modern times it has been suggested that De la Cloche's mother may have been Marguerite De Carteret, daughter of the Seigneur of Trinity ; but the only arguments advanced for this are very unconvincing. (I) In 1656, ten years after the Prince's visit, Marguerite married Jean De la Cloche ; so, if she had an illegitimate child, he might have taken his stepfather's name. But this is no proof that she ever had such a baby. (II) Part of a page has been removed from the Register of Trinity Church for 1648. This may have been done for any one of a dozen different reasons ; but can have nothing to do with the baptism of any son of the Prince, for 1648 was two years after the Prince had left the island, and in those days babies were baptized a week after their birth. (III) Marguerite's brother, Josué, became a Parliamentarian, and this may have been because his sister had been seduced by the King. This is the weakest argument of all. The De Carterets were not all Royalists. François of La Hague (q.v.) was for a time a Parliamentary Commissioner and his son Philippe (q.v.) one of Cromwell's Jurats. Whereas Josué (q.v.) was an unprincipled scamp, who cared only for his own interests, and was Royalist when the Royalists were winning, and only Parliamentarian when they were defeated. One statement in the forged letters effectually clears Marguerite of suspicion. James claimed that his mother's rank entitled him to the throne, which must mean that she was of royal blood. The Naples impostor named a 'Lady Mary Stuart' as his mother.

The most reasonable conclusion to come to about James is that he was probably a Jerseyman, but that there is no ground for believing either that Charles was his father or Marguerite De Carteret his mother.

[The letters are reprinted in Barnes' *Man of the Mask.* See also Boero's *Istoria della Conversione di Carlo II.* 1863 ; Lord Acton's *Essays and Reviews.* For the Naples impostor see Andrew Lang's *Valet's Tragedy.* His later conviction on the subject will be found in the *Westminster Review* Feb. 1903, and in his article in the *Encyclopaedia Britannica,* 1911.]

LANDER, JOHN HELIER (1868–1944), Portrait Painter. (The 'St' before the Helier was a later addition). Son of William Lander, bootmaker, and Emily Rule. Born in Belmont Road 19 Oct. 1868. Lillie Langtry (q.v.) gave him his first paint-box. As a small boy he was always painting, which seemed to his father such waste of time, that it was strictly forbidden. But he continued surreptitiously in the early morning before his parents were awake. At fifteen he was apprenticed to a watch-maker, but, when his father found that people were buying his son's pictures, he withdrew his opposition, allowed him to have paint- ing lessons, and exhibited his pictures in the shop. When sixteen he went to London with an introduction to Sir John Millais (q.v.). He called so early that he was invited to stay to breakfast, and between mouthfuls of kipper Sir John advised him to buy a broom and sweep a crossing before he attempted to earn a living with a paint-brush. Nevertheless he persevered, spent a year in Calderon's Art School in Hampstead, and then went to Julien's famous atelier in Paris, where he studied under Bouguereau and Fleury. Three year's work in the Royal Acad- emy Schools followed.

In 1892 he returned to Jersey, gave lessons in painting, and became Art Master at the Ladies' College, where he met his wife, Beatrice Hewart, sister of Lord Chief Justice Hewart, who was mathematical mistress. He began to paint portraits of local people. Two in the Masonic Temple, of Col. E. C. Malet De Carteret and Dr. John Le Cronier, belong to this period. His family have a portrait of himself, painted when he was sixteen, which might well be the work of a mature artist. His ambitious picture of the *Assize d'Héritage* was bought by Miss Westaway (q.v.) for £400 and presented to the Royal Court. This included portraits of all the prominent people in the island, for each of which he made a preliminary sketch. For a time he experimented in different styles. He did a number of Jersey landscapes, and some genre pictures in the style of Millais. His first Academy picture, *Violets* (a Jersey flower-girl) was accepted in 1894. This was followed by *Topsy* (a child whom he found in French Lane) in 1895, and *The Chorister* (a red-headed choir-boy) in 1898 ; but then he concentrated on portraiture. His first Academy portrait was that of *Captain Philip Falle* in 1899.

In 1905 he moved to London, and built a studio in the Boltons, Hanley Gardens, where he remained till he was bombed out in 1940. He now began to exhibit frequently in the Paris Salon. He received the Hon.Mention of the Salon in 1910 for his *Portrait of Mrs. Guy Repton* and the *Médaille d'Argent* in 1923 for his *Portrait of the Prince of Wales* in polo kit (now in the Manchester Art Gallery). He found an enthu-siastic admirer in a fellow-Freemason, General Abadie, whose portrait he had painted, when he was Lieut.-Governor of Jersey. He secured many commissions for him from his military friends. He painted most of the British Generals in the First World War, including Earl Haig, Viscount Ypres (now in the Cavalry Club), Sir William Robertson, Sir H. Smith Dorrien, and Sir Philip Chetwode. His portrait of Major Con-greve V.C. was specially praised by the critics, when exhibited in the Academy. For T. B. Davis (q.v.) he painted George V at the time of his jubilee (exhibited in the Salon 1934). The original hangs in the Howard Davis Hall in Victoria College, and he made five replicas, which Davis presented to the College he had founded in South Africa, to Canada House, to Australia House, to New Zealand House, and to Guernsey. Lander also painted Edward VIII for the Hon. Society of Master Mariners, and he and a fellow-Jerseyman, Edmund Blampied R.E., R.B.A., collaborated, as Landseer and Millais had sometimes done, to paint for *The Illustrated London News* the picture of George VI in his coronation robes, which now hangs in the Bristol Art Gallery. Other portraits of Royalty depicted the Duke of Kent in tennis kit and the Princess Royal (both now in Marlborough House), Queen Mary (now in the Doncaster Art Gallery), and Queen Elizabeth. Other distin-guished sitters were General Dawes, the American ambas-sador, (the picture is now in the Embassy), Lord Chief Justice Hewart and Lord Justice Bankes (both in University College,

Oxford), L.R. Farnell, Vice-Chancellor of Oxford (in Exeter College), the first Archbishop of Wales, Lord James of Hereford (in the Hall of the Middle Temple), Lord Sackville (in Maidstone County Hall), Lord Cornwallis (in Freemasons' Hall), Sir Louis Dane, Governor of the Punjab (in the Lawrence Memorial Hall at Lahore), Prince Prajadhipok (later King of Siam), the Jam Sahib of Nawanagar, and Mr. Walter Edge, American Ambassador in Paris.   One of his most successful efforts was his portrait of Sir William Vernon (q.v.), Bailiff of Jersey, now in the Royal Court.   Other local pictures of his are portraits of Edward Binet, E.T. Nicolle (q.v.) and Lady Otway in the Barreau Art Gallery.   He was a Founder Member of the Modern Society of Portrait Painters in 1908.   This held annual Exhibitions, till killed by the First World War. After the War he helped to found the London Society of Portrait Painters.   He was elected a member of the Royal Institute of Painters in Oils.   He died suddenly at his home in Witley, Surrey 12 Feb. 1944 aged 76, leaving two sons and a daughter. [Information from friends and family.]

LANGLOIS, PHILIPPE, known in America as ENGLISH, PHILIP (1651—1736), Merchant in Salem.   Son of Jean Langlois.   Born in Trinity 1651, and baptized in Trinity Church 30 June, Sir Philippe De Carteret, Seigneur of St. Ouen's, and his wife being godparents.   In 1670 he crossed the Atlantic to seek his fortune, and joined a group of Jerseymen who had settled in Salem on the Massachusetts coast.   There he translated his name into Philip English.   He lodged with a merchant, William Hollingworth, whose only daughter, Mary, he married in 1675.   In the same year his father-in-law was killed fighting the Indians, and Philippe inherited his fortune.   He now began to build ships, and in 1676 revisited Jersey in his ketch, *Speedwell*, with a cargo of dried cod, and returned with a shipload of Jersey boys and girls as 'indentured apprentices'.   The girls were bound to him for seven years, and he let them out as domestic servants ; the lads, who were bound for four years, were hired out as seamen, a usual arrangement in those days. He prospered greatly, and became, says Paine in *Ships and*

Sailors of Old Salem, "perhaps the richest man of the New England Colonies", owning twenty-seven ships, two of which traded regularly between Salem and Jersey, taking out cod and rum and molasses, and returning with Jersey stockings, French brandy, and more apprentices. He owned two wharves and warehouses, and built for himself, overlooking the harbour, a magnificent gabled mansion, in what is still called English Street. His daughter, Susannah, married Captain Touzel, a Jerseyman who commanded one of his trading vessels. In 1692, at the height of his prosperity, the Salem witch-panic broke out. An ex-Congregational Minister began to hold mysterious, secret meetings after dark, and it was whispered that he was forming a Church of the Devil. On 21 April Philippe's wife was arrested "for high suspicion of sundry acts of witchcraft". A week later a writ was issued for the arrest of Philippe : but he had had warning, and had fled from the State. His house however was sacked by the mob, and all the goods in his warehouses were confiscated by the Sheriff. After a month, hearing that his absence was prejudicing his wife's trial, he returned and gave himself up. Twenty of those accused of witchcraft were executed, and feeling ran so high that few of the other suspects could hope for acquittal. So Philippe planned an escape. On Sundays the prisoners in Boston Gaol were marched under escort to the Congregational Meeting House for Service. On the Sunday before Philippe and his wife were to go to Salem for trial a band of men hustled the warders back into the building. Two fast horses were waiting with shoes reversed to mislead pursuers, and Philippe and Mary escaped to New York, where the Salem writ did not run. Here Mary died of her privations in prison ; but later, when the excitement faded away, Philippe returned to Salem. There had always been a feeling that he was innocent, and the Governor was said to have been privy to his rescue. He rebuilt his business ; but he never forgave the Puritans. In 1725 he was imprisoned "for non-payment of his assessment for the support of the Minister of Salem". His defence was that he belonged to the Church of England, and was a member of the Anglican congregation that worshipped at Marblehead across the river, and that the only reason why he did not attend "so constantly as his inclination led him" was that the ferryman refused to work on Sunday. His niece Jane Langlois "at

present of Salem but born in the isle of Jersey" testified: "From
my arrival in Salem five years and six months since, I have
lived in the house of my uncle. He always professed to belong
to the Church of England at Marblehead, and he and I went
very frequently to the said church together". The Governor
eventually ordered his release. He then tried in vain to get
permission to establish in Salem an Episcopal congregation.
But apart from this controversy he seems to have been respected ;
for he was twice elected to public office. One of his bills of
lading dated 1707 shows the pious imprint of his generation.
It begins: "Shipped by the grace of God in good order and
well-conditioned in the sloop the *Mayflower*, whereof is Master
under God John Swasey" ; then follows a list of cargo ; and
it ends, "And so God send the sloop to her desired port in
safety. Amen". He died in 1736. [*Bull XIII* ; *Historical
Collections of the Essex Institute* 1860 and 61 ; Perley's *History
of Salem* ; *New England Historical and General Register.*
Vol. XXXV.]

LANGTRY, LILLIE, *née* LE BRETON (1853—1929). She
was baptized Emilie Charlotte, but from childhood was called
Lillie. Youngest child of Dean William Corbet Le Breton
(q.v.) and Emilie Davis Martin. Born in St. Saviour's Rectory,
13 Oct., 1853. Her father was strikingly handsome, and her
mother was described by Charles Kingsley as the most bewitch-
ingly beautiful creature he had ever seen ; Lillie inherited her
parents' good looks. When fourteen she received her first offer
of marriage from a son of Archbishop Longley, an officer stationed in Jersey. In Nov. 1873 her brother married a Miss Price.
Among the wedding guests was Edward Langtry, a well-to-do,
young, Belfast widower, whose first wife, Laura Price, had been
a relative of the bride. He had come to Jersey in his 200
ton yacht, *Red Gauntlet*, and gave a dance at the Yacht Club
as part of the wedding festivities. Here he and Lillie met,
and after six weeks were engaged. They were married in
St. Saviour's Church, 9 March, 1874.

During her first London season Mrs. Langtry's beauty caused
an amazing sensation. She was acclaimed as the world's

loveliest woman. She was painted by Millais, Watts, Whistler, Poynter, Burne Jones, Leighton, and Frank Miles. Oscar Wilde published a poem, *The New Helen,* in her honour, and to show his adoration slept one night on her doorstep. Famous hostesses competed for her presence at their dinner-tables. Her photograph was on sale everywhere. Langtry coiffures, Langtry hats, Langtry shoes, Langtry scent became the fashion. She was taken up by junior members of the Royal Family, and could be seen riding daily with the Prince of Wales in Hyde Park. Richard Le Gallienne wrote of her : — "To have been the representative of Beauty in one's own time, its very symbol, is a peculiarly aristocratic form of immortality. Such fame has been Mrs. Langtry's. Born into an age of great symbolic personalities, as Tennyson meant Poetry, Gladstone Politics, Mrs. Langtry meant Beauty personified ; and almost instantly she meant that, not only for London drawing-rooms, but for the world". This was true. Her portrait was tacked up in many a backwoodsman's cabin, and, when a new city was founded in Texas down by the Rio Grande, the cowboys named it Langtry after her. She revelled in her popularity ; but her husband hated it. "He was", she writes, "an extremely shy man, who had spent his life, since leaving Oxford, in outdoor country sports, and he felt like a fish out of water". He stuck it for a time ; but then went off on long fishing-expeditions to Ireland and America, leaving his wife to her own devices. For several Seasons her triumph lasted. Then something happened which caused Society to drop her. She strenuously denied later the widespread report that at a garden-party she had slipped a strawberry ice down the Prince of Wales' back (she was notoriously fond of practical jokes) ; but, whatever her offence, she was ostracized. As soon as this was known, tradesmen began to press for payment, and she discovered that her extravagance had made her husband bankrupt. Bailiffs took possession of her house ; and she fled to Jersey.

After a time she returned to London, where a friend pointed out a new path to fame. Henrietta Labouchere, an ex-actress, wife of the editor of *Truth,* believed that Lillie might win success on the stage. She booked her to play in *She stoops to conquer* at a charity performance at the Haymarket, and drilled her remorselessly in her part ; but she never succeeded in making her more than a second-class actress. Her beauty and notoriety however always drew a crowd. The Bancrofts engaged her for a Haymarket comedy. Then came a provincial tour. At Manchester admirers unharnessed the horses, and dragged her carriage through the streets. At Glasgow the students escorted her to the station with a torchlight procession. Next Mrs. Labouchere arranged for her a tour in the United States. Here her publicity-agent filled the papers with her portrait ; and, wherever she went, theatres were crowded. A young, New York millionaire, named Gebhard, became her devoted admirer, and gave her amazing presents, the most luxurious travelling-coach ever seen on American railways, a Californian ranch of 6,000 acres, and a well-stocked racing-stable. This chapter in her life lasted five years, during which she became a naturalized, American citizen. Then Gebhard married, and she returned to England.

Here Abingdon Baird, another millionaire, laid his fortune at her feet, and provided her with the *White Ladye*, the most palatial yacht yet built. But Baird died, and she had grown tired of the rich Bohemians, who had been his friends. She resolved to fight her way back into Society via the race-course. She entered into a racing partnership with Lord Rosslyn, which caused his young wife to appeal to the Prince of Wales. He protested, not to the husband, but to Lillie, who consented to drop Rosslyn, and thus renewed after twenty years her friendship with the Prince. She then started racing-stables of her own, and in 1897 won the Caesarewich with an Australian horse, Merman ; and the Prince publicly escorted her into the Jockey Club enclosure. On that race she won £39,000. On the same day her husband lay dying in a Chester workhouse.

In 1899, when forty-six, she married a young guardsman of twenty-eight, Sir Hugo Gerald de Bathe. The wedding took place in St. Saviour's, Jersey, on 27 July ; and they settled in a small cottage at Beaumont, which she called Merman. But she soon returned to London and the Stage. She bought the dilapidated Imperial Theatre, once part of the Westminster Aquarium, and spent over £50,000 on lavish redecorations ; but neither she nor anyone else could persuade theatre-goers to find their way to it ; and after a few years it passed out of existence. In 1918 she retired from the Stage, and built a villa at Monte Carlo. Here she died on 12 Feb., 1929, and her body was brought, as she had desired, to Jersey to be buried at St.

Saviour's. She had one daughter, Jeanne Marie, who in 1902 married Sir Ian Malcolm. A portrait of Mrs. Langtry by Sir Edward Poynter and a pencil drawing by Frank Miles are in the S. J. Museum. She bequeathed to the Museum among other things her clock, her dressing case, her mirror, and a collection of her stage-jewels, including the scarabs which she wore as Cleopatra. [Her autobiography, *The Days I Knew* : articles in the *Anglo-Norman Review*, Feb-Sept 1930 : newspapers of the period.]

LE BAS, SIR HEDLEY FRANCIS (1868—1926), Publisher. Son of Captain Thomas Alfred Le Bas (Merchant Service). Born at La Retraite, Samarès, 19 May, 1868. Educated at Parlett's School. On leaving school he ran away from home, and enlisted in the 15th. Hussars. Here he distinguished himself as a rough-riding corporal, and as a reformer of Army canteens. One of his duties was to buy food for his squadron. He discovered that better and cheaper food could be bought in the village than in the canteen; so he went out marketing every day. The canteen steward reported him to the colonel. As a result of Le Bas' disclosures an inquiry was ordered into all Army canteens, and the whole system reorganised. After serving his seven years, he left the Army, and became debt collector to Messrs. Blackie and Co, Publishers. He was a man of immense energy and push. After two years he was made Manager, and by 1899 had obtained sufficient financial backing to establish a publishing business of his own, the Caxton Press. This developed on a large scale the idea of subscription publications, and was very successful. In advertising his books he became an expert in publicity ; and, when the First World War broke out, he freely placed his knowledge at the Government's disposal. He was largely responsible for the advertising campaign for recruiting Kitchener's Army, and the later one for selling War Savings Certificates ; then for the Prince of Wales' Relief Fund and the Vienna Relief Fund. All this work was honorary, but in 1916 he was rewarded by being created Knight of Grace, St. John of Jerusalem. After the war he edited the *Lord Kitchener Memorial Book*, and was Honorary Organizer of the Lord Kitchener National Memorial Fund. In his later years his chief interest was interviewing candidates for Kitchener Scholarships and watching their careers. He died at Reigate, 25 March 1926. [Information from his sister. Article in *The Kitchener Scholar*, Nov. 1926].

LE BOUTILLIER GEORGE (1783—1867), Merchant. Son of Jean Le Boutillier and Rachel Le Geyt. Born in Trinity, Jersey, 1783. Married Elizabeth Le Maistre. Had four sons, Charles, born 1811, George, born 1813, James, born 1814, Thomas, born 1816, and three daughters, Eliza, Mary, and Ann. In 1804 he established a drapery business in Guernsey, and took a prominent part in local politics. His great work was the rebirth of Elizabeth College, founded and endowed by Queen Elizabeth in 1573. At the end of the eighteenth century it was almost dead. In 1799 it had only one pupil. Le Boutillier, who had sons of his own, decided that it ought to be set on its feet again. In spite of great indifference among the authorities, he investigated its history and finances, and, when a new Lieutenant-Governor, Sir John Colborne, arrived in 1821, he laid before him a carefully thought out plan for the entire reorganization of the College. The Governor appealed to the Dean, who was Visitor of the College, and, as the Dean moved slowly, in 1823 he ordered a Public Inquiry, which resulted in a new Charter being obtained in 1825, and new buildings begun in 1826. The school reopened with forty scholars, the first two names on the Register being sons of the Lieutenant-Governor, the next three numbers being given to sons of Le Boutillier in recognition of what the College owed to him. He was responsible for the introduction of gas into the island ; and then embarked on an ambitious scheme, the building of the Le Boutillier Arcade (later called the Commercial Arcade).

"Before his time", said the *Gazette de Guernesey*, "the old Town was like a nut without a kernel. The Grand'rue skirted the Harbour, but between it and the new streets there was nothing but gardens. He conceived the idea of linking the

Market Place with the Grand'rue by removing and levelling what was almost a mountain, and connecting the new district with the Platon by means of a flight of steps. The present site of the Arcade was then terraced gardens ; and he opened the thoroughfare that he needed by demolishing the house of Mons. Robin in the Grand'rue. The Arcade then arose, and a new commercial centre was created" (*Gazette,* 24 July, 1867). But the expense ruined him, and in 1838, when 55, he emigrated to Cincinnati, were he was soon joined by his three sons. Here he built up a large and prosperous merchant's business, and his sons opened branch houses in Philadelphia and New York. He returned to Jersey in 1864 a very rich man, and three years later on 17 July 1867 he died in his native parish of Trinity in his eighty-fourth year. The *Gazette de Guernesey* calls him "a man of novel ideas, one of those ardent spirits who conceive and inaugurate vast undertakings, a master mind that left its mark on every place it passed through". The *Elizabeth College Register* calls him "one of the greatest benefactors that ever came to this island". [Authorities quoted above.]

LE BRETON, CLEMENT MARTIN (1852—1927), King's Counsel. 5th son of Dean Corbet William Le Breton and brother of Lillie Langtry (q.v.). Born at St. Saviour's Rectory, 1852. Educated at Victoria College and Sandhurst. Ensign, Northumberland Fusiliers, 1870. Lieutenant, 1871. Retired through ill-health, 1874. Barrister, Inner Temple, 1879. K.C. 1904. Military Services (Civil Liabilities) Commissioner, 1916. Arbitrator in Industrial Disputes for the Ministry of Labour, 1917. O.B.E. 1918. Recorder of Sudbury, 1918. Chairman of the Shirtmaking and Tailoring Trade Boards, 1918. Died 1 July, 1927. Married Alice Jones, daughter of Lord Ranelagh, and had one daughter, Alice May, who married Wilfred Bloye,

LE BRETON, FRANCOIS (1739—1802), Dean of Jersey. Grandson of Dean Thomas Le Breton (q.v.) and fourth son of Thomas Le Breton, Seigneur of La Hague (for 20 years

Constable of St. Peter's) and Alice Anley. Born 1739, and baptized in St. Peter's Church 20 Feb. Entered Winchester College 1753. Matriculated at Oxford from Jesus College 1754. Entered Pembroke as a Morley Scholar 1757. Graduated from New College B.A. 1760. M.A. 1765. During one of Dean Payn's (q.v.) frequent absences from the island Le Breton, his godson, acted as Curate-in-charge of St. Mary's, and in 1765 he succeeded him as Rector. In 1775 he was appointed Dean, and in 1777 became Rector of St. Saviour's. In the political struggles of the time he first supported Jean Dumaresq (q.v.) and the Magots, and from 1779 to 1786 his name is found on all the anti-Lempriere petitions sent to the Privy Council. In 1779, when Charles Lempriere (q.v.) as Lieutenant-Bailiff refused to put a motion to the States that had been proposed and seconded, the Dean "with much warmth" moved that the States appoint a Judge Delegate to take Lempriere's place, so that business might proceed (*Documents relating to Political Differences*). But later he changed his views. In 1790 the *Gazette* called him a "champion of Charlotism". In the same year he complained to the Court that he had been assaulted by Philippe Dumaresq (q.v.), one of the Magot leaders, who had seized him by the collar as he left his vestry (G.). Toward the end of his life the Church was disturbed by the rise of Methodism. He was more friendly to the new movement than most of his fellow-rectors. In 1794 he presented to the States the petition of the Methodist militiamen against Sunday drill, and in 1798 protested strongly against the States' action in banishing all militiamen who refused to drill on Sunday. He died in July 1802, and was buried on the 9th in St. Saviour's churchyard. He married Elizabeth Penrose, and had ten children, of whom Thomas (q.v.) became Bailiff, and Philip succeeded his father as Rector of St Saviour's.

LE BRETON, PHILIP HEMERY (1806—1884), Preserver of Hampstead Heath. Eldest son of Rev. Philippe Le Breton, Rector of St. Saviour's, and Susanne, daughter of Clement Hemery, Constable of St. Helier's. Born 1806. Educated at Cogan's School, Walthamstow with Benjamin Disraeli.

Solicitor in London, 1828—51. Barrister, 1854. Revising Barrister for West Surrey. Lived in Hampstead, 1851 till death. Member for Hampstead of Metropolitan Board of Works, 1859—1879. By his initiative and perseverance he secured after many difficulties Hampstead Heath for the public. Presented with public testimonial in recognition of his services, 1871. Died, 1884. He married Anna Letitia Aikin, the authoress (See *Dic. Nat. Biog.*), who published among other books *Memories of Seventy Years* by one of a Literary Family. They had eight children. [*Barnes' Records of Hampstead.*]

LE BRETON, THOMAS (1680—1728), Dean of Jersey. Son of David Le Breton, merchant and ship-owner of St. Helier's, and Marie, daughter of Gilles Du Pin, merchant, of St. Lô, Normandy. Born 1680, and baptized in the Town Church, 16 March. Educated at a school in Southampton. He obtained a grant from the Don Baudains and matriculated at Pembroke College, Oxford, 1695, at the age of fifteen ; B.A. 1699. M.A. 1702. Became Fellow of Exeter 1702. Was appointed Rector of St. Mary's, Jersey, 1706, and resigned his fellowship the following year. He soon took a leading part in the disputes then raging between the Rectors and the Royal Court. (See *Le Couteur, Clement*). In 1712 the aged Clement Le Couteur appointed him Vice-Dean, and two years later he succeeded him as Dean. He died at St. Mary's 5 Oct. 1728, and a Latin inscription in the church proclaims the fertility of his genius, the culture of his mind, his vast erudition, and his knowledge of many literatures. He married Marie, daughter of Jurat Raulin Robin. His only son, Thomas, became Constable of St. Peter's and an Advocate.

LE BRETON, SIR THOMAS, senior (1763—1838), Bailiff. Eldest son of Dean François Le Breton (q.v.) and Elizabeth Penrose. Born 29 Sept. 1763. Educated at Winchester College, 1777—83. Entered Jesus College, Oxford, 1785 ; migrated to Pembroke, 1784 ; Fellow of Pembroke, 1784—90. B.A. 1787. At Oxford he was known as 'handsome Tom'. In 1786 he won the Chancellor's Prize for Latin verse on the rather un-promising subject, A Picture in Glass. He returned to Jersey, became Cornet in the Royal Jersey Troop (the Militia cavalry), and studied for the local bar. He was admitted Advocate 1799, and in 1802 was appointed Attorney-General. The Court however refused to register his Letters Patent on the ground that he had been recommended by the Lieutenant-Governor, who by an Order of James I. was forbidden to interfere in the ap-pointment of Officers of Justice. But the Privy Council des-cribed their refusal as "high contempt of his Majesty's Royal Authority". (O.C.). Le Breton took a leading part in 1808 in preventing the swearing in of Thomas Anley (q.v.) as Jurat, and in the unsuccessful attempt to get the method of appointing Jurats altered. (See his evidence printed in Report of the Royal Commissioners, 1811.) In 1816 Lord Carteret, the non-resident Bailiff, made him his Lieutenant. Two years later a scandal nearly wrecked his career. A blacksmith threatened to sue him for damages for adultery with his wife. Le Breton paid him £800 sterling to drop the matter. This became known, and eight Jurats reported to the Privy Council that they refused to attend any Court over which he presided. Thus no quorum could be ob-tained, and the judicial business of the island was brought to a standstill. They also printed a pamphlet, Copy of the Repre-sentations of Eight Jurats touching the conduct of Thomas Le Breton. The Council however severely blamed them for "inter-rupting the administration of justice" (O.C.), and apparently took no notice of the charges against Le Breton. He lived down this scandal, and in 1826 appeared before the Privy Coun-cil as Deputy of the States to complain about the encroachments of the French on the local oyster fisheries, and, while in London, was knighted (20 April 1825). In June 1826 Lord Carteret died, and Le Breton's appointment as Lieut.-Bailiff automatically expired. His opponents now hoped to get rid of him. The post of Bailiff had been hereditary in the Carteret family for 166 years, and Jersey assumed that the new Bailiff would be one of Lord Carteret's nephews. The editor of the Chronique declared that, if the Marquess of Bath were chosen, he meant to make Jurat Anley his Lieutenant. But to everyone's surprise Le Bre-ton himself was appointed Bailiff. He was sworn in 7 Sept.

1826, the first Bailiff for 120 years to live in Jersey. He held office for 4½ uneventful years, and resigned in 1831. "He has been accused of indolence", wrote the *Jersey and Guernsey Magazine* in 1831, "but his indolence, we believe, was the inactivity which ill-health sooner or later seldom fails to superinduce". He died at Bagatelle on 11 March 1838. He married in 1790 Anne, sister of Dean Hue, and by her had four children. Thomas (q.v.), Jean, François, and Anne Corbet. His first wife died in 1798. He then married Marguerite, daughter of Clement Hemery, Constable of St. Helier's. By her he had four more children, Clement (who settled in Buenos Aires, and became the father of Tomaso Le Breton, Argentine ambassador in Paris during the First World War), William, Eliza Margaret, and Maria. His portrait by Lawrence was presented to Pembroke College, Oxford, by his granddaughter, Mrs. Thorne. A print of it is in the S.J. Museum.

[Local newspapers ; Pycroft's *Oxford Memories* ; Jordan's *National Portrait Gallery of Illustrious Personages.* No. XVI. 1830 ; a *Life of Sir Thomas Le Breton* to be published by Craddock and Joy was advertised in the *Jersey Loyalist,* 1826, but never appeared.]

LE BRETON, SIR THOMAS, Junior (1791—1857), Bailiff. Eldest son of Sir Thomas Le Breton (q.v.), and Anne Hue. Born, 1791, and baptized in the Town Church, 13 July. Since Jersey Law was based on the Old Coutumier of Normandy, all the best Jersey lawyers took the Law course at Caen University ; but in Le Breton's case the Napoleonic wars seemed to make this impossible. He obtained however an American passport under the name of David Burger, and took the full course without being detected as a British citizen. When Napoleon visited the University, the young 'American' was presented to him. He returned to Jersey in 1810, and was sworn in as an Advocate, though barely nineteen. In 1813 his father secured his appointment as one of the two Receivers-General. In 1820 he was one of the founders of the *Constitutionnel,* which became the chief mouth-piece of the Laurel Party. In the same year he was promoted Colonel of the Town Battalion of the Militia. He had joined this regiment as Lieutenant in 1806, when only fifteen, had become Captain in 1817, and commanded it for thirty years.

His promotion from junior Captain to Colonel was resented by some of his fellow-officers, and one of them, Captain Aaron De Ste Croix junior, sent a protest to the War Office. This caused much ill-feeling, which was accentuated by a further quarrel over the trial of Queen Caroline. On the Queen's acquittal De Ste Croix illuminated his house, for which the *Constitutionnel* rebuked him. De Ste Croix thought that Le Breton had written the article, and stopped him in the Square, saying, "I would spit in your face, if you were worth the spittle". This led in Dec. 1820 to a duel on Samarès Marsh. At the second exchange of shots De Ste Croix was severely wounded, and his life was despaired of, and Le Breton fled to Granville to escape arrest. De Ste Croix however recovered, and Le Breton returned. The matter however did not end here. De Ste Croix publicly accused Le Breton of having unfairly used rifled pistols in the duel. The Lieutenant-Governor held an inquiry, and Le Breton was completely exonerated (*Constitutionnel*. 7 Sept. 1822). In 1824 he became Attorney-General.

In 1834 he had a serious clash with Major-General Thornton, the Lieut.-Governor. Thornton without consulting Le Breton appointed as Major in the Town Battalion, an Irish Lieutenant on half-pay, who was living in the island. Le Breton protested in writing that the passing over of regimental officers in favour of outsiders discouraged the best type of men from taking commissions in the Militia. Thornton suspended him from his command, and reported him to the Royal Court for insubordination. (The correspondence is printed in the *Constitutionnel*, 2 Aug. 1834). The Court however decided that his letters "contained nothing reprehensible". In this protest he had the whole island behind him, and more than two thousand people subscribed to buy a magnificent sword of honour, which was presented to him in July 1835 "to commemorate his patriotic and successful defence of the privileges of the island against the attempted encroachments of Major-General Thornton". When Queen Victoria visited Jersey in 1846, he as senior colonel was in command of the Militia, and rode at the head of the procession. Like most Le Bretons he was a strikingly handsome man, and both the Queen and Prince Albert were impressed by him. He was knighted at St. James's Palace 12 Feb. 1847.

He had hoped to become Bailiff, when his father resigned in 1831, but had been disappointed. When however Sir Jean De Veulle (q.v.) died in 1848, he at last secured this post ; but his nine years of office were not very successful. He failed, as his predecessor had done, to enforce order in his Court, and outrageous scenes between rival Advocates were habitual. Even his own paper, the *Constitutionnel*, in its obituary notice lamented his lack of firmness. A reserve, which was regarded as haughtiness, kept him rather friendless. "He was far from being a popular man", said the *Nouvelle Chronique*, "and he showed no desire to become one". In September 1857 he had a paralytic stroke, and died on 24 November, and was buried in St. Saviour's churchyard. He had married Frances, daughter of Thomas Jekyll Rawson of Oakover Hall, Stafford, but she died a year or two after marriage, and they had no children. His portrait hangs in the Royal Court. [Local Newspapers.]

LE BRETON, WILLIAM CORBET (1815—88), Dean of Jersey. Eldest son of William Le Breton and Jane Hue, sister of Dean Corbet Hue ; nephew of Sir Thomas Le Breton, senior, Bailiff ; grandson of Dean François Le Breton. Born at St. Helier's 1815, and baptized in the Town Church 17 March. Educated at Winchester College, where he was fag to Lord Selborne, who once beat him severely on the head with a frying-pan for burning his bacon. Matriculated at Pembroke College, Oxford, as Morley scholar at the age of fifteen ; B.A. 1835 ; M.A. 1837. Fellow of Exeter 1837—42. Ordained Deacon 1839, and Priest 1840 in the Diocese of Oxford. From 1845 to 1850 he was Curate of the now demolished church of St. Olave's, Southwark, at the south end of London Bridge. On the death of Dean Hemery all the Jersey clergy petitioned that his successor might be someone who had worked in the island ; nevertheless Le Breton was appointed (1850) Dean and Rector of St. Saviour's. In 1875 he was transferred from St. Saviour's to St. Helier's. H.E. Le V. dit Durell wrote of him: — "His commanding presence, his genial personality, his suave manners, his gentle nature, his eloquent and poetic language tended to command admiration. He was the admired of all admirers, a gentleman in the best sense of the world. Even in Piccadilly people turned round to look at him". *(Men I have known).* "At one of Queen Victoria's levées", wrote his daughter, "Sir John Pennefather walked up to him and said, 'When you joined the Church, Sir, there was a deuced fine sergeant-major spoilt' " *(The Days I knew).* He took little part in the work of the States, and no interest whatever in local politics ; but in social life he was immensely popular. In 1880 however rumours began to circulate about him, which forced him to leave the island. For the last eight years of his life he lived in England, leaving his parish and deanery in charge of Philip Alfred Le Feuvre, the Vice-dean. He died in London 28 Feb. 1888, and was buried at St. Saviour's. He had married at St. Luke's, Chelsea, in 1842 Emily Davies, daughter of William Martin, and had seven children, Francis Corbet, Clement Martin (q.v.), Trevor Alexander, Reginald, Maurice, William, and Emily Charlotte (See *Langtry, Lillie.*).

LE CAPELAIN, JEAN (1812—48), Water-colour Painter. Son of Samuel Le Capelain and Elizabeth Anne Pinkney. Born in St. Helier's 5 Oct. 1812. He had no regular art instruction, but developed a very pleasing individual style, somewhat after the manner of Turner, in which he made liberal use of the play of light through mist. He cared little for exact detail, but delighted in atmospheric effects suggesting the mystery of Nature. His pictures have been described as rhapsodies in colour. He explains his aim in the preface to his *Album* of the Queen's visit: — "Surrounded by the sea, Jersey is almost every night surrounded by mist, which the rising sun in dissolving tinges with prismatic colours. From the eastern coast is seen the splendour of sunrise, the cold, white light of dawn creeping up the dark sky, extinguishing the pale starry fires amid its rosy light. As the mists disappear, each object becomes more defined. As day advances, the sea, true mirror of the sky, reflects its darker blue. Along the western coast the glowing colours of the setting sun are reflected from each rocky headland, blending their rich hues with the pearly tints of the rising moon. In the drawings these varied effects of sunrise, sunset, twilight, moonlight,

and storm are given". His work was by no means confined to
Jersey. Many of his pictures are Scottish views, e.g. *Sunrise
over the Clyde', 'Rainstorm on Loch Ness', 'A Highland Storm'.*
Others were painted in Wales. But the bulk of his work was
done in his own island. When Queen Victoria visited Jersey in
1846 the States decided to present her with an album of Jersey
views, and commissioned Le Capelain to paint them. He produced twenty-five water-colours, six of the royal visit and nineteen
of local scenery, which were magnificently bound in red morocco,
and accepted by Her Majesty. These were lithographed and
published in book form, *The Queen's Visit to Jersey, drawn by
J. Le Capelain, published by Philip Falle, Jersey, 1847.* In
some copies of the book Le Capelain himself coloured the lithographs. This volume led to his receiving a commission from the
Queen to paint a series of pictures of the Isle of Wight. While
working on these, he developed tuberculosis of the lungs. Treatment in France failed to check this, and he died in Hill Street
on 17 Oct. 1848, aged 36. He was unmarried. His studio was
at the top of the Calvados Hotel at the corner of Church Street
and Hill Street. Immediately after his death an effort was
made to found a permanent Le Capelain Gallery as a memorial
to him. About £210 was subscribed. This however was not
sufficient to build a Gallery ; so two of his oil paintings and
sixteen of his water-colours were purchased, and entrusted to
the Constable of St. Helier's to be the nucleus of a future collection. A miniature of him, painted by himself, is in the S.J.
Museum, and also a bust. Lord Portsea has a fine collection of
his pictures. Others are in the Town Hall, in Rozel Manor,
and in the Barreau Art Gallery. [Local Newspapers.]

LE CORNU, CHARLES PHILIP, C.B. (1829—1911), Colonel,
Royal Jersey Militia. Youngest of four sons of Philip Le Cornu
of Vinchelez de Haut and Marie, daughter of Daniel Le Geyt.
Born at Vinchelez de Haut, St. Ouen's, 13 July 1829, and
educated at Southampton. In 1847 he became Ensign in the
North-West Regiment of Militia, but was soon transferred to
the Artillery. In 1869, when he was in command of the 1st
N.W. Battery, his men presented him with an address and

sword of honour. In 1873 he became Adjutant-General of the Militia with brevet rank of Lieut.-Colonel. In 1881, when the Militia was reorganized, he was appointed Assistant-Adjutant-General, a position which he held till 1896. He became Major in 1877, Lieut.-Colonel in 1881, and Honorary Colonel in 1885. At the Diamond Jubilee (1897) he was made a Companion of the Bath. On the death of Sir James Godfray he was appointed aide-de-camp to Queen Victoria, and later to Edward VII and George V; he attended the Queen's funeral and King Edward's coronation in this capacity.

He sat in the States as Deputy for St. Peter's from 1875 to 1881, and took a prominent part in the construction of the New Markets and the new Beaumont Road. All his life he was interested in agriculture. As early as 1851 he acted as a judge in the Royal Jersey Agricultural and Horticultural Society's shows, and was Secretary of the Agricultural section from 1857 to 1867. In 1864 he introduced the Herd Book. From 1870 to 1872 he was President of the Society. He belonged also to the Royal Agricultural Society of England, and judged cattle at many of its shows. Twice he won the Essay Prize of this Society; in 1859 for a pamphlet, *Agriculture in the Channel Islands*, and in 1869 for one on *The Potato in Jersey*. He also published a third on *The Jersey Dairy Industry*. He was an Honorary Member of the English Jersey-Cattle Society and of the British Dairy-Farmers' Association, and a corresponding member of the Société Nationale d'Agriculture de France. In 1884 he received from the French Government the Croix de Mérite Agricole.

He was a foundation member of the Société Jersiaise, its President 1882–1905, and its Président d'Honneur till his death. He contributed many articles to its Bulletins, and his granddaughter presented to the Society his collection of Jersey papers and contracts. He was a fellow of the Society of Antiquaries and a member of the Société Française d'Archéologie. He took great interst in St. Peter's Parish, where (9 Dec. 1871) he bought from Thomas Henry Pipon the fiefs of La Hague, Blanc Eperon, Nobretez, and Niesmes. The restoration of the church was due to his initiative, and he published an account of its history and architecture. He was a prominent Churchman, and a frequent speaker at Interdecanal Conferences.

He was one of the outstanding Jersey personalities of his day.

It was he who conceived in 1870 the idea of holding a Channel Islands Exhibition, and it was largely his energy and enthusiasm that made it a success. He died 27 June, 1911, and was buried at St. Peter's. He married in 1858 Anne, only child of Lieutenant-Colonel Philip Helleur R.J.M. ; and left one son, Charles Lambert Helleur (d. 1922), and four daughters, Anne Mary Helleur, Emily Lambert, Mary Le Geyt, and Alice Maria Lambert, wife of F.W.S. Le Maistre (q.v.). [Local newspapers.]

LE COUTEUR FAMILY. The Le Couteurs are found established at St. Mary's as soon as our Records begin. The Assize Roll of 1309 shows Colin Le Costour as one of the Principaux of the Parish, and in 1324 his son Robert was one of the 'Electores'. In 1534 Jean Le Couteur was Centenier of St. Mary's, and he was succeeded by his son Philippe. Philippe's son, grandson, great-grandson, and great-great-grandson were all Constables of St. Mary's, and no less than eight members of the family have filled that office. From this branch sprang Dean Philippe Le Couteur (q.v.), Dean Clement Le Couteur (q.v.), and François Le Couteur (q.v.), the militant Rector of St. Martin's. In the 15th century two younger sons of Thomas Le Couteur of St. Mary's moved to other parishes, and established branches there, which survive to the present day. Nicolas settled in St. Peter's and Thomas in St. John's. From the latter branch came Lieut.-General John Le Couteur (q.v.) and Sir John Le Couteur (q.v.).

LE COUTEUR, CLEMENT (1631—1714), Dean. One of the four sons of Jacques Le Couteur, Receiver-General, and Esther Botterel. Three of them became Jersey Rectors, and two of them Deans. Clement was born in 1631, and baptized in St. John's on Dec. 19. A letter among the Clarendon Papers shows that in 1654 he was a Royalist exile in Breda. We next hear of him at the Restoration, when Oxford gave him an M.A. degree on 15 Dec. 1660. He then was described as of Christ

Church, but this was probably one of many honorary degrees granted about this time to Royalists by the King's orders. In 1661 he became Rector of Little Mongeham, Kent, and in 1662 of Sedgebrook, Lincoln. In 1663 he returned to Jersey as Rector of St. John's, and in 1664 married Jeanne, daughter of Jurat Josué De Carteret, Seigneur of St. Jean la Hougue-Boëte. In 1672 he suceeded his brother Philippe (q.v.) as Dean. His first twenty-five years of office seem to have been peaceful. In fact he was blamed for being too pacific. Philippe Falle (q.v.) bitterly reproached him for not supporting him in his fight with the Seigneur of Trinity to secure for the Rectors the right of appointing the Regents of the Grammar Schools. But toward the end of the century he became involved in stormy controversies with the Royal Court.

In 1698 Hugh Grandin, Rector of St. Peter's, announced a Communion Service for Christmas Day. Philippe Anley, the Constable, objected, as the Canons only required a Communion once a quarter, and stood at the church door, forbidding people to enter. The Rector reported him to the Ecclesiastical Court, and the Dean excommunicated him and one of the Chuchwardens. They appealed to the Royal Court, accusing the Dean of issuing "a mandate containing many ignominious and scandalous statements contrary to their honour and reputation". For this, on Feb. 25 1699, the Dean was sent to prison. (Acts of the Court at this period do not specify the length of the sentence.) Then followed a long series of clashes between the Ecclesiastical Court and the Royal Court as to their respective powers. In 1703 the Seigneur of St. Ouen's accused Jean Tourgis, Greffier of his Seigneurial Court, of revealing confidential papers belonging to the Manor. Not content with dismissing him from his post as Greffier, he brought the matter before the Royal Court, which deprived Tourgis of his position as Lecteur (Parish Clerk) of St. Ouen's. The Dean claimed that the dismissal of Lecteurs was a matter for the Ecclesiastical Court, and reinstated him. The Seigneur appealed to the Bishop, who supported the Dean. The case was then taken before the Privy Council, which did not settle the dispute between the two Courts, but granted Tourgis the Queen's Pardon, and so restored him to his post as Lecteur (O.C.)

In 1704 the Bishop of Winchester made an appeal to the Privy Council about the state of affairs in Jersey: — "Such hath been the usage and behaviour of the Laity toward the Clergy that they have frequently assaulted their persons, and shewed many indignities and contempt to them, both in private and public, even when sitting in their Ecclesiastical Court. The inferior sort of people do frequently throw dust, stones, etc., upon the Dean and Clergy, while sitting in their Court, which, altho it cannot be personally imputed to the said Bailiff and Jurats, because not actually executed by them, yet it doth flow undoubtedly from their ill example of daily contempt of the Clergy" (*Le Geyt Note-Book* among S.J. MSS).

Pews were frequent matters of dispute. These might seem purely an ecclesiastical problem, but they were regarded as private property, and the Royal Court claimed that, like other forms of private property, they were under its jurisdiction. In 1705 there was a dispute about three pews in St. Lawrence's church. The case came before the Ecclesiastical Court, but the Royal Court peremptorily forbad the Dean to interfere — "We forbid you in the Queen's Name to disturb any of the parties in the said case or to allow them to be disturbed in the Ecclesiastical Court". The sequel is not recorded. But in 1706 in the Dean's own church of St. John, Jean Le Couteur changed his open seat into an enclosed pew, and by so doing obstructed the entrance to the pew of Josué Ahier, who appealed to the Ecclesiastical Court, which ordered Le Couteur to reduce the size of his pew. When he refused to recognize the authority of the Ecclesiastical Court, the Dean threatened to excommunicate him, unless he shortened his pew. He then appealed to the Royal Court, which fined Ahier, and forbad him to disturb Le Couteur further. A week later Le Couteur complained that Ahier had again disturbed him, and Ahier was committed to prison, where he remained two years. The Dean in March 1708 ordered Le Couteur's excommunication to be read from every pulpit. On the Saturday the Royal Court sent a message to all the Rectors forbidding them to read this. When they persisted, they were all arrested, taken before the Court, and fined, part of the fine being given to the excommunicated man.

Meanwhile a complicated controversy about tithes had been going on with the Queen's Receiver. The tithe of corn had once belonged to certain Norman Abbeys. Under Henry V this had been confiscated by the Crown. But in 1607 Royal Commissioners had decided that the Clergy still had a right to tithe from land that had been '*désert*' (i.e. uncultivated) in the days of the monks, but which had been brought under cultivation since. The Rectors complained that the Receiver was taking many tithes that rightly belonged to them. The Crown Officers resented this complaint. In 1703 Jean Dumaresq. Rector of St. Helier's, was sent to prison for "having uttered many calumnious words against the honour and reputation of the Lieut.-Governor". In 1706 Edouard Payne, Rector of St. Ouen's, was sent to prison on the complaint of the Receiver for "having in the presence of the Constable and Officers of the Parish spoken many malicious words tending to prejudice the Queen's interests and the honour and reputation of her officers". The Dean had made a proposal to try to end this controversy. It was difficult to prove at what date each field came under cultivation. So he suggested that, as the Receiver always farmed out the tithes to someone for a fixed sum, he should in future farm them out to the Rectors, who would then collect all the tithe, and pay the Receiver the agreed price. The Privy Council however rejected this plan (O.C.).

Le Couteur ruled his clergy with a firm hand. In 1700, when St. Ouen's was vacant, he arranged a rota to take the services. When the Rector of St. Mary's turn came, the Constable locked him out, and invited the Rector of St. Lawrence's to officiate, which he did. For this the Dean suspended the intruding Rector, forbidding him to preach or administer the sacraments, till he had made humble submission before the Ecclesiastical Court. Philippe Falle (q.v.) had done good work for the Church in the fight for the Grammar Schools ; but the Dean could not regard him with approval. The curse of the Church in England at this time was pluralities. A man might be Rector of several parishes, from which he drew the income, leaving all the work to a Curate. The Jersey Canons categorically forbad this ; but they had been interpreted merely to mean that no one might hold more than one living in Jersey. This left permissible the far more undesirable practice of holding one in Jersey and one in England. Falle, though Rector of St. Saviour's, had a living in the Diocese of Lincoln, and had not set foot in the island for twelve years. Edouard Dauvergne (q.v.), Rector of St. Brelade's, was also Rector of Great Hallingbury, Essex, and had been away for eleven years. De la Place, Rector of St. Lawrence's, had been ten years absent in an English parish. Le

Couteur determined to stop this. In Jan. 1706 he summoned all three before his Court, and, when thy did not appear, deprived them of their Jersey Rectories. They appealed to the Bishop ; but he upheld the Dean's action.

A storm of controversy surrounded the old Dean to the end. One of his last official acts, when he was eighty-two, was to issue a Prohibition to be read from every pulpit : — "Whereas it is notorious that in all the parishes the Church Trésor is used to pay the drummers and trumpeters of the Militia, for feux-de-joie, and many other secular purposes" (even when there was a lawsuit in 1706 between the Clergy and the Civil Court, in many parishes the Trésors were used to pay the costs of the Civil Court) "while the churches are left without repair and without their necessary ornaments, so that most of them seem more like caverns than Houses of God, and rain comes through the roof to the great inconvenience of worshippers ; they are neither whitewashed nor cleaned, nor are the aisles paved ; and the seats are broken ; nor is there in any church a font for the administration of Baptism as the Canons require" ; he therefore inhibited any Rector, Churchwarden, or Treasurer from paying or passing for payment any part of the Church Trésor to meet the expenses of the Civil Court in an appeal then impending.

He died in 1714, and was buried on Oct. 6 in St. John's Church. He had three sons, Aaron, Philippe, and Josué, who all died childless, and six daughters, four of whom married De Carterets. Jeanne married Charles, second son of Helier De Carteret, Seigneur of La Hougue ; Elizabeth married Charles, Seigneur of Trinity ; Anne married Amice, Seigneur of Vinchelez de Bas ; Esther married Edouard, Seigneur of St. Jean La Hougue-Boëte.

LE COUTEUR FRANCOIS (1744—1808), Rector, Patriot, Expert in Cider. Son of Jean Le Couteur, and grandson of François Le Couteur, Rector of St. Martin's, 1717—1765. His mother was Elizabeth Payn, sister of Dean Payn. He was born in St. Saviour's 1744 ; entered Jesus College, Oxford, as exhibitioner 1762 ; became Jersey Fellow of Exeter 1764 ; B.A. 1767. He was Curate of Shrewsbury for two years. He was

then starting as tutor to a rich youth on the tour of Europe,
when he broke his thigh, an accident which left him lame for
life. In 1771 he resigned his Fellowship on marrying Elizabeth
Perrochon of St. Helier's. In 1776 he became Rector of St.
Martin's. His share in capturing the French rear-guard at La
Rocque at the time of the French invasion of 1781 was long
remembered. A contemporary letter in the Library of the
Société Jersiaise says: — "Monsieur Le Couteur, Rector of St.
Martin's, brought down two cannons, which he had bought
and furnished with ammunition at his own expense after the
attack of the first of May (i.e. the Prince of Nassau's attempt
to land French troops in St. Ouen's Bay in 1779), and, having
joined the Glasgows, he showed Captain Campbell where the
French had landed, and urged him to attack them. But the
Captain, who had received positive orders to the contrary,
hesitated, feeling that he could not take responsibility for such
action without orders from the Commander-in-Chief. At last
a message came from Major Peirson saying that he was going
to disobey orders. In consequence of this and the persuasion
of Mons. Le Couteur the Captain ordered his Grenadiers to
charge the enemy with the bayonet, which they did, killing
and wounding twenty, and taking the rest prisoners". The
Société has also Le Couteur's own account of this day in a
letter written to Madame De Carteret of Trinity Manor, who
was then at Southampton: — "At half after seven in the morning I was suddenly awakened by one of the servants informing
me that the Alarm guns were firing all round the island. We
set immediately about preparing the cannon and getting ready
for the field. We had scarce begun when a man informed me
that a number of vessels were lying at anchor off St. Clement's.
I dispatched a servant to go to the heights and inform himself
with his own eyes what number of them were there. A few
minutes after came Lauges, the gunsmith, all out of breath, and
told me he was just escaped from St. Helier's, that the town
was full of French troops, that the Governor and his lady were
prisoners, and that himself had narrowly escaped with his life,
one of the soldiers having made a push at him with his bayonet,
and wounded him in the breast, upon which he opened his
shirt and showed me a wound. We moved toward Fort Conway in Grouville Bay to join a detachment of the East Regiment
and the Glasgow Volunteers. I then being on horseback

proceeded to reconnoitre their shipping ; and, it appearing to me that there might be some chance of setting them on fire, I returned to encourage the troops to march that way and endeavour to effect this. They were some time in doubt what step to take ; however after some deliberation they proceeded. We had not gone far when word was brought that the enemy had taken possession of a battery opposite their ships, and were there collected in force. The Grenadiers of the Glasgows separated in three platoons to attack them. I drew up my artillery upon an eminence to cover their retreat. The brave fellows soon put an end to the contest, though not without considerable loss. We then perceived that the ships were out of our reach, and the Commanding Officer having thought proper to return to the Fort (i.e. Fort Conway) with his corps, I remained with some of our own people to cannonade a boat that was coming to take off some of the French that had taken refuge among the rocks, which I had the pleasure of driving back without effecting her purpose, causing the enemy to the number of fourteen to be taken prisoners. Soon after Mr. Snow passed from Town to the Fort, I joined him. Conceive my astonishment, when I understood that he was sent as an express from the Governor with a shameful written capitulation to order all troops to suspend hostilities. Yet I did not entirely lose hope, though I lost all moderation. Fired with indignation I told the troops that I knew them by their late deportment to be too brave ever to submit to such preposterous terms, that Mr. Corbet was no longer Governor, since he was a prisoner, that, should they not march to the relief of St. Helier's, it would be an indelible blot upon their character, that I would go myself as a guide at the head of 300 of their men. As I was thus pleading the cause of honor, there arrived an express from the 95th Regmt. with a scrap of paper written with a pencil : — "Make haste to come to our assistance. We are going to engage". That to my inexpressible joy determined them to march".

In 1782 Le Couteur was appointed Vice-Dean. In 1783 by inheritance from his uncle he became Seigneur of La Malletière and of the Fief au Sauteur. In 1789 he moved from St. Martin's to become Rector of Grouville, the parish in which his new estate was situated. On 1 March 1799 he made a speech in the States, which he published, denouncing the narrow, winding, muddy lanes, which were the only means of communication in the island, and advocating the construction of military roads, for which he drew up a detailed plan. The credit for the modern road-system has been given entirely to General Don, but he did little more than carry out Le Couteur's suggestions.

In 1790 he founded the first Jersey Agricultural Society, and became its President. Its objects were improvements in road-making, cider-making, the construction of ploughs, the making of potato-flour, and the fattening of cattle. Members also pledged themselves to wear suits of Jersey-spun cloth (*drap d'ici*) with the hope of establishing a cloth-spinning industry in the island. At this time Jersey was producing annually over two million gallons of cider, and its export was the chief item in the local trade. Le Couteur was convinced that by scientific methods the yield could be increased and the quality improved. For thirty years he had been making experiments in the selection of apples, methods of grafting, transplantation, pruning, protection against pests, types of cider-presses, methods of clarification, etc. In 1801 he published the results of his research in his *Aperçu sur les Cidres à l'usage des Habitans de Jersey*. A second considerably enlarged edition appeared in 1806 ; and in 1808 an English translation was issued by the Board of Agriculture, *A Treatise on the Cultivation of Apple Trees and the Preparation of Cider, translated from the French of the late Rev. Francis Le Couteur, A.M.* He had previously published *Parallèle de la Culture des Grains et de celle des Pommiers rélativement à l'île de Jersey*, 1800. In spite of his many nonclerical interests he was evidently a good Rector. The *Gazette de Jersey* said of him at the time of his death: — "His solid, unostentatious piety, his freedom from every taint of worldliness, his scorn for frivolity, his kindness toward the poor and unfortunate, made him loved and respected by all". The Memoir prefixed to the English translation of his book on cider declared, "As a clergyman no one ever discharged his duty more conscientiously. He was in fact rather the Father than the Rector of his parish".

He died of typhus on 15 May 1808. He married Elizabeth, daughter of Jean Perrochon and had four children of whom the eldest, Francis John became Solicitor-General. [*Memoir* prefixed to the English translation of his book on Cider ; two articles in *St. Martin's Parish Magazine* 1898 ; Payne's *Armorial* ; MSS. *in Library of Société Jersiaise*.]

LE COUTEUR, JOHN (1760—1835) Lieut.-General. Son of
Jean Le Couteur of Les Buttes, St. John's, and Marie Bertault.
Born at Les Buttes, 26 Aug. 1760. Educated at Guildford
Grammar School. In 1780 he obtained a commission as Ensign
in the 95th. Foot, then stationed in Jersey. This was Peirson's
Regiment, and, in the following year, when Rullecourt invaded
the island, Le Couteur marched his men from St. Peter's to St.
Helier's, and took part in the battle. Four days later he was
transferred to the 100th. Foot as Lieutenant, and sailed with it
to India. He served in operations against Hyder Ali, and led
two forlorn hopes. Later his regiment joined the army fighting
'Tippoo Sahib', the Moslem Ruler of Mysore, and in 1782 they
were shut up in Nagur, and forced to surrender. The officers
were marched in chains naked for twelve days, and then imprisoned with legs in irons on a diet of rice and water, till peace
was made in 1784. "Souls released from Purgatory", wrote Le
Couteur, "could not experience more delicious sensations than
we enjoyed on obtaining our liberty". He published an account
of this compaign in *Letters from India* 1790.

In 1785 he was promoted Captain, but his regiment was
disbanded, and he was placed on half pay. He returned to
Jersey, and at once took an active part in local life. He became a
Centenier of St. John's, and, as that parish, through a disputed
election, was eight years without a Constable, for part of that
time he was Chief of Police. He identified himself with the
Magot Party, and helped the Dumaresqs (See *Dumaresq,
Jean*) to establish the *Gazette de Jersey* (See *Alexandre,
Matthieu*), and frequently contributed to it. In 1787 he
became Adjutant of the North-West Regiment of Militia. In
1790 he was elected Jurat. In 1792 he bought Belle Vue, St.
Aubin's, from Jean Dumaresq, and in 1793 married Dumaresq's
eldest daughter, Marie. In the same year he was appointed
Brigade-Major of the Militia, and in 1795 resigned his Juratship
in order to devote himself wholly to his Militia duties. Jersey
was expecting another French invasion, and Lieut.-Governor
Gordon had described the Militia as "an undisciplined rabble".
Under Le Couteur's vigorous handling matters rapidly improved.
Meanwhile his work in Jersey did not cause him to miss promotion in the Regular Army. In 1795 he was gazetted Captain
in the 11th Foot; in 1797 Major in the 16th; he was then
recalled for a time for regimental duties in Scotland, and in 1799

returned to Jersey as Inspector of Militia, a post which he held for the next twelve years. He now introduced against strong opposition the system of 6 a.m. drill for all boys of thirteen and upward, drills at which he himself was almost always present.

His tombstone in St. Brelade's Church reveals another task entrusted to him. It says, "He controlled the secret service in the French Revolution with Georges, Pichegru, and Larochejacquelein". Larochejacquelein, the Vendéan leader, was shot in 1794. The Republican General Pichegru joined the Royalists in 1795. Georges was the Chouan leader Cadoudal, whose revolt began in 1793. So it must have been in those years that Le Couteur handled the Jersey end of the help which England was secretly giving to all enemies of the Revolution. It is not clear whether he was working with the Duc de Bouillon (See *Dauvergne, Philippe*) or whether their work overlapped.

In 1808 he was promoted Colonel in the Army, and in 1811 Major General. He then laid down his work in the Militia, receiving the thanks of the States and a piece of plate of the value of a hundred guineas. He was placed on the staff in Ireland, and later sent to command a Brigade in Jamaica. In 1815 he was appointed Lieut.-Governor of Curaçao and its dependent islands, a Dutch colony off the coast of Venezuela, which was then in British hands. When this was restored to Holland, he returned to Jersey to his old home, Belle Vue. Here, according to his tombstone, "God blessed him with many years of health, peace, and contentment, which he devoted chiefly to the study of the Scriptures". He died at Belle Vue 23 April 1855. He had two sons, John (q.v.) and Gordon Thomas (b. 1801, d. 1817). [Memoir in *Guernsey and Jersey Magazine*, 1838 ; Sullivan's *General Don.*]

LE COUTEUR, SIR JOHN (1794–1875), Colonel, A.D.C. to William IV and Victoria, Fellow of the Royal Society, Agriculturist. Eldest son of Captain (later Lieut.-Colonel) John Le Couteur (q.v.) and Maria Dumaresq. Born at Belle Vue, St. Aubin's, 21 Oct. 1794. In 1808 he entered the Royal Military College. Here during an attack of pleurisy he shared a sickroom with George Fitzclarence, illegitimate son of the Duke of

Clarence, the future William IV, who was being nursed by Mrs. Jordan, his mother. In this way Le Couteur came in touch with Court circles. In 1810, when the second son, Henry Fitzclarence, was dismissed from the Navy in disgrace, the Duke put him under Le Couteur's care at the Royal Military College, with such good results that the Duke promised, "If ever I can be of service to you, you need only remind me of this".

In Nov. 1810, when 16, he was commissioned as Ensign in the 96th. Regiment, then stationed in Jersey, and in Nov. 1811 was promoted to a Lieutenancy in the 104th. Foot, and ordered to join his Regiment at New Brunswick. Immediately afterward war broke out with the United States, and his experiences included a nine-hundred miles' march through snow-covered forests and three years' confused forest fighting on the Niagara frontier alongside of Indian allies who scalped the slain. To control these Sioux braves in their own woodlands was no light task for a lad of eighteen. "The Indians were very savage", he writes in his Diary, "one tomahawked an American close to me during the parley". And again, "Indians are ticklish friends to deal with. I refused to give a half-drunken Indian a hide he coveted, over and above the meat which had been issued to his tribe. He snatched his tomahawk, and made a motion as if to cut me down. Self-preservation made me place my drawn sword to his throat".

When the American War ended and Waterloo was won, drastic cuts were made in the Army, and Le Couteur's regiment was disbanded. At twenty-two he found himself a Captain on half pay. He returned to Jersey, married his cousin Harriet Janvrin in 1818 (Her mother and his mother were sisters, both being daughters of Sir Jean Dumaresq), and settled in Le Bocage, close to his old home, Belle Vue. He threw himself strenuously into local life. In 1821 he was appointed Aide-de-camp to Sir Colin Halkett, the Lieut.-Governor, with the local rank of Lieut.-Colonel, and in 1829 he became Colonel of the West Regiment of the Militia. As member of St. Brelade's Roads Committee he persuaded it in 1824 to adopt Mc.Adam's new system of road-making. (Mc.Adam's Essay was only published in 1819, and the Parliamentary Committee which investigated his theories did not report till 1827 : so St. Brelade's must have been one of the first places where macadamized roads were tried.) In 1826 he became Constable, an office which he held till 1835, when he was elected Jurat. He was a very active member of the States. He proposed and secured the purchase of the first life-boat. The States put him in charge of the construction of the new road from St. Helier's to St. Aubin's. He secured the removal of the Militia cannons from the Churches, where they had always been kept, and the building of Arsenals, and also the abolition of Sunday elections.

In 1830 William IV came to the throne, and Le Couteur reminded him of his promise. The King at once appointed him his aide-de-camp for Jersey. He went to England to receive his commission, and evidently made a good impression, for five days running he was invited to dine at the royal table. On the last occasion he persuaded the King to add the word Royal to the title of the Jersey Militia. When Victoria came to the throne, she renewed his appointment as Aide-de-camp, and, when she visited Jersey in 1846, he was responsible for escorting her round.

When his father died in 1835, he moved to Belle Vue, and the same year was chosen Jurat after one of the most fiercely contested elections on record, the slogans of the other side being "Down with Militarism". "We want no Soldiers to judge us". But he got in by a two to one majority. In 1836 he persuaded the King to grant the King's Plate to be run for at the Jersey Races, an act which brought him a severe rebuke from his Quaker friend, Elizabeth Fry. In 1840 he began a long fight for the building of a breakwater at Noirmont, which would have made St. Aubin's the chief port of the island, but the interests of St. Helier's were too strong for him. In 1842 he was appointed Vicomte, a post which enabled him to put into practice some of Elizabeth Fry's theories of Prison Reform. In 1850 he was transferred from the command of the West to that of the Town Regiment.

He was a man of wide interests ; a geologist, perfectly happy on his travels, if he could wander about with a hammer, chipping off specimens of rock ; an amateur painter, who carried his sketch-book wherever he went, and, whenever in London, spent long days in the picture galleries. But his main hobby was horticulture and agriculture. In his first garden at Le Bocage, he records in his Diary, "Planted one Dahlia Purpurea, a Mexican plant, believed to be the first Dahlia brought to Jersey". At Belle Vue he experimented with many foreign bulbs and plants. He founded the Jersey Agricultural and Horticultural

Society (François Le Couteur's earlier Society had died of politics), and became its Secretary. For many years he made a careful, scientific study of wheat, and his book, *On the Varieties, Properties, and Classification of Wheat*, (1st edition 1836, 2nd 1872), was regarded as of such value, that in 1845 he was elected a Fellow of the Royal Society. His other writings were, *On the Use of the Jersey Trench Plough* 1842 ; *On the Rise, Progress, and State of Agriculture in Jersey* 1852 ; *The Rifle, its Effects on War* 1855. He gave valuable information to the Royal Commission of 1859 on the duties of the Vicomte, the administration of the Prison, and the laws of the island, specially the unsatisfactory state of the law regulating the tenure of real property. In March 1872 failing sight compelled him to resign the offices of Adjutant-General of Militia and A.D.C. to the Queen ; and in August his services were rewarded with a knighthood.

He died at Belle Vue in 1875, and was buried at St. Brelade's. He had two sons, John (born 1820), who died young, and John Halkett (born 1826), Lieut.-Colonel of the Coldstream Guards, who also died before him, and three daughters. Harriet (born 1819), Mary (born 1822), who married John Mannoir Sumner, eldest son of the Bishop of Winchester, and Sophia (born 1832) who died in 1844. The chief authority for his Life is his own voluminous diaries preserved at Belle Vue.

LE COUTEUR, JOHN DOLBEL (1883—1925), Painted-Glass Expert. Son of Philip Edward Le Couteur and Matilda Stratton Brice. When ill-health forced him to give up work in Lloyd's Bank, Jersey, he began about 1904 to take an interest in mediaeval painted-glass. He moved from place to place, and made himself thoroughly familiar with the glass of Canterbury, Exeter, Wells, Bristol, Fairford, the Cotswold churches, Gloucester, Tewkesbury, Salisbury, and Oxford. Everywhere he made friends with glass-painters and glass-specialists. During a stay at Great Malvern he helped to relead the windows of the Priory Church. He then settled at Winchester, where he made an exhaustive study of all old glass, ecclesiastical and domestic, in the city, and in 1920 published the result in his book, *Ancient Glass in Winchester*. At the invitation of the Dean he supervised the rearranging of the mediaeval glass in the great west window of the Cathedral. In the *Antiquaries' Journal* (Oct. 1924) he described how with one of the college boys he discovered and reconstructed part of St. Swithin's Shrine in the Cathedral. At his death on 13 Aug. 1925, he left a second book, *English Mediaeval Painted Glass*, ready for publication. It appeared in 1926. Though he had no scholar's training, he was recognized as a master of his subject. At his death appreciative notices of his work appeared in many papers, including the *Times*, *Guardian*, and *Notes and Queries*. [Memoir by G.M. Rushforth, in Le Couteur's *English Mediaeval Painted Glass*.]

LE COUTEUR, PHILIPPE (c. 1623—71), Dean. Son of Jacques Le Couteur of Le Câtelet, St. John's, Receiver-General, and Esther, daughter of Clement Botterel, Constable of St. Ouen's. Born about 1623. He was fifteen, when his father died, leaving six sons, all under age, the eldest an idiot, and one daughter. Their mother was appointed their *tutrice*. The *Clarendon Papers* contain a letter (19 Dec. 1646) from Sir E. Hyde to the Bishop of Derry, who, since being driven from his see, was acting as Chaplain to the English merchants at Antwerp, recommending "the bearer, Mr. Cooter, as a candidate for orders to fill a vacant benefice in the island". On 27 Feb. 1648 he was inducted as Rector of St. Mary's, which had been for two years Rectorless, since the tragic death of Jacques Bandinel (q.v.). Le Couteur's neatly kept Registers are the earliest that survive in this parish. He soon became a personality in the island, much in demand for funeral sermons and important baptisms. When Parliament recovered Jersey in Oct. 1651, he did not at once fly. His Registers show that he officiated regularly for the next four months. On 7 March he baptized the son of François De Carteret of Vinchelez de Haut in St. Brelade's Church ; but then his name drops out of local records. He spent the next nine years in France as a Minister of the Eglise Réformée, sitting in Synods and in every way recognized as a Huguenot Pastor. For part of this time he had charge of a Church in Caen, and for part he was Domestic Chaplain to the Maréchale de Turenne, whose husband, though a Protestant,

was Marshal of France.   She was a formidable *Grande Dame*.
A contemporary writes: — "Her virtue and piety are not
more memorable than her exact precautions to preserve the
privileges of highness and the precedence she claims above the
Duchesses" (Des Maizeaux' notes on Bayle).   But her Chaplain
seems to have got on well with her.   The *Jersey Church
Calendar* said in 1889: — "A collection of autograph letters
written 1659—62 existed not many years ago at La Hougue
Boëte Manor, addressed to him by several eminent ladies
of the Court of Louis XIV, the Maréchale de Turenne, the
Princess de Bouillon de la Tour d'Auvergne, with many others.
These letters are couched in terms of warmest friendship and
esteem for his talents, and character."

At the Restoration the Governor, the Earl of St. Alban's,
wrote to the States (28 July 1660), urging them to recall the
banished Ministers, and "to desire them from me and the whole
country to return to their Churches or to any they shall like
better, especially Mr. Cousteur" (O.C.).   Le Couteur chose St.
Martin's, from which the Parliamentarian, Pierre D'Assigny (q.v.
App. I.), had just been ejected.   On 3 July 1661 he was also
appointed Dean, an office that had remained vacant for sixteen
years since the death of David Bandinel (q.v. App. I.).   He was
sworn in on 23 Nov.   (His Patent and Oath are printed in *A.E.*),
and preached his first sermon at St. Martin's on the following
day.   The Church Register says: — "Almost all the island
Noblesse were present, and a great crowd of hearers from all
parts of the country".   In Sept. 1662 he married at Quevilly,
Rouen, Geneviève, daughter of Maximilien de Langle, Huguenot
Pastor at Rouen.   The lady was evidently rich, for by the marriage contract she assigned him £2,000, if she should predecease
him.

There had always been jealousy between the Ecclesiastical
and Royal Courts, and it was not till 14 Dec. 1663 that he
ventured to revive the former, but from that date onward it sat
weekly in the Town Church.   There was still considerable resistance to the restoration of Anglicanism.   Jean De La Place,
Rector of St. Mary's, refused to abandon his Presbyterian ways
and resigned.   His brother Pierre De La Place, Rector of St.
Ouen's, refused to take the oath of canonical obedience to the
Bishop, and was deprived.   Thomas Poingdestre, Rector of St.
Saviour's, was three times summoned before the Court for re-

ceiving to Communion those who did not conform. Jean Bichard was cited for saying that it was idolatry to communicate kneeling, Simon Lesbirel for calling the Church of England Service the Mass. Five years later we read: — "Philippe Le Feuvre, having repented of the scandal he had caused by speaking of the Communion Service as the Mass was sentenced to publicly confess his sin in St. Clement's Church on the following Sunday". Every week the Court dealt with a long list of moral offences, girls with illegitimate babies, and married couples whose first child had been born too soon after marriage. In each case the sentence was to do penance during the Sunday Service. Marie Lesbirel was punished for going to a masquerade dressed as a man, Jean Du Pré, Churchwarden of St. Mary's, for coming to church the worse for drink, and forgetting to remove his hat. The Regent of St. Mannelier was excommunicated for immorality, and deprived of his school. Alice Giffard was summoned for pretending to cure the sick with magical words ; and there were endless disputes about family pews. From time to time the Court issued long proclamations to be read in every Church. One of these ordered every communicant to receive the Sacrament kneeling. Another gave regulations for Baptism. This must always be administered on the first Sunday after birth, and none but regular communicants could be accepted as godparents.

Le Couteur died childless on 30 June 1671, and was buried in St. Martin's churchyard. He was succeeded as Dean by his brother Clement (q.v.). By his will (printed in *Bull.* IV) he left almost everything to his wife "in recognition of the help she has given me in health and often in sickness" with regret that he could not make better provision for "one who is so dear to me". [Authorities quoted above.]

LE CRAS, ABRAHAM JONES (1798—1869), Agitator. Son of Abraham Le Cras. Born Nov. 1798. "I was born in Salisbury", he told the Commissioners, "of a Jersey family". By the time he was twenty he was living in Jersey. In 1818 he announced in the local papers: — "A.J. Le Cras, Plain and Ornamental Penman, gives instruction in Penmanship, Arithmetic, English Grammar, and Geography at his Academy in Broad

Street". In 1819 he was offering to teach "Stenography in Six Lessons". He next turned his Academy into a junk-shop, and began to advertise for old rags and bottles. He then became a vendor of quack medecines, proclaiming the virtues of his Stomachic Candy, Medicinal Snuff, Pectoral Pills, and specially his Essence of Life, "the most universal remedy known". But his skill with his pen extended beyond the realm of ornamental penmanship. He could write racy, trenchant English, and he became Jersey's most prolific pamphleteer. He investigated with amazing industry the island's constitutional history. "For forty years", he told the Commissioners. "I have made the laws of the island my study. I have made a compilation of about 3,000 Orders in Council and from five to six thousand Acts of the Court. Those are the means by which I have acquired my information".

From these researches he evolved the startling theory that Jersey's claim to possess home rule was "founded on fraud and usurpation" (*Letter to Lord Palmerston*) ; that astute local officials in the past to increase their own power had bamboozled Commissioners sent over from England into recognizing bogus rights and privileges entirely without foundation ; that legally Jersey was subject to the British Parliament and the English Courts in exactly the same way as the Isle of Wight. "The States are not a provincial Parliament or a local Legislature, but a Municipal Council" (*Constitution of Jersey*). "They have no legislative powers. Their power is confined exclusively to matters usually cognizable by town corporations" (*Laws of Jersey*). "Their power is restricted to making bye-laws for roads, markets, harbours, pumps, taverns, and so on" (*Origin of the States*). "The law-making power for Jersey resides in Parliament, and nowhere else" (*Supplemental Memorial*). "The States have no more right to make laws for Jersey than I have" (*Commissioners' Report*).

There were now more than 15,000 English residents in the island, and they formed a colony quite detached from the Jersey people (e.g. "Between Jerseymen and the British there is very little social intercourse". Coghlan's *Handbook to Channel Islands*, 1843. "English Society in Jersey is quite distinct from the native Society. Intercourse is limited and infrequent". Payn's *Queen of the Isles*, 1840). Of this large group Le Cras now made himself the spokesman. Many of them had been annoyed at discovering that the local laws were different from those they would have found, if they had settled at Weymouth or Leamington. Le Cras' erudition was impressive to laymen, though lawyers like the Royal Commissioners, when he laid it before them, swept much of it aside as irrelevant antiquarianism. In 1830 a group of Englishmen advanced money which enabled him to publish a weekly newspaper, *The English and Foreign News*, which later adopted the portentous name, *The Jersey and Guernsey News, or General Advertiser for the Channel Islands, and Naval, Military, Commercial, Political, Agricultural, Scientific, and Literary Register*. In the following year he started a second paper, *The Patriot*. The *Patriot* appeared every Tuesday and the *News* every Friday, and each continued publication till 1849. He also published an annual calendar, *The Englishman's Almanack*. He had now a three-decker pulpit from which to preach his gospel of salvation from Jersey institutions, and to thunder against the States, the Royal Court, and the Honorary Police. He found however that Jersey journalism had its exciting moments. He was more than once arrested for libel. In 1842 he was horsewhipped in the street by someone he had criticized, and again in 1846 by the owner of a café that he had called a gambling-den. In 1839 he put his theories in more permanent form, and published through Longman's of London a book of 400 pages, *Laws, Customs, and Privileges in the Island of Jersey*.

In 1840 he won his first battle. He challenged the right of the States to naturalize aliens, a power they had exercised for centuries. The Law Officers of the Crown in England decided that this was illegal, and the States had to petition her Majesty in Council to ratify all the letters of naturalization that they had granted. This was done, and thus all doubts were dispelled as to the nationality of the persons who had obtained these letters. He then began to campaign vigorously against the Honorary Police, demanding "the introduction of an English police with an English superintendent". In 1844 he formed the British Protection Society, which published a list of tradesmen who were members of the Police, in order that English residents might boycott their shops.

In 1846 he started stirring up Parliament to assert its supposed powers. He persuaded Roebuck, M.P. for Bath, who had lived in the island, to move in the House of Commons that the House should appoint a Committee of Inquiry into the Criminal Law of Jersey. The Government refused to permit this, but promised a Royal Commission. This was a triumph for Le Cras. The English barristers, Ellis and Bros, sent as Commissioners, according to the *Nouvelle Chronique,* "knowing nothing of our habits, our customs, or our needs, regarded as evil everything that was not English". They did not agree to all Le Cras' demands—"It was urged upon us", they said, "to recommend measures little short of an absolute adoption of English law and an annexation of the island to an English circuit"—but they accepted many of his proposals. They recommended the appointment by the Crown of three paid Judges to take the place of the Royal Court and the Jurats, and the formation of "a paid police force independent of the Parochial Assemblies". It is impossible now even to tabulate all Le Cras' activities ; for example, between February and September he organized six petitions, one to the Privy Council for the immediate formation of the new Police system, another to the Home Secretary for the throwing open of the local Bar to all who wished to be Advocates, a third to the House of Commons against the transportation of Jersey criminals, then three more to the Home Secretary, about the treatment of lunatics, the procedure of the Court, and the law on trust-property—all in obedience to his slogan, "Keep the ball rolling". Nor did politics absorb all his energy. By 1844 he had become a Swedenborgian. In 1847 he published in London a book *On the Philosophy of a Divine Revelation,* and in 1848 he was one of the founders of the New Jerusalem Church in Victoria Street.

On 19 February 1848 his youngest son, Claudius Alphonso Weston Le Cras, who had managed his printing works, died in his 25th year, and in June 1849 Le Cras dropped both his newspapers. In 1850 he left Jersey, and went to live near Wimborne, alleging that Alderbury Lodge, the house he had bought in Les Vaux, "was assessed through party spirit at an exorbitant rate, for which there was no remedy, and that there was no security for his life through the corruption and irresponsibility of the police" (*Petition to Privy Council*). But by Aug. 1853 he was back at Alderbury Lodge, and again in the thick of the fray. He produced a stream of pamphlets, e.g. *A letter to Lord Palmerston.* 1853 ; *The Origin and Power of the States,* 1855 ; *Jersey, its Constitution and Laws,* 1858 ; *The Laws of Jersey and some existing Abuses*, 1858, and two larger books, *Manorial Rights in Jersey*, 1856, and *The Constitution of Jersey*, 1857. In 1858 he sent to the House of Commons a petition with 329 signatures asking for the abolition of the Royal Court, the appointment of the three Judges recommended by the Commissioners, and a new Commission "to inquire into the civil, municipal, and ecclesiastical laws in force in the island". Twelve months later he followed this up with a similar petition bearing 410 signatures. This was presented by George Hadfield, M.P. for Sheffield, with a long speech on "the unsatisfactory state of the laws of Jersey" ; and the result was the appointment of a new Royal Commission. Le Cras prepared for its arrival by forming a Jersey Reform Committee of eight English residents, which produced a *Memorial of the Jersey Reform Committee* of 96 pages, and then a *Supplemental Memorial* of 104 pages, beginning with a demand for the three paid Judges, "and that none but strangers to the island be in the first instance appointed", and ending with the suggestion, "It is desirable that a Bishopric be established in the Channel Islands, and that the Episcopal See be in St. Helier". Le Cras' examination before the Commissioners took the best part of five days, and fills 54 closely printed pages of the *Report*, which put forward 88 recommendations, including the appointment of the three Judges. The States referred this last proposal to the twelve Parish Assemblies, and, when these had all rejected it, adopted a policy of passive resistance. So Le Cras found a new parliamentary ally in Serjeant Pigott, M.P. for Reading, who in February 1861 asked the Home Secretary whether the Government intended "to bring in any Bill to amend the laws of Jersey". Sir George Lewis replied that "it was not the habit of that House to legislate on the internal concerns of Jersey". In spite of this Pigott in May introduced a Bill "to amend the constitution of the Court of the island of Jersey" ; but, after a long debate on its second reading in June, under strong pressure from the Government he withdrew it. In May 1862 he returned to the attack, but Grey again pleaded that the States should be given time. As they still did nothing, in 1864 John Locke, M.P. for Southwark, reintroduced Pigott's Bill, and this time it reached the Committee stage before it was withdrawn. The States then took a plebiscite of the island on the question of substituting paid Judges for the twelve Jurats. Le Cras worked hard to whip up voters, but it became manifest that his views had hardly any local backing. Only 180 votes were recorded in favour of the change. After this defeat he took little further part in public life. He died on 8 May 1869. He had married Maria Goodwin, and had three sons. His portrait appears in the Panthéon Jersiais No. 1. [His own writings ; *Reports* of the two Commissions ; Hansard ; local newspapers].

LE GALLAIS, PHILIP WALTER JULES (1861—1900), Cavalry leader. Grandson of Jurat Philip Le Gallais, and son of Edmund Le Gallais of La Moye and Léonie Metz of Luxembourg. Born, 17 Aug., 1861. Educated at Victoria College and in Germany. In 1881 he passed through the Jersey Militia into the 8th Hussars, and in the following year he went with his regiment to India. He became Captain in 1888, Adjutant in 1893, Major in 1897. From 1891—3 he was Aide-de-camp to the Commander-in-Chief, Bombay. In India he gained fame as a polo-player. His regimental team, in which he played No. 1, three years running reached the final in the Inter-regimental Tournament, and for the next two years won the Tournament. He was also a brilliant steeplechase-rider. In 1897—8 he served under Kitchener in the Nile Campaign. He was mentioned in dispatches after the Battle of the Atbara.—"Major Le Gallais' squadron gallantly charged the Dervish horsemen, forcing them to fall back"—and again after the Battle of Omdurman. He was given the brevet rank of Lieut.-Colonel, and received the Egyptian medal with two clasps. He remained in Egypt till 1900, when he went to the South African Campaign. He became Assistant-Adjutant-General to Ian Hamilton, and accompanied that General on his march to Pretoria. He was then given a mounted infantry command, and sent in pursuit of De Wet. He overtook him near Bothaville on 5 Nov., and in the five hours' fight which followed was shot through the left breast. De Wet described him in his book, *The Three Years' War,* as "without a doubt one of the bravest English officers I ever met". The choir-stalls in St. Brelade's church were given by his fellow-officers in his memory, and the States placed a commemorative tablet over the door of the Town

Church. [Burleigh's *Conquest of the Soudan : The Times' History of the War in South Africa:* Dooner's *Last Post,* and *British Sports and Sportsmen.*]

LE GEYT, CHARLES WILLIAM (1733—1827), Captain in the Army, first Postmaster in Jersey. Grandson of Philippe Le Geyt, junior, Lieut.-Bailiff, and eldest son of Charles Le Geyt (Seigneur of Saval, Colonel of the South Regiment of Militia, Constable of St. Helier's, 1726—33, Commissioner for Prizes) and Marthe De La Faye. Born in St. Helier's, 1733, and baptized in the Town Church, 4 May. He entered the Army, and in 1759 commanded a company of Grenadiers at the Battle of Minden. When the Seven Years War ended in 1763, he was placed on half pay, being then a Captain in the 63rd Regiment of Foot. On 7 April 1763, he married in St. Anne's, Soho, Elizabeth, eldest daughter of Dr. John Shebbeare, the notorious pamphleteer (See *Fiott, Nicolas*). He returned to Jersey, and soon became prominent in island politics on the anti-Lempriere side (See *Lempriere, Charles*). It was he who put Shebbeare in touch with Fiott. After the Revolt of 1769 Shebbeare stayed with Le Geyt at St. Saviour's (Aug. 1770) to collect material for his *Oppressions of the Islanders of Jersey.* In the following year Le Geyt was busy collecting signatures to a monster petition to the Privy Council demanding a Royal Commission to investigate complaints from Jersey. This petition he himself took to London in Feb. 1772.

In 1795 the English Post Office at last established a postal service with the Channel Islands, and a friend in London secured Le Geyt's nomination as Postmaster in Jersey. He knew nothing about this, and was astonished by the arrival at his house in Hue St. of a sack of letters and a warrant announcing his appointment. However he accepted the post, and held it for twenty years. The mail cutter crossed once a week. For the first three years there was no delivery ; but everyone had to call at Le Geyt's house for letters. This apparently kept him busy. "I breakfast at eight", he wrote in 1795, "to be ready to open at nine. I take one hour for dinner, which, I hope, will not be thought too much ; and nine in the evening is surely not too early to shut the Post Office, when, having no assistant except on mail-days, I have been from nine in the morning on my legs, and of course exhausted with fatigue" (*Bull.* XII). In 1798 he engaged an old woman to deliver letters in the Town, but it was not till 1829 that there was a country delivery.

In 1815 Le Geyt, being then 82, resigned his post in favour of his son. The old veteran died in 1827 at the age of 93. By his first wife, Elizabeth Shebbeare, he had two sons, Charles William, Major in the 45th Regiment, and George John. By his second wife, Marie Nicolle, he had three children, George William, who suceeded him as Postmaster, Pleydell Dawney, and Charlotte Ann. [*Bull.* V. & XII. Messervy's *Journal.*]

LE GEYT PHILIPPE (1635—1716), Lieutenant-Bailiff, Commentator on Jersey Law. Eldest son of Philippe Le Geyt, Jurat, and Jeanne Seale. Born in the Vingtaine of Mont à l'Abbé, St. Helier's, 1635, and baptized in the Town Church on 26 April. His boyhood was spent in the turmoil of the Civil War. He saw his home plundered by Parliamentarians, and the furniture destroyed. His Royalist father was in Elizabeth Castle, when it surrendered in 1651, and to escape confiscation of his property compounded by paying two years' income. The lad went to the Huguenot University at Saumur, and then took the Law course at Caen and Paris. He returned to Jersey, where his father, no longer a Jurat, had been living quietly under the Commonwealth Regime. At the Restoration his father resumed his seat on the bench, and Philippe was appointed Greffier (27 Sept. 1660), a post which his father had held before him ; and, when his father died, he was elected without opposition to succeed him as Jurat (20 Jan. 1670). In the following year he went as one of three Deputies to represent the States before the Privy Council. The Council had sent some Orders meant to improve the administration of justice. The Court had given them a trial, and found them unworkable. An appeal to the Council had secured only slight alterations. So this deputation was sent. After waiting fifteen months in

London, they returned with nothing accomplished. Sir George
Carteret (q.v.) wrote that he had done his best to secure an
interview for them, "but the attention of the Lords of the
Council is absorbed by the War and by great questions of
state now under discussion, and they have no time for less
important matters".

In 1676, when John Poindexter (q.v.) resigned the post of
Lieutenant-Bailiff, Le Geyt was appointed in his place. This
was no sinecure, for Sir Edward De Carteret, the Bailiff (q.v.),
was Gentleman Usher of the Black Rod, and his Court duties
kept him from the island. His successor, Sir Philippe De Carteret (q.v.), also appointed Le Geyt his Lieutenant, and, when
Sir Philippe died, he acted as Judge-Delegate during the interregnum ; so that for eighteen years he was Chief Magistrate of
the island and President of the States. He was the best Jurist
that Jersey has produced with a profound knowledge of Roman
Law, of the old Norman Coutumiers, and of the precedents of
his own Court. From the moment he became a Judge he
abstained (an unusual thing in Jersey both before and since)
from taking part in politics, lest he should be suspected of
partiality. In 1686 he presented to St. Helier's Church a silver
Baptismal Dish. (Fonts had not been used in Jersey since the
Reformation).

The Revolution of 1688 threw upon him a difficult task.
There were grounds for thinking that James II had some idea
of holding the island, as his brother had done, even if he lost
England. He appointed a Roman Catholic Lieut.-Governor,
and garrisoned Elizabeth Castle with Roman Catholic troops.
But Le Geyt quietly insisted that the local Militia should be
admitted to help to defend the Castle ; and, when the Prince
of Orange landed in England, a Protestant Regiment was sent
to Jersey, and the Roman Catholic soldiers were disarmed.

When Edward De Carteret (q.v.) became Bailiff in 1694, Le
Geyt asked to be relieved of his work as Lieutenant ; but he
retained his Juratship till 1711. He now had leisure for writing.
He had already in 1692 composed his *Procédé des Commissaires
Pyne et Napper,* a work invaluable to Jersey historians. His
other most important writings were his *Traité des Témoins*
(1696), which Sir Robert Marett considered his greatest claim
to the gratitude of posterity ; *Remarques sur quelques Loix et
Coutumes de l'Ile de Jersey* (1697) ; *Traité des Commissaires*

Royaux (1698) ; Traité des Crimes, in the course of which he
urges schoolmasters to take their pupils to see every execution
to impress on them a horror of crime ; and *Sentences et Questions.* He wrote also many shorter treatises on various legal
points. His last work was a series of *Méditations Chrétiennes.*
The treatise on *Priviléges, Lois, et Coutumes de l'île de Jersey
et Règlements Politiques,* commonly known as the *Code Le
Geyt,* a work of great merit, was almost certainly his work,
though his authorship has been questioned. He never married,
and in old age he lived with his nephew Philippe Le
Geyt. He died on Jan. 31st, 1716, and was buried in
the Town Church. His friend Baptiste Sorsoleil, Rector of St.
Lawrence, summed up his character thus : — "He was a man
of the old-fashioned school of virtue. In him knowledge,
courtesy, and probity were inseparably joined to love of religion
and zeal for justice". For many years his writings circulated
only in manuscript copies, but in 1841 the original manuscripts
were bought by Dean Jeune (q.v.), and offered by him to the
States, who printed them in four volumes: — *Les Manuscrits
de Philippe Le Geyt, Ecuyer, Lieutenant Bailli de l'Ile de Jersey,
sur la Constitution, les Lois, et les Usages de cette Ile.* 1846.
His portrait hangs in the Royal Court. [Memoir by Sir Robert
P. Marett prefixed to *Les Manuscrits. Eloge de Monsieur Le
Geyt,* by J.B. Sorsoleil. 1716. *Dic Nat. Biog.*]

LE GROS, AUGUSTUS ASPLEY (1840—77), Dialect poet.
(At his baptism his second name was registered as Asplet, his
mother's surname, but he always spelt it Aspley.) Son of
Edouard Le Gros and Mary Elizabeth Asplet. Born at St.
Helier's of a St. Lawrence family, 14 April 1840. Having lost
both parents, he was brought up by his maternal grandfather at
Allandale, Beaumont. He was educated at Victoria College
and then studied law for several years in the office of John
Coutanche, Solicitor ; but his interest in farming led him to
give up this, and to work his grandfather's land at Beaumont.
He was an active member of the committee of the Royal Agri-
cultural and Horticultural Society, and in 1865 became its
Secretary. In 1875 he was unanimously elected Constable of

St. Peter's, and in 1875 he was made a Jurat. This election too was almost unanimous, his two opponents receiving only 8 and 3 votes. In the States he was always on the side of progress, and in Court he was recognized as a scrupulously impartial and conscientious Judge.

From boyhood he had been an enthusiastic student of Jersey history. He joined many of the archaeological Societies of Normandy and Brittany, and it was largely due to his initiative that in 1873 the Société Jersiaise was founded. He became its first Secretary, and continued this work till his death. "He did more than anyone else", said the Annual Report of 1878, "to make it what it is today". He began to compile a Dialect Dictionary, which was continued by Thomas Gaudin, and eventually completed by a committee of the Société, and published as *Glossaire du Patois Jersiais*. He had a real gift for poetry, and wrote many poems in French and English and the Dialect. He published *Poems for Home and Fireside*, London, 1863, and *Poems*, London, 1868, and for eight years (1868—75) he printed an annual volume, *La Nouvelle Annaie, Pièches originalles en Normand-Jerriais*, containing dialect poems by himself and his friends. Other poems of his can be found in Pitts' *Patois Poems of the Channel Islands*, and annually from 1865 to 1877 in the *Almanach de la Nouvelle Chronique*, and also occasionally in the Chronique *Almanach*. Many of his poems reveal a deeply religious nature, and he was President of the Young Men's Christian Association. He published also *Mont Orgueil Castle: its History and Ruins*, and *La Bastaude à l'école de Maitresse Europa*, a translation into dialect of an English skit on the international situation. He died at the age of thirty-seven on 3 Dec. 1877, and was buried at St. Peter's. He married (I) Eliza Jane, daughter of Philip Payn, (II) Alice Marguerite Collas, by whom he had one daughter, Marie Louise. An excellent drawing of him appeared in *La Voix des Iles*, 26 April 1873. [Local Newspapers.]

LE HARDY, SIR CHARLES Senior, (1680—1744), Vice-Admiral. Grandson of Jean Le Hardy, Solicitor-General in Jersey, and 2nd. son of Philippe Le Hardy, Commissioner of Garrisons in Guernsey, and Mary Filleul of St. Helier's. Born in Guernsey, 1680. A naval officer, who rose steadily in his profession, till he became a Vice-Admiral, a Knight, and a Lord Commissioner of the Admiralty, though he never saw a gun fired in action. This is no imputation on his courage ; but his ship always happened to be elsewhere, when fighting was in progress. He entered the Navy at fifteen (30 Sept. 1695) as a volunteer on the *Pendennis*, which his cousin, Thomas Le Hardy (q.v.) commanded. After serving on the *Portsmouth* and the *Sheerness*, he was (28 Feb. 1701) promoted Third Lieutenant of the *Resolution*. In Dec. 1702 he was appointed to the *Weymouth*, and two years later to the *Royal Anne*. On 27 Nov. 1705 he was given command of the *Weazel* (6 guns). In 1706 he was transferred to the *Swift* (14), in 1709 to the *Dunwich*, in 1711 to the *Nonsuch* (50), in 1713 to the *Weymouth* (60), in 1718 to the *Guernsey* (50), in 1720 to the *Defiance* (60), in 1726 to the *Grafton* (70), then to the *Kent* (70), and in 1727 to the *Stirling Castle* (64). In Feb. 1738 he was appointed to the command of the *Carolina*, the royal yacht, which George II used for his voyages to and from Hanover, a position which he held for twelve years. In 1736 both King and yacht nearly went to the bottom of the North Sea. The King insisted on sailing in the teeth of a gale, and the furniture from the royal suite had to be thrown overboard, before the yacht could get back to harbour. On 6 April 1742 Le Hardy was promoted Rear-Admiral, and knighted. On 7 Dec. 1743 he was advanced to the rank of Vice-Admiral, and a few days later was appointed one of the Lords Commissioners of the Admiralty. In 1744 he was given command of a squadron to convoy a fleet of storeships to Lisbon. Having accomplished this, he resumed his seat at the Admiralty, and died suddenly a few months later on 27 Nov 1744. He married Elizabeth, daughter of Josiah Burchett, Secretary of the Admiralty, and had three sons, Josiah, Governor of the Jerseys, North America, John, Rear-Admiral, and Charles (q.v). Admiral, and four daughters, Mary, Elizabeth, Charlotte, and Margaret [*Dic. Nat. Biog.*]

LE HARDY, SIR CHARLES Junior (c. 1716—80), Admiral. Son of Sir Charles Le Hardy senior and Elizabeth Burchett.

Born about 1716. He entered the Navy in 1731, and received
his commission as Lieutenant in 1737. In 1741 he was promoted
Captain, and given command of the *Rye* (24 guns), and spent
a year cruising off the coast of Georgia. In 1744 he commanded
the *Jersey* (60), and in June that year was appointed Governor
of Newfoundland. He only held this post for a few months,
and then was recalled to England. On the return voyage some
of the ships in his convoy were captured. For this he was court-
martialled, but honourably acquitted. In 1745, still in the
Jersey, he had a three hours' fight with a French man-of-war,
La Sainte Esprit, in the Straits of Gibraltar, and crippled her,
but she escaped into Lisbon. For the next two years he continued in the Mediterranean. In 1755 he was knighted and appointed Governor of New York. It was a time of intense political
agitation. The previous Governor had committed suicide in
despair of being able to quell the rising spirit of independence.
And Le Hardy hated his job, and kept importuning the Home
Government to entrust him with some naval expedition (See
Sullivan's *History of New York State*). In 1757 he was promoted Rear-Admiral of the Blue, and ordered to put out to sea
with all the ships he could collect to escort the transports that
were to attack Louisburg ; but his fleet was caught in a hur-
ricane ; many of the ships were dismasted, and all he could
do was to bring the crippled vessels back to England. In 1758
he was made Rear-Admiral of the White, and ordered back to
New York to make arrangements for a second attack on Louisburg. During the blockade of Louisburg his flagship, the *Royal
William* (84), sank four French men-of-war, the *Apollo* (50),
the *Fidèle* (56), the *Chèvre* (16), and the *Biche* (16), and captured the *Echo* (52). In 1759 as Vice-Admiral of the Blue he
was Second in command of the Channel Fleet under Sir Edward
Hawke, and for the next three years his squadron and Sir
Edward's took turns in the ceaseless watch off Brest to prevent
the shattered remnant of the French Navy putting out to sea.
In 1762 he was promoted Vice-Admiral of the White, and in
1767 was one of the supporters of the canopy at the Duke of
York's funeral. In 1770 he was Admiral of the Blue, and in
1771 was appointed Governor of Greenwich Hospital. In 1774
he was elected M.P. for Portsmouth. In 1778 he became Admiral of the White, and in 1779 he was made Commander-in-
Chief of the Channel Fleet. This appointment was severely

criticized. The Earl of Bristol moved a vote of censure in the House of Lords, declaring that the Government had driven so many distinguished officers from the Service, that it "was now under the necessity of dragging forth Sir Charles Hardy from that repose which was suited to his time of life in the government of Greenwich Hospital, and compelling him at an age unfit for active service to undertake a task that may require the greatest activity ever displayed by a British seaman" (*Annual Register*). On this cruise Le Hardy had on board the *Victory* Benjamin Thompson, an American expert in ballistics, who obtained permission to accompany the fleet that he might make experiments in improving naval guns, and his day-by-day Diary has been reprinted in *The Naval Miscellany*, vol. III. Of Le Hardy Thompson wrote: — "Though he is sometimes a little positive, he is good-natured to a fault, and it would make you die of laughing to see him kick my hat about the deck, and attempt to be facetious and playful". (For a full discussion of this cruise see Introduction to Vol. III of the *Sandwich Papers*.) On 8 May 1780 he had an apoplectic fit at Portsmouth, and died. He married twice, first Mary, daughter of Bartholomew Tate, then Catherine, daughter of Temple Stanyan. He had three sons, George, Charles, and Temple, and two daughters, Susan, and Catherine. [The fullest account of his life (with portrait) is given in the *Naval Chronicle* Vol. 19.]

LE HARDY, CLEMENT (d. c. 1494), Bailiff and Lieut.-Governor. Son of Drouet Le Hardy, Jurat and Lieut.-Bailiff. In 1483 he was elected Jurat. On 12 Oct. in that year Henry Tudor, Earl of Richmond, last survivor of the House of Lancaster, who was living in exile in Brittany, put to sea on his first attempt to win the throne of England from his Yorkist rival, Richard III; but "the greatest wind that ever was" scattered his little fleet. When he reached Poole, he found the shore lined with troops to resist his landing. After waiting in vain for his other ships, he withdrew, and landed in Normandy, and was back in Brittany by 30 Oct. So far all contemporary authorities agree. But later a tradition survived in Jersey that on his way to Normandy he spent some days in the island.

Poingdestre, writing in 1682, speaks of his "having passed by Jersey, when he fled into France" (*Caesarea*). Falle wrote in 1694: — "Whether out of design or forced by contrary winds, he put into this island, where he lay concealed, till he found an opportunity to get over" (*Account of Jersey*). On the monument of Sir Thomas Le Hardy, erected in Westminster Abbey in 1732, the full story is told. It declares that Sir Thomas "was descended from Clement Le Hardy, who was made Lieut.-Governor, and had the office of Bailiff, or Chief Magistrate, of the island, with the Seigneurie de Meleche, conferred upon him for life by Henry VII as a reward for the most important service he had rendered him, when Earl of Richmond, after the disappointment he had met with in his first attempt upon England, when, being separated from the rest of his fleet by a storm, he landed privately in Jersey, intending to stay there, till he could obtain leave from the French King to come into his dominions, and was sheltered at the house of the said Clement, who protected him, and conveyed him safely to Normandy at the hazard of his own life, notwithstanding a proclamation from Richard III for apprehending the said Earl had been published in the island". (The inscription is printed in full in Payne's *Armorial*.) This evidence is admittedly late ; and against it may be quoted, not only the silence of all English authorities, but the fact that the *Chroniques de Jersey*, written in 1585, says nothing of the King's visit. On the other hand there are indications that the story may be true: — (I) On the way from Poole to Normandy Henry would pass Jersey, and he may well have thought it wise to make sure of the attitude of the French King before putting himself in his power. (II) If so, his visit to Jersey must have been secret, for Harliston, the Governor, was a wholehearted Yorkist. (III) As soon as Henry became King, Le Hardy was made Bailiff. (IV) Henry showed a quite unusual interest in Jersey. In 1486 he issued a Charter confirming the islanders in their privileges and rights. In 1494 and 1495 two long Orders in Council dealt with details of administration. He even appointed for the first time a Tabellion for Mont Orgueil. (V) The silence of the *Chroniques* may be due to the fact that the author, writing in the reign of Henry's grand-daughter, did not wish to admit that his heroes, the De Carterets, were then on the Yorkist side, and that it was an anti-De Carteret family that received the fugitive King.

In Feb. 1486 when Harliston, the Yorkist Governor, after a six months' siege surrendered Mont Orgueil, Matthew Baker and David Philip, two Esquires of the King's Body, who had been Henry's companions in exile, and were now high in his favour, were appointed Joint Governors, and Le Hardy was made Bailiff in the place of William Hareby, Harliston's stepbrother. We hear little of his term of office, except that he consistently supported Baker, who became Sole Governor in 1488. De La Croix prints documents (*Jersey: ses Antiquités*) which seem to show that he gave a judgement, which Royal Commissioners later decided to be unjust, in favour of the Governor in a dispute about mills in the Valley des Vaux ; and, when a long quarrel between Baker and Philippe De Carteret (q.v.), Seigneur of St. Ouen's, who had married Harliston's daughter, came to a head, and Baker trumped up a charge against him of conspiring to betray island to the French, Le Hardy committed De Carteret to Mont Orgueil without allowing bail, till the matter should be decided by ordeal of battle.

But a great storm, which wrecked a large Spanish ship off the Corbière, proved his undoing. The Seigneurs took full advantage of their right to wreckage. The Chronicler says that the hall of St. Ouen's Manor was half filled with bottles of sweet wine. And Le Hardy was tempted to secure some of this spoil for himself. "Matthew Baker had made Clement Le Hardy, the Bailiff, his Lieutenant, whereby he was so mightily puffed up, that his head was quite turned. Once, when the Lady of St. Ouen's addressed him as Gossip (*Compère*) instead of saying, Monsieur the Lieutenant or Monsieur the Bailiff, he swelled with importance and snarled, 'Zounds (*Dea*), Madam! Do you not know who I am?' She replied right courteously, 'Are you not my gossip, Clement Le Hardy?' 'Certainly not', he retorted, 'Am I not the Lieutenant and the Bailiff of Jersey?' 'Yes', said she, 'and you will be the first to be turned out'. And in truth no long time after this Baker fell out with him over some Spanish wines and other wreckage washed up on the beach, whereof a great amount was found on the King's fiefs which Le Hardy had retained for his private profit. Therefore Baker cast him into prison, where after a while he died covered with lice and vermin" (*Chroniques*). As Baker ceased to be Governor early in 1495, Le Hardy's fall probably took place in 1494. Thomas Lempriere was Bailiff in March 1495. In the Extente

of 1489 Le Hardy was registered as holding in his own right
the Fief of Crapedoit at St. Clement's and in his wife's right
the Fief Astelle in Grouville. He married Guillemine, daughter
of Jean Lempriere, Seigneur of Rozel, and had four sons, Edouard, who was a Jurat in 1524, Jean, who settled in Dorset, (and
became the ancestor of the Dorsetshire Hardys, including Thomas
Masterman Hardy, Nelson's captain, and Thomas Hardy, the
novelist) Richard, a priest, and Guillaume.
[Authorities quoted above.]

LE HARDY, THOMAS (d. prob. 1463), Rector of St. Martin's.
Son of Jurat Clement Le Hardy, who married a sister of Sire
Guillaume Lalague. His two brothers, Clement and Drouet,
both became Jurats. He is first mentioned as Rector of St.
Martin's in 1432. In 1442 he bought the Fief of Mélèches from
Jean De Carteret, in whose family it had been for nearly 150
years. In 1461, during the Wars of the Roses, Pierre de Brézé,
Seneschal of Normandy, sent a force which seized Mont Orgueil. In 1463 Le Hardy was arrested on a charge of plotting
to expel the Norman garrison. The evidence at his trial (printed
in full in *Bull* X) tells a good deal about him. Since his parents
married in 1381, and his brother Drouet was 72 in 1463, Thomas
must have been an elderly man at the time of his arrest. As
his duties included the Services in St. George's Chapel in the
Castle and in the Chapel of Rozel Manor as well as those in
St. Martin's Church, he had an Assistant Priest living with
him, spoken of as his Chaplain. Other members of his household
were his twelve-year-old cousin, Michel Payn, a manservant,
and a lad of fifteen. He rode about his parish on a mule.
Renaud Lempriere (q.v.), Seigneur of Rozel, was his closest
friend, and he was a frequent guest at the Manor.
    On the Thursday in Holy Week 1463 he went to say Mass
in the Castle, and Carbonnel, the Norman Captain, asked him,
as he understood English, to hear the confession of an English
prisoner. This was John Hareford or Hereford, one of Warwick
the Kingmaker's men from the garrison of Calais, who had been
captured in St. Ouen's Bay, while on a plundering raid. At Le
Hardy's trial it was alleged that during this interview he had told

Hareford that he too was a Warwick partisan, and had pointed out his house from the battlements, and had offered to hide him, if he could escape, till he could be smuggled to England. In Easter week Lempriere and his wife and Le Hardy dined with Carbonnel at the Castle. Hareford was also present. After dinner, so it was said, Le Hardy and Lempriere met Hareford in a court near St. George's Chapel, and asked him whether he needed funds, and offered him 100 crowns, if one night he would leave open the Rochfort sallyport, a small gate in the N.E. Corner of the Castle. This they strenuously denied. At Whitsun Le Hardy went to Normandy, and returned with news that Warwick had driven the indomitable Queen Marguerite, the heart and soul of the Lancastrian party, out of England. De Brézé was her cousin, and it was strongly suspected that he had seized the Castle with her connivance. This blow to the Lancastrians suggested that Jersey might now get rid of the Normans. The prosecution declared that on 11 Aug. Le Hardy met Hareford, who had been released on parole, at Rozel Manor, and read him letters from England reporting the formation of four new Yorkist armies, and also a letter from Guernsey, promising sixty men to rush the Castle, when he should open the gate. Le Hardy also agreed to Hareford's additional demand that Carbonnel should be his prisoner. On Sunday the 21st after Mass at St. Martin's Le Hardy invited two officers of the French garrison to dinner (the prosecution implied that he hoped to draw them into the plot), and the party spent the afternoon in the Manor gardens. After Vespers there was another meeting in the Manor of Hareford, Lempriere and Le Hardy, when, so it was alleged, a written agreement was signed and sealed. Obviously Hareford must have been acting from the first as a spy for the Normans ; for most of this information can only have been obtained through him.

Two days later both Le Hardy and Lempriere were arrested. On 10 Dec. they were brought up for trial before Carbonnel, du Vieuxchastel, Marshal of the Castle, and Guillaume De St. Martin (q.v.), a pro-French Jerseyman, who was Attorney-General. The trial lasted ten days. We have the depositions of the witnesses ; but unfortunately the last page of the manuscript is missing ; so we do not know the result. Lempriere however was apparently acquitted, for he was killed four years later helping to besiege the Castle ; but it looks as though Le Hardy was condemned, and his estates confiscated, for we find no later reference to him, and a contract among the Le Maistre MSS. shows that on 1 May 1465 Raulet De St. Martin, brother of the Attorney-General, was Seigneur of Mélèches.

LE HARDY, SIR THOMAS (1666—1732), Rear-Admiral. Son of Jean Le Hardy, Solicitor-General, and Marie, daughter of Richard Dumaresq. Born in St. Martin's 1666, and baptized in St. Martin's Church 13 Sept., Sir Thomas Morgan, Governor, and Thomas Jermyn, Lieut.-Governor, being his godfathers. He entered the Navy, says Charnock, "under the patronage of Admiral Churchill, to whom he is said to have been clerk, who procured him to be appointed a Lieutenant". At the Battle of Cape Barfleur in 1692 he was First Lieutenant on the *St. Andrew* (96 guns), commanded by George Churchill. In the following year he was given command of the *Charles*, fireship, from which he was transferred to the *Swallow Prize* (18), stationed at Guernsey to protect the Channel Islands. In Sept. 1695 he was appointed commander of the *Pendennis* (48). In the great naval reductions that followed the Peace of Ryswick (1697) he escaped being put on half pay, and in 1698 was given the *Deal Castle* (24), in 1701 the *Coventry* (50), and in 1702 the *Pembroke* (64). In 1700 he sold all his Jersey property to Charles Le Hardy (q.v.) and Charles Dumaresq.

In 1702 war broke out again with France over the succession to the Spanish throne, and the *Pembroke* was part of the great fleet sent to capture Cadiz. When this attack failed, Le Hardy was ordered to protect some transports which stopped at Lagos for water. Here Beauvoir, Le Hardy's Chaplain, a fellow-Jerseyman, went ashore. The French Consul, mistaking him for a Frenchman, boasted to him that the Spanish Plate-fleet, the richest that had ever left the Main, had evaded the British, and slipped safely into Vigo Bay. Beauvoir verified this, and collected further details, and carried the news to Le Hardy, who weighed at once, and, though the main Fleet had had two days start, and its destination was unknown, "though the head of his ship was loose, which endangered his mast, his ship leaky, and himself and his men reduced to two biscuits a day, notwithstanding the pressing instances of his men to bear away for England" (Charnock), he overtook it. Sir George Rooke, the Admiral, steered at once for Vigo, burst the boom, and destroyed the whole treasure fleet. Some of the spoil had been landed, but thirteen million pieces-of-eight fell into British hands. After the battle Rooke sent for Le Hardy, and asked him whether he knew that he was liable to be shot for leaving without permission the transports at Lagos. He replied, "I should be unworthy to hold my commission, if I held my life as anything, when the interest of my country requires me to hazard it". Rooke then gave him the honour of carrying the news to Queen Anne, who knighted him, and presented him with a thousand guineas. In Jan. 1703 he was given command of the *Bedford* (70), in which he took part in the drawn Battle of Malaga (1704), losing 74 killed and wounded. In December he was appointed to the *Kent* (70), in which he saw plenty of active service. In July 1707 he was ordered to escort 200 sail outward-bound for Lisbon. They sighted six enemy ships, but Hardy, thinking his duty lay with his convoy, did not attack. For this he was court-martialled, and honourably acquitted. and Sir John Leake, President of the court-martial, selected him to be First Captain of his flagship, the *Albemarle*.

The jealousy often caused in the Navy by promotion is illustrated by a paragraph in the *Life of Captain Stephen Martin*, written by his son. Martin had hoped to become First Captain, but was only made Second Captain under Hardy. Whereupon his son wrote: — "Sir Thomas was disagreeable to him and most unqualified for that post. He had been raised by Admiral Churchill from being Captain's Clerk to be a Captain, at which time he was so wholly ignorant, he did not know one rope from another. What little experience he got, after he was made Captain, served only to make his ignorance more conspicuous. To these disqualifications were added the most unhappy disposition, wholly composed of pride and ill-nature, which he showed by his outward behaviour and by a malicious grin ever upon his countenance. It was impossible to live a day with him without observing many ill-natured actions, ever being full of flaring taunts not to be endured by men of spirit. Add to all this he was a coward, having no sense of honour, though he had received the honour of knighthood, not for good behaviour but for being the messenger of our success at Vigo". His critics were not satisfied. They challenged the verdict of the court-martial in the House of Commons and in the House of Lords, which appointed a committee of inquiry. This reported that "he had fully justified himself and done his duty in every respect". In 1708 he was appointed to the *Royal Sovereign* (100), from which he was transferred to the *Russell* (74). In May 1710 he was elected an Elder Brother of Trinity House. In Jan. 1711 he was promoted Rear-Admiral of the Blue, and given the task of blockading the privateers in Dunkirk. In April he was returned as M.P. for Weymouth. In 1712, in ignorance of the fact that peace negotiations were in progress, he fought and captured six French vessels off Finisterre, only to find that Marlborough had fallen, a truce had been made, and therefore they could not be reckoned as prizes. In 1715 he was Second-in-command of the fleet sent to the Baltic to intimidate Sweden. But after the Jacobite rising of 1715 all officers suspected of sympathy with the Pretender were dismissed, and he was one of the victims. It is said that he was reinstated later, and promoted Admiral of the Red ; but, if so, it was on a reserved list, for his name does not appear in the list of flag-officers of 1727. He died, 16 Aug. 1732, and was buried in Westminster Abbey, where there is a pretentious monument to his memory on the south side of the west door. He married Constance, daughter of Col. Henry Hock, Lieut.-Governor of Plymouth, and three children survived him, Thomas, Charlotte, and Constance.

[*Dic. Nat. Biog.* ; Clowes' *Royal Navy* ; Charnock's *Biographia Navalis* ; *Naval Chronicle* 1808 ; Calender's *Sea Kings of Britain* ; the long inscription on his tomb is given in Payne's *Armorial* ; a full account of his court-martial is in *Annals of Queen Anne's Reign*, Vol. VI.]

LE HARDY, THOMAS (b. 1771   ), Miniaturist. Son of Thomas Le Hardy and Françoise Dumaresq. Born in St. Saviour's 1771, and baptized in St. Saviour's Church 20 June. Sir John Le Couteur (q.v.), wrote in his Diary on 30 April 1790: "Spoke to Mr. Philippe Jean (q.v.), the miniature painter, and found he would assist Mr. Le Hardy's son in his line, if he came to Town" ; and again on 7 May "Called on Mr. Jean,

and carried him Mr. Le Hardy's drawings. He promised he
would assist in bringing him forward". Le Hardy evidently
came to London, and in 1793 he exhibited in the Royal Academy a Portrait of a Boy. Between that year and 1807 he exhibited 21 miniatures in the Royal Academy and 4 with the Society of Artists. Among the celebrities whom he painted were
Philippe Dauvergne, Duc de Bouillon (q.v.), Dr. Daniel
Dumaresq (q.v.), Ignaz Pleyel, the composer, Johan Salomon, the
violinist, William Barrymore, the actor, Sir Henry Gould, the
judge, Dr. Osborn, the accoucheur, Edward Miller, the organist,
John Moody, the actor, Wilhelm Gramer, the violinist. A miniature by him of Capt. J. Fiott is in the S.J. Art Gallery. Engravings were sold of many of his paintings, most of which were
engraved by himself. Long says in his *British Miniaturists:* —
"Le Hardy's style varied considerably. His miniatures are well
drawn, and express a good deal of character. Some are soft in
treatment, others bolder ; some somewhat French in manner,
others more English". Pasquin's *Critical Guide to the Royal
Academy of 1796* calls his miniature of Dr. Samuel Arnold, Organist of Westminster Abbey, "a good smiling likeness. This
eminent composer looks as if in the act of letting off a pun".
Two of his miniatures are still exhibited in the Victoria and
Albert Museum —'The Rev. A.K. Thomas D.D.' and 'A Youth'—
and the latter is reproduced as one of the illustrations in the
catalogue. He did not confine himself to miniatures. The
National Portrait Gallery has a portrait by him of Horne Tooke
the agitator, measuring 29 inches by 24. Le Hardy's portrait was
painted by Dahl and engraved by Faber. In 1802 a J. Le Hardy,
probably his younger brother Jean (b. 1776), shared his studio,
and exhibited miniatures in the Royal Academy till 1807.

LE MAISTRE, FRANCIS WILLIAM SYNGE (1859—1940).
Artist, second son of the Rev. George Le Maistre M.A. and
Augusta, elder daughter of Dr. Alexander Low of Maison du
Coin, St. Brelade, was born at St. Aubin's, and educated at his
father's school there, then at Reading School, and Brighton Col-
lege, where his father became a master. He then went to King's
College, London, to study medicine ; but showed his interest

in art from the beginning by spending all his spare time in Art Galleries. He eventually gave up his medical studies, and, living with his aunt, Miss Low, in London, took up painting as his life's work. After his aunt's death he came to live with his parents at Maison du Coin, and he remained in Jersey for the rest of his life. He was specially interested in seascape, and had a studio built at the Corbière where he could study waves. In 1907 he married Alice, youngest daughter of Col. C. Le Cornu of La Hague Manor, and, after living at Graystones, St. Aubin's, built Grey Gables at the top of Mont au Roux. This house was sold later, and then he built Windward House, where he resided from 1925 till his death.

He exhibited for many years at the Annual Show of the Royal Institute of Oil Painters to which he belonged, and in 1905 had a picture hung on the line at the Royal Academy. One of his seascapes painted on commission for the Royal Empire Society was much admired by the King and Queen, and he painted one of the tiny pictures for Queen Mary's Doll's House. Two of his Jersey scenes, La Pulente Bay and St. Brelade's Bay, were reproduced by the Medici Society. Four of his pictures are in the Société Jersiaise Art Gallery, three are hung in St. Brelade's Church Hall, and many others are in private collections in the island.

By his will he left to the Parish of St. Brelade several of his pictures and the offer of Windward House, that it might be converted into a Parish Hall, with a picture gallery in the grounds ; but he died in May 1940 within forty days of making this will, and therefore by Jersey Law it was held to be invalid. His wife survived him only three weeks.

LE MAISTRE, THOMAS (1714—1800), Palaeologist. Little is known about him. The St. Saviour's Church Register shows that he was the son of Jean, the son of Jean, the son of Abraham, that he was baptized on 14 March 1714, married to Jeanne Falle on 7 July 1751, and buried on 9 July 1800. He was sworn in as Centenier of St. Saviour's on 14 July 1774. A MS. volume of verse in the Société Jersiaise Library shows that he was fond of composing French poetry, largely on religious themes.

But his chief claim to remembrance is a row of hand-written volumes in the Société's library still redolent of the snuff that he used as he wrote. What Thomas Rymer did for England, collecting in his *Foedera* every ancient charter and historic document that he could lay hands on, Thomas Le Maistre with equal diligence did for Jersey. He unearthed charters, contracts, acts of the court, licences, wills, and letters patent, musty old pachments stored away in mouldering muniment chests, and copied them out in his beautifully clear writing. This was his life's work. He began his first volume, so he tells us, in Sept. 1748, and, having finished it in Oct. 1764, took it to Diélament Manor, where "in the presence of the Jurats of the isle, the Attorney-General being present" it was "put under the seal of the isle" (the green cord to which the seal was fastened is still on the book), each official paper having first being compared word for word with the original by the Greffier. As a St. Saviour's man he was specially interested in his own parish. He transcribed Lists of Services due from tenants of the King's Fief, an older Burial Register than any now in the Church safe, a list of pre-Reformation endowments of the Church, and deeds of sale showing what happened to them at the Reformation, and a mass of papers about St. Mannelier Grammar School. He toiled on, volume after volume, till thirteen large folios had been filled and one smaller book. In his last volume he tells us that he made the index "on 31 May 1796, being then 82 years old". Many of the documents he copied, Chevalier's *Journal*, for example, the *Extentes*, and the *Acts of the States*, have been published since his day. But much remains unprinted, a mine of information for historians of the island.

LEMPRIERE FAMILY. This family originated in the Cotentin, where they possessed a small Fief de l'Emperière at Crosville, near St. Sauveur-sur-Douve. They spread to other parts of Normandy, and established branches elsewhere. Toward the end of the 13th century a colony of them appeared in Jersey. In the Extente of 1274 a Willelmus dictus Imperator (i.e. Guillaume dit l'Empereur) is mentioned as a Jurat, holding a Fief in the parish of St. Helier known as the Fief of Guillaume l'Empereur. At the time of the Assize of 1299 a Raoul or Ralph Lempriere held this Fief, which consisted of thirty acres, and was known as the Fief ès Empereres. Other members of the family appeared before this Assize. Matilda, daughter of the late Guillaume Lempriere, sued Raoul for certain rentes, and Guillaume Lempriere, son of Guillaume, sued Raoul's sureties for 10 *livres tournois*. Jourdan Lempriere was fined for an assault, and Guilbert Lempriere was prosecuted for unjustly detaining a common, and in another case a Philippe Lempriere was appointed an arbitrator. The Raoul mentioned above is said in Payne's *Armorial* to have been a son of Jean de Lempriere, Seigneur of Pont Ruilly, near Bricquebec in the Cotentin ; but this seems only a guess and a bad one. The French genealogist d'Hozier, who deals fully with this branch of the family, knows nothing of any such son ; and, when Raoul's grandson Raoul (q.v.) bought Rozel Manor the objection was raised that he was a Breton, and therefore incapable of holding land in Jersey. The elder Raoul is more likely to have been a son of Guillaume, the first holder of the Fief ès Empereres, who probably belonged to a branch of the family that had settled in Brittany. Raoul built a *colombier* (dovecot) on his Fief ; but this was a privilege granted only to a limited number of manors, and at the Assize of 1304 he was ordered to pull it down. He ignored this order ; so, when Justices Itinerant visited Jersey in 1309, he was prosecuted. "Ralph comes and offers our Lord the King a rent of one pound of pepper to be taken every year for ever, so that he and his heirs may enjoy the dovecot ; and it is allowed" (*Assize Roll*). By 1331 he was dead, for at the Assize in that year his son Thomas (who also held the Fief Torney in the same parish) was sued for not having paid the pepper. He pleaded that he had pulled down his father's dovecot ; but the Justices decided that the fine had been promised for ever, and therefore must still be paid. This Fief was long ago absorbed into the Fief of Mélèches, but the pound of pepper continues to be paid today by the tenant of the latter Fief. Thomas' son Raoul (q.v.) bought Rozel Manor. [Leturcq's *Généalogie de la Famille de l'Emperière* ; article, Ancienne Généalogie in *Bull* V ; *Extente* 1274 ; *Extente* 1331 ; *Assize Roll of* 1309 ; Payne's *Armorial*.]

LEMPRIERE, CHARLES (1714—1806), Lieut.-Bailiff. Eldest son of Jurat Michel Lempriere, Seigneur of Diélament. Born 1714, and baptized at St. Saviour's, 29 Aug. On 23 Aug. 1733, when eighteen, he married his first cousin, Elizabeth, only daughter of James Corbet, Seigneur of Rozel. As her father had been drowned in the wreck of the Hynde, by this marriage he became Seigneur of Rozel. On 1 Aug. 1741 he was sworn in as Solicitor-General. In this office he spent most of his time fighting Jean Le Hardy, Attorney-General, about their respective rights. This dispute began in 1741, and was not finally settled till 1749, when the Privy Council ruled that the Attorney-General "is the superior officer and the proper person to carry on all suits in which the King's Interest is concerned" (O.C.). While waiting for his case to be tried, Lempriere spent much time in London, and made influential friends, including Earl Granville, the non-resident Bailiff, and William Sharpe, Secretary of the Council.

The Lemprieres had long been the leading democratic family in the island. Charles' great-grandfather, Michel (q.v.), had been Cromwell's Bailiff ; his grandfather, another Michel, had been one of five Jurats deposed for sedition ; and at first Charles followed the family tradition, and was the outspoken champion of the island's rights. "Damnation to the Governor was drunk in all companies and success to honest Charles Lempriere" (Shebbeare). On the death of Philippe Le Geyt junior (q.v.) he was appointed by Lord Granville, the Bailiff, as his Lieutenant. The Court protested that he was not a Jurat, but Granville refused to revoke his appointment, and the dispute ended by Lempriere being elected a Jurat (O.C.). He was sworn in as Lieut.-Bailiff 13 Nov. 1750, and for thirty-one years, as Granville never visited Jersey, presided over the Court and the States.

His position was strengthened by the support of relations. At the time of his appointment his father, his father-in-law, and a first cousin, were Jurats ; in 1761 and 1762 two brothers-in-law were also raised to the Bench. In 1758 he secured the appointment of his brother Philippe (q.v.) as Attorney-General. Entrenched behind this family group his democratic sentiments evaporated, and he ruled as an autocrat, issuing ordinances through his Court, and punishing in the same Court all who protested. Moreover he was charged with using his power to feather his own nest.   Shebbeare (*Oppressions*) gives a long list of accusations.

Resentment against his methods was increased by the unpopularity of his brother Philippe), who, when Receiver-General, had made enemies among the farmers by the ruthless way in which he exacted the uttermost farthing of the King's dues, and the feeling that it was useless to appeal to the Court, because his Jurat relations would decide in his favour.   Moreover the poor suspected the brothers of artificially keeping up the price of corn, and therefore of bread, to increase the value of their wheat-rentes.   Among more influential people too exasperation was growing.   In 1759 Lempriere began his long quarrel with Fiott (q.v.), a man as rich and obstinate as himself, and though in the opening rounds Fiott was worsted, and in 1764 sent to prison for contempt of court, his constant appeals to the Privy Council called attention in England to the discontent in Jersey.   A group of half-pay officers too, who were living in the island, among whom Moyse Corbet (q.v.), Philippe Fall (q.v.), and Charles Le Geyt (q.v.) were prominent, became active opponents of the Lemprieres.   In 1770 they were reinforced by the arrival at Trinity Manor of Philippe De Carteret (q.v.) the circumnavigator, who threw himself heart and soul into the anti-Lempriere movement.

The first breach in the Lempriere position was the election as Jurat in 1767 of Philippe De Carteret of Mont au Prêtre, a definite opponent of their rule.   But a far more alarming explosion was approaching.   An openly revolutionary movement sprang up among the working people.   Food was scarce, and notices mysteriously appeared on the walls warning ship-owners that "whoever shall presume to take cattle or other provisions on board for export, their vessels will be burnt or otherwise destroyed".   In April 1768 the States forbad the export of corn ; but next year the harvest was good, and this Act was repealed. A great outcry arose: — "The Lemprieres are exporting our corn again to make it scarce and dear".   A mob of women boarded a corn-ship in the harbour, unloaded it, and sold the corn on the quay, paying the money to the owners.   A month later on 28 Sept. 1769, hundreds of men from the eastern parishes swarmed into the Royal Court, where the Assize d'Héritage was sitting.   Advocate Poingdestre described the scene: — "A great number of people armed with clubs forced their way into the

Court, threatening the Magistrates that, if they did not comply with their demands, they would not let them go, lifting their clubs from time to time, and striking on the benches ; and, notwithstanding the Rioters were granted every demand, they seemed not yet satisfied, but broke into the inner Court with such rage and fury, that this deponent did not expect the Court to escape with their lives" (*Bull.* XIII). The official Report to the Privy Council declared: — "A numerous body of Rioters, armed with large Clubs, forced themselves by violence into His Majesty's Court at a time when the Lieut.-Bailiff and Jurats were sitting, and not only obstructed the proceedings, but illegally extorted by most daring threats several Extraordinary Acts greatly derogatory to His Majesty's Authority" (*O.C.*). That this was a carefully planned rising is shown by the Thirteen Demands that had been prepared beforehand. These included the reduction of the price of corn to 20 sols per cabot, of crown tithes to 20 sous per vergée, and of the value of the sol to 4 liards, the abolition of the Seigneur's claim to enjoy for a year and a day the property of persons dying without heirs of their bodies, the banishment of foreigners, the expulsion of Revenue Officers who were on their way from England, the release of Philippe Larbalestier, and permission for Nicolas Fiott (q.v.) to return without penalty. When once these Acts were registered, the people dispersed quietly.

The next two days passed peacefully. On the Sunday the Acts were proclaimed in eleven of the twelve Churches. But on that day some rumour caused the Jurats to take fright. With Lempriere at their head they fled to Elizabeth Castle. Here on 6 Oct. he called a meeting of the States, which authorized him to go to London with his brother and two Jurats to report to the Privy Council. The Council ordered the extorted Acts to be erased from the Court records, sent a detachment of the Royal Scots to restore order, and instructed their commander, Colonel Bentinck, to report on the cause of the trouble. This shrewd Dutchman formed an opinion unfavourable to the Lemprieres. Humiliation after humiliation now fell on the Lieut.-Bailiff. On 15 June 1770 the Council ordered proceedings against the rioters to be dropped ; on 19 Dec. they received the King's Pardon ; in March 1771 the Pardon was extended to all whom Lempriere had arrested since the Riot ; in June Fiott too received the King's Pardon. In 1770 Lempriere saw his brother-in-law Ricard lose his post as Receiver-General, and in 1771 his brother Philippe allowed to resign the Attorney-Generalship, and, most mortifying of all, his cousin Moyse Corbet, his most active opponent, created Lieut.-Governor. The power to legislate was entirely taken away from the Court, and entrusted solely to the States. In the same year Lempriere resigned the Colonelcy of the North Regiment, stating that he could no longer command rebels (Messervy's *Journal*). Monster petitions asking for reform poured in to the Privy Council ; and now his enemies began to use the printing-press against him. Corbet's *Griefs de l'Ile de Jersey* was published in 1770. In 1771 and 1772 devastating attacks appeared from the pen of John Shebbeare, a notorious pamphleteer, who had been hired by Fiott: — *An Authentic Narrative of the Oppressions of the Islanders of Jersey* ; and *Tyranny of the Magistrates of Jersey demonstrated from Records of their Courts.* In 1773 an anonymous pamphlet, *Anecdotes relating to the Island of Jersey*, was believed to be by Colonel Campbell, who had been Lieut.-Governor 1762—1766.

Philippe Lempriere left Jersey, never to return ; but Charles stood his ground. He still had the Royal Court behind him, and a majority in the States, and a strong backing in the country. In 1770 he began to rebuild Rozel Manor. (Since his father's death he had been living at Diélament.) But now a new opponent appeared. Jean Dumaresq (q.v.), a brilliant young Winchester scholar, returned from France full of enthusiasm for the new democratic ideals that were stirring that nation. He determined to smash Lempriere's policy of government by a junta of Jurats. The two men became leaders of bitterly hostile parties, the Charlots or followers of Charles Lempriere and the Jeannots, who came to be called the Magots, the followers of Jean Dumaresq. Dumaresq was a born demagogue, an adept at every trick for stirring up popular fury ; and year by year Lempriere saw himself losing ground. Every election was fiercely contested by methods legal and illegal, neither side hesitating to resort to bribery and intimidation ; and at last a time came when almost all the Constables were Magots. As most of the Rectors voted with Dumaresq, this gave him a majority in the States. The struggle then became one between the States and the Court. But even here Lempriere saw defeat looming ahead. The increasing Magot vote at each election for Jurat showed that his enemies would soon capture the Court also. In 1781 he yielded to the inevitable, and went to England to resign in favour of his son, William Charles (q.v.). Thus he was out of the island at the time of De Rullecourt's invasion. So long as William Charles lived, his father was always behind the scenes, supporting and advising him. Even after his son's death in 1790 he remained the head of his party, mercilessly attacked by the *Gazette* as "the Baron of Bo-bo-bo". He lived to see the Royal Court become predominantly Magot and his enemy Jean Dumaresq Lieut.-Bailiff ; but he did not live to see the swing of the pendulum bring his party back to power under their new badge of the Laurel. He died in Rozel Manor 27 Aug. 1806, aged 92 "in full possession of all his faculties" (Burial Register. St. Martin's). His children were Charles (b. 1741), Sophie, (b. 1751), William Charles (b. 1754), Thomas (b. 1756), and Philippe (b. 1761). Two portraits of him are preserved in Rozel Manor, one painted when he was a boy of about ten, the other when about sixty. [All that can be said against Lempriere is set out in Shebbeare's *Oppressions*. Messervy's *Journal* gives an account of the Revolt by a Lempriere supporter. MSS. in the S.J. Library throw additional light on this. See also *Bull.* IX and *Ordres de Conseil*. For his struggle with Dumaresq see *A Collection of Petitions and Answers of the States and Royal Court relative to Political Differences*, 1788. Also *Gazette passim*.]

LEMPRIERE, CHARLES, (1818—1901), Writer and Politician. Second son of Dr. John Lempriere, compiler of the *Classical Dictionary*. Born 1818. Educated at Merchant Taylors and St. John's, Oxford. Matriculated 1837. B.C.L. 1842. D.C.L. 1847. Called to the Bar, Inner Temple, 1844. Travelled in Egypt and the Levant for various financial groups. In 1850 became Central Agent of the Conservative Party. In 1861 was sent by Sir Moses Montefiore to Mexico, then in a state of turmoil, to safeguard, as far as possible, threatened British interests. Travelling by way of the United States, he wrote *The American Crisis Considered*, 1861, a strong defence of the cause of the South. In the following year he published *Notes on Mexico*, which had a large circulation. In 1865 he returned to political work in England. In 1866 he stood for Winchester,

but was defeated. In 1867 his political services were rewarded
by the Colonial Secretaryship of the Bahamas. Here his Tory
views made him unpopular. He was accused of interference in
elections. His house was sacked, and he was forced to resign.
He went to the United States, and worked under Horace Greeley
as a writer on the *Tribune*. On Greeley's death he organized
in 1872 a Colony of young Englishmen at Buckhorn in Western
Virginia on lines suggested by Tom Hughes ; but this was a
failure, and the colonists were half starved. He returned to
England in 1879, and for the next ten years travelled widely in
the employ of financial syndicates. He died in 1901. His portrait is in Rozel Manor. [*Dic. Nat. Biog.*]

LEMPRIERE, CLEMENT (1683—1746), Cartographer and Artist. Eldest son of Thomas Lempriere of St. Helier's and Joan
Beach. Born 1683 and baptized in the Town Church on 18
January. Of his early life we know nothing, except that he was
a Captain, though in what service is uncertain. The usually
accurate Thieme says, "by profession a ship's captain"; but
his obituary notice in the *Gentleman's Magazine* calls him
"captain of a marching regiment". He evidently travelled, for
his sketches include views of Scotland, Portugal, Minorca, and
Bermuda ; but we cannot date his movements by them, for
many of them were not published till after his death. His earliest publication seems to have been a map of *The Roads between
Innersnait, Ruthvan, and Fort William in the Highlands* 1725.
Two years later he was appointed Draughtsman to the Civil
Branch of the Ordnance Office at a salary of £100 a year with
an office in the Tower, a position which he held till his death.
His next publication was *A Calculation of the Times of all
Eclipses for upward of twenty years*, 1738. That year he was
specially busy. He published *A Map of Bermuda or the Summer Islands from a survey by C. Lempriere* ; nine seascapes
with warships, engraved by W.H. Toms ; and also *A General
and Particular Prospectus of the Islands of Jersey, Guernsey,
Alderney, Serc, Arm, and Jethou, drawn on the spot by A.
Bastide and finished by C. Lempriere*. (Copies of these pictures
are in the S.J. Museum.) He followed this next year with a

series of *Views of Lisbon*, engraved by Fourdrinier, and sixteen sketches for the copper-plate engravings in Pine's *Tapestry Hangings of the House of Lords*. As the tapestries were destroyed in the fire of 1834, these drawings are the only record of them that survives. In 1740 he published *A Plan of the City of Lisbon*. He died 9 July 1746 (*Gentleman's Magazine*). After his death were published: — *A Plan of the Tower of London* 1750 ; *A New and Accurate Survey of the Island of Minorca* 1753 ; *A New and Accurate Map of Jersey* 1755 ; *A View of the City of Lisbon before the late Earthquake* 1756 ; and a number of single views. His portrait was painted by T. Frye and engraved by J. Faber junior. A copy is in the S.J. Museum. [Thieme's *Lexikon der Bildenden Künstler* ; Chamberlayne's *State of Great Britain* 1745.]

LEMPRIERE, JAMES (b. 1654), Captain R.N. Son of Clement Lempriere and Elizabeth, daughter of Jacques Bandinel (q.v.), the Rector of St. Mary's, who died from injuries received when escaping from Mont Orgueil. We have discovered only two events in his life. Lediard's *Naval History*, written in 1734, records: — "Rear-Admiral Dilkes on 22 July 1703 received orders from the Council to look for a Grand Partie said to lie in Cancale Bay. The 25th. he anchored off the south west port of Jersey, and sent Captain Chamberlain of the *Spry* to the Governor that he might learn the best intelligence. The Governor sent him Captain James Lempriere and Captain Thomas Pipon who were well acquainted with that coast ; by whom being informed of a fleet of 40 sail plying to windward to get to Granville, the Rear-Admiral upon consultation with the pilots decided to sail immediately, that he might attack the enemy by break of day next morning. Accordingly, 26th. July by daylight, perceived the enemy at anchor about a league to the westward of Granville, who upon their approach set sail and stood for the shore. The Rear-Admiral followed them as far as the pilots would venture, and found them to consist of 25 merchant vessels and three men of war. He then manned all his boats, and his ships did the same. By noon he had taken 15 sail, burnt 6 and sunk 3. The rest stood so far into a bay between Avranches and Mont St. Michel, that the ships could not attack them. Thereupon, the 27th, it was resolved to go into the Bay with the *Hector,* the *Mermaid* fireship, the *Spry,* and a ship of six guns taken the day before from the enemy, and all the boats of the squadron. This was performed between 10 and 11 in the morning, the Rear-Admiral being present accompanied by Captains Fairfax and Legg, also Captains Lempriere and Pipon. The enemy had three men of war, one of 18 guns, which they burned themselves, one of 14 guns, which Mr Paul of the *Kent* set on fire, and a third of 6 guns which was brought off. Seventeen more of the merchantships were destroyed, so that of the whole fleet only four escaped". For his work on this occasion the Queen presented Lempriere with a special gold medal inscribed: — "Her Majesty's award to Captain James Lempriere for his zeal in her service and his successful conducting ye Squadron commanded by Rear-Admiral Dilkes, who destroyed a considerable number of ye enemy's merchantships under convoy of men-of-war on their own coast. True to my trust".

Lempriere was then appointed Intelligence Officer for the French coast near Jersey. His orders ran: — "Instructions for our trusty and well-beloved Captain Lempriere, given at our Court at St. James the first day of Feb. 1704. As soon as you have received instructions from our Commissioners for the Exchange of Prisoners you shall with all expedition prepare some vessel proper for the transporting of prisoners, and, that you may have frequent occasions to repair to St. Malo for the *particular service* we expect from you, you must use such a vessel as is not capable of carrying many prisoners at one time. You are to give notice to our Lieut.-Governor of either of our islands immediately on your return, desiring his assistance to forward with all expedition to one of our principal Secretaries of State such intelligence as you may have gotten at St. Malo, and in case there be an opportunity of annoying the enemy by any of our ships of war or privateers, you are to give notice thereof to our Lieut.-Governor, that he may give such instructions thereon as he may judge proper. You are to endeavour to get intelligence on all matters at St. Malo or elsewhere on the coasts of France, particularly what ships are fitting out there, when they will be ready to sail, and what the design may be on which they are to proceed. In case there be any expense in procuring the same intelligence, you shall be allowed the same". He married Ann

Durell and had five children, James, who became Constable of St. Helier's and Jurat, John, George, Clement, and Elizabeth, who married Philip Nicolle, Rector of St. Clement's.

LEMPRIERE, JEAN (JEHAN) (d. 1534), Seigneur of Rozel, Lieut.-Governor, Acting Joint-Bailiff. Only son of Renaud Lempriere (q.v.), Seigneur of Rozel, and Katharine Camel. We first hear of him in 1463 as one of the two "beautiful children", for whom their mother pleaded, when their father was arrested on a charge of conspiring against the French Occupation of the island (*Bull.* X). The father was killed in 1468 during the siege of Mont Orgueil, and the mother married Edmund Weston. Jean was brought up at Rozel with his step-brothers, the future Sir Richard Weston (q.v.) and Sir William Weston (q.v.). When he came of age, he entered into possession of the property. In 1487 he is mentioned as a Jurat. In December 1500 on the death of Thomas Overay he was appointed by the King "to have the government of our island of Jersey and of the soldiers therein, until we appoint another Captain" (Patent in *Bull.* V). He held this post till July 1502, when he was ordered to hand it over to Sir Hugh Vaughan (*Bull* V). During his term of office he carried out extensive repairs to the walls of Mont Orgueil, and complaints were made to the Commissioners in 1515 that "by malice and subtlety, contrary to all right," he had made the island pay 300 crowns toward the cost of the work, when as executor to Overay's estate he had ample to meet all expenses (*Report of Commissioners of Henry VIII*). On laying down office however he secured from the States a glowing testimonial that "he had governed so honestly and well, maintained such discipline among the troops, and so scrupulously preserved and obeyed the ancient customs of the island, that all the inhabitants were well content with him and his good government" (*Bull.* V).

In Feb. 1523 he was acting as "Captain's Deputy" in Guernsey. Among the State Papers of Henry VIII is a long letter from him stating: — "I have taken two new gunners into wages. There are forty men of the island, archers and arbalesters, sworn to come to the Castle, whenever I order them. They are doing their duty, fortifying their bulwarks, and making good watch day and night. I have bought the artillery that came from Flanders, and put it into the hands of the workmen who make the guns". He was busy organizing an espionage system to collect information about movements of French troops and ships: — "Two young merchants have come to buy sheepskins and wool, and I have promised them, if they will do what I desire, they shall have liberty to sell and buy as much as they desire. I have given them money, and told them to inquire all the news of France. They will go hence to Rouen to buy merchandise, so as to avoid suspicion, and will return here. I wish you could obtain a safe conduct from the King for one or two boats to carry cider and wine. By them I should be able constantly to gather news". There had been trouble with some English ships anchored off St. Peter Port: — "The men of the island are much displeased at the complaint made by Trubleville against the island, since he went to the King. They showed him perfect cordiality in the island, and he has done all that he could against it. He remained a full month watching the harbour, where he has done great mischief both to the King's subjects and to strangers. I warned him in a friendly way, then threatened, then arrested him, and put him and his petty Captains in the Castle, telling him I would keep him there, until I knew the King's pleasure, if he did not restore the goods he had plundered ; on which they promised to make restitution, and I let them go" (*Letters & Papers of Henry VIII*).

His work in Guernsey had kept him out of the long struggle raging in Jersey between Vaughan and the Bailiff, Helier De Carteret (q.v.). He was not one of the eight Jurats who had petitioned Wolsey against being required to obey De Carteret. But in Aug. 1524 he was recalled to Jersey to act as Joint-Bailiff: — "Forasmuch as there is matter of variance depending betwixt Sir Hugh Vaughan and our well-beloved Helier De Carteret, for the appeasing of which we have determined to call the same before us at Westminster, Know that, to the intent that our subjects shall have justice indifferently administered to them, We, having good confidence in our well-beloved Sire Richard Mabon, Dean, and our well-beloved John Lempriere, Gentleman, do appoint the said Dean and John Lempriere jointly to have custody of the Register Rolls and Seal of the Bailiff, Furthermore giving them full power and authority entirely and wholly to have the administration of justice within the isle during the variance betwixt the aforesaid parties, *videlicet* in Civil Cases only. In Criminal Cases, as the Dean is a spiritual person, and may not in that behalf meddle, we authorize John Lempriere only to have the ordering of Justice" (Patent printed in *Prison Board Case*). Their official title seems to have been "Judge-Delegates commissioned and empowered by our Sovereign Lord the King and his worshipful and discrete Council to act in all causes civil and otherwise pertaining to the office of Bailiff" (Act printed in De La Croix' *Jersey*). They held office till Nov. 1527, when they were superseded by Jasper Pen. Later the Council decided that their appointment had been unconstitutional and Lempriere was ordered to repay to De Carteret all fees he had received. In 1531 he was one of a Royal Commission, consisting of two Jerseymen and two Englishmen, appointed to inquire into complaints against Sir Hugh Vaughan (*Bull. VI*). He was rewarded by a grant from the funds of the dissolved monasteries. He died childless on 10 April 1534, and his sister Catherine, wife of Dominic Perrin, inherited his estate. Thus Rozel passed to the Perrins for four generations. [Authorities quoted above.]

LEMPRIERE, JOHN (1765—1824), Classical Scholar. Second son of Charles Lempriere of Mont au Prêtre and Susan Collas. Born at Les Monts Noirons, Mont au Prêtre, St. Helier's, 3 Aug. 1765. Educated at St. Mannelier's Grammar School and at Winchester. Matriculated at Pembroke, Oxford, as a Morley Scholar, 17 Jan. 1786. In 1788, while still an undergraduate, he was ordained ; he became Assistant Master at Reading Grammar School under Dr. Valpy (q.v.) ; and he published the Classical Dictionary that made him famous, *Bibliotheca Classica, a Classical Dictionary, containing a full account of all the Proper Names mentioned in Antient Authors*. The Preface is dated, "Pembroke College, Nov. 1788". To modern scholarship the work seems superficial, but it showed an astonishing knowledge of the Classics, and proved immensely popular. No schoolroom was complete without it. It passed through edition after edition, in 1792, 1797, 1801, 1809, 1815, 1818, and each edition was enlarged, and it was translated into French and Latin. A new edition was published as late as 1888. In 1789 he visited his parents in Jersey. The *Gazette* described him as "a young man, a native of this island, the son of a farmer in the parish of St. Helier, who has been only lately ordained, and is now here for some weeks on a visit". Dr. Dupré asked him to take the services in the Town Church on 2 Aug. This was an Election Sunday, and party feeling between Magots and Charlots was very bitter. The Town was predominantly Magot, and Lempriere preached an outspokenly Charlot sermon. He printed it later in Guernsey (The S.J. Library has a copy.), *Sermon prêché dans le Temple de St. Helier, 1789*). Some who heard it declared that the printed version had toned down the more offensive passages ; but enough remained to explain what followed. He not only warned his hearers, "Close your ears to the fulsome appeals of the so-called Friends of Liberty. There are no such persons. Their actions prove it. Their faces look innocent, but their hearts are full of guile" ; but he made a vicious personal attack on the private life of the Magot candidate for the Juratship, a namesake of his own, Jacques Amice Lempriere, who was known to have home difficulties. He chose as his text, which he repeated again and again in the course of his sermon, "If a man know not how to rule his own house, how shall he govern?" This so incensed the congregation that many of them greeted him as he left the church with hoots and hisses, and then with clods of earth, and the young Divine was chased through the streets by a howling mob. In the evening he was burnt in effigy. Next day he appealed to the Royal Court for protection, declaring that his life was in danger, while a crowded Town's Meeting in the Town Church ordered him to be prosecuted at the expense of the parish (See *Gazettes* for 1789). He escaped however from the hornets' nest that he had stirred up to the calmer atmosphere of Oxford.

On 14 January 1790 he took his B.A., and the following year became Master of Lever's Grammar School, Bolton, Lancashire. In 1792 he took his M.A., and was appointed Head Master of Roysse's Free School of the Blessed Trinity at Abingdon, at a stipend of £98 a year, being then Curate of Radley.

In the same year he published the first volume of an annotated *Translation of Herodotus*. He remained Head Master for seventeen years, but he was not a success. The Education Commission of 1818 reported: — "During his time the number of scholars on the foundation never exceeded two, was generally one, and often none" (*Education Report* 1819). There may have been in addition a few fee-paying day-boys who were not Foundation Scholars, and at one time he had six boarders ; but the School only just remained alive. In 1793 he added to his duties the Readership of St. Nicholas' Church ; but in 1796 the Vestry complained to the Bishop of Salisbury that Evening Prayer was not read daily, and that sometimes Lempriere dropped the Sunday Morning Service in order to serve his Radley curacy. The Bishop ruled that this was excusable, as the Reader's stipend was only £27 a year ; but the Vestry refused to pay anything, unless full duty was performed. In 1799, as Lempriere had received no money for two years, he closed the Church, and for a time St. Nicholas was without Services. In 1800 he was appointed Vicar of St. Helen's, the old Parish Church. In 1808 he published his *Universal Biography, containing a copious account, critical and historical, of the life and character, labours and actions of eminent persons of all ages and countries, conditions, and professions.* (A second edition appeared in 1812.) He resigned his Abingdon Head-Mastership at Michaelmas 1809, and became Head-master of Exeter Grammar School at a salary of £40 a year and a house ; and in 1811 he exchanged his Abingdon Vicarage for the Rectory of Meeth, Devon. In 1823 a dispute with the Trustees led to his retirement from the School. He stated his side of the case in two publications, *A Vindication of Exeter School* 1818 and *A Petition to the House of Commons on the Conduct of the Trustees of Exeter School with Notes and Observations* 1820. In 1823 he became Rector of Newton St. Petrock, Devon. On 1 February 1823 he died of apoplexy in Southampton Street, Strand. He married three times: — (1) Lucy, daughter of Francis Willince, by whom he had ten children, one of whom, Everard, succeeded him as Rector of Meeth; (2) Elizabeth, daughter of John Deane, by whom he had three sons, one of whom, Charles, became Fellow of St. John's, Oxford, (3) Ann, daughter of Edward Collingwood, who died childless. There is a portrait of Lempriere in the Library of St. John's College, Oxford, and another in

Pembroke College. The latter is reproduced in Preston's *St. Nicholas, Abingdon.* [*Dic. Nat. Biog.* ; Macleane's *History of Pembroke College, Oxford* ; Preston's *St. Nicholas, Abingdon* ; *Gentleman's Magazine* 1824.]

LEMPRIERE, MICHEL (1606–71), Bailiff. Younger son of Jurat Hugh Lempriere, Lieut.-Bailiff, Seigneur of Diélament, by his second wife, Jeanne Herault, daughter of Jean Herault, Greffier (not, as *Armorial* says, sister of Jean Herault, Bailiff). Born, Dec. 1606. He was educated at the Huguenot University of Saumur, where he had imbibed the democratic ideas that lay at the root of Calvinism. In Jan. 1637 he was elected Jurat. He was then living in 'the Big House at Maufant', St. Saviour's, in which his grandfather had lived before inheriting Diélament. This house with its 156 vergées, "because it was the most important in the Vingtaine of Maufant" (Chevalier), was known as Maufant Manor, and Lempriere is called in the Rolls of the Court Monsieur de Maufant.

When the Long Parliament met, and grievances were being ventilated, he was one of a group of Jerseymen who went to Westminster to protest against the actions of Sir Philippe De Carteret (q.v.). "Certain gentlemen of the island", he wrote, "being in London, and hearing that Sir Philip was also come into that City, and knowing by woeful experience what tyrannies he had committed in that island, knowing also that for certain he would prove false to Parliament, framed Informations and presented them to Mr. Prynne to be read in the House of Commons" (*Pseudo-Mastix*). But Prynne, who had been kindly treated by Sir Philippe, when a prisoner at Mont Orgueil, suppressed their petition, and, when at last it was presented to the House of Lords, defended De Carteret so skilfully that their accusations were dismissed as "exhibited through malice rather than upon just grounds". (See article *Dumaresq, Henri*).

In Aug. 1642 the Civil War began, and in Feb. 1643 De Carteret definitely declared for the King. Shortly after, Charles Maret (q.v.) arrived in Jersey with an Order from Parliament (issued 16 Feb.: printed in Hoskins), appointing Lempriere, who

was back in the island, and four other Jurats Commissioners
"to apprehend the person of Sir Philip De Carteret, to suppress all tumults raised in defence of him, and to suspend from
office all confederated with him". When the States met in
March, Lempriere read a copy of his commission, and ordered
Sir Philippe to go to Westminster to answer the charges against
him. De Carteret adroitly asked for the original, and, as Lempriere had not brought it, ruled that the States could not discuss copies. Lempriere then tried to leave, but soldiers posted
at the door stopped him "with halberds pointed at his breast
and swords drawn" (*Pseudo-Mastix*). News however arrived
that the St. Saviour's and St. Clement's Militia were marching
on the Town ; so Sir Philippe hurriedly closed the meeting,
and retired to Elizabeth Castle.

For the next eight months the whole island except the two
Castles was ruled by Lempriere's Committee. The Castles
were besieged, but otherwise he showed extreme moderation.
The families of the Royalist leaders remained undisturbed in
their homes. The Royalist Vicomte, Laurens Hamptonne (q.v.),
moved about the island freely performing his duties. Royalist
Rectors, like Etienne La Cloche (q.v.), still occupied their pul-
pits. For three months the Castle soldiers bought provisions in
the Market, though this was stopped when De Carteret began
to bombard the Town.

Sir Philippe died on 23 Aug., and three days later Major
Lydcot arrived as Parliamentary Lieut.-Governor. On the 29th.
the States met and swore in Lempriere as Bailiff "in virtue of
an order of the two Houses of Parliament" (*Bull.* V) with the
time-honoured oath beginning: — "You acknowledge our Sovereign Lord Charles to be under God sole and supreme Governor of all his dominions". The Parliament Party even in
England was not yet Republican. It professed to be fighting
to deliver its King from evil counsellors. Lempriere then administered the oath to Lydcot as Lieut.-Governor. The two
men were however soon at loggerheads. Friction between
Governors and Bailiffs was endemic in Jersey, and in this
case it was inevitable, for the Governor was a soldier anxious
to establish martial law in war-time, and the Bailiff a Jerseyman
determined to maintain the island's constitution. "Ye Lieut.-
Governor", wrote a Lydcot supporter, "seeing that ye keeping
of ye Civil was very prejudicial to ye safety of the Island did

with the advice of the well-affected forbid Lempriere to keep it any longer, until the State was settled in better order ; but Lempriere and ye rest would never obey. They caused the States of the Isle to be assembled, whereof the major part were Malignants, against the advice of the Lieut.-Governor" (De La Rocque MSS). Lydcot, says Chevalier, "rode roughshod over the Royal Court, declaring the capture of the castles to be more important than fooling with Jurats". Religious differences arose. Jersey Presbyterians were alarmed at the spread of Independency and Anabaptism. Moreover the Castles seemed impregnable, and after eight months' siege the Militia grew weary and eager to return to their farms. When George Carteret (q.v.) landed at Mont Orgueil with Royalist reinforcements, the Parliament leaders were powerless to resist. Two days later (21 Nov.) Lydcot and Lempriere slipped out of Havre-des-pas by night "with many well-affected gentlemen in a little frigate to Guernsey, and then to England" (*Pseudo Mastix*).

Carteret proclaimed all deeds and contracts sealed by Lempriere null and void, and had them collected and burned by the hangman in the Market. On 11 Feb. 1644 Lempriere was degraded from his Juratship. On 4 Oct. 1645 he was tried in his absence by Royal Commissioners, found guilty of high treason, and condemned to be hanged whenever arrested, and meanwhile to be hanged in effigy, to have his property confiscated, his house razed, and his timber felled, as a sign of infamy to all posterity. The timber was used in St. Aubin's Fort and Elizabeth Castle. Lempriere remained eight years in London, at first in deep poverty, so that it was reported in Jersey that he had to beg his bread. In 1646 he wrote of "our great and almost intolerable sufferings by the space of three years and above" (*Pseudo-Mastix*) ; but toward the end of his stay he found employment in Worcester House, the office of the trustees for the sale of the King's property. At the Restoration he was accused of having been the man who "brake the King's crown and took the jewels out of it" (*S.P.*). In 1646 he raised enough money to print *Pseudo-Mastix, the Lyar's Whipp*, a bulky pamphlet, written by Henri Dumaresq (q.v.), Abraham Herault and himself (reprinted in *Bull.* II), to refute Prynne's defence of Sir Philippe De Carteret in *The Lyar Confounded*. During his exile he maintained a secret correspondence with Jersey and unceasing appeals to Parliament to take steps to recover the island. This agitation caused much anxiety to the King's Party. In March 1647 the Prince of Wales wrote: — "Being advertised by intelligence from London that those seditious fugitives do pretend to have a firm correspondency and a party in the island ready to joyne them, we have commanded our trusty servant Sir George Carteret to use the greatest industry for the discovery of such ill-affected persons as may be justly suspected" (S.P.). The result was a large batch of deportations and imprisonments.

When the Battle of Worcester ended the Civil War in England, Parliament at last had time to attend to Jersey. On 20 Oct. 1651 a force landed in St. Ouen's Bay too strong for Carteret to withstand, and with them came Lempriere. Mont Orgueil capitulated on 4 Nov., and Elizabeth Castle on 15 Dec. Lempriere resumed his old position as Bailiff. Carteret had carried off the Island seal contrary to the terms of surrender, but a threat to confiscate his property made him send it back from Brittany. In Feb. 1652 Lempriere wrote to the Speaker that he had purged all Royalist officers from the Militia and all Royalist officials from the administration: — "I have caused to be elected in each parish a Constable, Centeniers, Vingteniers, and Sermentés, who for the most part have suffered for the Commonwealth either by exile, fines, or imprisonment" (Report printed in Hoskins).

He was a hard-worked and conscientious official. Durell, who had examined the Court Books, wrote: — "The Records were better kept in his time than ever before. The judgements of the Court were in general unexceptionable" (Durell's *Falle*). One piece of work was thrown upon him that no previous Bailiff had performed. All marriages were now civil marriages, and he had to officiate. A typical entry runs: — "16 Dec. 1653. Samuel Le Four and Marguerite Maugier were married in Grouville Church, that it to say Michel Lempriere, Bailiff married them according to an order of the English Parliament". Sometimes this was supplemented by a religious service, e.g. "3 May 1654, Jacques Wittel and Marie Bertram of this parish were married. Monsieur the Bailiff married them. Afterwards on the same day Mons. Bonhomme, Minister of the parish, married them a second time in church" (St. Helier's Register).

Lempriere's eight years as Bailiff were full of troubles and anxieties. First he had the thankless task of billeting the English Parliamentary troops on the French-speaking population, who resented having to receive them. Then came grave misgivings about the future of the constitution. In those years of radical reorganization no one could foresee what the wild men of Westminster might be planning, whether the island would be absorbed into the English system, or what strange code or institutions might be thrust upon it. In 1652 Parliament appointed a County Committee for Jersey (S.P.). In Feb. 1652 Lempriere sent the Speaker a long *Account of the Civil Government of Jersey* to "dissipate the aspersions which some beyond the seas have already cast upon his government intending to obtain the setting up of their own conceits" (Hoskins). He also deputed Jacques Stocall (q.v.), his nephew, to go to Westminster "for the enlarging of the summary"; and Stocall on his arrival printed his own very rosy *Description of the Excellent Civil Government of the Island of Jersey* for distribution among members of Parliament. The danger passed, but next came the difficulty of persuading the overworked Commonwealth Government to provide new Jurats. The Royalist Jurats had been dismissed : Dumaresq was out of the island ; Herault remained the only one who could assist Lempriere. In 1651 the Council of State had ordered "no election of any Jurat until Parliament has taken order therein". Petitions were constantly sent urging the Council "to settle a course of justice in Jersey". One in 1652 from the twelve Constables and others spoke warmly of Lempriere as "a gentleman endowed with many rare abilities, who has kept an equal balance of Justice betwixt ye soldiers and islanders, and likewise hath with dexterity and wisdom made many atonements of difficulties which have arisen betwixt party and party with indefatigable care and labour", but declared that he seemed "much discouraged in that he cannot fully satisfy the People in the administration of Justice". In 1654 Cromwell appointed by his own mandate eleven new Jurats ; but some of these refused to take the oath ; so at last in 1657 an election of Jurats was permitted. It is noteworthy that, though "the eternizing of offices in one family" had been one of the charges against De Carteret, the new Jurat-list included Lempriere's brother Nicolas, nephew Hugh, his cousins Jacques and Benjamin, and his brother-in-law Philippe De Carteret of La Hague, while Aaron Stocall, another nephew, became Solicitor-

General, and Daniel Norman (q.v.), a connection by marriage, became Vicomte. In 1655 Lempriere's own position as Bailiff had been regularized by new Letters Patent (O.C.), his earlier appointment having been made in the name of Charles I.

In the same year he was nominated one of five Commisioners for Compounding. The Royalists' estates had not been confiscated as those of the Parliamentarians had been, but the owners were allowed to compound by paying not more than two years' income (O.C.). This entailed laborious inquiries into the value of every property, and led to a hot dispute with Charles Maret, the Receiver (q.v.), who probably demanded higher fines that his department might benefit. He "notoriously affronted" the Bailiff, and was imprisoned in Mont Orgueil, until he gave security for future good behaviour. But graver troubles lay ahead. A new Governor arrived, Colonel Robert Gibbons, an arrogant, high-handed soldier. The Army was now top-dog in England, and its officers had small respect for civilians appointed by Parliament. According to the *Articles of Impeachment exhibited against Col. Gibbons*, published in 1659, "he bastinadoed and misused to the endangering of their lives several of the inhabitants, committing them close prisoners without the knowledge of the Jurisdiction, amongst others the Constable of St. Saviour's"; he allowed his troops to plunder the farmers' fields and orchards ; he imprisoned the Constable of St Brelade's for searching a soldier's house to find a stolen sheep ; he interfered in elections, permitting no candidates but those of whom he approved ; he introduced the press-gang, which was contrary to many island charters ; and his officers found a profitable amusement in impressing well-to-do Jerseymen for Jamaica, and then allowing them to buy their freedom for a heavy ransom. Against all this Lempriere struggled in vain, and, when he protested to London, he was "very much threatened". In the midst of these troubles in 1657 he married Sara, daughter of François De Carteret of La Hague, a lady twenty-four years his junior.

In May 1660, when news arrived of the Restoration, he fled to Coutainville in Normandy, and his estate was given to a John Nicolls "in lieu of the place of clerk of the Privy Council in Ireland granted and then withdrawn" (S.P.). But this time his exile did not last long. Charles owed his throne to Presbyterians, and the new Parliament passed an Act of Oblivion.

Under this on 9 Nov. Lempriere obtained a pardon "for all political acts or ecclesiastical transgressions committed in connection with any of the wars either by himself or his supporters". He returned to Jersey, and recovered his property, but took no further part in public life. He found it however hard to submit to those who had superseded him. The new Court felt little sympathy for the old Republican. In 1662 Jean Bailhache sued him for 333 crowns, and he was condemned to pay. He appealed to the Privy Council, who not only dismissed his appeal, but awarded the Bailiff and Jurats £40 sterling as damages for his "injurious and ceaseless calumniations" (O.C.). Three months later Susanne Dumaresq claimed seven quarters of wheat *rente*. Again the Court decided against him ; and again he appealed. But he had lost his temper, when the case was tried in Jersey. "He did, whilst the Justices were assembled, breake into high and unseemly passions, speaking disdainfully and scornfully against the Lieutenant-Bailiff and Justices there assembled, saying some or one had done false and horrible things, and calling Mr Elias Dumaresq des Augrès, one of the Justices, 'Foolish Fellow', scornfully repeating what he said as despiseable and ridiculous in a most unhansome, uncivil, and unbeseeming manner". (O.C.). For this he was sentenced to make in the Court the following public apology: — "I, Michael Lempriere, do hereby testify before you the Magistrates of the Isle that my behaviour towards you was uncivil and irreverent at such time as you were met about the business of Mrs Susan Dumaresq and myself, and that I much misbehaved myself therein, and was in too great a passion. And I hereby beg yr pardon for the same". If he refused to do this, "their Lordships do impower the Bailiff to commit the said Lempriere to prison, there to remain till he doth make the said submission in the form aforesaid" (O.C.).

He apparently settled in St Helier's, for his children, all born after the Restoration, were baptized in the Town Church ; and he was buried (14 Feb. 1671) in the Town Church. He had two sons, Michel, who inherited the Fief of Diélament from his cousin, and Philippe, and three daughters, Marie, Sara, and Judith. [Chevalier's *Journal* ; *Pseudo-Mastix* ; *Bull.* VIII : and authorities quoted above.]

LEMPRIERE, NICOLAS (1611—67), Physician, Cromwellian Jurat. Son of Jurat Hugh Lempriere, Seigneur of Diélament, and Jeanne, daughter of Jean Herault, the Greffier. Born 12 Dec. 1611. Educated at Merchant Taylors' School 1627—8 and King's College, Cambridge 1629. He took his M.B. *Lit. Reg.* (i.e. by Royal Mandate) in 1636 and his M.D. at Caen in 1639. In 1641 he was practising in London in Sermon Lane. When the Civil War began, he was drawn into politics on the Parliamentary side, and in 1649 was appointed one of the Contractors to sell the lands and goods of the King and Queen (*A.O.*). In July he was sent to take an inventory of 102 horses, "part of the late King's personal estate" (*S.P.*). In 1650 he was a Trustee to sell the Fee-Farm Rents formerly belonging to the Crown (*A.O.*). In 1651, after the recovery of Jersey by Parliament, Michel Lempriere, his brother, the Cromwellian Bailiff, wrote to the Speaker: — "Dr Lempriere, who hath been very painful, and is still careful for the good of this poor island, is perfectly well acquainted with the government of the country and integrity of the people. He is able to recommend unto Parliament some able persons who are fit in this island to serve really and truly the Commonwealth" (Hoskins). In 1652 he was busy "selling the Castles, Parks, etc., belonging to the late King" (*A.O.*). In August he was one of the six members of the County Committee for Jersey (*S.P.*). He was now living in the island, and in February 1655 was nominated as a Jurat by Cromwell, but was not sworn in till October 1657. But in that year England again claimed him, and he became an "Assessor for the County of Surrey for raising the sum required from the county" (*A.O.*). At the Restoration he was pardoned under the Act of Oblivion, and resumed his medical practice. In Dec. 1664 he was elected Honorary Fellow of the College of Physicians. In his will, dated 1667, he describes himself as "of St. Botolph's, Bishopsgate". Like the Guerdains (q.v.) and other Jersey exiles, he had apparently become an Anabaptist, for his daughter Sarah was not baptized till she was twenty-four. [*Merchant Taylors' Register ; Acts and Ordinances of the Interregnum ; State Papers Domestic.*]

LEMPRIERE, PHILIPPE (1718—87), Attorney-General, brother of Charles Lempriere (q.v.). Son of Jurat Michel Lempriere,
Seigneur of Diélament, and Jane Corbet. Born in Diélament
Manor 1718, and baptized 9 July. "When a lad he was destined to the sea, and placed under the tuition of a master of
a bark, who traded between London and Jersey" (Shebbeare) :
but he soon gave this up, and till his marriage lived in his
father's house. In 1739 he married Julie Catherine de Varignon,
daughter of Brigadier General d'Apremont, and moved into his
wife's house at St. Lawrence. In the following year however
he settled at St. John's, where he became Colonel of the North-
West Regiment of Militia. In 1747 he was sworn in as an Advocate. In Jan. 1750 he became Receiver-General. At this time
it was the custom for the Receiver-General to contract to pay
a fixed sum annually to the Lieut.-Governor, who thus was
relieved of the trouble of dealing with hundreds of small debts,
and everything above that figure went into the Receiver's pocket.
Lempriere was accused of being the harshest collector the island
had ever known, always insisting on the payment of the uttermost farthing. Moreover, since most of the King's Revenue
consisted of wheat rentes, the Receiver's profits rose and fell
with the price of corn, and Lempriere and his brother, the Lieut.-
Bailiff, were accused of taking steps to keep corn, and therefore
bread, dear for the benefit of their own pockets. A third charge
was that, since most of the fines inflicted by the Court went
to the King's Receiver, his Jurat relations made these as high
and as numerous as possible.

He gradually accumulated other posts. He was Commissary-General for Jersey and Guernsey, Store-keeper, Barrack-
master, Paymaster of the Ordnance. He received 8/6 a day
for taking charge of the Invalids, a force of veterans stationed
in the island as a supplementary garrison. During the Seven
Years' War he was Agent for the Sick and Wounded and
Agent for Prisoners of War. Serious criticism was made against
his work in this last capacity. In 1758 Colonel Forrester, Commander-in-Chief in Jersey, reported that he had "received informations of many and great abuses in the treatment of prisoners
of war, not only with regard to their provisions, straw, and other
necessaries, but of outrageous maltreatment committed by persons
acting under Philip Lempriere". He then visited the prison
camp, and found these accusations true. He brought the matter

before both the Royal Court and the States, but in each case the
Lieut.-Bailiff replied that they had no authority over the camp.
Forrester could not even get a Jurat to take affidavits from the
prisoners that he could forward to the Commissioners (Sheb.).

In 1758 Lempriere became Attorney-General. He now had
to resign his post as Receiver. It would have been too scandalous for the Public Prosecutor and the Receiver of the fines
to be the same person ; but he secured the post for his brother-
in-law, Edouard Ricard, and it was openly asserted that
Ricard was only a screen behind whom Lempriere remained
the real Receiver. About this time too his wealth increased
rapidly through his partnership in the very successful privateer,
the *Charming Nancy*. In Dec. 1764 he inherited the Fief de
Chesnel from his grandmother, née Françoise De Carteret.
In 1769 came the Anti-Lempriere Revolt (See *Lempriere
Charles*). An armed mob invaded the Court, and compelled
the Jurats to make Acts at its dictation. The Jurats took refuge
in Elizabeth Castle, and from there sent the two Lemprieres
and two Jurats as Deputies to the Privy Council. But the
English Government now realized that all was not well in
Jersey. After Colonel Bentinck's investigation on the spot many
changes were made. Among others Ricard was removed from
his post as Receiver-General, and the old system of farming
out the office abolished. Henceforth Receivers were officials
with a fixed salary, who had to pay to the Lieut.-Governor all
that they received. In 1771 appeared Shebbeare's *Authentic
Narrative of the Oppressions of the Islanders of Jersey* in which
all that could be said against the Lempriere Administration was
collected and set down in detail. Philippe resigned the Attorney-Generalship, and left Jersey never to return. He built
a house at Woodbury, Devon, where he died in 1787. The
four children of his first wife died young. By his second wife
Maria Weekes, he had no children. [Literature as in *Lem-
Priere, Charles*.]

LEMPRIERE RAOUL (RAUF, RALPH, RADULPHUS),
d.c. 1378, Bailiff, Seigneur of Rozel. Son of Thomas Lempriere (See *Lempriere Family*), Seigneur of the Fief ès
Empereres in St Helier's. In 1337 he is mentioned as one of

the garrison of Gorey Castle. In the following year he was one of eight men-at-arms, who under Jean de Barentin with 43 bowmen and 22 servants sucessfully defended the Castle against the French Admiral Béhuchet (*Bull* III). In 1341 and 1342 he was still on duty in the Castle. In 1348 he became a Jurat, and in Sept. 1357 he issued "as Bailiff of our Lord the King in the island of Jersey" a proclamation fixing the rate of exchange of an English crown at 13/4 *tournois* (*Cart.*).

In 1356 the French had raided Guernsey, and captured Castle Cornet. In the following year Lempriere joined a party of Jerseymen, who with Sir Renaud de Carteret (q.v.) set out to try to recover it. "After a severe combat they took the Captain of the Castle, who ransomed himself for 80,000 florins. They might have taken those florins in aid of their expenses ; yet they surrendered the Captain without ransom in return for the surrender of the Castle" (*C.R.*). After its recovery William Le Feyvre, a prominent Guernseyman, "was slain as a traitor and adherent of the enemy by common assent of the armed men" (*C.R.*). This caused deep resentment in Guernsey, and Nicolaa, his wife, secured the arrest of all responsible. Neither Lempriere nor De Carteret had been present at the court-martial or the execution, but before the Guernsey Court they took full responsibility, declaring that they were "as blameworthy as any of those impeached" ; "whereupon the Bailiff and Jurats adjudged them to the King's Prison to be detained till justice were done on them" (*P.R.*). The Deputy-Warden of the Isles crossed to England to try to secure their release ; but they remained prisoners in Castle Cornet till March 1359, when, "because they were not at the killing or consenting to it", they received the King's Pardon (*P.R.*). Lempriere then resumed his work as Bailiff till 1564, when he took up again his old position as Jurat.

Meanwhile Philippe De Barentin (q.v.), Seigneur of Rozel, after a scandal in which his wife was involved and a murder by his two sons, had decided to leave the island and sell his property. This included, not only Rozel, but the Manors of Samarès, Diélament, Longueville, and La Hougue Boëte, and the smaller Fiefs of Patier and Maufant at St Saviour's, of Buisson and La Fosse at St Helier's, of Grochy and Burrier at St Martin's, of Le Homet at St Clement's and Ponterrin at Trinity. Lempriere and his brother-in-law Guillaume Payn (they had married the two daughters of Geoffroi Brosdefer) decided to buy the lot for a promise to pay De Barentin annually £200 sterling as long as he lived. His relations however furiously contested the sale. In Oct. 1362 they declared that De Barentin was a leper, and therefore by Jersey law a dead man, incapable of alienating his property (*Bull* V.). When this plea failed, they remembered that Raoul's great-grandfather had come from Brittany. Though the family had been in Jersey for four generations, they were still regarded by some as foreigners who were forbidden to acquire property in the island. A Latin genealogy, ascribed to Dean Soulemont (1534), contains the note, "Lempriere and Payn were Bretons and aliens" (*Bull.* V.). This was put right by paying a fine of £70 sterling to the King, and on 8 May 1368 they received a "Pardon to Ralph le Emperer and William Payn of their trespasses in acquiring in fee from Philip de Barentyn the Manors of La Rosell and Sant Marey (i.e. Samarès) without the King's licence, and a Grant that they may hold the Manors as acquired" (*P.R.*). Meanwhile they had registered at the Royal Court in January a contract by which they had bought out any possible claims of the Lovel family, children of De Barentin's daughter (*Bull* V.) ; and in June the *Cour d'Héritage* admitted them to make *comparence* as joint Seigneurs of the Fiefs (*Bull* V.). But the struggle was not yet over. De Barentin's nephew, Pierre Payn, Rector of St Brelade's, next claimed the *retrait lignager*, by which according to Norman law, if a man sold his property, any of his heirs could buy it back for the price paid. He failed, because he did not make his claim within a year and a day ; but the King's Receiver then demanded the Manors under the *retrait féodal*, by which the Seigneur had the same privilege as the heirs, and on 8 May 1369 the Council issued a "Grant in fee to Walter Huwet, Warden of the Isles, of those lands in Jersey, which Ralph Lempriere and William Payn lately bought from Philip Barentyn, and of which the *retrait* belongs to the King according to the custom of that country, because Walter in the King's name offered to pay Philip as much as Ralph and William paid him, no one of the blood of Philip suing for the purchase of the lands within a year, whereby the lands have fallen to the King" (*P.R.*). This was followed by a long and immensely complicated lawsuit, the course of which cannot be followed from the facts that have survived. Among the Close Rolls in

Nov. 1378 is a Writ of Supersedeas (a writ commanding a stay of legal proceedings) addressed to the Bailiff and Jurats "in favour of William Payn and Drouet Lempriere (Raoul's son), joint tenants of lands in Jersey, as they have done homage to the King" (*C.R.*) ; but eighty years later the case was still dragging on (See De la Croix, *Jersey*). The writ of Supersedeas shows that Raoul was dead by 1378. In 1382 Drouet and Payn divided the property, Drouet taking as his share Rozel, Longueville, La Hougue Boëte, and Patier. Besides Drouet, Raoul had a daughter Jeanette, who married Pierre Le Marchant of Guernsey. [*Calendar of Patent Rolls* (*P.R.*) ; *Calendar of Close Rolls* (*C.R.*) ; article 'Ancienne Généalogie' in *Bull* V ; De la Croix's *Jersey, ses Antiquités* ; other authorities quoted above.]

LEMPRIERE, REGINALD RAOUL (1851—1951), Seigneur of Rozel, Jurat. Only son of Rev. William Lempriere, Seigneur of Rozel and Diélament, and Julia Anne, daughter of Thomas Wayne. Born 8 Dec. 1851, at Wolverstone, near Ipswich. In 1859 his father inherited Rozel Manor, and the family moved to Jersey. Reginald Raoul entered Winchester College, 1864 ; Christ Church, Oxford, 1870, and transferred to Hertford College, Oxford, 1873. B.A. 1875. In 1873 he became Lieutenant in the East Regiment of the Militia, and was promoted Captain in 1881. He was called to the English Bar at the Inner Temple in 1875, and practised for a time, then becoming private secretary to Sir R. Herbert, Permanent Under-Secretary of State at the Colonial Office. He was offered an appointment in the Fiji Islands, but decided to return to Jersey, where he became an Advocate in 1880, and Constable of St Martin's 1880—3. In 1894 he was elected Jurat, but resigned the same year on being appointed Vicomte, a post which he held till 1917. In 1918 he stood for election as Deputy of St Helier's (No. 2 District), but was defeated. In the same year however he was for the second time elected Jurat.

He took deep interest in everything connected with the island, knew its history and constitution intimately, and was specially keen on agriculture and the navigation of local waters. He protected the Ecréhous from French interference by building houses on Marmotier and Blanque Ile and frequently visiting the islands. As a member of the Société Jersiaise he obtained from the States in 1894 a vote of £100 to enable the Chevalier manuscript to be transcribed, and as President from 1918—20 he took a leading part in acquiring the Hougue Bie. He wrote valuable articles for the Society's *Bulletins*, e.g. La Carrière d'Edouard De Carteret (V. 205) and L'occupation de Jersey par le Comte de Maulevrier (X. 102). He was an authority on French poetry and English literature of the 17th and 18th centuries, and was proud of his library. He had a good knowledge of the Jersey dialect. He was noted as an after-dinner speaker and a witty story-teller. One of his exploits in his youth had been to ride on horseback down the Snow Hill steps. The varied nature of his interests can be seen from the fact that in addition to the public posts already mentioned he was President of the Royal Agricultural and Horticultural Society, the Island Cricket Club, the Jersey Dog Club, the Jersey Race Club, the Jersey Drag Hunt, the Jersey Rowing Club, the Gorey Regatta Club, the Jersey Radio Society, and the Jersey Motor Association, which was formed at his suggestion. He was Rear-Commodore of the Royal Channel Islands Yacht Club, and also a Freemason. By the conditions of his feudal tenure the Seigneur of Rozel, when the King visits Jersey, is bound to meet him on his horse in the sea up to his saddle-girths, and to act as his butler, while he is in the island. Lempriere could not fulfil the first condition literally on the occasion of the King's visit in 1921, as he landed in the harbour, but he met him at the quayside, and served him with punch at Mont Orgueil. When he asked permission to resign his Juratship in 1929 owing to advancing years the King conferred on him the order of Commander of the British Empire.

He married at Paris in 1891 Clementina Justina Fanny, Baroness von Güttlingen of Stuttgart, and had three daughters, Yvonne, who married (1) Charles Robin of Steephill and (2) Major Christopher Riley, son of the Seigneur of Trinity, Roselle, who became the wife of Captain R.J.B. Bolitho, and Olga. He died on 4 Sept. 1931 ; and with him ended the male line of the Lemprieres of Rozel. [*Bull.* XII 13. Local newspapers.]

LEMPRIERE, RENAUD (REGNALDUS) (1418—1467), Seigneur of Rozel. Eldest son of Jean Lempriere, Bailiff, and Jehanette Le Lorreur : great-grandson of Raoul Lempriere (q.v.), who bought Rozel. In 1461, when England was paralysed by the Wars of the Roses, Mont Orgueil had been surprised by Norman troops, sent by Pierre de Brézé, Count of Maulevrier, Seneschal of Normandy. This was not a clear-cut foreign invasion, for de Brézé, though a vassal of the French King, was first cousin and staunch supporter of Marguerite of Anjou, Henry VI's Queen. Things were going ill with Henry and the Lancastrians, and there is reason to believe that the Queen had ordered Nanfan, the Lancastrian Warden, to hand over the Castle to de Brézé to secure the islands as a refuge for the royal family in case the Yorkists should win. De Brézé assumed the title Lord of the Isles, and, though he failed to secure Guernsey, for seven years all Jersey submitted to his rule. (The Chronicler's statement to the contrary is discussed in the article *De Carteret, Philippe.*). In spite of traditional hatred of the French, Lancastrian sympathizers could hardly refuse obedience to their Queen's cousin. Lempriere and most of the other Seigneurs took an oath of fealty. Le Cornu's refusal to take the oath for the Fief Levesque at St Mary's and the confiscation of his land (*Bull* VI) is the only exception recorded.

But in 1463 Lempriere was arrested for plotting to expel the French. The depositions of the witnesses at his trial (printed in *Bull.* X) give details of his life. He is described as a man of about 45, so was born about 1418. He became a Jurat in 1442. His household at the Manor at the time of his arrest consisted of his illegitimate son Jehan, always referred to as "the bastard of Rozel", old enough to play tennis and to drink with the men, Renaud's gallant young wife of 22, Katherine, daughter of John Camel of Shapwick near Blandford in Dorset, their two "beautiful children", Jean and Catherine, and Renaud's fifteen-year-old niece Guillemine, daughter of his dead brother Jehan. He was a keen fisherman, a chess-player, took pride in his gardens, which every visitor was taken to admire, and had a tennis court in his barn (for real tennis, not lawn tennis, played, not over a net, but against the walls). Mass was said daily in the Manor Chapel, and on Sundays the Seigneur and his household attended both Mass and Vespers in St Martin's

Church. Thomas Le Hardy (q.v.), Rector of St Martin's, was his closest friend.

At his trial both sides agreed on certain facts. In Easter week 1463 Guillaume Carbonnel, the Norman Captain of the Castle, lunched at Rozel Manor, and invited Lempriere and his wife to dine on the following day. The Seigneur went alone, but the Captain sent a message that they would not sit down without Katherine ; so she followed. He received her effusively, and said that she must talk with his "goblin", a fellow-countryman of hers, an English prisoner named John Hareford or Hereford. He was a retainer of Warwick the Kingmaker, one of the garrison of Calais, who had been captured on a plundering raid in St Ouen's Bay. He came of good family, and was a cousin of Thomas Wynchels or Wynsselo (probably Winslow), an Englishman, who had married a relative of the Lemprieres. He professed to know Katherine's father and many mutual friends. At his suggestion she persuaded the Captain to remove his fetters, and herself helped to unshackle him. Later Hareford was allowed to roam about the island on parole, and became a frequent visitor at the Manor. On Whit-Monday there was another dinner-party at the Castle to meet the Captain's wife, who had arrived from Normandy. Lempriere and Katherine were present, and the Lady of St. Ouen's. On 11 Aug. Hareford arrived at the Manor with a bitten thumb, rather the worse for drink. He had got roaring drunk on the previous day, St. Lawrence's Day, at the Fair in St. Lawrence's parish, had fought with "a country lout", who had bitten him, and he had put himself to bed in a pig-trough, till Raulin Payn took him home for the night. He offered to exchange his jet rosary for one on Katherine's girdle, and she consented, till he said he had stolen the black one from a merchant at Gorey. Four days later on the Feast of the Assumption they all met again at a dinner given by du Vieuxchastel, Marshal of the Castle, to the Confraternity of our Lady, and Katherine invited Hareford to come next day and help with the harvest. He worked for an hour with the reapers, and then invited himself to dinner. In the afternoon he went fishing with Lempriere, though the latter "told him many times that he did not want his company". They returned late, and Hareford slept at the Manor. On the following Thursday he arrived again, while the Seigneur and his wife were dining, and sat down at table with them. On the Sunday he came to Mass at St Martin's, and returned to the Manor for dinner. He then had a game of chess with Lempriere, and, when the rest of the family went to Vespers, played tennis with the Bastard and four other young men for a gallon of beer a set, and then they adjourned to St Martin's tavern to drink their winnings. When the Bastard returned, his father thrashed him for staying out so late.

All this sounds trivial enough; but at the trial a sinister interpretation was put on many of these details. The prosecution alleged that before the Easter dinner-party Le Hardy had sounded Hareford at confession as to whether he would help to oust the Normans from the Castle, and that after the dinner he and Lempriere had offered him 100 crowns, if on a certain night he would leave the Rochefort sally-port open. They swore that they had had no private conversation with the prisoner that day, but two witnesses declared that they had seen the three conferring together in a little court in the Middle Ward, and that Lempriere had been overheard cursing the garrison for stealing some of his sheep, and "that false traitor, Guillaume De St Martin" (q.v.), de Brézé's Attorney-General, "who brought the French to the island, and sold us like meat on a butcher's stall". It was also alleged that at Hareford's visit after St Lawrence's Day he had been shown a letter from Guernsey promising sixty men to rush the Castle on the night the postern was left open, and that the harvesting episode was only a cloak for another conference at which the agreement for a hundred crowns had been signed and sealed, and entrusted to Katherine to keep. Much of this information can only have come from Hareford himself, who was obviously being used by Carbonnel as a spy and *agent provocateur*. The striking-off of his irons had evidently been a cunningly devised trick to rouse Katherine's interest in the prisoner. Lempriere had had many warnings. The Lady of St. Ouen's had told Katherine that Hareford had tried to play De Carteret a dirty trick; a French man-at-arms had cautioned Lempriere that the Englishman was a bad lot; Le Hardy's assistant priest had advised him not to allow the prisoner to come so often to his house; but he had only replied, "If John comes to see me, I cannot throw him out".

On 23 Aug. John paid his final visit, and followed Katherine into the kitchen, asking why he did not get a warmer welcome.

Then the Captain arrived, and she sent to the harvest-field for her husband. Carbonnel told him that a dying prisoner had made a confession implicating him, and that he must come to the Castle to confront him. The Marshal followed almost at once with a troop of soldiers, and searched the Manor for letters from Guernsey, finding only some not very compromising correspondence about a lawsuit and a cloak. Le Hardy was arrested the same day, and the two men were kept in prison till 10 Dec., when they were brought before a tribunal consisting of Carbonnel, du Vieuxchastel, and Guillaume De St Martin (q.v.) the Attorney-General. The examination of witnesses lasted ten days, one and a half of which were occupied in cross-examining Katherine. Hour after hour this girl of twenty-two faced her inquisitors, swearing "by the passion of Christ" and "as she hoped for Paradise", that her husband was innocent of all the charges against him. "Might she be damned for ever in Hell with the irrevocably lost", if all Hareford's stories were not a pack of lies. The prisoners also strenuously denied the accusations. Nevertheless the evidence leaves a strong suspicion that the plot was a real one. Unfortunately the last page of the manuscript is missing; so we have no record of the result of the trial. But Lempriere must have been acquitted; for four years later in 1467, when Harliston blockaded the Castle by sea, and Philippe De Carteret (q.v.) besieged it by land, the Chronicler writes, "During the siege many gentlemen and men of property in the island were slain and wounded, among others the Seigneur of Rozel" (*Chroniques*); and De Soulemont's genealogy (*Bull* V) has the note: — "Regnaldus Lempriere, killed in an assault on the Castle". A Latin document quoted by De La Croix (*Jersey*) gives the actual date: — "During that siege on the eve of Corpus Christi (i.e. the Wednesday after Trinity Sunday) Reginald Lempriere was killed during a certain assault". Soon after his death Katherine married Edmund Weston, one of Harliston's men-at-arms, and became the mother of Sir Richard Weston (q.v.) and) Sir William Weston (q.v.). Lempriere's son Jean succeeded him as Seigneur, and on his death without direct heirs his sister Catherine became Lady of Rozel. She married Dominic Perrin of Guernsey, and thus the Manor passed for a time to the Perrin family. [Authorities as quoted.]

LEMPRIERE, THOMAS, Seigneur of St Jean La Hougue Boëte, Bailiff 1495—1514. Son of Raulin Lempriere, Seigneur of La Hougue Boëte, and grandson of Jean Lempriere, Bailiff, Seigneur of Rozel. His mother was Jeanette Nicolle. In 1482 he was elected Jurat. In 1492 on his father's death he became Seigneur. An Inquest Report of 27 March 1495 (*Bull.* III) shows that by that date he had been appointed Bailiff. About 1502 his house in Morier Lane (now the Hill Street end of Halkett Place) was burnt with disastrous results for future historians of the island. At an inquest into the property of Geoffroi Wallis (q.v.), held in 1532, twelve old men testified "that they knew of a truth from what they had seen and from common knowledge that about thirty years back a house in St Helier's belonging to Thomas Lempriere, then Bailiff, was accidently destroyed by fire; that in it were the Privileges, Confirmations, and ancient Rolls, Records, and Registers of the island, and that these were burnt with the house" (Report printed in De La Croix' *Jersey*). On 10 Nov. 1509, on the accession of Henry VIII, Lempriere was reappointed Bailiff with a stipend of 20 francs *tournois* a year (*Letters and Papers of Henry VIII*).

In July 1502 Sir Hugh Vaughan had been appointed Governor. He was a Welshman of low birth, a favourite with Henry VII in the days of his exile. He allied himself closely with the De Carterets of St. Ouen's, and after a time, according to the Chronicler, "gave himself up to so lewd a life that he was wont to seize young girls by force; wherefore they durst not walk alone on the roads for dread of him. Furthermore, if he claimed any man's heritage, he would send a soldier from the Castle to fetch him to produce his title-deeds, and, as soon as he saw them, he tore off the seal, and broke it in pieces. Moreover he beat divers persons so sorely, that oft times they were in no small danger of death" (*Chroniques*). The charges were fully confirmed at a Commission of Inquiry in 1531. (See Article, 'The Chroniques in the light of Contemporary Documents', in *Bull* XIII). His conduct grew so outrageous that in 1513 Lempriere crossed to England to complain to the King. Thereupon Vaughan deprived him of his office, and appointed Helier De Carteret (q.v.) in his place. Lempriere's protest however caused the appointment of a Royal Commission to inquire into the state of affairs in Jersey; but the two Commissioners, who were

Englishmen, were easily hoodwinked by Vaughan and the De
Carterets, and produced (1515) a whitewashing Report. "Through
the influence of the Seigneur of St Ouen and his brothers all
was hushed up for a time" (*Chroniques*). They even turned
the tables on Lempriere by discovering that his own conduct
had not been blameless. While Jurat, he had owned a tavern,
contrary to law. For twenty years as Bailiff he had illegally
levied for himself a fee of 2 shillings on every sale of land. He
was wrongfully detaining certain rentes belonging to Jehan Journeaux. And he had occupied the water-mills of Ponterrin,
Quetivel, and Tostain without any title (*Report of Commissioners
of Henry VIII*). His later career is difficult to disentangle from
that of two namesakes. When a Thomas Lempriere is mentioned in the Records, it is hard to say whether it is the ex-
Bailiff, or his son, or a cousin of Rozel. He married Jeanette,
daughter of Jurat Guille Hamptonne, and had six children,
Thomas, who succeeded him as Seigneur of La Hougue Boëte,
Clement (q.v.), who became Bailiff, Nicolas, who became a
Jurat, Katherine, Peronelle, and Jeanne, who married Jean
Dumaresq, Seigneur of Samarès. [Authorities quoted above.]

LEMPRIERE, THOMAS (1756—1825), Colonel R.J.M. Third
son of Charles Lempriere (q.v.), Lieut.-Bailiff, and Elizabeth
Corbet. Born in Diélament Manor 16 Sept. 1756. Educated
at Oxford. In 1776 at Earl Granville's death he inherited in
right of his mother a fourth part of the Fief of St Ouen's. In
1780 his father admitted him an Advocate of the Royal Court.
On the morning of the Battle of Jersey (6 Jan. 1781) he was
awakened at Rozel by the sound of alarm guns and the clanging
of the church bells. He struggled into his uniform, and rode
off toward St. Helier's. Half way he met the Solicitor-General,
who reported that the Town was in the possession of the enemy
and the Lieut.-Governor a prisoner. William Charles Lempriere, his brother, tells the rest of the story in a letter to their
father: — "The instant my brother heard that some of our troops
were forming on Gallows Hill, he immediately went to join
them. The 95th Regt. had not yet arrived, and he went at
the desire of the Commanding Officer of the 78th to hasten

the march of the St. Martin's Division, who, for want of orders,
had marched toward Grouville, having heard that the enemy were
in those quarters. As soon as he returned, he found Major
Peirson at the head of the 95th, to whom he offered his services,
which the Major very politely accepted. During the whole
action my brother kept near the Major, and on horseback to be
more ready to carry any orders that might be found necessary.
He was only two or three yards from the Major, when he was
killed. Toward the close of the action he received a shot which
entered at the right shoulder, and passed nearly through the
centre of the back. The officers of the Regulars allow that he
displayed marks of great courage ; but he certainly exposed
himself more than prudence required" (*Bull.* V). "I had
strength", wrote Thomas, "to reach the house of Mons. Gosset.
I cannot tell you what care and attention I have received from
that worthy family" (*ibid.*).

Two months later, when William Charles was appointed
Lieut.-Bailiff, and resigned the post of Deputy-Commissary of
Musters for the troops in Guernsey and Jersey, Thomas succeeded him at a salary of six shillings a day. He now lived in
St John's, and in 1784 he and John Arthur competed for the
Constableship. Arthur won by ten votes, but Lempriere challenged the result, and the Court ordered a new election (*A.E.*).
Both sides appealed to the Privy Council, and for eight years
the Parish was without a Constable. In 1792 however, as
neither party had taken any steps to be heard, and as Lempriere
had left the parish, and so was no longer eligible, the States
ordered Arthur to take his seat (*A.E.*). In the stormy politics
of the period Lempriere took an active share. On the eve of
an election for Constable, the *Gazette* reports, "Monsieur the
Commissary and his servant rode through the parish all night,
begging and imploring everyone to vote for their candidate".
At a St John's Parish Assembly in 1787 he jeered at Jurat Le
Maistre, Seigneur of La Hougue Boëte, "putting his face within
four inches of his nose". Le Maistre knocked him down. Lempriere prosecuted him, but the Court refused to convict (*G.*).
Some of his fellow-officers in the Militia (he was Major in the
North Regiment) felt strongly that, instead of prosecuting, he
should have challenged his opponent to a duel, and wrote to
the Lieut.-Governor threatening to resign their commissions, if
he were not removed. This was reported in the *Gazette*. The

result was that when he and Philippe Dumaresq (q.v.), owner
of the *Gazette*, met in the Market Place, there was a furious
fight with canes and fists and finally a rough-and-tumble in
the mud (See article *Dumaresq, Philippe*). Most of his
own regiment however stood by him. A meeting of officers
passed a resolution with only two dissentients that "The Corps
of Officers taking into consideration the behaviour of Thomas
Lempriere Esq in a late dispute with Edward Le Maistre Esq,
Senior Jurat of the Bench, and having maturely examined the
whole circumstances of the case, are of opinion that his conduct
on the above occasion is not derogatory to the character of a
gentleman" (S.J.MSS.). Lempriere retained his commission,
and in 1795 became Colonel of the Regiment. In 1788 there
was another fight at St John's. On the eve of all Parish Assemblies each Party held a dinner. Both were eager to secure
the vote of a new-comer. Lempriere took him by the arm, and
tried to lead him to the Charlot dinner. Philippe Durell protested that he had promised to dine with the Magots. "From words
they came to blows. The fight lasted some time. At last the
combatants were separated, and Mr Lempriere retired with his
face blood-stained and battered" (G.).

Meanwhile in 1787 he had become involved in a quarrel with
Charles Lempriere (q.v.), his father. In the previous year he
had bought from his uncle Philippe (q.v.), who was now living
in Devon, the Fief of Chesnel and its dependencies. But, when
Philippe died, Charles claimed this estate as his brother's principal heir, alleging that the pretended sale had been a fraud
devised to keep him out of part of his inheritance ; and he
won his case. Thomas then moved to Town, and eventually made
his home in La Motte Manor, the house in which Corbet (q.v.)
had been seized. He was now a busy Advocate ; but he lost
no opportunity of trying to improve his position. In 1795 and
again in 1798 he tried hard to secure the post of Receiver-General. In 1798 he applied for the position of Storekeeper of the
Ordnance. In 1800 he approached Lord Townshend, Lord
Cornwallis, and Sir Charles Morgan asking them to secure his
appointment as Solicitor-General. Their polite refusals are
among the MSS. in Rozel Manor. In 1820, when a rumour
arose that Lord Carteret, the aged Bailiff, was about to resign,
Lempriere again wrote many letters asking influential acquain-
tances to support his candidature, but Major-Gen. Gordon, the

Lieut.-Governor, wrote to Lord Townshend, the Governor, "Mr Lempriere would be among the last I should recommend for so responsible a situation" (Beresford MSS in Public Library).

In 1806 after losing within a few days his wife and a daughter, he gave up his colonelcy. Col. Le Couteur wrote: "From circumstances of the most distressing nature in Col. Lempriere's family he has felt himself obliged to resign the command of the North Regiment" (Rozel MSS). In 1816 he resigned his position as Advocate. In his later years he became very studious. The *Gazette* said of him at his death: — "He had a perfect knowledge of the learned languages as well as French and English, in which his style was clear and elegant. He investigated unremittingly the laws and customs of his land, and knew them through and through. He could decipher ancient manuscripts with ease, and was such an enthusiast on this subject that he often spent whole days reading the old Rolls of the Court. One can safely say that no man in the island knew our legal procedure better". J.A. Messervy adds, "He was very erudite, a distinguished antiquary, and an eminent genealogist". He married (14 Oct. 1783) Elizabeth Charité, daughter of Rev. Samuel Beuzeville, and had eleven children, of whom the eldest was Vice-Admiral George Oury Lempriere). He died after three days' illness in 1823, and was buried in St Helier's on 5 July. His portrait in blue uniform with red lapels and silver facings, yellow waistcoat, lace cravat and cuffs and powdered wig, painted by Mason Chamberlin, and one of his wife by the same artist hang in Rozel Manor. [Authorities quoted above.]

LEMPRIERE, WILLIAM (d. 1834), Traveller and Medical Writer. Third son of Thomas Lempriere of Jersey, British Consul at Faro, and Mary Garnaut of Lisbon. He entered the Army Medical Service, and in 1789 was attached to the garrison of Gibraltar as Regimental Surgeon's Mate in the 11th Foot. In September of that year General O'Hara at Gibraltar received a letter from one of the Sultan of Morocco's sons, who was going blind, asking that an English doctor might be sent to treat him, offering in return "a liberal reward" and the release from slavery of ten shipwrecked British sailors. "Impelled by that impetuous curiosity which is natural to youth" Lempriere volunteered to go. He landed at Tangier on 14 Sept., and escorted by two negro cavalrymen rode on mule-back 550 miles down the coast to Mogador, and then another 130 miles to Tarudant, where he found the Prince. After five weeks' treatment his patient's sight definitely improved. But the old Sultan Mahomet XVI grew nervous lest this foreign doctor might be poisoning his son ; so the Prince was hurried off on pilgrimage to Mecca, and Lempriere sent 120 miles over the Atlas Mountains to Marrakesh. Here his medicines were handed to Moorish physicians to analyze. No notice was taken of his requests to be allowed to return to Gibraltar. Then the Sultan's favourite wife was poisoned by her rivals, and he was called in to attend her. By pretending that the necessary drugs could only be obtained in Europe, at last he secured permission to leave the country. He got back on 27 March 1790. In 1791 he published in London an account of his adventures, *A Tour from Gibraltar to Tangier, Sallee, Mogodore, Santa Cruz, Tarudant, and thence over Mount Atlas to Morocco, including a particular account of the Royal Harem.* Among the subscribers were Dr. Bandinel, Netherbury, Dorset, John Lempriere, British Consul at Faro, Charles Hilgrove Hammond of Trinity College, Oxford, and Arthur Atherly Hammond of St. John's, Oxford. This book had a tremendous success. It reached a second edition in 1793, a third in 1800, a fourth in 1808 and a fifth in 1813. A German translation, *Reise von Gibraltar nach Marakko* was published in Berlin in 1792 and reprinted in 1798, and a Portuguese translation, *Viagens da Gibraltar a Marrocos* appeared in Lisbon in 1794. In 1792 Lempriere was sent to the West Indies where he spent five years as Surgeon to the Jamaica Light Dragoons. On his return he published two books, *Practical Observations on the Diseases of the Army in Jamaica during the years 1792–7*, and *On the Situation, Climate, and Diseases of Jamaica and on the most probable means of Suppressing Mortality among the Troops and Europeans in Tropical Climates, 1799.* He took his M.D. at Aberdeen in 1799. His next station was the Isle of Wight, where he was Physician-General to the Troops. While here he published a *Report on the Medicinal Effects of an Alumnious Chalybeate Water lately discovered at Sandrocks in the Isle of Wight, 1812*, and *Popular Lectures on the Study of Natural History and the Sciences,*

delivered before the Isle of Wight Philosophical Society, 1830.
He left the Army with the rank of Inspector-General of Hospitals, and died at Bath 24 July 1834. [*D.N.B. Gent. Mag.*
1834. His own works.]

LEMPRIERE, WILLIAM CHARLES (1754—1790) Lieut.-
Bailiff. Second son of Charles Lempriere, Lieut.-Bailiff (q.v.).
Born at Diélament Manor, 5 July 1754. Matriculated at Ox-
ford from Hertford College 1773, but did not take a degree. He
returned to Jersey, was sworn in as Advocate of the Royal
Court 1776, and became an officer in the North Regiment of the
Militia. Toward the end of 1780 his father, who had been
Lieut.-Bailiff for thirty-one years, decided to resign, if he could
secure the appointment of his son as successor. They crossed
to England, and so were out of the island during De Rullecourt's invasion. The transfer of office was arranged. On 4
Aug. 1781 he was sworn in as Jurat and Lieut.-Bailiff, and on
the same day presided over the Royal Court. On 22 Aug. he
presided over the States. His father then transferred Diélament
Manor to him.

He inherited the fierce fight between Charlots and Magots
(See articles *Dumaresq, Jean* and *Lempriere, Charles*) ; and
Jean Dumaresq, the Magot leader, who had driven the father
from office, prepared to do the same for the son. First blood
was drawn by Lempriere. In May 1782 Dumaresq presented
his bill for expenses as Deputy to the Council in the dispute
about Jacques Pipon (q.v.). Lempriere opposed payment,
and on appeal to the Council succeeded on the technical
ground that the proposal had not been lodged au greffe. In
July the States appointed Dumaresq their permanent Deputy
to the Council, but Lempriere refused to fix the island seal to
this act, with the result that, when Dumaresq arrived, the Council would not receive him. Half the members of the States then
signed a protest refusing to attend any more meetings, till the
Council had considered their difficulties. Lempriere had a
haughty manner, which did not conciliate opponents, who nicknamed him Bec-en-l'air. In their petition to the Council they
alleged (I) that he had frequently refused to summon the States
when urged to do so by members: (II) that, when the States

did meet, he had refused to put to the vote motions that had been proposed and seconded: (III) that he had "frequently at Meetings of the States cast most indecent reflections on the character and understanding of members". In his reply Lempriere frankly admitted the first two points, asserting that the Civil Government of the island rested with the Royal Court, that the function of the States was merely to give advice when asked, that only the Court had any right to demand a meeting of the States, and that, though by the Code of 1771 no new law could be made without the States' consent, there was nothing in the Code to say that the Court was bound to adopt any law the States might pass. He added: — "The Clergy and Constables have no right to make motions properly so called. When they have anything to ask, it must be by way of petition, like all other private persons. If a motion is proposed by persons incompetent to propose it, the Lieut.-Bailly is bound to refuse it".

This statement clearly defines the difference between the parties. Dumaresq regarded the States as a local Parliament. Lempriere regarded it as a consultative committee, whose advice the Royal Court was by no means bound to accept. In his correspondence with the Council Lempriere always refers to the States as "a subordinate assembly", whereas Dumaresq calls it "the assembly in which the whole legislative power of this country under his Majesty in Council resides". In July 1784 the States met again to answer certain questions submitted by the Council. Lempriere had now found a new way of thwarting his opponents. Before the reply, which had been drawn up by a committee, could be read, he left the chair, and so brought the meeting to an abrupt conclusion. The majority of members however signed the reply individually, and handed it to the Lieut.-Governor to forward to the Council. After many delays the Council on 2 June 1786 gave its decision on the points at issue. It declared that "the feuds and animosities that have so unfortunately disturbed the island of late years have been created by a contention for power between the States and the Royal Court, and both sides have been tempted to exceed the bounds of their rights", that Lempriere's claim to be able to refuse to put to the vote any motion he disliked was "arbitrary and dangerous and would throw the whole legislative power into the hands of one man", but that Lieut.-Bailiffs did possess the right to decide when and how often the States should meet. A petition in Nov. 1786 showed that Lempriere was still continuing his practice of leaving the chair, and so closing the meeting, whenever something displeased him.

Meanwhile in 1784 Dumaresq had found a new weapon. His brother Philippe (q.v.) with Mathieu Alexandre (q.v.) had brought the first printing press to Jersey, and begun to publish a monthly *Magasin de l'Ile de Jersey*. In July 1785 there appeared in it a Letter from Mirza to Zadig. Mirza had been wrecked on the island of Yeseri (Jersey), and taken by a native named Tevris (Sivret) to the Council of Twelve (Royal Court). Then followed this description of Lempriere: — "The seat that is higher than all the rest is occupied by a young man entirely without experience, whose father resigned the post of Cadi in his favour. His face is enough to show his character. He uses his power to oppress the people, following his father's advice, who is the wickedest man in the world. While he lives, Yeseri will be in slavery". Lempriere ordered the arrest of Alexandre, the printer, on a charge of "publishing an infamous libel calculated to stir up sedition", and then took a singular revenge. He called up the case from time to time, examined a few witnesses, asking whether they had read the Letter, and who they imagined the Cadi to be, and then adjourned it, so that it dragged on for years, and was only ended by Lempriere's death in 1790.

In 1786 Dumaresq replaced the monthly *Magasin* by a weekly *Gazette de l'Ile de Jersey*, a far more vivacious and spiteful sheet, which published by no means impartial accounts of the secret meetings of the States, and harried Lempriere without mercy. In Jan. 1788 he and eight Jurats complained to the Privy Council of "incendiary harangues and publications of evil-disposed persons". "This venom is spread over the island by a weekly paper called *The Jersey Gazette*". "The inflammatory insinuations, daily sounded in the ears of the undiscerning, will convince your Majesty that it has become impracticable for your Royal Court to administer Justice without the risk of an actual insurrection".

By Jan. 1789 Lempriere was suffering from consumption, but in April he crossed to England to resist before the Council Dumaresq's latest plea for Trial by Jury. He became however too ill to appear, and in September returned to Jersey unable to attend to any duties. He then went to the South of France

hoping to recover his health. In November he obtained the
King's permission to resign his Juratship, though he retained
his office of Lieut.-Bailiff till his death. He died on 1 May
1790 in the town of Pézenas in Languedoc. In 1782 he had
married Elizabeth, daughter of Matthieu Gosset, and had four
children, Philippe Raoul, later a Jurat, William Charles, a Captain in the Royal Horse Artillery, who distinguished himself
at the taking of Washington, Elizabeth, and Mary. His portrait hangs in Rozel Manor.

[*Ordres du Conseil*, Vol. IV ; *Petitions, Representations, and
Answers of the States and Royal Court relative to Political Dif-
ferences* ; *Magasin de Jersey* and *Gazette* passim. *Actes des
Etats.*]

LE ROSSIGNOL, WALTER AUBIN (1873—1945), Indian
Judge. Son of John Mauger Le Rossignol, Governor of the
Gaol, and Mary Ann Rachel Aubin. Born in St. Helier's, 3
April 1873. After a brilliant career at Victoria College (1884—
91), in the course of which he carried off the Gold Medals for
Classics and Modern Languages and French and the Queen's
History Prize, he passed First into the Indian Civil Service
direct from School. He went up to Exeter College, Oxford,
with a Channel Islands Scholarship, and in due course arrived
in India, where he eventually held a succession of high judicial
posts, retiring as Senior Puisne Judge in 1926. Archibald Campbell wrote: — "He was quite the most eminent and efficient
Judge of the Chief Court and the High Court that I have
known, and I was in a good position to know, for I was Registrar for many years, and have had the reading up of the Law
Reports since I retired. And apart from judging his was one
of the best brains in our Service". He married Jeanne Dugand,
daughter of a Methodist Minister, and had two daughters, Jeanne
and Yvonne. He died at Eastbourne 11 Aug. 1945.

LERRIER, DURELL (1814—76), Jurat. First President of the
Société Jersiaise. Second son of Josué Lerrier and Elizabeth,
daughter of Francis Gautier ; nephew of Dr Philip Lerrier, in
whose house Rullecourt (q.v.) died. Born at St Helier's 25
Dec. 1814. Educated in the private school kept by Edouard
Durell (q.v.) at St. Saviour's. He inherited from his mother
property in Grouville, and in 1840 was elected Constable's Officer of that parish. In 1843 he became Procureur du Bien
Public, and in 1845 Constable. In 1853 he was elected Jurat,
only two votes being cast against him in the whole island. He
came to the Bench with a thorough knowledge of Jersey law,
which had for years been his favourite study. It was said at
his death that no judgement of his had ever been overthrown.
A studious, modest, retiring man, he seldom spoke in the States
owing to an impediment in his speech. In 1865 he was appointed Lieut.-Bailiff. He was one of the founders of the Société Jersiaise, and became its first President. The *Voix des
Iles*, a paper published by the French proscrits, which as a rule
rather sneered at all Jersey officials, grew unexpectedly genial,
when it wrote of Lerrier: — "How gentle his face! How pensive
his mien! He seeks no salutes or deference. Far from it! He
shuns all fawning flattery. He is Modesty personified ; though
when occasion requires, he can be as polite as a Spaniard. But
on the judgement-seat he is quite a different person ; still kindly,
courteous, gracious, but no longer bashful. When he presides
in the Bailiff's absence, everyone knows that each must speak
in his turn, and that no one may interrupt. If ushers shout
Silence, it is only from habit, for there are no disturbances. Advocates do not promenade the Court as if in the Royal Square.
The Lieut.-Bailiff allows no liberties. Physically he is a handsome old man, tall and benignant, eager to be of service to anyone except young women on the prowl for an old husband"
(28 June 1875). He died in his house at Grouville 14 June
1876, and was buried in Grouville churchyard. [*Bull.* I.]

LE SUEUR, PIERRE. (1811—1853), Constable of St Helier's,
Youngest son of François Le Sueur, blacksmith. Born November 1811 in Broad Street (then La Grand'Rue), in a house op-

posite the spot where his obelisk now stands. Educated at Le
Gros' School. At 15 he became clerk in the lawyers' office of
Le Gallais, the Deputy Vicompt, and Hugh Godfray, which
was the headquarters of the Laurel party. In 1835 he persuaded
his father to let him go to Paris to study law under Beaufils
who had trained François Godfray. On his return to Jersey
Le Gallais and Godfray obtained from the Bailiff his nomination
as one of the six Advocates. He was sworn in, 10 Dec. 1836,
but returned to Paris to complete his studies. He began to
practise in Jersey in Oct. 1837. If the Laurel Party thought
they had gained a brilliant recruit, they were disappointed. He
surprised everyone by identifying himself with the Rose Party.
One of the Rose leaders was fighting against ruin. Edouard
Durell (q.v.) was facing a serious charge ; and the young Advocate made his name by the dogged ingenuity with which for
four years he fought every inch of the ground, while the whole
island looked on. Henceforth he was engaged in every big
case, and almost always had François Godfray (q.v.) as opponent. No two men could be more different. Godfray was all
rage and rhetoric, sweeping away opposition with thunderous
perorations. Le Sueur was always cool, concise, and quietly
persuasive. He was amazingly clever. He undertook cases apparently hopeless, and generally found some loop-hole through
which his client could escape. In the Durell case he never
came to grips with the question whether his client was guilty,
but he argued that the Ecclesiastical Court, which had suspended him, had exceeded its powers. In his next big case,
when a brandy-merchant named Whitfield was accused of
defrauding the Impot of over £ 4,000, he made no attempt to prove
his client's innocence, but proved that the law under which he
was prosecuted had lapsed and had never been renewed. As
an Advocate he was greatly in demand and earned a large
income.

But his main work was done as Constable of St Helier's. In
1839, when Perrot (q.v.) became a Jurat, Le Sueur was unanimously elected to succeed him. It was a proof of his popularity
that the Laurel Party did not even put up a candidate. He
also succeeded Perrot in taking over the direction of the *Chronique*, the leading Rose newspaper. He was re-elected Constable
in 1842, 1845, 1848, 1851. The work that he did for the Town
was invaluable. When he took control, its sanitary condition

was appalling. The better streets poured their sewage into open water-ways. In the poorer districts there was no sanitation whatever. He started to make a complete system of underground sewers. This was costly, and the rate-payers grumbled loud at the expense ; but he stuck to his guns and carried the whole scheme through. He prosecuted slum-landlords, until they made their property decently habitable. Old streets were widened. A Fire Brigade formed. The names of the streets were posted up and the houses numbered. In 1849 the *Jersey Times,* by no means a Le Sueur paper, said: — "Since the first drain was commenced in 1845, improvement has followed improvement in rapid succession, so that one who had visited these islands in 1843, and now returned among us, would scarcely believe that he was in the same town". And his fellow-townsfolk appreciated what he had done. In 1848 he was presented with a handsome gift of plate; a four-branched candelabrum, two vases, and a silver salver, bought by 1200 subscribers and costing £330.

The work of Constable was no sinecure ; in addition to the routine work there were special emergencies. In 1846 he was responsible for the management of the immense crowds that poured into town for the visit of Queen Victoria. In 1847 he had to face an ugly riot. The price of bread was causing discontent among the poor. The men working on the new La Haule Road suddenly downed tools and marched on the Town. They visited every yard and workshop and compelled others to join them. Le Sueur got his Centeniers and Vingteniers together in time to repel an attack on the Royal Court and to make some arrests. The crowd then set off for the Town Mills. Le Sueur hastily swore in special constables and followed. But the mob had broken into the Mill, thrown the flour out of the window, and was returning to Town with two vans of corn. Le Sueur climbed into the first van, and challenged anyone to move it, and the rioters slunk away. The second van was not recaptured without a fight. Then the Governor sent troops, and order was restored. Le Sueur however was not content with prosecution and repression. Next day he opened a Fund for the relief of distress, and within a few hours received over £200. In 1849 he had a more dangerous fight. Cholera reached Jersey from France, and in spite of the new sanitation the epidemic assumed alarming proportions. On the Constable fell the responsibility of making arrangements to cope with the disease.

And all the time he was a leading member of the States, and in 1846 was appointed Treasurer. Because of his legal knowledge every new law was submitted to him for the final drafting. Reformer though he was, when Le Cras' (q.v.) Reform Committee began to agitate for the Anglicizing of all Jersey institutions, Le Sueur became a strenuous defender of the island's constitution. For years he had been overworking, and on 16 Jan. 1853 he died quite suddenly, when only 41. Over 400 people followed him on foot to his grave in Green Street Cemetery, and the obelisk in Broad Street was erected by public subscription to his memory. On 12 March 1873 the States paid a joint compliment to the two life-long opponents by this resolution: — "The States have decided to order the painting of oil portraits of Pierre Le Sueur and François Godfray, two men who as members of this assembly have rendered great services to the country, and have always shewn themselves animated by patriotic sentiments in defending its institutions whenever they were seriously threatened". These portraits hang in the Royal Court.

[Local newspapers. Abraham Mourant's unfinished *Biographie de Pierre Le Sueur*.]

LE VAVASSEUR DIT DURELL, DAVID (1729—75), Vice-Chancellor of Oxford University. Son of Thomas Le Vavasseur dit Durell and Mary, sister of Jurat Charles Hilgrove. Born in St Helier's 1729, and baptized in the Town Church 21 November. He matriculated at Oxford from Pembroke College 1747, took his B.A. 1750, and his M.A. 1753. He became Tutor of Hertford College, and in 1757 at the early age of 27 was made Principal. This was quite irregular, as by the Statutes the choice was confined to Westminster students of Christ Church, but no one seems to have challenged it. All through his Principalship he quietly ignored out-of-date Statutes to the great advantage of his College. He took his B.D. in 1760 and his D.D. in 1764. In 1765 he became Regius Professor of Greek, and in the same year was elected Vice-Chancellor of the University. In 1767 he became Prebendary of the Twelfth Stall at Canterbury, and was presented to the valuable Chapter

living of Ticehurst in Essex. In the following year he became
involved as Vice-Chancellor in a controversy that attracted
nation-wide attention. The Methodist movement had reached
Oxford, and six undergraduates of St Edmund Hall were accused to him by their Tutor of holding prayer-meetings in their
rooms, in which they indulged in "the absurdity of extempore
prayer", and of "venturing to dispute their Tutor's opinions in
his lectures on the Thirty-Nine Articles". In March 1768 Durell
as Visitor of the Hall held a Public Inquiry, and solemnly expelled them from the University. A flood of pamphlets poured
from the press. In one Sir Richard Hall remarked: — "It is to be
hoped that, as some have been expelled for extempore praying,
we may hear of others being expelled for extempore swearing".
Some commended Durell. Horace Walpole had no pity for
the "sanctimonious rascals", and when Boswell said to Johnson, "I am told they were good beings", he replied, "A cow is
a good thing in a field, but we turn her out of a garden"; but
the general opinion was that Durell had acted unjustly. In
1770, as he was travelling to Jersey by France to avoid the long
sea passage, he was arrested at Carteret as a spy, but after a
short detention he was set free (Messervy's Journal). He was
an ardent advocate of a new translation of the Bible. He
published *The Hebrew Text of the Parallel Prophecies of Jacob
and Moses with translation and notes together with the Sama-
ritan-Arabic Version of those passages and Four Dissertations on
points connected with these Prophecies*, 1763, and *Critical
Remarks on the Books of Job, Proverbs, Psalms, Ecclesiastes
and Canticles*, 1772. He died in Oxford 16 October 1775, and
was buried in the churchyard of St. Peter in the East under the
shadow of St. Edmund Hall. [Hamilton's *Hertford College:
Dic. Nat. Biog.*: Ollard's *Six Students of St. Edmund Hall*.]

LE VAVASSEUR DIT DURELL, EDOUARD (1781—1848),
Local Historian. Born in St. Helier's, Dec. 1781 ; son of
Edouard Le V. dit Durell and Elizabeth Le Breton. Educated
at Exeter. He obtained a grant from the Don Baudains, and
entered Pembroke College, Oxford, 1799, B.A. 1803, M.A. 1809.
From 1812 to 1814 he was Curate of Broad Rissington, Glouces-

tershire. For a short time he was Classical Master at Norwich Grammar School under Edward Valpy (q.v.). Then in 1815 in partnership with another clergyman he started a school at Bodmin, Cornwall. In 1818 he described himself as Curate of Withiel, Cornwall. In 1819 he was appointed Rector of St Saviour's, Jersey. Apparently some charge had been brought against him in Cornwall, for the Bishop of Winchester refused to institute him, until an Inquiry had been held. This however exonerated him, and he became Rector.

Abraham Mourant describing the States at that period wrote: — "The Rectors are the passive part of the Assembly. Most of them never speak in debate. They never bring forward a Bill. They never take any initiative". (Biographie de P. Le Sueur.) Durell broke this tradition. His active mind and keen intelligence made him plunge with enthusiasm into the political strife. He joined the Rose Party, and there was hardly a meeting of the States at which he did not make three or four speeches, often highly provocative ones, which infuriated the Laurelites. In 1823 he became Editor of the *Gazette*.

In 1836 two of his leading parishioners charged him with sodomy. It is impossible to pass this over in silence, for the Durell case for five years divided the island into factions. Whether he was guilty or innocent no one can now say, for the main question was never decided. His friends strenuously maintained that he had been 'framed' by political opponents. Certainly party passion ran strong, and a Rose Rector in a Laurel parish was intensely unpopular ; but he had only himself to blame, if he was thought guilty. He sued one of his accusers for slander, but, when the first three witnesses had been heard, abandoned the case. Dean Hue summoned him before the Ecclesiastical Court, but he refused to attend or make any defence, and the Dean suspended him, until the case was decided. His Churchwardens insisted that he should sign a bond promising to cease to take the Services and appoint a Curate, or forfeit £1500 to the poor. The States removed him from all committees, and he absented himself from the States' meetings. But he ignored the Dean's sentence and his pledge to the Churchwardens, and continued to read the Service in an empty church.

In 1857 Pierre Le Sueur (q.v.), a brilliant young Advocate just admitted to the Bar, undertook his defence. He put forward the plea that the Ecclesiastical Court could only deal with matters specifically entrusted to it by the Canons of 1623, and that the offence with which Durell was charged was not one of these ; and the Royal Court decided that he was right. This left the Dean powerless ; and the Royal Court shrank from dealing with the case itself, for at this time the penalty for this crime was death. So in 1838 the St Saviour's Parish Assembly decided to sue for the £1500. Le Sueur pleaded that the bond was illegal, and dragged out the case for two years with constant appeals on technical points, till the Parish grew tired of this endless litigation, and decided to drop the case. Durell claimed this as a rehabilitation, and resumed his seat in the States. Meanwhile Dean Hue had died, and Jeune (q.v.) had become Dean. He saw at once that this scandal must be settled, and appealed to the Privy Council against the decision of the Royal Court that the Ecclesiastical Court was not competent to deal with it. The Council decided (1840) that the Ecclesiastical Court was competent ; and Jeune summoned Durell before it. This time he did appear with Le Sueur. While denying the major charge, he admitted that his conduct had caused scandal, and on this ground (10 May 1841) he was suspended for five years, and a Curate put in charge. He still put up some show of resistance, locking the Church and refusing to give up the keys, but he was persuaded to submit, and retired into private life. At the end of the five years he made no attempt to resume his position. (A detailed account of the case is given in Mourant's *Biographie de Pierre Le Sueur*. The charges against Durell are printed verbatim in *Recueil des Pièces Authentiques relatives aux Poursuites vers le Rév. Ed. Le V. dit Durell.*)

Durell's chief claim to remembrance is the new edition he published of Falle's *Account of the Island of Jersey*. Before the storm burst, he had for years been collecting material. It is a pity that he never wrote an entirely new History, for his research had been painstaking and thorough. He had listed all the orders in Council ever sent to the island. He had plodded laboriously through the Records of the Royal Court. He had discovered Chevalier's *Journal* (See *Chevalier, Jean*). He had borrowed many old manuscripts preserved in Jersey families. But he contented himself with adding over two hundred pages of notes to Falle. "I have fallen", he wrote in the Preface, "on evil men and evil times, and it is even extraordinary that I have brought this work to a conclusion, while struggling with the severest trials. Oppressed with the dejection of a wounded spirit and trodden down by unmerited vituperation, I have been numbered among the children of misfortune". The book was published in 1837 as *An Account of the Island of Jersey by the Rev. Philip Falle to which are added Notes and Illustrations by the Rev. Edward Durell*. Other publications were *Charitable Visits to Philip George Jolin, executed for the murder of his father, with an account of his Trial and Execution,* 1829; *The Royal Album, a series of Lithographs* (of the Queen's visit) *from drawings by P. J. Ouless with Descriptions in prose and verse by the Rev. Ed. Durell*, 1847; and *A Picturesque and Historical Guide to the Island of Jersey*, 1852. The latter was the best of the local guides, and was often reprinted.

Durell also wrote poetry. In 1818, in his Curate days in Cornwall, he published an enormous elegaic poem, *The Triumph of Old Age*, "occasioned by the death of Mrs Gilbert of the Priory, Bodmin". Other published poems were: — *Janvrin's Tomb, a Poetical Legend of Olden Time*, 1840; *An Ode on the Visit of Her Majesty, Queen Victoria, to Jersey*, 1846 ; *An Elegy to the Memory of Charles Rouse Durell M.R.C.S. by his afflicted Father*, 1847. And the local newspapers frequently contained poems from his pen both in French and English.

He died of paralysis in his house in Windsor Road on 23 Feb., 1848, and was buried in St. Saviour's churchyard. He married Mary, daughter of Thomas Anthoine, and had five sons and a daughter who married William Duheaume, Rector of Trinity. A portrait of Durell appeared in the *Crapaud*, May 1835. [Local Newspapers.]

LE VAVASSEUR DIT DURELL, HENRY EDWARD

(1845—1921), Advocate, Attorney-General. Son of Henry Edward Le Vavasseur dit Durell, Grocer, of Beresford St., and Rachel Sullivan. Born in St. Helier's 13 Nov. 1845. Educated at Victoria College (1855—9), Coutances Lycée, and Caen University. Called to the Bar by the Middle Temple June 1868, and admitted to the Jersey Bar 12 Sept. "He had a gift of real eloquence", wrote C.T. Le Quesne K.C. "which was displayed most effectively in criminal cases. When he was in the full stream of his argument, drawn up to his full height, arrayed in his red robe, skilful and varied in gesture and in modulation of voice, he was impressive both to see and to hear". Three of his cases deserve mention. In 1873 the Jersey Mercantile Union Bank failed, and its chairman, Jurat Josué Le Bailly, was arrested for embezzlement. The trial lasted eleven days, one of which was entirely occupied by Durell's speech for the defence. This dealt so clearly and exhaustively with immensely complicated financial transactions that, though he could not save his client from well earned penal servitude, his own reputation was once for all established. In 1884 an old master-gunner from the Castle named Venner was accused of murdering an eating-house proprietor. The case against him seemed overwhelming; he was seized with the pistol in his hand; yet Durell's three hours' speech so impressed the jury that twenty-four gave a verdict of Not Guilty. In 1886 he undertook the defence of Philip Gosset, the States' Treasurer, who for twenty-eight years had been defrauding the island. Durell's mastery of all the details of his intricate financial juggling, as shown in his cross-examination of witnesses even more than in his closing speech, was a marvellous intellectual feat, and secured for the prisoner the comparatively light sentence of five years. Nor was he less effective in appeal cases in the awe-inspiring atmosphere of the Privy Council. Into every case he undertook he threw himself heart and soul. At the close of the Venner trial tears were streaming down his cheeks. Once he overstepped the mark. In 1891 he was suspended from practising at the Bar for four months for writing an indignant letter to the press about a matter that was still *sub judice*.

In 1872 in his first attempt to enter the States as one of the Deputies for St. Helier's he received what he described as "a fearful licking"; but in 1875 he succeeded, and at the next five elections was returned at the head of the poll, securing in 1892 the largest number of votes ever recorded. In 1896 he became Constable of St Helier's, and carried out many improvements at La Collette and the Parade. In 1899 he was appointed Solicitor-General, and was promoted Attorney-General in 1912. With his tall upright carriage, piercing eyes, and heavy moustache he was one of the best known figures in the Town, and a dog of the whippet breed was his constant companion. For some years the leading articles in the *Chronique* were written by him. He held strong religious views of a somewhat old-fashioned type, and was a prominent member of the St. Paul's congregation. When the King and Queen visited Jersey in 1921, much of the preparatory work fell on his shoulders, and the strain proved too heavy. Immediately after the visit he took to his bed, and died on 25 July. His first wife, Hannah Renouf, whom he married in 1885, died childless. In 1914 he married Winifred Mary Hooper, by whom he had two children. After his death the Jersey Society in London printed his lecture *Men I have known.* [Local newspapers ; C.T. Le Quesne's Introductory Note to *Men I have known.*]

LE VAVASSEUR DIT DUREL, JEAN (1625—1685), Dean of Windsor. Son of Jean Le Vavasseur dit Durel of St Helier and Susanne, daughter of Nicolas Effard, Rector of St Saviour's. Born at St Helier's 1625, and baptized in the Town Church 18 May. Entered Merton College, Oxford, aged 15, 1640. In 1643, when Oxford was garrisoned for the King, he withdrew to Caen, and took his M.A. there in 1644. His thesis, *Theoremata Philosophiae rationalis, moralis, naturalis, et supernaturalis* (Caen 1644), was the first of his published books. He then took a two years course in Divinity at Saumur, and wrote one of the *Disputationes* published by President Placens. In 1647 he returned to Jersey in Presbyterian Orders, and became Chaplain to Elizabeth Castle under Sir George Carteret (q.v.). In 1650 he went to Paris, and received Anglican Orders on Trinity Sunday from the Bishop of Galloway in the Chapel of the British Ambassador, being ordained Deacon and Priest on the same day. (See article *Brevint, Daniel*). In March 1651 he became Acting Rector of St Ouen's, during the exile of Etienne La Cloche (q.v.). When the Parliamentarians reoccupied Jersey in October, he withdrew to Elizabeth Castle with Sir George. The latter realized that the Castle could not hold out indefinitely ; so he sent Poindexter (q.v.), and then Durel, to Paris to the King to ask for instructions. They returned with orders to surrender on the best terms obtainable.

Durel spent the next nine years in France, first with the English exiles in Paris, than at St Malo. He was invited to act as Minister of the Huguenot Temple at Caen, and to become Chaplain to the Landgrave of Hesse ; but he accepted the post of Chaplain to the Duc de la Force, father of the Princess of Turenne, in whose household Brevint (q.v.) was Chaplain. At the Restoration in 1660 he was offered the choice of the Rectory of St Helier's or St Mary's in Jersey ; but he preferred to go to London. As an ordained Minister of both the Huguenot and the Anglican Church his ambition was to unite the numerous Huguenot congregations in England with the Church of England. The King gave him the use of a Chapel in the Savoy, where the Services would be in French, but the Prayer Book would be used, and the authority of the Bishop of London recognized. The wearing of the surplice was not to be enforced. The opening Service was held on 14 July 1661, and Durel quickly gathered an elegant and distinguished congregation, consisting largely, as the Registers show, of French Protestant nobles and their families who were in exile, a number soon to be swollen by the Revocation of the Edict of Nantes. But the majority of London Huguenots refused to dally with Prayer Book or Prelates, and maintained the full Presbyterian system in their Threadneedle Street Chapel. At first Durel used an old French Prayer Book issued in 1616, when Bandinel was made Dean of Jersey. But the entire revision of the English Prayer Book, which was completed in Feb. 1662, made a new translation necessary. Durel was entrusted with this task. On 6 Oct. 1662 the King ordered that his translation, as soon as it was completed, should be the only one used in Jersey, Guernsey and all Huguenot Churches that conformed to the Church of England (S.P.). The Bishop of London's Chaplain passed it for publication in April 1665 ; but it did not appear till 1667, its title being, *La Liturgie, c'est à dire le Formulaire des Prières Publiques, de l'Administration des Sacrements, et des autres Cérémonies et Coûtumes de l'Eglise, selon l'usage de l'Eglise Anglicane.*

This book remained in use with certain modifications in every Jersey church for more than two hundred years.

The Act of Uniformity made a Latin Prayer Book also needed for use in the Universities and at Convocations. This translation was first entrusted to Earle, Bishop of Salisbury, and Pearson, later Bishop of Chester ; but Earle died, and his manuscript was lost in the Great Fire, and Pearson was too busy to carry through the work ; so this task also was handed to Durel, a high compliment when England was so full of good Latinists. His book appeared in 1670 with the title, *Liturgia seu Liber Precorum Communium et Administrationis Sacramentorum aliorumque Rituum atque Ceremoniarum Ecclesiae juxta usum Ecclesiae Anglicanae.* Of this at least seven editions were printed in the next thirty-four years.

Durel had been made Rector of Overton, Hants. in 1661 and in 1677 Rector of Great Haseley, Oxon. Meanwhile honours were pouring in upon him. In 1662 he was appointed Chaplain to the King. In 1663 he became Prebendary of Salisbury, in 1664 Canon of Windsor, while still continuing his work at the Savoy Chapel. In 1668 he was made Prebendary of Durham. On 28 Feb. 1670 Oxford conferred on him the degree of D.D. On 27 July 1677 he was installed as Dean of Windsor, and on 9 Nov. as Registrar of the Garter; and shortly after he was also made Rector of Witney. He seems to have been a rich man, for the Treasury books show that in 1671 he lent to the King £ 15,000 sterling. He published many books of theological controversy directed against Nonconformists ; among others, *The Liturgy of the Church of England Asserted* 1661; *A View of the Government and Public Worship of the Reformed Churches beyond the Seas* 1662 ; *Sanctae Ecclesiae Anglicanae adversus iniquas atque inverecundas Schismaticorum Criminationes Vindiciae* 1669. He married on 21 Sept. 1664 in the Temple of Quevilly, Rouen, Marie de Langle, daughter of the Huguenot Pastor. He died on 8 June 1683, and was buried in St. George's Chapel, Windsor. [Wood's *Athenae* ; Marshall's *Latin Prayer Book of Charles II* ; *Dic. Nat. Biog.*]

LE VESCONTE, HENRY THOMAS DUNDAS (1813—48), Lieutenant R.N., Arctic Explorer. Only son of Commander Henry Le Vesconte and Sarah Wills. Born at Netherton, Devon, and baptized at Combe-in-Teignhead on 15 July 1813. He entered the Navy as First Class Volunteer on the *Herald* (26 guns) in 1829; was appointed Midshipman on the *Britannia* (120) in 1832, and was transferred to the *Endymion*

(44) in 1834, in which ship he saw active service in the war with China. Here he distinguished himself by helping to silence a battery on the island of Anunghoy on 23 Feb 1841, to capture the last fort protecting the approaches to Canton on 13 March, to capture the city itself on the 18th, and to destroy the whole line of defences on the 26th. For these services he was promoted Lieutenant in June 1841. He served in the *Hyacinth* (18) on the East India station, and then in the *Clio* (16) off the coast of Africa. In 1844 he was appointed to the *Superb* (74) in the Channel Squadron. In 1845 the Government decided to send an expedition to discover whether there was a passage from the Atlantic to the Pacific round the north of America. Two vessels, the *Erebus* and the *Terror*, were specially fitted out, and the veteran explorer, Sir John Franklin, who had already led three Arctic enterprises, was put in command. Clowes writes, "The flower of the Navy volunteered, and the pick of these was chosen" (*History of the Royal Navy*). The *Erebus* was commanded by Captain Fitzjames, under whom Le Vesconte had served on the *Clio*, and he specially asked to have him as Lieutenant, and Le Vesconte thought himself fortunate to be selected. The expedition left the Thames on 19 May, and on 4 July reached the Whalefish Islands off the coast of Greenland; where the transport, which was carrying part of their stores, handed these over and left. On 28 July the Captain of a whaler spoke to them as they were moored to an iceberg in the middle of Baffin's Bay. After that they were never seen again. A brief report, found later under a cairn of stones, showed that that summer's work was a failure. They sailed 150 miles up Wellington Sound, but then were turned back, probably by impenetrable ice. They retraced their course to Beechy Island, where the grave-stones of three of the crew and over 600 empty meat tins marked the site of their winter camp. In the summer of 1846 they tried another channel, now called Franklin Strait, and at first made good progress, but in September the ships were caught in drift ice, and could not be extricated. They had to winter on board. In the summer of 1847 the ice failed to melt; Franklin died; and another winter had to be spent on the ships. In April 1848 it was decided to try to march to the northernmost station of the Hudson Bay Company 1,200 miles away. Weakened by scurvy they set off, dragging boats on sledges, and their route was

traced later by the skeletons of those who fell by the way. Le
Vesconte reached Point Hall about 150 miles from the ships,
where a skeleton, believed to be his, was found, and sent to
England, and buried before the Franklin Expedition Memorial
in the Painted Hall, Greenwich. His comrades struggled on
for a few days longer, and perished at Starvation Cove. His
portrait is in the Royal Naval Museum. A pen and ink sketch
which he made showing the *Erebus* and *Terror* at anchor off
Whalefish Island (this was brought home by the transport) is
in the S.J. Museum, together with a silver fork bearing his
name, which was bought back from some Eskimos. Two pro-
montories within the Arctic Circle bear his name, Le Vesconte
Point in Baillie Hamilton Land and Point Le Vesconte in King
William Land, which was one of the points he passed on his
last march. [*Bull.* XII; Cyriax' *Franklin's Last Arctic Expedition;* O'Byrne's *Naval Biographical Dictionary.*]

LUCE, JOHN (1758—1827), Commander R.N. Eldest son of
Lieut. John Luce R.N., and Elizabeth Matthews of Bishop's
Waltham. Born in St Helier's 5 Nov. 1758. Educated at
the Greenwich Naval School. He joined the merchant service.
He made many voyages to Honduras, where there was a Jersey colony; but later on the advice of his godfather, John
Thomas Durell, Solicitor-General, he joined the Navy. He
served for a time in the small squadron protecting the Channel
Islands, and then in the West Indies. He was present at the
conquest of Martinique in 1793, and then joined the *Crescent*
(36 guns), commanded by Capn. Saumarez, on which almost
all the crew were Channel Islanders. Being then Master's Mate,
Saumarez strongly recommended him for a commission. He
went to London, and by the help of Paul Le Mesurier, a
Guernseyman who was M.P. for Southwark, secured permission to sit for examination. He passed, and rejoined his ship
in time to distinguish himself in the capture of the *Réunion.*
Thereupon he was appointed Lieutenant (1758). His ship was
now ordered to co-operate with the Chouans, who had risen
against the Republicans in Brittany. In this his knowledge of
French made him useful. He often landed in disguise, and

took long adventurous journeys ashore to interview the Chouan leaders in their secret hiding-places, and after the disaster of Quiberon Bay he arranged for the escape of many of the defeated army. When Saumarez was appointed to the *Orion* (74 guns), he took Luce with him as First Lieutenant. At the Battle of St Vincent in 1797 Luce boarded the Spanish three-decker *Salvador del Mundo* (112 guns), and received her surrender. He took the prize back to Spithead, and, we are told, "so abundant were the preserved meats found on board, that the victors fared sumptuously every day". He was rewarded by a commission as Commander. This however brought his active service to an end; for a cannon shot, which had blown his speaking-trumpet out of his mouth at the Battle of St Vincent, had left him deaf, and he had to retire. In 1800 he married at Gosport a Miss Scarvel, whom he had met in the West Indies, and he built for himself a cottage at Walworth, where he died on 7 May 1827. He left no children. [Memoir in *Guernsey and Jersey Magazine*. April 1837. Ross' *Memoirs of Admiral de Saumarez*.]

LYS, PHILIPPE (1763—1826), Signals Officer. Third son of Jean Lys, Harbour Master, and Susanne Skibo. Born in St Helier's in 1763 and baptized in the Town Church on 15 July. In 1802 he was appointed Signals Officer on the Mont de la Ville. In the following year the building of Fort Regent was begun. On 4 June 1804 at 6 p.m. he was on duty in his look-out, when he noticed soldiers rushing headlong down the Hill. He was told that smoke was pouring from the vent-holes of the powder-magazine. It was the King's Birthday, and at noon a royal salute had been fired from the Hill, and a careless gunner had put back in the Magazine an imperfectly extinguished length of the nitre-impregnated rope, with which the cannons were fired. Taking with him Edouard Touzel (q.v.), a carpenter, and William Pulteny, a private of the 31st, he ran to the Magazine. Touzel burst open the door, and flung out armfuls of burning fuses, which Lys and Pulteny removed to a safe distance. They then fetched water to extinguish the fire. (For fuller account see *Touzel, Edouard.*) The

States voted Lys a reward of 5,000 *livres* (about 300 guineas) and a gold medal suitably inscribed. In the following year he was appointed Inspector of Artillery on the Staff of the Militia, an appointment which he held till his death. In 1813 he was promoted Major. He married in 1785 Marie Messervy, and had nine children, one of whom, John Stephenson Lys, became Rector of Alderney. [Stead's *Gazette*, 9 June 1804; De La Croix' *Ville de St Hélier; Annual Register* 1804; Johnson's Book of Heroes ; Yonge's Book of Golden Deeds.]

MABON, RICHARD (d. 1543), Dean of Jersey. In a deed leaving an endowment for masses to be said for their souls (*Bull.* 1925) he described himself as native of the parish of St. Saviour's and son of Colin Mabon and Tassine. (In the *Extente* of 1528 Colyn Mabon appears as holding land belonging to the Fief of St. Germain in St. Saviour's). Richard inherited from his father land on the Fief of Grainville at Longueville, adjoining which he built a house long known as the Maison de Mabon (*Extente* of 1668), in which he lived before becoming Rector of St. Martin's. He also possessed land at St. Martin's on the Fief of La Queruée. We first hear of him, when the Coutances Register records on 22 Nov. 1509 the appointment of Dominus Richard Mabon, Priest, to the Deanery of Jersey. There was evidently some difficulty about this, for on 28 Jan. 1510 the Register records the confirmation of his appointment. On 10 June another entry states that he has been appointed Dean, as though nothing had been said about it before ; but on 1 Oct. the appointment of Nicolas Levesque as Dean of Jersey is recorded. De La Croix prints a deed dated 7 Aug. 1512 creating him Dean ; and the Coutances Register shows that he was again made Dean on 2 May 1514, this time describing him as "Curé of St Martin's". Why he should have been appointed five times in four and a half years is nowhere explained.

In 1515 Thomas Mallet is mentioned as Dean. Probably this was the time when Mabon made the long, arduous, dangerous, and expensive pilgrimage to Jerusalem. On his return he built on the Hougue Bie the Chapel which stands there still. From early times this great mound, which covers the tomb of a prehistoric chief, had been the centre of semi-pagan superstition. In the 12th. century an attempt had been made to christianize it by building the little chapel of Notre Dame de la Clarté on the top. This however had apparently fallen into ruins. The mound was on Mabon's property ; so he now restored the Chapel and added a new one. In the deed mentioned above he says, "Richard Mabon, Curé and Rector of St. Martin's, Pilgrim, having returned from the Holy Sepulchre and the Jerusalem pilgrimage, has built in honour of the Assumption of the Virgin Mary, of our Lady of Loretto, and of Monseigneur St. Michael on a spot named Houguebye a Chapel called Notre Dame de la Clarté, and adjoining the said Chapel at the east end another little Chapel, like an Oratory, called Jerusalem, in honour of the Passion of Jesus, and underneath this another little Oratory, like a sepulchre, more or less resembling the Holy Sepulchre at Jerusalem, so far as Sire Richard could make it". His hope was that this would become a place of pilgrimage. The only account of his efforts comes from two prejudiced Calvinists, to whom every Papist was a rogue and impostor.

"The said Priest", wrote the Chronicler in 1585, "was an idolater and a great maker of images, who caused the poor to believe many lies and rascalities, so that they would bring him offerings. He made simple folk believe that the Virgin often appeared to him near the said Chapel". A later chronicler (*Bull* 1925) says, "The image of Notre Dame de la Hougue Bie held out one hand for offerings. This hand was pierced, so that the coin fell into a money-box, and was so arranged that the hand and arm made a movement which seemed to thank the donor". This simple mechanical device no doubt encouraged offerings, but can hardly have been meant to deceive anyone ; yet the writer says, "Thus the superstitious and ignorant poor were still further exploited, and Mabon enriched himself at the expense of all who came to see the pretended miracle". Later, he adds, the people grew tired "of making this impostor opulent with the riches of Mammon", so he invented a new miracle, and hung candles by wires from the roof, and pretended that they were burning in mid-air. But charges like these were the stock-in-trade of the baser type of Reformers in their campaign against pilgrimage centres.

On 22 Dec. 1519 Mabon was reappointed Dean. A struggle

was now raging between Helier de Carteret (q.v.), the Bailiff,
and Sir Hugh Vaughan, the Governor. Mabon sided with
Vaughan. On 13 July 1552 the Governor wrote to Cardinal
Wolsey that Mabon was coming to London to visit him, and
that his views might be accepted as those of the island (S.P.).
On 19 July Mabon sealed with the Dean's seal a petition from
eight Jurats asking for the dismissal of De Carteret (Bull. 1912).
On 22 Aug 1524 Mabon and Jean Lemprière, Seigneur of Rozel,
were appointed to act as Joint Bailiffs, till the matter of variance
betwixt Sir Hugh Vaughan and Helyer Carteret be appeased ;
though in criminal cases Lemprière was to act alone, "for as
moch as the seid Dean is a spiritual pson and may not in that
behalf medel" (Patent in *Prison Board Case*). On 3 and 8
Oct., 1524 we find Mabon presiding over the States, and he
retained the office of Bailiff till 1527. De La Croix prints a
contract passed before him on 18 July of that year.

In 1528 he had an unpleasant adventure. His successor as
Acting Bailiff was Jasper Pen, an Englishman. He on his way
to Jersey met some Spaniards in Southampton, and sold them
a cargo of Jersey wheat, for which he received £40. When
they reached the island, they could not find either their corn
or the Bailiff. So they decided to seize the ex-Bailiff as hostage.
They raided St. Martin's Rectory in the middle of the night, gave
Mabon no time to dress, marched him in front of them to the
beach wearing nothing but his shirt, so that his legs and feet
got full of thorns, and kept him prisoner on their boat, till he
paid them the £40, a debt which he never could recover from
Pen (*Chroniques*).

On 31 May 1553 by an Act passed before the Royal Court
he handed over the Hougue Bie and its Chapels with adjoining
land as endowment to two priests, Jacques Amy and Lucas
Falle, who were to say Mass in the Chapels. When they died,
successors were to be appointed by his heirs, or, if they failed
to do so, by the Rector of St. Martin's (Bull. 1925).

Of his next seven years we know nothing. He apparently
retained the Rectory of St. Martin's, but he ceased to be Dean,
for from 1534 to 1541 this office was held by Thomas De Soulement (q.v.). On 20 May 1542 however he was appointed Dean
for the seventh time. He then apparently began to build another
Chapel close to St. Martin's Church, for in 1740 the Churchwardens petitioned the Ecclesiastical Court, stating that there

was a Chapel adjoining the north-east of the Church, commonly called 'la Chapelle Mabon', which according to tradition Dean Mabon had built ; that probably he had never finished it, as it appeared never to have had a roof ; that at the time of the petition it was in a state of ruin, part of its gable having fallen during the previous autumn ; that it never had been or could be used for Divine Service ; and that its ruins were a disfigurement to the Church ; they therefore asked permission to demolish it.

Mabon's plans were probably interrupted by death. At the end of May 1545 he is mentioned as alive in the Rolls of the Cour de Catel ; but on 14 June 1543 Jean Mourant, son of his sister, Marion, appeared before the Court to claim as heir all the property that Mabon had possessed at his death. [Authorities mentioned above.]

MAJOR, DOROTHY (1628—76), Protectress of England. Toward the end of the 15th. century Jean, son of Jean Mauger of Handois, Jersey, settled in England. His grandson and great-grandson, both named John (The family now spelt its name Major), became Mayors of Southampton. The latter's son Richard bought Hursley Manor, four miles south of Winchester. Oliver Cromwell, seeking a wife for his son Richard, rejected "the offer of a very good marriage", "as I see not that assurance of godliness", and selected Richard Major's twenty-year old daughter Dorothy, "whose virtue and godliness has so great a place in my heart that I think not to neglect anything that may consummate the business". After somewhat lengthy negotiations about her dowry she and Richard were married in Hursley Church 1 May 1649. In 1658 Oliver died, and Richard was proclaimed Lord Protector, and Dorothy was installed in Whitehall as Protectress of England. At the restoration in 1660 Richard escaped to France, leaving at Hursley his wife and three young children and a baby as yet unborn. She never saw him again, though she devised secret ways of sending him money in his exile. She died at Hursley 5 Jan. 1676 [Payne's *Armorial* ; Cromwell's *Letters* ; Ramsey's *Richard Cromwell.*]

MALET DE CARTERET, CHARLES EDWARD (1869–1942), Bailiff. Second son of Col. Edward Charles Malet De Carteret (q.v.), Seigneur of St. Ouen's, and Elizabeth Poingdestre. Born at Mon Plaisir, near St. Aubin's, 26 July 1869. Educated at Victoria College, at Westminster School (1881–3), and at Oxford Military College (1884–6). Passed into Sandhurst first on list of Cavalry cadets. In 1888 he was gazetted to the Inniskilling Dragoons, with which regiment he served in Natal and Zululand. Being unable to continue to meet the expenses of a crack cavalry regiment, he resigned on the return of the troops to England, and turned to Law, though he also became a Captain in the Artillery of the Royal Jersey Militia. He was called to the Bar (Inner Temple) in 1896, and to the Jersey Bar on 27 Aug. 1898. He practised for a time as an Advocate, and in 1903 became Receiver-General. In 1912 he was appointed Solicitor-General, and in 1925 Attorney-General. He was a scholar with a quick discerning mind, and a fluent speaker. In 1931 he became Bailiff. He was probably the most self-effacing man, who ever occupied this office. His entry in Who's Who held the record for brevity. It consisted merely of the dates of his appointments as Solicitor-General, Attorney-General, and Bailiff. He lived in an undistinguished boarding-house. When sent an invitation to the King's Silver Jubilee, he could not be persuaded to use it. And, though failing eyesight would soon have made his retirement inevitable, his resignation in 1935 was undoubtedly hastened by a desire to escape the ceremonies of the Prince of Wales' visit. He had become a Freemason when nineteen, and after holding many offices in the Order, in 1914 succeeded his father as Provincial Grand Master. He died unmarried in the Millbrook Nursing Home on 28 Jan. 1942, and was buried at St. Ouen's. [Local Newspapers, specially *Evening Post* 1.5.31.]

MALET DE CARTERET, EDWARD CHARLES (1838–1914), Seigneur of St. Ouen's. Grandson of Jean Mallet, Rector of Grouville, and second son of John Mallet, an old East India Civil Servant, and Jane Anne, eldest daughter of Philip Le Maistre, Seigneur of St. Ouen's. He was born at Paignton,

Devon, 1 March 1838, and educated in England and France. In 1855 he was gazetted as Lieutenant by purchase to the 88th Regiment, the Connaught Rangers, and later transferred to the 25th, the King's Own Scottish Borderers. He served in the Crimea, and in India during the Mutiny, earning the medal and clasp for Central India. On the death of his elder brother in 1856 he became Seigneur of St. Ouen's, and in 1859 assumed by sign manual the name of Malet de Carteret. (When Robert, Lord Carteret, died childless in 1776, St Ouen's Manor passed to Jane Ann Le Maistre, great-great-grand-daughter of François, son of the famous Sir Philippe. The next two Seigneurs were therefore Le Maistres. When this male line also became extinct in 1848, John Paignton Mallet, and then Edward Charles Mallet, inherited it as sons of the eldest daughter of the last Le Maistre Seigneur.)

In 1861 he married Elizabeth, daughter and heiress of Abraham Poigndestre of La Vieille Maison, St John's, whom local papers declared to be the richest man in the island. He then left the Army, and settled in Jersey. While still an officer in the Regulars, he had taken a commission in the Jersey Militia. In 1857 he had become a Lieutenant with leave of absence in the South-West Regiment. Now in 1861 he was promoted Captain, and in 1863 he became Lieutenant-Colonel. In the same year he was transferred to be Lieutenant-Colonel of the North-West (the St. Ouen's) Regiment. He was Aide-de-camp to three successive Lieut.-Governors. In 1866 he was elected Deputy of St. Ouen's, and was re-elected in 1869. In May 1886 he was elected Jurat, and claimed as Seigneur of St. Ouen's the seat on the Bailiff's left, as senior Jurat. After examination of precedents this claim was granted. He was Lieut.-Bailiff from 1889 to 1901, and acted as Juge-Délégué from 1898 to 1899 between the resignation of Sir George Bertram as Bailiff and the appointment of Sir William Vernon. In the States he was a frequent speaker, and exercised much influence, as most of the country members followed his lead. He was for a long time President of the Defence of the Island Committee.

He was a prominent Freemason. He had been initiated at Colchester in 1859, and in 1869 was installed as Provincial Grand-Master of Jersey. Knocker's *Freemasonry in Jersey* says of him: — "His rule over the Province extended over a period of 45 years, and toward the end of that time he had the distinction of being the Senior Provincial-Grand-Master under the English Constitution. Those 45 years were marked by great changes for the better in the status of Freemasonry in Jersey. At the commencement of them the Craft was far from strong either in numbers or finance, while it was occasionally rent by internal dissensions, and in addition the irregular French lodge (see *Baudains, Philippe*) working in its midst was a constant source of anxiety. At the end of his reign a far more pleasing picture can be presented of a fraternity strong in numbers and finance, and firmly settled down to a state of harmonious usefulness". He remained in office till his death.

He devoted many years and much money to the restoration of St. Ouen's Manor, the interior of which was in a ruinous state, when he inherited it. With Adolphus Curry as architect the building inside and out was skilfully repaired. The grounds were put in order, and, so that the lane past the Manor might become a private avenue, the land on which the present main road runs was transferred to the Parish. The work on the house was finished in 1904, and then the Manor Chapel of St. Anne, which had been used as a barn, was restored, and 'reconciled' by the Bishop of Winchester on 5 May 1914. Colonel Malet de Carteret was President of the Société Jersiaise from 1906 to 1914. He died on 2 Sept. 1914, and left four children. Reginald (b. 1865. Jurat 1915—35), Charles Edward (b. 1869. Bailiff 1931—5), Marie, and Margaret (m. Charles L.H. Le Cornu of La Hague Manor).

MANLEY, MARY DE LA RIVIERE (1673—1724), Playwright and Novelist. Daughter of Sir Roger Manley, who was Deputy-Lieutenant-Governor of Jersey 1667—74. She was born on 7 April 1673, most authorities say in Jersey, but Pope in his *Literary Correspondence* (1735) says "at sea between Jersey and Guernsey". At all events her infancy was spent in Mont Orgueil. Her mother died the following year, and her father then brought his five children to England on his appointment as Governor of Landguard Fort, Suffolk; so not much more than a year of her life was passed in Jersey. Sir Roger died when she was sixteen, and she was trapped into a bigamous marriage with her cousin John Manley, a man 25 years older than herself, whose wife was still alive. He deserted her, and she became a protégée of Barbara Villiers, Duchess of Cleveland, the King's Mistress. When she quarrelled with her, she began to write plays, which outrivalled in grossness those of the obscenest playwrights of the period. She became the mistress of Sir Thomas Skipworth of Drury Lane, a married man with many children, and persuaded him in 1696 to put on one of her plays, *The Lost Lover*, at his theatre ; but it was damned on the first night. Another, *The Royal Mischief*, produced the same year at Lincoln's Inn Fields, was hardly more successful. She next became the mistress of John Tilly, Warden of the Fleet, and in 1705 was arrested as an accomplice in the forging of a marriage certificate to obtain for an unmarried girl a widow's dower from a rich estate, but she was released. In the same year she published her first political novel, *The Secret History of Queen Zarah*, a very thinly disguised libel on that great Whig lady, Sarah, Duchess of Marlborough. Her most notorious book, *The Secret Memoirs of Several Persons of Quality from the New Atlantis, an Isle in the Mediterranean*, was published in 1709. In this the islanders, whom she accused of scandalous vices, were obviously to be recognized as members of the Whig Ministry. She and her printer, John Barber, whose mistress she now was, were promptly arrested ; but there was enough truth in some of her accusations to make the Ministry unwilling to wash its dirty linen in public, and in 1710 the prosecution was dropped. Other unsavoury books of the same type followed, *Memoirs of Europe by Eginardus, Secretary to Charlemagne*, in 1710, and *Court Intrigues in the New Atlantis* in 1711. The Tory Party now adopted her as one of their pamphleteers. In 1711 she succeeded Swift as Editor of *The Examiner* (he described her to Stella as "very homely and very fat"). Political pamphlets, plays, and novels poured from her pen. In 1714 she published her highly-coloured autobiography, *The Adventures of Rivella, or the History of the Author of The New Atlantis*. In 1717 a tragedy of hers, *Lucius, the first Christian King of Britain*, was a Drury Lane success. "Loose in her life and venomous in her pen", writes Sergeant in *Rogues and Scoundrels*, "licentious and deadly bitter, she has no close parallel among women". The *Times Literary Supplement* said of her (11 December 1924): — "Her joy in salacious detail could not save her novels from incredible

dullness. Her mind was incapable of decency and her spirit
of anything great". Her only importance lies in the fact that
some of the mud she threw stuck. Churchill in his *Life of
Marlborough* and Trevelyan in his *Reign of Anne* declare that
Macaulay was influenced by her libels, and that his unpleasant
picture of Marlborough's character was accepted by later his-
torians. Mrs Manley died on 11 July 1724, and was buried at
St. Benet's, Paul's Wharf. [Her autobiography as above ; *Dic.
Nat. Biog.* ; *Encyc. Brit.* ; Sergeant's *Rogues and Scoundrels* ;
Jerrold's *Five Queer Women*.]

MANUEL, HENRI LUCE (1818—75), Dialect Poet. Grandson of Matthieu Manuel, native of Beziers in Languedoc, who
had settled in Jersey, and son of Henri Manuel, Tanner, and
Betty Jenny Pickstock, daughter of Captain Pickstock (q.v.).
Born in 1818, and baptized in the Town Church on 21 June.
From 1839 to 1846 he was Constable's Officer at St Helier's.
In his last year of office he went with Centenier Le Cronier
to arrest a brothel-keeper at Gorey. The stalwart virago stabbed Le Cronier to death, and pursued Manuel, a little man,
down the street with the blood-stained knife. In 1842 he was
appointed Registrar for St. Helier's. In 1844 he was admitted
a Notary. In 1846 he became Surveillant ; and from 1858—72
he was Procureur du Bien Public. Toward the end of his life
he became a partner in the English and Jersey Union Bank.
As a young man, he made an unfortunate incursion into journalism. He allowed his name to appear as proprietor of a new
English paper, the *Jersey Gazette*, though the real owners were
a group of men who preferred to remain anonymous. In April
1840 the paper called Jean De La Croix (q.v.), editor of the
Constitutionnel, a 'penny-a-liner'. De La Croix came to Manuel's house, and violently assaulted him. In June the paper
made an absurd attack on one of Dean Jeune's sermons, accusing him of advocating the assassination of Queen Victoria.
Jeune sued him for libel, claiming £1,000 damages, but after
several hearings the case seems to have been dropped. But
Manuel was more in his element as the moving spirit in various
cultural Societies. He was Secretary of the Société d'Emu-

lation, which offered an annual £10 prize for the best essay on some subject connected with Jersey. The prize essay in 1843, Tréhounais' *L'histoire, la topographie, la constitution, les moeurs, et le langage de Jersey*, was considered so useful that it was printed at the Société's expense. In 1850 Manuel was Secretary of the Committee that tried to establish a permanent Exhibition of Le Capelain's pictures. In 1871 he was Secretary of the Loan Section of the Channel Islands Exhibition, and the exhibits that he lent himself showed that he had been a diligent gleaner of local relics. They included a collection of the earliest Jersey newspapers, of old local caricatures, of old proclamations, and of Jersey bank-notes. But his chief fame rests on his dialect poems, which he always signed merely L. Twelve of these will be found in Mourant's *Rimes Jersiaises*, and several in the *Nouvelle Année*. He published *Queur de Femme en chinq scènes*, two brochures of *Rimes et autres Poésies Jersiaises*, and a fourth called *La R'connaissance et autres Rimes Jersiaises*. His predecessors had mostly chosen topics of rustic life and humour, but Manuel was more ambitious. He loved elegaic themes, in which the predominant note is a wistful melancholy, e.g. 'L'apprèche de la mort', 'L'n'ya rein qui sait sur dans cette vie'. He died in his house in Duhamel Place on 2 Dec. 1875. He married Elizabeth De Veulle. His portrait appears in the Panthéon Jersiais, No. 1.

MARCULF, SAINT. See Appendix I.

MARET, CHARLES (c. 1618—66), Receiver-General. Eldest son of Jean Maret of Trinity, Receiver-General, and Marie Machon. At the beginning of the Civil War in March 1643 he brought to Jersey from the Close Committee the Order appointing five Commissioners to arrest Sir Philippe De Carteret (q.v.). He then "assisted the Committee with all his power in rebellion against His Majesty's fortresses" (Indictment at his trial). On 26 Sept. he was sworn in as Parliamentary Receiver.

On 5 Oct. the King at Oxford issued a warrant for his arrest. On 21 Nov. he fled to London, when the Royalists recovered the island. In 1644 his father was arrested for receiving letters from him. In 1645 he was condemned to death in his absence for high treason. Meanwhile he was hanged in effigy and his goods confiscated (*Bull.* III).

In 1646 he brought to Guernsey to Sir Peter Osborne, who was holding Castle Cornet for the King, an offer from the Earl of Warwick of generous terms of surrender. "He waited in a small boat flying a white flag midway betwixt Town and Castle, till Sir Peter sent his shallop to demand his errand. He had brought two bottles of wine, one Spanish, the other claret, with which to regale those who came for his dispatches. They drank to the King and Parliament, and then toasted one another. When the bottles were empty the men from the Castle returned to refill them to show that they too had no lack of wine ; and they brought them back and drank healths as before. Meanwhile Sir Peter mustered his troops, and told them the terms offered, and asked if they were still willing to keep the Castle with him. The greater part made answer that they would guard the Castle with their lives" (Chevalier). So Maret's mission failed.

In 1651, when Parliament had recovered Jersey, he resumed his work as Receiver. On 2 Aug. 1652 he was appointed a member of the County Committee for Jersey (*S.P.*) and on 13 Aug. one of the four Commissioners for Compounding (*S.P.*). He now quarrelled violently with his colleagues. He "notoriously affronted" Michel Lempriere, the Bailiff (q.v.), perhaps because he thought him too lenient in fixing the fines which Royalists paid to recover estates, fines which came to Maret's department ; and Lempriere imprisoned him in Mont Orgueil, till he found security for future good behaviour. In July 1655, when a new Commission for Compounding was appointed, Maret was left out, and Col. Gibbon the Governor was ordered to "take into your own hands the accompts of Charles Maret, the present Receiver of our Revenue" (*O.C.*). This led to another explosion. On 29 Nov. Gibbon wrote to Cromwell: — "Since my last gave you an accompt of the dangerous letter of Mr Maret, I secured him, and so he remains, refusing to give security to live peaceably toward the Government and those entrusted here". (The offensive letter was apparently written to

Philippe Messervy, Seigneur of Bagot, who was arrested at the same time.). Gibbon added that he has learnt "of Maret's giving public affronts, as now, to all formerly in authority here, as Major Littcot and Major General Heane. The man is of a very ill conversation as well as levellingly stubborn. I beg your Highness' pleasure concerning him" (*Rawl. MSS.*).

At the Restoration in 1660 Maret fled to Coutainville in Normandy, taking his ledgers with him. These he eventually restored, for in 1665 the Lieutenant-Governor was authorized to "examine and pass Chas.Maret's accounts". He was then allowed to return to Jersey under the Act of Indemnity. He died in 1666, and was buried in Trinity churchyard on 6 Aug. He married Sara Streeter, but left no children. His brother was his heir. He presented a silver Communion Cup to Trinity Church. [Chevalier's *Journal*; *State Papers*.]

MARET, PHILIPPE (d. 1637), Attorney-General; second son of Charles Maret of Trinity and Marguerite, daughter of Noel Le Cerf. Born in Trinity. Educated at Merton College, Oxford, with assistance from the States, who contributed (*A.E.*) 24 crowns to send him there. He took his B.A. degree in 1598. In 1600 he was offered the post of Regent of the new College proposed by Laurens Baudains (*A.E.*), but this came to nothing. He was then with Sir Walter Ralegh, who came to Jersey as Governor in Sept. 1600. A State Paper speaks of him as "bred as a scholar at Oxford, whence he came to Sir Walter Ralegh for a while, and then went into Spain" (*Conway Letters*). Bailiff Herault wrote in 1616, "He has been brought up in Spanish seminaries, got pernicious maxims, and refuses to give an account of his faith"; "He will not receive the Sacrament and abjure his religion learned among the seminaries" (*S.P.*). His own complaint in 1617 was that he had been persecuted for a long time by the Elders and Consistory of St. Helier's and suspended from the Sacrament. Perhaps it was for his stay in Spain that he received help from Anthony Poulet; for in 1605 the King's Receiver, as agent for Sir Anthony's heirs, sued him for £31, which Sir Anthony had given him for the prosecution of his studies; but Maret was discharged from the action.

On his return to Jersey Sir John Peyton, the Governor, made him Solicitor-General (1607—1613), King's-Receiver (1609—1615), and Attorney-General (1613—1616). He was of contentious disposition. In June 1605 he was fined for accusing Nicolas Effard, Rector of St. Saviour's, of owing money in Oxford. Words of his in Court offended all the Rectors, and led to a lawsuit, which was prolonged, till both parties asked for the Governor's arbitration. The action which caused his suspension from office in 1616 shows the same spirit. At a meeting of the Court it was discovered that a paper belonging to the case to be tried had been removed by Maret. The Bailiff sent the Denunciator to fetch him, but, though he was in the Market Place outside, he refused to come. The Denunciator was sent again, and Maret said that, if they wanted him, they must sub-poena him. For this contempt Bailiff Herault (q.v.) proposed that Maret be punished. Philippe De Carteret (q.v.), as Senior Jurat, was giving his opinion, when Maret entered with his hat on, interrupted him, and said that he had an accusation to bring against De Carteret, whose men had come to his house by night to assassinate him. (What had really happened was that a cousin of De Carteret's, while drinking with Maret, had challenged him to fight.) Sir Philippe stopped speaking, and asked for redress. The Jurats ordered Maret to ask pardon of God, the King, and the Court for his contempt ; and fined him fifty crowns for insulting De Carteret, the money to be used for repairing the Court. As he refused to pay, he was suspended from office as Attorney-General, and ordered to appear within forty days before the Privy Council. He pleaded that the Court had no power to suspend him ; but before the Council his behaviour was so obstreperous, that he was committed to the Gatehouse. On his return to Jersey he told the Court that his case had not been tried ; but the Bailiff produced a letter from the Secretary of the Council, showing that he had been ordered back to acknowledge his offence. This he refused to do ; so he was imprisoned in Mont Orgueil. Thence he sent a petition to the King, asking that his case might be heard before the Commissioners, Conway and Bird, who were coming to the island. Before them he brought charges of tyranny and corruption against the Bailiff. But their verdict was that all his charges were unfounded, that many of his other statements were false (e.g. he had complained that he was "fettered and manacled in

close prison", whereas he had been allowed to walk freely on
the ramparts and to invite his friends to dinner), and that the
whole trouble "sprung from certain haughtie fashions and insolent behaviour of his own".

In the struggle between Anglicanism and Calvinism Maret,
as one of the Governor's men, was anti-Presbyterian, and represented the Episcopal side at the inquiry before the Council in
1614. When Herault died, Maret and Sir Philippe De Carteret
were rivals for the vacant post. Maret had the backing of Buckingham, the King's favourite, but King Charles honoured a promise made to De Carteret by his father, and in 1626 Sir Philippe
became Bailiff. Maret was elected Jurat in 1629. His election
was disputed, and he complained that the Lieut.-Bailiff, acting
for Sir Philippe De Carteret, had hindered him from taking his
seat; but he remained Jurat till his death in 1637. He seems
to have kept in favour with the Governors, for in 1632 he was
appointed by Sir Thomas Jermyn Lieut.-Governor.

In 1628 he married Martha Lempriere, widow of Elie Dumaresq
of La Haule, and came to live at La Haule. He had one son,
Philip Maret (born 1628, Jurat 1671—76), a Parliamentarian, who
died unmarried (*Bull.* III). The father bought in 1628 the Fief
des Arbres from his stepsons Edouard and Elie Dumaresq.
Brevint refers to him in his Journal as "*Mons. Philippe Maret,
un des hommes de la Chambre de Présence*". [MSS. in Société
Jersiaise' Library; *Calendar of State Papers, Domestic, Ad-
denda; Acts of the Privy Council; Actes des Etats; Dic.
Nat. Biog.*]

MARETT, PHILIP (1792—1869), New England Merchant and
Banker. Son of Captain Philip Marett of Boston U.S.A., and
Elizabeth Cunningham, and grandson of Philippe, third son of
Pierre Maret of La Haule. Philippe, the grandfather, emigrated
to New England, but returned to Jersey, where he died in 1760.
His son, the second Philip, went back to Boston, but corresponded
regularly with his Jersey cousins. The third Philip was born in
Boston 25 Sept. 1792. He was intended for the Law, but enter-
ed business at an early age, and as partner in the firm of Plymp-
ton, Marett, and Dorr and as President of the New England

Bank amassed a large fortune. As Portuguese Vice-consul for Massachusetts and New Hampshire he became involved in a famous Admiralty case. A Portuguese merchantman and a U.S. schooner each mistook the other for a pirate. Shots were exchanged, and a prize crew took the Portuguese vessel into Boston. Marett in the name of the Portuguese Government sued the Admiralty for damages, and was awarded 20,000 dollars. Appeal was made to the Circuit Court and then to the Supreme Court. Extremely intricate questions of international law were involved, and the leading Attorneys in America were briefed on one side or the other. Eventually the damages were disallowed. Politically Marett was a prominent member of the National Republican Party, which opposed President Jackson's administration ; and in Religion he was a devout Unitarian of the Channing school. On retiring from business he settled in New Haven, where he died 22 March 1869. He married Martha, daughter of Josiah Knapp of Boston, and had one daughter, Ellen Martha, who married Arthur N. Gifford of New York. He left a life-interest in his fortune of 700,000 dollars to his wife and daughter, and on the death of the latter in 1890 it was divided by his direction into six parts to be used for the New Haven Hospital, the aged poor, the care of the feeble-minded, the Orphan Asylums, Yale College, and the foundation of a Free Library. His daughter also left over a million, most of which went to charities. The archway leading to St. Aubin's Church was erected by his trustees in his memory, and they also gave the two small windows at the west end of the Church. [Baldwin's *Brief Memorial of Philip Marett.* New Haven.]

MARETT, PHILIP JANVRIN, (1879—1939), Lieut.-Colonel R.A.M.C., Bacteriologist. Elder son of Col. James R. Marett and Fanny White. Born in India 1879. Educated first at Cheltenham College, then at Victoria College (1894—7). He gained an entrance scholarship at Westminster Hospital, and qualified M.R.C.S., L.R.C.P. in 1904, being awarded a Beit Research Scholarship. He joined the Royal Army Medical Corps in 1905, and made bacteriology his special study. He served in the South African War, and was twice stationed in

Malta, where he did successful work on sand-fly fever. At the outbreak of the First World War he went to France with the British Expeditionary Force, and was first responsible for the sanitary organization of the base at Rouen. Later he commanded a casualty clearing-station in the forward area, and then was appointed Consulting Bacteriologist to the British Forces in Italy. Finally he became Sanitary Officer for the whole of France, and was awarded the Croix de Guerre. After the war he left the Army for family reasons, and in 1922 became Medical Officer of Health for Jersey. He threw himself into this work with great energy, organizing a new Public Health Department and a States' Bacteriological Laboratory, and training his staff to a state of high efficiency. Diphtheria cases dropped from 155 in 1922 to 9 in 1929, and this was largely due to his system of detecting and isolating carriers. Another subject of which he made a special study was tuberculosis. This caused 69 deaths in 1922, but only 28 in 1937. He founded the Chest Clinic in 1931, and the fine Overdale Isolation Hospital was opened in 1934. He died in Bon Air Nursing Home on 23 July 1939, and was buried at St. Saviour's. He married in 1904 Eliza Prangley, and left two sons, Philip Lee Prangley of the R.A.F. and Rupert Richard Figus of the Wellington Regiment, and one daughter Violet Irene Mignon, wife of Ian P. Henderson.

MARETT, SIR ROBERT PIPON (1820—1884), Bailiff. Dialect Poet. Eldest son by a second marriage of Peter Daniel Marett, Major in the Madras Infantry of the old East India Company's Service, and Mary Ann, elder daughter of Thomas Pipon, Lieut.-Bailiff. He was born at St. Peter's 20 Nov. 1820, and educated at Mc.Mahon's School, La Motte Street. He then went to Caen University and later to the Sorbonne in Paris. He was admitted an Advocate of the Royal Court 1845; but in 1846, owing to the ill-health of his mother, the family went to Blois. One life-long hobby of his was building. "Balbus who built a wall", writes his son, "was not in it with him" (*A Jerseyman at Oxford*). And here he found scope for it by helping in the construction of the English Church. On his return to Jersey he entered the arena of local politics, and took a leading part in founding and directing *La Patrie,* a weekly newspaper in French started in the interest of Constitutional Reform, which ran from Jan. 1849 to Dec. 1855. Some of his poems in the Jersey dialect first appeared in its columns, under the nom-de-plume of Laelius. His poems are witty, and show a perfect knowledge of the island tongue. Some of the best known, which are still recited, are *La Fille Malade, Le Vier Garçon, La Buonne Femme et ses Cotillons, Les Vielles Filles, L'Amoureux,* and *La Picagneresse.* François Victor Hugo, struck by the beauty of *La Fille Malade,* reproduced it in his *Normandie Inconnue.* The inscription placed by Jurat J. G. Falle over the entrance to the Museum of the Société Jersiaise (of which Sir Robert was a Founder and President) is from a poem in his honour by a Guernseyman, Mr. Lenfesty.

Sir Robert's interests were many-sided. He could repeat most of *Paradise Lost,* had an intimate knowledge of Dickens and Thackeray, and could recite large portions of Virgil and Horace. He illustrated poems which he wrote to amuse his old school-fellow Josué Falle (q.v.) on his voyage to Canada. Bertrand Payne (q.v.) was indebted to him for much genealogical and historical information reproduced in the *Armorial.* Sir Robert also edited in 1846 the four printed volumes of *Manuscripts of Lieut.-Bailiff Philip Le Geyt,* the seventeenth century jurist, adding a Preface on the life of the author.

In 1853 he stood for the Constableship of St. Helier's as a Reform Candidate who was neither Rose nor Laurel, but was defeated; three years later however he was elected without opposition. His Constableship was of short duration, as he became Solicitor-General in 1858 ; but he was instrumental in acquiring for the parish what are now the Parade, the Lower Park, and the People's Park, and in widening Cheapside and the sea-front to First Tower. In the middle of last century there was no Police Court and no Petty Debts Court. Everything including Militia matters had to he dealt with by the Royal Court, and there was hopeless congestion. Though the Reform Party agitated, the majority of the States refused to remedy this evil. So the Home Government took the unconstitutional step of legislating for the Island by three Orders in Council establishing a Police Court, a Petty Debts Court, and a Paid Police. The Royal Court declined to register these Orders, and the States appealed to the Privy Council to get them recalled. When the case was heard, besides the States two other sections of island opinion were represented, one which wished the Orders to become law, and a larger section which wanted the Orders withdrawn on the understanding that the States would introduce legislation on the same lines. Marett was one of the counsel representing this last group, and the Council adopted the line he urged, and advised the withdrawal of the Orders on the understanding that the States would legislate. He also gave full and valuable evidence before the Royal Commissioners appointed in 1846 to inquire into the state of the Criminal Law, and again before the Royal Commission of 1860.

In 1866 on the death of Attorney-General Dupré (q.v.) he succeeded to that position; and, while Attorney-General, prepared and passed through the States the Loi sur la Propriété Foncière, one of the greatest legal reforms of the century. It was the culmination of many years' work, and was passed against strong Conservative opposition. The creation of the Rentes Publiques des Etats was his idea, and its adoption was largely due to his advocacy. He was keenly interested in Elementary Education, and took an active part in starting St. Brelade's Central School, then a Church School. He also submitted a design for the new Harbour at St. Helier's. In April 1880 he succeeded John Hammond as Bailiff. A knighthood followed on 31 May. But his health then began to decline, and for two years before his death, he could only carry on his duties from his study. He died 10 Nov. 1884 at La Haule Manor, the residence of his wife's sister, where he and his family had lived since a fire in 1874 had destroyed Blanc Pignon, the property he had bought in 1859 from Major Elie Pipon. He married in July 1865 Julia Anne, youngest daughter of Philip Marett of La Haule Manor, a distant cousin, and left one son, Robert Ranulph (q.v.), later Rector of Exeter College, Oxford, and three daughters, Philippa Laetitia, Julia Mary, and Mabel Elizabeth. [H. E. Le V. Durell's *Men I Have Known;* Obituary notices in Jersey newspapers of 1884.]

MARETT, ROBERT RANULPH (1866–1943). Rector of Exeter College. Anthropologist. Only son of Sir Robert Pipon

Marett, Solicitor-General and later Bailiff (q.v.), and Julia Anne
Marett of La Haule. Born at Blanc Pignon, La Haule, 13 June
1866. Educated at Victoria College. In 1884 he won the senior
Open Exhibition at Balliol College, Oxford. He soon attracted notice as a Latinist. In 1886 he took first class honours in
Classical Moderations, and in 1887 won the Chancellor's Prize
for Latin Verse, one of the blue ribbons of the University. The
subject set was 'The Islands of the Blessed', and Marett made
his poem a paean in praise of Jersey: 'Why seek the Happy
Isles in imaginary Homeric realms, when they exist today in
the English Channel?' This was typical of the patriotism that
was his all his life. He swept up other prizes in passing, became
Secretary of the Union, and crowned his undergraduate career
by taking First Class Honours in the School of Literae Huma-
niores in 1888. He then meant to follow his father's footsteps
as a lawyer. In 1885 he was called to the English Bar as a
Member of the Inner Temple, and to the Jersey Bar in 1891.
But in the same year Exeter College called him back to Oxford
as Fellow and Tutor. He became Dean of his College in 1892,
Sub-Rector in 1893, and Rector (i.e. Head) in 1928, a position
which he held till his death. His first subject was Philosophy,
and his lectures on Plato crowded the College Hall; but in 1893
he carried off another of the big University prizes, the Green
Moral Philosophy Prize, and this proved the turning point of
his life. The subject set was 'The Ethics of Savage Races',
and in preparing this essay he plunged into a hitherto unexplored
region in which henceforth he worked with boundless enthusiasm. Oxford at this time hardly recognized the existence of
such a science as Anthropology, and like all pioneers Marett
had to face criticism. It seemed almost treason for a Philosophy
Tutor to divert his pupils' thoughts from Greek culture to the
dingy byways of prehistoric barbarism. But he stuck to his
guns, and forced his University to recognize the importance of
his new subject. In 1910 Oxford appointed him Reader in
Social Anthropology. For twenty years he was Secretary of the
Oxford Committee for Anthropology and Director of the studies
of all who took up this subject. He was indefatigable with his
pen. *Custom is King* lists 88 of his articles in learned periodicals. He contributed to the *Encyclopaedia Britannica* the
articles on Animism, Anthropology, Mana, Prayer, Primitive
Religion, Ritual, Spell, Supernaturalism, etc. He also wrote

articles for *The Encyclopaedia of Religion and Ethics,* and the
article on Sir E. B. Tylor in the *Dictionary of National Biography.* His own books were *Anthropology and the Classics,*
1908 (translated into German 1910); *The Threshold of Religion,*
1909 (enlarged edition 1914); *Anthropology,* in the Home University Library, 1912 (translated into Swedish 1919, into Spanish
1931, into Chinese 1931.); *Psychology and Folklore* 1920; *The
Diffusion of Culture* 1927 ; *Man in the Making* 1928 ; *Spencer's
Last Journey* 1931 (with T. K. Penniman); *Faith, Hope, and
Charity in Primitive Religion* 1932; *Spencer's Scientific Correspondence* 1932 (edited with T. K. Penniman); *Sacraments of
Simple Folk* 1933; *Thoughts, Talks, and Tramps: A Collection
of Papers by Sir Everard Im Thurn,* edited with Memoir 1934;
Head, Heart, and Hands in Human Evolution 1935; *Tylor,*
in Modern Sociologists Series, 1936. He was widely in demand
as a lecturer. He was Frazer Lecturer at Cambridge, Gifford
Lecturer at St. Andrew's, Lowell Lecturer at Boston U.S.A.,
Donellan Lecturer at Trinity College, Dublin. He was President of the Folklore Society 1913—18, of the Sociological Institute 1932—35. In 1913 he took his Doctorate of Science at
Oxford, and in 1937 his University gave him the honorary degree
of Doctor of Letters, and in the following year St. Andrew's
made him a Doctor of Canon and Civil Laws. On his seven-
tieth birthday twenty anthropologists combined to publish a
volume of essays to commemorate his work with the title *Custom
is King.*

But, though Oxford was his workshop, Jersey was his home.
He never lost his love for or his interest in his native land.
When in Jersey he constantly attended the Chefs Plaids
d'Héritages to renew his oath as Advocate. He made La Haule
Manor, which he inherited from his mother, a treasure-house of
Jersey pictures, books, pamphlets ,and manuscripts. He writes
in his Autobiography: — "A scheme had long been in my
mind to establish some sort of University College in Jersey, an
integral part of which would be to hold an annual Summer
School, where English (and Americans) could meet Continental
folk and especially French students; Jersey providing an ideal
liaison. A strong Committee of the Société Jersiaise was actually formed to work out the details; but there did not seem to
be anyone on the spot who had the experience and connections
necessary to ensure a successful start, if I were not present to

lend a helping hand". He was delighted when discoveries in his own subject came to light in the island. In 1910 and 1911 he did strenuous manual work helping to excavate the Levalloisian cave at La Cotte, and twice nearly lost his life through a fall of rock. When local funds were exhausted, he obtained grants from the British Association to employ skilled quarrymen to continue the work. He was President of the Société Jersiaise 1929—31. Shortly before his death he published his autobiography, to which he gave the characteristic title, *A Jerseyman at Oxford*. He married Nora, daughter of Sir John Kirk. His eldest son John Ranulph de la Haule retired from the Navy as Lieut.-Commander, but was recalled at the outbreak of war, and was lost in the aircraft-carrier, *Glorious*. His other children were Robert Hugh Kirk, Philippa Susanne, and Joyce Elizabeth. He died 18 Feb. 1943. [Autobiography ; Character-sketch by L.H. Dudley Buxton in *Custom is King*.]

MARTEL JEAN (1694—1753), Brandy Merchant. The Martel family are found in Jersey as early as 1229 *(Lettres Closes)* and in St. Brelade's from 1525. Jean, 7th child of Thomas Martel (Diacre of St. Brelade's, a merchant who had made voyages in his ship *La Fidélité*) and of Marthe Heraut, was born in March 1694. He worked for seven years in Guernsey in the counting house of Lau Martin. Then he and a friend, Jean Fiot, in 1720 set up in business as English Merchants at Bordeaux. This proved a failure, and in 1727 they had to come to terms with their creditors. But in 1720 Martel had also opened a business of his own as Brandy Merchant at Cognac. This was more successful. He developed a large export trade to the Channel Islands, where the Jersey and Guernsey smugglers were his best customers, and carried his brandy to England and America and indeed all over the world. As a side line he imported into France Jersey-knitted stockings, collected for him by his mother. He married twice. His first wife, Jeanne Brunet of Cognac, died childless. He then married her cousin, Rachel Lallement, by whom he had 4 sons and 5 daughters. He died on a voyage on 23 Jan. 1753, leaving his young wife, who was only 33, to bring up their large family, of whom the eldest was 14, and to manage the business. She however proved to be a first-class business woman, and under her direction the firm became the leading house in the trade, a position it never lost. [Firino. *La Famille Martell*].

MESNY, WILLIAM ((1842—1919), Chinese General and Plant-collector. Son of William Mesny, cobbler, and Marie Rachel Nicolle. The Mesnys are an Alderney family, but William's father had settled in Jersey, and he was born in Trinity 9 Oct. 1842. At twelve he went to sea. The only record of his early years is some doggerel verses of his own: —

A sailor for years I ploughed the rough sea,
And Africa's hot clime I tested.
India's tall palaces also I've seen ;
Australia's rich shores I have visited.
At last to the Chinese Empire I came,
And thought that no more I would travel ;
So on shore I did go to seek glory and fame.

This was in 1860. As a lad of eighteen he deserted his ship, and made his way to Hong Kong. Here he quickly learnt the language, and made many Chinese friends among the merchant class, and had several narrow escapes from marriage, for the prestige of Britain then stood high, and there was keen competition among fathers to secure a British son-in-law.

China was rent with civil war, and the Tai-ping rebels looked as though they might overthrow the Manchu dynasty. Both sides were recruiting foreign mercenaries. Mesny returned to Shanghai, and tried to raise a company for the Emperor's service. He enlisted a band of scallywags of all nationalities, but on the night they were to sail, being overheard speaking French, he was arrested by a party of French marines, who were rounding up naval deserters, and his company left without him.

Navigation on the Yang-tse was then very dangerous. Fighting was going on on both banks ; the ports were constantly changing hands ; and each side seized any cargoes it could lay hands on. Ordinary commerce was at a standstill ; so big profits could be made by any boat able to run through the danger zone. Bags of salt bought for a dollar at Shanghai sold for thirteen dollars at Hangkow. Mesny embarked on this business, first in a small sailing-boat, the *Rob Roy*, then in a Chinese junk. He also made what he calls "a few very successful speculations in the arms trade". Once his boat was seized by Imperialists, and he was wounded in two places. Once he was captured by Tai-pings, who fixed his ransom at 100,000 dollars, "a princely price", he says, "for a poor Jerseyman". At first he was treated badly, but, when his captors discovered that he could play Chinese tunes on his four-octave flutina, their behaviour entirely altered. After six months not unpleasant captivity he was rescued by a British gunboat.

In 1863, when Robert Hart became Inspector of Chinese Customs, Mesny obtained a place in that service. But, when Gordon was lent to the Chinese Government to command a force that was to suppress the Tai-pings, Mesny served under him as Lieutenant ; and, when Gordon returned to England in 1865, Mesny remained in the Chinese Army. He volunteered for service in Szu-chuan and Kuei-chon in 1868, and in 1889 was decorated with the Hua-ling Plume, and promoted Colonel. In the following year he was awarded the decoration of the Pao Hsing (the star of China). In 1873 he became a Major-General, and was created Ying Yang Pa-t'u-lu (Penetrating Knight of the Pa-t'u-lu, the Chinese equivalent of the French *Légion d'honneur*). In 1880 he was decorated for three generations San Tai Kao Feng. He volunteered for service in Hsin-kiang, and went to Hami. In 1882 he served in Shansi as Adviser on Foreign Affairs, and the nineteen great industrial works undertaken by the Viceroy Chang Chih-tung were planned by Mesny, and authorized by imperial rescript. About this time he married a Chinese lady named Han, by whom he had a son Hu Sheng (born 11 March 1885) and a daughter, Marie Wan-er, who married an Englishman, F.H. Watson, and had two children. He now became a Mandarin of the First Class, always wore Chinese dress, and a magnificent pigtail, and was said to be the only European who could speak Chinese without a foreign accent.

At intervals between official duties he travelled from end to end of China, penetrating into districts that no European had ever entered before. For example in 1877 he made the twenty months' journey, which his companion Capt. W.J. Gill has described in *The River of Golden Sand*, from Ching-tu, the capital of Szechuen, across the Tibetan tableland to Talifu, the capital of Yunnan. After a visit to Jersey he made another three thousand miles' journey in 1879 from Canton in South China to Kashgar in East Turkestan. On these travels he acquired fame as a plant-collector, and supplied Hance the botanist with a number of new specimens.

In 1883 he volunteered for active service, and was sent to Yunnan, and in 1884 to Foochow. In 1885 he was in charge of the two arsenals at Canton. In the following year he was promoted Lieut.-General. He went to North An-hui twice on Famine Relief in 1889 and 1890. In 1895 he began to publish in Shanghai a chatty magazine, *Mesny's Miscellany*, entirely written by himself, full of information that he had gathered on his travels about Chinese customs, plants, cities, etiquette, superstitions, secret societies. Its pages show that he still kept in touch with his native island, for he constantly reprints verses and paragraphs copied from the *Jersey Observer*. He never abandoned his British citizenship, and was Fellow of the Royal Geographical Society, of the Royal Historical Society, and of the Imperial Institute. He died at Hankow 11 Dec. 1919, aged 77. [*Mesny's Miscellany* ; Family information.]

MESSERVY, CHARLES (1849—1925), Colonial Office Official. Son of George Messervy of Mont Cantel, Rouge Bouillon and Charlotte Augusta Louisa Bolt. Born in St. Helier's 27 Aug. 1849. Educated at Victoria College. While still at College he won a £5 prize offered by the States for the best design for the College gates. He worked at the bench in his uncle's shipyard at Gorey, and then entered the office of Philip Brée, States' Architect. On passing into the Civil Service he was sent to the West Indies, where his appointments were: — Assistant Colonial Engineer, Lagos 1870 ; Assistant Superintendent of Public Works, Barbados 1881 ; Director of Public Works, Grenada and Windward Islands 1885 ; Member of the Legislative Council, Grenada 1891 ; Justice of the Peace for St. Lucia and Member of the Legislative Council 1895 ; Commissioner and Justice of the Peace for the Falkland Islands 1898. On retiring from the Service he returned to Jersey, and opened an office in St. Helier's. He was one of the architects respon-

sible for the restoration of Trinity Manor. In 1918 loss of sight
compelled him to retire from business. He died at St. Ouen's,
4 Nov. 1925. He married in 1875 Emilie De Faye, sister of
Philippe De Faye, the Composer, and had nine children.

MESSERVY, DANIEL (1721—75), Diarist. Elder son of
Daniel Messervy of Mont au Prêtre and Anne, daughter of
Jurat Josué Pipon of La Moye. Born in St. Helier's 1721, and
baptized in the Town Church 4 Aug. One grandfather had been
Attorney-General, the other Lieut.-Bailiff. His uncle was Vice-
Dean, his grandmother a De Carteret of St. Ouen's. So Daniel
was soon drawn into public office. When twenty-two he became
Churchwarden of St. Helier's ; when only thirty-two he was
sworn in as Jurat (9 Feb. 1754). A collection of his papers, in
the S.J. Library, gives an intimate peep into the life of a well-
to-do man of the period.

His father had died in 1729, and, when Daniel came of age,
he was at first pretty lavish with his money. He ordered from
London presents for his lady friends, ear-rings for one, silver tea-
spoons for another, a silver cream-jug for a third, for a fourth a
shagreen case, "silver at both ends, wherein be sizars, penknife,
bodkin, and a scale" ; for a fifth he sent a little box "to be en-
cased in pinchbeck with Bristol stones, and a little Cupid to be
painted on the top". He ordered also a portrait of himself: —
"Have it done prettyly, and don't spare cost". He bought his
clothes from a Cannon-Street tailor. His barber's bill shows
that he had a man in to shave him every day. His pots of
pomatum and the dressing of his wigs cost him over a pound a
month.

On the other hand he had schemes for gaining money. He
took shares in more than one privateer. He sent boats to the
Newfoundland fisheries. He exported Jersey-knit stockings to
England, and trounced his agent, if he sold them at too low a
price. He constantly invested in lottery tickets, and grumbled
because he drew nothing but blanks.

On 7 June 1742 he married Jeanne, only daughter of Daniel
Valpy dit Janvrin of St. Brelade's, and by doing so became involved in a long, vexatious law-suit. Twenty-six years before,

his bride's great-grandfather had died, and the old gentleman's
two sons had quarrelled over the division of his property. The
Court sent the matter before the Greffier for arbitration : but,
when a preliminary award was given, the loser appealed to the
Privy Council on technical points. The Council dismissed the
appeal, and the case went back to the Greffier. So many new
documents were then produced, that the Greffier sent the parties
back before the Royal Court. The Court's decision was appealed against to the Council, and reversed, and the Court ordered to finish the case quickly, and finally to determine the
accounts. Both sides then became obstructive, and refused to
produce evidence. Meanwhile the original litigants died, and
their children inherited the quarrel. Messervy's bride represented
one side, and a Mrs. Mary Melvil the other, "that clamorous
woman", Messervy called her, apparently with justice, for the
Court remarked that the case would make more progress, if she
would "proceed to business, instead of breaking out into injurious invectives, as she hath too often done, and if she would
be guided by her counsel". In 1748 the matter went again before
the Greffier, and again reached a deadlock. In 1757 she complained to the Privy Council that she could not get justice, and
the Court was ordered to come to a decision. In 1760 it decided
in Messervy's favour, but in 1763 the Council reversed this
judgement. This did not end the matter. Mrs Melvil now
claimed interest on the money out of which she had been kept.
Messervy fought this to the Privy Council but again lost. The
case had lasted forty-eight years.

When Messervy became a Jurat in 1754, he joined the party
of Charles Lempriere (q.v.), and remained a good party man.
He chiefly distinguished himself by persistently pressing for the
fortification of the Town Hill, were Fort Regent now stands,
"your favourite hill", Charles Lempriere calls it in one of his
letters. In 1758 Messervy wrote, "I am glad our friends have
cast a favourable eye on the Town Hill, as this will make some
impression on those who found it ill that I spoke so much in
its favour". But his public work was hampered by ill-health.
He seems to have been subject to periodical nervous breakdowns,
and he was obviously a valetudinarian. The amount of drugs
that he swallowed is incredible. We have several of his doctor's bills. One for 1752 runs: — "Jan. 5. A bottle of anodyne.
Jan. 6. A vomit. Jan. 7. A bolus. Jan. 8. A bottle of cordial.

Jan. 9.   A bolus. Jan. 10. A bolus. Jan. 11.   12 pills:"—and so the record goes on for weeks, varied only with an occasional bleeding or blistering.   Sixteen years later the story is still the same:— "Jan. 15. 4 stomachic pills. Jan. 15. A nervous julep. Jan. 17. Stomachic mixture. Jan. 18. Purgative pills. Jan. 19. A dozen nervous pills". He writes to England for "Dr Lowther's Nervous Powders with directions, also a bottle of Mrs. Holt's Elixir for the Palsy, and seven packets of Major's Cephalic Snuff with a book of its cures".   He paid long visits to Bath and Dinant to take the waters.

Through ill-health he was absent from Court for most of 1769, and so missed the famous revolt of 28 Sept., when his fellow-Jurats fled for refuge to Elizabeth Castle ; but the Trinity rioters called at his house on their way to Town, and demanded cider, "which one could not refuse at a time when a crowd of nearly three hundred was passing every moment".   The excitement stimulated him to start a *Diary* which he kept for almost three years (Published by S.J. in 1896).   He claimed a sick man's privilege, and took no part in public events, but sat at home recording the rumours and reports that were brought to him. He writes with the contempt of an oligarch for *"la popupallace"*, "men of low degree, day labourers, common people" ; but he recognizes that the trouble was due to the failure of the States to regulate the sale of corn fairly.   He managed to secure copies of all the petitions and counter-petitions that were circulating. Everyone came to see him, members of what he calls the Party of the Grumblers (*Grondeurs*) as well as his own colleagues, even Thomas James Gruchy, leader of the Trinity revolt: — "He said that the people were like devils, openly clamouring for four lives. I asked whether mine was one of them. He answered, No. You need not be nervous. It is the Lieut.-Bailiff, Mons. Pipon of La Moie, the Seigneur of St. John's, and the Deputy-Vicomte (George Benest)". Colonel Bentinck commander of the newlylanded troops, called on him. So did Philippe De Carteret (q.v.), just back from his voyage round the world.   So did David Durell (q.v.), Vice-Chancellor of Oxford, released from a French prison.   Among others a young Ensign of the Scottish troops came to dine and stay the night: — "He is a great genius. He brought us a book of his own poems, of which he may well be proud. He recited one that he wrote when only thirteen". This was Thomas Erskine, the future Lord Chancellor.   The *Diary* gives a graphic picture of the life of three eventful years. On 19 Dec. 1770 an Order in Council permitted Messervy to resign his Juratship on the ground of ill-health. In 1775 he died, and was buried in the Town Church on 5 March. He lived in the house on Mont au Prêtre, later called Linden Hall from the avenue of linden trees that he planted in 1751. He had five children, Daniel, who on the death of Earl Granville became through his great-grandmother one of the Seigneurs of St. Ouen's, François, who worked under the Duke of Bouillon as director of the operations of the naval flotilla protecting the Channel Islands (the S.J. Museum has a cup presented to him in recognition of his courage at the wreck of the *Nymphe* off Boulogne), Philippe, an officer in the 18th Foot, Jeanne, the Janneton of the *Diary*, and Anna Elizabeth. [*Journal de Daniel Messervy* with note on his life: MSS in S.J. Library.]

MESSERVY, ELIE, (d. 1626) Rector of St Peter's. Son of Helier Messervy, Constable of St. Clement's, and grandson of Richard Messervy, Jurat. His importance lies in the fact that his nomination as Rector of St. Peter's was the first step in the overthrow of the Presbyterian regime in Jersey. Under Elizabeth and for the first part of James I's reign successive Governors had been content to appoint to Rectories only those recommended by the Presbyterian Colloquy, the quarterly meeting of Ministers and Elders. Sir John Peyton decided to challenge this custom. When St. Peter's Rectory was vacant in 1615, without waiting for the Colloquy to meet, he appointed Elie Messervy, the first student whom the Don Baudains had supported at Oxford. But Messervy, before he left the University, had been episcopally ordained by the Bishop of Oxford, and the Colloquy refused to receive him, unless he would sign the Calvinist Book of Ecclesiastical Discipline. This he refused to do, and appealed to the Privy Council, who wrote: — "The King's Majesty, having out of his Princely care settled the Churches in his dominions in uniformity of government, as hath particularly appeared in reducing Scotland to the ancient custom used in the Church since the time of the Apostles (i.e. Episcopacy), and finding that only the Churches of Jersey and Guernsey are not yet established with that government. His purpose was to order some course for the redress of those things that are loose and unsettled there: which, while His Majesty had in consideration, there hath been offered an occasion by a petition presented in the name of Elias Messervy, student in the University of Oxford, admitted into Holy Orders after the manner of the Church of England, who was presented by the Governor to a benefice, but cannot obtain the approbation of the Ministers of the Colloquy to be admitted thereunto, unless he take upon him a calling after the Rite received among them, and so relinquish that he hath attained by his ordination in England" ; the Council therefore ordered the island "to make choice of able and sufficient persons, as well of those that embrace the present ecclesiastical government as of such as dislike it, and to send them over hither, furnished with such reasons as they have for strengthening their part, to settle a conformity according to the government of the Church of England or to dispense therewithal and to tolerate another form". When the delegates, of whom Messervy was one, had arrived and been heard, the Council ordered Messervy to be at once admitted to his benefice "there peaceably to exercise the form used in the Church of England" ; but the matter was eventually settled by a compromise. The Colloquy Minutes say that on 15 July 1614 he received the right hand of fellowship after agreeing to the request made to him by the Elders of St. Peter's not to make any change in the services, i.e. to continue to use the Huguenot Prayer Book. The wider result of this Inquiry was the restoration in 1620 of the Anglican system and the reappointment of a Dean. According to Herault, the Bailiff (q.v.), this would have been done sooner, "had it not been for the vaunts of Elie Messervy of the power the Dean would have to the prejudice of the people's liberties". In 1614 Messervy added to his duties those of Chaplain of Elizabeth Castle. He married in 1617 Marie Balleine of St. Peter's, and had two daughters, Marguerite and Marie. He died of plague, 7 October 1626, and was buried in St Peter's. [Minutes of the Colloquy. *State Papers, Domestic. Messervy Genealogy.* De Schickler, *Eglises de Refuge.* Le Quesne, *Constitutional History of Jersey.*]

MESSERVY, JAMES ALFRED (1859—1921), Genealogist.
Son of Rev. Thomas George Messervy (Eglise Réformée) of
Coie Terrace and Estelle Françoise Guillaume. Born 1859.
Educated Victoria College 1869—1877. Went to College at
Vire, Calvados. Took his B. ès L. at Caen and his B.Th. at
Montauban. Became Minister of the Eglise Réformée at Mon-
tilly (Orne) 1885. Married in 1893 Carolina Léonie Augusta,
daughter of Frédéric Auguste Quirin, Minister of Gries (Bas
Rhin). In 1894 he returned to Jersey. He became Editor of the
Bulletins and Publications of the Société Jersiaise. Among other
valuable contributions that he made to Jersey historical knowledge were his Lists of Governors, Lieutenant-Governors, Bailiffs, Jurats, Rectors, Constables, Attorneys-General, Vicomtes,
Solicitors-General, Receivers-General, and Greffiers, with biographical notes on each ; his long series of *Notices sur quelques
Anciennes Familles Jersiaises* with genealogies, which appeared
in the *Bulletins*, and his carefully edited edition of Chevalier's
Journal and of the *Actes des Etats*. He also edited for the States
the first five volumes of the printed edition of the *Ordres du
Conseil*. In all this work, which was done with meticulous accuracy, he was greatly helped by his wife. He died in 1921.

MESSERVY, MAXIMILIEN (1616—1645), Coiner. Eldest son
of Jean Messervy, Seigneur of La Hougue, Constable of St.
Saviour's, and Sara De Carteret (sister of Jurat François De
Carteret, Seigneur of La Hague) ; brother of François Messervy ; grandson of Aaron Messervy, Lieut.-Governor. Born
in St. Saviour's, 25 July 1616. His father died in 1634, and
on becoming of age in 1637 he inherited the Fiefs of La
Hougue, Patier, ès Verrants, and Petit Rozel. But they were
heavily encumbered with debt. According to a statement made
to the Privy Council in 1640, "his father and grandfather died
deeply indebted to divers persons in the isle, which debts petitioner has in most part discharged" (*S.P.*). To do this he sold
La Hougue in 1638 to Jean Le Hardy. In 1639 by the help of
a bribed maidservant he carried off to Normandy an heiress of
seventeen, Collette, daughter of Jurat Benjamin De La Cloche,
Seigneur of Longueville. (The story is told in the La Cloche

Memoirs, *Bull.* II.) He married her at St. Lô. On his return
he sued Amice De Carteret, Seigneur of Trinity, calling on him
"to demolish a mill lately erected contrary to law to the great
prejudice of petitioner, who holds the Mill of Ponterrin". The
case was carried to the Privy Council, where De Carteret pleaded
that as Lieutenant-Bailiff he could not leave the island. (*S.P.*)
How the matter ended is not recorded. In 1640 Messervy was
again appealing to the Privy Council. Some of his father's creditors refused "to take either houses, lands, wheat or money
rentes at the usual rate, and do now with eagerness and extremity
prosecute him to make a general cession of his estate of purpose
to make a prey thereof to the perpetual infamy of his family".
Sir Philippe De Carteret, his wife's uncle, backed him up in
this, and by his influence he obtained an order compelling the
creditors to accept the rentes he offered. (*S.P.*).

Unfortunately he now discovered too easy a way of escaping
from financial difficulties. He became an exceedingly skilful
coiner. Later, when some of his coins were submitted to goldsmiths of the City of London, they declared them to be "the
most artificial counterfeiting of silver that they ever saw" (*Lyar
Confounded*). In Oct. 1640 Sir Philippe was forced to arrest
him and his brother François for passing counterfeit Spanish
pistoles and pieces of eight. Maximilien pleaded that he had
received them from a Norman to whom he had sold some horses,
but, when his house was searched, "the melting pot, mould, met-
als sophisticated with false silver and gold were found in his
study, which I myself saw". (*id.*). The case caused great scandal,
for the young men were related to the best families in the island ;
and, after eight months' imprisonment in Mont Orgueil, influential friends managed to secure for them the King's Pardon,
June 28. 1641 (*O.C.*).

On his release Maximilien again found himself in financial
difficulties. He sold Petit Rozel to Jean Le Hardy and ès-Ver-
rants to Thomas Poingdestre, Rector of St. Saviour's, and then
lapsed with François into "his old trade of coining false gold
and vending it in Normandy and the island. Sir Philip upon
proof thereof sent officers to apprehend them, but they escaped
by night in a small boat into France, and not long after into
England. Upon these coiners' arrival at London they, siding
with Sir Philip's opposites, complained of great injuries he had
done them for their good affection to Parliament" (*Lyar Con-*

founded). Prynne, the Puritan lawyer, who had been befriended by Sir Philippe when he was a prisoner in Mont Orgueil, heard of this, and informed the Close Committee of their character. He writes, "I employed one to find out their lodging, which he did at last, informing me that they were full of money, and that Maximilian had offered a small ingot of gold. Whereupon, conceiving that they had set up their coining trade, I procured a warrant from Justice Hooker to search their lodgings, which was delivered to Master Stone, a constable of St. Clement's, who, standing at their door, heard them telling money on the table ; after which, he knocking at the door, Maximilian offered to escape out of a garret window, but at last they were both apprehended" (id.). In Maximilien's trunk a mould was found and implements for coining, and in a room above some counterfeit coins "so cunningly sophisticated with alchemy salts that they shewed like silver". Politics at this time did not hesitate to interfere with justice, and Messervy by appealing to political friends nearly turned the tables on the forces of law, and almost got Justice Hooker arrested as a Royalist for issuing a warrant against him. But Prynne again intervened, and the two coiners were committed to the Gatehouse to await the next Sessions.

But, before this time came, Lydcot's expedition to Jersey was planned (Aug. 1643), and their friends urged so strongly the help that their local influence would give, that they were released to accompany it. This Maximilien did, though his brother remained in England. In Jersey Maximilien distinguished himself by the violence of his advice, urging that Mont Orgueil should be stormed, even though it meant the loss of five hundred men. When after three months Lydcot and most of the Parliamentary leaders fled, Maximilien remained, perhaps presuming on the fact that George Carteret, the new Governor, was his cousin. But in March 1644 Captain Carteret had him again arrested for coining. Whether this was a new charge, or the old one from which he had previously fled, is not clear. He was kept in prison till 2 Aug. 1645, when he was brought up before the Royal Commissioners, and condemned to be hanged. The sentence was carried out the same day. His body was handed to Thomas Poingdestre, Rector of St. Saviour's, who buried it in St. Saviour's churchyard, and became the Guardian of his two children, Philippe, aged 4, who became Deputy-Vicomte, and

32

Sara, aged 2. During his life-time Maximilien had given to St. Saviour's Church a silver baptismal bowl. [Chevalier's *Journal ;* Prynne's *Lyar Confounded ; Ordres de Conseil ; Généalogie de la Famille Messervy.*]

MESSERVY, NATHANIEL (d. 1758), of Portsmouth, New Hampshire. Second son of Clement Messervy and Elizabeth Jones. His grandfather, Clement Messervy, had emigrated from Jersey to America before 1673, when he appears on the roll of Portsmouth taxpayers. He was probably the son of Jean Messervy of Gorey and Marie Machon. Nathaniel became a prominent ship-builder at Portsmouth and a man of wealth. In 1745 he was made Lieut.-Col of Col. Moore's New Hampshire Regiment, gathered for the reduction of Louisburg, "the Gibraltar of America", then held by the French. Between the landing-place of the troops and a commanding position in the rear of the fortress was a morass supposed to be impassable. But Messervy, the shipbuilder, conceived the idea of making wooden floats, on which cannon could be dragged across the swamp. Sledges 15 feet long and 5 feet wide were constructed, and for fourteen nights under the cover of fog his men up to their knees in mud dragged the guns to a height commanding the city. This manoeuvre took the French so entirely by surprise that they surrendered with little resistance. In the following year Messervy was one of the twelve purchasers of the Mason Patent in New Hampshire ; this was the origin of his vast ownership of land. In 1749 he built at Portsmouth for the British Government the frigate *America* (44 guns). In 1756 a regiment of 700 men was put under his command to operate against the French near Lake Champlain, but the attack was not made, and the regiment was disbanded. He seems however to have distinguished himself during this campaign, for his family preserved a pair of silver sauce-boats, inscribed: — "From the Right Honourable the Earl of Loudoun, Commander-in-Chief of his Majesty's Forces in North America: to Col. Nathaniel Messerve of New Hampshire in testimony of his Lordship's approbation of his good services at Fort Edward in the year 1756". In 1758 he went again to Louisburg in command of a company of carpenters, probably to build a log-road across the swamp. Here most of his men caught small-pox, and he and his son Nathaniel both died on 28 June. He had married Jane Libby, and had four sons and seven daughters. One of his sons, George, was Collector of Customs at Boston, when the tea was flung into the harbour. After the Revolution he left America and settled in England. [*Généalogie de la Famille Messervy.*]

MILLAIS, SIR JOHN EVERETT (1829—96), President of the Royal Academy. Millais was not born in Jersey, but his family had lived in the Island from before the Extente of 1331. His father, John William Millais of La Coie House, St. Helier's, was an officer in the Jersey Militia. But he moved for a time to Southampton, and there on 8 June 1829 the boy was born. When he was four, the family returned to Jersey. He had only two day's schooling. On the second he bit his master's hand, and was expelled. After that, he was taught by his mother. But he did receive drawing lessons from a Mr. Bessel, and quickly proved himself an infant prodigy. A collection of drawings made when he was seven was shown in the Royal Academy of 1898. At eight he gained the Silver Medal of the Society of Arts. His parents then moved to London, and put him in Sass' Academy, the best art school of the time. When eleven he was admitted a student of the Royal Academy, and during the next six years carried off innumerable medals and prizes. At sixteen he was getting so many commissions from dealers, that he was paying the greater part of his family's household expenses. At seventeen his first picture was accepted for the Royal Academy Exhibition.

He was born in an execrable age artistically, without any shred of the fine tradition that helped to make a Titian, a Rembrandt, or a Velasquez. But his natural gifts were so immense, that they overrode all defects of teaching, and every influence that threatened to cramp them. His early pictures were historical scenes, pained in conventional style, full of violent action, *Pizarro seizing the Inca of Peru, Elgiva seized by the soldiers of Odo, The Benjaminites seizing the Women of Shiloh.* But he soon outgrew that style, and with his friend Holman Hunt formed what they called half in fun the Pre-Raphaelite Brother-hood, a group of young rebels, who spoke scornfully of Sir Sloshua Reynolds and Landseer's 'Monkeyana menagerie', and as he said, "had but one idea, to present on canvas what they saw in Nature". It was a search after sincerity, an escape from fashionable conventions, and it led to a storm of criticism. When in 1849 Millais exhibited his *Christ in the Home of His Parents*, a picture recognized later as a masterpiece, the *Times* called it "loathsome"; *Blackwood's Magazine* remarked, "We can hardly imagine anything more unpleasant", and Dickens denounced it as "mean, odious, revolting, and repulsive", and declared that the kneeling Mary was "so horrible in her ugliness that she would stand out from the rest of the company as a monster in the lowest ginshop in England". A dealer was bold enough to buy it for £ 140 ; but in 1920 it was resold for 10,000 guineas. These Pre-Raphaelite days were a time of struggle, during which Millais was glad to paint portraits for £ 2, and by 1859 ruin stared him in the face. He decided that he must change his style, and give the public what it wanted. "A physician sugars his pills, and I must do the same". He left Pre-Raphaelitism behind, and gradually became the most pop-ular painter in England. Everyone has seen reproductions of his *Vale of Rest* (1859), *The North-West Passage* (1874), *A Yeoman of the Guard* (1876), *Nell Gwynne* (1882), *St. Stephen* (1895). His *Greenwich Pensioners at Nelson's Tomb* (1868), *The Boyhood of Raleigh* (1870), and *The Princes in the Tower* (1878) hang in a thousand school-rooms. He now grew fantas-tically rich. This was the painters' Golden Age. Rich men everywhere were buying works of art. In 1867 Millais calcu-lated that he was making £ 100 a day by his water-colours alone. In the eighties he confessed, "Last year I made forty thousand, and it would have been more, if I had not taken a longer holiday than usual in Scotland". For he could afford to rent now expensive shootings in the Highlands. Here in tweeds and a deerstalker cap he was a typical sportsman. No artist has ever slain more stags or landed so many salmon.

There was admittedly no deep thought or symbolism in his pictures. His subjects were generally commonplace, and often nauseously sentimental. But his drawing and colouring were almost perfect. One characteristic of his work was his exacti-tude in detail. It is said that every leaf and fern in his landscapes is botanically correct. If the paper in the jailer's hand in *An Order of Release* (1855) is examined closely, it will be seen to bear the signature of T. Hilgrove Turner, who was Lieutenant-Governor of Jersey in 1815. Before painting the picture he secured from Jersey an actual order for a prisoner's release, and copied it even to the signature. Thirty-five years after *Sir Isumbras* had been painted, someone pointed out a mistake in the horse's harness. He took the picture back to his studio, and set this detail right. But his main greatness lay in the fact that he broke the bonds of conventionality that were strangling British Art, and infused new life into it.

His output was enormous, at least 350 large easel paintings, and numberless black and white drawings. Only Turner among English painters left more work behind him ; and his versatility was amazing. Lucas Stone said, "He was a dozen artists. There were a dozen Millais". He excelled as a portrait painter. Most of the famous men of his time, Gladstone, Salisbury, Beaconsfield, Ruskin, Irving, Tennyson, Cardinal Newman, John Bright, Thomas Carlyle, John Leech, Sir Arthur Sullivan, Lord Shaftesbury, Sir James Paget, the surgeon, sat for him. And he constantly introduced portraits into his other pictures. His father appears as Joseph in *Christ in the Home of His Parents*, and as the man with the napkin in *Lorenzo and Isabella*. The Huguenot in the famous picture of that name is Arthur (later General) Lempriere. Effie in *Effie Deans* is Mrs. Langtry. As a landscape painter he was equally successful. All his landscapes from *Chill October* to *Halcyon Weather* are actual portraits of landscape. He never idealized, never moved a tree to get a better effect; but selected what he wanted, and then painted it exactly as it was. One curious fact in a painter who had spent his childhood in Jersey is that in none of his major pictures did he introduce the sea. In his *genre* pictures his favourite subject was a pair of tragic lovers. In *The Huguenot* and again in *The Black Brunswicker* a young man going out to die is saying farewell to a maiden. *The Proscribed Royalist*, hidden in a tree, is kissing his lady's hand. In *The Romans leave Britain* a legionary is giving a last embrace to a British girl. But often, instead of thinking out a subject of his own, he was content to illustrate a passage from a poet. *Rosalind and Celia*, *Ferdinand lured by Ariel*, and *Ophelia* are illustrations of Shakespeare, *Mariana* and *Swallow*,

Swallow of Tennyson, *Lorenzo and Isabella* and *St. Agnes'*
Eve of Keats. *The Woodman's Daughter* illustrates a poem by
Coventry Patmore. A subject that appealed to him irresistibly
was a pretty child. Everyone knows *Bubbles*. This was his
grandson, Willie James, and he sold it to the *Illustrated Lon-*
don News, and was furious when he found that the purchaser
had resold it to advertise Pears' Soap! *Cherry Ripe, Little*
Miss Muffet, Cinderella, My First Sermon, My second Sermon,
Sleeping, Waking were hardly less popular. The Société Jersiaise possesses a delightful example of Millais in this mood, *A*
Picture of Health, a portrait of his little daughter Caroline.

He also did an immense amount of black and white illustration, and this alone, had he never touched a brush, would have
won him a great reputation. He delighted in wood-block work,
and was the founder of the modern school of book-illustrators.
He illustrated Trollope's novels and Dickens' *Old Curiosity*
Shop ; and magazines like *Once a Week* and *Good Words* are
full of his brilliant drawings. He tried hard to get wood-block
workers accepted as eligible for the Royal Academy.

The remaining facts of his life can be briefly told. In 1853
he became an Associate of the Royal Academy ; in 1863 a
Royal Academician. In 1880 Oxford honoured him with the
degree of D.C.L. In 1885 he was created a Baronet. In 1895
he revisited Jersey. In 1896 he succeeded Leighton as President of the Royal Academy. In the same year he was found
to be suffering from cancer in the throat, and on August 13th
he died. He was buried close to Leighton in St. Paul's Cathedral, and his pall-bearers were Holman Hunt, Sir Henry Irving,
Viscount Wolseley, and the Earl of Rosebery. In his youth
everyone was struck by his beauty. "His face", wrote Rossetti,
"is as the face of an angel". Marcus Stone said of him,
"He was as beautiful as an Apollo". And to the end of his
life he was strikingly handsome. He married in 1855 Euphemia
Chalmers Gray. (She is Virtue in *Virtue and Vice*, and the
lassie bringing the pardon in *The Order of Release*.) She had
previously been John Ruskin's wife, but had obtained under
Scottish Law a decree of nullity. By her he had seven
children. To the end of his life he was always proud of his
Jersey origin, and delighted to greet his Jersey friends in Jersey
French. [*Life* by his son, J. G. Millais. Spielmann's *Millais*
and his Works ; Baldry's *Millais, his Art and Influence* ; Arti-

cles in *Dictionary of National Biography*, and in *Encyclopaedia Britannica*. Bayliss' *Five Great Painters* ; Gaunt's *Pre-Raphaelite Tragedy*. The story of his marriage is told in James' *Order of Release*.]

MONAMY, PETER (c. 1670—1749), Marine Painter. Horace Walpole, a contemporary collector of pictures, wrote in his *Anecdotes of Painting:* — "Peter Monamy, a good painter of sea pieces, was born in Jersey, and from his circumstances had little reason to expect the fame he afterwards acquired, having received his first rudiments of drawing from a sign-and-house painter on London Bridge. But, when Nature gives real talents, they break forth in the homeliest school. The shallow waves that rolled under his window taught young Monamy what his master could not teach him, and fitted him to imitate the turbulence of the ocean." (The famous old houses on London Bridge were not pulled down till 1756.)

His apprenticeship ended, his first independent commission was to help to decorate the wall of a gallery in the Vauxhall Pleasure-Gardens. Here he painted pictures of 'Admiral Vernon's Capture of Porto Bello', 'The Taking of the San Joseph', 'The Victory of the Mary Rose over Seven Algerine Pirates', and 'Sweet William's Farewell to Black-eyed Susan'. These were quickly recognized as no ordinary sign-painter's work, and were later engraved by Fourdrinier. A mezzotint of the last, a sentimental illustration of Gay's popular ballad, had an immense sale, and was pinned up in innumerable sailors' cabins. The ill-fated Admiral Byng then employed Monamy to decorate his coach with ships and naval trophies.

But his ambition was to paint on canvas. He took as a model the work of the younger Van de Velde, whom Charles II had brought to England to be Court Marine-Painter, and he copied his style so closely, that pictures by the two artists have often been confused. A Monamy in the Dulwich Gallery was long attributed to the Dutchman, and a Van de Velde in Hampton Court once was labelled Monamy. It is said that dealers used to buy his pictures, and resell them as Van de Velde's with the result that some provincial galleries still exhibit Monamys over the Dutchman's name.

He specialized in nautical scenes, a subject which English painters had almost wholly neglected ; and scores of his pictures bear such titles as 'Ships at Sea', 'A Calm Day' (reproduced in Chatterton's Old Sea Pictures), 'A Fresh Gale', 'A Sea Storm', 'Moonlight', 'Sundown at Sea', 'Ship running before a Rising Gale', 'Night and a Ship on Fire'. Four characteristic seascapes of his are in the S.J. Art Gallery. His naval pictures probably outnumbered the purely nautical ones. Many of these are in the Macpherson Collection, which now belongs to the nation. These include 'A Man of War saluting' (reproduced in colour in Chatterton's Old Sea Pictures), 'H.M.S. Royal George' (reproduced in the same work in black and white), 'H.M.S. Lion', 'Man of War receiving an Admiral', 'Man of War under Weigh', 'A fleet at Sea'.

Chatterton rather strangely wrote of him (op. cit.): — "His aim was to please and mollify, to attract rather than grip. Sea life with him is not shot and shell, fighting and tussle, but pleasant contemplation on a summer's day, where the advent of gales or heavy seas would be sacrilege". This is true of some of his pictures ; but he also delighted in battle-pieces. Many of these had a Channel Islands interest: e.g. 'The Taking of the Princesa' by Captain Durell (q.v.), 'The Capture of the Mars' by Captain Saumarez. Another Channel Island picture was 'A Ship in Distress', representing the loss of the Victory in the Race of Alderney. The finest picture he ever painted was 'The Battle of Solebay' (reproduced in Mathew's British Seamen.) In Kensington Palace several of his pictures of sea-fights hang in the King's Gallery.

In those days, when so many Englishmen had been to sea, nautical painting was an extremely technical business. No picturesque suggestion of white sails and blue sea would pass muster. Every sail must be correctly cut and correctly set ; every spar, shroud, stay, brace must be exactly right, before it would satisfy that sternest of critics, the sailorman. So far as we know, Monamy had never been to sea ; but he passed this test triumphantly. His ship-knowledge seems to have been perfect. No rope is ever out of place. The smallest details of his ships and their rigging are meticulously accurate.

His skill as an artist is highly praised by experts. Of one of his sea-pieces at Hampton Court Redgrave writes: — "Though much cracked, it is beautifully painted, showing a fine quality of texture with great precision of touch. The work might puzzle the best painters of such subjects to rival" (*Century of Painters*). "His execution is good", writes Chatterton (op. cit), "his technical ability as an artist high ; his colouring is delightful". The chief criticism passed on his work is that he was sometimes tempted to paint on too large a scale. He was at his best on a moderate-sized canvas. Though he never reached the topmost rank, he holds an assured place high among the lesser Masters.

Though almost exclusively a marine painter, his most popular pictures were not wholly sea-scapes. None has been reproduced more often than his '*Old East-India Wharf*', now in the Victoria and Albert Museum. Warehouses occupy the left of the picture ; merchandise is strewed about ; coopers are packing cases ; the masts are a mere detail. Of this Redgrave says: — "It is almost identical with the work of some of the Dutch artists, and aptly illustrates the gradation from cold monochrome tints till warmer colour in the foreground is reached, grey being used in the shadow-colour in the distance, cool brown in the mid-distance, culminating in warmer brown and even a reddish tint in some foreground tiles, the whole being laind on in such clean sharp washes and with such transparent pigments, that it might have been executed a century later, when the art was at its full excellence in England" (*Dictionary of Artists*). Another picture frequently reproduced is '*Bristol*', now in the Bristol Art Gallery. Here again, though masts of ships in the river appear on the left, the main interest of the picture lies in the houses and the busy street. A third favourite is '*The Embarkation of Charles II at Scheveningen*', now in the Dublin Gallery.

His portraits show Monamy to have been a man of attractive appearance. In Horace Walpole's collection was one, often reproduced, described as 'Monamy showing a sea-piece to his patron, Thomas Walker'. In this the figures are by Hogarth, the seascape by Monamy. Another portrait, etched by Bretherton, is in the S.J. Museum. A later portrait by H. Stubly, now in the possession of Mrs. Marett of La Haule, was engraved in mezzotint by J. Faber junior. Monamy lived during his later years on the riverside at Westminster, where he died in straitened circumstances early in February 1749. In 1761 the Incorporated

Society of Artists voted ten guineas to his widow out of the proceeds of their first Exhibition at Spring Gardens. [Authorities quoted above, and *Mariners' Mirror*, Vol. I.]

MORANT, PHILIP (1700—1770), Antiquarian. (He matriculated as Mourant, but after 1734 spelled his name Morant). Second son of Steven Mourant and Mary Filleul. Born at Les Pigneaux, St. Saviour's, 6 Oct. 1700. Educated at Abingdon Grammar School. He obtained a grant from the Don Baudains and matriculated at Oxford from Pembroke College, Dec. 1717: B.A. 1721: M.A. 1724: Ordained 1722. In 1729 he took his M.A. at Cambridge as a member of Sidney Sussex College. From 1722 to 1732 he was Curate of Great Waltham, Essex, where he helped his Vicar, Nicholas Tindal, to prepare a new edition of Rapin's *History of England*, and to translate De Beausobre and Lenfant's *Commentary on St. Matthew*. He attracted the notice of Bishop Gibson of London, through whose influence he became Chaplain of the English Church at Amsterdam, 1732— 1734. The same patron secured for him a bewildering succession of Essex livings, Shellow Bowells, 1733, Broomfield, 1734, Chignal Smealy, 1735, St. Mary at the Walls, Colchester, 1737. Wickham Bishops, 1743, Aldham, 1745. His main work however was that of an antiquarian. In 1748 he published his *History and Antiquities of Colchester*. He followed this with his great *History and Antiquities of the County of Essex*, 1st vol. 1760, 2nd vol. 1768. In 1768 he was entrusted by a committee of the House of Lords with the preparation for the press of the ancient Rolls of Parliament, an arduous task for which his knowledge of Norman French specially qualified him. The *Rotuli Parliamentorum* between 1278 and 1413 were edited by him. He was a friend of Philippe Falle, the historian (q.v.), who added to a second edition of his *Caesarea or an Account of Jersey*, 1734, a long dissertation "by the hand of my ingenious Countryman, Mr Mourant", *Remarks on the 19th. chapter of the 2nd. book of Mr Selden's Mare Clausum*. Other writings of his were: — *The Cruelties and Persecutions of the Romish Church Displayed*, 1728 ; *The History of England by way of Question and Answer*, 1737 ; *An Account of the Spanish Invasion of 1588 by Way of Illustration to the Tapestry Hangings in the House of Lords*, 1739 ; *Geographia Antiqua et Nova*, 1742 ; and all the articles marked C in the 1st edition of the *Biographia Britannica*. In 1753 he wrote to the Governors of the Don Baudains expressing gratitude for the help given him by the Fund in his youth, and offering either to repay all that he had received, or to found an exhibition for Jersey lads at Oxford. The Governors suggested that, instead of creating a separate exhibition, he might increase the endowments of the Don Baudains, and he adopted this course. In 1755 he was elected a Fellow of the Society of Antiquaries. He married Anne Stebbing of Great Tey, Essex, and had an only daughter, Anna Maria, who married Thomas Astle, Keeper of the Records in the Tower of London. Morant died in South Lambeth, where he was living to be near his work at the House of Lords, on 25 Nov. 1770, and was buried in Aldham Church, of which he was still Rector. His portrait shows a keen-looking, portly man in a wig with a very large aquiline nose. [*Dic Nat. Biog., Essex Review*, Jan. 1894. *Trans. Essex Archaeolog. Sy.*, Vol. II. Maclean's *History of Pembroke College*.]

MOURANT, ABRAHAM, (1831—78), Ecrivain, Editor of Jersey books. Son of Jean Mourant and Anne Maria Filleul. Born 1831, and baptized at Grouville 13 March. After working in an écriviain's office he studied law at Rennes. On his return in 1857 he was appointed an écrivain, and became the leading solicitor in the island. He was an ardent member of the Rose Party, a supporter of Pierre Le Sueur (q.v.), and a frequent contributor to the *Chronique* and *Nouvelle Chronique*. In 1858 he published an edition of the anonymous Jersey classic, written in 1585, *Les Chroniques de Jersey*. The only existing edition was one published by G.S. Syvret in Guernsey in 1837, based on an eighteenth century manuscript discovered in Sark. Mourant collated this with five Jersey manuscripts, and added an essay on the date and value of the work. In 1860 he edited a new edition of the 1771 *Code of Laws for the Island of Jersey* with an index showing which laws had been abrogated, which superseded, and which were still in force, and an Appendix

of new laws confirmed since 1771. In 1861 he published his
Biographie de Pierre Le Sueur. In 1865 he issued his fourth
book, *Rimes et Poésies Jersiaises,* a well-chosen selection of
verses by Sir Robert P. Marett (q.v.), H.L. Manuel (q.v.),
Esther Le Hardy, Philippe Asplet and other dialect poets.
Meanwhile he took an active part in public life. He was
Centenier of St. Helier's 1864—7. Deputy of Grouville 1872,
and Constable of Grouville 1875. He had just been re-
elected to this office in 1878, when he died on 20 June. In
1877 he had started the *Jersiais,* the second newspaper of that
name, but it only lived a year. He married Louisa Mary
Syvret, but died without children.

MOURANT, PHILIPPE (1771—1845), Printer and Newspaper Proprietor. Son of Philippe Mourant and Elizabeth
Pirouet. Born in St. Helier's 1771, and baptized in the Town
Church 22 July. The first Jersey newspaper, the *Gazette,* was
established by Mathieu Alexandre (q.v.) in 1786 to support
the Magot Party. In 1792 their opponents, the Charlots, started
the *Soleil de l'Ile de Jersey.* They fell out with their first
printer, François Jeune, and entrusted the paper to Mourant.
The *Gazette* remarked: — "Last Saturday Lady Press gave
birth to a puny monstrosity. The father seems unaccountably
happy, and, since he cannot endow the little gutter-snipe *(mal-
otru)* with either beauty or talent, he has decided to dazzle
us with its title. In spite of its deformity he has named it the
Soleil de Jersey. The baby's health is deplorable. The doctors
say it cannot live a year". As a matter of fact the *Soleil* outlived the old *Gazette,* which died in 1797.
    That year an Englishman, John Stead, "formerly engaged in
His Majesty's Printing Office in London", set up a Printing
Press in Jersey. Between him and Mourant there was fierce
rivalry. Stead published in 1797 an *Almanach Historique,
Utile, et Curieux,* continuing a series begun by Alexandre in
1785. Mourant responded with a similar almanac with exactly
the same title. In Sept. Stead took over the moribund *Gazette.*
He immensely improved its appearance under his management,
but it lacked local interest, consisting mainly of cuttings from

French and English papers. On 23 Sept. Stead announced that he was about to publish an English Gazette. The following week the *Soleil* said: — "Philippe Mourant informs the public that he is publishing a newspaper in English containing all the most interesting news, the price of the funds, and the arrivals and departures of Jersey vessels". If these papers ever appeared, no copy seems to have survived. In Jan. 1799 Mourant dropped the *Soleil*, and, entering into partnership with Angot, the printer of the old *Gazette*, substituted a *Gazette de l'île de Jersey*, using exactly the same title Stead had already appropriated. For the next thirty-five years the rival papers ran side by side with precisely the same format and title, the only distinguishing mark being the final note, "Published by Philippe Mourant" or "Printed by J. Stead".

Journalism had its dangers. In 1802 the Peace of Amiens had patched up a truce between Napoleon and England. In the following Feb. Mourant was arrested for publishing observations "tending to disturb the friendly relations between His Majesty's Government and the French". As however these proved to be only extracts from English papers, the Court contented itself with expressing its "entire disapprobation of this outrage", and discharged him with a warning. In 1817 two naval Lieutenants quarrelled "when under the effects of wine", and John Goldie challenged Alexander Bisset to a duel. Bisset ignored the challenge ; so Goldie persuaded Mourant to publish the correspondence, after receiving a guarantee that Goldie would be responsible "for any ill consequences". Bisset sued Mourant for £5,000 damages for libel, and he then found that Goldie had sold his property in the island, and possessed nothing on which he could distrain.

But on the whole Mourant conducted his paper with discretion. In early years it had no leading articles, expressed no opinions, steered clear of party politics, and was purely a news-sheet. And, while the War lasted, foreign news was more important than local happenings. His translations however from English papers were sometimes amusing. Once Dr Valpy (q.v.), the famous Headmaster, sent him an advertisement of Reading Grammar School, asking him to turn it into French. He did, and 'Reading School' appeared as *'Ecole de Lecture'!* But in the course of years the character of the paper varied with the Editor employed. From 1813 to 1816 it was chiefly interested in the banquets, routs, and assemblies of the people it called *les Fashionables*. Then *les Fashionables* entirely dropped out, and full reports were given of sessions of the States and Court. Among the Editors were Edouard Le Vavasseur dit Durell (q.v.) and Jean De La Croix (q.v.).

In 1825 Mourant undertook the publication of a new weekly. An English paper, the *British Press*, had been started in 1822, and its tone infuriated Jerseymen. So Mourant announced, "A Society of English and Jersey gentlemen has resolved to publish a weekly paper under the name of the *Jersey Loyalist*. The Proprietors are resolved to suffer no misrepresentations against this island to go out into the world unchallenged." In their opening article they said, "We have seen our Laws and Constitution ridiculed, our Public Functionaries vilified. We are thorough determined haters of whoever shall insult our country". The *British Press* was edited by Michael Rafter, a swashbuckling Irishman. He had been a Colonel in the Columbian army ; so the *Loyalist* nicknamed him Don Ferdinando. "We are sorry to inform our readers", it said, "that the malady of Don Ferdinando continues to increase, and we are afraid that his keepers will be obliged to remove him to the cells of Bedlam. We have however enough of the milk of human kindness to open a subscription at our office toward defraying the poor gentleman's travelling expenses to that asylum" (28.11.25). But there was as yet no public for two English papers. The five French journals provided all that Jerseymen needed. And in Feb. 1831 the *Impartial* printed in its Deaths column: — "Died on Monday last at its residence in the Royal Square the *Jersey Loyalist* at the end of a decline endured for five years with exemplary patience".

In 1796 Mourant was appointed Printer to the States, and for thirty-nine years produced all official publications. He also printed many books for use in the island, including Frs. Le Couteur's *Aperçu sur les Cidres* 1801, *Le Voyage de Bethel* 1809, a devotional manual used by most Jerseymen in preparation for Holy Communion, *Le Rapport des Commissaires Royaux concernant le Mode de choisir les Jurés* 1813, and *The Representation of Eight Jurats touching the conduct of Thomas Le Breton, Lieut.-Bailiff*. 1818.

In Nov. 1830 Mourant stood for election as Centenier of St. Helier's. For some reason this contest aroused intense ex-

citement as a trial of strength between the Rose and Laurel
Parties, which had superseded the old Magots and Charlots.
When Mourant, who was the Laurel (or Conservative) candidate, won by 126 votes, his supporters dragged out the parish
cannon, and acclaimed his victory with salvoes, and flags surmounted with bunches of laurel were flown, we are told, from
at least three hundred windows. At the end of three years
however he did not stand for re-election.

In March 1835 he announced that his *Gazette* would cease
publication. It had been outstripped by its younger rivals, the
Chronique, the *Constitutionnel*, and the *Impartial*, which spoke
of it patronizingly as *la Grand'mère*. Henceforth he devoted
himself to his bookshop in the Square, the largest in the Channel islands, with its circulating library of over 3,000 volumes.
He died on 31 July 1845, "the *Doyen* of local publicists". "He
was endowed", said the *Chronique*, "with a benignity that
recalled bygone days". He had married in 1793 Elizabeth
Pickstock, and his children were Betsy (b. 1794), Marie (b.
1798), Nancy Olive (b. 1802), Janey (b. 1803), Philippe Dupré
(b. 1804), Esther (b. 1806), and Edouard (b. 1808). [Local
newspapers.]

MOWAT, JOHN LANCASTER GOUGH (1846–94), Fel-
low of Pembroke College, Oxford. Third son of James Mowat,
Wesleyan Minister in Jersey, and Elizabeth Lancaster. Born
in Peter Street. St. Helier's, 25 Sept. 1846. Educated at the
Wesleyan Collegiate Institution, Taunton. While here he gained a prize for a poem on *Thermopylae*, which he printed, 1864.
He won a Channel Islands scholarship at Exeter College, Ox-
ford, 1865. Took a first in Classical Moderations, 1867, and
a second in the Final Schools, 1869. B.A. 1869. M.A. 1872.
Became Fellow of Pembroke, 1871, Lecturer, Senior Bursar
and Junior Dean, 1872, Proctor, 1885, Curator of the Bodleian
Library, 1889 till his death. He was also Bursar of Lincoln
College. He was an antiquarian, a botanist, and a great
pedestrian. In 1882 he edited an old Latin Glossary, *Sinonoma
Bartholomei*, and in 1887 a medico-botanical glossary, *Alphita*.
In 1892 he published his *Notes on the Oxfordshire Doomsday*.

He completely explored the line of the Roman Wall between England and Scotland, and in 1885 published *A Walk along the Taufelsmauer and Pfahlgraben*. He hanged himself in his rooms in Pembroke College on 7 Aug. 1894 during a fit of temporary insanity.

NEEL, JEAN (d. 1497), Co-founder of St. Mannelier and St. Anastase. The Latin epitaph on his tomb in Arundel tells that he was born in Jersey ; that he devoted himself to the seven arts ; that he graduated at Paris ; that he became Treasurer to William of Waynfleet, Bishop of Winchester (who died in 1486) ; that he became Dean of Prince Arthur's Chapel ; that he shed lustre on his native land by founding two schools, in which grammar should for ever be taught ; and that he died on 5 March three years short of the year 1500. (Dean of Prince Arthur's Chapel meant Senior Chaplain to the Household of the nine-year-old Prince of Wales. Other Jerseymen held posts in that Household. Thomas De St. Martin, Seigneur of Trinity, was Premier Usher, and Edouard De Carteret was Gentleman-Carver). The only other fact known about him is that in 1488 he was Master of Arundel College, for in that year the *Calendar of Inquisitions* mentions a "messuage called Ryvers in Fittleworth, Sussex, held by John Neel, Master of the College at Arundel". This was a College founded in 1380 by Richard, Earl of Arundel. It consisted of a master, seven priests, three deacons, three sub-deacons, two acolytes, seven choristers, two sacrists, with three yeomen and two grooms to wait on them. And their duty was to say Masses daily in the church of St. Nicholas, Arundel, for the souls of the Earl's parents.

The two Grammar Schools were founded in conjunction with a fellow-Jerseyman, Vincent Tehy (q.v.), Merchant of Southampton. On 15 November 1496 Henry VII granted a charter: "To our well-beloved Jean Neel, Dean of the Chapel of our dearest son, Arthur, Prince of Wales, and to Vincent Tehy, Merchant of Southampton, we grant licence to found two schools in our island of Jersey on such sites as shall be found convenient with two Masters and two Ushers, if need require, to instruct the boys of the island in Grammar (in those days this always meant Latin Grammar) and in the other lesser liberal sciences according to the constitutions laid down by the aforesaid Vincent and Jean, the Masters to be appointed by the Dean and Clergy of the island. Moreover we grant leave to Jean and Vincent, notwithstanding any Statute of Mortmain to the contrary, when the schools are erected, to endow them with an annual rente of 60 quarters of wheat, and we grant leave to any, who are willing to do so, to contribute to increase this to 260 quarters. And we will that neither our Governor nor any other island officials save the Dean and Clergy shall in any way intermeddle with appointments to these schools".

The Founders decided to use part of their gift to increase the endowment of St. Mannelier at St. Saviour's (See *Jehan Hue*), and to use the rest to establish a similar school for the eastern parishes, which they attached to a Chapel of St. Anastase, which stood in a lane leading down to St. Peter's Valley. This was an appropriate link, for St. Anastase, a monk of Mont St. Michel, who became a hermit on the neighbouring islet of Tombelaine, was, we are told, "very learned in Greek and Latin". The Founders' Statutes required that school should last from six in the morning till six at night, and that the education should be entirely free. Both schools lasted till the middle of the nineteenth century, but were always crippled by lack of adequate funds, for no benefactors came forward to increase the endowments, as the Founders had hoped. Today the endowment is used for scholarships at Victoria College. Neel died on 5 March 1497, only four months after the Charter had been granted. [The Charter is printed in Falle's *Account of Jersey*; Neel's epitaph will be found in Durell's notes on Falle.]

NICOLLE, EDMUND TOULMIN (1868–1929), Vicomte. Honorary Secretary of the Société Jersiaise. Son of Edmond Nicolle, Optician, and Matilda Caroline Tibot. Born in St Helier's, 19 Sept. 1868. Educated at Victoria College. His first ambition was to be a journalist, and he joined the staff of *The Jersey Express* as reporter. In 1890 a new paper, *The Jersey Reformer*, was started. To this he contributed serio-comic skits on Eminent Jerseymen, in one of which he rashly suggested that a member of the Harbours Committee might be receiving a commission on the cement used in the harbour works. This led to his leaving the island hurriedly to escape arrest. Later, when the outraged Jurat had consented to treat this article as a juvenile escapade, Nicolle returned and entered the office of E.B. Renouf, Solicitor, who encouraged him to read for the law. He went to London to study, and was called to the Bar (Middle Temple) in 1894, and the same year was admitted an Advocate of the Jersey Royal Court. He was still a keen reformer, and helped to found the short-lived Progressive Party, which demanded drastic changes in the island's constitution. In 1895 he was elected a Centenier of St. Helier's, and proved a terror to evil-doers, running to earth several elusive criminals, including a French coiner, who had established a mint in Sand Street. In June 1899 he made his first attempt to enter the States, over-ambitiously standing for the Constable-ship of St. Helier's in opposition to the veteran Philippe Baudains (q.v.), who had held office for fifteen years. Nicolle was badly beaten. The same year he stood again for a vacant Town Deputyship, and was again defeated. In August 1900 however at a by-election he secured a seat as Deputy. At the General Election of 1901 his programme was the substitution of an elected Municipal Council for the Parish Assembly, and he was returned as senior Deputy at the head of the poll. But in 1904 he lost his seat. His previous poll of over a thousand shrank to 474, and out of six candidates he came only fifth. At the next election in 1907 the Town was divided into dis-tricts, and Nicolle was elected one of the Deputies for the Sec-ond District, and he retained his seat in 1910, 1913, and 1916. In 1917 he was appointed Vicomte.

His most enduring work however was wholly unpolitical. In spite of great personal popularity he seldom persuaded the States to adopt the reforms he advocated, though these grew far less sweeping than in his Progressive Party days. But in 1898 he became a member of the committee of the Société Jersiaise, and in 1901 was elected an Honorary Secretary, a post which he held for twenty-eight years till his death. R.R. Marett wrote of him: — "He found the Société académique ; he

left it national.   Founded by a group of enthusiasts with antiquarian and scientific leanings, it has come about largely by
Nicolle's personal influence that every person of light and leading in the island reckons it a public duty to support it".   When
he became Secretary its membership was 148 ; when he died
it was 639.   But he was far more than an energetic official.
He was a great research-worker.   His early interests were mediaeval, and the *Cartulaire des Iles Normandes,* which he edited
with R.R. Marett (q.v.) and Guy de Gruchy (q.v.), and his
book on *Mont Orgueil Castle* are models of historical accuracy.
Then the excavation of the cave-dwelling at La Cotte, the
transference of many dolmens into the Société's keeping, and
the purchase of La Hougue Bie in 1919 drove his investigations
back into Prehistory.   He became the recognized expert on all
phases of the island's past, and, as the *Bulletins* show, could
write with equal ease and authority on The Bronze Age in
Jersey (*Bull.* VIII), The Attack on Jersey in 1406 (*Bull.* X),
or The Jersey Revolution of 1769 (*Bull.* IX).   It was an odd
paradox, that he, whom political opponents pilloried as an anti-
patriotic Jerseyman out to destroy all the venerable institutions
of his country, should prove the most ardent lover of all that
was ancient in the island.   In 1927 the French Government
recognized the debt French *savants* owed to his researches by
making him an *Officier d'Instruction Publique,* and in 1928
he was elected a Fellow of the Society of Antiquaries of
London.

He had many other interests.   As an expert horticulturist he
was a judge at Rose Shows. He was one of the founders of the
Jersey Rowing Club.   As a musical enthusiast he was President of the Orchestral Society and of the Jersey Philharmonic
Society.   He was President of the Jersey Law Society.   Indeed
there were few cultural organizations of which he was not at
least a Vice-President.   He even possessed a surprising knowledge of the higher mysteries of the culinary art.   He died at
Merman, Beaumont, 13 Aug. 1929, and was buried in St.
Saviour's churchyard.   He left to the Société £3,000 by will
and among other legacies his valuable collections of books and
pamphlets on the Channel Islands.   He married in 1897 his
cousin Jeanne Marie, daughter of Adolphe Nicolle, but had
no children.   His portrait hangs in the Barreau Art Gallery.
Among his publications were: — *Jersey Chronology* (Jersey

1892), a revision of Ansted and Latham's *Channel Islands* (London 1893) ; *A Description of Jersey* (Illustrated Guide Books, Brighton) 1896 ; *An Account of Queen Victoria's Visit to Jersey* (Jersey) 1896 ; *Recent Prehistoric Researches in Jersey* (Guernsey) 1911 ; *L'Exploration de la Grotte Paléolithique dans la Baie de St. Brelade* (Le Mans) 1912 ; *Mont Orgueil Castle, its History and Description* (Jersey) 1921 ; *L'Administration des Iles Normandes et leur Rapport avec le Cotentin* (Caen) 1925 ; and *The Town of St Helier (Jersey)* 1931. The last was published after his death from notes found among his papers. A list of his contributions to the S.J. *Bulletins* is printed in *Bull.* XI. Other articles include one on "The Judicatures of the Channel Islands" in *The Brief* 1895, and another on 'The Neutrality of the Channel Islands in the 15th, 16th, and 17th centuries' in the *Journal of the Society of Comparative Legislation* 1920. [Local newspapers. S.J. Bulletins.]

NICOLLE, HOSTES (d. 1564), Bailiff. Son of Jean Nicolle, Seigneur of Longueville, and Catherine, sister of Helier Gosselin, Bailiff of Guernsey (q.v.). He was not a member of the old-established Nicolle family of Jersey. His great-grandfather, John Nichol, was a Cornishman (one of the Nichols of Penvose), who had been Gentleman-Porter of Mont Orgueil, and had bought Longueville in 1480. Here his neighbours spelt his name Jerseywise as Nicolle. His son, Hostes the elder, was Jurat in 1501 ; and the latter's son, Jean, father of Hostes the younger, was Vicomte 1527—35, and Attorney-General 1533—45. Hostes junior inherited Longueville on his father's death in 1545, became Gentleman-Porter of Mont Orgueil in 1551, Constable of St. Saviour's in 1558, and Attorney-General till 1561, when on 8 March he was sworn in as Bailiff. It is noteworthy that Sir Hugh Poulet wrote to the States, "I have appointed Hostes Nicolle". The appointment was made by the Governor, not by the Crown. (The letter and Nicolle's oath are printed in *Actes des Etats*).

Nicolle, as was natural in a nominee of Poulet, belonged to the Protestant party. At one of the first sessions over which he presided the Court ordered all Breviaries and Legendaries (i.e. Lives of the Saints) to be burnt ; and a year later a man who was found to possess a Breviary was sentenced to bring a cartload of wood to the Market Place at his own expense, and publicly burn the book. It was also under Nicolle that the first two witches were burnt in Jersey. He only held office for three years, but during that period important things happened. It was to him that Elizabeth granted her Charter (June 1562), confirming all the privileges previously accorded to the island, including freedom from import duties at British ports, from English taxation, and from of the Courts at Westminster. He also received the Elizabethan Commissioners, who in Oct. 1562 issued Ordinances to secure safer guardianship for orphans' property, to establish a Registry of Wills, and another for transfers of real property, to shorten the duration of lawsuits, to regulate weights and measures, and to compel the Constables to enforce decrees of the Royal Court, all of which Nicolle and the Jurats accepted and confirmed. In 1563 he had to cope with a serious outbreak of plague, brought to the island by Jersey soldiers, who had been fighting in France to help the Huguenots. The death-rate was so heavy, that the Court met in St. Saviour's Church to avoid entering the Town.

He is however chiefly remembered by the Chronicler's story of his death: — "There was a poor man, whose house and land adjoined that of the Bailiff. This land the Bailiff coveted, but he knew not how to get it. One day however he bade his servants choose two of his finest sheep. These they slew, and at his behest carried to the house of ...., who was by trade a butcher. (The name is missing in all surviving manuscripts, and was probably torn off the original from which these copies were made. Tradition calls him Antoine). Next day he roused the Constable and his officers, and bade them search the butcher's house ; and there they found the sheep dead and hanging in a stable, where the Bailiff's servants had put them. The man was at once arrested, and brought into Court, and without any defence condemned to be hanged that day, though he was in nowise blameworthy. Thereupon, as the hangman put the rope round his neck at the door of the Court, he said to the Bailiff before everyone, 'I summon you to appear within forty days before the just Judge of all to answer to God and me for the injustice you have done'. And on the thirty-ninth day Hostes Nicolle, the wicked Judge, fell dead by the wayside,

as he was returning from Town". There is no other evidence
to support or refute this story ; but the *Chroniques* was written
in 1585, only twenty-one years after Nicolle's death. C.B.
Bateman, Seigneur of Longueville, writing about 1860, gives
three versions of the legend, which were current in his day
(*Bull.* XI), but these are of no importance compared with the
Chronicler's almost contemporary account. At that time the
Bailiff's ghost was still believed to gallop round the manor.
He was buried in St. Saviour's Church 10 June 1564. Bateman's statement (*Bull* XI) that the Church Register asserts that
he was buried "in the cross-roads like a dog" is incorrect. The
entry runs, "Hostes Nicolle, gentleman, Seigneur of Longueville,
Bailiff of Jersey, was buried in the middle of the chancel of the
church (*enfouy au milieu du coeur de l'église*)." He married
Ysabel, daughter of Jurat Edmond Perrin, Seigneur of Rozel,
and had five children, John (b. 1555, d. 1563), Hugh (b. 1556),
Marguerite (b. 1557, d. 1560), Nicolas (b. 1558), and a second
Marguerite (b. 1560). Hugh was only eight, when he succeeded
his father. Thirty-one years later he was forced by debt to sell
the manor and retire to England. [Authorities quoted above.]

NICOLLE, JEAN (1599—c1668), Vicomte. Younger son of
Nicolas Nicolle of St. Martin's and Jeanne, daughter of Pierre
Dolbel. Born 1599, and baptized in St. Martin's Church 28
June. In 1616, when seventeen, he joined the staff of Lord
Dorchester, English ambassador at the Hague, and remained
with him sixteen years, rising to be his Secretary. Letters of
the period frequently mention him as John Nicholls ; e.g. Thomas
Locke wrote in 1625 to Sir Dudley Carleton at the Hague, "As
I was going to send these, John Nicholls being now on his
departure" (*S.P.*). In 1627, when Dorchester was in England,
and Nicolle presumably in Jersey, Conway asked Sir Philippe
De Carteret (q.v.) to "send some discreet man into France to
gain intelligence with promise of good pay", and Sir Philippe
chose Nicolle (*S.P.*). In the following year he returned with
Dorchester to the Hague. In 1632 Dorchester died, and Nicolle
had to seek new employment. The following letter of his to Sir
Francis Windebank, Secretary of State, is a study in place-

hunting: — "My Lord of Holland, when I sued for the French Secretary's place, objected no manner of impediment therein, only that I spake too late, it being already bestowed ; whereupon I was induced to petition for the reversion of the Bailiff's place in Jersey, which, though his Majesty did not then grant me, he promised I should have, when it fell void ; but for that I may wait long, Sir Philip De Carteret having got three lives therein conferred on his house. Lord Dorchester becoming suitor to his Majesty, when Mr Warwick obtained a reversion of the Signet, that it might rather be bestowed on me, was denied. Being afterward suitor for a filazer's place (the officer who filed writs) at the Court of Common Pleas, I was likewise refused. So, having failed in all I ever sued for, being poor and needy, I am forced to implore your mediation with his Majesty for some consideration, either the reversion of the place of Assistant to the Master of Ceremonies, or, unless it be too great presumption, of a Clerk's place at the Council, or, in case none of the above be thought practicable, that somewhat be allowed me yearly for intelligence I shall send you from foreign parts, or at least that a blank I have under his Majesty's signature for a Baronet may be filled" (S.P.). At the same time he was asking the Marquis of Hamilton to get him the Clerkship of the Peace for the County of Middlesex (S.P.). But all these hopes came to nothing. In 1646 he was collecting information for Sir George Carteret in Paris. In Feb. 1647 Sir Edward Hyde wrote from Jersey: — "Mr Nicholls, heretofore Secretary to Lord Dorchester, sends constant intelligence from Paris" (Clarendon Papers). Chevalier wrote in April: — "Mr Jean Nicolle returned to Jersey from Paris, where Sir George had sent him as agent to glean news at the Court of the Prince, and send word of all that was happening. He wrote to Sir George every week. He also received 20,000 livres tournois, which the Prince had borrowed from gentlemen in Jersey, when he was there. This Nicolle received from the Queen's Treasurers a little at a time as they could spare it. He had been more than six months in France. He brought back some arms with him". The Clarendon Papers add that he also brought for Hyde, "six fair pyes of lamprey". He then became Deputy Judge of the Jersey Admiralty Court that dealt with prizes brought in by the privateers, and in 1650 Supreme Judge. In 1648 he drew up a long Memorial (printed in Hoskins) concerning the Failure of

Sir George Carteret's Design upon Guernsey through the Obstinacy of Sir Baldwin Wake. In Sept. 1648 Carteret sent him to Holland to report what was taking place in the Prince's Court there. He returned in November with news that the Prince meant to visit Jersey. In June 1649 he went with Carteret to Paris to arrange for the Prince's visit. When the royal party arrived in September Nicolle was made Gentleman of the Bedchamber to the young Duke of York, the future James II. He left Jersey with the Duke in Aug. 1650 ; but was back again in Feb. 1651, when he married in St. Brelade's Church Sir George's eldest sister, Anne, widow of Jurat Thomas Seale. When the Roundheads recovered Jersey in October, he remained in the island, living in his wife's house at La Moye, and there three of his children were born. But he still visited France, and in 1654 quarrelled with his brother-in-law. A letter among the *Clarendon Papers* says: — "Challenges have passed between Sir George Carteret and Mr Nicolls about, as is supposed, the coining of some false gold in Jersey". This possibly refers to the ill-starred attempt to establish a mint at Trinity. At the Restoration he was appointed Vicomte, and was sworn in April 1661 ; but he did not allow these duties to tie him to the island. He was the first Vicomte to appoint a Deputy. In May he went as Deputy of the States to the Privy Council to protest against the tax on foreign boats visiting the island (A.E.). He resigned in 1668. As his burial does not appear in any local register, he probably died in England. He had at least four children, George (b. 1651), Elizabeth (b. 1653), Rachel (b. 1655), who married Jean De Carteret, Seigneur of Vinchelez de Haut, and Anne, who married Jurat Elie Le Montais. [Authorities mentioned above.]

NORMAN, DANIEL (d.c. 1668), Vicomte. Younger son of Jean Norman of St. Lawrence and Lucasse Benest. In the Civil War he was an active Parliamentarian. At his trial it was stated that he had assisted with all his power in the siege of the Castles, and that he had seized the salt provided for the King's troops. He fled to England when the Royalists recovered the island in Nov. 1643. In 1644 Carteret had all his corn carried to Elizabeth Castle. He was tried in his absence for high treason in 1645, and sentenced to death. Meanwhile he was hanged in effigy, and his goods confiscated. Carteret cut down his trees for the repair of Elizabeth Castle. De La Rocque states that Norman, like other of the Jersey exiles, became an Anabaptist. In 1649 'Daniel Norman, Merchant of the Isle of Jersey' is mentioned as one of the six contractors for the purchase of the King's Property (*Acts and Ordinances*) ; and in 1651 he was still employed in Worcester House, the office of the Trustees for the Sale of the Royal Estates. That year he returned to Jersey with the Parliamentary expedition that reconquered the island, and he helped to reorganize the Militia. Michel Lempriere, the Parliamentary Bailiff (q.v.), wrote to the Speaker: — "Col. Heane at our first coming did put the Militia at the disposing of Col. Stocall (q.v.), Capt. Norman, and myself" (Hoskins). On 31 Aug. 1653 the Council of State removed Edouard Hamptonne from his office of Vicomte and resolved "that Capt. Daniel Norman, a person of known integrity and good affection, be appointed by Parliament Vice-Count or Sheriff, he being willing to go over and execute that place" (*S.P.*). His fees were fixed at "five sols for adjournments and significations of Orders from the Bayliffe and Justice, as likewise for sale of goods, and nine sols for all seizures and executions upon goods" (*O.C.*). For some reason he was not sworn in till April 1657. At the Restoration he withdrew to England, where he died, apparently about 1668. He married Marthe, sister of Doctors Aaron and Denis Guerdain (q.v.), and had one daughter, Martha, who married Nathaniel White, a London surgeon. [Chevalier's *Journal* and authorities quoted above.]

OULESS, PHILIP JOHN, (1817—85), Local Artist. On 7 Jan. 1787 Philippe Joseph Oulez, a Frenchman from Paris, married in St. Andrew's Guernsey Elizabeth Noel, daughter of Jean Noel of St. Saviour's, Jersey. They came to Jersey to live, but, in the years that followed Rullecourt's invasion, the island did not welcome Frenchmen. The Lieut.-Governor ordered him to leave, and, when he still tarried, he was arrested on 20 Jan. and commanded to depart within eight days. He slipped back again ; for a year later he was again banished. Either he or his wife was very persistent, for they returned once more, and their son Philippe Jean was born in St. Helier's in 1787. In 1789 an influentially signed certificate declared that P. J. Oulez, Fencing Master, had lived in Jersey for two years, and that his conduct had been irreproachable. Soon after, he went to live in Coutances, where he became a member of the Municipal Council. In 1795 he led a rising of the Jacobins in Coutances, in consequence of which he was imprisoned on a charge of terrorism, but later released. His wife seems to have divided her time between Coutances and Jersey. In 1817 the husband visited Jersey, and made an extraordinary will leaving to his son 44,000 francs, which he said the French Government owed him for his services. After this the breach with his wife became permanent, and he lived at Coutances with a Frenchwoman, by whom he had several children. Meanwhile the son, Philippe Jean, grew up in Jersey, and became the leading auctioneer in the island. He married Susanne Blampied. Their son, Philip John, was born in St. Helier's on 7 April 1817. He studied painting in Paris, and then established himself in Jersey as a "Portrait, Landscape, and Marine Painter" and as a Teacher of Painting. Portraits of ancestors painted by him hang in many Jersey homes. Jersey ship-owners commissioned him to paint pictures of their ships, and many specimens of this side of his work hang in the Museum. The Barreau Gallery also has two of his larger oil-paintings, Gorey Races 1849, and St. Aubin's Bay 1875. He published Albums of Local Views, among which were *Scenic Beauties of the Island of Jersey*, 1840, *The Royal Jersey Album*, 1847, (pictures of Queen Victoria's visit), *Jersey Illustrated*, 1874, *The Death of Major Peirson*, 1881, *The Ecréhous*, 1884. He also illustrated Le Gros' *Mont Orgueil* and Durell's *Picturesque and Historic Guide* to Jersey. While not a great artist, his work is of real value for its extraordinarily accurate observation of details of the shipping, costume, and life of the period. His sketch books are in the possession of the Société Jersiaise, and some of the best sketches are reminiscent of those of the old Dutch Masters in their sailor's view of things. He married in 1839 Catherine, daughter of Henry Savage and Marguerite Selous of St. Brelade's, and had three sons, Philip Daniel, Captain R.N., William Walter, the Royal Academician (q.v.), Clarence, a photographer, and a daughter, Florence. He died at 53 New Street on 22 June 1885.

OULESS, WALTER WILLIAM (1848—1933), R.A. Portrait Painter. Son of Philip John Ouless (see above), and Catherine Savage. Born in St. Helier's 21 Sept. 1848. Educated at Victoria College. Entered Royal Academy Schools, when seventeen. His first picture was accepted for the Academy Exhibition in 1869. He was elected A.R.A. in 1877 and R.A. in 1881. He began as a painter of pictures with a story behind them. His first Academy pictures were called *He was a stalwart knight*, *Home again*, *Sad tidings*, *An incident in the Revolution*, *Sympathy*, and *Dorcas visiting the poor*. His picture of *David and Goliath* hangs in the Hall at Victoria College. But he soon realized that his strength lay in portraiture. His portraits of John Bright, Thomas Hardy, and Sir George Scharf hang in the National Portrait Gallery. Other well-known portraits of his are those of Cardinal Newman (now in the Oratory, Birmingham), Cardinal Manning, Lord Roberts, Lord Kelvin, the Duke of Cambridge, the Prince of Wales (1900), Lord Lister, Lord Stanhope, Lord Selborne, John Morley, Charles Darwin. He also painted a bevy of Victorian Bishops, including the Archbishop of York (Thomson), the Bishops of Lincoln (King), London (Jackson), Norwich (Pelham), Oxford (Mackarness), Worcester (Philpott), St. Alban's, Chichester, Truro, and Llandaff. His own portrait of himself he bequeathed to the Société Jersiaise. R. Muther in his *History of Modern Painting* (III.170) writes of him: — "Among portrait painters Walter Ouless will probably merit the place of honour immediately after Watts as an impressive exponent of character. He has assimilated much from his master, Millais,—not merely the heaviness of colour, which often has a disturbing effect in the latter, but also Millais' powerful flight of style. The chemical expert, Pochin, as Ouless painted him in 1865, does not pose in the picture, nor allow himself to be disturbed in his researches. It is a thoroughly contemporary portrait, one of those brilliant successes which later arose in France also. The Recorder of London, Mr. Russell Gurney, he likewise painted in his professional character and in his robes of office. In its inflexible graveness and earnest dignity the likeness is more than the portrait of an individual : it seems the embodiment of the English Bar resting on the most ancient traditions. His portrait of Cardinal Manning had the same convincing power of observation, the same large and sure technique. The soft light plays upon the ermine and the red stole, and falls full on the fine, austere face". He married Lucy Maitland Chambers, daughter of Doctor T.K. Chambers, Physician to the Prince of Wales. He died in London on 25 December 1933. His daughter, Catherine, became a distinguished painter. One of her Academy pictures, *Sunset on the Dorset Coast*, is in the Barreau Gallery. He had two other daughters, Evelyn Ursula and Margaret Olivia.

PAYN, FRANCOIS (1699–1775), Dean. Son of François Payn, Seigneur of La Malletière, and Elizabeth, daughter of Jurat Raulin Robin. Born in Grouville 1699, and baptized in Grouville Church 6 April. Entered Pembroke College, Oxford, as Morley scholar 1718. B.A. 1721. Fellow of Jesus College 1722. M.A. 1723. In 1725 François Parain de Durette, a Huguenot refugee, who for twenty-two years had been Chaplain to General Gore's regiment, was appointed Rector of Trinity, though he continued to serve with the troops ; and in 1728 on the recommendation of the Governor he was appointed Dean. The States protested that he was not a Jerseyman, and the appointment was cancelled. The choice then fell upon Payn. He was sworn in 3 July 1729, and instituted as Rector of St. Mary's. He held the Deanery for forty-six years, the longest period on record, but for much of this time he was absent from the island. During his first year he spent eleven months in England, and in each of the next three he took nine months' holiday. He then stayed in Jersey for six years, but followed this by four years' absence. A three months' visit was followed by two years' non-residence, and in the next eleven years he was only seven months in the island. He probably spent his time in one of his English livings. From 1729 he was Rector of Wigginton, Oxon. From 1730 to 1739 he was Rector of Furtho, Northants., a parish containing two farms and two cottages. From 1739 to 1756 he was Rector of Swerford, Oxon. Perhaps an early experience as Dean gave him a dislike for Jersey. In 1730 an alteration in the currency caused a fierce riot. The country people, finding they would have to pay six liards instead of four for every sou they owed, flocked into Town with pitchforks and cudgels, and invaded the

Royal Court. For some reason the new Dean was one of the persons against whom they were specially incensed. (Perhaps he had said something ill-advised in a sermon.) A contemporary writes: — "Seeing the danger that threatened, he crawled under the benches of the Court, and got out at the backdoor. He went into Harper's house, who kept a tavern behind the Court, and, taking his brother's great coat that was there and Harper's cap, jumped out at a back window, ran up the Town Hill, and made unto the Castle. Some of the people saw the Dean get into Harper's house, and, thinking he was still there, ransacked the whole house. They went likewise to a chamber that he had at Mr. Aire's, imagining he might be there, but the bird had flown" (*Bull* V). In 1764 he at last settled down in Jersey, and in 1765 became Rector of St. Martin's. Five years later he was in trouble with the Governor. Messervy wrote in his *Journal*: — "The Dean is always a meddler and anxious to know everything. He never refuses to marry anyone, even marrying Roman Catholics to Jersey women, provided they pay him well, which is a heavy burden to the island, for these Catholics. when they have many children, often desert them and leave them to be supported by the parishes. Though he is Chaplain to the Castle, and so in a sense a subordinate of Col. Bentinck the Lieut.-Governor, he was rash enough to go to Mons. Jean Hue and ask him if he could get him a copy of the *Middlesex Journal*". (There had been another riot in the Town, and copies of this paper which criticized Bentinck had been confiscated.) "Hue said that he could not procure one, as they had all been destroyed, but the Dean pulled one from his pocket. He told Hue that he had heard on good authority that the Receivership had been sold to Bentinck and Corbet to share half and half. Hue told the Colonel what the Dean had said, and he in a fury took an affidavit from Hue before the Jurats, and began to take steps to sue the Dean for slander. Payn, fearing that he would lose his Deanery and Chaplaincy, got friends to intercede for him with the Colonel, but he remained inflexible. At last Payn wrote a letter to the Colonel apologizing for the scandal he had caused, and this letter was read to the States in the presence of the Colonel". Messervy evidently disliked Pain. The *Armorial* says: — "His erudition and piety together with his influence at Court rendered his long life a pleasure and a benefit to all with whom he came into contact". At the time of his death he was

a Fellow of the Royal Society. He died 8 April 1775, and was
buried in Grouville Church, where there is a monument to his
memory. He married Jane, daughter of Ralph Brideoak, Archdeacon of Winchester, and had one daughter Jane.

PAYNE, JAMES BERTRAND PAYEN (1833—1898), Genealogist. Son of James Payne of Holmesdale, St. John's Road.
Born 8 April, 1833. Educated privately. About 1849 he went
to England and learnt something about book-production from
his relative, the publisher Charles Tilt. He returned to Jersey
on his father's death in 1856, and it was then that his interest
in the heraldry and genealogy of the island began. In 1859 the
family moved to London, and he sent out his first prospectus
of the *Armorial.* That same year he met Charles Moxon, and
their friendship led to Payne joining the Moxon Publishing
House, which since 1830 had issued the works of most of the
Poets of the day. At first he was literary adviser, and later he
became Manager of the business for Mrs. Moxon. In 1859 he
published Part I of *An Armorial of Jersey, being an Account,
Heraldic and Antiquarian, of the chief Native Families with
Pedigrees, Biographical Notices, and Illustrative Data ;* in 1860
a second issue of Part I and Part II ; in 1862 Parts III and IV ;
and in 1865 Parts V and VI. Though later research has ine-
vitably discovered a number of mistakes, due to the fact that he
trusted too much to family information, which he did not verify
from Church Registers and Court Records, his work remains a
monument of patient industry. He always looked forward to
further editions corrected and brought up to date, but lack of
funds prevented this. Payne continued the traditions of the
House of Moxon by publishing the works of Tennyson, Brown-
ing, and Swinburne. When Swinburne wrote his *Poems and
Ballads* in 1866, he refused to omit certain pagan passages which
mid-Victorian taste considered unfit for publication. John Morley denounced them in the *Saturday Review,* and Payne withdrew the book from circulation ; whereupon Swinburne transferred all his books to a rival publisher. Tennyson left the firm
in 1869, and in 1871 it went bankrupt. In 1873 Payne had a
lawsuit with Mrs. Moxon, and the costs ruined him. Meanwhile

in June 1869 he had been elected Chairman of the Metropolitan Conservative Association, and in November that year tried to start a Junior Conservative Club, but, as often happened, his plans were too grandiose, and after a short and stormy existence the Club collapsed. (The story is told in *The Junior Conservative Club* by S.R. Mayer.) Payne next edited *The King of Arms*, a weekly journal of family history and heraldry. As a genealogist he was a strong supporter of legitimist claimants to thrones, and in 1873 joined the English Carlist Committee to assist Don Carlos in his claim to the throne of Spain. In 1874 he went to Spain, became a Colonel in the Carlist Army, and was present at the Battle of Tolosa and the siege of Irun ; but he was disgusted with Don Carlos' incapacity and the crowd of needy adventurers with whom he had to associate, and he returned to England. From 1878 to 1888 he lived in chambers in the Temple, and worked at *The Roll of High Sheriffs*. From 1884 to 1885 he edited *Colburn's United Service Magazine*, but left it to organize the National Union Club as a meeting place for all who opposed Gladstone's Home Rule Bill. He was a life-long contributor to the Press. A series of articles that he wrote for the *Jersey Independent* in 1861 were published by W.H. Smith & Son in book form as *A Gossiping Guide to Jersey*, and this passed through several editions. He contributed to the *Gentleman's Magazine* in 1866 an article on Jaques De La Cloche (q.v.), the alleged son of Charles II, which he republished as a pamphlet. Four years later he edited Haydn's *Dictionary of Biography*, and wrote the text for a book of humorous drawings by Moyr Smith, *The Anglican Mysteries of Rome*. In 1874 he issued anonymously the libretto of an extravaganza entitled *St. Helier ye Hermit*. For a pamphlet written in 1872, *England, Russia and Persia*, the Shah conferred on him the Order of the Lion and the Sun ; while another pamphlet, *The Turkish Crisis*, in 1876 gained for him from the Sultan the Order of the Medjidie. No Jerseyman ever collected such an array of titles. He describes himself on the title-pages of some of his books as Knight Commander of the Legion of Honour, Knight Grand-Cross of the Royal Order of Isabella the Catholic, Knight Commander of the Royal Order of Charles III, Knight of the Eagle of Este of Modena, Knight of the Royal Order of Francis I of the Two Sicilies, Knight of the Nichan-Iftichar of Tunis, Fellow of the Royal Geographical Society, Fellow of the Genealogical Society

of Great Britain, Member of the Royal Institution, of the Royal
United Service Institution, of the Royal Society of Literature,
of the Geographical Societies of London and Paris, of the His-
toric-Genealogical Society of New England, of the Société de
l'Histoire, of the Institut Historique de France, of the Gens de
Lettres de Paris, Honorary Member of the Societies of Antiquaries of Normandy, Sweden, New Jersey, Massachusetts, and
New York, Freeman of the Worshipful Company of Bookmakers.

He had many ambitious schemes for future publications. He
advertised as 'In Preparation' an *Armorial of Guernsey*, uniform
with the *Armorial of Jersey*, a *Universal Peerage* "to embrace
the history of all the Noble Houses of Europe with Pedigrees,
Arms, Biographies, and Portraits", an *Armorial of Europe* ("Many
thousand bearings are already obtained and classified".), a
*Baronetage of England, Scotland, and Ireland, existing and
extinct* ("The command of the Norman Archives by the Author
by special permit from the Prefect of La Manche renders this a
favourable juncture for the compilation of his work".), a new
edition of Wace's *Roman de Rou, an Illustrated Dictionary of
Heraldry, a Universal Encyclopaedia of Heraldry, The Biographies
and Genealogies of all the Sovereigns of the World, A Roll of the
British Clergy, Monograms, and how to draw them, The Spanish
Question, containing a careful analysis of the rights claimed by
Don Carlos*, and *The Anglo-American Armorial, containing the
arms, lineages, and biographical data of American families of
English extraction.* None of these however was ever completed.
Payn was a man of striking appearance. Doré took him as model
for King Arthur in the illustrated edition of the *Idylls of the King*.
He married in 1864 Zoe Taylor, and left one son, De Vinchelez
Payen Payne, Editor of many school editions of French authors.
The father added Payen to his name in 1874 at the request, he
said, of the Norman branch of the family. [Memoir by his son,
prefixed to his *Lecture on Jersey*, published by the Jersey Society
in London.]

PEIRSON, MAJOR FRANCIS.   See Appendix I.

PERROT, CLEMENT (1786—1849), Independent Minister and Journalist. Born in St. Helier's 1786, and baptized in the Town Church 23 Aug. Among the Huguenots who had found refuge in Jersey about 1740 was a Madame Harivel, widow of a St. Quanten watchmaker, and her six children. One of her daughters, Jeanne Susanne, visited Cork, where she married Perrot, son of another Huguenot exile. She brought her husband to Jersey, where they opened a bakery in Hill Street. Their son, François, married Elizabeth Hooper in 1781 ; but he and his wife both died in 1800, leaving seven children, François (q.v.), Philippe, Clément, Pierre (q.v.), George, Esther, and Elizabeth, to be brought up by their widowed grandmother, Jeanne Susanne. She was a keen woman-evangelist, who conducted religious meetings in farm-houses in various parishes, and she used to take the boys with her. Under her influence François and Clement both became Independent ministers. Clement went to Dr. Bogue's Independent Theological Academy at Gosport, where his brother, François, had been trained ; and in 1808 preached at the opening of his brother's Chapel in Halkett Place. He remained in Jersey as his brother's assistant, taking charge of the work in the country districts. He was largely responsible for the building of the Independent Chapel at St. John's in 1810.

After the restoration of the French Monarchy in 1815 complaints arose as to persecution of the Protestants in Southern France. Perrot was sent there as an independent investigator, and his Report led the British Government to intervene, and to secure for the Huguenots freedom of worship. He then became Principal of the Independent Theological College at Rotherham in Yorkshire, a post which he held for nearly twenty years, during which he trained large numbers of Ministers, many of whom became famous. In 1835 he returned to Jersey, became Minister of the Chapel at St. John's, and took private pupils to train for the ministry. Independent Ministers in those days were often keen politicians ; and the Perrot brothers took a leading part in local politics as supporters of Pierre Le Sueur (q.v.) and the Rose Party. In January 1845 Clement became editor of a new English paper, *The Jersey Herald* (the second paper with this name) at a salary of £2 a week. The object of the paper was twofold. On the one hand it was to be Reformist in opposition to the *Constitutionnel* ; but on the other it was to defend the Jersey constitution against the attacks of A. J. Le Cras (q.v.) and his

Jersey News. "When men without principle gain a miserable livelihood by printing with astounding impudence every calumny which malice can invent against the States, the Court, and the Police, and when leading journals of the metropolis in ignorance of their falsehood give these a wide circulation, the urgent necessity for a newspaper devoted to the defence of the laws and institutions of our country is felt by every good citizen". A long series of Letters, signed Caesariensis, which Perrot wrote for his paper on all sorts of subjects, historical, literary, topical, and political, attracted wide attention, and these were often cut out and preserved in scrap-books. But the paper only lived two years. In 1848 Clement suceeded his brother, François, as Minister at Halkett Place, but died 25 April 1849.

PERROT, FRANCOIS (1782—1848). First Noncomformist Minister in Jersey. Eldest son of François Perrot and Elizabeth Hooper. Brother of Clement (q.v.) and Pierre (q.v.). Born in St. Helier's 1782. His parents died in 1800, leaving their seven children to be brought up by their grandmother. She was an ardent Evangelist, who used to conduct cottage meetings in various parts of the island, and took the boys with her. François, the eldest, sometimes preached at these meetings, and in 1802 went to Dr. Bogue's Theological Academy at Gosport to be trained for the Independent ministry. Here he had as fellow-students Angell James, the Birmingham preacher, and Robert Morrison, the famous missionary to China. He returned to Jersey, and held meetings in the Long Room in the Square. A Religious Revival began, and a number of his converts decided to form an Independent Church (the name then used by those who later called themselves Congregationalists). In 1807 he bought some plots of meadow land in Halkett Place, and built a red brick Chapel (opened 1808), the first Noncomformist place of worship in the island. (The present Chapel stands on the same site). His brother Clement (q.v.) came to share his work and a second Chapel was built at St. John's. In 1811 François married Susanna Maria Sharp of Romsey, Hants. She introduced Sunday Schools into the island,

and had established six, when she died in 1819 as the result of a fall at a Sunday School prize distribution. In the next few years Chapels were built at St. Aubin's, St. Clement's, St. Peter's, St. Saviour's, and in Guernsey, and all these remained under the supervision of Perrot. For forty years he continued his work, and his influence extended beyond the circle of his own congregations, for, like many Independents in those days, he was a keen politician, and took an active part on the Reform side in the municipal life of the town. He died 7 Oct. 1848. His only son, Clement, died in 1832 at the age of eighteen. [Jack's *One Hundred Years at St. John's Independent Church.*]

PIERROT, PIERRE (1789—1843), Founder of the *Chronique.* Jurat. Third son of François Perrot, and brother of Clément and François (see above). Born in St. Helier's 23 Jan. 1789. Unlike his brothers he went to sea. Here he must have shown unusual capacity, for in 1805, though only sixteen, he was prize-master on the Jersey privateer, the *Hope,* on which Jean Syvret (q.v.) was second in command. His job was to take captured ships to Jersey. In that year the *Hope* was wrecked near the mouth of the Loire, and the crew made prisoners. Perrot was taken to Valenciennes, where his knowledge of French and English got him the job of interpreter to the commandant of the depot for English prisoners. "This allowed him", wrote Syvret, "to leave the barracks when he liked", and he used his stay to improve his education. In 1811 he managed to escape, made his way to the coast, put out in an open boat, and after great privations was picked up by an English frigate, and returned to Jersey.

In 1814 with a friend, Pierre Chevalier, — they were both only 25 — he founded the *Chronique* newspaper; but in 1818 his partner died suddenly, and he was left in sole control. He edited the paper for the next twenty-five years. The three local news-sheets, Stead's *Gazette,* Mourant's *Gazette,* and the *Gazette de Césarée,* were produced on the paste and scissors principle. The proprietors subscribed to a number of French and English newspapers, cut out paragraphs they thought interesting, pasted them together, and handed them to the printer to reprint. They added no comment and little local news. Perrot had been accustomed in France to papers which led public opinion, and he aimed at providing one of this type in Jersey. But he took some time to get into his stride. The opening numbers were extremely dull, and the circulation stuck at about 300. Then he grasped the fact that the way to attract notice was to start a crusade. He launched a series of campaigns, first a much needed one against the Jersey paper-money, for in those days almost anyone could call himself a banker, and print an unlimited number of his own bank-notes. He followed this with an attack on the Militia Drill-Sergeants, then one on the method of appointing officers in the Militia, then one on the permits which had to be bought before anyone could buy coal. In this way he made everyone buy his paper. Many rival sheets were started, the *Constitutionnel*, the *Impartial*, the *Jersiais*, the *Miroir*, but none was able to oust the *Chronique* from its leading place. You might buy one of the others as an extra, but you had to subscribe to the *Chronique* to see what Perrot was saying. But this fighting policy kept him constantly in a hornets' nest. Life became one long libel-suit after another. The Drill-Sergeants sued him for libel ; so did the Dénonciateur; so did the road-contractors ; so did Dean Dupré (q.v.). Nor was this the worst penalty. Many who were annoyed at his leading articles preferred a horse-whip to a lawsuit. He was a little man — rival papers called him "le petit pierrot", and "our pocket O'Connell" — and the *Chronique* often reports that he had been waylaid and assaulted in the street. But he seems to have accepted this philosophically as one of the risks of his trade.

The *Chroniques* supported the Rose Party (it always headed its local news with a spray of roses), and in 1830 this Party chose him as its candidate for the Constableship of St. Helier's. At his first attempt he was beaten by François Godfray (q.v.) in a fiercely fought election, in which a record number of votes were polled; but in 1833 he defeated Godfray by 45 votes. In 1837 he was re-elected unanimously. Before becoming Constable he had been for seventeen years Constable's Officer, and as an active member of the Parish Assembly had secured the paving of many streets and the removal of the slaughter-houses from the centre of the town to the quay. As Constable his first problem was finance. His predecessor had left the parish

burdened with debt. Perrot succeeded in paying off a large
part of this, although he built the Arsenal and carried out many
street improvements. When a vacancy occurred on the bench
of Jurats in 1839, he was unanimously elected. On becoming
a Judge he entirely withdrew from party politics, and handed
over the *Chronique* to Philippe Huelin. In the States he
became one of the most influential members. Twice he was
chosen to represent them before the Privy Council, and the New
Harbour was largely due to his energetic advocacy. As one
paper said at his death, "The plans for the Harbour would
probably still be slumbering peacefully in the Greffe, had it
not been for the perseverence of Judge Perrot". He died 5 Jan.
1843, after a long illness, during which States' Committees met
in his bed-room, so that they might still have his advice. At
the time of his death a public subscription had just raised
£ 200 to present him with a service of silver plate in recognition
of his services ; but he did not live to receive it. He had married Catherine Waters, and left five children all under age. Of
these George Frébout Perrot became later a Centenier and editor
of the *Chronique* and a well-known writer in the dialect under
the pseudonym Hibou. Pierre Perrot's portrait was published
in the *Chronique*, 14 Jan. 1914.

[Manuel's *Memoir of Pierre Perrot*, published by the Société
d'Emulation ; Obituary notice in the *Chronique* 7 Jan. 1843 ;
Local Newspapers.]

PHILIPPES DE GORREQUER, SIR GEDEON (1781—

1841), Colonel. The Philippes de Gorrequer were originally
Bretons. In 1742 Jacques Guillaume Philippes de Gorrequer
of Brest settled in Jersey, and married Anne Syvret of St.
Ouen's. Their son Gédeon married Susanne Raven of St. Brelade's ; and their son Gédeon was born at St. Brelade's 1781.
He entered the Army as Ensign in the 18th Royal Irish Regiment 1797, and a year later was promoted Lieutenant. In 1801
he served with distinction against the French in Egypt, and for
"gallant conduct before the enemy" received from the Sultan the
Imperial Ottoman Order of the Crescent. In 1804 he obtained
his company in the 18th, and went with his regiment to the

West Indies. In 1809 he was aide-de-camp to Major-General Montresor during the occupation of Sicily. In 1814 he was still acting in the same capacity during operations against the French near Genoa. In a dispatch dated 14 April General Montresor wrote: — "The enemy made an obstinate resistance, but Col. Bruce's brigade, having opportunely debarked, was conducted into action by my aide-de-camp, Captain Gorrequer, which decided their defeat". For work in this campaign Gorrequer was promoted Brevet-Major, and received from the Prince Regent the Knighthood of the Royal Guelphic Order, and from the Kings of Sardinia and the Two Sicilies respectively the decorations of Knight Commander of the Order of St. Maurice and St. Lazarus and of the Order of St. Ferdinand and of Merit.

When Napoleon was banished to St. Helena in 1815, Gorrequer went there as aide-de-camp to Sir Hudson Lowe, the Governor, and became Military Secretary. He is one of our chief authorities for life in the island, and figures largely in contemporary memoirs. Sir Hudson Lowe wrote: — "A detailed correspondence addressed to His Majesty's Government reports the occurrences of almost every day during the five years that Napoleon remained under my custody. The greater part of the conversations with Bonaparte or his followers was immediately noted down with an ability and exactness which reflect the highest credit on my Military Secretary. This gentleman was not only a perfect master of the French language, but possessed a memory equally remarkable for accuracy and tenacity, and was therefore eminently qualified to report the conversations at which he was present". In 1819, while still at St. Helena, Gorrequer was promoted Brevet-Lieut.-Colonel. After Napoleon's death in 1821 he rejoined his regiment, and served in the Ionian Islands. In 1826 he became full Lieut.-Colonel on half pay, and settled in London. In 1837 he became Colonel of the 4th (King's Own) Regiment. He retired shortly afterwards. He died suddenly 18 July 1841, and was buried in Kensal Green cemetery. He never married. His portrait is in the S.J. Museum. [Bull VI. 200.]

PICKSTOCK, THOMAS (1765—1800), Privateer. Son of
Thomas Pickstock, Sergeant in 99th Regiment, and Jeanne Le
Feuvre. Born in St. Helier's 1765, and baptized in the Town
Church 2 June. As a young man, he was in charge of a King's
cutter at Portsmouth. Finding this not adventurous enough, he
returned to Jersey, and entered the service of Messrs. J. & C.
Hemery, who owned several privateers. In 1792 he was in command of the *Queen* and in 1798 of the *Herald*. James' *Naval
History* describes a fight of his on 25 Feb. 1798: — "As the
British privateer schooner, *Herald* of Jersey, Captain Thomas
Pickstock, was cruising off the Neapolitan coast, three French
privateers commenced a furious attack on her. Captain Pickstock by an animated address so inspirited the *Herald's* crew,
that after an action of three hours' duration the *Herald* beat off
all three of her opponents, leaving them with shattered hulls,
and a loss of thirty killed and wounded, while the British vessel
had the good fortune not to lose a man. The *Herald* was only
of 80 tons, and mounted ten guns, 3, 4 and 6 pounders, with a
complement of 28 men, whereas the largest of the French privateers mounted 5 long 18 pounders, and the other two 4 eight-
pounders each. The united crews of the three must have
amounted to at least 180 men. On the night of the action a
felucca with 22 men suddenly appeared alongside the *Herald*
with a view of carrying her by boarding, but a well-directed
broadside from the *Herald* sent the felucca and all on board to
the bottom. On his arrival at Naples Captain Pickstock received from all ranks the highest marks of attention. The Duke
of Sussex, who was then in Naples, twice honoured Capt.
Pickstock with an invitation to breakfast, and presented him
with a hanger of considerable value, marked with the initials of
his Royal Highness ; and one of the Prince's suite gave a pair
of pistols to the gallant privateersman. The latter also received
great attention from Sir William Hamilton, the British envoy.
The brave crew of the *Herald* did not pass unnoticed : as the
British merchants at Naples raised by subscription and distributed them 200 dollars". The hanger with the initials A.F.,
i.e. Augustus Frederick, is now in the S.J. Museum. In March
1799 the Jersey Chamber of Commerce subscribed 500 livres to
present a piece of plate to Captain Pickstock for rescuing the
brig *Princess Royal* from the hands of the enemy off the coast
of Newfoundland, but he never returned to Jersey to receive

the gift. In April 1800 he died of yellow fever at Surinam (Dutch Guiana). His son was for many years Judge of the Supreme Court in British Honduras. His daughter, Betty Jenny, became the mother of Henri Luce Manuel (q.v.). (*Guernsey and Jersey Magazine*, Jan. 1837).

PIPON, HENRY (1843—1924), Major-General. Governor of the Tower. Second son of Col. James Kennard Pipon, Seigneur of Noirmont, and Elizabeth, daughter of James Collier M.P. He joined the Royal Artillery from Woolwich in 1861. His first active service was during the Fenian Raid on Canada in 1866. During the Afghan Campaign of 1879—81 he served in the Royal Horse Artillery, and was present at the actions of Shutagandau and Charasia and the operations at Kabul. On the famous march to Kandahar he was Adjutant R.A., and took part in the Battle of Kandahar, receiving the medal with three clasps, the bronze star, and three mentions in despatches. From 1896 to 1900 he was Colonel on the Staff in Bengal, and in 1900 was made a Companion of the Bath. In 1900 and 1901 he commanded the R.A. in the China Field Force, and was again mentioned in despatches. This was his last active service. In 1903 he was appointed Assistant Inspector of Remounts at Headquarters and in 1905 Deputy Assistant Director. In 1909 he became Resident Governor (Major) of the Tower of London, living in the King's House, in which the Guy Fawkes conspirators were examined. He took the keenest interest in the historic buildings, which for the next fourteen years were under his care. He retired in 1923, and died on 14 Jan. 1924. He married Louisa Anne, daughter of Admiral Sir William Edmonstone, and had five daughters, Mary, Emma, Georgina, Evangeline, and Geraldine.

PIPON, JACQUES (1746—1814), Receiver-General. Second son of Thomas Pipon (son of Thomas, son of Jacques) of St. Aubin's and Anne, daughter of Michel Lempriere, Seigneur of

Diélament. Born in St. Aubin's in the house on the quay now called Amblève House in 1746, and baptized in St. Brelade's Church 22 March. He was the centre of the first big fight betwen the Charlots and Magots. His mother was a sister of Charles Lempriere (q.v.), the Charlot leader, but he married in 1767 Esther Dumaresq, sister of Jean Dumaresq (q.v.), leader of the Magots ; so he had links with both camps ; but he joined the Magots. On 11 Jan. 1772 he was appointed Receiver-General, an office which he held for nearly forty-three years. In 1776 he was elected Constable of St. Brelade's, and no one opposed his swearing-in. When however he was re-elected in 1779, the Court refused to administer the oath on the ground that the offices of Receiver and Constable were "egregiously incompatible". A new election was ordered, at which Pipon was re-elected by an increased majority. The Court then referred the question to the Privy Council and meanwhile ordered the senior Centenier to represent the parish in the States. But, when he took his seat, the Magots carried a motion that, as the Constable of St. Brelade's had not been summoned, the Assembly was incomplete, and could not proceed to business. Charles Lempriere, the Lieut.-Bailiff, retaliated by refusing to summon any more meetings of the States. This brought the business of the island to a standstill ; so General Conway, the Lieut.-Governor, appealed to Pipon, and he consented to stand aside, till the Council had given a decision. A new election was held, and his brother-in-law, Edouard Remon, became Constable. In Nov. 1781 the Council decided that the two posts of Constable and Receiver were not incompatible, and in 1782 Pipon was re-elected Constable. He was elected again in 1785, 1788, and 1791. He died 16 Sept. 1814, and was buried at St. Brelade's. He had four daughters, Anne who married Jacques Pipon (son of Thomas, son of Josué), Esther, who married Lieut. John Gordon R.N., Mary, who married Philip, son of Sir Jean Dumaresq. and Elizabeth, who married, (1) Peter Schooles (2) John Nesbit. [*Magasin de l'île de Jersey* 1784—5, *passim ; Collection of Petitions etc. relative to Political Differences.*]

PIPON, JOHN PAKENHAM (1849—1899) C.B., C.M.G. Captain R.N. Youngest son of Col. James Kennard Pipon, Seigneur of Noirmont, and Elizabeth, daughter of John Collier M.P. Born in Malta 10 Jan. 1849. Educated at Wellington College. He entered the Navy in 1862, obtained his commission as Sub-Lieutenant in 1868, and was promoted Lieutenant in 1872. He served as Lieutenant with the Naval Brigade during the expedition up the Perak River against the Malays (1875—6), and for this he obtained the Perak medal and clasp. He was Lieutenant on the Royal Yacht *Victoria and Albert* (1878—80), and was then promoted Commander. While Commander of the *Penelope* his ship took a leading part in the bombardment of Alexandria and the operations which followed in the Suez Canal (1882), and he received the Egyptian medal with clasp, the Khedive's bronze star, and the 3rd class of the Order of the Medjidie. As Commander of the *Ranger* (1884—7) he had some strenuous weeks in 1885 protecting with his guns the hard-pressed garrison of Suakin. During the Burmese War (1886—7) he commanded the Naval Brigade, and after the annexation "in subsequent operations against the Dacoits the *Ranger*, Commander Pipon, did long and arduous work. Three of his officers and Pipon himself patrolled the waters of Upper Burmah in steam launches for a considerable period, and had several skirmishes with Dacoits. Commander Pipon was deservedly promoted Captain. 1 Jan. 1887" (Clowes' *Royal Navy*). In 1890 he was appointed Captain of the *Magicienne*, and in the following year became British Consul at the Portuguese port of Beira in East Africa through which all the Mashonaland trade had to pass. Serious difficulties had arisen here both with the Portuguese and the Boers, and Pipon's work was rewarded by a C.M.G. In 1894 he was gazetted to the *Sirius*, and was the senior officer on the south-east coast of America, when British lives and property were endangered by the revolution in Rio de Janeiro. He received a C.B. at the Diamond Jubilee, and in 1899 was appointed A.D.C. to the Queen. The same year he became Captain of the *Caesar* on the Mediterranean station, but died in London 6 May, and was buried at Southsea. He married in 1881 Alice Elizabeth, daughter of Murray Johnson of Sandgate, and had two sons, who both entered the Navy, James Murray and Henry Cecil Brand. [*Bull.* VI ; *Times* 8.5.99.]

PIPON, JOSUE (1655—1728), Lieut.-Bailiff. Eldest son of
Edouard Pipon of La Moye, Constable of St. Brelade's and
Elizabeth, daughter of Daniel Gruchy, Rector of St. Mary's.
When he was accused of having begun life as a trooper, his
friends replied: — "He is a gentleman of good family, and had
University learning, and, being a person of capacity and merit,
was taken into favour by his Grace the Duke of Hamilton, and
commanded a troop of horse in the reign of King James II. It
is true he rid some time in his Lordship's troop, which is a Gentleman's post, and, his Grace having particular regard for him,
he was soon preferred to a commission. But the cares of his
estate requiring his presence in the island, he left the Service,
and was pitched upon by the Hon. Edouard De Carteret, then
Bailiff, to be Greffier" (*Answer to the Bailiff's Complaint*). He
apparently returned to the island about 1691, in which year he
married at St. Brelade's Elizabeth Dumaresq of des Augrès (not
Elizabeth Chevalier, as the *Armorial* says). In 1693 he was
elected Constable of St. Brelade's, and in 1694 was sworn in
as Greffier, an office which he held for six years. In 1695 the
Court decided that the posts of Greffier and Constable were
incompatible ; so he resigned his Constableship. In 1701 he
was elected a Jurat.

In 1702 his first wife died, and in the following year he married Elisabeth, widow of Philip Lempriere of Diélament, and
sister of Philippe Pipon (q.v.) of Noirmont. The latter was
Receiver-General, and in 1704 he leased to his new brother-in-
law the tithes of St. Mary's, which were part of the Crown
Revenue. A dispute arose over these tithes, and Philippe declared that he had been swindled out of £100. He could not deprive
Josué of them, for he had leased them for as long as they were
under his control. So he resigned all his rights over this parish,
and then persuaded the Governor, to whom they reverted, to
dismiss Josué. The quarrel became furious. When the two
men met in Town they drew swords, and had to be parted by
bystanders. One night Philippe with his brother and his brother-
in-law Thomas Pipon (q.v.) waylaid Josué and wounded him.
The feud lasted fourteen years, during which each man did his
utmost to injure the other.

Meanwhile Josué had become involved in a much wider
struggle. He was now the leading member of the States, and
three times was sent to England as the States' Deputy, once to

protest against the appointment of Custom House officers for
Jersey, once to urge the British Government to bring pressure
on France to remove its embargo on Jersey stockings, and once
to try to establish free trade between England and Jersey. He
was also leader of the Opposition to Sir Charles De Carteret
(q.v.), the Bailiff. In 1711 Sir Charles complained to the Privy
Council: — "Joshua Pipon, one of the Jurats, a person of ambitious and unquiet spirit and extremely desirous of power and
to be head of a Party, prevailed with four other Jurats, viz. John
De Carteret, Elias Dumaresq, John Durell, and Charles Poingdestre (all being cousins german of Pipon by marriage or otherwise), to combine with him in setting up the power of the Jurats,
derived from the People, against the Power of the Bailiff, derived
from her Majesty, and, having by threats and other indirect
means procured his brother-in-law Philip Dumaresq to be elected
a Jurat, he has thereby gotten a majority of the acting Jurats
into his Combination". In 1711 the Bailiff instructed the Lieut.-
Bailiff to nominate Thomas Pipon (q.v.) as Deputy Greffier,
but the majority of the Jurats refused to swear him in, and
"Joshua Pipon did in a seditious manner address himself in a
loud speech to the People telling them they had the privilege
of choosing their Judges, that the Bailiff was not of their putting
in, and that they ought to desire a deliverance from an arbitrary
and despotic power". On another occasion, when the Bailiff
fined an Advocate for interrupting the Court, "Pipon rose in a
very tumultuous manner, and in defiance of the Bailiff's authority ordered the Greffier not to record the fine, and a day or two
after, to encourage the Advocate in his further contempt of the
Bailiff, declared that the said Advocate should be protected by
the Court". The whole matter was thrashed out in 1713 before
the Privy Council, and Pipon won a notable victory. The verdict was "that the complaint be dismissed and Sir Charles
De Carteret do forthwith pay unto the defendants five
pounds" (O.C.).

In 1715 Sir Charles De Carteret died, and Lord Carteret, the
new Bailiff, appointed Pipon his Lieutenant. As Lord Carteret
never visited the island, for the next thirteen years Pipon presided
over the Court and the States. This appointment seems to have
been a wise one. He was just, tactful, and conciliatory. Old
enmities were laid aside. By Lord Carteret's efforts he even
became reconciled to his brother-in-law Philippe. In 1718 the

sore point of the £100 was submitted to the arbitration of the
Governor and Crown Officers, who decided that Josué had been
right. In 1720 Philippe wrote: — "Lord Carteret of his goodness has rescued us from our enemies, so that those who were
our greatest are now our friends. I speak of Mr. Pipon". The
chief difficulty that Josué had to cope with was a monetary crisis.
The high rate of exchange in France had drained the island of
gold and silver coins, and nothing was left but liards (half far-
things). This brought trade almost to a standstill. The difficulty was partially overcome by the issue in 1720 of paper notes
to the value of 50,000 *livres tournois*. The best act of his mag-
istrature was the prohibition of the sale of pauper children by
the Parishes to be exported to France. In 1722 with two partners he bought from Lord Carteret the Fief of Vingt Livres.
He died in 1738, and was buried at St. Brelade's on 21 July.
By his first wife he had two children, Anne (b. 1693) and Jean
(b. 1696), who became Greffier. By his second wife he had
eleven, Jeanne and Elisabeth (b. 1703), twins, who died young,
Elisabeth (b. 1704), Jeanne (b. 1706), Josué (b. 1707), who became Jurat and Lieut.-Bailiff, Thomas (b. 1709), Jacques (b.
1711), Rachel (b. 1712), Marie (b. 1714), Catherine (b. 1715), and
Edouard (b. 1717). [Letter Books of Philippe Pipon ; *Humble
Representation of Sir Charles Carteret* with *The Defendants
Answer to the Bailiff's Complaint* ; *Ordres du Conseil*.]

PIPON, PHILIPPE (1671—1726), Seigneur of Noirmont. Eldest
son of Elie Pipon of St Peter's and Jeanne Le Sueur. Born
1671. Though he never did anything outstanding, his career is
worth recording as an illustration of the life of a well-to-do
Jerseyman of the period. In 1693 he was a merchant in London,
dealing largely in Jersey stockings, in which, he says, the trade
was *extrêmement triste*. So he dyed 2,000 pairs, and sent them
to Lisbon, where they sold at a good profit. He then developed
this Portuguese business, sending out boats laden with stockings,
which returned with wine and raisins. He also did much miscellaneous business for friends in the island, including the paying
of school-fees for children at school in England. His own investments were not gilt-edged. He had for example high hopes

of a fortune from a silver mine in Devon. He carried through the long and complicated negotiations, by which his father in 1695 bought Noirmont Manor from Lord Carteret for £700 sterling.

In 1696 his father died, and Philippe inherited Noirmont. He also succeeded his father as Receiver-General. In Nov. 1699 he married Elisabeth, the young widow of Philippe De Carteret, Seigneur of Rozel, and daughter of James Carteret (q.v.), the New Jersey rebel. His home life seems to have been very happy, and his wife's letters are full of affectionate references to her husband. She backed him up loyally in all his struggles, and wrote long appeals for support to her De Carteret relations. Looking through his wife's papers he discovered that her father had been made a Landgrave in Carolina with a barony of 12,000 acres, and that through her American mother she was heiress to part of Manhattan Island (now the most valuable land in New York) ; but for thirty years this property had been unclaimed, and was now difficult to identify. For the rest of his life Pipon was making vain attempts to recover his wife's inheritance.

In 1700 he was elected Constable of St. Brelade's. He soon became entangled in a long series of bitter quarrels with his neighbours. The first was with Jean Le Couteur, who in 1701 complained to the Court that "his life was in danger from the blows and threats of Philippe Pipon, who had assaulted him on the highway" ; but Pipon had friends on the Bench, and the case was dismissed. In 1702 Le Couteur and his son were fined for libelling Pipon. In 1704 Le Couteur summoned him for "wresting by force a gun out of the hands of the Plaintiff's son, while he was shooting rabbits on ground of which Le Couteur senior is the undoubted proprietor". The Court decided that, as Seigneur, Pipon had exclusive shooting rights over the whole Fief ; but on Appeal the Privy Council reversed this judgement (O.C.). In 1705 Le Couteur challenged Pipon's right to appoint Charles Dumaresq Seneschal of his Seigneurial Court on the ground that he subfarmed from Pipon some of the Crown revenues. Dumaresq was a Jurat, and for the way he did this Le Couteur was ordered to ask pardon on his knees. He refused, and was imprisoned ; but the Privy Council liberated him. When Pipon appointed Philippe Anley Seneschal in 1715, Le Couteur refused to pay his dues, because Anley had been fined for smuggling wool into France. The Court decided in Pipon's favour, but again Le Couteur appealed. The case was not heard till 1617, and this time Le Couteur lost : but for four years the Seneschal had been unable to collect any dues.

Another feud was that with his distant cousin Josué Pipon (q.v.) of La Moye. It began with a quarrel over the St. Mary's tithes. Tithes in Jersey are part of the Crown Revenue, and Philippe as Receiver had leased to his cousin the tithes of that parish for as long as they were under his control. But a dispute arose about certain payments, and Philippe declared that he had been swindled out of £100. When later the question was submitted to arbitration, the Governor and Crown Officers decided that Josué was in the right ; but for fourteen years Philippe shouted to the world that this cousin was a rogue and a thief. To get his revenge Philippe resigned his rights over St. Mary's parish, and persuaded the Governor to whom they reverted to dismiss Josué. At least twice the cousins came to blows. Once, when Philippe was waiting for friends to escort him across the sands, as he was carrying a large sum of money, Josué arrived and bumped his horse into him and nearly dismounted him. Philippe struck the horse with his cane, and the two men, one a Jurat and the other the Receiver, sprang to the ground and drew their swords ; but bystanders separated them. On another occasion Philippe and some friends waylaid Josué, and in the scrimmage Philippe ran him through the arm with his sword. Edouard Carteret, Lord Carteret's brother, tried in vain to reconcile them. "Let him burn", wrote Philippe, "those memoirs which he has told me he keeps concerning me to leave to his children, as if to entail an everlasting hatred among us". In 1715 Philippe had the mortification of seeing his enemy appointed by Lord Carteret Lieut.-Bailiff. At last in 1718 Lord Carteret succeeded in persuading them to bury the hatchet.

A third feud was with Pierre Seale, whom Pipon describes as "a very strong-headed man who neither forgives nor forgets". He had been Constable 1690—3, and was Colonel of the South-West Regiment. In 1708 Seale raised the *clameur de haro*, because Pipon was building for himself a house, which blocked the approach to Belle Croute. When the Court delayed a decision, Seale appealed to the Privy Council. Then he complained to the Court that "on a Monday, the day when merchants gather on the Public Quay at St. Aubin's to transact business, Philippe Pipon arrived, boiling over with rage, and assailed the Plaintiff with abuse and calumny, and, having a sword at his side and a thick cane in his hand, he attacked the Plaintiff, who is an elderly man and had neither sword nor staff, and would have continued to strike until life had fled, if someone had not seized his arm. And not content with having beaten the Plaintiff almost senseless, he shook his cane saying, 'This cane has been used on many others, and will be on many more' ". The Court gave Pipon a week to reply, and he left the island. When he returned, Seale renewed the charge, and three years after the assault the case was heard ; but the Jurats were divided, and the Lieut.-Bailiff refused to give his casting vote. Seale appealed to the Council, who ordered the Court to settle the case. Five years after the assault Pipon was fined, but the Court disallowed Seale's claim that by the Coutumier of Normandy "If the Lord of a Manor lay violent hands upon his Vassal he shall lose all homage, rents and duties due to him". He appealed again, and eleven years after the original offence the case was still hanging fire, and Pipon was pleading that he was covered by the King's General Pardon. Meanwhile Seale had found a new point of attack. Pipon owned a house in St. Aubin's, and in 1716 Seale claimed that the steps leading to it were on his ground. Twice the Court viewed the property, and ordered the steps to be removed ; but, when Pipon tried to rebuild them on the other side, Seale again raised the *clameur de haro*.

It would be wearisome to follow all Pipon's quarrels. Many were due to his dogged determination to exact the uttermost farthing of his seigneurial rights. Once, when a ship was wrecked in Belle Croute, the Admiralty claimed it as a prize, but Pipon asserted that all wreckage belonged to him as Seigneur. Long before the matter was settled, the wreck had broken up, and was worthless to either party. He confessed that his perpetual litigation was partly his own fault, and pleaded in excuse his possession of "the Pipon temper". "I am sorry", he wrote to Edouard Carteret, "that the violentness and ungovernableness of my temper have been the occasion you could not befriend me as much as you could otherwise have done, but the fault was not wholly mine". He did however undoubtedly escape many of the penalties of his violence by the fact, while his wife lived, he had behind him the powerful De Carteret interest.

In 1710 he had a clash with one group of Jurats. "Philip

Pipon having without provocation grossly affronted three of the Jurats, the only three then in Court, the Bailiff and the Lieut.- Bailiff were often applied to for justice, which cause they protracted for months, and then transmitted to the Council, in order, as is supposed, to shelter Pipon from justice, in hopes that on account of the extraordinary charges they would drop their suits. The countenance given to the said Pipon hath encouraged him to further abusing. On 12 Oct. 1712 Sir Chas. Carteret (the Bailiff), instead of coming to Court to have justice done to the Jurats, chose rather to go to Pipon's house; and Pipon, coming back from the place, where he had entertained his guests, rode through a small town singing and roaring at the head of them, as if he had bid defiance to Justice" (*Case against Sir Chas. De Carteret*). Now however he overstepped the mark. He so outrageously insulted Jurat Dumaresq in Court, that he was sentenced to beg pardon on his knees ; and, when he refused, was committed to prison. He escaped this by appealing to the Council ; but his appeal was dismissed, and he was forced to return and make the humiliating apology.

In 1718 he hoped to become himself a Jurat. He wrote confidently that he was sure of a 500 majority, and, if Lord Carteret would recommend him, it would be over a thousand. Lord Carteret ordered the Lieut.-Bailiff to support Pipon's candidature, though he added, "I hope, if he secures this post, he will behave without passion, forgetting all the petty quarrels that have made him so many enemies". But the Bailiff's backing did him more harm than good. Voters resented Lord Carteret's interference, and Pipon was beaten by Michel Lempriere of Diélament by 1595 to 1382.

He was almost always in financial difficulties ; and he owned that, if Lord Carteret had not allowed his wife a pension, he could not have carried on. As Receiver he was constantly apologizing to the Governor for being in arrears. He said that he received his dues in liards, which were worthless in England, and no other coins were obtainable. But the trouble was not only difficulty in transmission. When Sir Thomas Jermyn, the Governor, died in 1703, he left to the Poor of the island all the money due to him that was still in Pipon's hands. This amounted to £682 sterling. But the Constables found it very hard to get this out of him. In 1707 he still owed them £136 (*A.E.*). At last General Lumley, the new Governor, grew so dissatisfied that in 1716 a new Receiver was appointed. In 1722 Pipon had to fly from the island for a time to escape his creditors ; and, when he died, his son wrote, "The small estate, which he has left, is overwhelmed with debts".

After many attempts to recover his wife's inheritance through agents in America, he set out in 1724 for New York to look into things for himself. But he returned in 1725 unsuccessful. "There is no justice", he wrote, "to be expected from these gentlemen". His son wrote later: — "Ever since my father's return he has been in a decaying and languishing condition". One ambition however was gratified. In April 1725 he was elected a Jurat. But he did not live long. His stormy life ended in a characteristic fashion. He dropped dead on 6 June 1726 in the midst of a violent quarrel with his brother, the Constable of St. Peter's, about money which his brother had advanced to pay Philippe's son James's expenses at Caen University. He was buried in St. Brelade's Church. Of his ten children seven survived him, James, who succeeded him as Seigneur and became a Jurat, Elie who settled in New York, Philippe, Jean, Jeanne, Delaval, and Louise. [The S.J. Library possesses many manuscripts concerning him, including four Letter Books into which he copied every important letter that he wrote. See also Notice sur la Famille Pipon in *Bull.* VI and *Groans of the Inhabitants of Jersey*.]

PIPON, PHILIP GOSSET, C.B. (1824—1905), General. 4th son of James Pipon, Seigneur of Noirmont, Commissary-General H.M.F., and Elizabeth Dobbyn, daughter of Nathaniel Hodges. Born at Noirmont Manor, 11 April, 1824; died at La Motte House, St. Helier, 3 Nov., 1905; and buried at St. Saviour's. He was educated at St. Mannelier School, and then went to Woolwich. In 1842 he entered the Royal Artillery, and his battery went to Canada, where he married in 1849 Sophia, daughter of John Ashworth, Deputy Assistant Commissary-General of Quebec. On his return to Europe he was stationed at Fort George in Scotland, and was then sent to the Crimea, taking part in the whole campaign from 1854 to 1856. For this he received the Crimean medal with 3 clasps, the Turkish and

Sardinian medals, and also the order of the Medjidie. His next
post was Ceylon, whence he returned with his family via
the Cape in 1864. The next few years he spent in Canada, and
was awarded the Fenian medal for the part he played in the
suppression of that raid in 1866. In 1870 he was in Ballincolig,
near Cork, and in 1874 went to Barrackpore as Colonel commanding a Brigade. He received the C.B. for his services, and
returned from India in 1876 to Woolwich, where he held the
post of Inspector and Purchaser of Horses for the Artillery for
five years. On his retirement in 1881 with the Rank of General,
he settled in Jersey with his family at La Motte House. His
wife predeceased him in 1897. He left two sons, both of whom
settled and married in Canada, and two daughters who died in
Jersey in 1939 and 1940. [*Bull.* VI.]

PIPON, PHILIPPE (1771–1829), Captain R.N. Son of Thomas
Pipon of La Moye, Attorney-General (q.v.), and Jeanne Pipon.
Born at St. Brelade's 14 June 1771. He entered the Navy, and
served under Admiral Russell on the *Diana*. Though only a
middy he was entrusted by the Admiral in 1792 (perhaps because
of his knowledge of French) with the delicate task of landing
at San Domingo, and demanding from the French Revolutionary
Government, that was then in power, the life of a British Officer, whom they had condemned to death. In 1801 he was in
command of a force of boats, that rowed into the harbour of
Corunna, boarded the *Neptuno*, a new Spanish man-of-war of
20 guns, a gun-boat, and a merchant vessel, and towed them out
to sea under a heavy fire. Admiral Cornwallis wrote in warm
terms of "the merits of Lieutenant Pipon, who directed the
enterprise with most becoming spirit and address". He was
promoted Commander in 1802, and appointed to the *Kite*. He
was again mentioned in dispatches for sailing into the harbour
at Granville during Admiral Saumarez' bombardment, and silenc-
ing the guns that were threatening to destroy Saumarez' flagship, which had grounded on a shoal. Later he commanded
the *Rose*, and was advanced to post rank in 1808, and appointed
to the *Daphne*. For the next five years he was employed in the
Baltic, and then sailed in command of the *Tagus* to the South

American station. Here in June 1814 after a 250 miles' chase
he overhauled the new French frigate, the *Cérés,* on her first
cruise, shot away her mainmast, and added her to the British
Navy. He then rounded Cape Horn in search of an American
frigate that was harrying our whalers. On this voyage he
visited Pitcairn Island, and found the descendants of the Mutiny
of the *Bounty.* In 1824 he was appointed to the *Britannia,* and
then his name drops out of the Navy List. He died in Jersey
on 7 Dec. 1829, and was buried at St. Brelade's. He married
Elizabeth, daughter of Sir John Dumaresq, in 1802, and had two
sons, Philippe (b. 1811) and Robert (b. 1814). [Marshall's *Royal
Naval Biography* ; James' *Naval History of Great Britain.*]

PIPON, THOMAS (1678—1735), Constable of St. Brelade's.
Son of Jacques Pipon of St. Aubin's and Jeanne Le Brocq. He
was baptized in St. Brelade's Church on 5 March 1678. According to a statement before the Privy Council he was "bred
up to the sea", but later settled as a merchant in St. Aubin's.
Between the Pipons of Noirmont and the Pipons of La Moye
there was a bitter feud. Thomas belonged to the La Moye
branch, his father having been a younger son of Jurat Thomas
Pipon of La Moye; but in 1705 he married Susanne, sister of
Philippe Pipon of Noirmont, and henceforth always sided with
his brother-in-law. In 1708 he succeeded his brother as Constable of St. Brelade's, and held office till 1713. A fierce quarrel was now raging between his brother-in-law and Jean Le
Couteur (See article *Pipon, Philippe),* and Thomas got involved in it. An Act of the Ecclesiastical Court in Dec. 1708
declares that "Thomas Pipon, while selling as Constable the
corn due to the poor and the trésor in St. Brelade's Church at
the close of Divine Service, presumed to insult, abuse, and
slander Jean Le Couteur in a most outrageous manner, and even
enforced his abuse with oaths, thus profaning the Church and
causing great scandal in the parish. The said Pipon, having
argued at length on many preliminary points, withdrew declining
to recognize the authority of the Court, though ordered to remain
and hear his sentence. He is therefore excommunicate". On
the following Sunday his sentence was read from the pulpit:

"He is severed from the Body of Christ as a septic limb *(un membre pourry)* and all the faithful are commanded to shun his company". This had the curious result of excluding him not only from the Church Services but from the Parish Assemblies, which were then always held in Church. At the following Easter the Ecclesiastical Court refused to swear in the St. Brelade's Churchwardens, because an excommunicated man, the Constable, had voted at their election.

In 1710 he joined his two brothers-in-law Philippe and Jean in waylaying one night his cousin Jurat Josué Pipon (q.v.) on his way back from Town, and wounding him with a sword. Thomas was arrested, but Philippe slipped out of the island, and his friends on the Bench postponed the trial till he should return. In 1711 Thomas became the cause of a constitutional crisis. The Greffier had to leave the island on business, and it became necessary to appoint a Deputy to take his place. The Bailiff, Sir Charles De Carteret (q.v.), instructed the Lieut.-Bailiff, Charles De Carteret of Trinity, to nominate Pipon. The majority of the Jurats refused to accept him, as he was a defendant awaiting trial, and knew nothing of Court procedure; but the Lieut.-Bailiff walked out of Court, thus closing the proceedings. The following week the same thing happened. At the third meeting of the Court, when the Lieut.-Bailiff and three Jurats left, the other Jurats remained and swore in Edouard La Cloche, the Registrar, who had acted as Deputy-Greffier several times before. The Bailiff indignantly appealed to the Privy Council, who decided that "such person as the Bailiff shall appoint be sworn in". So Pipon took the oath. La Cloche however then refused to give up the books, and a new lawsuit was begun to recover them. Before this was tried however the real Greffier returned and resumed his duties.

PIPON, THOMAS (1756–1801), Compiler of the 1771 Code. Son of Jurat Josué Pipon of La Moye and Rachel Hocquard. Born 1756. In 1761 he was sworn in as Advocate, and in 1768 was appointed one of the two trustees of the new General Hospital. When Colonel Bentinck was sent to Jersey after the riot of 1769, one task given him was "to select a proper Collection of the most useful and necessary Laws out of that immense Chaos of them now confusedly scattered through the many Books of the States and the different Courts, to be established by way of a permanent system for the Political Government of the country, by which means every individual will know how to regulate his Conduct, and be no more obliged to live in continual dread of becoming liable to punishments for disobeying Laws it was morally impossible for him to have knowledge of" (*A.E.*). Bentinck appealed to the States to appoint someone with a good knowledge of local law to help him, and they selected Pipon. He borrowed the manuscripts of Philippe Le Geyt (q.v.), and by their help and by piecing together Orders in Council, Acts of the Court, *Règlements* of the States, precedents from cases decided in Court, and fragments from the old *Coutumier* of Normandy, he produced the first Code of Jersey Law. Bentinck said, "I cannot without ingratitude pass by doing justice to Mr. Pipon's superior judgement and indefatigable application with the most anxious zeal for the true interest of his native country, as I have experienced daily the strongest proofs of them during the whole course of this very laborious task" (*A.E.*). On 6 Sept. 1770 Bentinck presented the Code to the States, and after much discussion it was sent up on 20 Oct. to the Privy Council for approval. In Dec. the States appointed Pipon their Deputy to explain the Code to the Council, allowing him a guinea a day for his expenses. On 28 March 1771 the Council approved the Code, and declared that "all other Laws heretofore made in the Island shall be henceforward of no force and validity" (*O.C.*) Pipon was rewarded for his work by being made Attorney-General. He was sworn in on 4 April.

In 1770 he was Captain of the La Moye Company of the South-West Regiment of the Militia, and in 1778 became Colonel of the Regiment. When the French invaded Jersey in 1781, Corbet (q.v.), the Lieut.-Governor, was captured, and sent for Pipon as senior Crown Officer to sign with him the capitulation. Pipon however ignored the message, and led his regiment to St. Helier's. In the battle which followed they charged up Broad Street into the Market Place (now the Royal Square), and played a leading part in the victory.

In 1786 the Magot Party appealed to the Privy Council for leave to establish Trial by Jury in civil and criminal cases. After much correspondence the Council, bewildered by the intricacies of Jersey Law, in 1789 commissioned four Jerseymen, of whom Pipon was one, to draw up a statement of the actual procedure in the Jersey Courts (*A.E.*). The result was two valuable reports, one by Pipon and John Thomas Durell (*Statement of the Mode of Proceeding in the Royal Court of Jersey*), representing the Charlot point of view, the other by Jurat James Hemery and Jean Dumaresq (q.v.), representing that of the Magots. In 1797 Pipon was sent as Deputy of the States to the Privy Council to support various Acts dealing with tumultuous assemblies, taverners, and the duty on spirits. In Jan. 1801 he was appointed Lieut.-Bailiff; but he died in Dec., and was buried on 11 Dec. at St. Brelade's. He married Jeanne, daughter of Thomas Pipon of St. Aubin's, and had ten children, of whom Josué became Solicitor-General, James Receiver-General, John Constable of St. Peter's and Philip Captain in the Navy. [Authorities quoted above.]

PIQUET JOHN (1825—1912), Local Botanist. Son of Jean Piquet and Elizabeth Le Marquand. Born at St. Helier's, 16 March 1825. He was apprenticed, when 12 years old, to John Ereaut, chemist in St. Helier's, and after five years' apprenticeship stayed on as assistant for another five, his hours being from 6.30 a.m., to 11 p.m., the whole ten years without a holiday. In 1847 he opened a chemist's shop of his own, and this business continued till his death. His chief hobby was Botany. Between 1855 and 1865 he made a collection of Jersey seaweeds, which he presented to Dr. Henri Van Heurck of Antwerp, when the latter was writing his *Prodome de la Flore des Algues Marines des Iles Anglo-Normandes*. He became the recognized authority on local flowering plants and ferns, accompanying English botanists when they visited the island. In 1896 the Société Jersiaise published his *Phanerogamous Plants and Ferns of Jersey*, a list of 721 species, exclusive of varieties ; which was followed by a supplement in 1898 of 24 more species. All had been collected by himself. He was one of the Founders of the Jersey Swimming Club, and continued to bathe in the open sea in summer till he was 86. He died on 5 Sept. 1912, and was buried in Mont à l'Abbé Cemetery. [*Journal of Botany*. December 1912.]

POINDEXTER, JOHN (1609—1691). 2nd son of Edouard
Poindexter of the Fief ès Poingdestre (Grainville Branch) and
Pauline Ahier. Born at Swan Farm, just behind Grainville,
St. Saviour's, in 1609. Died at St. Saviour's on 2 Sept. 1691,
and buried in the Church. He entered Pembroke College, Cambridge, as sizar in 1626, and in 1628 obtained a grant from the
Don Baudains ; he took his B.A. degree in 1630, and his M.A.
in 1633. He then went to Exeter College, Oxford, as Gentleman
Commoner, from Oct. 9 1635 to Nov. 1636, and was admitted
as a Jersey Fellow of Exeter on 14 Aug. of that year. According
to the Journal of Benjamin La Cloche he was tutor to the children of the Earl of Pembroke in 1636, and, whilst tutor, in 1638
he gave to St. Saviour's Church, of which his younger brother,
Thomas, became Rector in June of that year, two silver cups for
Holy Communion (*Bull*. II). In 1641 he was ordained Deacon
at York. He was with Sir Philippe de Carteret in Elizabeth
Castle during the siege in 1643.

In 1648 he was expelled from his Fellowship, because he was
a Royalist ; but the pretext given was his long absence. (Boase,
Register Exon). In 1651, when the Parliamentary forces reoccupied the island, he was with Sir George Carteret (q.v.) in
Elizabeth Castle. Carteret sent him to Paris to ask for instructions from the King. After four weeks he returned with orders
to make the best terms possible (*Bull* II). He helped to draw up
the conditions of surrender. He seems to have lived quietly in
Jersey under Parliamentary rule. He rejected Hyde's suggestion
that he should act as Latin Secretary to the exiled King. He
was godfather to a baby in St. Saviour's Church in 1654. John
Gibbon, the antiquary and herald, cousin of the Parliamentary
Governor, consulted him. In 1656 the Council of State referred
a legal case to him as an expert in Jersey Law. From 1656 to
1657 he was one of the Procureurs for the Parish of St.
Saviour's.

At the Restoration he returned to Oxford, staying with the
Warden of Merton and tutoring the son of the Earl of Carnar-
von. In 1669 he was appointed Lieut.-Bailiff. He had stipulated with Sir Edward de Carteret to be his Lieutenant, and,
since to be qualified he must be a Jurat, a Sign Manual was
issued recommending his election. Owing to an alleged infor-
mality (*Armorial*) he retired from the position of Lieut.-Bailiff
in 1676, but remained a Jurat.

He wrote (1) *Caesarea or a Discourse of the Island of Jersey*, the original of which is in the British Museum, the Harleian Collection, No. 5417. It was presented by Poindexter to James II. Falle (q.v.) drew largely from it for his *Account of Jersey*. It was published by the Soc. Jers. in 1889. (2) *Les Commentaires sur l'Ancienne Coutume de Normandie*, edited by the Société des Gens de Droit, and published with a life of Poindexter by E.T. Nicolle in 1907. (3) *Les Lois et Coutumes de l'Ile de Jersey* (Soc. des Gens de Droit 1928). (4) *Remarques et animadversions sur la Nouvelle Coutume de Normandie* (Unpublished).

Falle in his *Account of Jersey* says of Poindexter: "He was esteemed one of the best Grecians in the University, able to restore and give a new edition of Hesychius, the Lexicographer, which was long expected from him. The beautifullest Greek types of the Stephens scarce excelled his handwriting in that language. It was, indeed, a disadvantage to him to act on so narrow a Theatre as this little Island, where he had not scope to exert his talents ; yet even that makes for his honour, as on the contrary nothing can be more despicable than a man placed in a large scene of action and wanting capacity to fill it with dignity".

Some of his emendations of the Greek poets still exist in MS. (*Armorial* 322), Poindexter's monument is in St. Saviour's Church with an inscription in Latin, probably by Falle: — "In omni scientiarum genere eruditissimus utriusque praesertim juris peritissimus, Graecanicis literis ita doctus, ut priscis illis Athenis oriundum natum diceres—Regiis Partibus semper addictissimus".

He married in 1659 Anne, daughter and co-heiress of Laurens Hamptonne, Vicomte of Jersey, and left one son and one daughter. [Authorities mentioned above.]

POINGDESTRE, CHARLES HENRY (1829—1905), President of the British Academy at Rome. Son of John Henry Poingdestre and Caroline Harris Poingdestre. Born in St. Helier's 1829, and baptized in the Town Church 20 March. For more than thirty years he lived and worked in the Via Babuino, Rome and for twenty years was President of the British

Academy there, the famous Art School, founded by Sir William Hamilton, when he was Minister in Naples, and endowed by George IV and Queen Victoria. His favourite subjects were scenes from Italian peasant life or from the wild life of the Campagna, e.g. buffaloes trying to escape from the flies among the reeds and bulrushes. Among his Royal Academy pictures were *A Sketch in the Farmyard* (1850), *The Road from the Marble Quarries* (1862), *The Quarries at Carrara* (1871), *The Valley of the Anio* (1872), *An Unfortunate Recognition* (1873), *The Roman Cattle-Market* (1873), *Flies* (1875). He then exhibited every year till 1901. He was a well-known figure in Rome, to be seen any night in the Caffè Greco, the great resort of artists, sitting with his hat tilted over his eyebrows, siping his *caffè nero*. The *Athenaeum* described him as "a man of very taciturn and reserved temperament, but a worthy friend to all artists in need". He frequently visited Jersey, and some of his Academy pictures were painted at 7 Royal Crescent: e.g. *The Poultry Market at Rome* (1880), *An Italian Fair* (1884), *A Continental Express* (1887). The last, which depicts some donkey boys, was presented by him to the Société Jersiaise. He also painted some charming pictures of Jersey scenery. In his old age he settled in Sussex, and produced delightful landscapes of the Arun valley and the neighbourhood of Arundel. He died quite suddenly in Victoria Mansions, London, 26 Oct. 1905. Lord Portsea has a fine collection of his pictures.

POULET, SIR AMIAS, Governor. See Appendix I.

POULET, SIR ANTHONY (1562—1600), Governor. Builder of Elizabeth Castle. Second son of Sir Amias Poulet, Governor (q.v. App. I), and Margaret, daughter of Anthony Hervey. The Commissioners, Pyne and Napper, state that he was "born in the island". Before he was twenty-one he was Captain in Elizabeth's Guard. He came of age in 1583, and married Kateryn, only daughter of Sir Henry Norris of Rycote, who had been Elizabeth's guardian during the reign of Mary. In the same year on 17 Aug. his father made him Lieut.-Governor, to replace his uncle, George, who had been appointed Bailiff. Eighteen months later Sir Amias was sent to be custodian of Mary, Queen of Scots, and never returned to Jersey. For five years Anthony was in sole charge. This was a grave responsibility for so young a man. Elizabeth's aid to French Huguenots and Netherland rebels had brought England to the verge of war with both France and Spain. The Governor of Guernsey wrote : — "These islands will be attempted and taken, unless great regard be had to them. This is resolved both by the French and Spanish Kings to make them places of magazine to annoy England" (S.P.D.) ; and Anthony secured from the Privy Council munitions, men, and money. But with the scattering of the Armada this anxiety seemed for the moment to have passed.

Internal squabbles however caused even greater difficulties. In 1587 he got drawn into a dispute between his uncle the Bailiff and three Jurats (See *Poulet, George,* Ap. I and *De Carteret, Jean).* The latter as a climax to their quarrel were collecting signatures for a petition to the Queen, asking for the abolition of the Cour Extraordinaire, alleging that the Bailiff transferred cases there, because he got higher fees. Anthony imprisoned the three Jurats in Mont Orgueil for attacking a constituted Court and petitioning the Queen without first approaching the Governor and States. His act was definitely unconstitutional. He had no power to imprison without trial. His father wrote to the Bailiff : — "I wish that my son and you had taken another course. I do not find it felony or treason that the inhabitants should make a complaint to Her Majesty and procure the signs of such as are grieved. I think my son was ill-advised and worse counselled, when he committed these men to prison, for he exceeded the bounds of his commission, which forbiddeth to imprison, but only in martial matters. These things belong to you and the Justices, and not to the Lieutenant, whose place is to see your orders executed, and not to make himself a party" (Letter in Le Geyt).

This case aroused such indignation, that, when Sir Amias died in 1588, a strong effort was made to prevent Anthony from becoming his successor. "The people", wrote the Rector of St. Brelade's, "were divided into contrary parties, one saying that they would have my Lord Seymour for Governor, the other Mr. Anthony Poulet" (*Le Geyt*). "The Justices and the States", said the Royal Commissioners, "with uniform consent dispatched one of the Court for Anthony Poulet to be Governor" (*id*). The leader on the other side was Jean De Carteret (q.v.) of Vinchelez de Haut. He had just been released from the Marshalsea Prison, where he had been lying for contempt of court, and had reached the coast on his way home, when he heard of the death of Sir Amias. He hurried back to London, and laid before the Council a series of charges against Anthony, which they decided to be "injurious and slanderous and proceeding from some former spleen", and he was sent back to the Marshalsea, "till he submit to their Lordships and Anthony Poulet" (*id*). By letters from prison he stirred up a great agitation in Jersey. "Carteret and his confederates combined themselves into a new league and solicited from house to house to seek by petition for some other to be Captain. What insolent behaviour, riding, and assembling to alienate the subjects' minds from obedience to Her Majesty's Lieutenant! They made themselves patrons of the lewd and unruly people within the Isle, so that the Lieutenant was forced to keep his Guards about him" (Commissioners' Report). Nevertheless in 1590 Anthony was appointed Governor, though he had to pay a stiff price for the post. Among the Hatfield MSS. one runs : — "20 Feb. 1590. Sir Anthony Poulet grants unto Her Majesty a yearly rent of £300 charged upon divers manors of his in Devon, Somerset, and Dorset, during such time as he shall enjoy the office of Governor of Jersey and all the profits thereof". He was sworn in before the Royal Court on 4 July.

Meanwhile De Carteret had returned again to the attack, and sent to the Council a fresh list of eighteen accusations, of which the most serious were that Anthony had sold cannon from Mont Orgueil for his own profit, and that, when the Armada was preparing, he had sold corn to Spain. The Council decided that these must be investigated on the spot, and sent to Jersey Dr. Tertullian Pyne and Robert Napper as Royal Commissioners. Their Report, issued on 15 March 1590, was a complete vindication of Poulet. The cannon proved to be obsolete ones discarded long before by a Royal Commission, and bought by his father as scrap iron. The corn was only a ton that he had put on a Jersey boat sailing to Bayonne, which the captain was to sell

there, and bring home trinkets for Mrs. Poulet ; but a storm had
driven the boat into San Sebastian, where the Spaniards had
forced it to unload. The other charges proved equally frivolous,
and De Carteret was forced by the Council to make an abject
public apology, "promising that hereafter I will lay aside all
malice and factions, and behave myself as becomes a dutiful
subject toward the Magistrate set in authority by the Queen"
(Le Geyt).

   In 1592 the Spanish danger flared up again. Twice the St.
Martin's churchwardens entered in their accounts : "For candles
burnt in church during the alarm about the Spaniards". In July
1593 Poulet wrote to Lord Burghley : — "What we most heark-
en after is what the Spanish fleet doth. It is thought they will
come to take Paimpol, which is but twelve leagues from us.
If they come so near, it is not unlike these isles shall be visited,
which maketh us stand on our guard" (*Hatfield MSS*). But
again the peril passed. About this time Poulet's tendency
toward highhandedness once more got him into trouble. In the
same letter to Burghley he said : — "One of our English Soldiers
was so bruised by a very bad fellow of this isle that the poor man
lived not above nine days after ; whereupon action is intended
against the offender, who deserveth no favour in so vile and
notorious an act. I hear he intendeth to be a suitor for a
pardon from Her Majesty. All honest men of the Isle desire
greatly to see exemplary punishment done upon this evil member" (*Hatfield MSS*). The Council asked for further particulars
about the culprit, Michel Poingdestre. Poulet replied : — "He
is hated generally throughout the Isles, for his cruel conversation
and corrupt dealing, even from his youth. Though he hath
gone about to produce testimony of good behaviour, it is manifest
that those who signed are bad and vile people. The man is of
wealth, and the Lord having by virtue of his indictment put both
lands and goods into Her Majesty's hands, I hope she will
advise to bestow this escheat rather upon the strengthening of
this place than permit so evil a member to enjoy it" (*id*). But
a letter from the Council then gave the story as stated by
Guillemyne, Poingdestre's wife : — "Her husband by chance
meeting Robins, a soldier, while gathering a herb called Wracke,
as the inhabitants are yearly accustomed to do, on occasion of
speech falling out, though one understood not the other, the
soldier, presuming on his youth and strength, took Poingdestre,

who was aged about 75 years, suddenly by the neck. But his foot slipt, and he had the fall without any apparent hurt, as he himself confessed. A few days after the soldier dying, occasioned by evil diet or some other like cause, Poingdestre is by malicious practice indicted. Good testimony is exhibited of the continual peaceable conversation of this old man, and that there was no secret malice betwixt the parties, never having seen each other before. It is very unprobable that a man of his years would attempt revenge on so lusty a young soldier". The Queen was present at the Council and was "in pity much moved with this poor old man's distress". Poulet was ordered to release him immediately on bail, and to take no further proceedings, till he had sent a further report (O.C.). Five weeks later another Order in Council rebuked Poulet for still keeping Poingdestre in prison, adding, "He is not such an evil man as you writ, being, we are informed, of long time employed by yourself as farmer of the tithes. We have cause to think this matter more hardly carried against him than is conscionable. We straitly command you not to proceed further in this cause, till we be better informed. You shall be directed from here. In the mean time set him at liberty on good bail, and suffer him to have possession of his lands and goods" (O.C.). Poulet then climbed down, and wrote : — "I rather wish Poingdestre's conversion than his overthrow. I do not seek his blood, but shall be glad if the Queen will pardon him, provided his wilfulness be bridled" (S.P.D.). In 1594 he was infuriated by the failure of a small experiment. He brought over a number of hares from England, and released them in the island, hoping they would breed (Bull II), but, in spite of stringent prohibitions by the Royal Court, the local sportsmen exterminated the lot.

His great work however was fortification. His father and grandfather had spent large sums in strengthening Mont Orgueil, and at first he continued this. Paul Ivy, a military engineer, was sent over to help him. The fourth gateway still shows the arms of Elizabeth and the date 1593 with the Poulet arms on one side and Anthony's on the other, impaled with those of his wife, Kateryn Norris, and the initials APL : KN. But Ivy had come to feel that their work was wasted. In Aug. he wrote to Lord Burghley : — "Were it not for the loss of the great charges Her Majesty hath bestowed upon this place, I durst not be of opinion that one penny should be bestowed upon it, for it is so evil-situated a place as it cannot possibly be worse" (*Hatfield MSS.*). On receiving this the Council wrote to Poulet: — "We have been informed that the Castle is very ill-seated, and lieth subject to a mighty hill but 400 feet distant, and so overtopt by it, that no man possibly can show his face in defence of this side next the hill, which giveth us good cause to think Her Majesty's charges already employed to be to small purpose. We therefore require you to deal with Mr. Ivy, and, having his advice, to consider what were meet to be done, that neither Her Majesty nor the inhabitants be put to any idle expense" (*Nicolle*). After further correspondence the Council decided (March 1594) "not to be at any further charge in fortifying the Old Castle", but to concentrate all resources on building a new one on the Islet off St. Helier's (*Hatfield MSS*). This was no new idea. In 1550 the Council had ordered "the making of a bulwark on the Islet according to a plan sent unto you" (*O.C.*). The project had been revived at the time of the Spanish Armada (*A.E.*), but nothing had been done. But now Poulet and Ivy tackled the task vigorously. The Queen contributed £500, the States £400, and agreed to provide at least 100 workmen. They began work even before the final Order was received, for in July 1593 Poulet was asking for "a warrant to the Woodward of Hampshire for 100 tons of oak, a warrant to take up lime about Portsmouth, and a warrant to press a causeyman" to make a causeway between the Islet and the shore (*Hatfield MSS*). By July 1594 such good progress had been made, that he was asking for "men and munitions for the new Fort, it being high time the place was munitioned and guarded" (*id.*). But perhaps it had been pressed forward too rapidly, for in July 1596 he reports that "the great abundance of waters which have fallen this summer did make ruins to the new Fort", and a later memorandum showed that a large amount of munitions and clothing had been spoilt by the flooding of the cellars (*id.*). But the work went forward, and was almost finished by the time of Poulet's death, though extensions were made by later Governors. His arms, impaling those of his wife, are at the side of Queen Elizabeth's gate.

In 1595 he asked to go to England "to give account of his two years' service", and on this visit he was knighted ; but, though only thirty-three, his health had begun to fail. In March 1596 he sent Sir Robert Cecil a note "scribbled in London"

regretting that he was unable to wait on him "by reason of some
infirmity" (id.). He returned to Jersey ; but in Nov. he wrote
from Somerset that he was "unable from illness to undertake the
journey" to London (id.). In May 1597 he wrote again that he
had started to take ship for Jersey, when an infirmity to which
he had been subject for three years took such hold upon him
that it was only with great difficulty that he reached his home at
Hinton (id.). He did get to Jersey later ; but in Aug. he writes,
"Having spent this summer upon my charge here, though with
difficulty and impairment of health, and finding my health
requires counsel of a physician, which this place does not afford, against my will I beg you to obtain my licence to return to
England for some time" (S.P.D.). In Aug. 1599 he writes that
the Queen has ordered him to stay in Somerset, till he is fully
recovered (Hatfield MSS). On 22 July 1600 he died, and was
buried at Hinton St. George beneath a sumptuous Renaissance
tomb (Photograph in Proceedings of Somerset Arch. Sy Vol.
LXXIV) with life-size effigies of Sir Anthony in plate-armour
with a six-inch beard, moustache, and curly locks, and his wife
in Elizabethan Court-dress with Paris head-dress richly decorated
with jewels and pearls ; on the sides of the tomb are figures
of their ten children kneeling in prayer. These were John (q.v.),
who became Lord Poulet, Amyas, Henry, Thomas, who died
when twenty, Philip, Elizabeth, Anne, Margery, who married
John Sydenham of Combe, Somerset, Susannah, who married
Sir Peter Prideaux of Netherton, Devon, and Margaret. [State
Papers Domestic ; Calendar of Hatfield MSS. ; Manuscripts
of Le Geyt ; Ordres du Conseil ; Actes des Etats ; Nicolle's
Mont Orgueil ; Collins' Peerage.]

POULET, GEORGE, Bailiff.   See Appendix I.

POULET, SIR HUGH, Governor.   See Appendix I.

POULET, JOHN, Dean. See Appendix I.

POULET, LORD JOHN (1586—1649), Cavalier. Eldest son
of Sir Anthony Poulet (q.v.) and Kateryn Norris. Born 1586.
As his father became Lieut.-Governor in 1583, and apparently
did not leave the island for the next six years, John was almost
certainly born in Jersey, though this cannot be proved, as the
Town Church Registers only begin in 1596, and the Register
of St. George's, Mont Orgueil, is lost. His father died, when
he was fourteen. He matriculated at University College, Oxford,
in 1601, but did not graduate. In 1603 he obtained a licence to
travel abroad. He became a Cavalry Colonel in 1608, and in
1610 entered as a Student of the Middle Temple. In the same
year he was elected M.P. for Somerset at a by-election, but
three months later this Parliament was dissolved. Poulet's
family seat was in the village of Hinton St. George, Somerset.
Edmund Peacham, the Rector, who had been appointed by
Poulet's grandfather, was an outspoken Puritan. Already in
1603 he had been accused of "uttering in a sermon seditious
and railing words against the King" (S.P.D.). In 1614 he was
again arrested for high treason. Poulet, as patron of the living,
was suspected of complicity, and was twice examined before the
Council, but managed to clear himself.

In 1618 he was Sheriff of Somerset, and in 1621 M.P. for Lyme
Regis. In 1625 Charles I visited him at Hinton, and at the
King's request Poulet entertained for nearly a year the defeated
Huguenot Admiral, the Duc de Soubise. In 1627 he was created
Baron Poulet, and took his seat in the House of Lords. Immediately after this however he was in trouble again. To provide
money for the Fleet the King resolved to disafforest Neroche
Forest near Ilminster, of which Poulet was Keeper. A letter
from the King states: — "A rumour of this has stirred up some
of the underkeepers to raise opposition, and they stick not to say
that his Lordship doth animate them herein. The King is not
apt to believe every report, and would be glad to believe better
things of Lord Poulet. Take knowledge that this is the King's
own words, intended for the service of the commonwealth,
wherein he requires Lord Poulet's assistance, and shall measure
his affection by the success of the business" (S.P.D.).

The storm however blew over. Letters in *S.P.D.* show him living in Hinton with occasional visits to London, sending presents of Cheddar cheese to his friends in Town. He still kept in touch with Jersey. In 1629 he wrote to Lord Dorchester, "begging his favour for Sir Philippe De Carteret (q.v.) and that poor island, and Mr. Louveraine, the preacher, now in England, also one more of that island, Jean Nicolle (q.v.), some of whose countrymen conjecture that he has less credit with you than he used to have" (*S.P.D.*). Five months later he wrote again sending "thanks for favours conferred on Sir Philippe De Carteret". In 1631 he sent one of his daughters to Whitehall to be touched for the King's Evil. He evidently had little faith in the effect of "His Majesty's most blessed hands", for he made arrangements for her burial in London; but she miraculously recovered. "The return of the child", he wrote, "with so much amendment hath much revived a sick father" (*id.*). Like his father and grandfather he was still a Puritan, and in 1633 he joined other Justices of the Peace in petitioning the King against the revival of Church Ales (*id.*).

In 1635 he appeared in a new capacity. A strong Channel Fleet was assembling to protect British commerce from the French and Dutch, and Poulet was given command of the *Constant Reformation*, a vessel of 40 guns with 250 men. Even here he maintained his reputation for hospitality. In June one of his officers records: — "My lady Poulet and other ladies and many gentlemen and gentlewomen of great quality came aboard, and were nobly feasted and entertained" (*id.*). On 23 Sept. Poulet was knighted at sea with his eldest son John on board the *Mary Honour* by Lord Lindsay, the Lord High Admiral. His naval career however was cut short. In the same month he was taken ill, and had to return home.

When the Civil War broke out, it was assumed that the Puritan traditions of his family would make him a Parliament man; but he joined the King's side. Parliament voted him a delinquent, and issued a warrant for his arrest. Meanwhile he had retired to Sherborne Castle, and, when that was evacuated, to Wales. Here he was taken prisoner, but after a few weeks released. He then raised 2,500 men round Oxford, and led them into Dorset. In Jan. 1644 he took and burnt Lady Drake's house at Ashe, and then besieged Lyme Regis. In June the town was relieved by Essex, and Poulet withdrew to Exeter. He remained in that city as Commissioner till its surrender in April 1646. He was sent a prisoner to London, a very sick man, and on the intercession of Fairfax was allowed to live in his own house at Chiswick. He was released on payment of a fine of £2,742, plus £1,500 to Lady Drake for burning her house, plus an annuity of £250 to Lyme Regis for the soldiers maimed in its defence. He died on 20 March 1649, and was buried in Hinton Church, where a stately chapel was dedicated to his memory. He married in 1614 Elizabeth, daughter of Christopher Kenn, and had three sons and five daughters. His eldest son John, who succeeded him, was the first to bring to Jersey the news of the King's execution (Chevalier), and was one of the defenders of Elizabeth Castle. The Anne Poulet who married Carteret La Cloche, Seigneur of Samarès, and was buried in St. Saviour's Church on 18 April 1663, was probably Lord Poulet's grand-daughter. [*Dic. Nat. Biog.* and authorities quoted above.]

ROBIN, CHARLES (1745—1824), Merchant in Gaspé. Youngest son of Philippe Robin and Anne Dauvergne. Born in St. Aubin's 1743, and baptized in St. Brelade's Church 30 Oct. The Robins and Pipons were connected by marriage, and the two families had formed a firm, Robin, Pipon, and Co. to trade with Newfoundland, which had long been a British colony. In the year that Charles was born his uncle Thomas had nearly lost his ship, while returning with "dry fish, oyle, and passengers" (*Bull* XI). By the Treaty of Paris in 1763 Canada passed from the French to the British, and the firm resolved to make a bid for the trade on the Canadian coast south of the St. Lawrence. This had been largely in the hands of merchants of St. Malo. In 1766 Charles was sent to spy out the land. The vast, desolate Gaspé peninsula seemed an unlikely place for fortune-making, but the shallow waters teemed with cod, for which there was an unlimited demand in all Catholic countries, and there were possibilities of trading in furs with the Indians. So he reported favourably, and in the following year returned with a cargo of goods to barter with the Red-skins. He landed at Paspebiac, where he built a wooden house and warehouses. "When Char-

les Robin came to Gaspé", writes the historian of the district,
"the fishing was scattered in small establishments and without
organization. Though his purpose was to seek locations for new
establishments, the outcome was the development of a concern
with interests so wide and influences so commanding as practically to consolidate and control the entire business without
serious competition for nearly a century". (Clarke's *Sketches
of Gaspé*.) The S.J. possesses a Journal which he kept for the
information of his partners (*Bull* XI). He obtained a permit
from the Governor of Quebec "to make a treaty with the
savages" ; so he travelled up the St. Lawrence to find the Indian
Chief, with whom he bartered goods for furs. Then came a
heavy blow. His firm had ignored the new Navigation Act,
which required Jersey boats sailing for America to clear outward
from an English port. In May 1767 the *Endeavour*, coming
with additional stores, was arrested and taken to Halifax. In
the following year his two remaining boats were confiscated
with all goods on board. Nevertheless he carried on. The
Company bought new boats, and a profitable trade in fish was
opened with Spain and Portugal. Many Jersey lads were
brought out to work in the fishing. Robin wrote that he preferred those from St. Ouen's, as they were not spoilt by town
dissipations. The American War of Independence (1775—82)
introduced new difficulties. Rebel privateers watched the coast.
Charles' brother, Jean, who had established a branch of the
firm at Arichat on Cape Breton Island, where there is still a
village named Robins, narrowly escaped capture. In 1778 privateers seized two of Charles' ships at Paspebiac itself, and he
had to spend the night hiding in the woods. A month later
yet another of his boats was captured. Yet the business continued to grow. In June 1777 he shipped to England furs worth
over £1,000, and ten tons of whale and cod oil.

In the autumn of 1778 he returned to Jersey, where he remained
for nearly five years, and became a Captain in the South-West
Regiment of the Militia, and took part in the Battle of Jersey
(1781). After the Battle he was given command of the boat
which the States bought to watch the French coast and guard
against future surprise (*A.E.*).

In 1783 the Robins and Pipons decided to divide their business. The original firm concentrated on their Newfoundland
trade, while the Canadian stations were transferred to a new

Company, Charles Robin & Co. This was evidently a friendly arrangement, for all the shareholders in the new concern were Robins or Pipons. Charles returned to Canada to take charge. At first he was discontented. In 1784 he grumbled in a letter, now in the S.J. Library: — "There's no slave in the West Indies, but has much more time to himself, and enjoys life better than I do. If I was clear of the business, all the treasures in the world would not tempt me to undertake it again". He considered his salary of £150 inadequate—"None of the Jersey gentlemen would do half the work for that sum"—though of course he also received as partner his share of the profits. But on the whole he evidently enjoyed hard work. He opened a second centre at Percé in Gaspé Basin, 70 miles north of Paspebiac. He spent much of his time afloat in small half-decked boats, trading with scattered settlers and Indians, and keeping an eye on the fishing. In 1786 he wrote that he had that year exported 2,200 ton of salt cod and 1,000 casks of salmon. Nicolas Fiott (q.v.) and other Jersey merchants set up rival establishments on the coast to try to secure a share of the trade, but Robin beat them out of the field, and after a few years was left in sole possession.

He introduced the truck system, paying the fishermen for fish caught, half in cash and half in goods from the Company's stores. As the cash eventually found its way back to the stores, this was very profitable to the Company, and the system lasted ninety-nine years ; but it was severely criticized. In bad seasons most fishermen ran into debt with the stores ; and this put them entirely under Robin's thumb. "The inhabitants", wrote Abbé Ferland, a missionary on the coast, "are completely dependent on the House of Robin. When they try to shake off their bondage, and carry their fish to other markets, they are threatened with a summons for debt, and forced to expiate their bid for freedom by a long penance. The fisherman is always in debt to the proprietors, always at their mercy, liable, whenever his debts reach a point where they cannot be repaid by fishing, to serve without wages on one of the Company's ships, and make a voyage to Europe" (*Nouvelle Relation de la Gaspésie*).

In autumn 1802 Robin returned to Jersey "old and overfatigued" (Letter to nephew), leaving six commissioners in charge. "Very strict regulations govern them", wrote Abbé Ferland, "entering into the minutest details of their daily life, even spec-

ifying what dishes may be placed upon their tables. Their pay
is small, but no master was ever served more faithfully. The
interests of the Company become identified with their own.
Every second year three of them winter in Jersey to report".
Robin settled at St. Aubin's, where he died 10 June 1824. He
left £2,000 to build a new wing to the Hospital, and £1,000 to
provide a Chaplain. He never married. [Authorities quoted
above.]

ROMERIL, FRANCOIS AMICE (1804–73), Journalist. Son
of George Romeril and Elizabeth Luce. Born in St. Helier's
in 1804, and baptized in the Town Church on 22 May. He
lived in Paris from 1825 to 1830, and for some time was part-
proprietor of an exhibition of performing serpents. Hence rival
journalists later nicknamed him "the menagerie-man", and declared that his snakes' venom had got into his pen. On returning to Jersey he found that his brother Charles had become a
printer, and was planning a number of new papers and magazines. François Amice joined him, and in 1831 started a weekly
paper, *L'Impartial, Journal Politique, Anecdotique, Commercial,
et Littéraire*. In spite of its name its politics were vehemently
Rose. Its opening article said: — "Soon you will see the haughty
Laurel bow its proud head in the mire, crushed by the People's
scorn". In 1838 he launched a second paper, *Le Jersiais, Journal
des Intérêts du Peuple*, which ran in double-harness with the
Impartial, one appearing on Wednesday and the other on Saturday. In 1844 he amalgamated his papers, dropped the name
Le Jersiais, and issued a Wednesday and a Saturday *Impartial*.
In 1840 he published an English paper, *The Jersey Gazette*, but,
when sued for libel, denied that he was either owner or editor,
protesting that he was merely the printer. In the same year his
son Charles added a fourth paper, *Le Miroir*, to the Romeril
group. The father was one of the stormy petrels of Jersey journalism. In 1840 he was thrashed in the street twice in a single
day by members of the Le Quesne family for a sarcastic article
on the retirement of Jurat Le Quesne. He prosecuted them ; but
two months before he had wriggled out of a libel action brought
by Dean Jeune (q.v.) by pleading that the Dean had sued Fran-

çois Romeril, whereas he was François Amice. His assailants now escaped by pleading that they were charged with assaulting François Romeril, who, so the Court had decided, did not exist. In 1842 he was tilting against the Hospital administration. The three sons of Edouard Sullivan, the Director of the Hospital, waylaid him, and, according to the *Chronique*, "Jean Sullivan knocked him down with a blow of his fist, and then administered sound correction with a whip" ; but, according to the *Miroir*, Romeril had the best of the tussle: — "When Sullivan stopped, Romeril made for him, armed with a life-preserver, a whalebone implement with a ball of lead at each end. His brother ran to his rescue, and received a blow on the head, which would have cracked a skull less thick than his ; but at the cost of a bruise and the loss of his hat he enabled the hero of the whip to escape". Thus did pressmen fight their battles in the middle of the nineteenth century. It was useless to appeal to the Court ; for Jurats did not like journalists, and, if provocation was pleaded, awarded infinitesimal penalties. In 1845 Romeril went bankrupt and sold the *Impartial,* and became editor of the *Chronique* till 1854. His brother-in-law, Philippe Huelin, then founded the *Nouvelle Chronique,* and Romeril moved to the new venture as editor. He died in Birmingham on 20 April 1873. His portrait appears in Panthéon Jersiais, No. 1.

RULLECOURT, BARON DE, Soldier of Fortune. See Appendix I.

SAUNDERS, ARTHUR CHARLES (1861—1938), Jersey Historian. Son of C.B. Saunders, Nurseryman, of St. Saviour's Road, and Jane Elizabeth Durell, who was descended from Admiral Philippe Durell (q.v.). Born 1861. Educated at Victoria College, Avranches College (France), and King's College, London. Entered H.M. Customs. Became Collector of Customs 1900. Retired 1921. On returning to Jersey he became Honorary Librarian of the Société Jersiaise, and published five books on Jersey History:— *Jersey in the Eighteenth and Nineteenth Centuries*, 1930 ; *Jersey in the Seventeenth Century*, 1931 ; *Jersey in the Fifteenth and Sixteenth Centuries*, 1933 : *Jersey before and after the Norman Conquest of England*, 1935 ; *Jean Chevalier and his Times*, 1936. He died in 1938.

SELOUS, ANGIOLO ROBSON (1805–83), Dramatist. Son of Gideon Selous and Sophia Anne Lokes, brother of Henry Courtenay Selous (q.v.), Artist, and uncle of Frederick Courtenay Selous (q.v.) Hunter, and Edmund Selous, Naturalist. He began life on the London Stock Exchange, but soon abandoned finance for literature. His first book, *Tales by a Rambler*, was published in 1836. This was followed in 1850 by his first play, *The Templar*, produced at the Princess' by Charles Kean, who took the leading part. The following year Kean produced *The Duke's Wager* at the same theatre, and again he and Mrs. Kean were the hero and heroine. *Hamilton of Bothwell Haugh* was produced by Phelps at Sadler's Wells in 1855, Phelps himself playing Hamilton ; and, when it was revived later, this part was taken by Henry Irving. When touring theatrical companies visited Jersey in the sixties and seventies *Hamilton of Bothwell Haugh* was always their star piece. Next came *The Borgia Ring* at the Adelphi in 1859 and *Light and Shadow* at the Princess' in 1864. But his great success was *True to the Core, a Story of the Armada* at the Surrey in 1866. This won a prize for the best nautical drama, and roused intense patriotic enthusiasm, when taken on tour to most of the provincial theatres. His last play was *Aesop or the Golden Bubble*, staged in 1879. His niece described him as "a man of most polished and courtly manners", and added, "There was little in which he did not excel. He had a beautiful voice, and was a charming singer, often accompanying himself on the guitar, and was a well-known dramatist. I remember the first night of his *True to the Core*, when we all went across the river to the Surrey Theatre, and helped with our feet and umbrellas in the general enthusiasm. He was also a charming artist. We have a perfect gem of his, *Don Quixote in his Study*". The *Era* spoke of "his silvered hair, his fierce snow-white moustache, his dignified, old-world, courtly bearing". He married Emily Sherborn, and had five children, Percy Sherborn, Emily, Alice, Constance, and Harold, who became first Mayor of Nelson, Canada. [Nicoll's *Later Nineteenth Century Drama* ; obituary notice in *The Era* ; family information.]

SELOUS, FREDERICK COURTENAY (1851—1917), Hunter, Author and Explorer. Son of Frederick Lokes Selous, Chairman of the Stock Exchange, and Ann Sherborn ; grandson of Gideon Selous of La Moye, Jersey. Born in Regent's Park, London, 31 Dec. 1851. Educated at a Preparatory School at Tottenham and at Rugby, where he distinguished himself by his love of mischief and perpetual trespassing in pursuit of birds' eggs. When sixteen he left school and spent two years in Switzerland and Germany to learn French and German. From the latter country he had to make a hasty flight to escape arrest for knocking down a forester, who caught him poaching eggs in a bird-sanctuary. At his prep. school he had been found sleeping on the dormitory floor to harden himself, so he said, because he meant to be a hunter, and he had not outgrown this ambition. His father wished him to be a doctor, and he began to study medicine ; but in 1871, when he was nineteen, he sailed for South Africa, and made his way to Matabeleland. Lobengula, the King, amused at his boyish appearance (most would-be big-game hunters were bearded grizzled Boers), scornfully gave him permission to shoot anywhere in his dominions. For the next ten years he made a living by shooting elephants for their ivory and collecting natural history specimens for museums. In 1881 he paid a visit to England, and published his first book, *A Hunter's Wanderings in Africa*, which ran through five editions. He returned with many commissions from museums and trophy-dealers, and, while fulfilling these, visited parts of the interior that had never been explored, contributed articles to the *Journal of the Royal Geographical Society*, and was rewarded by the Founder's Gold Medal, the highest honour the Society can bestow. In 1890 he entered the service of the British South Africa Company, and acted as guide to the pioneer expedition to Mashonaland, which forestalled the Portuguese, and secured that country for Britain. His second book appeared in 1893, *Travel and Adventure in South East Africa*. He fought and was wounded that year in the Matabele Campaign ; and at its close returned to England, bought a house in Surrey, and married, and had a long controversy in the *Times* with Labouchere, who accused the colonists of cruelty toward the natives. He returned to Matabeleland with his wife in 1896, and settled on a farm, when the Native Rising took place ; large numbers of colonists were murdered, and the rest had to fight for their lives. He published an account of this in *Sunshine and Storm in Rhodesia*. He then settled down at home, and supported himself by his pen, but made hunting expeditions to Armenia, Newfoundland, and the Rockies. His later books were : — *Sport and Travel East and West*, 1900 ; *Recent Hunting Trips in British North America*, 1907 ; *African Nature Notes and Reminiscences*, 1908. When the First World War broke out, in spite of his age he obtained a commission as Captain in the Legion of Frontiersmen, served in the East African Campaign, was awarded the D.S.O., and was killed in action on 4 July 1917. Though he lived a life of adventure, his character was quite unlike that of the typical adventurer. He was a man of simple tastes, gentle manners, and extreme modesty, who hated being lionized and loved to be alone with nature. He married Marie Katherine Gladys, daughter of Canon Maddy, Vicar of Down Hatherley, Gloucestershire, and had two sons, Freddy, killed in action 1918, and Harold Sherborn. His memorial tablet and bust stand beside the statue of Darwin in the South Kensington Museum. The most important Game Reserve in Africa is the Selous Reserve in Tanganyika. An antelope, *limnotragus selousi*, is called after him. [Millais' *Life of F. C. Selous* ; *Dic. Nat. Biog.*]

SELOUS, HENRY COURTENEY, (1802—90), Painter and Children's Author. (His name was originally Slous, but about 1831 he and his brother adopted the spelling Selous). Son of Gideon Slous of La Moye, Jersey, and Sophia Lokes. Born at Deptford, 1802. He was admitted as student at the Royal Academy 1817, and next year exhibited his first picture in the Academy Exhibition, *Portrait of a Favourite Cat*. He gained the silver medal for drawing from life, and before he was twenty had won two gold and two silver medals from the Society of Arts. Twenty-six of his pictures were hung in the Academy, and twenty-one in the British Institute. He first gained fame as an animal painter with *A White Fox from the North Pole* (1819), *Hare and Leverets* (1820), etc. Then for a time he took to portraits ; then to landscapes, *A Misty Morning, A View near Dorking*, etc. But eventually he settled down to the large historical pictures that were then popular, *The Battle of Ascalon, Guttenberg showing his first experiment in printing to his wife, The Murder of Rizzio, The Charge of the Heavy Brigade at Balaclava*, etc. In 1843 he entered the competition for paintings to decorate the new Houses of Parliament, and gained a prize of £100 for his cartoon (15 feet by 10) of *Boadicea haranguing the Iceni*. In the following year he exhibited his great fresco, *Alfred submitting his Code of Laws to the Witenagemot* (now in the Law Institute), which showed how thoroughly he had mastered this difficult process. Other pictures that attracted attention were his great *Crucifixion* (now in the Sheffield Art Gallery), his *Opening of the Great Exhibition of 1851* (now in the Victoria and Albert Museum), and two large paintings of *Jerusalem Ancient and Modern*, which were exhibited in all the great cities of the country. His last Academy picture was *Cassio wounded*, exhibited in 1874.

From 1843—45 he was principal painter to Burford's Panorama in Leicester Square, then one of the show places in London, a circular building with its wall covered with an immense picture 130 feet in length, made realistic by special lighting and solid objects placed in the foreground, so that the spectator standing in the centre had the illusion of looking at real scenery. For this he produced *The Island of Hong Kong, The Ruins of Baalbec, Naples by Moonlight, The City of Athens, The Attack on Sebastopol, The Arctic Regions, The Ruins of Pompeii, The Lakes of Killarney, The Battle of Alma*, and at least ten others. He also did a great deal of book-illustration, some of his most important commissions being Cassell's *Bible, The Pilgrim's Progress, The Holy War, Shakespeare's Works, and Kingsley's Hereward the Wake*.

Meanwhile under various noms de plume such as Aunt

Eleanor and Auntie Cae, this versatile artist was writing successful children's books, which ran through many editions, *Granny's Story Book, Gerty and May, Sunny Days, The Young Governors* (this was reprinted as late as 1909), *The New Baby,* and *Children of the Parsonage* (this was illustrated by Kate Greenaway). Selous was also an excellent violoncello player, and a first-rate amateur actor. He married Elizabeth Bone, grand-daughter of Henry Bone, R.A., by whom he had four daughters. He died at Beaworthy, North Devon in his 88th year on 24 September 1890. [Bryan's *Dictionary of Painters and Engravers.* Obituary Notice, *Athenaeum.*]

SINEL, JOSEPH (1844–1929), Local Naturalist and Archaeologist. Youngest son of Philip Sinel, wholesale tobacco merchant, and Charlotte Babot. Born in St. Helier's 13 Dec. 1844. When fifteen he entered Voisin and Co.'s Furniture Department, where he rose to be Manager ; but even in those early years his main interest was Zoology. His spare time was spent at low tide among the rocks of St. Clement's Bay, where the wealth of marine life in the pools so fascinated him, that he determined to devote his life to Natural Science. He resigned his position at Voisin's, and started business as a taxidermist. While living at Samarès, he made with John G. Romeril the large collection of wild birds of Jersey, now in the Museum. His lectures in the Prince of Wales' Rooms roused much interest in local zoology, botany, and geology, and he lectured regularly in the Guille Allès Museum, Guernsey, and at the Summer Camps of the Society of Friends in England. Papers which he contributed to *Science Gossip* brought him English correspondents, many of whom crossed to Jersey to obtain his help in collecting specimens. Charles Darwin and A. Russel Wallace frequently wrote to him about topics of Marine Zoology. With his son-in-law, James Hornell, he built in 1891 a Biological Station at Havre-des-pas with aquarium tanks for the study of marine life and the supply of living specimens to students. For some years this was successful, but the opening of similar establishments in England, subsidized by Government, forced it to close. His next venture was an attempt to revive the local Oyster Fisheries. A Jersey Oyster Culture Company was formed, and quantities of spat from Auray were placed in cage-traps near Green Island ; but the site proved insufficiently protected against storms, and the enterprise failed. Later he spent much time in an attempt to extract osmiridium from the local diorite, but this too proved a financial failure. In 1906 the Committee of the Société Jersiaise consulted him on the rearrangement of the Museum. He drew up a Report, which the Committee adopted, and in 1907 made him Curator of the Museum, a post which he held till his death. Most of the zoological exhibits are his handiwork. In 1910 the Société commissioned R.G. Crawford to paint his portrait, and this is now in the Art Gallery. During the last twenty years of his life he turned his attention to Prehistory, and took an active part in the explorations made by the Société, on most of which he contributed valuable papers to the *Bulletins*. Sir Arthur Keith wrote of him : — "Mr. Sinel has read the history of his beloved island as it is written by the sun, the wind, the sea, and the frost, and of its ancient inhabitants as it is told by their relics ; and he has obviously read aright". (Foreword to *Prehistoric Times*.) He frequently visited Carnac, Brittany, and helped to arrange the Prehistoric Museum there.

In his later years his inquiring mind was attracted by Psychical Research, and he spent much time experimenting in Telepathy and kindred subjects. Among his publications are: — *The Complete Guide to Jersey*, 1896 ; *Fishes of the Channel Islands*, 1906 ; *An Outline of the Natural History of our Shores*, 1906 ; *Crustacea of the Channel Islands*, 1906 ; *Notes on the Lizards of the Channel Islands*, 1907 ; *The Reptilia, Batrachia, and Mammalia of the Channel Islands, their Origin and Modification by Isolation*, 1908 ; *The Relative Ages of the Channel Islands*, 1908 ; *The Geology of Jersey*, 1912 ; *Prehistoric Times and Men of the Channel Islands*, 1st edition, 1914, 2nd edition, 1923 ; *The Children's World of Wonders* (3 vols), 1924 ; *The Sixth Sense, a Physical Explanation of Clairvoyance, Hypnotism, Dreams, and other Phenomena usually considered Occult*, 1927. He also contributed the section on Geology to the 3rd edition of Ansted and Latham's *The Channel Islands*, 1893, and many articles to the *Transactions of the Guernsey Society of Natural Science and Local Research*. He died in St. Helier's, 2 April 1929. In 1868 he married Elizabeth Du Feu, and had a son, Joseph William, who died in 1927, and a daughter, Charlotte Elizabeth, who married James Hornell. [*Bull.* XI. 223.]

SINNATT, FRANK STURDY, C. B., D. Sc., F. R. S. (1880–1943), Fuel Research Chemist. Son of Francis Sinnatt and Sarah Sturdy. Born in Les Grands Vaux, St. Helier's, 4 May 1880. Educated at the College of Technology, Manchester. Became Head of the Fuel Section of that College, Lecturer on Fuels in Manchester University, and Director of the Lancashire and Cheshire Coal Research Association. From 1924 to 1931 he was Assistant Director of Fuel Research in the Government Department of Scientific and Industrial Research, and in 1931 he became Director. In 1919 he was made a Member of the Order of the British Empire and in 1935 a Companion of the Bath. He was Doctor of Science (Manchester), Fellow of the Institute of Chemistry, and Fellow of the Institute of Physics. In 1938 he was elected a Fellow of the Royal Society. He was on the Councils of the Institute of Mining Engineers, of the Institute of Fuel, and of the Colliery Owners' Research Associat'on. He was Member of the Safety in Mines Research Board, of the Coal Utilization Association, and of the Royal Swedish Institute for Engineering Research. He commanded the Manchester University Officers' Training Corps till 1922 ; and published a large number of scientific and technical papers on coal. He married Louise Midgley Badger ; and died 27 Jan. 1943.

SIVRET, THOMAS (1751–90), Rector of St. John's. Son of Thomas Sivret, Constable of St. Martin's, and Louise, daughter of Henry Le Cras of St. Lawrence. Baptized at St. Martin's 11 Jan. 1751. His father died, when he was five, leaving the family badly off. The boy was educated at St. Mannelier Grammar School, and then studied by himself, until he was able to pass the Bishop's Ordination Examination. In 1779 he became Rector of St. John's. (His brother George was Constable of the parish 1781–4). In the early days of the struggle between the Charlots and the Magots many of the Rectors were eager partisans of the democratic party. "The Clergy", wrote W.C. Lempriere (q.v.), the Lieut.-Bailiff, to the President of the Council (22.6.1784), "are the great patriots of the day, who conscientiously sacrifice every consideration to what they call Liberty, that is the pleasure of throwing everything into confusion by their ill-fated interference in Politicks. Your Lordship will no doubt admire their zeal when you know that on Sunday they marched in a public Market Place with blue cockades in a disgraceful and undignified manner, huzzaing for Liberty like Bacchanalians, and wearing the badge even in the Pulpit, no doubt with a view of inspiring their auditors with Christian meekness and moderation. The effect of this unclergymanlike behaviour with the populace is to be dreaded. That frantic zeal which they inspire is of the worst and most ungovernable kind, and I am convinced it will be necessary to apply a speedy and efficacious remedy to an evil, which might become at length uncurable" (Rozel MSS.). Of these ultra-political parsons Sivret was the most demonstrative. He was the orator of the Magot Party. A big man of magnificent presence with "a voice like the booming of the waves" (*Magasin*), he thundered forth sonorous periods, which were by no means empty rhetoric, but full of pith and sting. His Party used its new printing-press to multiply copies of his orations, and spread them broadcast through the island. "Like a true athlete", said *La Patrie* later, "he fought against the powers of darkness, and shone forth as a champion among those early Reformers, who dared to make a frontal attack on the innumerable abuses in the laws that governed us". In 1787 he was involved in a dispute with Dean François Le Breton. The Canons ordered the Rector, Surveillants, and Principaux to appoint a schoolmaster in every parish. The Dean interpreted this to mean that no one else was allowed to teach. George Ahier, who had opened a school in Trinity, was summoned before the Ecclesiastical Court, and ordered to close his school. Sivret denounced this as "nothing less than an attempt to keep the people in ignorance and barbarism", and described the judgement as "odious and infamous". But he himself took pupils in his Rectory ; so he was summoned before the Court as an unlicensed schoolmaster. The case attracted wide attention. His defence was that he did not claim to be Parish

Schoolmaster, but that he had a perfect right to instruct children entrusted to him. He was eventually acquitted, and his School became a flourishing one. He also crossed swords with William Le Marchand, Bailiff of Guernsey, who had published over the signature A.B. an anonymous attack, on the Magots in general and Sivret in particular. Sivret replied with a witty Open Letter to the Bailiff appealing to him to discover and punish the author of these atrocious libels. He followed this up with an *Examen de la Lettre de A.B. aux Anticharlots* 1788. So his life went on, an unbroken series of controversies and orations, till he died on 16 Jan. 1790, and was buried in St. John's Church. He married Anne, daughter of Edward Le Maître, Seigneur of La Hougue Boëte, but had no children. [*Gazette, passim* ; Dorey's *Notice Biographique sur le Rev. Thomas Sivret* ; articles in *La Patrie*, May 1850.]

STOCALL, JACQUES (1620—65), Parliamentarian. The family descended from a Nicolas Stocall, one of the garrison of Mont Orgueil under Henry VIII, who married a De Ste Croix. Their son John became a Jurat, and lived in "the great house of Stocall" in the Market Place. His younger son, Aaron, settled at Longueville, St. Saviour's, and became Constable. Aaron's son, Aaron, who was also Constable, (1629—45) married Elisabeth, sister of Michel Lempriere (q.v.), Parliamentary Bailiff. Jacques, their eldest son, was baptized in St. Saviour's Church 10 Jan. 1621. In March 1643, when Michel Lempriere went to the States to arrest Sir Philippe De Carteret (q.v.), Jacques, his nephew, marched the St. Saviour's Militia into Town to support him ; but Sir Philippe heard of this move in time, and withdrew to Elizabeth Castle. In Nov., when the Royalists recovered Jersey, Stocall fled with Lempriere to England, and his father's property was confiscated (5 Nov. 1644) by the Crown. In De La Rocque's MS. (undated, but between 1647 and 1651) it is said, that, while in Jersey, he had been arrested on suspicion of coining, that in England he had become an Anabaptist, and that he was then teaching French to the young Duke of Gloucester, son of Charles I, a boy of about ten. In 1651 he was employed at Worcester House, the office of the trustees for the sale of the King's Property. In Oct., after eight years' exile, he sailed with Blake in the expedition that recovered Jersey for Parliament. "He voluntarily ventured himself with the first at the landing", wrote Lempriere to the Speaker, "and hath been very serviceable in assisting the Parliament's forces. I cannot but recommend to your Honour his abilities and good endowments, most particularly for the twelve learned speeches he made to the twelve parishes, when the inhabitants subscribed the engagement, when he shewed most ingeniously the great difference of the late and the present Government" (Hoskins). His first task was the reorganization of the Militia, which Carteret had filled with Royalist officers. These were deprived of their commissions, and new officers appointed. "Col. Heane at our first coming", wrote Lempriere, "did put the Militia at the disposing of Col. Stocall, Capn. Norman, and myself". (ibid). Meanwhile Lempriere feared drastic changes in the island's constitution. This Jersey Parliamentarians were quite as determined as their opponents to resist. He wrote (Feb. 1652) a long *Account of the Civil Government of this Island* (printed in Hoskins) and gave it to his nephew to take to the Speaker, adding, "I refer the enlarging of this summary to this gentleman, Colonel Stocall ; he is also able to recommend unto Parliament some able persons, who are fit in this island to serve really and truly the commonwealth". In London Stocall published (March 1652) a 14 page pamphlet addressed to Lieut.-Gen. Fleetwood, *Freedom or the Description of the Excellent Civill Government of the Island of Jersey, by James Stocall Esq, Collonel of a Regiment of the Trained Bands of the said Island, consisting of 1,500 men,* giving a very rosy picture of the Jersey constitution, leading up to the conclusion: — "There is no need of change in the form of the Civil Government", though it "might be desired" for the islands to have "a Representor or two in Parliament to the end of a speedier expedition of necessaries unto our people". He returned to Jersey, but occupied no official position except that of Colonel of the East Regiment of Militia (St. Saviour's, Grouville, and St. Clement's), which he held till the Restoration. His brother Aaron became Solicitor-General. He died about 1665. His wife's name was Lucie. [*Bull* IV ; Hoskins' *Charles II in the Channel Islands.*]

SYVRET, JEAN (1784—1862), Seaman. Prisoner of War. The
story of his life, written by himself in his old age, gives a vivid
picture of the life of a Jersey sailor of this period. Elder son
of Philippe Syvret, a sea captain, and Anne Hue. Born at
St. Lawrence 21 Nov. 1784. When a baby he was adopted by
his mother's aunt, Rachel Hue, widow of John Belin of St.
John's. At fourteen he went to sea on a Jersey privateer, transferring later to a larger one belonging to the Janvrins. This
cruised off the West African coast, and Syvret rose to be prize-
master, and brought back many captured vessels to Jersey.
When peace came in 1802, he sailed to Newfoundland ; but,
when war was resumed, he left the cod, and returned to privateering. In 1804 he was second in command of the Jersey
privateer *Hope*. Off the Spanish coast they met two other privateers, also from Jersey, the *Phoenix* and the *Marquis of
Townshend*. While the captains dined together on the *Phoenix*,
Syvret entertained the second officers on the *Hope*. The three
young men took out their long-boats to attack some French
luggers near the shore, but were chased by hidden French
warships, and Syvret had to beach his boat. He and his crew
were captured by Spaniards, and marched two hundred miles
to prison at Corunna. Here he made a hole in the prison wall,
seized a Spanish boat, and put out to sea ; but was soon recaptured. Eventually he was exchanged, and sent to neutral Portugal, whence he got a passage home on a Jersey privateer, the
Union. He at once joined another privateer, the *Commerce*,
but was wrecked off the barren isle of Le Pilier, near the mouth
of the Loire in Sept. 1805, and again taken prisoner. The crew
was marched south for several days to Sables d'Olonne, where
they turned north, and marched to Nantes. On leaving Nantes
Syvret with Le Gallais, another officer, took advantage of a
turn in the road, when for a moment they were out of sight of
their escort, and made a dash for freedom, and hid among the
heather. With only the north star as guide they crossed Brittany
to St. Malo, getting food from sympathetic peasants by pretending to be deserters from the French navy. They obtained a passage on a Swedish vessel, but were discovered at the last moment,
and thrown into prison. From this they escaped with the help
of two French criminals by taking an impression of the gaoler's
key, and cutting one of their own. They went to Cancale, hoping to steal an oyster-boat, but failed. They then tried Gran-

vile, where they found a priest who had been a refugee in Jersey.
He arranged with a fisherman to take them to Chausey, but that
night the port was closed, and no boats allowed to leave.

In Jan. 1806, they were recaptured. Syvret was now suffering severely from exposure and cold, and for a time was in
Hospital. When better, he was sent to Valenciennes, a depot
for English prisoners of war, where he met many Jerseymen.
Thence he was moved to Metz, where he received a letter and
money from his family. Later he was moved to Verdun. Here
he was fairly comfortable. He received a regular remittance
from home, and was allowed to live in the town, and go where
he pleased, having only to report twice a day for roll-call. Napoleon stopped for an hour at Verdun, and Syvret was close
to him as he re-entered his carriage ; but he was not cheered
by the Emperor's little speech, "Gentlemen, so long as I remain
Emperor, there will be no exchange for you". After two years
at Verdun Syvret spent five at Saarlouis. Here the prisoners
formed a school among themselves, in which Syvret taught
navigation, and they held a Service in their school every Sunday. He had now come to feel that Napoleon would never
be defeated, and that he would spend the rest of his life in
France. He met and married (31 Oct. 1810) a French girl,
Jeanne Antoinette Tortorithy, and for three years lived happily
with her parents. But then came the retreat from Moscow.
Orders were given to move all prisoners further from the frontier.
Syvret was transferred to Bapaume, leaving his wife behind.
Here he and another Jerseyman, Jean Le Gresley of St. Ouen's,
broke through a bricked up door in the ramparts and made their
way for nine days through deep snow to Namur, where they
found the army of the Allies. They were picked up by Cos-
sacks, and taken before the Russian general, Baron Ferdinand
von Wintzingerode, who gave them a passport for Holland.
At Willemstad they found an English naval brig, which landed
them at Deal ; and Syvret eventually got back to Jersey on 5
March 1815 after nearly ten years' absence. Here his wife
joined him. The rest of his manuscript is less interesting, being
largely a record of family squabbles about the division of his
mother's property. He went back to the sea, and for twenty
five years commanded various Jersey trading vessels. In 1829
he was wrecked in the Bay of Biscay, and taken for a second
time to Corunna. In 1841 he obtained his pilot's certificate,

and for ten years acted as a Jersey pilot. He then opened a School of Navigation, and notes that many of his pupils obtained a Captain's first-class certificate. He died on 19 May 1862. and was buried in Green Street Cemetery. He had seven children, two born at Saarlouis, and five baptized at St. Lawrence. His autobiography, *Abrégé de la Vie de Capitaine Jean Syvret*, will be published by the Société Jersiaise. As he tells us that his sight failed in his old age, it was probably dictated, which would account for the unconventional spelling. His trick of interpolating English words into his French narrative evidently puzzled his amanuensis, who spelt rubbish *robige*, cottage *catige*, boastswain *bausoin*, blunderbus *blanderbouches*, midshipman *macchickman*, and wrote of a heavy sea that it *nous jeta sur nos biemins* (beam-ends).

TEHY, VINCENT (fl. 1469—98), Part-Founder of St. Mannelier and St. Anastase. The Tehys were a Jersey family. In the Assize Roll of 1309 there is a Pierre Tehy at St. Peter's and a Jean Tehy at St. Helier's. Henry VII's Charter mentions Pierre Tehy as one of five Jerseymen who distinguished themselves in the recapture of Mont Orgueil. In later documents St. Helier's Manor-house was spoken of as *la maison de Tehy*. Vincent is first mentioned in 1469 as Burgess and Water Baily of Southampton, a post which he held till 1471. Under Edward IV he was Collector of the fifteenth and the tenth granted by the laity of the town to the King, and on the accession of Richard III he received the usual General Pardon for all deficiencies. In 1474 he was Sheriff, and he was twice Mayor in 1484 and 1498, and the *Book of Fines* during his Mayoralty shows him to have been an exceedingly active official. He was a merchant in a large way of business. In 1484 he and his partners acquitted some London merchants of £1,200 in return for an acquittance of 1086 sacks of wool, and some years later he joined with others in exporting 150 bales of cloth. On 15 November 1496 Henry VII granted a licence to Jean Neel and Vincent Tehy "to make, found, and establish two schools in our island of Jersey with two Masters and two Ushers, if need be. under them for the education of boys living in the island in

Grammar (which in those days always meant Latin Grammar)
and the other inferior liberal branches of learning." For an
account of this foundation see the article *Neel, Jean.* [Falle's
Account of Jersey ; Davis' *History of Southampton* ; *Historical
M.S.S. Commission, Report XI* ; Chapman's *Black Book of
Southampton.*]

THOREAU, HENRY DAVID (1817—1862), American naturalist, moralist, and philosopher. He was born in Concord,
Massachusetts, 21 July 1817, and in 1846 he borrowed an axe,
and went off into the woods to build himself a shack. He
wanted to try by doing without all unessential things to discover
what it is that makes life worth living ; and at the end he felt
able to write, "I truth discern, who knew but learning's lore".
His book *Walden* became an American classic. Details of his
life can be found in the *Encyclopaedia Britannica,* in Salt's
Life of Thoreau, and in Sanborn's *H.D. Thoreau* in the "American Men of Letters" Series. He died in 1862. This note
merely points out that he came of Jersey stock. His grandfather
John Thoreau, son of Philip Thoreau of St. Helier's and Marie
Le Gallais, his wife, was born in St. Helier's, and emigrated
to New England in 1754, and married a Scottish lady named
Burns. Their son, John, married Cynthia Dunbar, daughter
of a New England clergyman ; and their son, Henry David,
was the famous writer. Thoreau's Journal for April 21 1855
alludes to three letters given by his aunt, Maria Thoreau, which
contain all the family history of which he was aware on the
paternal side. This aunt Maria outlived all the American
Thoreaus, and at her death in 1881 this branch of the family
became extinct. The mother of Lord Du Parcq, Sophia Thoreau,
who died in 1940, was descended from an elder brother of the
John who emigrated.

TOUZEL, EDOUARD (1782—1815), Carpenter. Son of
Edouard Touzel and Esther Le Cordier. Born in St. Helier's

1782, and baptized in the Town Church 20 Jan. A man of unusual physical strength (in his last illness four men could not hold him in bed, and he had to be fastened with ropes), but according to the *Chronique*, of a singularly kindly and gentle disposition. On 4 June 1804 St. Helier's was holiday-making in honour of the King's birthday. At noon an immense crowd had gathered on the Town Hill, where Fort Regent was being built, to see the Royal Standard hoisted in the presence of the Lieut.-Governor and his staff and the royal salute fired. At six the Lieut.-Governor was giving a dinner-party and a ball in the Town below, and Edouard Touzel with his brother Thomas was dismantling the flagstaff on the Hill erected for the mid-day ceremony, when Philippe Lys (q.v.), the Signals' Officer, called to him that the powder-magazine was on fire. Cannon were still fired by lengths of rope soaked in nitre to make them burn slowly, and a careless gunner of the Invalids had put one of these 'matches' smouldering back into the magazine, in which were 209 barrels of powder and many boxes of cartridges and charged hand-grenades, and here it had set fire to a heap of other 'matches'. Lys sent Thomas into the Town to fetch the keys and warn the Lieut.-Governor, and with Edouard, and a private of the 31st, William Pulteney, rushed to the danger-spot. Touzel broke down the palisade round the magazine, burst two padlocks, and went inside. He heaved out several chests of powder that were close to the fire, and then, "encouraging the others with most gallant words", he flung them armfuls of glowing fuses, which burnt his hands and face, and then extinguished the rest with water which they brought. When the work was almost done, he collapsed overcome by fumes. He was only just in time. Next day the Constable reported that two boxes filled with horns of powder were found to have been badly charred, and that even the roof-beams were scorched.

Touzel's fellow-townsmen were not slow to show their gratitude. A public subscription bought fourteen quarters of wheat-rente to be paid to him and his descendants for ever. He was made Sergeant-Major of the Town Battalion, and presented with a silver-mounted sword, which he was authorized to wear. And the States voted 5,000 livres (about 300 guineas) to be paid him from the public funds, a similar sum to Lys, and a pension of £12 a year to Pulteney, and presented each with a gold

medal suitably inscribed. "The States feel it their duty", ran
the Act, "to pay this tribute of gratitude to these three intrepid
men, who, realizing that the explosion would certainly demolish
part of the Town and destroy many inhabitants, decided without hesitation to risk almost certain death in the heroic hope
of saving their fellow-citizens". For some reason Durell be-
littles their exploit, describing the Act of the States as "fulsome
and ridiculous", and suggesting that the smouldering match
would never have reached the powder. "Few persons were acquainted with the true state of things, and these few were
equally interested to increase their claim to remuneration by
impressing the public with a deep sense of the extreme danger
to which they had been exposed" (*Historical Sketch of Jersey*).
But this was not the opinion of contemporaries. Touzel died
24 May 1815, aged only 33. [The fullest account is the Constable's Report, printed in Stead's *Gazette*, 9.6.1804. The Act
of the States and the Testimonial presented to Touzel by the
parish are in De La Croix' *Ville de St. Hélier*. See also *Annual
Register* 1804 ; Johnson's *Book of Heroes* ; Yonge's *Book of
Golden Deeds*.]

TURNER, SIR ADOLPHUS HILGROVE, Kt. (1846—1911),
Attorney-General. Only son of Adolphus Turner, British
Chargé d'Affaires at Monte Video and Eliza McNeill of Cush-
enden, County Antrim. Grandson of General Tomkyns Hilgrove Turner (q.v.), Lieutenant-Governor. Born in Grouville,
3 Sept. 1846. He was educated at Christ Church, Oxford,
taking honours in Law and History. B.A. 1870. M.A. 1877.
He was President of the Union, 1870. In early life his favourite
sport was mountaineering. In 1881 he was called to the Jersey
Bar, and the same year he became Deputy of Grouville, being
re-elected in 1884. While Deputy he was one of a deputation
sent by the States to England to submit to the Home Authorities the historical evidence which proved the Ecréhous to be
British territory. The Memorandum was drawn up by himself.
In 1887 he received the thanks of Lord Salisbury for a "very
able Reply" to the Report of the French specialists on this
question. He had been appointed Solicitor-General in 1884, and

was made Attorney-General in 1899. In 1894 he received the silver medal of the Royal Humane Society for saving the lives of two visitors at Plemont. He was knighted among the Coronation honours in 1911. He was a devoted Churchman, always interested in education, and a keen horticulturist, whose gardens at Gouray Lodge, where he lived with his mother, were charming. He never married. He died suddenly of heart-failure on 13 Dec. 1911. He had not been well, and had been abroad for his health, but was able to lecture on his travels to the St. Helier's Literary Society two days before his death. He is buried in La Croix Cemetery, Grouville.

TURNER, SIR TOMKYNS HILGROVE (1764—1843), General. Lieut.-Governor. Eldest son of Richard Turner M.D., and Madeline Hilgrove (She was a daughter of Jurat Charles Hilgrove, who was son of Charles, Constable of St. Helier's, 1697—1703, who was son of Thomas, licensed taverner in St. Helier's, 1645, who was son of William Hilgrove of White Parish near Salisbury, a soldier in a regiment stationed in Jersey, who had settled in the island, and married Alice Romeril). The future General was born according to his tombstone on 12 Jan 1764. When he died, both the *Chronique* and the *Jersiais* described him as "a native of this isle". In his first speech after his appointment as Lieut.-Governor in 1814 he said that he was proud to be able to say that he was a Jerseyman (*Chronique*). In 1815, when the States passed a vote of thanks to him, the mover said, "Our country should congratulate itself on having given birth to so distinguished a man" ; so his birth in Jersey may be accepted as a fact, though his name does not appear in any Baptism Register. Perhaps his father disapproved of infant baptism.

He obtained a commission in the 3rd Foot Guards in Feb. 1782, and was promoted Lieutenant and Captain, Oct. 1789. He went to Holland in Feb. 1793 with the Brigade of Guards, and fought in the Battle of St. Armand and at the capture of Valenciennes. Here he found his wife. Elizabeth Wordsworth, Principal of Lady Margaret Hall, Oxford, whose family intermarried with the Turners, tells the story: — "He was present in

1793 at Valenciennes at an attack on a convent, whence two
youthful sisters, not nuns, were being torn to be given over to
some red republicans. One of these sisters, Esther by name,
charmed him so much that he offered to marry her himself, and
did so. She was but seventeen. No one knows what became
of the other. A portrait of the former still in existence represents
her as a beautiful young girl with wayward little curls of dark
hair and a lovely pose of head. Her eldest daughter, Madelon,
was baptized in a cellar by a priest in a smock frock" (*Glimpses
of the Past*). For the next fourteen months Turner's regiment
was continuously in action, at the siege of Dunkirk, the battles
of Cateau and Tournay, and the retreat behind the Waal.
He specially distinguished himself at the Capture of Fort St.
André in Oct. 1794.

He was promoted Lieut.-Colonel, Nov. 1794, and Brevet-
Colonel, Jan. 1801. In this year he went to Egypt. In March
his regiment landed at Aboukir under heavy fire, and captured
the French guns at the point of the bayonet. After five months'
strenuous fighting he was present at the capitulation of Alexandria in September. For his services he was made Knight
of the Order of the Crescent by the Sultan and Knight of the
Order of St. Anne by the Czar. One article of the Capitulation required all curios collected by the French Institute to
be handed over to the British. Turner was a keen antiquary,
and the reception of these museum treasures was entrusted to
him. Among them was the famous Rosetta Stone, discovered
by French troops when demolishing a wall, which provided the
clue to the deciphering of the hitherto unreadable Egyptian
hieroglyphics. Menou, the French General, tried hard to retain
this, saying that it was his private property, but Turner insisted.
"When first I saw the stone", he wrote, "in General Menou's
house in Alexandria, it was covered with soft cotton cloth and
double matting. When the French understood that we were
to possess the antiquities, the covering of the stone was torn
off, and it was thrown on its face, and the excellent wooden
cases of the rest were broken off. I made several remonstrances,
but the chief difficulty I had was on account of this stone.
Lord Hutchinson gave me a detachment of artillerymen and a
'devil-cart' with which I went to General Menou's house and
carried off the stone amid the sarcasm of numbers of French
officers and men. We were the first British soldiers who en-

tered Alexandria. Having seen the other remains of Egyptian
sculpture sent on board the *Madras*, I embarked with the Rosetta Stone, determined to share its fate, on the *Egyptienne*, and
arrived at Portsmouth in Feb. 1802" (*Archaeologia*. Vol. XVI).
The stone was placed in the British Museum.

In 1803 Turner was Assistant-Quartermaster-General of the
Home Forces, and in 1804 was promoted Brigadier-General.
In 1807 he was sent to South America to help in the attack on
the Spanish Colony of Buenos Ayres, but before he arrived
the attempt had failed. In 1808 he became Major-General,
and was given command of a Brigade in London. In 1811 he
was made Colonel of the 19th Foot (Yorkshire 1st Riding), a
post which he held till his death. In the same year he became
Private Secretary to the Prince Regent (later George IV), one
of his duties being to take charge of foreign royalties who
visited the country. In May 1814 Oxford made him a Doctor
of Civil Law. On 23 June 1814, he was appointed to succeed
General Don (q.v. Appendix) as Lieut.-Governor of Jersey ; on
28 July he was knighted by the Prince Regent ; and on 8 Oct.
was sworn in before the Royal Court. One of his first duties
must have pained him as an antiquarian. The military authorities considered the mediaeval chapel of Notre Dame des Pas
on the Mont de Ville a danger to the newly-built Fort Regent
as affording cover to an attacking enemy, and he was ordered
to blow it up. Before doing so he sent a sketch of it to *Archaeologia* (Vol. XXVII). A ticklish problem arose in the Militia.
General Don had appointed a Philip Mourant Lieutenant of
the Town Batteries. For some reason, probably connected with
party politics, his fellow-officers published an advertisement in
the local papers : — "The Officers having been informed that
Mr. Philip Mourant has obtained a commission in the batteries,
it has been unanimously resolved never to acknowledge, receive,
or act with the said Philip Mourant as an officer of the corps".
Exactly how Turner solved the problem does not seem to be
recorded ; but his settlement gave general satisfaction. On 19
Dec. 1815, the Parish Assembly of St. Helier's passed by a
large majority a vote of thanks to him for "his firmness in maintaining the royal prerogative and supporting Mr. Mourant" ;
and on 27 Dec. the States unanimously thanked him for "the
moderation, wisdom, and firmness" he had shown, and expressed
a hope that "under his conciliatory and liberal rule the unhappy

political dissensions, which have so long divided the island, may for ever disappear". In 1816 however the Government decided that, now that peace was secured, a Lieut.-General (Turner had been promoted to that rank in 1815) was no longer needed in Jersey, and in spite of strong petitions from the States he was recalled.

In 1825 he was made Governor of the Bermudas, and remained there for six years. In 1830 he was promoted General, and on his return to England was made a Knight Grand Cross of the Royal Hanoverian Guelphic Order and a Groom of the Bed-chamber of the Royal Household. About 1835 he returned to Jersey. Twenty years before, while still Lieut.-Governor, he had bought from Josué Falle a house with grounds on the Fief de Vaugalème, Grouville. From time to time, as opportunity offered, he had bought adjoining strips of land. Now he and his wife made this their home. In 1835 the Board of Ordnance put him in charge of Mont Orgueil. He appointed a veteran artillery-sergeant caretaker, made a charge of sixpence for admission, and used the proceeds for repairs. He cleared away the debris surrounding St. George's Chapel, and discovered the coffins of two sixteenth-century Governors. He died 6 May, 1843, and was buried at Grouville. His wife survived him for twenty years, and died, blind but vigorous to the last, 15 Sept. 1863. His eldest son, Frederick Henry, became Colonel of the 3rd regiment of Guards. His second daughter, Charlotte, married Henry Octavius Coxe, Bodley's Librarian. General Turner published *A short Account of Ancient Chivalry and a Description of Armour*, 1799, and a translation from the French of Warnery's *Thoughts and Anecdotes, Military and Historical*, 1811. He also contributed articles to *Archaeologia*, e.g. his account of the acquisition of the Rosetta Stone, mentioned above, a Deciphering of the Inscription on Pompey's Pillar at Alexandria (Vol. XV), Two Views of a Cromlech near Mont Orgueil, drawn by himself (Vol. XXVIII). Portraits of General and Lady Turner hang in the S.J. Museum. [*War Office Records*: Jersey Newspapers: *Dic. Nat. Biog.*: *Annual Register*: Canon's *Records of the 19th Regiment*: *Gentleman's Magazine* 1843, 1844.]

VALPY, ABRAHAM JOHN (1787—1854), Classical Scholar and Publisher. Second son of Dr. Richard Valpy (q.v.). Born at Reading 1787. Educated at Reading Grammar School, and at Pembroke College, Oxford. Matriculated 1805, B.A. 1809, M.A. 1811. Before he left school he published a volume of *Cicero's Letters* which passed through five editions, and, while still an undergraduate, a collection of *Latin Poems* by himself. In 1811 he became a Fellow of his College. But his ambition was to become a famous printer of the classics, like Aldus and Stephanus in the past. With this object he bound himself as apprentice to a London printer, became a liveryman of the Stationers' Company, and acquired a printer's business in Tooke's Court, Chancery Lane. His first great speculation, a new edition of Stephens' *Thesaurus Graecae Linguae* in thirteen volumes, which had taken several years to prepare, was killed by a brilliant but cruel review in the *Quarterly Review* by Blomfield, later Bishop of London. Undismayed however, Valpy gathered round him a group of classical scholars, and, beginning with Plautus, Aesop, and Eutropius, issued an immense number of school classics with English notes and vocabularies, many of them edited by his father, his uncles, and his brother Francis. Sallust, Terence, and the Iliad were edited by himself. He also started *The Classical Journal*, which ran for 40 volumes, and a weekly literary paper, called *The Museum*. In 1818 he began the stupendous task of issuing a carefully revised edition of the *Delphin Classics* in 143 volumes. This proved a great success, the last volume appearing in 1830. Another notable achievement was his *Family Classical Library*, 52 volumes of translations of the classics. Whatever he planned, he planned on a gigantic scale. His chief personal contribution to scholarship was his edition of Tacitus in five volumes, first published in 1812, and frequently reissued. But he did not confine himself to Greek and Latin. He wrote *Rules for the pronunciation of the French Language* 1821, and he published an immense series of *Sermons by Divines of the Church of England*, an *Epitome of English Literature*, a 15 volume edition of Shakspere, and a serial *National Gallery of Painting and Sculpture*. He adopted as trade-mark the Greek digamma, which he placed, not only on his books, but on the panels of his carriage. In 1838 he retired from publishing with a comfortable fortune, and became a Director of the University Life Assurance Company.

He married Harriet, daughter of the Rev. S.T. Wylde of Burrington ; but he had no children. He died in his house in St. John's Wood Road, 19 Nov. 1854. [*Dic. Nat. Biog.* with literature there quoted. *Annual Register* 1854.]

VALPY, EDOUARD (1764–1852), High Master of Norwich. Fourth son of Richard Valpy of St. John's and Catherine Chevalier, and brother of Dr. Richard Valpy (q.v.), Headmaster of Reading. Born at St. John's 1764, and baptized in St. John's Church on 8 March. Educated at Bury St. Edmund's Grammar School, where his brother Richard was then Second Master, and at Trinity College, Cambridge. Admitted Sizar 1781. Readmitted as Ten Year Man 1788. B.D. 1810. From 1781 to 1810 he was his brother's assistant at Reading, serving at the same time the church of Stanford Dingley, Berks. In 1810 he applied for the High-Mastership of Norwich. It was a closely contested election, and he only gained the post by the Mayor's casting vote. "He determined", wrote Dr. Cox, an old pupil, "to make by means of this appointment a name and a fortune ; and, when once he had come to a determination, he was not easily turned from it. His ambition was to supersede all the existing Suffolk and Norfolk Grammar Schools ; and in two or three years scholars were obtained from all parts of Norfolk, Suffolk, and Cambridgeshire, and even from places far beyond, notably from London, Surrey, and Middlesex". This was certainly a feat. When he took over the School, the boys numbered eight. By the end of two years he had 180 boarders and more than 100 day-boys. And his scholastic successes were remarkable. Under him the school turned out an unusually large number of boys, who made their mark later in various spheres of life. Among his pupils were James Martineau, the famous Unitarian divine, Henry Reeve, editor of the *Edinburgh Review*, George Henry Borrow, author of *Lavengro*, Sir James Brooke, Rajah of Sarawak, Sir Vincent Eyre of Indian Mutiny fame, Sir Archdale Wilson, the captor of Delhi, David Hodgson, the landscape painter, John Lindley the botanist, R.M. White, Rawlinsonian Professor at Oxford, and a large number of Fellows of Oxford and Cambridge Colleges. But it is still a debated point whether he was a great Head Master. He was a merciless flogger. "He secured his fame", writes H.W. Saunders in his *History of Norwich Grammar School,* "by terrorization and mental torture". "For five years", writes Dr. Cox, "my life was little else than a continual round of torture. On one ever-to-be-remembered morning he flogged me so brutally and so long, because I missed a word in saying the Greek irregular verbs, as to be unable to wield his cane any longer". Martineau tells how he had to lend his back as a horse, while Valpy birched Borrow for one of his escapades among the gipsies. But Henry Reeve defends him: — "Mr. Valpy was a man of keen and sensitive temperament, passionately devoted to classical literature. It surprises me to think how much he combined genuine poetical enthusiasm with the drudgery of class teaching. When the dullness of his scholars failed to reflect the glowing spirit of their guide, he may have lost his temper ; but schoolmasters are human, and Mr. Valpy suffered from gout". Of the sternness of his discipline there can be no doubt. Another old boy writes: — "No Quaker Meeting was ever so still as the School when he was present". And one set of School verses begins: —

> "Norfolk dunces, wont to tremble
> Under Valpy's birchen rule".

But on the credit side of the balance can be set three facts: a number of his old pupils formed a Valpeian Club, and dined together annually till 1866 ; after his death his old boys put a stained-glass window in the School Chapel in memory of him ; and one of the city streets has been called by his name. In 1829 however the Corporation appointed a Committee to investigate the conduct of the School, and Valpy indignantly resigned. But even then they presented him with a handsome piece of plate.

In 1819 he had become Examining Chaplain to Bishop Bathurst, and the Bishop had presented him to the living of Thwaite All Saints, which he held till his death. In the same year the Corporation appointed him Vicar of St. Mary, South Walsham. He was also Vicar of Swardeston from 1819 to 1822. His best known book was his *Elegantiae Latinae or Rules and Exercises illustrative of Elegant Latin Style,* pub-

lished in 1803. This ran through ten editions in his life-time.
In 1815 appeared his critical edition of the *Greek Testament
with English Notes* in three volumes ; of this he issued an
enlarged edition in 1826. He married Anne, daughter of Thomas
Western of Great Abington, Cambridgeshire, and widow of
Chaloner Byng Baldock, Vicar of Milton Abbey, Dorset. He
had one son, Edward John Western Valpy. He died at South-
town, Yarmouth, 15 April 1832. Henry Reeve wrote of him: —
"His manners were to the last degree refined and elegant. His
Jersey origin was perceptible in a slightly foreign peculiarity
of address". [*Dic. Nat. Biog.* ; Saunder's *History of Norwich
Grammar School ;* articles in *The Norvicensian,* the School
Magazine, in 1879.]

VALPY, RICHARD (1754—1836), Headmaster of Reading.
Eldest son of Richard Valpy of St. John's and Catherine Chev-
alier. Born in St. John's Jersey 7 Dec. 1754. His first school
was St. Mannelier. When ten, he was sent to Valognes in
Normandy. Five years later he passed on to Southampton
Grammar School, and then to Guildford Grammar School.
While there, he published his first book in 1772, *Poetical Blos-
soms or a Collection of Poems, Odes, and Translations, by a
Young Gentleman of the Royal Grammar School, Guildford.*
He all but entered the Navy, "but", says the *Gentleman's
Magazine,* "the entreaties of his mother dissuaded him", though
he never lost his love for the sea. His next ambition was the
stage. He got as far as Garrick's house, seeking an engagement,
when with the uplifted knocker in his hand his heart failed him
and he beat a retreat. Then scholarship claimed him. He matriculated at Oxford from Pembroke College as a Morley Scholar
in 1773, and obtained a grant from the Don Baudains in 1774.
He took his B.A. in 1776, his M.A. in 1784, his D.D. in 1792.
In 1777 he was ordained, and appointed Second Master of Bury
St. Edmund's School. In 1781 he became Head Master of Reading Grammar School, a post which he held for fifty-five years.
The school, though it had produced Archbishop Laud, had fallen
into low water, but Valpy rapidly made it one of the foremost
schools in England. "The Doctor", says Mrs. Sherwood, author
of *The Fairchild Family,* who often stayed in his house, "was

a very handsome man, dark and rather thickset, excessively warm in his manner, talking learnedly without affectation, and equally easy with all the world". B.B. Bockett, an old pupil, wrote: — "The Doctor was of about middle stature, but most unwilling to appear less than his full height by the slightest stoop or bend in his gait or walk". He enlarged the Boarding House, and installed as Matron "a lady from Jersey, Mademoiselle Patriarche, whom the boys nicknamed Splatterdash, who could not speak English distinctly, whose business it was to wash the little boys, to laugh with the big boys, and to mend all the stockings" (Mrs. Sherwood) ; he also built a large new schoolroom at his own expense. Boarding fees were fifty guineas a year with an entrance fee of five guineas ; and, when the town protested that the name of the school was the Reading Free School, he pointed out that the old endowments were not sufficient to enable him to engage a staff ; and his critics were silenced, when they saw the school draw fresh families to the town for their sons' education.

From among his pupils sprang great scholars, like Dobree, Professor of Greek at Cambridge, and Bulkeley Bandinel (q.v.), Librarian of the Bodleian, bishops like Jackson of London and Jeune (q.v.) of Peterborough, judges like Sir William Bolland and Sir Thomas Talfourd. His visits to Jersey every summer ensured that a number of Jersey boys were always among his boarders. Like most schoolmasters of that period he was a mighty flogger. His nickname was Dr. Wackerback. And a Reading poet wrote of

"Valpy, who caned the Classics in
Through many a schoolboy's tender skin".

And not schoolboys alone. Mrs. Sherwood tells how one night, when his party had returned from Jersey, his daughter Carteretta had to share her bed with a Guernsey girl. "They began to pinch and scratch and make such a noise that the Doctor heard them in the next room, and snatching up his cane instantly appeared, and without ceremony administered punishment with much good will to the offenders". Yet he inspired in his pupils an intense affection. Miss Mitford might call him "vainer than a peacock", but Judge Talfourd described him as "a polished gentleman and scholar, who by consummate tact, prepossessing manners, and affectionate treatment drew around him disciples from every part of the empire". Another ex-pupil, B.B. Bockett, who wrote as 'Oliver Oldfellow', tells in *Our School* stories of his old headmaster ; how imposing he looked to a schoolboy's eye astride his charger at the head of the Yeomanry in his three-cornered hat and full canonicals as Chaplain to the Troop ; how he tossed half-crowns into the Thames to encourage the boys to dive ; how the French Professor mysteriously disappeared after questioning the purity of Valpy's Jersey-French.

To Valpy the main purpose of education was to turn out classical scholars, boys to whom Latin and Greek were as familiar as their mother tongues. But he did not cling to traditional methods. He revolutionized the teaching of the classics. He was the first man to teach Latin in English, and the school books, which he wrote for Reading, were adopted by most of the Public Schools in England. The chief prize of each year was his guinea for the best original Greek play. Every third year the School according to its Statutes was visited by the Vice-Chancellor of Oxford, the Provost of St. John's, and the Warden of All Souls'. This was a great occasion. Imitating Winchester and anticipating Bradfield, the boys presented plays by Sophocles or Euripides in Greek costume. He partially retired from the Head Mastership in 1830, his youngest son taking his place, but he continued to teach the upper sixth, and exercise some control. For many years his old scholars dined together annually in London ; and still in the school-chapel the boys thank God daily for "the memory of Richard Valpy".

In 1787 he became Rector of Stradishall, Suffolk ; but he only visited his parishioners at Easter and Christmas. To atone for this neglect he wrote for them *An Address from a Clergyman to his Parishioners, 1811*, which became a best-seller in the religious world. He was correcting the proofs of the 8th edition on his death-bed. Of his other publications his classical school-books brought him the widest fame. His Latin Grammar (*Elements of the Latin Language, 1782*) and Greek Grammar (*Elements of the Greek Grammar, 1805*), his *Greek Delectus, 1815*, and *Latin Delectus, 1816*, passed through innumerable editions, and were used for many generations. His *Elements of Mythology: a concise History of the Pagan Deities, 1815*, was also often reprinted. He continued to publish poetry. His *Poetical Chron-*

ology of Ancient and English History 1793 became almost as popular as his classics. His *Poems, Odes, Prologues, and Epilogues spoken at Reading School,* 1804, were regarded as models for this type of versification. In spite of prejudice against the Theatre among many families from whom he might hope to draw pupils he remained a firm believer in Play-acting as a form of education. He published a large number of Plays adapted for performance by schoolboys. Some of these were classical, e.g. The *Aulularia,* the *Amphitruo,* the *Rudens,* and the *Captivi* of Plautus. Others were by English dramatists. His adaptation of Sheridan's *Critics,* interspersed with patriotic interludes of his own, raised £130 for the orphans of seamen killed at the battle of Camperdown. Even more successful were his adaptations of four Shakspere plays, *King John, Henry IV,* part II, *Henry VI,* part III and the *Merchant of Venice.* The fervent anti-Gallican speeches, which Valpy put on the lips of Shakspere's characters, made the first of these so popular, that it had a run at Covent Garden, and "was performed in almost every town in Great Britain and Ireland".

Valpy also gained considerable fame as a preacher. He published *Two Assize Sermons with Notes* in 1793 ; a *Sermon at the Anniversary Meeting of the Royal Humane Society* in 1802, which passed through six editions ; and two volumes of *Sermons preached on Public Occasions* in 1811. His theology was that of an unusually broad churchman, and a pamphlet denouncing him as a heretic was answered by his admirer Dr. Butt in *The Practice of Liberal Piety Vindicated.* The *Dictionary of National Biography* says that he twice refused a bishopric. On his visits to Jersey he was in great demand as a preacher. In 1824 he raised £40 for the National School by a sermon in the Town Church, and he frequently preached for the Bible Society.

In addition to his educational interests he was a Radical politician. In 1795 he was accused of sedition for denouncing Pitt's Bill for suppressing seditious meetings ; and after the passing of the Reform Act in 1832, he took a prominent part in a monster open-air banquet, when 7,000 citizens sat down at tables in the streets, and he prayed that the enfranchisement of the people might turn to noble uses.

He married first Martha Cornelius of Guernsey, by whom he had one daughter, Carteretta Cornelia. By his second wife, the beautiful Mary Benwell of Caversham, who was adored by many generations of schoolboys ("Illness was almost a pleasure to the boys", says Oldfellow, "for they knew well who would nurse them, and how tenderly"), he had ten children, Richard (b. 1783), Abraham John (q.v.), Gabriel (Rector of Bucklebury. Berks.), Anthony Blagrove (Captain R.N.), William Henry (q.v.), Francis Edward Jackson, (who succeeded his father at Reading, but was not a success, and eventually became Rector of Garvestone, Norfolk), Mary, Frances, Elizabeth Blanche (who married Philippe Filleul q.v.) and Penelope Arabella.

Valpy died in his eldest son's house in Kensington, 28 March 1836, and was buried in Kensal Green Cemetery. His portrait was painted by Opie. A statue was erected to his memory in St. Lawrence Church, Reading, and a bust of him is in the Société Jersiaise Museum ; but the best idea of him can be gained from the caricatures in *Our School*. [Child's *Reading in the Early Years of the Nineteenth Century* ; Cooper's *Some Worthies of Reading* ; 'Oliver Oldfellow's' *Our School* ; Darton's *Life and Times of Mrs. Sherwood* ; Russell's *History of King Edward's School, Southampton* (with portrait) ; Macleane's *History of Pembroke College* ; Coate's *History of Reading* ; *Dic. Nat. Biog.*]

VALPY, WILLIAM HENRY (1793–1852), New Zealand Settler, son of Dr. Richard Valpy (q.v.) and Mary Benwell. He was born and educated at Reading, and at fourteen entered the Navy. But he did not like the sea ; so an exchange was arranged with his brother Anthony, and he went to Haileybury to prepare for service with the East India Company. He arrived in India as Writer in 1812, became Collector at Cawnpore in 1820, and in 1833 Magistrate at Sarun. He retired in 1837 being then Commissioner of Revenue at Benares. He settled in Cheltenham, where he took a leading part in establishing a Training College for Teachers. But his health had suffered through his stay in India, and he was advised to leave England. At this time the lately formed New Zealand Company was appealing for emigrants to establish a colony there, and Valpy decided to go. He travelled in state as a rich man with a large staff of farm and household servants, and in 1849 he landed at

Otago, where there was a small settlement of whalers. He selected a farm of 120 acres, south of Dunedin, and also acquired land on the flat. He built a fine stone mansion on the lines of an English Manor House, with a flour-mill and a saw-mill, the machinery for which he had brought from England, and there he farmed in English style with the help of a Bailiff, and entertained the whole neighbourhood like a Squire at his annual Harvest Homes. He soon became one of the leading figures in the infant colony. Besides the farm he had runs at Horseshoe Bush and Waihola (the latter under his son, W.H. Valpy, who with two shepherds made a famous pioneer ride of exploration from Christchurch to Otago, crossing the broad rivers in their paths by means of rafts of flax sticks). "Valpy was a good employer", says the *Dictionary of New Zealand Biography*, "and a man of the highest public spirit. Highly cultured and having had long administrative experience, he was a valuable asset to the community, but he was too refined and sensitive for the conditions of a young colony". In 1850 he gave offence to his neighbours by accepting a seat on the nominated Legislative Council, which the settlers boycotted, because they were demanding self-government ("Nomination is not Democracy") ; but he never took his seat, for, before the Council met, he died on 25 September 1852. In many ways he showed that he inherited his father's liberal views. He advanced money to buy the plant to establish the *Otago Witness*, that the Colony might have a newspaper ; and, though an Anglican, he supported strongly the Presbyterian Minister, Thomas Burns, the poet's nephew, in his social, political, and educational work. [Barr's First Decade of Otago: Roberts' *Southland in 1856*.]

VARDON, HENRY WILLIAM (1870–1937), Professional Golfer. Fourth son of Philip George Vardon, gardener, of Grouville, and Elizabeth Augustine Bouchard. Born at Grouville, 9 May, 1870. Educated at the village school by Boomer, father of the two golfers, Audrey and Percy Boomer. He did not distinguish himself there. "I was", he confessed, "the dunce of the school". In 1877 a golf-course was laid out on Grouville Common, and some of the village boys became interested in the game, playing with home-made clubs and large white marbles on a course of their own construction ; but Vardon only joined them occasionally. "Up to the time when I was twenty", he wrote, "I played so little golf that I can remember almost every round as a red-letter event. We were a big family of six boys and two girls, and at the age of twelve I went out to work collecting seaweed, which brought a nice few pounds a year into the family exchequer. When thirteen, I entered a doctor's service as page-boy,. and for four years had virtually no golf at all. When seventeen, I went as gardener to Major Spofforth, brother of the 'demon bowler'. Major Spofforth was keen on golf, and now and again he took me out to play. Apart from this my golf was limited to Bank Holidays". About this time his brother Tom, who was learning club-making at St. Anne's on-Sea, (he later became professional to the Royal St. George's Club, Sandwich) won £20 in a tournament. This turned Vardon's thoughts to golf as a profession. Hearing from his brother that a greenkeeper was wanted for new links being laid out on Lord Ripon's estate near Harrogate, he applied, and got the job (Nov. 1890). On the strength of this he married at All Saints' Jessie Bryant of St. Helier's. A year later he became professional to the Bury Club. He first attracted notice by his play for the Open Championship at Sandwich in 1894, when he finished fifth. This won him an invitation to a professional tournament at Pau. On his return he became professional at Ganton, Yorkshire. In 1896 he won for the first time the British Open Championship. In the following year he lost it to H. H. Hilton, an amateur ; but he won it again in 1898 and 1899. "During those two years", wrote Bernard Darwin, "he was winning nearly all the tournaments there were to win, and murdering his enemies in exhibition matches. He made a triumphant tour through Scotland, and that dour country had to admit that England had the best of it. His play was, as Andrew Kirkaldy said, 'enough to break the heart of an iron horse' " (*Playing the Like.*) Next came an all-conquering tour of 20,000 miles through America in 1900, and the winning of the Open Championship there. "I consider", he wrote, "that at that time I was playing better golf than I had ever played before, or have done since" (*C.G.*). The papers hailed him as the Golf King in letters an inch deep, and his visit gave a great impetus to American golf. But he admits that he overtired himself, and

that his play suffered. In the next three British Championships
he finished second, but in 1905 he regained his old position.
Then his health broke down, and he had to enter a sanatorium.
He made a good recovery, but it was some time before his golf
recovered. In 1911 however he won the German Open Championship, and followed this by winning the British Open
Championship for the fifth time. In 1914 he won it for the
sixth time. Then came the War, during which competitions
ceased, and his house at Totteridge was destroyed by a German
bomb. When the War was over, Vardon's championship days
were over too. But he remained a popular and successful golf
coach. He died in 1937. Bernard Darwin, no mean authority,
wrote of him: — "I cannot believe that anyone ever had or will
ever have a greater genius for hitting a golf-ball than Harry
Vardon". He published, *The Complete Golfer*, 1905 ; *How to
play Golf*, 1912 (each of these ran to 21 editions) ; *Progressive
Golf*, 1922, and *My Golfing Life*, 1933. His clubs and medals
are in the S. J. Museum. [His autobiography, *My Golfing
Life* ; *The Complete Golfer* and *Progressive Golf* also give
particulars of his career. Bernard Darwin has an essay on him
in *Playing the Like*.]

VERNON, SIR WILLIAM HENRY VENABLES (1852–
1934), Bailiff. His grandfather, Lieut.-Col. the Hon. Henry
Vernon, Grenadier Guards, of Mayfield Hall, Derbyshire, had
married Grace, daughter of Edward Coke, niece of the Earl of
Leicester. The Anti-Corn-Law agitation and the Chartist riots
caused many families to leave the Midlands, and Sir William's
grandmother, then a widow, came to Jersey, and settled in
St. Peter's House. Her only son, Edward Henry, a Lieutenant
in the Navy, married at St. Brelade's in 1851 Louise Sophie
Charlotte, daughter of Jean Gédeon René de Joux, a Minister
of the Swiss Church, who had received Anglican orders, and
had kept a school in Hemery Row since 1829. Sir William,
their only child, was born at La Profonde Rue, Trinity, 1 Jan.
1852. His father was wounded in China, and died soon after.
When his mother remarried, the child remained in Jersey in his
grandmother's care. He spent his early years in the island, and

in a schloss near Heidelburg, and, after his grandmother's death, with an uncle at Nuttal Priory, Nottinghamshire. Later he went to Touraine to perfect his French, and then entered the University of Toulouse. Here he had a brilliant career ; B. A. 1868 ; Licentiate in law, 1871 ; Prizeman in Judicial Composition and in Roman Law, 1869,70, and 71 ; Medallist, Literary Composition, 1871. His family wished him to enter the diplomatic service ; so he came to Jersey meaning to sell St. Peter's House ; but Bailiff Hammond (q.v.), a friend of his father, and Sir Robert Marett (q.v.), his grandmother's legal adviser, persuaded him to join the local Bar, which he did in 1873. He was elected Constable of St. Peter's in 1875, but only held office for a year, as in 1876 he was appointed Greffier, a post which he held for fourteen years. In the same year he took a commission in the Militia as Lieutenant in the East Regiment, being transferred later to the Artillery, and becoming Captain in 1881. In 1880 he became Solicitor-General, in 1885 Attorney-General, and in 1899 Bailiff. On the day he was sworn in there was a great display of bunting in the Town and on the ships in the harbour ; the engines of the Jersey Railways, of which he had been Chairman, were gaily decorated ; and St. Peter's bells rang from early morning. He was knighted by King Edward in 1903, and made a Knight of the British Empire by King George V in the States Chamber on 12 July 1921, when the King visited the island. In 1923 the University of Caen conferred on him the honorary degree of Docteur en droit after the holding of the Semaine Normande in Jersey. His portrait, painted by John St. Helier Lander (q.v.), which hangs in the Court, was subscribed for by the general public, and presented to him in 1928 on the jubilee of his connection with the Royal Court.

Sir William was one of the most brilliant jurists the island has known. He always gave a clear analysis of cases brought before him, and rarely allowed Advocates to wander from the point. He ruled the States Assembly with dignity, and kept debates in order. He displayed unfailing courtesy to all, high and low, rich and poor. He was a good linguist, and could speak the Jersey dialect fluently. He sailed his yacht, the Wyvern, the last built in St. Aubin's, under the Commodore's flag of the Royal Channel Islands Yacht Club, as far north as the Hebrides and as far south as the Mediterranean. A much travelled man, conversant with many subjects, he was always listened to with interest on topics of social or public importance. In his early years he had been a successful breeder and exporter of Jersey cattle. He was Treasurer of the Société Jersiaise 1884—6, and President 1923—5. He published nothing under his own name but his *Thèse* at Toulouse, but the voluminous *Case for the Crown* in the Prison Board Case 1891—4 was prepared by him as Attorney-General, and is a work of great historical and constitutional value. He resigned the post of Bailiff in 1931 owing to advancing age, and died in St. Peter's House 23 Jan. 1934. He was buried at St. Saviour's. He had married in 1880 Julia Matilda, daughter of Philip Gosset of Bagot. [Local newspapers.]

VOISIN, FRANCOIS (1816—94), Merchant. Eldest son of François Voisin of St. Lawrence and Elisabeth Gibaut. Born in St. Lawrence 1816 and baptized 2 June. The Voisins were a family of Huguenot origin, who had been farming in St. Lawrence for 130 years ; but François, when twenty, opened in April 1837 a small shop in King Street with, as his first advertisement announced, "a great assortment of drapery, haberdashery, silks, hosiery, and gloves just arrived from the London market". King Street was then a narrow crooked lane, on to which opened the backyard doors of the houses in Broad Street and the Square. Its old name had been Rue de Derrière, and it was still often called Back Street. Voisin's was only a tiny back-street shop ; but it prospered. In the following year he took over the shop next door as a Men's Department. Later he acquired the property on either side and a large strip of land in the rear.

But quite early he formed the theory that the most important part of a shop is its buying department. Having trained his assistants, he left the selling entirely in their hands, while he wandered about the world buying goods for them to sell. He was easily the most travelled Jerseyman of his generation. With a few belongings tied up in a red cotton handkerchief he made his way through all the countries of Europe, and even to Asia and America. His Diary shows him choosing shawls at Paisley,

ribbons at St. Etienne, textiles at Berne and Basle, buying silks
at Lyons, linen at Belfast, lace at Malines, fancy goods in the
Black Forest. He visited regularly the great fair at Nijni-
Novgorod in Russia to select his furs, and even journeyed to the
East in search of silks and damask.

In 1878 having made his fortune he handed over the business
to two of his sons, and in April was elected without opposition
Constable of St. Helier's. He completed the laying out of the
Parade and West Mount, begun by R.P. Marett (q.v.), but
left unfinished by his successors. At the close of his term of
office in 1881 he would not stand again ; but built for himself
a house on the top of West Mount, where he lived till his death
on 20 April 1894. He married Jeanne Catherine, daughter of
Pierre Bishop, and had eleven children, of whom Edward became
Constable of St. Lawrence [*Jersey Express* 26 Ap. 1894 :
Through Six Reigns.]

WACE (fl 1135—1174), Norman Poet. The name Robert
sometimes given him arose through a mistranslation of a line
in his *St. Nicolas*. He says that he wrote this "*a l'oes Robert
le fitz Tiout*", "for the use of Robert, son of Tiout". Huet
(*Origines de Caen*) misread this as "*Robert le fit tout*", "Robert
made it all", and assumed that Wace's name was Robert, and
later writers followed him. In his own writings he merely calls
himself Maistre Wace or Maistre Guace, and the few contemporaries who mention him give him no other name. This
may have been his Christian name, a French form of the
Teutonic Wazo, and he may not have had a surname, for in his
day surnames had not become universal. On the other hand
charters printed in Dupont's *Histoire du Cotentin* show that
Wace was a surname in Jersey in the twelfth century ; one in
1180 speaks of a Richard Wace of St. Helier's ; and Vasse
became a common surname in the island later. The statement
that his mother was a daughter of Tosteins, the chamberlain of
Duke Robert I, rests on no firmer foundation than a suggested
emendation of a difficult line.

We know neither the date of his birth nor that of his death ;
but he tells us, "Three King Henries I saw and knew, and was

a 'Clerk lisant' in their time" (R.R.). He was therefore already ordained, a cleric without clerical duties who devoted himself to literature, before Henry I died in 1135, and he was still writing in 1170, when Prince Henry was crowned in the lifetime of Henry II. He was born in Jersey ("En l'isle de Gersui fu nez". R.R.), and, while still young, was sent to Caen to be educated ("A Chaem fui portez, Illoques fui a letres mis"). Here there were two famous schools, Lanfranc's religious seminary and Arnoul's school for secular learning. Later he studied for a long time in France, perhaps at the University of Paris ("Puis fui longues en France apris"). Then he returned to Caen, and earned his bread by writing 'romances', i.e. poems, not in Latin, but in the Romance tongue ("De romanz faire m'entremis Mult en escris e mult en fis"). The Anglo-Norman Renaissance was then at its peak. A leisured class had grown up eager for books in their own language. Three of Wace's early poems have come down to us, all on religious subjects. The first is a fragment, 420 lines from his Vie de Ste Marguerite. In this he confesses that he has merely translated into Romance verse a Latin prose life ("Ci faut sa vie, ce dit Guace, Qui de latin en roman mist, Ce que Thodimus escri"). The second is La Conception Nostre Dame, a translation of a Latin tract describing how the Feast of the Conception became the Fête aux Normands. The third, La Vie de St. Nicolas, is also a translation from the Latin. He remained at Caen doing this kind of work for many years. ("A chaem lungues conversai").

Then came his first great poem. In 1147 Geoffrey of Monmouth had taken the reading world by storm with a wonderful work of fiction, his Latin History of the Kings of Britain. He tells how after the fall of Troy Brutus, grandson of Aeneas, travelled to Britain, and founded New Troy (London). As he tells of the reigns of his descendants, we meet with Lear and his daughters, Merlin the Enchanter, and for the first time we find the Celtic legends of King Arthur woven into the ideal figure of a hero king. Wace read this, and turned it into a Romance poem of 16,000 lines, the Roman de Brut. But he did more than paraphrase Geoffrey's Latin prose. He added a wealth of picturesque detail, some of which, he says, he gathered from Breton sources ; so that his poem is an important link in the chain of Arthurian legend. In Wace we hear for the first Time of the Round Table and of the hope that Arthur will

return. And he in his turn inspired the first great English poet,
for almost all the material in Layamon's *Brut* is derived from
Wace. He finished the *Roman de Brut* in 1155. (*M C L et
cinq ans Fist Mestre Wace cest romanz*"), the year after Henry
II came to the throne, and according to Layamon dedicated it
to "the noble Eleanor, the high King Henry's Queen".

Now, perhaps through this poem, Wace came into touch with
the Court. Caen was one of Henry's favourite cities. Here he
built a palace in which he often stayed ; and Queen Eleanor
became the poet's patroness. "Frank is Eleanor", he writes,
"and debonair, and wise" (*R.R. Chron. Asc.*) In 1160 he received a commission to write "for the honour of the Second
Henry" a metrical chronicle of the Dukes of Normandy from the
time of Rollo (he gives the date. *Chron. Asc.*), and he was
given a canonry at Bayeux as a retaining fee. "Henry caused
me to be given a prebend at Bayeux. May God reward him
for it. And many another gift he gave me" (*R.R.* 173). His
name now appears occasionally in Church documents. In the
Livre Noir of Bayeux a letter from the Bishop, dated 1169, refers
to 'Wacius canonicus', and a charter of 1174 mentions Was-
cius in a list of the city clergy. From this royal commission
sprang his second great poem, the *Roman de Rou*. This, like
its predecessors, was based on Latin originals, the Chronicles of
Dudo of St. Quentin and William of Jumièges ; but here again
he amplified the story from so many other sources, documentary
and traditional, that his poem is a valuable mine of historical
evidence, specially for the Norman conquest of England. But
Wace was a leisurely writer. In 1174 the King awoke to the
fact that the poem he had ordered fourteen years before had not
yet been completed, and with justifiable impatience he transferred the commission from Wace to his rival, Benoit de Ste.
Maure. We last see the old Canon in his lodgings at Bayeux
a soured and disappointed man. Queen Eleanor, his patroness,
is disgraced and in prison. "Dead is our old nobility, and
perished with it is largesse". His hands are frozen, and he
cannot afford a fire. He is driven to pawn his belongings.
(*Chron. Asc.*) So he throws down his pen, and leaves his poem
unfinished. "Here ends the book of Maistre Wace. Let anyone
who wishes finish it". (*R.R.*). The unfinished poem presents
many interesting problems. Most of it is in Wace's favourite
metre of rhymed eight-syllable couplets, like Scott's : —

The way was long ; the wind was cold ;
The minstrel was infirm and old.

But two sections (one of which, called the *Chronique Ascendante* because it tells the story backward, covers the same ground as part of the rest of the poem) are in the twelve-syllable Alexandrine metre, "that like a wounded snake drags its slow length along" (Pope). Had Wace begun to rewrite the whole poem in a new metre, or were the Alexandrines meant to be a preface to the rest? A scholarly edition of the *Roman de Rou* is needed. The French edition by Pluquet is described by Gaston Paris in *Romania* (IX) as "in every respect a deplorable work, in which insincerity argues with ignorance—a literary fraud", while Andresen's German edition is dismissed by Paul Meyer as "very bad". [The best accounts of Wace are V. Payen-Payne's *Wace and the Roman de Rou*, one of the Occasional Publications of the Jersey Society in London, Kate Norgate's article in *Dic. Nat. Biog.*, Professor Salmon's article in *La Grande Encyclopédie*, Du Meril's chapter in *Etudes sur quelques points d'Archéologie et d'Histoire littéraire*, Gaston Paris' article in *Romania* Vol. IX, and Philpot's *Maistre Wace.* Payen-Payne gives a full bibliography, and Kate Norgate a shorter one.]

WAKE, SIR ISAAC (1581—1632), Orator and Diplomatist. Second son of Arthur Wake, the famous Puritan Canon of Christ Church, Oxford, who, when deprived of all his preferments in England, had been offered by Sir Amias Poulet the Chaplaincy of Mont Orgueil, where he found sanctuary for eighteen years.

Isaac was born in 1581 in St. Martin's ; entered Christ Church, Oxford in 1593 ; graduated B.A. in 1597 ; was elected Fellow of Merton in 1598 ; took his M.A. 1603 ; and in 1604 became Public Orator to the University. Wood says of him: — "He had his pen more at command in the Latin, English, and French tongues than any of his time in the University. His speaking was majestic ; but he employed his time more in reading political and civil matters than in philosophy or the great faculties. He was a man of exquisite learning, strong parts of nature, and a most refined wit. He was put upon speeches at all receptions and funerals". James I however found his style soporific, for comparing the Orators of the two Universities he said: "When Wake of Oxford speaketh, his utterance and matter are so grave that I am apt to sleep, but Sleep of Cambridge never speaketh without keeping me awake".

In 1609 Wake abandoned the University for a diplomatic career, and became Secretary to Sir Dudley Carleton, British Ambassador to Venice. In 1615 he was appointed Ambassador to the Court of Savoy, a post which he held for sixteen years. He was knighted in 1619, his escutcheon bearing the title, "Ambassador Extraordinary in Savoy and Piedmont, Ordinary for Italy, Helvetia, and Rhetia, Select for France". He was employed on many delicate diplomatic missions, to mediate an alliance between Savoy and the Swiss States, to support the candidature of the Duke of Savoy for the Imperial Crown, to secure the help of Venice for the recovery of the Palatinate, and to mediate between the King of Denmark and the Duke of Savoy. In 1623 he was in England, and married Anna Bray, stepdaughter of Sir Edward Conway, Secretary of State. In 1624 he was elected M.P. for Oxford University. He attended Parliament regularly for some months, but then returned to his work in Italy. In 1631 he was appointed Ambassador to the French Court, and was about to succeed his old chief Carleton as Secretary of State, when he died in Paris in 1632. He published a number of his Latin Orations, including his welcome to James I on his first visit to Oxford, and his funeral tribute to Thomas Bodley, founder of the Bodleian Library; several books on foreign politics, e.g. *The Thirteen Cantons of the Helvetical League; The State of Italy; The Proceedings of the King of Sweden;* and a volume of sermons. *Disquisitions upon the Nativity of our Saviour Jesus Christ.* [*Dic. Nat. Biog.*; Wood's *Athenae Oxoniensis; Cal. State Papers.*]

WALDEN, ROGER (d. 1406), Archbishop of Canterbury. Walden's right to a place in this Dictionary is not unchallengeable, for Adam of Usk, the contemporary Welsh Historian, says: — "Him the town of Walden in Essex saw exalted from a butcher's son" ; Fuller too in his *Worthies* (pubd. 1662) made him a native of Saffron Walden. But Adam is not the most accurate of historians, and the birth at Walden may be only a guess from his name. On the other hand several points confirm the Jersey tradition that he was one of the Jersey Vauldens, whose name had been anglicized as Walden. Indeed the French Chronicler who wrote *Lystoire de la Traison et Mort du Roy Richard* calls him the Archbishop of Canterbury "qui avoit nom Vauduin". All authorities agree that his origin was humble and obscure. Thomas of Walsingham says: "From a little pauper (*pauperculus*) he rose to be Treasurer of England" (*Hist. Ang.*) ; and the *Annals of Richard II* call him "a man utterly illiterate", which probably merely means that he had no University degree. He is first heard of in July 1371, when he was appointed to the Rectory of St. Helier by the King, "the Bishop of Coutances being the King's enemy" (*Foed*). It was quite common for English clerics to snap up Jersey livings, when England was at war with France, livings which they never visited ; but Walden came to Jersey, and remained there till 1385. In Dec. 1371 he became Commissioner in Jersey to inquire into the concealed goods of aliens (*P.R.*). In 1374 Lord Percy presented him to the Rectory of Kirkby Overblow, Yorkshire, and in 1376 he added to this the Rectory of Fenny Drayton, Lincolnshire (*P.R.*) ; but to each of these he merely appointed a Curate, and stayed on in Jersey. In 1578 he was appointed by two English clerics their attorney in Jersey (*P.R.*). In 1382 he was entrusted by the King with the guardianship of Philippe De Carteret, the young Seigneur of St. Ouen's, till he should come of age (*Foed.*). In 1383 and 1384 he was Sub-warden of the Isles under Sir Hugh Calverley (Treaty Roll). It is difficult to picture an Essex butcher's son ministering contentedly to parishioners who spoke nothing but Norman-French ; and it is impossible to believe that a young ecclesiastic as able and ambitious as Walden proved himself to be, one moreover who evidently had considerable influence at Court, would have been content to remain for fourteen years in a backwater like Jersey ; but both mysteries are easily explained, if Jersey was his native home.

In 1335 he seems to have left the island, for, when he exchanged the Rectory of Fenny Drayton for that of Burton in Kendale, he was described as one of the King's Clerks (P.R.). He was still however employed on a good deal of Jersey business. In 1586 he received Jean De St. Martin's recognizances after his escape from Gorey Castle (C.R.). In 1588 Colette Nicolle of Jersey and William Arnaud were ordered to appear before him in the Church of St. Martin's Vintry, London, to pass a transfer of land (C.R.). He now began to accumulate ecclesiastical benefices. In 1587 he was appointed Archdeacon of Winchester. He became Rector of St. Andrew's Holborn in 1591. He held prebends at Lincoln (1389), Salisbury (1389), Gloucester (1391), Exeter, and Lichfield (1394). Dean Hook rather naïvely pictures him meditating on verses from a Psalm inscribed on his stall at Lincoln ; but in those days Church appointments were regarded merely as sources of income to provide salaries for the King's officials. Walden at this time was certainly not chanting Psalms in any Cathedral. His duties were purely secular. In Oct. 1378 he was Captain of Mark near Calais. In December that year he was appointed Treasurer of Calais, "to abide there on the King's service for the safeguard of the town" (C.R.), a post which he held till 1392. In 1388 we hear of him leading a cattle-raid into French territory, and a little later he was spoken of as "our Captain in the parts of Picardy". In 1391 he was made High Bailiff of Guisnes ; and the following year he was recalled to be Secretary to Richard II. Adam of Usk quite truly said of him that he was "better versed in things of the camp and the world than of the Church or the study". In 1395 he became Treasurer of England, and to provide him with a salary the King appointed him also Dean of York.

Meanwhile trouble had been brewing between Richard and a group of Lords, led by the Earl of Arundel and his brother, Archbishop Arundel of Canterbury. In 1397 the King by a *coup d'état* overthrew this opposition, and Archbishop Arundel was banished from the country. To depose an Archbishop was no simple matter ; but the Pope obliged the King by translating Arundel against his will to St. Andrew's, and then appointing Walden to the vacant see. He was consecrated on 5 Feb. 1398. He then received "in consideration of his great labours and expenses in the office of Treasurer of England, and whilst he was with the King and his army in Ireland and Scotland" a General Pardon and Discharge from all claims that could be brought against him (*P.R.*). Of his acts as Archbishop we know little, for at his deposition his Register was destroyed, to show that his successor did not admit the legality of any of his proceedings. We know however that his enthronement was conducted with great magnificence, the King himself being present, that he entertained the Court again, when the King came to pray at the shrine of St. Thomas before sailing for Ireland, that he presided over the Convocation that added the Festivals of St. David, St. Chad. and St. Winifred to the Calendar. In March 1399 he was appointed Papal Legate (*C.R.*).

He was now at the height of his power. But that Lent William Norham, a hermit, ordered him in the Name of God to give up his Archbishopric, and to counsel the King to amend his life, "else both he and the King would suffer such retribution, that the ears of all who heard thereof would tingle". Walden suspended him from celebrating Mass, and sent him to the King, who after hearing his denunciations committed him to the Tower, "where he remained", says the chronicler, "till he saw his prophecies fulfilled" (*Annals*). In July Henry of Bolingbroke landed in England ; Richard was deposed ; and Bolingbroke became Henry IV. Arundel had returned with Henry from exile, and reclaimed his archbishopric. The Pope quashed the Bull in Walden's favour, declaring that it had been issued through misinformation ; and Arundel was restored to his see. "Now" says Fuller, "was Roger Walden reduced to Roger Walden, as poor as at his first beginning". Yet even his enemies spoke well of him ; and Arundel secured his pardon from the King.

In Jan. 1400 he was suspected of knowledge of a plot to restore Richard, and committed to the Tower. "The insurgents were brought before the Justices. The laymen were drawn and hanged ; the clerics drawn and beheaded. The Bishop of Carlisle was imprisoned and deprived of his bishopric. Roger Walden alone was excused" (Continuator of the *Eulogium*). By July he was sufficiently restored to favour to be granted two tuns of Gascony wine yearly from the King's cellar (*P.R.*). In Feb. 1401 he was granted "full restitution of all his manors, lands, rents, and possessions, from which he was expelled for certain crimes against the King's Majesty, whereof he has been acquitted" (*P.R.*). In 1404 on the death of the Bishop of London Archbishop Arundel, "nobly reflecting on his worth, or

his want, or both" (Fuller), persuaded the Pope to 'provide'
Walden to that see, and after considerable difficulty gained the
King's consent.   On 30 June 1405 he was installed ; but a few
months later he fell ill, and on 5 Jan. he died in his episcopal
residence at Much Hadham, Herts.   His body lay in state in a
new chapel which he had added to St. Bartholomew's Smithfield
and he was buried in St. Paul's.

His career had not been one that would have led us to expect
all men to speak well of him.   Yet such was the case.   Adam of
Usk wrote: — "This Roger was a modest man, pious and courteous, whose speech was always profitable and his words well-
chosen".   J. Prophete, another contemporary, spoke of "his moderation in prosperity and patience in adversity".   Archbishop
Arundel declared: "No Bishop was ever more devout, more
temperate in success, more resigned in affliction, more amiable
toward all, more full of grace and virtue".   But his name became
a proverb for the fickleness of fortune.   Trussell calls him "the
tennis-ball of Fate".   Adam of Usk says that he proved the
maxim, "Quick gains are soon lost".

The British Museum possesses a manuscript *History of the
World* in Latin, which is said by its title to be by "Roger Walden, Bishop of London" ;   and this authorship is accepted by
Wylie and Hook ;   but Professor Tait in the *Dic. Nat. Biog.*
declares that this title was not added till the 16th century, and
that the manuscript itself must be older than the time of Walden.   [*Dic Nat. Biog.* and authorities there quoted ;   Hook's
Lives of the Archbishops, appendix to vol. IV ;   Wylie's
Henry IV.]

WALLIS (or WALSH), GEOFFROI (d. 1471), Seigneur of
St. Germain.   (The spelling of his surname varies.   A contract
of 1363 in De La Croix' *Jersey* calls his grandfather Valis.   In
Jurat-lists his father thrice appears as Walich.   A letter from
the Bailiff in *Bull* IX refers to Geoffroi as Wallisch.   The
Royal Court called him Walysse, Walsche, Walich, and Walsh.
His cousins, when claiming his estate spelt their name Walsh.
The Inquest of 1532 used the form Wallys.)   His grandfather,
Geoffrey Wallis, a Dorset man of good family, settled in the

island, when he married a Jersey heiress, Eléanore De Chesney, widow of the Seigneur of Handois. He had a son, Raulin, who became a Jurat. Raulin's son, Geoffroi, inherited through his grandmother the fiefs of Handois in St. Lawrence, Paisnel in St. John's, Morville in St. Ouen's, and Grainville in St. Saviour's. These four fiefs now began to be considered as one, and were called the Fief of St. Germain from the house Les Saints Germains at St. Lawrence in which the family lived. It was one of the largest fiefs in the island, containing 210 ver-gées. Geoffroi married Katherine, only child of Jean De Vin-chelez, who inherited the Vinchelez estates. He was a soldier, and in the Wars of the Roses followed the banner of Warwick the Kingmaker, being one of the private army, which the Earl maintained, who all wore the badge of the ragged staff, and according to Holinshed ate six oxen daily for breakfast. In 1457 Warwick as Lord of the Isles made him Captain of Castle Cornet, Guernsey (*Bull.* IX). In 1464 he was appointed Survey-or of the Scrunity in the Port of Poole (*P.R.*). The Chronicler says that he accompanied Warwick on his embassy to Spain (*Chroniques*) ; but, as Warwick never went to Spain, this prob-ably means the embassy to France in 1467, which caused the breach between Warwick and Edward IV. In 1468 Wallis was back in Guernsey as Lieut.-Governor. In 1470 he followed the King-maker from the Yorkist to the Lancastrian side, collected his Jersey tenants, and joined the force which landed with War-wick at Dartmouth in September and restored Henry VI to the throne. But in March 1471 Edward IV landed again in York-shire. On Easter Day, April 14, the armies met at Barnet. War-wick made his mounted men send their horses to the rear to show there would be no retreat. When they were outflanked and defeated, their heavy armour made escape impossible. Wal-lis fell with his leader. Some of his more lightly armed billmen made their way to Southampton. At an Inquest on the Estate later Jean Mourant testified that "he had been present at South-ampton, when divers of Geoffroi's men were captured in that town by officers of the King and hanged for treason". Others more fortunate escaped home to Jersey (De La Croix' *Jersey*). Wallis' estates were confiscated. He had no children. His widow, who survived him for fifty years, married Philippe De La Hougue. At the accession of Henry VII some cousins claimed the estate, pleading that a Lancastrian King should not maintain a sentence of treason passed by Yorkists on a man who died fighting for the House of Lancaster. The litigation dragged on till 1552 ; but the Crown retained most of the property. [Article, The Family of Walsh, *Bull* X.]

WESTAWAY, JULIA (1820—1901), Benefactress. Daughter of Nathaniel Westaway, builder, who began in a small way of business, but died a very rich man in 1852. He married Anne Alexandre. He left three children, Harriet and Julia, who lived together, and John Nathaniel, a merchant. On the father's death there were quarrels over the division of the estate, and the dispute became so bitter that in Oct. 1861 Nathaniel put his sisters in the debtors' prison to enforce a claim for a small sum of interest, which he had established at law, but which they thought unjust. On 1 Nov. he even reduced them to 'short commons'. Bound by law to support them, he refused to contribute more than the minimum allowance of 3d. a day. In a week Julia's health broke down, and the ladies submitted and paid. But from that date neither held any communication with him or his family. Harriet died, but Julia lived to be 81. The voluminous evidence produced before the Privy Council later revealed a truly pathetic picture of a kind-hearted, charitable, but rather simple-minded old lady, bullied by a coarse, drunken, domineering house-keeper, and surrounded by a crowd of greedy sharks trying to get money out of her. In 1895 she made her will, leaving the bulk of her estate to provide (a) a crèche and day-nursery for babies, (b) a fund for *pauvres honteux* (poor who had never applied for parish relief) to be distributed at the discretion of the Constables and Churchwardens, (c) a fund to provide clothes and books for Protestant elementary schoolchildren. Six years later she died, 20 Sept. 1901, and left £92,000. Her brother's son John then claimed that the will should be set aside on the grounds that his aunt was "infirm in body and weak in mind", and that it had been made under "undue influence". This led to a long series of lawsuits ; but eventually (Feb. 1906) the Privy Council decided that "on the evidence the testatrix was of sound mind, memory, and understanding and there was no evidence of undue influence". And so the

Westaway Crèche and the Don Westaway were added to the island's charities. [Printed evidence at the lawsuit. Local newspapers.]

WESTON, SIR RICHARD (1469—1542). Courtier. Governor of Guernsey. In 1461 when England was rent by the Wars of the Roses, the French seized Mont Orgueil, and established themselves in Jersey. In Oct. 1468 Richard Harliston, Vice-Admiral of England, recaptured the castle after a nineteen weeks' siege. Among those killed during the fighting was Renaud Lempriere, Seigneur of Rozel. His widow, Catherine Camel (daughter of John Camel of Shapwick, Dorset), married one of Harliston's knights, Edmund Weston (son of Peter Weston of Boston, Lincolnshire). Their eldest son, Richard, was born in Rozel Manor (*Chroniques*) in 1469. Two facts fix the date. In 1519 he was one of the 'ancient knights' put in charge of the young Henry VIII, and we are told that these were all over fifty ; but his parents could not have married before May 1468, the month in which the siege began, during which his mother's first husband was killed.

The Westons were in high favour with the Tudor kings. In 1485, within a month of the coronation of Henry VII, Richard's father, Edmund, was made Governor of Guernsey "in consideration of good and gratuitous services performed with great labour and great personal cost", which suggests that he had helped to secure Henry Tudor his throne. Four months later he was made an Esquire of the Body. In 1502 we hear of Richard at Court. The *Privy Purse Expenses* make a note of £1.13.4 paid him "for the King's loss at disse" (dice), and a gain of £2 "for the King's loss at cheke" (chess). About this time he married Anne, daughter of Oliver Sandys of Shere, one of the Queen's gentlewomen.

When Henry VIII became King, Richard's rise was rapid. Even before the Coronation he was made Governor of Guernsey (his father was now dead), a post which he held for thirty-two years. In 1511 he became Lieutenant of the Castle and Forest of Windsor with lodgings in the Lieutenant's Tower. In the same year he was one of the commanders of the English archers sent to help to drive the Moors out of Spain. In 1514 he was knighted by the King, and in 1518 appointed a Knight of the Body, which meant being in constant attendance at Court, and was dubbed a Knight Commander of the Bath. In the same year, when peace was made between England and France, he signed as one of the witnesses. In 1519, when the gay, young sparks in attendance on the King were "discharged at the request of the Council", he was one of the "four sad and ancient knights", who took their place. "He was", says Frederick Harrison", a servant after Henry's own heart, brave, discreet, wary, magnificent, artistic, cosmopolitan, without troublesome scruples either in Church or State, a man without any feudal connections and with no dangerous ambitions". "He served for more than thirty-two years, and never lost the King's favour or resigned a single office till his last illness. He saw out all the changes in policy and religion ; he did homage to five of Henry's Queens ; he saw scores of his colleagues and his own son beheaded ; and yet he retained to the last the confidence of the King". "He was one of the able men of courage, brains, and culture, on whom the Tudors relied to break the teeth of the barons, personally unscrupulous, grasping, time-serving, self-seeking, but withal of unblemished credit and staunchly faithful to his master". "There is hardly a single State ceremony during Henry's reign in which he is not recorded to have had part" (*Annals of an Old Manor House*). He was a Judge in the Star Chamber. He was in attendance on the King at the Field of the Cloth of Gold. He was Treasurer of Calais, Under-Treasurer of England. He was sent to meet Anne of Cleves, when she landed, and to escort her to Rochester, where the King was waiting for her. In 1521 on the execution of the Duke of Buckingham he was granted the Manor of Sutton on the banks of the Wey in Surrey, and here he built the beautiful house that is still standing. Henry stayed with him in 1533 "huntyng the redd dere".

His only son, Francis, was brought up at Court, and made a Page, when he was fifteen. At nineteen he was one of the King's favourites, and figures frequently in the *Privy Purse Expenses*. These show £6 (the equivalent of £72 today) paid him for "iiii games which he wanne of the Kinge's Grace at Tennes at iiii angelles a game", £4—10s "lost to Weston at bowles", £46 (i.e. £550) "wonne off the King at Dyce", and £18 "lost by the King to Weston at Pope Julius' game". In 1530 he married Ann Pickering, an heiress to great estates in

Cumberland. In 1533 at Anne Boleyn's coronation he was made a Knight of the Bath and Gentleman of the Queen's Chamber. In May 1536 he was arrested as one of the Queen's lovers, and beheaded. In his last letter to his father he enclosed a list of his debts (chiefly gambling ones) "which I humbly desyre you to dyschardge". These amounted to £925, or about £12,000 of our money.

His execution did not affect his father's relations with the King. Sir Richard was present in the following year at the christening of the young Prince Edward and at the funeral of Queen Jane Seymour. In 1539 he was appointed Master of the new Court of Wards, which gave him control of the estates of all heirs of the King's tenants who were under age. He died on 7 Aug. 1542, and was buried in the Parish Church of the Trinity at Guildford in the chapel he had built for the purpose. [*Chroniques de Jersey* ; Harrison's *Annals of an Old Manor House* ; *Calendar of State Papers, Henry VIII* ; *Privy Purse Expenses* ; *Dic. Nat. Biog.* ; *Bull.* X.]

WESTON, SIR WILLIAM (1470?—1540), Last Prior of the Knights. Hospitallers in England. Younger son of Sir Edmund Weston and Catherine, widow of Renaud Lempriere (see previous article). The Jersey Chronicler wrote: — "A gentleman of Harliston's company, named Weston, after the death of the Seigneur of Rozel married the Lady of Rozel. To Weston and this lady two sons were born, one named William, the other Richard. They were both Knights. William was a Knight of Rhodes, and afterward Grand Prior of the Order in England. Richard was Captain of the Isle of Guernsey, and also a member of the King's Privy Council. Both were born in Rozel Manor". Sir William confirmed his birth in Jersey in a letter written in 1530: — "I, Sir Wm. Weston, do declare for matter of treweth that Nicholas Villiard, berer hereof, was borne in the parishe of St. Saviour's in the Isle of Jersey, in the which Isle I myselfe was borne" (*Bull* X.).

He joined the Knights Hospitallers of St. John of Jerusalem, an Order in which two of his uncles had been Turcopoliers (i.e. second in command to the Grand Master) and a third Lord

Prior in England. We first hear of Sir William in 1508, when
he arrived in Calais on a diplomatic mission (*Chron. of Calais*).
In 1510 he was at the headquarters of the Order in Rhodes. In
1520 he was Admiral of the fleet of the Knights of Rhodes,
and commanded the first ironclad on record, the *Great Carrack*,
which carried a crew of 500, and was provisioned for six months.
She was sheathed in metal, and said to be perfectly cannon-
proof. He was wounded in the famous defence of Rhodes (May-
Dec. 1522), when a thousand knights kept at bay the forces of
Solyman the Magnificent at the heyday of his power. In 1527,
through his brother's influence with Wolsey, he was appointed
Lord Prior of the Order in England. Their chief house was
St. John's, Clerkenwell, and the Prior ranked as first of the lay
barons in the Roll of Peers. "He was a kind of otter, a knight,
half spiritual, half temporal" (Selden's *Table Talk*). Sir William
took his seat in the House of Lords, and unlike his brother opposed the King's anti-papal policy. In 1540 his Order was
dissolved in England. He was granted a pension of £1,000,
an enormous sum in those days, five times the salary of the
Lord Chancellor, but he did not live to enjoy it. "Upon 7 May,
1540, being Ascension Day, the same day as the dissolution of
the House, he was dissolved by death, which strook him at the
heart at the first time he heard of the dissolution of the Order"
(Weever's *Funeral Monuments*). Fuller remarks, "His Hospital
and his earthly tabernacle were buried together, and gold, though
a great cordial, could not cure a broken heart" (*Memoirs*). He
was buried in a "fair marble tomb" in St. James' Church,
Clerkenwell. [*Chroniques de Jersey*: Harrison's *Annals of an
Old Manor House*: *Dic. Nat. Biog.*: Taafe's *Hist. of the Order
of St. John of Jerusalem*: *Letters and Papers of Henry VIII.*]

APPENDIX I

NON-JERSEYMEN WHO LEFT THEIR MARK ON JERSEY HISTORY

BANDINEL, DAVID (d. 1645), first Anglican Dean of Jersey. Contemporary writers call him an Italian (e.g. La Cloche, *Bull* II, Prynne, *Lyar Confounded*) ; so his name was probably Bandinelli. Payne's *Armorial* connects him with the Bandinelli of Sienna, a family which produced a Pope ; but no evidence for this exists. There was a small colony in London of Protestant refugees from Italy, who had obtained permission to establish an Italian Church there, and Bandinel probably came from this group. Of his early life we know nothing, except that later (1626) in a letter to Sir John Coke, he claims that Sir John knew him when he was "employed in the house of Mr. Verney" (*Cowper MSS. Hist. Man. Com.*). Toward the end of Elizabeth's reign he arrived in Jersey with a female relative, perhaps a mother or sister (an Esther Bandinel was godmother to one of his children), and an English bride, Elizabeth Stallenge, daughter of William Stallenge, Clerk of Naval Receipts at Plymouth. What brought him here is not known ; but in September 1601 he offered himself as candidate for the Ministry. The Church in the island was then Huguenot. The Colloquy Minute Book records, "David Bandinel, for whom the Church of St. Brelade has declared a particular affection, promises, if found worthy, to give himself entirely to the said Church, which is henceforth responsible for his support, till he is ready for the ministry". In October he was commissioned "to preach bareheaded in the church of St. Brelade" (Ordained Ministers wore *claque-oreilles* in the pulpit). In November he was "installed in his charge by the laying on of hands". On 2 Aug. 1602, he was naturalized as a British subject, his papers being signed by Sir Walter Ralegh, Governor.

He remained at St. Brelade's for twenty-seven years, during which seven children were born to him, Jacques (q.v.) (b. 1602),

Daniel (b. 1603), Anne, David (b. 1606), Esther (b. 1607), Thomas, Jean (b. 1610). Unfortunately the 'particular affection' of his parishioners did not last. In 1606 he was fined by the Royal Court for "cutting down certain trees under pretext of repairing the Presbytery without consent of the Constable". In 1607 the Constable summoned him for "defamatory words spoken by him and his wife, both in and out of the pulpit", Jean Guille summoned him "touching defamation", and Thomas Bibes "for forbidding him and his wife from Communion and for personall". In the same year came a fierce dispute with the local fishermen. He claimed a tithe of all their fish, wherever caught. They argued that they only owed it on fish caught in the bays of the parish. The case came before the Royal Commissioners, who decided, "Considering with how great danger ye fishermen do take their fish, considering also how needful it is yt said Minister be in some reasonable manner provided for, we adjudge that ye fishermen pay ye Minister a fifteenth part of all fish taken". But this did not end the quarrel. In 1608 Audrey Jehan was sentenced "to be flogged till blood ran" for speaking coarsely of this decree, when Madame Bandinel showed it to him.

But, apart from parish squabbles, a larger problem was disturbing the peace of the Church. Jerseymen liked their Calvinist services, and took pride in their Calvinist creed as far superior to "the superstitions of the Papists", but a revolt was brewing against the Calvinist discipline. Huguenots laid great stress on this. "Doctrine without Discipline", they said, "is a body without a backbone". By Discipline they meant careful supervision of the whole life of the community. In Jersey Elders were called Surveillants. Each was responsible for a vingtaine, and his duty was "to watch for scandals," and to summon offenders before the parish Consistory. Laymen resented these petty parochial courts and their ecclesiastical police ; yet everyone felt that a Church Court of some kind was necessary. Excommunication was still a powerful weapon against offenders, and someone must have the right to pronounce it. Then it was remembered that before the Reformation there had been a Dean and a Central Court. Some began to consider the possibility of reviving this, laymen in order to escape from their parish Consistory, Ministers because they hoped that it might strengthen Church Discipline. But no one dreamed that a Dean would bring all Anglicanism in with him. James I became King in

1603. He hated Presbyterianism ; but he was used to it in Scotland, and, finding it in the islands, he let it remain. "We ordain", he wrote, "that our said Isles quietly enjoy the Ecclesiastical Discipline there now established". But in 1613, when the Governor appointed the episcopally ordained Elie Messervy (q.v.) to the Rectory of St. Peter's, and the Consistory refused to receive him, the Privy Council ordered an Inquiry into ecclesiastical arrangements in the islands, and cited "those who support the present system and those who dislike it" to send representatives with reasons and papers. Bandinel was one of four Ministers chosen to represent the Calvinists.

No decision was reached however till 1618. In 1617, when two Royal Commissioners came to Jersey, one of their instructions was "to inquire touching the erection of a Dean ; what jurisdiction he should have ; who is to appoint him, the King, the Ministers, or the States ; whether our Book of Common Prayer might be placed in every church, that the people might become acquainted therewith". As a result of their Report the Council decided: — "It is ordered that a Dean be erected, his Majesty giving leave to the Governor and States *pro hac vice* to nominate three of the most grave and learned ministers there, out of which he may choose one" (*Acts P.C.*). The proposal to revive the Deanery caused much discussion in Jersey. Jurats feared that the new Court might prove a rival to their own. Opinion was so divided, that the States hesitated to make the three nominations ; and the Council had to act alone. Bandinel had evidently made a good impression, when he appeared as a delegate ; and by December he knew that he had been selected for the new post. All parties now began to prepare for the inevitable change. In Lambeth Library are two sets of Canons submitted by the island clergy. Both retain the Huguenot Service-Book and Presbyterian ordination, but accept the idea of a Leader to preside over Church Synods. They jib however at the word Dean. One calls him President, the other Moderator. The Bailiff wrote that the Jurats would submit to the King's wishes, if the Dean's power was curbed by a long list of restrictions. At last in Jan. 1620 the King wrote to the Bishop of Winchester and to the Governor and Bailiff: — "We have nominated our well-beloved David Bandinel to you, Bishop, willing you to admit him, and to you, Governor, Bailiff, and Jurats, to accept him as lawful Dean, and yield him assistance in the

exercise of his place" (S.P.). And, "in order that the Dean have
some power, and not be only in name admitted to that dignity,"
the King issued Twenty-Three Instructions to be followed till
Canons were compiled. The most important were: — "The Book
of Discipline shall be of no validity, neither shall lay Elders claim
jurisdiction in ecclesiastical causes. All Ministers hereafter admitted shall be ordained by some Bishop, but Ministers already
admitted shall retain their places, so as they be willing to conform to the Public Service now directed. The Book of Common
Prayer, translated into French, shall be used in the Public Service, but forbearance shall be shown in the use of the surplice,
the cross in Baptism, and the reading of the Apocrypha. In
every parish two of the discreeter sort shall be chosen Churchwardens to see that churches be kept in repair and to provide
things necessary for the Service of God. The Dean shall every
year visit the several churches, churchyards, and houses of the
Ministers to inform himself of decays and to receive information
of all neglect of duty in any Minister or Church Officer. The
Dean shall have probate of testaments of all that die in the
isle. The Dean on his arrival shall cause all Ministers to meet
and consider the Canons appointed within this Realm of England, and collect such of them as they think fit to be used in the
isle, and add others".

There were stormy scenes in the States, when Bandinel was
sworn in on 15 April, 1620, disputes as to whether his patent
should be handed to the Governor or Bailiff, whether he should
sit above or below the Jurats, whether he or the Bailiff should
retain the King's instructions. "Samuel De la Place, Minister
of St. Mary's, and Daniel Brevint, Minister of St. John's, rose
and protested against the oath Mr. Bandinel had taken, and
said they would not acknowledge him to be their Dean nor their
superior in anything, that the word Dean was not found in
Scripture, and that they had signed and sworn another Discipline" (S.P.). Then followed a squabble about expenses.
The Dean presented a letter from the Council: — "The business
concerning ecclesiastical affairs being now settled, the bearer,
David Bandinel, now Dean, having attended the accommodation
thereof, hath made suit to be assisted with our directions for the
satisfaction of the charges he hath sustained. Forasmuch as
the business concerneth the general good of the island, we
require you to take order for due payment according to his just

demands" (*Acts P.C.*). The States replied: — "We think it hard to be called on to bear the charges he was at for his own preferment. We think we should not bear the charges of one not chosen by ourselves, nor liked, being a stranger" (*S.P.D.*). The Council arranged a compromise. Bandinel withdrew his demand, and in return the States granted an exhibition to his son Daniel at Pembroke College, Cambridge (*S.P.D.*).

Jersey was now part of the Anglican Diocese of Winchester. From early times the islands had been under the Bishop of Coutances in Normandy. Edward II had claimed them for the Diocese of Exeter, and Henry VII had obtained Papal Bulls transferring them first to Salisbury, then to Winchester ; but these attempts failed. The Bishop of Coutances calmly continued his jurisdiction. In 1568 Elizabeth again conveyed them to Winchester ; but by this time they had become Huguenot, and would acknowledge no Bishop. It was now Bandinel's task to establish Anglicanism. He ordered the election of Churchwardens. Herault (q.v.), the Bailiff, forbad this. He had always sworn in the Huguenot Surveillants. "The temporal power," he wrote, "has always administered the oath to churchwardens. To retrench the Bailiff's jurisdiction without his being heard is very extraordinary" (*S.P.*). But the Council ordered the Governor to see that the elections were held, and summoned Herault to London "to show cause for his opposition". De la Place, Rector of St. Mary's, a staunch Presbyterian, absolutely refused to use the Prayer Book, and Bandinel deprived him of his living. When no one would fill his place, the Dean took charge of the parish himself, and for six years was Rector of St. Mary's and St. Brelade's. The French Prayer Book met with passive resistance from clergy and congregations. When Brevint (q.v.), Rector of St. John's, died thirty years later, Chevalier, himself a Church Officer in St. Helier's, wrote with evident approval: — "He accepted the Service Book much against his will. The Dean had great difficulty in getting him to use it. From the first he never read the responses, and set aside all ceremonies and vain repetitions" (*Journal*). Even in the Dean's two churches the congregations refused to kneel to receive the Communion. The compilation of Canons provoked much wrangling. When Bandinel at last persuaded the Clergy to agree to fifty-eight, and crossed to England to lay them before the Council, the Royal Court sent over three Jurats to op-

pose him. The Council however persuaded both sides to accept compromises, and in June 1623 the King affixed his Seal
(The Canons are printed in Falle's *Jersey*). On one point Bandinel showed the slimness of which he was often accused. The
21st Canon, as passed by the Clergy, ran: — "The Dean in the
Ecclesiastical Court shall decide all cases by the majority of the
votes of the Ministers present". But the Canon, which the
King sealed, merely says: — "The Dean shall ask the advice of
the Ministers present". He is bound to ask their advice, but is
not bound to take it.

Meanwhile Bandinel's parochial life pursued its tempestous
course. A storm broke out at St. Mary's. In 1626 Jacques Bandinel (q.v.), his eldest son, was ordained, and was appointed
Rector on his father's resignation. In July Madame Bandinel
came to stay with her son. The Constable, seeing her in church,
ordered the congregation to leave, and no more Services to be
held, on the ground that plague was raging at St. Aubin's, and
she might have brought infection. On the following Sunday
he "thrust her out of church with a halberd". Next Sunday
the Dean occupied the pulpit, and declared that such behaviour
was "more meet for Papists of Queen Mary's days than for
Protestants". The Constable reported him to the Royal Court
for treason, asserting that he had said, "We are living in a
worse reign than Mary's". The Privy Council took a serious
view of this, and wrote to the Royal Court (July 1627) : — "The
complaints against the two Bandinels must be further examined.
Take strict examination of those undutiful speeches alleged to
have been uttered". The Dean had to cross to England, before
he was finally cleared, the Council deciding that the controversy
arose through "a misinterpretation of the words of the said
Minister". On the return voyage (March 1628) the boat in
which he was travelling was captured by corsairs. He was
carried to Dunkirk, robbed, and released. He made his way
to Calais, whence he wrote asking for help, saying he was ill
and penniless (*S.P.D.*). By July however he was home again.

In March 1629 he resigned St. Brelade's to become Rector of
St. Martin's ; but he did not grow more popular. When the
spire of Trinity Church was struck by lightning Chevalier considered this a sign of God's displeasure at "the pontifical gran-
deur of the Dean, who was ruling with a rod of iron, making
himself head of all, and holding a sovereign Court within the

Church of Christ" (*Journal*). In 1635 his enemies made a determined attempt to ruin him. Catherine Bisson of St. Brelade's had an illegitimate baby. One of the Churchwardens of the parish charged Bandinel with being the father. The Bishop suspended him, and appointed two Commissaries to try him in his own Ecclesiastical Court. But the Court decided that the charge was "a wicked calumny without proof or probability", and the island seems to have accepted the verdict, for though during the next few years Bandinel was charged with almost every conceivable crime, nothing more was heard about the Bisson baby. In the same year he had a home tragedy. Daniel, his second son, had taken his degree at Cambridge, and married Jeanne Gervaise, but in 1635 he became a hopeless imbecile, and spent the last twelve years of his life in bed.

The Dean was now involved in a quarrel with the most powerful man in the island, Sir Philippe De Carteret (q.v.), who was both Lieutenant-Governor and Bailiff. How it began is not clear, but as early as 1628 Sir Philippe had sent to the House of Commons a petition, which is docketed, "Complaints against proceedings of David Bandinel, an alien, made Dean. Prays that a Commission may be issued under the Great Seal to inquire into the conduct of the said Dean". Nothing seems to have come of this. But in 1641 Sir Philippe was provoked into a step, which proved indefensible. When the Deanery was revived, the King had endowed it with the Great Tithes of St. Saviour's, which since the Reformation had been paid to the Crown. Now De Carteret as Lieut.-Governor claimed these on the strength of earlier Letters Patent, and sued Bandinel for all that he had received during the last twenty years. The Royal Court decided in the Dean's favour, and so on appeal did the Privy Council.

But, when in England on this business, Bandinel found in London a group of Jerseymen working to overthrow his enemy. A deputation led by Henri Dumaresq (q.v.) had brought to the Long Parliament Twenty-two Complaints against Sir Philippe. Bandinel joined them. But Prynne, the Puritan leader, had been kindly treated by De Carteret, when a prisoner in Mont Orgueil. To repay him he caused Bandinel and Dumaresq to be hastily summoned before a Committee of the House of Lords. When they could not produce on the spot witnesses to establish their charges, the Committee threatened "to commit them both

for their malicious, libellous articles, which they could not prove :
but by Sir Philip's importunity their commitment was taken
off" (*Lyar Confounded*). But the Dean got into further trouble.
The man who had suppressed Presbyterianism in Jersey was
ill-advised to call attention to his presence in Puritan London.
His old opponent Samuel De La Place (q.v.) was now in
London. The *Journal of the House of Commons* records : —
"Ordered that Mr. David Bandinel, Dean of Jersey, be summoned to appear here tomorrow morning to answer the petition
put in against him by Samuel De La Place of Jersey" ; and
on the following day, "The petition of Samuel De La Place
was read, and it was ordered that Mr. David Bandinel be sent
for as a Delinquent by the Serjeant at Arms, ant that the Petition be referred to the Committee that is to inquire after scandalous Ministers". Apparently he had been in communication
with Archbishop Laud, for Prynne writes : — "This Parliament
being assembled, and the Archbishop questioned, he met with
articles of complaint against himself for gross oppressions done
by him as Dean, for which he was committed to the Commons
House for two or three months to the Serjeant's custody" (*Lyar
Confounded*).

He returned to Jersey on the eve of the outbreak of Civil
War. Since De Carteret, though Puritan, had declared for the
King, Bandinel, the Anglican, joined the Parliamentarians, and
soon became their leader. "I hold the King's Commission",
wrote De Carteret, "to suppress the sedition-mongers, led by
Bandinel, the Dean. I charge him with high treason as ringleader of the rebels". In Chevalier's fable of the revolt of the
midges the Queen Midge is Bandinel. For the moment he
triumphed. De Carteret (Feb. 1643) took refuge in Elizabeth
Castle, and the Dean's Committee of Bien-affectionnés, as the
Parliamentarians called themselves, ruled all the island except
the two Castles. For eight months there was desultory war
between the castles and the island, a war fought partly by
cannon-balls, partly by proclamations. In the latter the Dean
was an adept. "I recognize in your letter", wrote De Carteret
to the Committee, "the pernicious knavery of the Dean. Every
line reveals the blackness of his poison pen. He thinks he is
playing the mountebank on a stall in the market to attract
customers to his quack medicines". But matters reached a deadlock. The Commitee had neither cannon nor storm-troops with

which to capture the castles, and these could easily be provisioned from the sea. The Militiamen grew tired of the siege, and longed to get back to their farms. Moreover the Bienaffectionnés were no longer a united family. Jerseymen were still Presbyterian at heart, though they had accepted Anglicanism. But Lydcot, the new Parliamentary Governor, was an Independent, disliking Presbyterians as much as he did Anglicans. Moreover Lempriere (q.v.), the Parliamentary Bailiff, Daniel Norman (q.v.), James Stocall (q.v.), and Denis Guerdain (q.v.) had during their exile in England become Anabaptists. And Anglicans and Presbyterians regarded Anabaptists as worse than Papists. The island seemed drifting into religious and social anarchy. At first the Committee had maintained strict order, and protected the property of its opponents; but gangs of roughs from the Town began to wander through the country districts looting Royalist houses. Bandinel decided that only peace could save the situation. He proclaimed a Fast "to pray for the restoration of peace between the King and his People". He had always been Royalist at heart. He had continued to pray for the King every Sunday, and, while besieging the King's castles, maintained that he was a loyal subject resisting an unrighteous Governor. When his enemy Sir Philippe died on 23 Aug., the Dean began to gravitate back to the side to which he really belonged. In October he wrote to Lady De Carteret offering his services as a peace-maker. His letter remained unanswered; but Lydcot heard of it, and ordered his arrest; and he had to go into hiding.

On 19 Nov. George Carteret (q.v.) landed at Mont Orgueil. Most of the Puritan leaders fled, but Bandinel remained, hoping to retain his position. On 5 Dec. his hiding-place was discovered, and he and his son, Jacques, were taken to Elizabeth Castle. At first they were treated leniently. Their friends were allowed to visit them. But on 30 June 1644, Carteret "made proclamation in the Market that David Bandinel, Dean, henceforth would be imprisoned more straitly, and that no one should visit him without leave from the Lieutenant or Porter, because he was suspected of informing his friends of what was happening in the Castle". On 2 July the Dean and his son were transferred to Mont Orgueil. "They were allowed by day to walk on the upper part of the Castle, and, when shut in at night, they spent most of their time playing draughts".

(Chevalier.). On 10 Feb. 1645 they tried to escape. "With a gimlet they succeeded in making holes in the plank of a door, and by boring the holes close together they broke the plank. The door led into another room next to the outer wall, and had a closet, into which, when they had removed some stones, they crept sideways. Here was a small narrow window at the top of the battlements. Through this they crawled with difficulty. Then by the help of a cord and napkins knotted together, which they fastened to a kitchen ladle fixed in a crack in the wall, they climbed down. They chose a night when it was blowing hard, and one could scarce keep one's feet, and trees were torn up by the roots. At the foot of the wall was a rugged rock, and at the bottom of this a steep slope down to the sea. The son descended first ; but the rope was too short, and he fell on the rock, injuring his limbs. Afterward the father tried to climb down. But the rope broke, and he crashed on the rock and lay senseless. When his son regained consciousness, he was amazed to find his father in so sore a state. At first he thought he was dead, but, finding a spark of life in him, he turned him on his back, and covered him with his cloak. Then he left him, and fled to hide himself. The father remained at the foot of the wall till broad daylight, when he was found by some of the garrison, and carried into the Castle. A message was sent to his wife, that she must come quickly, if she would see him alive. When she arrived, he made a slight sign that he recognized her, and next morning he died". On 13 Feb. he was buried in St. Martin's churchyard "under the thorn-tree". Chevalier's comment was : — "He who had been given the title of Venerable, to what an end had his misdeeds brought him ! He was a man of great ability, but he caused much misery to this poor country. He left no stone unturned to avenge himself on Sir Philippe. All the waters of the sea cannot wash out that stain. He came to this island a poor man, and at the end he wished to lord it over all. Thus was fulfilled the saying, Whosoever exalteth himself shall be abased". In April the Royal Commissioners laid a ban on all the family, excluding them for ever from holding any public office. But this had no effect. His son Thomas became Constable of St. Martin's, his grandson David a Jurat. His great-grandson George and two great-great-grandsons became Vicomtes. The General Hospital is built on land given by Philip Bandinel, Constable of St. Sa-

viour's ; and one of his descendants became Public Orator at
Oxford, and another Librarian of the Bodleian. [De Schickler's
Eglises du Refuge ; *Calendar of State Papers, Domestic* ; *Acts
of Privy Council* ; Prynne's *Lyar Confounded* ; Chevalier's
Journal ; Hoskins' *Charles II in the Channel Islands* ; Durell's
edition of Falle's *Jersey* ; *Dic. Nat. Biog.* ; Minute Book of
Colloquy (Cambridge University Library) ; Actes of Eccles.
Court (Jersey Greffe) ; Causes heard before Gardiner and Hus-
sey (S.J. Library) ; Grand of St. Saviour's tithes to Dean ;
(S. J. Library) ; a large number of papers in Record Office.]

D'ASSIGNY, PIERRE (fl. 1635—60), Rector. At his marriage
he was described as "Son of the late Daniel D'Assigny: born in
Authon in Perche" (now part of Eure et Loire). He had been
a monk: — "late a zealous popish monk, who deserted his orders, some say for incontinency" (Prynne. *Lyar Confounded*) ;
cf Chevalier: "an alien, who had been a monk, and changed
sides, God knows why" (*Journal*). On 6 Dec. 1635 he married
Marguerite Coutois, a native of Valenciennes, at the Huguenot
Church in Threadneedle St., London. She cannot have lived
long, for on 20 Nov. 1636 he married again, his bride being
Elisabeth, daughter of Nathanael Marie, Pastor of the Church.
In the interval between his two marriages he had been ordained
according to the Presbyterian rite, for at the second he is des-
cribed as "Minister of the Word of God". His wife's brother,
Nathanael Marie, who had died two years before, had been
Rector of St. Clement's, Jersey, and her knowledge of the dearth
of French-speaking clergy probably brought him to the island.
Here Sir Philippe De Carteret (q.v.) befriended him. "His
means were slender, when he arrived ; but the Seigneur of St.
Ouen's helped him with money, and procured for him the
Rectory of St. Helier's" (Chevalier). He was inducted on 30
Sept. 1638. Sir Philippe "did him the honour of standing as
godfather to one of his children". (This was Philippe, baptized
in the Town Church 2 Jan. 1639. Lady De Carteret was godmother). "He showed him every courtesy. The last time he
came to the Church, he went to call on D'Assigny's wife, who
was in child-bed" (*ibid*).

As Rector he proved very popular. "He had the hearts of the townsfolk entirely under his sway through his persuasive tongue" (*ibid*). When the Civil War began he became a rampant anti-Royalist. Chevalier gives several pictures of his war-time activities. In May 1643 Sir Philippe evaded the besiegers of Elizabeth Castle, and visited Mont Orgueil. "Hearing this the Committee assembled in D'Assigny's house to take steps to capture Sir Philippe, for they deemed he must pass the Town that evening on his way back to the Castle ; but therein they were deceived. D'Assigny urged that he must be captured dead or alive, and that this was a chance that must not be missed. So they sounded the tocsin, and beat the drums, and summoned the Vingtenier of the Town Vingtaine (Chevalier himself), who kept the keys of the magazine, where the pikes and cannon were stored, to give out pikes to the soldiers who were to arrest Sir Philippe. D'Assigny urged them to take the cannon too ; but the others did not agree". Chevalier however refused to surrender the keys ; so "a few days later D'Assigny and others brake open the magazine, and seized the pikes. They carried off the parish drums also, which the Constable had refused to give up, and put them all in D'Assigny's house, for he fain would have charge of everything" (*ibid*).

"30 Sept. On the night before Sacrament Sunday D'Assigny visited the Well-Affected house by house, and bade them immediately after Communion on Sunday afternoon bring spades to the Mont de la Ville, and build a fort to bombard the Castle that was bombarding the Town. Service ended, he harangued the people, alleging there was nothing wrong in defending themselves on that day, for the Sabbath was made for man, not man for the Sabbath, and he summoned them to the Hill to cut turfs for a redoubt. Then, leaving his gown in his house, he hastened to the Governor's residence, and fetched an armful of spades and shovels, which he distributed to the people who had come out of church, and were waiting in the Market Place : then he went back for more. This done, he went with them to the Mount, and set them to work, not stinting his own cider, which he bade them take with them to hearten them in their toil. However he could not persuade many except the Well-Affected, for the people were sorely shocked by sabbath-breaking on Sacrament Sunday" (*ibid*).

A month later news reached Town that Etienne La Cloche

(q.v.), the Royalist Rector, had returned to St. Ouen's, and was trying to persuade his parish to declare for the King. "At night D'Assigny ran from house to house, bidding men leave their beds and follow him, for St. Ouen's had revolted, and was coming to cut their throats. When he and his company reached St. Ouen's they brake down the church door and seized the cannon that were there. They burst open the vestry and its chests, and took the silver cups and some money, but, remembering that stealing these would be sacrilege, they placed them in a house near by. Next they went to the Seigneur of Vinchelez' house, to see if La Cloche was there; but he had fled. Nevertheless they sacked the house, smashing open cupboards and coffers. Everyone helped himself to whatever came to his hand; and D'Assigny, who was present, said one must needs chastise the refractory. Next day, as they came back to Town, he marched at the head of his company, holding a pistol on high, as though returning from a glorious victory" (id).

On 5 Nov. during the Sunday service the Castle Cannon fired a volley in honour of Guy Fawkes' Day. Thinking this a new bombardment the congregation moved towards the doors. D'Assigny, finding he had lost their attention, "left the pulpit without offering the prayers, and proceeded to baptize some babies. When the noise ceased, he remounted the pulpit, and gave out a psalm" (id). Next day he organized another "fox-hunt" for La Cloche through his relations' houses. By Sunday the 12th he saw that things were going amiss. In an angry sermon he denounced the divisions in his party's ranks, and challenged the faint-hearted to be gone. On the following Sunday Captain Carteret (q.v.) landed at Mont Orgueil. On the Tuesday St. Brelade's rose for the King, and seized St. Aubin's Fort. That morning D'Assigny was again on the Mount, "sword on thigh and pistol in hand", supervising the building of an earthwork, when he noticed boats passing between St. Aubin's Fort and the Castle, and realized that the Fort was lost. He rushed down into the Town crying, "Treason". But the Parliament men knew now that their cause was hopeless. That night the leaders left for England, and D'Assigny went with them. On 25 Jan. 1644 "Elizabeth Marie, wife of Pierre D'Assigny, fugitive rebel", was banished from the island. On 15 Oct. 1645 he was condemned in his absence by the Royal Commissioners to be hanged.

D'Assigny settled in Norwich. A number of French-speaking Walloon weavers had taken refuge there from their Spanish persecutors, and had been given the Church of St. Mary at Tombland to worship in. The Pastor of this, Dr. Guilleaume De Laune, was Mme. D'Assigny's uncle, her mother's brother. His Anglican leanings (Cambridge had given him dis D.D. for translating the Prayer Book into French) and his Royalist sympathies had made him unpopular in this Parliamentary town. When D'Assigny arrived, young, eloquent, the victim of a Royalist reaction, part of the congregation resolved to get rid of the uncle and make the nephew their Minister. At a "tumultuous meeting at which no Elder was present" on 15 April 1644 they deposed De Laune and elected D'Assigny. At the next Synod (the Governing Body of the French-speaking Churches), held in London in May, D'Assigny and De Laune each presented himself as the Pastor of Norwich. The Colloquy tried to make peace, declaring De Laune's deposition "unconstitutional according to our Discipline", but consenting to recognize D'Assigny as his Co-adjutor. This decision D'Assigny vehemently refused to accept, and left the Synod vowing he would never return. The Synod passed a resolution regretting his "violent, impetuous, and injurious behaviour not only toward individuals but toward the company as a whole", and warned Norwich not to receive him. His party however still supported him, and the unseemly struggle raged for six years. The next Colloquy in 1646 spent days debating the problem, and at last resolved: — "In view of the lawless misconduct of Pierre D'Assigny at the previous Colloquy and its continuance in an aggravated form, repudiating all authority ecclesiastical and civil, whereby disorders, factions, and tumults have ensued in the Church and City of Norwich, we degrade the said D'Assigny from the office of Co-adjutor and forbid him to exercise the sacred ministry, not only in Norwich, but in any Church affiliated to this Colloquy". D'Assigny's party ignored this sentence, and he continued to preach, and even fostered trouble in other Churches. In 1648 he visited Canterbury, and ordained a schismatic Pastor for a discontented minority there, who then stormed the Cathedral crypt, which had been given to the Huguenots to worship in, and ejected the regular congregation. Meanwhile in Norwich things went from bad to worse. Each party claimed the church building. Appeals were made to the local magistrates and even to Parliament. Prynne wrote that D'Assigny "hath quite ruined and dissolved the French Church in Norwich" (*Lyar Confounded*). At length however in 1650 De Laune's party won, and the local Consistory recognized him as their "ancient and legitimate Pastor".

In Oct. 1651 Parliament recovered Jersey, and D'Assigny returned. He was given the Rectory of St. Martin's, which was then considered the most important of the twelve, as Mont Orgueil was in its parish. Little is known of his doings here, but two Acts of the Court show that he had not learnt to keep out of quarrels. In Jan 1657 Thomas Bandinel, Constable of St. Martin's, was imprisoned for "speaking disrespectfully in the presence of the Court, and uttering many injurious words contrary to the honour of Mons. Pierre D'Assigny, calling him mutineer (*mutin*), a liar, and unworthy of his office". Three months later D'Assigny was sent to join him in the Castle for "assaulting on the high road François, son of Amice De Quetteville, and beating him black and blue with a stick". At the Restoration the Earl of St. Alban's, the new Governor, wrote (July 1660): — "As for Mr. D'Assigny, of whose forcible entry into his charge, irregular life, and scandalous doctrine I have been informed, you are to signify to him yt he forbear to preach any more in the island, and to take care yt the Parson House, Lands, and Tithes of St. Martin's be sequestred until further notice" (O.C.). He had probably already escaped to France. No more is heard of him ; but an Act of the Court in 1674 calls him "the late Mons. D'Assigny". His second wife, Elisabeth Marie, died early in his St. Martin's ministry, and was buried in the Church "in front of the pulpit under the table". By her he had at least four children, Philippe (b. 1639), Marius (q.v.), Jean (b. 1652: drowned at low tide in 1665), and Pierre (buried July 1656). On 20 Sept. 1654 D'Assigny married Marguerite Nicolle. Four of her children were : — Marguerite (b. 1655 : d. Jan. 1657), a second Pierre (b. Sept. 1656), a second Marguerite (b. 1657), and Sara, who married Philippe Mallet of Rozel and then Jean Messervy of Anneville. Mme. D'Assigny died at St. Martin's in 1688. [Chevalier's *Journal* ; *Colloques et Synodes* ; Hoskins' *Charles II in the Channel Islands* ; *Bull.* VII ; Moens' *The Walloons and their Church in Norwich* ; Schickler's *Eglises du Refuge en Angleterre* ; and authorities quoted above.]

DON, SIR GEORGE (1756—1832), Lieut.-Governor. Youngest son of Sir Alexander Don of Newton, Berwickshire. Born, 1756. Entered the Army in 1770, when only fourteen, as Ensign in the 51st Foot. Joined his regiment at Minorca. Promoted Lieutenant, 1774. Became Aide-de-camp to the Governor and Military Secretary. Made Brevet Major 1783 for his work as chief of staff during the siege of the Castle of St. Philip by the Spaniards. Appointed Major of the 59th Foot in Gibraltar, 1784. Purchased the lieut.-colonelcy of this regiment, 1789, and remained in Gibraltar till 1792. His regiment was then transferred to Jersey. He spent only nine months in the island, but left a good impression. As a rule the island paid little attention, as regiments came and departed ; but, when the 59th left, the *Gazette* said: — "No regiment has ever been more successful in winning the people's friendship. Colonel Don is loved and respected by all. A more urbane, kindly, courteous gentleman is inconceivable". The States presented him with a vote of thanks inscribed on parchment, acknowledging "the zeal he had shown in maintaining the discipline of the Militia".

He went with the Duke of York's army to the Netherlands as Deputy-Adjutant-General in 1793, and for his services was made Aide-de-camp to the King and promoted Colonel in 1795. When the army returned to England, Don remained in Germany as Military Commissioner with the Prussians, till he was promoted Major-General in 1798, and given command of the troops in the Isle of Wight. He commanded a brigade in 1799 in the Duke of York's unfortunate expedition to the Helder, which not only failed to drive the French out of Holland, but was forced to ask for an armistice. Don was sent with the flag of truce, and contrary to all laws of war was kept a prisoner till June 1800. He then rejoined the Staff at the Horse Guards as Deputy-Adjutant-General. In 1803 he was promoted Lieut.-General, and in 1804 became second in command of the troops in Scotland. When war broke out again, he was sent to North Germany to command the King's German Legion.

In 1806 he was appointed Lieut.-Governor of Jersey, which, though Trafalgar had eased the position, was still in danger of invasion. Before he landed, he sent the Government a long report (now in S.J. Library), based on his previous knowledge, on what should be done to strengthen the defences of the island. He was sworn in, 21 June. He at once showed extra-

ordinary vigour. He established a signalling system, by which,
if the French fleet left St. Malo, news could be flashed from a
look-out ship to Mont Orgueil, and thence, via Grosnez and
Sark, to Guernsey, where a British fleet was stationed. It was
found that a message could be passed from Mont Orgueil to St.
Peter-Port in a quarter of an hour, using flags by day and blazing
tar-barrels by night. He resolutely disciplined the Militia. After his first inspection he reported, "Five battalions out of the
six are totally unfit for service". He appointed sixteen additional drill-instructors. He built Drill Sheds in every parish,
so that the men might drill in all weathers. And by the help
of Colonel Le Couteur (q.v.) he made the whole force keen
and efficient. Every bay and possible landing-place in the
island was fortified. The plans for Fort Regent had been passed before he arrived ; but one of his first acts was to lay the
foundation stone, and he saw the Fort completed before he
laid down his command. But the best work that he did was
his road-making.

When he arrived, the only roads were narrow, tortuous lanes,
in winter knee-deep in mud, along which it was impossible
to move troops or artillery with speed. All contemporaries comment on this. "The roads are very bad", wrote Lyte, "and sunk
so low that they act as drains to the adjoining fields, and in
winter nearly impassable" (*Sketch of the Island of Jersey*).
"The roads", said Quayle, "are narrow, winding, and very intricate, sunk below the level of the land, flanked by enormous
mounds, crowded with trees overcanopying them. Carts meeting
cannot pass, but must back to the nearest gateway. To this
may perhaps be attributed the remarkable proficiency of the
population in swearing" (*Agriculture in the Islands.*). Don
determined to remedy this. It was no easy task. To carve new
roads was not only costly, but involved an enormous amount
of interference with private property, cutting slices off fields,
felling trees, even demolishing buildings. At first there was
a tremendous outcry. When Don rode about the country surveying, he had to be protected by soldiers.

His first road was the one by Longueville from the Town to
Grouville. This was held up by one farmer, who entrenched
himself in a field, and threatened to shoot the first workman who
removed a sod. Don himself took a spade, and dug through the
boundary bank ; and the farmer did not fire. The road was

finished in Dec. 1806, and the States decreed that "this spacious road, which replaces one that was very bad, sunken, narrow, and boggy", should be called the Route Don. It was paid for by an increase in the import duty on spirits. In March 1807 he began a road from St. Ouen's church to Beaumont, for which he obtained £1,000 from the British Government (opened May 1808). When this was finished, he undertook a third from St. Helier's to St. Aubin's (opened Nov. 1809). Hitherto the sands had been the only means of communication. As neither the States nor the Home Government would provide any more money, he paid for this partly by a public subscription, which he started with a gift of £100, partly, "knowing the Jerseyman's love of speculation", by a lottery.

Then his work was interrupted. In 1809 the Earl of Chatham, the non-resident Governor of Jersey (Don was only Lieut.-Governor), landed with the largest army that had ever left England on the Dutch Island of Walcheren with the hope of seizing Antwerp, Napoleon's naval base. Military and naval operations were muddled ; Chatham returned to England ; and Don was hurriedly sent to Walcheren to evacuate what was left of the army. On his departure the *Jersey Magazine* burst into verse : —

> Of all the chiefs that this blest isle e'er loved
> Justly thou wert by far the most approved.

The States voted 200 guineas for a piece of silver "in recognition of his great services to the island", and sent a strong letter to the Home Government urging that he might be allowed to return, when his mission was accomplished. At Walcheren Don found the army decimated by typhus. On 27 Oct. he sent 6,000 sick to England. On 30 Oct. he reported 1,300 fresh cases. On 12 Nov. he had 5,000 men in hospital. Yet in spite of ever-increasing pressure from Napoleon's generals he successfully embarked his last men on 6 Dec.

On 2 May, 1810 he returned to Jersey, and was presented with a gold-hilted sword by officers of the Militia. He at once resumed his road-making. In June he persuaded the Trinity Parish Assembly to agree to make a road from Bouley Bay to Town via Trinity Church, and he himself opened the subscription with a gift of 300 livres. (It is characteristic of him that when writing to Constables he always signed himself, 'Your

most obedient, humble servant.') This road caused trouble.
An idea had sprung up that the new roads exposed the Town
to sudden raids by the enemy. A printed leaflet in French
verse (in S.J. Library) declared that the old, narrow, winding
lanes were the Town's best protection. One Rector preached
from the text, "The broad road leadeth to destruction". When
Trinity had almost completed the work, the St. Helier's Parish
Assembly by four votes refused permission for the last section
of the road to pass through the parish. But the States overrode
the Parish Assembly, and the road was finished.

During the next four years the following roads were constructed, all under the personal supervision of Don himself, who,
though an infantryman, proved himself a skilful engineer, the
arrangement being that, if the parish contributed the land and
the stone, and carted the latter to the spot, the States would
pay the labourers and soldiers engaged in the actual road-
making: —

(1) From St. Brelade's Church to St. Aubin's by Mont Sohier.
(2) From St. Lawrence Church to Millbrook by Mont Félard.
(3) From St. Peter's Church to St. Aubin's by Mont de la
     Rocque.
(4) From St. Martin's Church to Town by St. Saviour's.
(5) From St. Mary's Church to Grève de Lecq.
(6) From St. Ouen's Church to St. Ouen's Bay by Mont
     Matthieu.
(7) From Rozel to Town by St. Martin's.
(8) From St. Brelade's Church to St. Ouen's Bay across the
     Quennevais.
(9) From Grouville Church to Gorey.
(10) From St. Martin's Church to Gorey.
(11) From St. John's Church to Carrefour Selous.
(12) From St. Mary's Church to Carrefour Selous.
(13) From the Dicq to Grouville Bay by St. Clement's Church.
(14) From Grouville Church to meet No. 13 at the foot of
     Verclut.
(15) From La Chasse de la Hougue to Bel Royal down St.
     Peter's Valley.

The above are printed in the order of construction. A number of connecting cross-roads were also made. Nor did this

exhaust his energies. During a great storm in Oct. 1812 the
sea poured through breaches in the sea-wall, flooded the Grouville marshes, and threatened 4,000 vergées of land in the
Longueville district with inundation. Don undertook the rebuilding of the entire sea-wall from St. Helier's to Gorey.

The food problem had been an anxiety all through the War.
Don believed that this might be solved by bringing more of the
unreclaimed land under cultivation. "In order to evince by
actual experiment", wrote Quayle in 1812, "the practicability
of bringing into culture the most arid and hopeless of these
wastes, he took into his own hands a portion of the Quennevais. He carried round his experimental 20 acres an earth fence
planted with whitethorn. A cottage and outhouses were built,
a kitchen-garden formed, and trees planted for shelter. The
vegetable earth, which had been overwhelmed by sand, was
discovered from six to ten feet under the surface. This was
removed to the surface, and the whole laid level. In Jan. 1812
ten vergées were sown with rye without any manure. In the
Spring buckwheat, peas, tares, and lucerne were sown, and
potatoes planted. In June white clover and sainfoin. The
motive for diversifying these experiments was to bring conviction to the incredulous that this bleak and dreary region is
really capable of producing a variety of plants. To this smiling
spot the General gives the appropriate term of the Oasis. All
its produce is of superior quality" (*Agriculture in the Islands*).

Don had one failure. Like some of his predecessors he tried
to alter the constitution of the island. The election of Thomas
Anley (q.v.) as Jurat alarmed him. With the support of Sir
Jean Dumaresq (q.v.), the Lieut.-Bailiff, he appealed for a
Royal Commission to inquire into the method of appointing
Jurats. The Commissioners reported in favour of his plan,
that they should be chosen by the States and Crown Officers
and not by popular election ; but this aroused such opposition
that the Privy Council did not adopt the recommendations.

This move however did not destroy his popularity. When
he left Jersey in 1814 to be Lieut.-Governor of Gibraltar, the
States paid him the most glowing tribute ever offered to a departing Governor: — "Surrounded as they are by lasting memorials of his love for their land, the States recognize that no
one ever won a better right to their esteem. He is one of that
small group of distinguished men, whose work has made an

epoch in the history of Jersey. In the short space of eight years he has changed the face of the country. He has made our coast-line bristle with forts, ramparts, and batteries, in which more than 600 cannon secure us from invasion. He has brought our Militia to its present state of perfection. In spite of obstacles which would have daunted a less determined man, new roads have been cut and old ones remodelled from one end of the island to the other. Works wisely conceived and rapidly executed have saved the richest part of our soil from inundation by the sea. His mind has been constantly occupied with plans to increase our prosperity, and to accomplish this he has not scorned to attend to the smallest details. Nothing could quench his ardour or turn him from his task. To these rare qualities his Excellency has added a marked consideration for this assembly and a most touching affability toward all classes of the population". The States invited him to have his portrait painted at their expense "by one of the ablest artists in England", that it might hang in their Council Chamber. He approached Sir Thomas Lawrence, but found that the sittings would take more ime than he could spare, so asked that the money might be spent on the new roads.

He ruled Gibraltar for seventeen years as vigorously as Jersey. The Colonial Hospital has a Latin inscription "to his eternal honour" as its founder. The Supreme Court and the Exchange Building were built under his auspices, and the Alameda Gardens laid out, and the Charter of Civil Justice instituted. He kept on good terms with the Spanish authorities, and was allowed to build a villa at San Roque on the Spanish side of the frontier, and to construct a road from his house to Gibraltar. In 1818 he became Colonel of the 56th, and in 1829 was transferred to the colonelcy of the 3rd, the Buffs. He was made a Knight Grand Cross of the Bath in 1820, a Knight Grand Cross of Hanover in 1823, and a Knight Grand Cross of the Order of St. Michael and St. George in 1825. He was also a Knight Grand Cross of the Prussian Order of Mérite Militaire. He died in Gibraltar, 1 Jan. 1852, and was buried in the Garrison Church (now the Cathedral), where a monument records his "sixty years of uninterrupted active service". In Jersey Don Street, Don Road, Don Bridge, and General Don's Farm retain his name. In 1872 the States commissioned a French sculptor, Robinet, who had taken refuge in the island, to cast

a statue of Don, and voted £1,000 for this purpose. After many
delays this was unveiled in the Parade in 1885. [*Dic. Nat.
Biog.*; W.G. Don's *Memoirs of the Don Family*; Sullivan's
General Sir George Don (second volume never published.);
articles by J. Le Bas in the *Chronique*, Aug. 1885.]

HELIER, SAINT (?about 550), Hermit. The Legend of St.
Helier is based on a statement in two Latin Lives of St. Marculf (one printed in the Bollandists' *Acta Sanctorum*, the other
in Pigeon's *Saints du Diocèse de Coutances*). Both call Normandy by its old name of Neustria, and so were probably written before the 10th century. They tell how in the reign of
Childebert I (511—558) Marculf (q.v.), a young noble of Bayeux, set out to convert the pagan Cotentin, and founded a missionary settlement at Nanteuil, opposite the islands now called
the Iles St. Marcouf. Each *Life* takes him to a Breton island.
One says: — "He summoned his brethren, and announced that
he was going to Brittany, and Romard, a holy Priest, asked
leave to accompany him. So they crossed the Breton country,
and came to an isle, which those who lived there called Agna.
Here they found a brother, named Eletus, who had long been
living a hermit life. Then those three holy men discussed the
guile of the Evil Spirits, and how by God's grace the Serpent is
always foiled; and they gave themselves wholly to fasting and
prayer. Therefore the crafty foe, seeing the island radiant with
three such shining lights, stirred up against it nearly three
thousand Saxon pirates. Now the isle, though rich in goods
and cattle, had not many inhabitants. One day the inhabitants
on their way to work saw the Saxon horde approaching, and
fled in panic to the cell where the three holy men were at prayer,
and cast themselves at Marculf's feet crying, 'Save us, or we
perish!' The Saint replied, 'Fear not, God will fight for you.
In His sight numbers are as nothing'. Cheered by these words,
they rushed on the foe, while Marculf, prostrate on the ground,
pleaded for Divine help. Now many say that the Isle had only
thirty inhabitants. The invaders were leaping into the surf,
and some had reached the shore, when a great gale swept the
ships out to sea, and smashed them to atoms, while the natives

slew all who reached the sands. When the Bretons heard of the miracles daily wrought by Marculf, crowds flocked to him, and he built a place of prayer on that isle, in which he placed monks to serve God".

The other *Life* tells the same story with variations: — "Wishing to live for a time a hermit life Marculf went with a Priest named Romard to an island called Agnus off the Breton coast (*Britannicae regioni quamdam adjacentem insulam quae Agnus vocabatur*). This isle was inhabited by a few serfs (*coloni*), among whom dwelt a man named Helibertus, a very ascetic man, who kept his body in subjection by ultra-rigorous fasts. Marculf and Romard shared his hut and his life of contemplation and self-discipline. One day three thousand Saxon pirates descended on the isle with all sails set and oars swinging. The natives, who numbered no more than thirty, fell trembling at Marculf's knees, crying, 'Father, save us', 'My sons', he said, 'to arms! The God Who overthrew Pharaoh and his host will fight for you. Forward! I promise you victory'. Relying more on the Saint's prayers than on their own strength, they killed all who landed, while those still on board were engulfed by the waves. The Lord of the Isle (*insulae dominus*), when he heard this, gave the Saint half the island, and here he built a monastery, in which he placed monks to form perpetually a Household of God". Marculf, then returned to Nanteuil.

Three points deserve attention: — (I) The island is not called Jersey, but Agnus and Agna. Other monastic writings however show that one of the Channel Islands was called Angia. *The Life of St. Samson* says that he sailed to "Lesia and Angia, islands of the sea". *The Miracles of St. Wandrille* states that an Abbot of Fontenelle was sent to an "island called Angia, which Bretons inhabit, adjacent to the Coutances country". *The Acts of St. Magloire* tell how the Saint was summoned to "the island of Angia near Sark". An island described as "near Sark", and "adjacent to the Coutances country" certainly sounds like Jersey, though the Bollandists suggest Herm, perhaps because the thirty inhabitants sound more reasonable there. So if (and this is only an assumption) Agnus, Agna, and Angia are the same, St. Marculf's biographer may have placed his hermit in Jersey. (II) The hermit is not called Helier, but Helibertus and Eletus. (III) The pirate story is practically the same as one told of St. Magloire in Sark. He too encouraged

the natives to resist. He too received from the Lord of the Isle
half the island as a gift. He too built there a monastery. Legends of two Saints with sowewhat similar names have clearly
become entangled. So the whole incident may belong to Sark,
not Jersey.

We hear no more of a Jersey hermit, till we reach the Passion of St. Helier (*Passio Sancti Helerii*), which cannot be
earlier than the eleventh century, since it speaks of Normandy
(Normannia), not Neustria. There are three Latin versions of
the *Passion*, one printed by the Bollandists, one printed by Pigeon, and one printed in Le Grand's *Saints de la Bretagne*.
There is also a French translation in an old Office Book at Rennes. They vary in details, but agree in their main story, which
is this: — When Childebert reigned, after the death of the
wicked Queen Brunehild, a childless couple lived at Tongres
(now in Belgium), Sigobard, the richest noble of the north, and
his lovely wife, Lutsegard. Though pagans, they begged St.
Cunibert to pray that they might have children, promising, if
his prayers were answered, to dedicate their firstborn to his
God. A son was born, but when Cunibert claimed him, they
would not let him go. Then the boy's legs began to wither;
and Sigobard, remembering the vow, took him to the Saint, who
healed him, and adopted him as his son, calling him Helerius.
Daily the old man and the boy chanted God's praise together,
living on barley-bread and greens seasoned with salt. Then
miracles began. Helier kept the garden. When hares ate his
cabbages he said, 'Let us share fairly' and drew a line across
the cabbage patch, which the hares never crossed again. One
day a hunter broke through the hedge to catch one of the hares,
but a branch pierced his eye, and he would have been blind,
had not Helier healed him. A woman with an issue of blood,
which no physician could staunch, ate some of Helier's greens
and was cured. A lad slept with his mouth open, and an adder
slipped down his throat. Helier made the sign of the cross and
the snake crept out ashamed.

Sigobard now wished to recover his son; so he sent two
henchmen, who cut off Cunibert's head. Helier however ran
away, and came to Thérouanne (south of Calais). Here in the
darkest corner of a disused church he made a private torture-
chamber, where he prayed night and day, standing on jagged
stones up to his knees in icy water with nails sharp as cobblers'

awls pricking his chest and back. People began to honour him as a Saint, specially when he had raised from the dead the child of a noble named Rotald. So, since admiration is bad for the soul, an Angel bade him go to Nanteuil in Normandy. On his way he cleansed a tainted spring by sprinkling it with salt. At Nanteuil he found St. Marculf, who baptized him. (A surprising statement. Why had not Cunibert done this long before? The mediaeval Church acknowledged no unbaptized person as a Christian ; yet here was one becoming a Saint, and even working miracles!) After three months Marculf gave him leave to be a hermit, and sent him to Jersey (Different MSS read Gersut, Gersuth, and Gersich) with Romard as companion. (In the earliest story Romard only came to Agna with Marculf).

They sailed from Genêts to Jersey, which had only thirty inhabitants. Here Helier healed a cripple with twisted legs, named Anscretil (other MSS read Ascretil, and Anchitil). Traces of this miracle can still be seen on the rocks (an indication that the writer was a Jersey resident. Indeed, who else would be likely to write the life of such an obscure local Saint?). Helier chose as home a cave in a crag cut off at high tide. Three years later Marculf visited him, and wept to see how worn he was with fasting. While Marculf was there, thirty pirate ships from the Orkneys threatened the island. The Saints prayed, and the pirates fought among themselves so fiercely that not one returned home. (There were three versions of this Viking story. In one the ships were smashed by a storm. In one the raiders killed one another. And Poingdestre in 1682 wrote of "an old French rime in which it is sayd that Sir Agobard, yt is a knight, was his father, and Elizambard his mother, and yt like Elishah he was wont to delude pirats, who came to invade ye island, soe as they could not see it".) Three days later Marculf and Romard returned to Normandy. Helier now cut down his meals to one a week, and grew so feeble that he could not walk more than a stone's throw.

Twelve years passed. Then Vandals (i.e. pirates from North Africa) occupied the whole island. They discovered Helier's cave through the twittering of the birds that congregated round it, and cut off his head. The bloodstain is still on the rock (another indication of local knowledge, referring probably to some red streak in the granite). Next day his pedagogue (*Pedagogus* ; who this was is not explained) found the corpse a hundred yards from the cave with its head in its hands, as though it had tried to carry it to the shore. He laid the body in a boat, and fell asleep for sorrow. When he awoke, the tide had carried the boat to Holland. One manuscript says "to a town called Hereuarde, where the Meuse and Rhine and Waal meet, and there it was buried on July 16th by Willibrod the Bishop in a noble mausoleum". Another says "to a town called Hermiarde ; and St. Gillebrius, the Bishop, had it taken to Struenarlensis, where he buried it on July 16th in a noble mausoleum". The old Office Book says, "It was carried to Hexvuarde, and buried at Stonenarleuse". None of these places can be identified.

Such is the story. The first thing that strikes a reader familiar with Lives of the Saints is that he has heard of every incident before. The childless couple vowing to dedicate their firstborn to God, the boy brought up by an old priest, is a story first told of Samuel. Twenty per cent of the Celtic Saints as boys were brought up by hermits. The story of the hares and the cabbages is told of St. Antony and St. Godric, while St. Firmetus struck the same bargain with a wild boar. Dozens of Saints saved hares from hunters, who, when they ignored a warning, were hurt, but later healed. One sensational version of this tale is told of St. Marculf, in which the huntsman was thrown from his horse and all his bowels gushed out, but the Saint gathered them together, and restored them to their place. The woman with the issue of blood has stepped out of the Gospel story. The boy who swallowed a snake in his sleep appears in the *Miracles of St. Hilary.* Celtic Saints according to their legends were always reciting the Psalter standing in icy water, St. Iltyd in Wales, St. Gwenael in Brittany, St. Erth and St. Neot in Cornwall, while St. Cuthbert did it in the sea, and the porpoises used to thaw his frozen toes with their breath. The poisoned spring cleansed with salt is one of Elisha's miracles. The betrayal of the cave by the twittering of the birds recalls innumerable legends of hermits and their feathered friends. The cells of St. Aventin, St. Galmier and St. Maixent were surrounded by swarms of song birds. St. Fructueux' hiding-place and St. Adjuteur's tomb were discovered in the same way. The head-carrying exploit on which St. Helier's office-hymn laid stress —

Mortuus propriis manibus
Cervicem detulit plus centum passibus,
In his own hands, though he was dead,
More than five score yards he carried his head. —

is attributed to no less than eighty-six other martyrs, including
St. Denis of Paris and the British St. Alban.

Indelible bloodstains were pointed out on many a site of
martyrdom, as for example at St. Winefride's Well. The
miraculous voyage to Holland is one of a large group of similar
stories. The world-famous pilgrimage to Santiago was based
on the belief that, when Herod beheaded St. James, Hermogenes
and Philetus rescued his body, and put it in a boat. "They then
fell asleep, and, when they awoke next morning, they found
themselves in Spain" (*Acta Sanctorum*). The *Passion of St.
Helier* is a mosaic of anecdotes told originally about entirely
different persons.

Moreover its chronology is absurd. St. Helier was born, we
are told "after the death of wicked Queen Brunehild, when
Childebert governed the Franks". This must be Childebert III,
who came to the throne in 695. But Helier became a disciple
of St. Marculf, who died in 558 ; and according to one account
he was buried by the famous eighth century Bishop Willebrod.
In other words he was baptized 150 years before he was born,
and buried, while still a young man, two hundred years later.

But, if we have to admit that the *Passion of St. Helier*, written at least five hundred years after the time when our hermit
is said to have lived, is a religious romance, composed purely
for edification, and not based on any historical research, what
evidence is there that St. Helier ever existed ? The *Lives of St.
Marculf*, much older works, assert, if Agna is Jersey, that there
was a hermit in Jersey in the sixth century, a thing in itself
highly probable, for the hermit movement was then at its height,
a reaction against the prevailing laxness and worldliness of the
Church ; and on scores of Islands off the Breton coast, and in
the isles of Chausey, could be found enthusiastic young men
determined to be total abstainers from luxury. But the strongest
argument is that in the twelfth century, when William Fitzhamon
founded his Abbey on the spot where Elizabeth Castle now
stands, he dedicated it to St. Helier (*ecclesia Sancti Helerii*).
He must have believed that there had been such a person

(though even here it can be argued that the church was really dedicated to St. Elerius, a well-known Welsh Abbot, or to St. Hilary, the famous Bishop of Poitiers, and that Helier was merely the French form which the name assumed in the island).

However, when the *Passion of St. Helier* was written, the Jersey hermit acquired a certain amount of fame. A chapel was built over what was said to be his cave. At Fruges, near Thérouane, a church was dedicated to him, and the village spring identified with the one he purified. A church at Rennes still bears his name, and one at Baubec, near Rouen. In the fifteenth century St. Helerus was added to the Calendar of the Augustinian Priory of Launceston in Cornwall (the monks on the Jersey islet were Augustinians). But St. Helier's name was not added to the Coutances *Breviary* till late in the seventeenth century, and it is not yet included in the *Roman Martyrology*, the official list of martyrs recognized by the Roman Church. The Bollandists class the *Passion of St. Helier* as a '*Légende peu sûre*', a legend on which little reliance can be placed. (*Analecta Bollandiana*.) [Authorities quoted above.]

MARCULF, SAINT (c. 484–c. 558), Missionary Monk. Two Latin *Acts of St. Marculf*, one in the Vatican, the other at Avranches, are our main source of information. Neither can be later than the tenth century, for they speak of Neustria, not Normandy. They vary in details, but agree in main facts. They state that Marculf was born at Bayeux, and names mentioned later show that this must have been about 484. The towns in North France were now Christian, but the country people still clung passionately to the worship of the old Gaulish gods. Marculf was the son of one of the conquering Franks, who had followed the example of his leader Clovis and become a Christian. The name Marculf (border wolf) is one of the wolf names of which the Franks were fond (cf Ranulf, Rudolf, Randulf, Regenwulf, Brunwulf, Adolf, etc.). When his wealthy parents died, Marculf gave away all his goods to the poor, in order to be free to go out as a wandering missionary to the pagans. When twenty-eight he rode out from Bayeux on his donkey, and after two years' free-lance work he arrived at Coutances.

Here St. Possessor, who was Bishop of Coutances from about 512 to about 524, took him into his household, and after a period of training ordained him Priest, and sent him out to continue his missionary work. He was a little man of fiery eloquence, and soon won disciples. Then, prompted by an Angel seen in a dream, he decided to gather these into a monastery. He rode to Paris to beg from Childebert I (511—558) land on which to build one, and the King granted him an estate at Nanteuil on the east coast of the Cotentin. Here he built an oratory with a cluster of wooden cells round it ; but every year he spent Lent in solitude on one of the islets off the coast, now called the Iles St. Marcouf.

The Avranches manuscript thus describes his visit to Jersey. It says that, feeling again the need for a time of solitude, he came with a venerable priest named Romard (another MS. reads Domard) "to an island off the Breton coast called Agnus". We know from other Acts of the Saints that one of the Channel Islands was called by a name which monkish chroniclers latinized as Agnus, Agna, Angia, or Augia. The *Miracles of St. Wandrille* state that an Abbot of Fontenelle was sent to "an island called Angia, which Bretons inhabit, adjacent to the Coutances country". The *Acts of St. Magloire* tell how that Saint was summoned to "the island of Angia near Sark". An island described as "near Sark" and "adjacent to the Coutances country" may safely be assumed to be Jersey. The account goes on: "This isle was inhabited by a handful of serfs (coloni), among whom dwelt a man named Helibertus, who was leading an ultra-ascetic life, and mortifying his flesh by over-rigorous fasts. Marculf and Romard shared his hut and his life of contemplation and self-discipline. One day a horde of Saxon pirates, numbering nearly 3,000, approached the isle with sails set and oars swinging. The islanders, who are said to have numbered no more than thirty (Does this refer only to those on the islet adjoining St. Helier's hermitage?), seeing them from afar were sore afraid not knowing what to do, or whither they could fly, as the sea hemmed them in. They ran for succour to the Blessed Marculf, and clinging to his knees loudly implored his aid. 'My sons', said the Saint, 'be strong and of a good courage. To arms! With intrepid hearts forward to meet the foe! I promise you victory. He Who overthrew Pharaoh and his host will fight for you'. Heartened by these words, and trusting not to their own strength but to the Saint's prayers, they charged right dauntlessly into battle with the pirates. Then was there bitter strife ; but by the grace of God and through the Saint's intercessions not one islander was wounded. Of the barbarians divers were slain and many were drowned in the waves, and none survived to bear the tidings to their own land. When the Lord of the Isle heard how thousands of the enemy had perished through Marculf's prayers, he rendered thanks to God, and gave into the Saint's keeping half of that isle. (Does this mean half Jersey or half the islet on which Elizabeth Castle stands?) Here the Saint built a monastery, wherein he placed certain brethren, who should form perpetually a household of God". This last sentence is important. If Marculf left behind him, when he returned to Nanteuil, a monastery of missionary monks, he was the true founder of the Christian Church in Jersey. St. Helier (q.v.) may have been here first ; but a hermit's religion is too self-centred to win converts. His whole aim is the salvation of his own soul. But Marculf was a missionary of repute, and the monks he left behind would have continued his work.

The story in the Vatican manuscript varies in certain details. Marculf comes to Jersey not seeking seclusion but converts. "He summoned his brethren, and announced that he was going to Brittany. 'I must preach the Word in other lands, for therefore was I sent'. Then a priest named Romard prayed to be allowed to accompany him. So they crossed the Breton country and came to an isle called Agna". Then follows their discovery of the hermit, who is called Eletus, their stay with him, and the arrival of the pirates. "One day the islanders on their way to work saw the Saxon horde approaching. They fled in panic to the cell where the three holy men were praying, and cast themselves at Marculf's feet crying, 'Save us or we perish.' The Saint replied, 'Fear not. Quit you like men. Be strong'. Then he made over them the sign of the cross, saying, 'God will fight for you. In His sight numbers are as nothing'. Heartened by these words they rushed on the foe, while Marculf, prostate on the ground, pleaded for divine help. The raiders were leaping into the surf, and some had reached the shore, when a great gale swept the ships out to sea, and smashed them to atoms, while the natives slew all who reached the sands. When the Bretons heard of the mighty deeds daily wrought by Marculf, crowds flocked to him, and he built a place of prayer in that isle, in which he placed monks to serve God".

Of the rest of his life little is told. Near its end he visited the King once more to get the gifts made to his monasteries duly confirmed by charter. On this visit he is said to have conferred on Childebert and his descendents the power which he himself possessed of curing scrofula by a touch. French Kings down to 1825 continued to touch for King's Evil. Edward III claimed to have received this gift through his mother, Isabella of Valois, and from his day till the accession of the House of Hanover English sovereigns also had fixed days when the sick were brought to them to be touched. Roman Catholics still invoke St. Marculf for scrofula. He returned to Nanteuil, where he died about 558. His Abbey, which was never more than a group of wooden huts built round a little Chapel, was burnt by Norsemen in the ninth century, and never rebuilt ; but the monks escaped with the body of the Saint to Corbeny, where his shrine became a famous pilgrimage centre. A mediaeval window in Coutances Cathedral shows St. Marculf in his boat setting sail for Jersey, St. Marculf embracing St. Helier, the three Saints praying, and the islanders fighting the pirates. [*Acta Sanctorum: Mémoires de la Société Académique du Cotentin.* Vol. X.]

PEIRSON, FRANCIS (1757—81), Officer in command of the troops at the Battle of Jersey. Eldest son of Francis Peirson, of Mowthorpe Grange, Kirby-Grindalythe, in the East Riding of Yorkshire, Major in the 36th Foot, and Sarah Cogdell of York. He was educated at the Warrington Academy, and on 16 July 1772, when only fifteen, he obtained a commission as Ensign in the 36th Foot, of which Lieut.-General Sir Richard Peirson, his cousin and godfather, was Colonel (Sir Richard's portrait is in the Barreau Art Gallery). The regiment was then in Jamaica, but Peirson remained at York as Recruiting Officer. As his father had a house in the city, this meant that he lived at home. On the regiment's return he joined it at Chatham in March 1774, and was promoted Lieutenant in September. In March 1775 he was back in York recruiting, and stayed there till Dec. 1776, when he rejoined his regiment in Ireland. In March 1778 he was appointed aide-de-camp to his godfather. In May 1779 he became Captain-Lieutenant in the 75th Foot : but in August, when a new regiment, the 95th Foot, was being raised, he was appointed Major, and sent back to York on his old job of recruiting. His career up to this point showed no special promise of distinction. Of his first eight years in the Army he had spent five, thanks to family influence, comfortably at home, or else acting as aide-de-camp to a relative.

Now however life became more strenuous. For the new regiment he was chief recruiting-officer, and other agents had to pass on their men to him. His father wrote: — "In October he began recruiting at York, and continued there till January 1780, receiving recruits from the different recruiting officers, and had not one officer to assist him. In March the regiment was moved to Leeds, and from thence to Plymouth, a march of above 300 miles. He had the sole command the greatest part of the march, and they were conducted to Plymouth with only the loss of three men by desertion, a remarkable thing, when it is considered that they were collected from England, Ireland, and Scotland. On April 6 the regiment was inspected by General Gray, and only seven men out of the whole rejected. Major Peirson raised 115 men himself, 20 of whom were Grenadiers. Not one man of his raising was rejected" (MS. in S.J. Library). On the following day, April 7, the officers received their commissions, and on May 21 the new regiment was given its colours. "I made them a discourse", wrote Peirson in his diary, "proper to the occasion".

On June 3 the 95th sailed for the Channel Islands. After dropping some of its companies at Guernsey, Peirson and the rest arrived in Jersey on the 13th. They remained for more than four months under canvas, and on November 1 moved into winter quarters at La Hougue, a large house with many outbuildings not far from St. Ouen's Bay, where eighteen months before the French had attempted a landing. Before Christmas the Colonel and Lieutenant-Colonel went home on furlough, leaving Peirson in command. On the morning of January 6, 1781, news came that a French force had landed in the night on the other side of the island, and captured the Town by surprise (See *Rullecourt*). Peirson "instantly beat to arms", wrote Harrison, his Adjutant, "and the 95th fell in with the greatest alacrity.

The artillerymen being absent, he helped to harness the horses with his own hands, that no time might be lost in moving the cannon". He marched four miles to Gallows Hill, the rocky height overlooking St. Helier's from the west, where he found five companies of the 78th Highlanders, who had withdrawn from the Town in time to avoid capture. They had been joined by the North and the South-West Militia Regiments and the St. Lawrence's, St. Saviour's, St. Mary's, St. Peter's, and St. Ouen's Battalions with their cannons, and by stragglers of the Town Regiment, who had been able to escape. Lempriere, a Militia officer, estimated the number as "nearly 2,000"; Lieutenant Boyne of the 95th said, "near 1,600". No one yet knew the number of the enemy.

The officers present held a rapid council of war. What might have been an awkward question of seniority was satisfactorily settled. Could Militia Colonels of many years standing put themselves under the orders of a very juvenile Major of 24? "Those who affirm", said Lempriere, "that the Militia put themselves under the command of the Regulars are mistaken. They merely agreed to co-operate with them, and waived their pretensions to rank for a time to avoid dispute". But there was a more serious problem. Captain Lumsden of the 78th had received from Corbet (q.v.), the Lieutenant-Governor, the order: — "The island being surprised, to save the Town from being destroyed and to obtain certain privileges for the inhabitants, the Governor has signed a capitulation. The troops are to embark with all the honours of war. The troops and militia are therefore to remain quiet, and hostilities are to cease". Corbet was Commander-in-Chief. Dare junior officers disobey? Peirson decided that everything depended on whether Corbet was a prisoner. He sent his Adjutant into the Town to discover. "The commanding officers agreed", said Harrison, "to send Ensign Boyne and me (I think it was about eleven o'clock) with a flag of truce to know if the Lieutenant-Governor was a prisoner or not". Yet a third point had to be settled. If it was decided to ignore Corbet's capitulation, what was the next step? "It was debated for some time", says one account, "whether the troops should not wait for reinforcements from England". But information dribbling out from the Town suggested that the number of French troops there did not much exceed five hundred; and Peirson insisted on immediate action.

Meanwhile he made skilful preparations. He arranged his
artillery on Gallows Hill to cover a retreat, if one should be
necessary. He sent an urgent message to the regiment at Grouville: — "Make haste. Come to our assistance. We are going
to engage". He ordered the light companies of the 95th and
the 78th and two companies of Militia to make a detour and
occupy the Mont de la Ville on the other sider of the Town, from
which it was possible to fire into the Market Place, where the
French were massed. Then, thinking his two officers were
detained too long, he dispatched another with a flag of truce
to demand an immediate reply. Rullecourt's answer was to
send Corbet on parole to insist on the observance of the capitulation. "On our return", said Harrison, who accompanied
him, "we saw the British troops advancing on the hill. On our
arrival the Major halted them. The Lieutenant-Governor said,
'Major, this has been a very sudden surprise. I was made
prisoner, before I was out of bed'. The Major answered, 'Sir,
give me leave to inform you that the 78th and 95th have not
been the least surprised'. The Lieutenant-Governor then read
a copy of the capitulation, and said he had done everything in
his power for the good of the service and the island ; and
further said that there were 1,000 French troops in and about
the Town, that two battalions of artillery were coming, and 600
or 6,000, I am not sure which, landed in a different part of the
island, besides 10,000 at St. Maloes waiting for orders. Major
Peirson asked him how he came to know this. The Lieutenant-
Governor said, the French General had given him his word of
honour that it was true. Major Peirson then told him that the
commanding officers were determined to die before they would
surrender. He then pulled out his watch, and asked the
Lieutenant-Governor how long he would require to go back.
He asked half an hour. Major Peirson would give him but ten
minutes, and told him at the expiration of this he would storm
the Town" (Evidence at Corbet's Court Martial. A very
similar description of this interview, given by Boyne, is quoted
in the article, *Corbet, M*).

He continued the story in an account given to Peirson's
father : — "When the Lieutenant-Governor and the French
officer had got some little distance, Major Peirson placed himself at the head of the Grenadiers, and drew his sword, and
flourished it over his head. From this signal the troops con-

cluded they were to engage. Instantly every cap and hat was off, and the troops gave three loud cheers, which caused the Lieutenant-Governor and the French officer to look back. Major Peirson marched the troops toward the Town with his watch in his hand, and finding that, if he marched on, he would attack before the expiration of the ten minutes, he halted a short time, and then cried, 'Follow me' ". Lumsden led his Highlanders, the South-West Militia regiment, and the St. Lawrence' and St. John's men up the Grande Rue (Broad Street). Peirson led the 95th and the rest of the Militia up the Rue de Derrière (King Street). The French awaited the attack in the Market Place (Royal Square). They had found the cannons of the Town Militia in the church, and placed them to cover each approach. But Rullecourt's artillerymen had failed to land through the turn of the tide, and his infantry evidently did not understand cannons, for, though they fired point-blank at the advancing columns, no one was hurt. Lumsden's men charged into one end of the Square up the Rue Trousse Cotillon (Church Street) ; almost simultaneously Peirson and his men swung into the opposite end through the narrow entrance now called Peirson Place ; while the troops sent to the Mont de la Ville poured in a withering fire from above. In ten minutes the victory was won. "The enemy", wrote Pirouet, "threw down their arms, and fled for refuge, some into the Court, some into the Beef and Corn Markets, the rest into any houses that they found open". But by this time Peirson was dead. He advanced up King Street "six paces in front of his regiment, and, when he appeared opposite the Pig Market, a cannon was fired, which did no harm ; but, as he reached the gable-end of the house of Monsieur Lerrier, he was struck in the right breast by a musket-ball, and died at the moment of victory". "Just before the French gave way", wrote Harrison, "a French soldier, who had planted himself at the angle of a wall, took fatal aim, and shot Major Peirson through the heart. He fell with his head against me. I took him out of the action with assistance, and got the Surgeon General to him, but all in vain. He died in my arms without speaking. His death was instantly revenged by a Jersey militiaman and a black servant of Captain Christy's of the 95th, both of whom rushed forward and shot the Frenchman".

Peirson was buried in the Town Church on January 19 with all the pomp and pageantry of a state funeral. At their first meeting after the Battle the States commissioned the elder Bacon to carve a memorial to be placed on the church wall ; they also sent a letter to Peirson's father : — "Convinced that we owe our present power of deliberating to the gallant behaviour of your son, who purchased our freedom at the inestimable price of his life, we think it our indispensible duty to express to you our sincere grief and condolence on so great a public and private loss". Peirson died unmarried ; but the British Government granted to his father a pension of £250 a year, and smaller pensions to his three surviving sisters. His best-known memorial is Copley's picture, The Death of Major Peirson, now in the National Gallery (painted 1783). His miniature by Philippe Jean (q.v.) is in the Barreau Art Gallery, and his watch in the S. J. Museum. [Pedigree of Major Peirson in *Bull* XIII 413 : Evidence of Boyne, Harrison, and Anley in *Proceedings at large in the Trial of Moses Corbet* : Harrison's account given to Peirson's father, *Bull* I. 319 & 362 : Lempriere's account, *Bull*. V. 269 : Poingdestre's account, *Bull*. XIII. 70 : Pirouet's account in Mourant's edition of the *Chroniques de Jersey* : Ouless' *Death of Major Peirson* : Perrot's *Surprise de Jersey* : Brachet's *La Dernière Expédition contre Jersey* : Rochfort's *Invasion of the Island of Jersey*.]

POULET FAMILY. The Poulets were an old West Country family, which by a series of marriages had acquired manors in Somerset, Devon, Wiltshire, and Hampshire. Members of the Hampshire branch became Marquises of Winchester and Dukes of Bolton. The senior Somerset branch had its seat at Hinton St. George, near Crewkerne. Amias Poulet of this branch was knighted in 1487 after the defeat of Lambert Simnel. Once, when Wolsey was a Somerset parson, Poulet is said to have clapped him in the stocks. He commanded troops in France in 1513, and later became Treasurer of the Middle Temple (See *D.N.B.*). His descendants for three generations played important parts in Jersey history. Two of his sons, Hugh (q.v.) and John (q.v.), became Governor and Dean ; two of his grandsons, Amias (q.v.) and George (q.v.), became Governor and Bailiff ; two of his great-grandsons, Anthony (q.v.) and Abra-

ham, became Governor and Attorney-General. Contemporaries
often spell the name Paulet, Pawlett, Pallet ; but Sir Hugh and
his brother John, the Dean, and his son George, the Bailiff,
always signed themselves Poulet, and that is the spelling on
Sir Hugh's tomb and that of the first Sir Amias. On Sir
Anthony's tomb it is Poulett. The family today spell the name
Poulett, and pronounce it Pawlet.

POULET, SIR AMIAS (d. 1588), Governor. Eldest son of
Sir Hugh Poulet (q.v.) Governor, and Philippa, daughter of Sir
Lewis Pollard. Since his brother George (q.v.), the third son,
was born in 1534, Amias cannot have been born later than 1532.
He came to Jersey, when his father was made Governor in
1550, and at once became his father's assistant. In 1551 he was
sent to London to report to the Privy Council that local officials
in Normandy refused to hand over six robbers who had escaped
from Jersey. The Council sent him to Paris with a letter to the
Constable of France ; the Constable gave him an order to the
Bailiff of La Foi ; and he returned to the island with his
prisoners (S.P.F.). In 1556 he was made Lieut.-Governor.
    Sir Hugh was often absent. In 1559—60 he was Vice-
President of the Council for the Welsh Marches ; in 1562 he
sailed with the English army to Havre. So Amias was often
for long periods in sole charge of Jersey. Elizabeth's reluctance
to admit the French right to Calais had brought the two countries to the brink of war. In 1559 news came from Normandy
that a French adventurer, named Glatigny, was preparing a
raid. A year later the Ambassador in Paris wrote, "Something
is in hand touching Jersey". So Amias did a little espionage
on his own account. He visited Brest and St. Malo, and counted
the ships and troops that were gathering there. But with the
death of the French King the immediate danger lessened, though
a letter from Amias to his father shows that eight years later
the friction with Normandy continued: — "Mr. St. Aubin has
been arrested by Mons. Boisrougier of Coutances, and after
fourteen days' imprisonment dismissed with the loss of a gos-
hawk and 20 ells of canvas. I wrote to this Monsieur for redress ;
but he answered, he was sorry he had dismissed his prisoner,
and that his stock was not better, advising me to look to myself,

as he hoped to pluck me out of my house, as he had the Captain of Alderney. If I had the Queen's leave, I would ask no aid but the retinue of this Castle to pluck him out of his house" (*S.P.D.*).

One obvious safeguard against French threats was to strengthen Mont Orgueil. For twenty-five years Poulet was trying to squeeze money out of Elizabeth's bankrupt purse for this purpose, advancing money of his own, and spurring on the builders. "Though I have husbanded Her Majesty's money well", he wrote in 1557, "I have been constrained to employ more than I received, and our walls want a third part yet" (*S.P.D.*). In 1563 he wrote: — "I am much deceived, considering the depth of the foundation, the height and thickness of the walls, if a greater piece of work hath ever been done for the like sum" (*Hatfield MSS.*). He wrote again in 1573: — "A strong piece of work, begun four or five years ago, lacks completion of one third. Four hundred pounds will be needed this year and four hundred next" (*S.P.D.*). The result was the mighty Somerset Tower, the central tower of the castle, completed just before he died.

One early trouble was the plague, brought back by his father's soldiers from Havre. "The plague is very sore in Jersey", wrote Carew in 1563, "specially in the Castle". And Poulet told Cecil that he could not meet the Commissioners in Guernsey, till the plague abated. "Indeed I dare not leave the Castle for fear of disorder by the soldiers" (*Hatfield MSS.*).

Like Sir Hugh, Amias was anti-Catholic, and, as soon as Mary died, he made no secret of his views, as the Somerset Tower bears witness, for its masonry contains smashed images of saints and altar slabs used as gun-platforms. But he did not see altogether eye to eye with his father. Sir Hugh was a Prayer Book Protestant, who wanted the French translation of the Prayer Book used throughout the Island. Amias was a Puritan, whose ideal was Calvin's Geneva. Commissioners were hunting heretics in every village in Normandy (1558), and refugees poured into Jersey, and among them Huguenot Pastors. As the island was short of clergy, Poulet appointed some of these to Rectories, and they began to use in their Services the Huguenot *Forme des Prières Ecclésiastiques*. This shocked Sir Hugh's Elizabethan love of order. He wrote to Cecil in 1560: — "I desire your opinion, which I will see observed, or that you write to John Poulet, my brother, the Dean, to whom the spiritual

affairs of the island appertain. Some order should be taken.
Most of the inhabitants dislike these devices in matters of
religion, set forth after the private fantasies of a few, chiefly
Frenchmen, contrary to Law" *(S.P.D.)*. But Amias, the man
on the spot, encouraged the Calvinizers. In 1562 he appointed
to the Town Church Guillaume Morise, Seigneur de la Ripau-
dière, a Huguenot minister from Anjou. "He was the first",
says the Chronicler, "to set up a real Reformed Church in
Jersey and to administer the Lord's Supper according to the
purity of the Gospel, at which Supper Mr. Amias Poulet and
most of the notables assisted ; after which with the Lieutenant's
assent he ordained Elders and Deacons, and formed a Consistory" *(Chroniques)*. Amias' brother George (q.v.) was one
of the new Elders. In 1567 Poulet visited London, and secured
Elizabeth's permission "to use such form of Service in the
Parish Church of St. Hyllerye as is accustomed in the French
Church in London, following the Queen's Book of Divine
Service in all other parishes of the isle without any alteration"
(Huguenot's Sy's Proceedings. Vol V.). He quietly ignored
however the second clause, and the Calvinist Book was soon
used in every Church in Jersey.

A new wave of persecution in France brought in 1568 a fresh
influx of Huguenots. Amias welcomed them, but Sir Hugh was
alarmed at this increase in the French population. "I approve
my son's zeal", he wrote, "in receiving these strangers, but I
cannot like their continued abode in the isle. They should be
passed on" *(S.P.D.)*. But in spite of occasional disagreements
father and son worked well together, and in Nov. 1571 Sir
Hugh surrendered his patent to Elizabeth, in order that Amias
might be made Joint-Governor with him. When he died,
Amias remained sole Governor.

Jersey now saw less of him. Large estates in Somerset demanded his attention. Even before his father's death he had
represented the county as Knight of the Shire in the Parliament
which met in 1571 *(Proceedings, Somerset Arch. Sy. Vol.
LXXXII)*. Part of each year was spent at Court, where in October 1575 he was knighted. Then came a new duty. "In
1576", writes the Chronicler, "he was bidden by the Queen to
be for three years her resident Ambassador in France. On
receiving this letter, he settled as speedily as he might the
business in the castle and island that he had in hand, and

then called the States together, and showed them the Queen's Order, and made Guillaume Lempriere, Seigneur of Trinity, his Lieut.-Governor" (*Chroniques*). He left Jersey with his wife and family on 26 June, waited in Guernsey for the three days' Synod, which established the Presbyterian system of Church government throughout the islands, and, after a short stay in England, crossed to France on 25 Sept., groaning at the size and pomp of his retinue, and on 13 Oct. presented his credentials to the boy King. His task was not easy. Elizabeth's tortuous foreign policy kept her ambassadors on thorns. What they were instructed to say one day might be repudiated the next. Poulet was given an embarrassingly free hand. "Her Majesty wishes you", wrote Walsingham, "in matters that concern her service to deal as you think fit, though you have no special direction, such trust she reposes in you" (*S.P.D.*). This sounded flattering, but meant that, if things went wrong, he would bear the blame. Poulet faced his difficulties stoutly. In Feb. 1577 the Venetian Ambassador wrote: — "The English Ambassador made a serious complaint to their Majesties, saying his Queen marvelled at the decision to extirpate the unhappy professors of the Reformed Religion. After many representations, that were almost threats, he said that his Queen had always been their Protector, and could not fail to help them" (*Venetian State Papers*). By August however the Huguenot position seemed hopeless, and Poulet was ordered to make peace ; but the Queen Mother, the formidable Catherine de Medici, "spake in a haughty tone, saying that to deny matters that were evidently true was only to aggravate the crime" (*id*). That month a rumour ran round Paris that Mary Queen of Scots had been killed, and that Poulet would be hanged in reprisal ; but the rumour proved false. In Jan. 1579 his eldest son Hugh lost his life through an accident in Paris, a brilliant lad of twenty-one, whom Sir Amias used as his confidential messenger (He left in manuscript a French Romance, *L'Histoire de la Duchesse de Savoye*). Another son or daughter must have perished in the same catastrophe, for both Walsingham and the Queen wrote to condole with him on the death of his "children" (*S.P.F.*). In Nov. his three years were up, and he wrote with relief, "I am Jack out of office, and I thank God for it" (*id*).

He returned to Jersey. In 1581 he was serving on a Commission in Guernsey, making grants to churches from money

raised by the sale of Church property there (*S.P.D.*). He spent
the winter of 1582 in his manor at Sampford Peverell (*id*).
In 1583 he was back in Jersey, and was present in the Royal
Court, when his brother George (q.v.) was sworn in as Bailiff,
and his son Anthony (q.v.) as Lieut.-Governor. He was now
in high favour at Court, and in 1584 was made a Privy Councillor. While ill in Jersey in 1585, he was summoned to be
custodian to Mary Queen of Scots. A desperately delicate
task! She was heir to the throne, and, if Elizabeth died, would
be Queen tomorrow ; but she was Elizabeth's deadliest foe,
and was conspiring with more than one group to hasten Elizabeth's end. She was lodged in the Staffordshire castle of
Tutbury, and there, as soon as he was well enough to travel,
Poulet took up his duties ; though later they moved into pleas-
anter quarters in Chartley Castle in the same county. But he
still kept in touch with Jersey. In July 1585 he wrote to Walsingham: — "Mont Orgueil is short of calivers and powder.
These threatening days require a better store" (*Letter Book*).
In Dec. he wrote again: — "My son Anthony says, Count
Brissac prepares ships. I fear the French may stir up new
enemies ; but living here a prisoner I cannot judge. If you find
truth in the report, pray desire Her Majesty to send men and
munitions" (*S.P.D.*). Four days later he suggests that "one or
two of Her Majesty's smaller vessels might be commanded to
attend there to bring advertisement of necessity, if any should
happen" (*Letter Book*).

His main task however was to thwart Mary's innumerable
wiles. She smuggled out letters in her dirty linen, and in false
bottoms to her beer barrels. She tried to suborn Poulet himself
promising, if she were Queen, to make his Governorship of
Jersey a semi-independent sovereignty with power "greater than
was ever before given to an English subject". "Poulet", says
Froude, "at once blighted any hope she had of corrupting him.
He replied that he would show her all respect and courtesy, but
must obey the orders of his Sovereign. Mary alternately raved,
cursed, wept, and entreated. Poulet was courteous, but firm.
She was allowed to walk, ride, or hunt, but always attended by
guards. No stranger was permitted to see her, and everything
that went out of the castle passed through Poulet's hands"
(*History of England*). Elizabeth applauded his vigilance. "Amyas", she wrote, "my most faithful and careful servant, God

reward thee treblefold for thy most troublesome charge so well
discharged. If you knew, my Amyas, how kindly my grateful
heart accepteth your spotless actions, performed in so crafty and
dangerous a charge, it would ease your travails" (*id*). One
thing however he would not do even for Elizabeth. When she
shrank from signing Mary's death-warrant, she sent a message
through Walsingham: — "She doth note in you a lack of that
zeal in her service that she looketh for, that you have not found
some way of shortening the Queen of Scots' life. She taketh
most unkindly that you should cast the burthen on her". Poulet
received this note at 5 p.m., and by six had sent off his answer: — "My goods and my life are at Her Majesty's disposition, but God forbid I should make so foul a shipwreck of my
conscience, or leave so great a blot on my poor posterity" (*Letter Book*). Poulet and Mary had now moved to Fotheringay.
He was one of the Commissioners at her trial, and was present
at her execution (8 Feb. 1587). She took his arm, as she
mounted the scaffold, saying, "Thanks, Sir Amias, this will be
the last trouble I shall give you". But she did not forgive him.
She sent a message through the Spanish Ambassador to the
King of Spain: — "She enjoined His Majesty on the day he
made himself master of England to recollect how she had been
treated by Amias Poulet" (*Spanish State Papers*).

Elizabeth was furious at his refusal to have Mary murdered,
"swearing by God's death that he was a dainty fellow, who
knew not what loyalty meant". Nevertheless he was too faithful a servant to lose. In 1587 he became Clerk to the Duchy
of Lancaster and Chancellor of the Order of the Garter. In
Jan. 1588 he was lodging in Fleet St., and dealing with a
dispute about Jersey tithes. In Feb. he was sent to the Low
Countries as one of four Commissioners to try to make peace
with Spain. Catholics resented his appointment. "Powlett",
wrote one, "is adjoined in commission, that hard gaoler of the
Holy Queen and Martyress. Man muses they are so shameless"
(*S.P.F.*). He lived just long enough to see the Armada defeated,
and died that year in London on 26 Sept., and was buried in
St. Martin's in the Fields in a handsome table-tomb supporting
his life-size effigy in plate armour (Photograph in *Proceedings
Somerset Arch. Sy.* Vol. LXXIV). The long epitaph signed
E.R. is said to have been composed by Elizabeth. When the
Church was rebuilt in 1728, the parishioners refused to readmit

the monument, and it was removed to Hinton St. George.

Sir Amias married Margaret, daughter of Anthony Hervey of St. John's Columb, Devon, and had three sons, Hugh (b. 1558), killed in Paris, Anthony (q.v.), who became Governor, and George (b. 1565), his brother's Lieutenant-Governor. (In 1593 Anthony wrote, "My brother will supply my place", and again in 1596, "I have received a letter from my brother, my lieutenant" (*Hatfield MSS*). This George must not be confused with his uncle, George, (q.v.) who was Lieut.-Governor earlier and later). He had also three daughters, Joan, who married Robert Heydon, Sarah, who married Sir Francis Vincent, and Elizabeth. At his death Sir Amias owned fourteen manors in Somerset, four in Devon, and a large house with an acre of land in Clerkenwell, which had belonged to his stepmother's first husband, Sir Thomas Pope. An engraving of his portrait is in the S.J. Museum, and is reproduced in Saunders' *Jersey in the 15th and 16th Centuries*. [*State Papers Domestic ; State Papers Foreign ; Catalogue of Hatfield MSS ; Venetian State Papers ; Dic. Nat. Biog. ;* Collins' *Peerage ;* Poulet's *Letter Book* when Ambassador, published by the Roxburgh Club. His letters while in charge of Mary have been edited by J. Morris ; other letters are in Thorpe's *Scottish State Papers*.]

POULET, GEORGE (1554—1621), Lieut.-Governor and Bailiff. Third son of Sir Hugh Poulet (q.v.), brother of Sir Amias (q.v.). Born 1554 (a petition from him in 1614 in *S.P.D.* states that he was then eighty). He came to Jersey, a boy of sixteen, when his father was appointed Governor. In their father's absence George's elder brother Amias acted as Lieut.-Governor, but on four occasions, when Amias also was summoned to England, George was sworn in as Lieutenant (*A.E.*). The Manor of St. Germain had been promised to his father, when Helier De Carteret should die. This happened in 1561, and Sir Hugh then passed it on to George. He lived there for a time, but then moved to St. Saviour's, where his wife was buried in 1574. In 1602 he was living at St. Lawrence, and in 1605 in St. Helier's.

In June 1562 he was one of five Royal Commissioners appointed to survey the fortifications, redress what was wrong in the administration of justice, and reform the grammar schools. In religion he was a Calvinist. When Guillaume Morise in 1565 set up at the Town Church what the Chronicler calls "the first real Reformed Church in Jersey", Poulet was one of the Elders ; and, when Hugh Perrin, Seigneur of Rozel, attacked the Huguenot innovations, the Consistory appointed Poulet one of its Attorneys "in all controversies before judges secular or ecclesiastical", and sent him to England to answer Perrin before the Bishop of Winchester. In 1567 he went to Guernsey as a Royal Commissioner to report on repairs to Castle Cornet, on whether the proposal to build a pier would endanger the safety of the Castle, and on what use should be made of the money raised by the sale of Church property (S.P.D.). About this time the Privy Council adopted a plan of not hearing in London appeals from the islands, but appointing local Commissioners to decide them on the spot. Again and again Poulet was employed for this purpose (P.C.). In 1579 he was once more a Royal Commissioner for Guernsey "for the redressing of sundry grievances, wherein the inhabitants complain" (P.C.).

In 1580 he married his daughter Rachel to Sir Philippe De Carteret of St. Ouen's in St. George's Chapel at Mont Orgueil. About this time Brevint records as a note-worthy feat of horsemanship: — "Mons. George Poulet on a Review Day descended on horseback from the summit of the Town Hill right down to the Churchyard" (Journal). In 1583, when gout compelled Jean Dumaresq (q.v.) to resign the Bailiffship, Poulet took his place. He was sworn in on 31 Aug., and his oath included the clause: — "You will defend the rights of the true Christian Church, and secure to the utmost of your power the destruction, annihilation, and abolition of the false Church of the Pope, and that all who despise the pure Word of God shall be condignly punished" (A.E.). He held office for nearly three years, and then, as Dumaresq's health had improved, resigned in May 1586 in his favour. But in less than a year Dumaresq, "crippled with infirmity", again retired, and Poulet once more succeeded him (Oct. 1586). He then got involved in a quarrel with three of his Jurats (The story is told in detail in Manuscrits de Ph. Le Geyt. Vol. IV). During the hearing of a codfish case, in which the Jurats were divided, Poulet said something which Helier Dumaresq resented as "a nasty insult".

The Bailiff reported this remark to the Council ; but Dumaresq apologized and was fined. He then however joined two other Jurats, Jean De Carteret (q.v.) of Vinchelez de Haut and Philippe Journeaulx, in attacking Poulet for transferring cases from the ordinary Courts to the Cour Extraordinaire, in which his fees were higher. They circulated a petition to the Council to abolish the Cour Extraordinaire, and began to collect signatures. Poulet appealed to his nephew Anthony (q.v.), the Lieut.-Governor, who imprisoned the three Jurats in Mont Orgueil. Meanwhile the Bailiff called together the remaining Jurats, the Advocates, and the States, and they unanimously voted that the Cour Extraordinaire was a necessity. Journeaulx and Dumaresq made their submission, but De Carteret appealed to the Council, and, though committed to the Marshalsea for "his factious proceedings", he returned so persistently to the attack, that eventually (Feb. 1591) two Commissioners, Robert Napper and Dr. Tertullian Pyne, were sent to Jersey to investigate his charges against the Poulets. Their verdict with regard to the Bailiff was: — "We find that George Poulet hath very well behaved himself, and hath in respect of his long continuance there good experience of their laws, and hath used both diligence and integrity in the said office".

In May Poulet was appointed Lieut.-Governor of Guernsey, and resigned the Bailiffship, and Jean Dumaresq resumed his old place. Five years later (1596) Dumaresq again asked for his discharge on the ground of ill-health, and for the third time Poulet became Bailiff. He now adopted a conciliatory policy toward his former opponents. His first Lieut.-Bailiff was Helier Dumaresq, and his second Jean De Carteret. In Oct. his nephew Anthony appointed him Lieut.-Governor, and, when Sir Walter Ralegh and Sir John Peyton became Governors, they too made him their Lieutenant ; so that for the next eighteen years he was both Lieut.-Governor and Bailiff. In 1602 his old quarrel with Jean De Carteret flared up once more. When De Carteret had a case before the Court, he refused to plead before Poulet and demanded another Judge. For this insult Sir Walter Ralegh sent him to the Castle. He then did his utmost to reconcile them "pointing out to De Carteret how grievous was his fault in not reflecting, before uttering such insults, that the Bailiff, when sitting on the Seat of Justice, represents the authority of the Prince. De Carteret, touched by these

remonstrances, freely acknowledged that he had grossly trans-
gressed in using such language. The Bailiff however was not
satisfied. So the Governor and States considered the matter
again, and judged the apology to be adequate, and urged the
Bailiff to accept it for the sake of peace and concord. Whereupon he agreed" (A.E.).

In 1609 he was appointed one of eight Royal Commissioners
"to diligently review the Laws of Jersey, to reduce them to a
more certain, clear, and perfect form, and to amend them, where
need should require" (P.B.C.). When he married the widow
of Hostes Nicolle (q.v.), he had become the guardian of her
three surviving children. In 1594, when his daughter's husband, Sir Philippe De Carteret, died, he secured from the
Crown at a stiff price the guardianship of her nine little children. At first he looked after their property well, but, as age
crept on, he grew careless, and, when Sir Philippe (q.v.), the
future Royalist leader, came of age, he complained bitterly of
the way the St. Ouen's estate had been neglected.

On 22 April 1614 Poulet asked leave to retire, pleading that
he was eighty years old, and had done fifty-six years' service as
Lieut.-Governor or Bailiff. In reply the King wrote to Peyton,
the Governor: — "We are pleased that our old servant, George
Poulet, shall now retire to his private ease, and it is our pleasure
hat you allow him £20 a year during life" (S.P.D.). But he
was still vigorous. In 1617 and in 1619 he was again sworn in
as Lieut.-Governor, and in the latter year, when a dispute arose
about the extradition of some prisoners to France, he crossed
to England to report to the Privy Council. "What has passed",
wrote Peyton, "I send by George Poulet, who has knowledge
of sixty years" (S.P.D.). He died in 1621, and was buried in
St. Saviour's Church on 17 Jan.

He married four times. His first wife was his cousin Elizabeth
Poulet. He married again in 1564 Ysebel, daughter of Edmund
Perrin, Seigneur of Rozel, and widow of Bailiff Hostes Nicolle.
She was the mother of Rachel (b. 1564), who married Sir Phi-
lippe De Carteret. She died in 1574. A third wife is mentioned
in the Town Church Burial Register: — "5 Nov. 1601 Cicille
Pollett, wife of the Lieutenant, was buried". Her children were
Abraham, who became Attorney-General in 1603 and died in
1605 (he married Esther, daughter of Jean De Carteret of Vin-
chelez de Haut, and had a large family), and Dorothy, who

married in 1609 Hugh Perrin, Seigneur of Rozel. On 8 Nov.
1604 Poulet married in the Town Church Lucrece Dabucy. By
her he had two children, Elizabeth, who died as a baby, and
Philippe, who lived to be seven.

[Authorities quoted above.]

POULET, SIR HUGH, (d.c. 1578), Governor. Eldest son of
Sir Amias Poulet of Hinton St. George and Laura, daughter
of William Kellaway of Rockbourne, Hants. From 1532 he
was a Justice of the Peace for Somerset, and in 1536 Sheriff for
Somerset and Devon. When the Northern Rebellion broke out
in 1537, he was summoned to attend on the King's person with
300 armed men (L.P.). On 18 Oct. he was knighted, and was
one of the knights in attendance at the christening of the future
King Edward VI (L.P.). In 1538 on the death of his father he
inherited the family estates, and bought from the King for
£1,000 the manor of Sampford Peverel, Devon (L.P.). At the
Musters of 1539 he provided from Hinton 40 fully armed men,
30 billmen, 20 archers with 5 tenants and 9 others (L.P.) ; and,
when a Council for the West was formed, he was appointed a
member. That year after the execution of the Abbot of Glastonbury he was made Administrator of the Abbey lands at a salary
of £20 a year ; and twelve years later he settled in the ruins
a colony of refugee Flemish Protestant weavers (*Huguenot
Society Proceedings*. Vol. XIII). In 1540 he was one of the
knights appointed to meet Anne of Cleves at Shooter's Hill
and escort her to the King. In 1543 he was summoned to sail
with the King to Flanders. The decisive moment in the siege
of Boulogne in Sept. 1544 was when he and his men stormed
the outwork known as the Braye (L.P.). He was made Treasurer
of the captured town, and his duties were not merely financial.
In June 1545 he captured and burned the town of Davourn ;
and a hill near Boulogne, which changed hands more than once
during the fighting, became known as Poulet Hill (L.P.). At
the accession of the boy King, Edward VI, in 1547 the Government called him home to be one of those responsible for "the
good order of the shires in the West" (S.P.D.). When the
West rose in 1549 against the Reformation changes, he was

Knight-Marshal of the Government's army, and, after the defeat
of the rebels at Sampford Courtenay, led the pursuit, and finally
crushed them at Kingsweston, near Bristol.

That year two things called the Council's attention to Jersey.
A French raid was repulsed by the Militia; and complaints
poured in against Cornish, Somerset's Lieut.-Governor. So on
5 Nov. Poulet was sent to investigate. He landed on Christmas
Eve, took up residence in Mont Orgueil, and summoned the
States to meet him. On 27 Dec. he reviewed the Militia in
order to test their strength. He inquired into the conduct of
Cornish, and dismissed him from his post. After three weeks
he returned to London, and presented his report to the Council
on 19 Feb. 1550. On 20 March he was himself appointed Governor for life, and was granted the Fief of St. Germain, "when
it shall come to the King by the death of Helier De Carteret"
(P.R.). He made one break with tradition. He did not live in
Mont Orgueil, but in the house of Philippe Quenault near the
Hougue Bie.

Much of his time was spent in fortification. Before he left
England he secured some of the Glastonbury lead for Mont
Orgueil. He pressed on the building of the great central tower,
which had been begun by Somerset. "He also", says the Chronicler, "strengthened well-nigh all the circuit of the castle walls,
repaired and raised the road that entered by the garden gates,
and fortified and enlarged the Rochefort Tower and the Douvres
and divers other parts of the Castle". (The Douvres were the
castle ditch, which he strengthened by repairing the loop-holed
palisade which surrounded it on the landward side.) "He obtained from the Queen many heavy cannon both of cast and
wrought iron" (Chroniques). He also transformed St. Aubin's
Tower into a Fort by building battlements round it. This work
cost more than he could squeeze out of the Queen's Treasury;
and he wrote in 1599 that he had advanced £1,400 out of his
own pocket. He also stiffened the Militia. "He held many
General Parades", says the Chronicler, "and drilled the men
hard, so that they would know how to man their bulwarks, for
he had been all his life a Captain expert in war". On one
point however he was beaten. His instructions were "to convey
the town of St. Helier's unto the hill above the same" (i.e. where
Fort Regent now stands), "which we be informed may with
little charge be made strong and defensible"; but, though the

Council wrote to the States, "We doubt not you be persuaded that your only commoditie and surety resteth therein" (*P.B.C.*), the townsfolk resolutely refused to move from their old homes.

The Chronicler attributes to him the wholesale destruction of pre-reformation ornaments: — "He was bidden to inquire into Obits and Masses and rentes bequeathed for Lights, Fraternities, and other unlawful things, also all Bells great and small, and Chalices, Ornaments, and Censers, and to pull down all Images and Idols in Churches and Chapels, likewise to demolish the Chapels themselves and the wayside Crosses and those in the Churchyards, and generally to extirpate, oust, and abolish all idolatry, bigotry and superstition" (*Chroniques*). But most of this work had been completed under his predecessor Somerset. In only remained for him to sell the church bells, leaving one for each parish (this brought in for fortification £171. 9. 0), to make careful search for any chalices or jewels the parishioners might have hidden, and to suppress any simmering discontent. In 1550 Jean Aubin, a Priest, and others were fined for "obstructing the Word of God and upholding the superstitions of Rome". In 1551 the Elders of Trinity Parish were ordered by the Vicomte to report to the Court all who murmur against the Word of God, and to inform the Jurats of the mockeries, disturbances, and popish acts that were still maintained in that parish. In 1553 Pierre Fallu was sent to the Castle for permitting his wife to take two rosaries to St. Peter's Church. But there seems to have been singularly little opposition to the Reformation changes, and therefore little repression. Poulet cannot have been regarded as a Protestant persecutor, or he would not have kept his post throughout the reign of Mary. The Chronicler praises his rule: — "He was a great lover of justice, and, while he was Governor, the island remained in perfect peace and tranquility. He kept the people bound together in complete unity and concord".

Much of his time however was spent in duties elsewhere. In 1553 he was sent to Alderney to investigate charges against the Deputy-Governor and to dismiss him, if he had "undiscreatly used himself" (*P.R.*). He still had duties in Somerset. In 1556 he received the thanks of the Council for "his travail taken this last summer in well ordering the West Partes" (*P.C.*). In 1559 and 1560 he was in Wales as Vice-President of the Council for the Marches (*S.P.D.*). In 1562, when the Huguenots surrendered

Havre to Elizabeth, she sent Poulet as "a man of wisdom and long experience" to advise the Earl of Warwick, the English commander (S.P.D.). He landed with £3,000 on 17 Dec., but the plague played such havoc with Warwick's troops that in July 1563 were forced to evacuate the city. Poulet secured some of the soldiers to strengthen the garrison of Mont Orgueil, but they brought the plague with them, and it spread through the island.

When he was absent, Poulet left his son, Amias (q.v.), in charge as Lieut.-Governor, and toward the end of his life he delegated his Jersey duties almost entirely to him. In May 1571 he surrendered his Patent to Elizabeth in order that he and Amias might be appointed Joint Governors.

He was Knight of the Shire for Somerset in the Parliament which met in 1572 (*Proceedings Somerset Arch. Sy.* Vol. LXXXII). The date of his death is uncertain. His tomb says that he died on 6 Dec., but the year is illegible. The bye-election, which his death must have caused, is not mentioned in Parliamentary records. The swearing-in of Amias as sole Governor is missing from the Acts of the Royal Court. The *Chroniques* says that Sir Hugh died "in 1572 or thereabouts" ; but this is too early. He took the Musters for Somerset in June 1573 (S.P.D.), and in May 1578 a warrant was issued to pay him £100 yearly for the repair of Taunton Castle (S.P.D.). But a document, which the Editor of the *State Papers* dates with a query "? Oct. 1578", speaks of his wife as a widow. The "Oct." must be wrong, for 6 Dec. 1578 is the earliest possible date for his death ; and this is probably correct. He was buried in Hinton St. George in a magnificent tomb, which he had prepared in his life-time, supporting an effigy of himself in plate-armour.

By his first wife, Philippa, daughter of Sir Lewis Pollard, he had five children, Amias (q.v.), who succeeded him as Governor, Nicholas, who settled in Somerset, George (q.v.), who became Bailiff, Jane, who married Christopher Copplestone, and Anne. In 1560 he married Elizabeth Blount, the wealthy widow of Sir Thomas Pope, founder of Trinity College, Oxford. Of her the document mentioned above gives the surprising information, "Lady Poulet, widow of Sir Hugh, has Mass commonly in her house" (S.P.D.). Other State Papers of the period refer to her as a Recusant suspected of harbouring Priests and

Jesuits in her great house in Clerkenwell, inherited from her
first husband. [*Chroniques de Jersey* ; *Letters and Papers of
the Reign of Henry VII* (*L.P.*) ; *State Papers Domestic*
(*S.P.D.*) ; *State Papers Foreign* (*S.P.F.*) ; *Acts of the Privy
Council* (*P.C.*) ; *Patent Rolls* (*P.R.*) ; *Appendix to Prison Board
Case* (*P.B.C.*) ; *Dic. Nat. Biog.*]

POULET, JOHN (d.c. 1580), Dean.   Second son of Sir Amias
Poulet of Hinton St. George and Laura Kellaway ; brother of
Sir Hugh Poulet (q.v.).   Educated at Oxford: B.A. 1530, M.A.
1532, Proctor 1534.   His father, when he died, left his property
to his eldest son Hugh, charging him to be loving to his brothers,
John and Henry, and to help them to preferment (Will in
Nicolas' *Testamenta Vetusta*).   When Hugh became Governor
of Jersey, he appointed John to the Rectory of St. Martin's.   On
30 Oct. 1553 the Bishop of Coutances' Register records: —
"John Poulet, Cleric, was admitted to the Parish Church of St.
Martin in the Isle of Jersey, vacant by the death of Charles
Mabson, the previous Curé, on the presentation of Sir Hugh
Poulet, Governor" (*Bull.* II).   A fortnight later however Philippe
Carey arrived at Coutances with a presentation signed by
Queen Mary ; but, as Carey was Rector of St. Andrew's Guern-
sey, and could show no licence to hold two parishes in plurality,
his claim was disallowed (*id*).   In an Order in Council of 31
March 1554 the Queen acknowledged that, when she nominated
Carey, she had forgotten that she had granted this right to the
Governor by his Patent (*O.C.*).   Poulet's appointment as Dean
probably also dates from 1553, but neither his Patent nor his
Swearing-in seems to be recorded.   He was Dean in June 1555,
when Richard Averty (q.v.), a Priest, was tried for infanticide.
Poulet made desperate efforts to save him, vesting him in a surplice, when he came up for trial, and claiming the case for the
Ecclesiastical Court ; but failed.   He slipped a surplice over
his head again, as he was being chained to a hurdle to be dragged to the place of execution ; this was stripped off, when he
reached the gallows.   He was more successful with another criminal.   A thief, Réné Le Hardy, had taken sanctuary in Trinity
Church.   He was haled before the Royal Court ; but on 28 Feb.

1558 the Dean demanded that his life should be spared, and the Jurats gave way. The earliest surviving book of the Acts of the Ecclesiastical Court begins in 1557. It shows Poulet busy disciplining four of his clergy who had married in the reign of Edward VI. On 20 March Jean Nicolle, Raoul De La Rocque Nicolas Esnouf, and Jean Vautier were sentenced to a week's imprisonment on bread and water for refusing to separate from their wives. On 10 April Nicolle and Vautier and their wives were threatened with corporal punishment, if they continued to meet. On 12 Nov. De La Rocque was ordered to walk barefoot in front of the cross in the procession in the Town Church on the following Sunday holding a lighted candle, and to remain kneeling in the penitent's place in the chancel throughout Mass. If he failed to do this, he was to be imprisoned on bread and water without any indulgence till Candlemas (i.e. for 13 weeks). On the other hand several laymen were prosecuted for not living with their wives, and others were threatened with imprisonment, unless they kept their wives in better order. Most of the cases however dealt with disputes about tithes, rentes due to Church trésors, wills, and breaches of promise of marriage. But secular cases were also tried before this Court, if a 'cleric' was involved, and even bell-ringers and sextons were regarded as 'clerics'. On 10 April 1557 Nicolas Robert was fined for "wronging a cleric by citing him before the Royal Court". So Poulet felt that he could not let the Averty case rest unchallenged. "Three years later in spite of the lapse of time his vindictive spirit did not soften, and he resolved to take vengeance at any cost on his brother, the Governor. He embarked for England to appeal to Queen Mary ; but, off the Corbiere, they passed an inward-bound boat. 'What news?' they asked. 'Good news', was the reply, 'Jezebel is dead'. So the Dean saw that his trip would be bootless, and asked to be put ashore" (Le Maistre MSS.).

Queen Mary died on 17 Nov. 1558. The Dean presided over the Ecclesiastical Court on 12 Nov. ; but from that moment his name disappears from the Act Book. At subsequent meetings Louis Gybault, Rector of St. Helier's, presided as Dean's Commissary. Poulet seems also to have ceased to officiate at St. Martin's, for an Act of the Royal Court in 1568 shows that at some previous date "Thomas Johanne, Minister of the Reformed Church", had been allocated to that parish. The Dean however continued to perform his other functions. In Jan. 1560 Sir Hugh

Poulet, when protesting to Cecil against innovations introduced by Huguenot Rectors, said: — "I desire you would write to John Poulet, my brother, parson of St. Martin's and Dean of Jersey, to whom the spiritual affairs of the island appertain" (*S.P.D.*). And again two months later: "The inhabitants of Jersey require to be led in matters of Religion by some order to the Dean" (*id*). In 1562 the Royal Commissioners restored to him the probate and registration of wills (*P.B.C.*), which had been transferred to a Lay Registrar in 1547 (see De La Croix' *St. Helier*). In 1563 Poulet bought the derelict Chapel of Notre Dame at Grouville, perhaps with the idea of making it a private oratory ; but he resold it six years later (*Le Maistre MSS.*). Among the *Hatfield MSS.* is one dated 1568, which says, "Every three years a Visitation is made by the Dean throughout all the parishes, whereat he receiveth of every Curate 6/8d." In 1569 however John After was appointed Dean of Jersey, Guernsey, Chausey, Alderney, and Sark. Yet even in 1574, when the Presbyterian system was virtually established in the island, the Royal Court still called him "Mons. le Doyen", when it appointed him an arbitrator ; and in the same year he was sued in another case as "the person responsible for the Schools" of St. Mannelier and St. Anastase. But the Synod of 1576 by its *Discipline Ecclésiastique des Iles de la Manche* finally transferred to the Calvinist Colloquy all functions hitherto performed by a Dean. Henceforth Poulet was merely a private person. His family were all Protestants, and he gradually became reconciled to Protestant ideas. In Sept. 1571 an Act of the Court states that he was in charge of St. Lawrence Church, where the Rector had died. He must therefore have been then using the Anglican Prayer Book. (He was probably living in that parish, for eight years before he had bought 30 vergées of land there.) In April 1572 he took charge of St. Brelade's during another vacancy, and continued to officiate there till Oct. 1574. Late in life (his son was still a minor twelve years after Poulet's death) he married Marguerite, daughter of Jean Lempriere, Seigneur of Trinity. He died about 1580. According to the Le Maistre MSS. he committed suicide. "It is said that he opened a vein in his foot in a warm bath, and thus ended his days". He left a son Hugh and a daughter Marguerite, who married Arthur Fortescue of Lyme Regis. [Authorities quoted above.]

RULLECOURT, PHILIPPE CHARLES FELIX MAC-
QUART, BARON DE (1744—81), Soldier of Fortune. Seigneur of Dainville, St. Cosme, Lagendronnière, etc. His father,
Charles Félix Macquart, Seigneur of Rullecourt, was Secrétaire
du Roi in the Chancellery of the Parliament of Flanders, and
senior Alderman (Echevin) of Merville. His mother was a
Spaniard, Marie Françoise Pélagie Philippo. An ancestor in
1456 had married a niece of Joan of Arc. Philippe was born
near Lille, 9 July, 1744. When seventeen, he fled from France
to avoid arrest. He joined a company of Flemish Guards in the
Spanish service, and in 1767 became a Captain in the Nassau-
Ysembourg infantry. In 1768 he was in Poland, where he was
sentenced to be hanged for theft, but escaped with a price on
his head. In July of that year he was back in France, where
he stole from a convent Marie Félicité, a young illegitimate
daughter of the Marquis of Argenson. The Marquis consented
to their marriage, and in 1769 secured for him a Captain's commission in the Royal Nassau Hussars. He became a Major,
but gambling debts forced him to fly to Russia, where he refused
command of a Carabineer company as beneath his dignity, and
returned to Poland. Here he became Colonel of the Massalsky
Regiment. From 1775 to 1780 there is a gap in his history, but
in some way he became a Commander of the distinguished
French Order of Notre Dame de Mont Carmel et St. Lazare.
Later it was believed in Jersey (See Poingdestre's and Le Couteur's letters: *Bull.* XIII and MS. in S. J. Library), that he had
been second in command in the Prince of Nassau's raid on the
island in 1779, but his name does not appear in any official
document. Wherever his fellow-countrymen mention him, they
give him a bad character. Bachaumont in his *Mémoires Secrets*
calls him "a roué in every sense of the word, over head and
ears in debt, and paying his creditors with sword-thrusts."

In 1780 he was in the service of the Prince of Salm-Kirbourg,
for a passport issued on 8 June states that the Prince was sending
him on business from Germany to Spain. About this time the
Chevalier de Luxembourg, hoping to succeed where Nassau
had failed, had obtained permission to raise a legion for the
conquest of Jersey. Argenson suggested Rullecourt as commander, and on 1 Oct. he received his commission as Lieut.-Colonel
of the Luxembourg Volunteers. This force, which was quartered
in the citadel at Havre, consisted of 950 men. About 300 had

been bought by Luxembourg from Nassau, and still wore the
blue uniform of the previous raid ; another 300 were a draft
from two Normandy Militia regiments ; about another 300 were
deserters condemned to the chain-gang, released from State
prisons on condition that they joined the legion ; the rest were
a motley collection of volunteers, including seamen in oilskin
hats, and two Germans in Uhlan uniform.   One of the officers
was an Oriental in a flowing robe and turban.   While his
officers licked them into shape by relentless drilling at Havre,
Rullecourt went to Granville, and arranged with Régnier, a
well-to-do smuggler with a house on Chausey, to collect boats
to carry them.   He then crossed to Jersey, disguised as a grain-
smuggler, and spent several days surveying possible landing-
places.   Meanwhile the attitude of his Government was very
hesitant.   Convicts had been released for him.   Three warships
had been ordered to act as his convoy.   But on the other hand
the Naval Commissaire at St. Malo received instructions from
Paris : — "The Ministry of Marine takes no cognizance of
Monsieur de Rullecourt's expedition.   You will regard it as a
privateering venture for which the King has no responsibility,
and you will act accordingly".   Its destination was kept secret.
The men were supposed to be the crew for a new privateer that
was coming from Texel.

Rullecourt led his men out of Havre on 19 Dec., and reached
Granville on the 27th, having left a bad reputation behind them.
"Like all troops of this kind", wrote de Lambert, "his corps is
composed of brigands".   Bachaumont calls them, "gallows-birds
who have plundered the whole countryside".   "This troop", wrote
an officer at Vire, "will long be remembered.   All along their
route they carried away turkeys, hens, ducks, hams, and sau-
sages".   At Granville Rullecourt put them at once on the waiting
boats.   He had hoped to surprise Jersey during the Christmas
festivities ; but the 29th found him still off Chausey detained by
contrary winds.   "We are suffering much", he wrote, "from
hunger, thirst (you have given us no water), cold, and sea-
sickness".   A sail on the horizon, mistaken for that of a British
frigate, sent them back to Cancale, but on the 30th they were
again off Chausey.   Here a north wind detained them till 5 Jan.,
while Rullecourt was on thorns lest his expedition should be
countermanded.   "The foe", he wrote, "I fear more than the

English, the winds, and the sea, is a recall, which our friends at Court will treat us to, if they can".

On the afternoon of the 5th the wind shifted, and he set sail. He had chosen La Rocque as his landing-place, the last spot where an invader was expected, for here jagged reefs, the Banc de Vielet, stretch out two miles to sea. But there is a channel between them known to local fishermen, and Rullecourt had a La Rocque fisherman as pilot, Pierre Journeaux, who had fled from the island two years before after killing a man with his fist. It was a dark night, with high-tide soon after midnight ; and at about eleven the twenty-six French boats sailed up the narrow water-way in single file to the Plat Rocque, where the little pier now is. There seems no truth in the report, current in the island later, that five of the boats were wrecked and 200 men drowned. But the disembarkation took longer than had been expected ; the ebb set in, and the seven rearward ships drifted south on the falling tide, and, to escape the dangers that engirt them, made for the open sea. In this way Rullecourt was deprived of nearly three hundred of his men and all his artillery.

Five hundred yards from the Plat Rocque stood the La Rocque Guardhouse. Here there should have been nine militiamen, one of whom should have been sentry at the door and one patrolling the shore ; but according to Corbet's report : — "The Chef de Garde was intoxicated and neglected to fix his sentinel on the battery. He sent no tide-patroles, which my orders strictly enjoined. He quitted guard himself before day, and suffered his men to follow his example in disobedience to the standing orders, which direct the night-guards not to quit their posts till relieved an hour after it is light". Thus no alarm was given. Rullecourt left a company at the battery to secure, if necessary, his retreat, and hurried by dark, inland lanes to avoid the Guard-Houses on the coast, (General Don's roads were not yet made) to St. Helier's, arriving undetected about 6 a.m.

Six hundred men seems an absurd force with which to invade an island garrisoned by about a thousand Regulars and three thousand Militiamen. If Rullecourt had been a Napoleon, he might have pulled it off. The three half-regiments were camped in different parts of the island. A lightning stroke might have overwhelmed each separately, before the others could join forces with it ; the Militia might perhaps have been dispersed before their mobilization was complete ; though even then it is hard to see what he could have done about Elizabeth Castle, before reinforcements poured in from England. But he trusted, not to military tactics, but to his power of bluff. He marched straight to the Market-Place (now the Royal Square). The Lieut.-Governor, Moyse Corbet (q.v.) was arrested in his house, and brought to the Royal Court. Here Rullecourt told him that the troops in the Market were only his advance-guards, that 4,000 others occupied all important points in the island, that 10,000 more would land before nightfall, that the regiment at Grouville had surrendered ; and he gave him the choice between signing an immediate capitulation or seeing the town (his own home town) sacked and burnt. "The French General", said one witness, "lifting up his arm, in a very peremptory manner said, 'Monsieur, I shall insist, I shall insist', and then added, he would give up the town to be plundered and laid to ashes". Another witness added, "He pulled out a watch, and said: — Take care. By such a time, if the articles were not signed, hostilities should commence". The bluff worked. After some resistance Corbet signed, and sent orders to all troops to lay down arms.

Rullecourt now regarded his victory as complete. The story may be apocryphal that he put on a red ribbon of the Order of St. Louis, which the King had granted him on condition that he conquered the island (this does not appear in the list of his effects drawn up after his death) ; but he issued a Proclamation in the name of the French King promising security of person and property and religious liberty to all inhabitants who remained quiet, but summary military execution to any who resisted. He ordered the Market to be held as usual, and the shops to open. He himself went into one ; and bought some ribbons. He invited the principal Jerseymen in the Court to dine with him that evening. But soon he was disillusioned. Elizabeth Castle took no notice of Corbet's order to surrender, and went on firing the alarm-gun. A sentry on the church tower reported that he could see troops assembling on the top of Gallows Hill. Taking Corbet with him, Rullecourt rode across the sands to the Castle to insist on the capitulation being obeyed ; but the guns opened fire, and they had to retreat. "The Baron", said Corbet, "returned to the Court House in a violent rage". He then sent Corbet on parole to interview Major Peirson (q.v. Appendix), who was in command of the troops on Gallows Hill. Peirson also refused to regard the capitulation as binding, and Corbet had hardly got back to the Court, when the troops burst into the Market. As Rullecourt stepped out of the Court House, holding Corbet's arm, he was struck by four bullets, and fell mortally wounded. According to one account (Captain Harrison's) he was signalling his surrender : — "The Baron came on to the steps, and held up a white handkerchief and three swords by the points, and threw them down". Ten minutes later his troops gave up the fight. He was carried into the house of Dr. Philippe Lerrier, where he died about six. Next morning he was buried with military honours in the Town Churchyard, his officers bearing the coffin. By March a pyramid had been erected over his grave with an inscription which ended : — "This is not so much a monument to an enemy as a warning, O Jerseymen, to you and your children to pay more heed to your safety" (*Courier de l'Europe*, 2 March, 1781). Its existence is confirmed by a letter from the Marquis of Argenson (12 Jan., 1782 : — "If during his life he had faults, he has fully atoned for them by a glorious death, as the enemy themselves have acknowledged by erecting a public memorial to him" (*Carnet de la Sabretache*, March 1907). When this was removed, nobody knows. The grave is now marked by a simple slab inscribed "Rullecourt. Jan. 6,1781." When an appeal was made for a pension for his widow, it was said, "The Baron leaves three children starving, as he had consumed all the property of their mother". His portrait is in the S. J. Museum which also contains several relics of him, including his snuffbox, his proclamation, and a certificate from the Prince of Luxembourg testifying to "his zeal, intelligence, activity, and most astonishing valour". [*Mémoire des Preuves servant à établir la Filiation et La Noblesse de Messire P. F. C. Macquart, Baron de Rullecourt :* Perrot's *Surprise de Jersey :* Brachet's *La Dernière Expédition contre Jersey:* Ouless' *Death of Major Peirson ;* Proceedings at Large on the Trial of Moses Corbet: Rochfort's *Invasion of the Island of Jersey:* Articles in the *Carnet de la Sabretache,* March 1907 and Jan. 1913.]

APPENDIX II

PERSONS WHO HAVE BEEN INCORRECTLY CLAIMED AS JERSEYMEN

BASIRE, ISAAC (1607—76), the eccentric Chaplain of Charles I, who travelled through the East to teach the Oriental Christians the Church of England Catechism and convert them to the Anglo-Catholic Faith. He has been claimed as a Jerseyman on the strength of an entry in Wood's Diary at the time of his death, "Born I think in Jersey"; but, when entering St. John's College, Cambridge, he described himself in the Register as *Rothomagensis Normano-Gallus*, a Norman-Frenchman of Rouen.

CABOT, SEBASTIAN (1474—1557), Navigator and Explorer. He was son of a Venetian, Giovanni Caboto, who settled in Bristol. Whether Sebastian was born in Venice or England is not certain. He told the Venetian ambassador, "I was born in Venice but brought up in England"; but he told Eden, "I was born in Bristol, and at four years old I was carried to Venice, and returned again after certain years". But he had no connection with the Jersey family of Cabot.

JACOB, HENRY (1608—52), the Sectary. Baker's *Caesarea* asserts: — "It is stated by Wood that he was born in Jersey". But this is not the case. Wood's *Athenae Oxonienses* says that Jacob's mother was "Sara, sister of John Dumaresq of Jersey", but that he himself "was born in the Diocese of London". His father had to fly to Holland, and there he was brought up; and there is no evidence that he ever set foot in the island.

KEMPENFELT, RICHARD (1718—82), the Admiral who
went down on the *Royal George*. He narrowly escaped being
a Jerseyman, for his Swedish father came to the island in 1718
to be Lieut.-Colonel of the Regiment a few months after his
birth, and in 1723 became Lieut.-Governor ; but his parents
were in Westminster, when Richard was born.

APPENDIX III

SOME JERSEY WORDS AND TITLES

[As this book goes to press (1948) changes are being made in the Jersey Constitution ; but the notes below represent the facts to the end of the German Occupation, 1940—45.]

ADVOCATE, *Avocat.* The name used, wherever a legal system is based on the Roman Code, for the lawyer who in England is called a Barrister. He was known in the *Old Coutumier* as a *Conteur.* Advocates have been attached to the Jersey Court from early times. (Nicolas Galicien, *Plaidator,* is mentioned in 1299.) The Ordinances of 1523 lay down the oath they must swear. Till 1860 their number was limited to six, and they were chosen without any test by the Bailiff ; but in that year the Bar was thrown open to any British subject who had lived ten years in the island and possessed the necessary English or French diplomas, or had passed a local law examination. Lists of Advocates since 1523 are printed in *Bulls* IX and XIII.

ASSIZE. A judicial inquiry conducted by Judges acting under special commission. Before the loss of Normandy in 1204 Jersey was visited triennially by Norman Judges. In 1218 Henry III ordered the Warden to hold Assizes, "as they were observed in the time of our grandfather", i.e. Henry II. But the Warden used to appoint Judges out of his local officials. This system favoured the local administration, and protests arose ; so in 1525 Justices Itinerant (q.v.) began to be sent from England. In 1531 this was discontinued, and the administration of justice left to the Royal Court (q.v.) with appeal to the Privy Council. The later plan of sending Royal Commissioners to inquire into complaints to some extent took the place of the old Assizes.

The Assize Rolls for 1299, 1304, 1309, 1320, 1323, and 1331 are preserved in the Record Office. The Roll of 1309 has been printed by S.J. Extracts from others will be found in *Second Report of Commissioners into the Criminal Law of the Channel Islands (Guernsey)*.

ATTORNEY-GENERAL. *Procureur-Général du Roi.*

A legal Officer of the Crown, appointed to plead the King's cause, to give guidance to the King's representatives, to advise the Royal Court on doubtful points of law, and to prosecute offenders. He has a seat in the States, and may speak, but not vote. He is legal adviser to the States. A list of Attorneys-General is in *Bull.* III.

BAILIFF. *Bailli.*

Chief Magistrate and President of the States. In early days the Warden of the Isles (q.v.), who was Military Governor, was often called *Ballivus*, and among other duties presided over the Court ; but by the beginning of the 13th century the Wardens had Bailiffs under them. In 1201 a Letter Patent speaks of "Peter de Préaux and his Bailiffs in Jersey and Guernsey". In 1235 a Close Roll addressed to the Warden adds, "The same instructions have been sent to the Bailiffs of Guernsey and Jersey". These early Bailiffs were merely Bailiffs of the Warden ; in 1213 they are called "the Bailiffs of Philip d'Aubigny". They were appointed, paid, and dismissed by him ; but, as the century progressed, their appointment was confirmed by the Crown, and in time they began to call themselves "the King's Bailiff". At first they assisted in all sides of the Warden's duties, but about 1290 under Otto de Grandison a division of work was established. His lieutenants who dealt with military and administrative matters were called Sub-Wardens (*Subcustodes*), and the name Bailiff confined to the one entrusted with judicial duties. Later still Bailiffs were appointed directly by the Crown. Then friction often arose between Bailiffs and Governors as to their respective powers ; so in 1617 the

Privy Council laid down the rule "that the charge of the military forces be wholly in the Governor, and the care of justice and civil affairs in the Bailiff". The Bailiff presides over the Royal Court, where however he has no vote, except a casting vote. He also presides over the Assembly of the States. Here he may temporarily suspend decisions by expressing his dissent, but, if he does so, he must state his reasons to the Secretary of State. A list of Bailiffs is printed in *Bulls* IV and XII.

BANON. By Jersey law, based on the old *Coutume* of Normandy, much private land was only private for six months of the year. From the end of harvest till March all land, not enclosed by a hedge from ancient times, was thrown open, and any parishioner might release his cattle to graze on it. This was known as the season of Banon. This right was recognized and enforced by the Code of 1771, and was again affirmed and regulated by an Act of the States as late as 1810.

CENTENIERS. The second rank in the Honorary Parochial Police. Originally, like Anglo-Saxon 'Hundred-men', they were responsible for the behaviour of about a hundred families. Now they are elected for three years by the rate-payers of the parish to be the Constable's chief assistants in all his duties. If the Constable is ill or absent, the senior Centenier takes his place as *Chef de Police*.

CHURCHWARDENS. *Surveillants*. Two Church officers in each parish appointed by the Ecclesiastical Assembly (if an election is contested, the Rector has the right to nominate one), not only "to keep the Church in repair, and to see that all things appertaining to the ministration of the Word and Sacraments be provided", but also during the seventeenth and eighteenth centuries "to search during Divine Service places suspected of gaming, taverns, and tippling-houses", and to present before the Ecclesiastical Court "all Papists, Heretics, and Schismatics, blasphemers, such as have recourse to wizards, incestuous persons, and drunkards" (*Canons of 1623*). The parochial poor-relief is still in the Churchwardens' hands, except in St. Helier's, where, since 1908, it is administered by a special Commission, on which however the Churchwardens have seats *ex officio*.

COLLOQUY, *Colloque*. Under the Calvinist regime a Church Court, composed of all Ministers in the island and one Elder from each parish, meeting quarterly to exercise judicial and legislative powers.

CONSISTORY. *Consistoire*. Under the Calvinist regime a weekly meeting of the Minister, Elders, and Deacons of the parish to transact Church business and enforce discipline, as in the Scottish kirk-session.

CONSTABLE. *Connétable*. A title which, beginning as the name of the head of the Imperial stables (*Comte de l'étable*), rose to be the designation of high dignitaries, the Constable of France, the Constable of Scotland, the Constable of the Tower. In Jersey the Constable is civic head of his parish, represents it in the States, presides over the Parish Assembly, and is head of the Police. In early days Constables often held office for life, but since 1621 a new election is held every three years. The position is honorary. Lists of Constables will be found in *Bull*. Vols. V, VI, VII, and XIII.

CONSTABLE'S OFFICERS. *Officiers du Connétable*. The fourth rank in the Honorary Parochial Police. Elected, formerly by the Parish Assembly, later by each Vingtaine, to help the

Constable, Centeniers, and Vingteniers in their duties. In 1804 the number was fixed at 24 for St. Helier's, 15 for St. Brelade's, and 12 for each of the other parishes.

COUSTEUR. See LECTEUR.

DEACON. *Diacre.* Under the Calvinist regime a Church officer "ordained to receive the offerings of the people after the sermon, and to distribute them according to the needs of the poor by the advice of the Consistory". The name survived the establishment of Anglicanism for a considerable time. Falle wrote in 1734: — "The Poor's Box is held by a Deacon at the Church-door every Lord's Day". The word Almoner, *Collecteur des Aumônes,* has now taken its place.

DEAN. *Doyen.* When Jersey was in the Diocese of Coutances, and still more when it was joined to Winchester, from its insular position it was rather out of touch with its Bishop. Hence from early times the Bishop entrusted to one of the clergy, known as the Dean, unusual administrative and judicial powers. Robert Merlin was Dean of Jersey in 1180 ; and *Bull.* IX prints a list of Deans since 1494. Under the Calvinist regime Deans disappeared for nearly half a century ; but the office was restored in 1620. The Dean's duties differ from those of English Deans. As Commissary-General of the Bishop he is Judge in the Ecclesiastical Court (q.v.). Like an English Archdeacon his duty is to visit each parish to inspect Church property. He issues marriage-licenses. He is appointed by the Crown, and preference must be given to a Jerseyman.

DENUNCIATOR. *Dénonciateur.* An executive officer of the Court, appointed by the Bailiff, and subordinate to the Vicomte. He served processes, and carried the mace before the Bailiff. In earlier days he proclaimed new laws at the Market Cross. From 1645 there were two Denunciators. A list of holders of this post since 1525 is in *Bull.* IX. The office was abolished in 1930. Most of the Denunciator's duties are now performed by an officer known as the *Sergent de Justice.*

DEPUTIES FROM THE STATES. Since the 17th century, when difficulties have arisen with the British Government, the States have appointed one of more of their members to represent them before the Privy Council. This has always been regarded as a high honour.

DEPUTIES TO THE STATES. *Députés.* To increase the representative character of the States, Deputies, elected for three years, were added in 1856, one from each country parish and three from St. Helier's. In 1907 the Town was divided into three districts, each returning two Deputies. As this book goes to press the number of Deputies is being increased. Lists of Deputies are in *Bulls* XIII and XIV.

ECCLESIASTICAL ASSEMBLY. *Assemblée Ecclésiastique.* The Parish Assembly (q.v.), meeting to transact Church business, with the Rector, instead of the Constable, in the chair.

ECCLESIASTICAL COURT. *Cour Ecclésiastique.* This Court is mentioned in 1291. It dealt with Church disputes, testamentary questions, and offences against morals. Before the Reformation it also claimed the right to try all clerics accused of crime. During the Calvinist regime it ceased to exist. After its reconstitution in 1623 it was largely a Court of morals, dealing with "blasphemers, adulterers, fornicators, drunkards, and profaners of the Sabbath", its weapons being excommunication and public penance. This side of its work was quietly dropped in 1838 ; but it still deals with cases of clergy discipline, disputes about church buildings, matrimonial cases, and separations *a mensa et thoro,* and the legitimization of children. It swears in Church officers, registers Notaries, and was the Probate Court of the island. The Dean is the Judge with the Rectors as Assessors, whose opinion he is bound to ask, but is not bound to adopt. From its judgements appeal lies to the Bishop of Winchester.

ECRIVAINS (*Scriveners*). Lawyers who do most of the work performed by Solicitors in England. Formerly admitted by the Bailiff without any test. Since 1867 they must have worked five years in an Advocate's or Ecrivain's office, and then have passed a local law examination.

EPERQUERIE. (*Esperkeria*). A Seigneurial right. Originally a drying place for conger to which all tenants of a fief were bound to bring their fish, just as they were bound to have their corn ground at the Seigneur's mill. Early in the 13th century it was extended to include the right of pre-emption.

ESQUIRE. *Ecuyer.* A much coveted title in Jersey about which there was frequent dispute ; for the island followed the French rule, by which Ecuyers were reckoned as the Third Order of the Noblesse (Lords, Knights, Esquires). An Ecuyer was one of the Noblesse. In Jersey it was at first reserved for Seigneurs of the greater fiefs. In 1712 it was extended to all Jurats. In 1786 a Guernsey Order in Council, registered in Jersey, granted it to all Militia officers above the rank of Lieutenant.

EXTENTE. A detailed statement of the Crown revenues from the island, drawn up parish by parish. The *Extentes* of 1274, 1331, 1528, 1607, 1668, and 1749 have been printed by S.J.

GENTLEMAN. *Gentilhomme.* Originally a man, not a nobleman, who was entitled to bear heraldic arms. Long after the word had become in England a mere expression of courtesy given to any one of good social position, Jersey stood rigidly by the older meaning, and added it to the name as a title, e.g. "Elie Dumaresq, Gent". In the 17th century it was extended to all Seigneurs and Officials of the Court, who did not possess the higher rank of Ecuyer. In the 18th century it became the jealously guarded prerogative of certain leading families. As late as 1829 the Court decided that François Le Montais "had the right to describe himself as Gent., because his family had borne this title from time immemorial". But the number of "Gents." was largely increased, when toward the end of the 18th century all Militia Lieutenants were designated in their commissions as "Gentlemen". The Title was also given to the eldest sons of Jurats.

GENTLEMAN-PORTER of Mount Orgueil, and, later, of Elizabeth Castle. A position of some dignity. Two Gentlemen-Porters of Mount Orgueil became Bailiffs and one a Vicomte. In the Civil War, when Sir Philippe de Carteret died in Elizabeth Castle, Hungerford, the Gentleman-Porter, assumed command. The Gentleman-Porter kept the keys of the Castle, was responsible for the opening and closing of the gates, and for the safe custody of all prisoners, political and criminal.

GOVERNOR. *Gouverneur.* Till 1471 there was only one Governor over all the Channel Islands; see LORD OF THE

ISLES, WARDEN OF THE ISLES ; but from the appointment of Harliston as *"Capitain et Gouverneur de Jersey"* Jersey had a Governor of its own. At first the Captains, as they were usually called, were heads of the civil administration as well as the military, but gradually the Bailiffs secured more power, till in 1617 Bailiff Herault (q.v.) obtained an Order in Council declaring that military matters were the province of the Governor and civil affairs of the Bailiff. The office often for long periods became a sinecure, the Governor seldom visiting Jersey, and leaving his duties to a Lieutenant-Governor. It was abolished in 1854. A list of Governors since 1471 is printed in *Bulls.* IV and V.

GREFFIER. Clerk and Registrar of the Court and Keeper of the Records. From the 13th to the 16th century he was called the *Clerc de la Cour.* He had charge of all archives of Court and States. Financial disputes and other matters were often sent before him as *Greffier Arbitre.* In the States his duties included drawing up in due form proposals and amendments, and drafting the final Acts. At one time he used to count the votes, and announce the results. Since 1931 he is known as *Greffier Judiciaire,* and a separate Greffier performs the duties connected with the States. The Ecclesiastical Court has always had a Greffier of its own. A list of Greffiers is in *Bull.* VIII.

JUDGE-DELEGATE. *Juge Délégué.* Someone, almost always a Jurat, chosen by the States to act as Bailiff from the death or resignation of one Bailiff till the swearing in of his successor. A list of Judge-Delegates is in *Bulls* IV and XII.

JURATS or *Jurés Justiciers.* Twelve honorary, elected Judges, who with the Bailiff form the Royal Court. "The problem of the origin of Jurats", writes Le Patourel, "is one of most baffling

in the history of the islands". There are two apparently con-
tradictory statements. At the Inquest of 1248 the islanders asserted that King John "instituted twelve sworn coroners (*corona-
tores jurati*) to keep the pleas and rights pertaining to the
Crown". A reorganization of island institutions must have
been necessary after the separation from Normandy, and many
in 1248 remembered the reign of John ; but Jurats are more akin
to "doomsmen" and other old Teutonic customs than to the
feudal ideas of the 13th century. And in 1309, when Justices
Itinerant demanded by what right Jurats were elected, the islands
replied that "their forefathers *from time immemorial* have always
been wont to have twelve Jurats from among themselves", who
"judge all causes, pleas, contempts, transgressions, and felonies,
except such as be too arduous". Does the earlier statement merely
mean that John made the existing Jurats coroners? The word
Jurati at first seems merely an adjective, 'bound by an oath', but
it soon established itself as a title. We read of 'the King's
Jurats', 'Jurats of the Assizes', 'Jurats of the Royal Court'. By
the middle of the 13th century their position is clear. In the
King's Courts all judgements were rendered and all fines assessed
by them. Even when Justices Itinerant visited the island, the
Jurats claimed to sit with them, and this claim was usually allowed. The method of election varied. In 1323 they were chosen
"by the King's officers and the *optimates* (magnates) of the
country". Maulevrier's Constitutions in 1462 order their election
by the Bailiff, Jurats, Rectors, and Constables. In 1600 instructions were issued, "according to the ancient and laudable customs of the isle", that the Constables should consult their Parish
Assemblies, and submit three candidates to the States, who
would select one of them. But from 1605 Jurats have been elected "by the plurality of votes of the common people of the isle".
Once elected they cannot resign without special permission from
the King in Council. A list of Jurats since 1274 is in Bulls. IV,
VIII, and IX. (See Le Patourel's *Mediaeval Administration of
the Channel Islands*, Havet's *Cours Royales des îles Normandes*,
and H.M. Godfray's paper L'Origine des Jurés-Justiciers in
Bull. III).

JUSTICES ITINERANT. The equivalent of the English Justices in Eyre (i.e. in *itinere*). See ASSIZE.

LECTEUR. In the mediaeval Church the Lecteur was an ecclesiastic in minor orders, who led the singing and read the epistle. In Jersey he disappeared during the Calvinist regime, but in England he survived the Reformation as the Parish Clerk, who still led the responses, and often read the lessons. The Canons of 1623 reintroduced him into Jersey after the English pattern. Each parish was ordered to appoint a *Clerc* or *Cousteur* "able to read calmly, distinctly, and intelligibly, and reasonably qualified to sing the Psalms." Falle notes in 1734 that the Lecteurs usually read the lessons, and Durell adds in 1837 that this was still the practice in his day. The last Lecteur, George Frederick Poole of Grouville, died in 1941.

LIEUTENANT-BAILIFF. *Lieutenant-Bailli.* Someone, generally a Jurat, nominated by the Bailiff to perform his duties, when he is ill or absent from the island. A list of Lieutenant-Bailiffs is in Bull. IV and XII.

LIVRES TOURNOIS. In early days the great Abbey of St. Martin at Tours had the privilege of coining money, and the City of Tours retained its mint till 1722. Its *livres tournois, sols tournois,* and *deniers tournois* were worth rather less than the *livres, sols,* and *deniers* minted in Paris. Till Oct. 1834 the *tournois* coinage remained the legal currency in Jersey. Fines inflicted by the Court were always reckoned in *livres tournois.* The Extentes show how the value of this *livre* varied when compared with sterling. In 1331 it was worth 5 shillings ; in 1668 1/6½ ; in 1730 1/5 ; in 1749 1/4 ; in 1835 9¼d. Of the lesser coins 12 *deniers* made a *sol* ; 20 *sols* made a *livre.*

LIEUTENANT-GOVERNOR. *Lieut.-Gouverneur.* When the island had a resident Governor, his Lieutenant was merely his deputy, performing his duties in his absence. But when, as often happened, Governors were non-resident, the Lieut.-Governor exercised all the Governor's powers. Since 1854 no Governor has been appointed, only a Lieut.-Governor. He commands all troops in the island. The States cannot meet without his consent. He can veto Acts of the States, but, if he does so, must states his reasons to the Secretary of State. Lists of Lieut.-Governors are in *Bulls.* II, IV, and V.

LORD OF THE ISLES. *Dominus insularum. Seigneur des îles.* During the 13th century the custom arose of providing an important person with an income by appointing him Lord of the Isles. He was usually non-resident. Prince John, afterwards King, and Prince Edward, later Edward I, held this post. Otto de Grandison was Lord for nearly fifty years, but only once visited the islands. They appointed Wardens (q.v.) to do their work. After a gap of nearly a century the sinecure was revived in 1415 for the brother of Henry V. The last of these Lords was Warwick the King-maker.

MILITIA. *Milice.* From early times Jersey must have had some force for repelling invasion. In 1337, at the beginning of the Hundred Years War with France, this was remodelled. Edward III ordered the Wardens to enrol all able-bodied men, to divide them into companies, to provide them with arms, and to appoint officers. For the next three centuries the organization was parochial, each parish having its own company. In 1665 these companies were united into three regiments, the East, the North, and the West. In 1678 for the first time the men were put into uniform, red musketeers'-cloaks. In 1771 the number of infantry regiments was increased to five, the North-West, the North, the East, the South, and the South-West ; a short-lived cavalry regiment was formed ; and the Artillery was made a separate corps in blue cloaks lined with scarlet. Service in the Militia was compulsory for all the able-bodied, and was unpaid. The age-limit varied at different times, but was usually from 17 to

65. In modern times reforming Lieut.-Governors made many changes, but the Militia survived more or less in its old form till 1929, when the War Office withdrew its grant, and the States made it a small volunteer force.

NOTARY. *Notaire.* An official commissioned to provide evidence as to the authenticity of important papers, e.g. to attest documents being sent to another country, and to take affidavits. In 1705, when Martin De Gruchy (q.v.) tried to practise in Jersey, English Notaries were appointed by the Archbishop of Canterbury. The Royal Court refused to recognize the Archbishop's authority, but an Order in Council compelled them to do so. In Jersey Notaries are still appointed by the Archbishop, and register their appointment in the Ecclesiastical Court.

PARISH ASSEMBLY. *Assemblée Paroissiale.* A meeting of all Ratepayers in a parish assessed above a certain figure. The Rector, Churchwardens, Almoners, members of the Honorary Police, and any Jurats or Crown Officers living in the parish are members *ex officio.* The Assembly fixes the rate, appoints minor officials, deals with matters of roads, drainage, lighting, and much of the business transacted in England by a Borough Council. The Constable presides.

PREVOT. Originally every Seigneurial Court had its Prévôt, appointed annually on some Fiefs by the Seigneur, on others by the Tenants, "to guard the rights of the Seigneur and the tenants, to make good all summonses and loyal records, and to pay the corn-rentes, *fermes,* and extracts". He had to enforce all orders of the Court and all bye-laws of the Fief. With the decay of the Seigneurial Courts these officials died out except on the King's Fiefs, where one is still appointed for each of the ten parishes that contain a Royal Manor. At very Assise d'Héritage the Prévôts du Roi hand in lists of persons who have died without direct heirs, of persons presumed to be dead, of wreckage, treasure-trove, and other information from which the King should benefit. In time their duties were extended to the collection of all amounts in their parish due to the King, whether the debtors lived on or off the Crown Fief, including fines imposed by the Royal Court. They also serve summonses in their parish. In two parishes, St. Ouen's and St. Clement's, which have no Crown Fief, these duties are performed by the Prévôts of the neighbouring parishes of St. Mary's and Grouville. (See printed *Proceedings in Privy Council between Attorney-General and Joseph Le Moignan* 1892).

PRINCIPAUX. Ratepayers assessed above a certain figure, and therefore entitled to attend the Parish Assembly. The figure has varied at different times and in different parishes.

PROCUREUR DU BIEN PUBLIC. A trustee, elected by the Parish Assembly, whose main duty is to pass deeds or contracts, to conduct parish law-suits, and to keep a watchful eye on the Constable's finance.

RECEIVER-GENERAL. *Receveur-Général des Revenues de Sa Majesté.* The Crown draws considerable revenues from the island. In 1331 the King owned seven manors inherited from the Dukes of Normandy. He received all fines imposed by the Court, the Great Custom on foreign ships using the anchorages, the Little Custom on foreign imports and exports, and innumerable feudal dues of fowls and wheat and eggs. In 1413, when Henry V confiscated the property of the alien priories, the Crown gained the income hitherto paid to great Norman abbeys,

including most of the wheat tithe.   At the Reformation many
endowments for masses and other ecclesiastical purposes were
seized.   Since the 13th century the King's dues have been collected by a Receiver.   A list of holders of this office is in *Bulls*
V and VII.

RECTOR. *Recteur*. The title of the incumbents of the twelve
ancient parishes has varied at different times. In the 13th century it was *Recteur* ; then it became *Curé-Recteur* ; then *Curé*.
In five volumes of the Coutances Registers (1487—1555) island
clergy are only three times called *Rector*, and in every other case
Curatus, i.e. *Curé*. After the Reformation the universal title
was *Ministre*, and this is the word used in the Canons.   In the
17th century the word *Recteur* began to reappear.   The Rectors
sat in the States ever since that Assembly existed.   Lists of
Rectors will be found in *Bulls*. Vols VII, VIII, and X.

REGENT. *Régent*. The usual mediaeval title in France for
a schoolmaster, given in Jersey to the Headmasters of the Grammar Schools of St. Anastase and St. Mannelier.

ROYAL COMMISSIONERS. *Commissaires Royaux*. Persons appointed from time to time by the Crown through the
Privy Council to visit Jersey to investigate complaints, and to
report.

ROYAL COURT. *Cour Royale*. The Court of Justice, composed of the twelve Jurats under the presidency of the Bailiff.
Its origin is bound up with the problem of the origin of Jurats

(q.v.). The *Cartulaire* shows it functioning through the 13th
century, but it was overshadowed by the triennial visits of the
Justices Itinerant, for whom all important cases were reserved.
The last of these visitations was in 1331, and in 1349 the Warden
was given "full power to judge and chastise evil doers and
exercise full jurisdiction in the King's name" (*P.R.*). Still
however disputes from the islands were taken before the King's
Bench at Westminster ; but in 1368 this Court declared itself
incompetent to deal with them (see Coke's *Institutes*), and henceforth they were left entirely to the Royal Court with right of
appeal to the Privy Council. In the 14th century the Court
divided itself into two tribunals, the *Cour d'Héritage*, dealing
with real property, and the *Cour de Catel*, dealing with chattels
and criminals. Two subsidiary Courts were added later, whose
duties were never very closely defined, the *Cour du Billet* and the
Cour du Samedi. The *Cour de Catel* was abolished in 1862.
In the lower Courts the Bailiff and two Jurats form a quorum.
Appeals from these lie to the Full Court, at which seven Jurats
must be present. In addition to its judicial powers the Royal
Court till the middle of the 16th century was the only legislative
body in Jersey. As the States began to gain power, Acts of the
States and Ordinances of the Court had equal authority. In
1771 an Order in Council withdrew from the Court all legislative rights. (See Havet's *Cours Royales*, Le Patourel's *Mediaeval Administration*.)

ST. ANASTASE. A free Grammar School at St. Peter's, established 1496 by Jean Neel (q.v.) and Vincent Tehy (q.v.). It
was closed in 1875. The endowment is now used for scholarships
at Victoria College.

ST. MANNELIER. A free Grammar School at St. Saviour's,
established by Jean Hue (q.v.) in 1477, re-endowed by Jean Neel
(q.v.) and Vincent Tehy (q.v.) in 1496. Descriptions of it in its
later days will be found in John Wesley's *Journal* and in W.L.
De Gruchy's *Reminiscences*. It was closed in 1884. Its endowment is now used for scholarships at Victoria College.

SEIGNEUR. The Lord of a Fief, the possession of which entitled the owner to claim certain Seigneurial Rights, relics of the Feudal System. Great Manors, like St. Ouen's and Samarès, had the right of *Haute justice*, in early times to condemn their tenants to death, later, if a tenant was sentenced by the Court, to hang him on the manorial gallows. The latter claim was often enforced as late as the 17th century, and in the case of Samarès was confirmed by Patent in 1695. Property of criminals hanged or transported was forfeit to the Seigneur. In the Middle Ages the chief burden on tenants was the *corvée*, the carriage of the Seigneur's wood, wine, and hay, wherever required ; but this had lapsed by the 16th century. *Eperquerie*, the first choice of all conger, had been commuted to *essiage*, a yearly tax of 6 sols on fishermen. Other rights lasted well into the eighteenth century, *vraicq*, the privilege of cutting seaweed ahead of other parishioners, *verp*, the fine on impounded cattle, *gravage*, one third of the goods washed up by the sea, *chasse*, the sole right to hunt or shoot on the Fief. On some Fiefs tenants had to bring their corn to be ground at the Seigneur's mill, and to keep the mill in repair. On some the Seigneur might build a *colombier*, and breed pigeons, which would feed on his tenants' crops. Seigneurs still claim the right to enjoy for a year and a day the revenue from the real estate of any tenant, who dies without direct heirs of his body.

SOLICITOR-GENERAL, more correctly ADVOCATE-GENERAL, *Avocat-Général du Roi*. First mentioned in the 16th century. A Crown Officer, who originally merely took the place of the Attorney-General, when the latter was ill or absent from the island. Since the creation of a Law Officers' Department in 1930, his position has become practically that of Assistant Attorney-General. He takes his full share of the chamber work of the Department, though the bulk of the Court work is still done by the Attorney. A list of Solicitors-General is in *Bull.* III.

STATES. *Etats.* Till the 16th century the Royal Court was the only legislative body in Jersey. Then the custom arose of sometimes calling in the Rectors and Constables for consultation. What began as a matter of courtesy became expected as a right. The Assembly of Jurats, Rectors, and Constables grew into a separate body. In 1549 a summons was issued to "the Estates of this island, that is to say the Jurats, Rectors, and Constables, to meet to have advice on matters which concern the common good". (The word Etats was in common use in France at this time. The French Parliament was called the *Etats Généraux*, and there were provincial *Etats de Normandie, Etats de Bretagne, Etats de Bourgogne,* etc.) For the next two centuries the island had two legislative bodies. Ordinances of the Court and Acts of the States were equally binding. In 1771 an Order in Council made the States the only body with power to legislate. It can make temporary regulations for three years without express permission from the Crown, but all permanent laws must be submitted through the Privy Council for the King's assent. The representative element in the States was strengthened in 1856 by the addition of Deputies. (See J.A. Messervy's Preface to *Les Actes des Etats*). Further drastic changes are being made as this book goes to press.

SYNOD. *Synode.* Under the Calvinist regime the annual meeting of all Ministers in the Channel Islands and one Elder from each parish, held in alternate years in Jersey and Guernsey.

TENANT. *Tenant.* A tenant on a Jersey Fief bore no resemblance to a tenant in England. He owned his own land, for which he paid no rent, but the Seigneur of the Fief could claim from him certain rights, which have varied on different Fiefs and at different periods. See SEIGNEUR.

VERGEE. A Jersey land-measure of about 2150 English square yard. Thus 2¼ vergées are roughly equivalent to an English acre.

VICTORIA COLLEGE. A Public School for boys, supported by the States, founded in 1852 to commemorate the visit of Queen Victoria to the island.

VINGTENIER. The third rank in the Honorary Parochial Police. Every parish (except St. Ouen's, where the sub-divisions are called Cueillettes) is divided into Vingtaines, originally containing about twenty families. In each a Vingtenier is elected to collect the rate (except in St. Helier's, which has now a paid collector) and to help the Constable and Centeniers to preserve the peace.

VISCOUNT. Vicomte. In ancient France a very high dignitary, the Vice-Count (cf Viceroy, Vice-President, Vice- Chancellor), who took the place of the Count or Duke, when absent. Later in Normandy a Viscount was appointed over each county, the Viscount of the Cotentin, the Viscount of the Avranchin, etc. A charter of 1179 shows a Viscount holding the King's Court in Guernsey (Cart.). In time the dignity of the name was forgotten, and the Viscount became a mere Court official. By the 14th century the Viscount in Jersey was the chief executive officer of the Court, appointed by the Crown to see that orders of the Court were carried out, to issue summonses, to make arrests, to keep prisoners in custody, to abate nuisances, to deliver seisin 'by the Viscount's rod'. He also acted as Coroner, and till 1885 the Public Markets were under his control. He read aloud Royal Proclamations in the Royal Square, was Comptroller of Weights and Measures and a member of the Prison Board. A list of Viscounts is in Bull. III.

VRAIC. A local seaweed, used for manure, and up to the 18th century dried and burnt as fuel. Two carefully regulated Vraic Harvests were held every year in February and June.

WARDEN OF THE ISLES. *Custos insularum.* *Gardien des Iles.* During the 13th, 14th, and 15th centuries two officials were often entrusted with the government of the Channel Islands, a Lord of the Isles (q.v.), generally non-resident, and under him a resident Warden. Frequently for long periods no Lord was appointed. Then the Warden was supreme Governor. A list of Wardens from 1198 to 1415 is in Le Patourel's *Mediaeval Administration of the Channel Islands.* The last Governor to bear this title seems to have been William Bertram in 1448.

APPENDIX IV

A BRIEF BIBLIOGRAPHY OF JERSEY HISTORY

A fuller list of authorities is given at the end of each article.

Cartulaire de Jersey, Guernesey, et les autres Iles Normandes: Recueil de Documents conservés aux Archives du Departement de la Manche 1025—1698. Société Jersiaise. 1919.

Jersey Prison Board Case: Memorandum prepared for the Privy Council by W.H.V. Vernon and H. Sutton. Eyre and Spottiswood. 1893. (The Appendix prints many documents illustrating the Constitution of Jersey from 1130.)

Documents Historiques relatifs aux Iles de la Manche tirés des archives conservées dans le Public Record Office à Londres. 1199—1244. Société Jersiaise. 1879.

E Rotulis Litterarum Clausarum Excerpta ad Insulas Normanniae Spectantia 1205—1327 (with French translation). Société Jersiaise 1893.

Extente des îles de Jersey, Guernesey, Aurigney, et Serk, suivie des Inquisitions dans Jersey et Guernesey 1274. Société Jersiaise. 1877.

Ancient Petitions of the Chancery and the Exchequer 1290—1454. Société Jersiaise 1902.

Rolls of the Assizes held in the Channel Islands 1309. Société Jersiaise. 1903.

Extente de l'île de Jersey 1331. Société Jersiaise. 1876.

Rapport des Commissaires de Henri VIII. 1515. Société Jersiaise. 1878.

Actes des Etats 1524—1800. Société Jersiaise.

Extente de l'île de Jersey 1528. Société Jersiaise. 1881.

Ordres du Conseil enregistrés à Jersey 1556—1867. Jersey: printed for the States.

Discipline ecclésiastique dans les îles de la Manche de 1576 à 1597 (edited by G.E. Lee), Guernsey 1885.

Chroniques de Jersey 1585. (Edition published by A. Mourant). Jersey, 1858.

The Chroniques de Jersey in the light of contemporary documents. A.J. Eagleston. S.J. Bull. 1936.

Extente de l'île de Jersey 1607. Société Jersiaise. 1880.

Journal de Jean Chevalier 1643—51. Société Jersiaise. 1906.

The Lyar Confounded. Wm. Prynne. London. 1645. (Reprinted in Almanach de la Chronique 1884).

Pseudo Mastix, the Liar's Whip. Michel Lempriere and others. London. 1646. (Reprinted in S.J. Bulletin 1888).

Freedome or a Description of the Excellent Civill Government of Jersey. London. 1652.

A Survey of the Channel Islands. Peter Heylin. London. 1656.

Extente de l'île de Jersey 1668. Société Jersiaise 1882.

Caesarea or a Discourse of the Island of Jersey. Jean Poingdestre 1682. Société Jersiaise. 1889.

A Survey of the Island of Jersey. Ph. Dumaresq. 1685. Société Jersiaise. 1935.

An Account of the Island of Jersey. Philippe Falle 1734. (Edition with notes by Edouard Durell). Jersey. 1837.

Extente de l'île de Jersey 1749. Société Jersiaise. 1883.

Journal de Daniel Messervy 1769—72. Société Jersiaise. 1896.

An Authentic Narrative of the Oppressions of the Islanders of Jersey. London. 1771.

A Code of Laws for the Island of Jersey. 1771.

Lois et Règlements non compris dans le Code de 1771. Jersey. Printed for the States.

Collection of Petitions etc. relative to Political Differences from 1779—88. Jersey. 1788.

A Chronology of Jersey. R. Mollet and E.T. Nicolle.   1935.

Série chronologique des Gardiens et Seigneurs des îles normandes de 1198 à 1461. Julien Havet. Paris. 1876. Cf corrections and additions in Le Patourel's Mediaeval Administration, and in H.M. Godfray's article in S.J. Bulletin. 1885.

Lists of Governors and Lieut.-Governors are given in Bulls 1901 and 1902 ; of Bailiffs in Bulls, vols. IV, VII, and XII ; of Jurats in vols. IV, VIII, IX : of Deans in vol. IX ; of Constables in vols. V, VI, VII, and XIII ; of Rectors in Vols. VII, VIII, and X ; of Attorneys-General, Vicomtes and Solicitors-General in vols. III and VII ; of Greffiers in vol. VIII ; of Advocates in vols. IX and XIII ; of Dénonciateurs in vol. IX ; of Deputies in Bulls 1938—41.

An Armorial of Jersey, being an account, heraldic and antiquarian, of its chief Native Families. J. Bertrand Payne. London. 1865.

Généalogie de la Famille Messervy. J.A. Messervy. Jersey. 1899.

Histoire du Cotentin et de ses îles. Gustave Dupont. 4 vols. Caen. 1870—85.

The Channel Islands.   Edith F. Carey.   London 1904.

A Constitutional History of Jersey.   Charles Le Quesne.   London. 1856.

The Town of St. Helier.   E.T. Nicolle.   Jersey. 1931.

La Ville de St. Hélier.   Jean De La Croix.   Jersey. 1845.

Les Etats.   Jean De La Croix.   Jersey. 1847.

Jersey: ses antiquités, ses institutions, son histoire.   Jean De La Croix.   Jersey. 1859.

Caesarea: the Island of Jersey: its History, its Antiquities, and Biographies of its Eminent Men.   London. 1840.

Les Cours Royales des îles Normandes.   Julien Havet.   Paris. 1878.

The Mediaeval Administration of the Channel Islands 1199–1399.   J.H. Le Patourel.   London. 1937.

The Importance of the Channel Islands in British Relations with the Continent in the 13th and 14th centuries.   D.T. Williams.   S.J. Bull. 1928.

Jersey in the Fifteenth and Sixteenth Centuries.   A.C. Saunders.   Jersey.

L'occupation de Jersey par le Comte de Maulevrier 1463. R.R. Lempriere S.J. Bull. 1924.

Mont Orgueil Castle: its History and Description.   E.T. Nicolle.   Jersey. 1921.

Les Eglises du Refuge en Angleterre.   F. de Schickler.   Paris. 1892.

Charles II in the Channel Islands.   S.E. Hoskins.   London. 1854.

The Channel Islands and the Great Rebellion.   M.F.H. Ellis.
S.J. Bull. 1937.

Jean Chevalier and his Times.   A.C. Saunders.   Jersey. 1936.

The Jersey Revolution of 1769.   E.T. Nicolle.   S.J. Bull. 1922.

Surprise de Jersey en 1781.   Maurice Perrot.   Paris. 1929.

Proceedings on the Trial of Moses Corbet.   London. 1781.

Jersey in the Eighteenth and Nineteenth Centuries.   A.C. Saunders.   Jersey. 1930.

Gorey Castle: Official Guide Book.   N.V.L. Rybot. Jersey. 1947.

The Islet of St. Helier and Elizabeth Castle.   N.V.L. Rybot. Jersey. 1947.

Jersey under the Swastika.   Ralph Mollet.   London. 1945.

The German Occupation of Jersey.   L.P. Sinel. Jersey.   1946.

The leading periodicals in the island have been:—

> Le Magasin de l'île de Jersey 1784—5.
> La Gazette de l'île de Jersey (pubd. by Alexandre and
>   Angot) 1786—97.
> La Gazette de l'île de Jersey (pubd. by Stead) 1797—
> La Gazette de l'île de Jersey (pubd. by Mourant) 1797—1835.
> Le Soleil de l'île de Jersey 1792—8.
> La Chronique de Jersey 1814—1917.
> The British Press 1815—1860.
> Le Constitutionnel 1820—76.
> L'Impartial. 1831—57.
> The Jersey Times 1832—5.
> The Jersey Times (2nd paper of that name) 1835—59.
> Le Miroir 1840—50.
> La Patrie 1849—55.
> La Nouvelle Chronique 1855—1917.

The Jersey Independent 1856—64.
The Jersey Express 1860—1901.
The British Press and Jersey Times 1860—1910.
The Evening Post 1897: still running.
The Morning News 1909: still running.
Les Chroniques 1917: still running.

See also the local Almanacs, specially those published by the Chronique from 1815, the Constitutionnel from 1821, the British Press and Jersey Times from 1843, the Patrie from 1850, the Nouvelle Chronique from 1856, the Jersey Express from 1862, the Evening Post from 1910.

ABBREVIATIONS

A.E.	*Actes des Etats*
A.P.C.	*Acts of the Privy Council*
App.	Appendix
Arm.	Payne's *Armorial of Jersey*
Asst.	Assistant
b.	Born
Bart.	Baronet
Bull.	*Bulletin* of the Société Jersiaise (The number following refers to the bound volume, not to the actual *Bulletin*)
c.	(*circa*) About
Cal. Inq.	*Calendar of Inquests*
Cart.	*Cartulaire de Jersey*
cf.	(*confer*) Compare
Ch.R.	*Calendar of Charter Rolls*
C.R.	*Calendar of Close Rolls*
d.	died
D.N.B. or	
Dic. Nat. Biog.	*Dictionary of National Biography*
e.g.	(*exempli gratia*) for instance
fl.	(*floruit*) Flourished
Foed.	Rymer's *Foedera*
F.R.	*Calendar of Fine Rolls*
G.	*Gazette de l'île de Jersey*
Gent. Mag.	*Gentleman's Magazine*
I.R.	*Extracts from Issue Rolls*
Kt.	Knight
L.P.	*Letters and Papers of Reign of Henry VIII*
l.t.	Livres Tournois (See App. III)
M.	Monsieur
Mme.	Madame
M.R.H.	*Material illustrating Reign of Henry VII*
O.C.	*Ordres du Conseil*
op. cit.	(*opus citatum*) the work previously cited

P.B.C.	Memorandum on Prison Board Case prepared for Privy Council
P.C.	Privy Council
P.R.	Calendar of Patent Rolls
q.v.	(quod vide) For further information refer to the article on this person
R.C.	Royal Court of Jersey
R.J.M.	Royal Jersey Militia
R.N.	Royal Navy
Rot. Chart.	Rotuli Chartarum
Rot. Lit. Claus.	Rotuli Litterarum Clausarum
Rot. Parl.	Rotuli Parliamentorum
S.J.	Société Jersiaise
S.P. or S.P.D.	Calendar of State Papers, Domestic
S.P.F.	Calendar of State Papers, Foreign

CHRONOLOGICAL INDEX

The dates after the names are those of the deaths of the persons described.

J. Carteret 1682
P. De Carteret (7) 1682
E. De Carteret 1683
J. Le V. dit Durell 1683
P. Dumaresq 1690
Poindexter 1691
P. De Carteret (8) 1693
Brevint 1695
E. De Carteret 1698
J. Lempriere c. 1704
C. Le Couteur 1714
C. De Carteret 1715
P. Le Geyt 1716
M. D'Assigny 1717
M. De Gruchy 1720
Janvrin 1721
Manley 1724
P. Pipon 1726
T. Le Breton 1728
J. Pipon 1728
T. Le Hardy 1732
T. Pipon 1735
Langlois 1736
E. Dauvergne 1737
Bartlet 1741
P. Dumaresq 1741
T. Durell 1741
J. Cabot 1742
P. Falle 1742
C. Le Hardy 1744
C. Lempriere 1746
F. Cabot 1748
Monamy 1749
Martel 1753
N. Messervy 1758
J. Carteret 1763
P. Durell 1766
Denton 1770
Morant 1770
D. Le Vav. dit Durell 1775
D. Messervy 1775
F. Payn 1775
R. Carteret 1776
C. Le Hardy 1780
Peirson 1781
Rullecourt 1781
"A. Dumaresq" c. 1785
Fiott 1786
P. Lempriere 1787
Sivret 1790
W. C. Lempriere 1790
P. De Carteret (9) 1796
M. De Gruchy 1797
Joyce 1797
J. Dauvergne 1799
I. Gosset 1799

T. Le Maistre 1800
Pickstock 1800
T. Pipon 1801
Jean 1802
F. Le Breton 1802
J. Bandinel 1805
D. Dumaresq 1805
C. Lempriere 1806
T. Le Hardy c. 1807
Alexandre 1808
F. Le Couteur 1808
Fall 1811
I. Gosset 1812
Burrard 1813
J. Pipon 1814
P. Dauvergne 1816
Corbet 1817
M. Dupré 1818
Touzel 1818
J. Dumaresq 1819
P. Dumaresq c. 1822
T. Lempriere 1823
E. Dupré 1823
J. Lempriere 1824
Robin 1824
Lys 1826
Anley 1827
C.W. Le Geyt 1827
Luce 1827
C. Dauvergne 1828
P. De Carteret (10) 1828
P. Pipon 1829
Don 1832
E. Valpy 1832
J. Dupré 1834
W. Lempriere 1834
J. Le Couteur 1835
R. Valpy 1836
C. Hue 1838
T. Le Breton 1838
Philippes de Gorrequer 1841
Anquetil 1842
P. Perrot 1843
De Quetteville 1843
T. Turner 1843
P. Mourant 1845
De Veulle 1848
W. Gosset 1848
Gruchy 1848
E. Le Vav. dit Durell 1848
J. Le Capelain 1848
H. Le Vesconte 1848
F. Perrot 1848
Blampied 1849
J. Bandinel 1849
Hemery 1849

C. Perrot 1849
Knapp 1850
W. H. Valpy 1852
Le Sueur 1853
C. Bertram 1854
A. J. Valpy 1854
T. Le Breton 1857
B. Bandinel 1861
C. Hue 1861
Thoreau 1862
Syvret 1862
A. De Gruchy 1864
De L'Estourbeillon 1864
J. W. Dupré 1866
Le Boutillier 1867
F. Godfray 1868
F. Jeune 1868
Le Cras 1869
P. Marett 1869
De La Croix 1869
Delagarde 1871
Romeril 1873
Filleul 1875
J. Le Couteur 1875
Manuel 1875
Lerrier 1876
H. Godfray 1877
Le Gros 1877
A. Mourant 1878
J. L. Hammond 1880
J. Hammond 1880
J. Bertram 1882
P. H. Le Breton 1884
R. Marett 1884
P. Ouless 1885
R. A. Gosset 1885
W. Le Breton 1888
H. H. Godfray 1892
Mowat 1894
Voisin 1894
Millais 1896
De Gramont 1897
J. Payne 1898
J. P. Pipon 1899
Le Gallais 1900
C. Lempriere 1901
Westaway 1901
J. G. Falle 1903

F. H. Jeune 1905
C. H. Poingdestre 1905
P. G. Pipon 1905
De La Haye 1906
G. O. Balleine 1906
P. Baudains 1908
Le Cornu 1911
A. Turner 1911
Piquet 1912
E. Malet de Carteret 1914
G. C. Bertram 1915
Joslin 1915
W. Mesny 1919
W. De Gruchy 1920
H. C. Balleine 1921
J. W. Godfray 1921
H. E. Le Vav. dit Durell 1921
J. Messervy 1921
Barreau 1922
Gavey 1923
Grandin 1924
H. Pipon 1924
J. D. Le Couteur 1925
C. Messervy 1925
Le Bas 1926
C. M. Le Breton 1927
De Faye 1929
Langtry 1929
E. T. Nicolle 1929
Sinel 1929
R. R. Lempriere 1931
G. F. De Carteret 1932
W. Ouless 1933
Bosdet 1934
Vernon 1934
Vardon 1937
S. Falle 1937
Bouillon 1937
Saunders 1938
P. J. Marett 1939
G. De Gruchy 1940
F. Le Maistre 1940
Davis 1942
C. Malet de Carteret 1942
R. R. Marett 1943
Sinnatt 1943
J. H. Lander 1944
W. A. Le Rossignol 1945

CLASSIFIED INDEX

The names under each heading are in chronological order.

ACTRESS
Langtry.

AGRICULTURISTS
Le Gros ; F. & J. Le Couteur ; De La Haye ; Le Cornu.

AMERICA
G. Carteret (Proprietor, New Jersey) ; P. De Carteret, 7 (Governor, New Jersey) ; J. Carteret (New Jersey ; Langlois (Salem) ; J. & F. Cabot (Salem) ; P. Dumaresq (Boston) ; N. Messervy (Portsmouth) ; Le Boutillier (Cincinnati) ; P. Marett (Boston) ; J. Bertram (Salem).

ARMY (See Soldiers)

ARTISTS
C. Lempriere ; Monamy ; Jean ; I. Gosset ; T. Le Hardy ; Le Capelain ; P.J. Ouless ; Millais, R.A. ; F.W.S. Le Maistre ; Barreau ; J.D. Le Couteur ; W.W. Ouless, R.A. ; Poingdestre ; Bosdet ; Lander.

ATTORNEYS-GENERAL
G. De St. Martin ; H. Nicolle ; E. De Carteret ; P. Maret ; P. Lempriere ; T. Pipon ; J. Dumaresq ; T. Le Breton (jnr.) ; T. Le Breton (jnr.) ; J.W. Dupré ; R. P. Maret ; G.C. Bertram ; Vernon ; A.H. Turner ; H.E. Le V. dit Durell ; C.E. Malet De Carteret.

AUTHORS (See Writers)

BAILIFFS & LIEUT.-BAILIFFS
R. De St. Martin ; J. De St. Martin ; G. De St. Martin ; R. Lempriere ; C. Le Hardy ; T. Lempriere ; H. De Carteret ; J. Lempriere ; H. Nicolle ; J. Dumaresq ; G. Poulet ; Herault ; P. De Carteret (3) ; M. Lempriere ; G. Carteret ; P. De Carteret (4) ; E. De Carteret ; Le Geyt ; P. De Carteret (5) ; P. De Carteret (8) ; E. De Carteret ; C. De Carteret ; J. Carteret ; C. Lempriere ; R. Carteret ; H.F. Carteret ; W.C. Lempriere ; T. Pipon ; T. Pipon ; J. Dumaresq ; T. Le Breton (snr.) ; J. De Veulle ; T. Le Breton (jnr.) ; J. Hammond ; R.P. Marett ; G. C. Bertram ; Vernon ; R. Malet De Carteret ; C.E. Malet De Carteret.

BARONS
J. Poulet ; F.H. Jeune.

BARONETS
G. Carteret ; P. De Carteret (8) ; C. De Carteret ; Burrard ; Millais.

BISHOPS
Walden (Canterbury & London) ; F. Jeune (Peterborough ;) G.F. C. De Carteret (Jamaica).

CAMBRIDGE
Esquire Bedell: H. Godfray.
Fellows: A. Guerdain (Queens') ; Hemery (Trinity) ; J.L. Hammond (Trinity).
Graduates: A. De Carteret ; Bisson (Corpus) ; A. Guerdain (Jesus) ; N. Lempriere

(King's) ; Poindexter (Pembroke) ; M. D'Assigny (per.lit. reg.) ; Morant (Sidney Sussex) ; E. Valpy (Trinity) ; H. Godfray (St. John's) ; G.C. Bertram (Trinity).

CANADA
Fiott (Gaspé) ; Robin (Gaspé).

CHARLOTS
C., P., W.C. & T. Lempriere ; T. Pipon ; D. Messervy.

CIVIL SERVANTS
D. De Barentin ; Walden ; De Soulemont ; Wake ; G. Carteret ; A. Guerdain ; J. Carteret ; D. Bandinel ; W. Gosset ; R.A. Gosset ; C. Messervy.

CIVIL WAR
Parliamentarians: Bisson ; P. De Carteret (6) ; De La Place ; H. Dumaresq ; A. & D. Guerdain ; M. & N. Lempriere ; C. Maret ; Norman ; Stocall ; P. D'Assigny.
Royalists: P. De Carteret (3) ; G. Carteret ; E. & E. De Carteret ; P. (4) & P. (5) De Carteret ; J. De Carteret ; Hamptonne ; E. La Cloche ; J. L. V. dit Durell ; J. Nicolle ; Poindexter ; J. Poulet.

CLERGY (See also Bishops, Deans, Rectors, Oxford Fellows & Schoolmasters)
Neel ; M. D'Assigny ; D. Dumaresq ; Knapp.

CONSTABLES
St. Brelade's: J., T., T. & J. Pipon ; J. Le Couteur.
Grouville: Lerrier ; A. Mourant.
St. Helier's: Anley ; F. Godfray ; P. Perrot ; P. Le Sueur ; R.P. Marett ; J.G. Falle ; W.L. De Gruchy ; Voisin ; P. Baudains ; H.E. Le V.dit Durell.
St. John's: P. Dumaresq.

St. Martin's: F. Godfray ; R.R. Lempriere.
St. Peter's: J. Dumaresq ; Le Gros ; Vernon.
St. Saviour's: F. Godfray ; H. Nicolle.

CRIMINALS
Averty ; H. Nicolle ; E. De Carteret ; M. Messervy ; J. De La Cloche ; A. Dumaresq.

DEANS
Faleyse ; G. De Carteret ; Mabon ; De Soulemont ; J. Poulet ; D. Bandinel ; P. & C. Le Couteur ; T. Le Breton ; F. Payn ; F. Le Breton ; E. Dupré ; Hue ; F. Jeune ; Hemery ; W.C. Le Breton ; G.O. Balleine ; S. Falle. Amy (Guernsey) ; J. Le V. dit Durell (Windsor) ; Brevint (Lincoln).

DEPUTIES
St. Helier's: J. G. Falle ; H.E. Le V. dit Durell ; E.T. Nicolle.
Grouville: A. Mourant ; A.H. Turner.
St. Ouen's: E.C. Malet De Carteret.
St. Peter's: Le Cornu.
St. Saviour's: F. Godfray.

EXPLORERS
W. Lempriere (Morocco) ; P. De Carteret (9) (Pacific) ; P. Dauvergne (Trinidada) ; H.T.D. Le Vesconte (Arctic).

FRANCE
Martel ; Rullecourt ; De l'Estourbeillon ; De Gramont ; Bouillon.

GOLFER
Vardon.

GOVERNORS & LIEUT.-GOVERNORS
D., G. & D. De Barentin ; C. Le Hardy ; J. Lempriere ; H., A. & A. Poulet ; P. De Carteret (3) ; G. Carteret ; P. De Carteret (4) ; Corbet ; Fall ; T.H. Turner.

GREFFIERS

Gosselin ; Le Geyt ; J. Pipon ; F. Godfray ; Vernon ; H.M. Godfray.

GUERNSEY

G. De Carteret (Prior of the Vale) ; R. De Carteret (Captor of Castle Carey) Wallis (Lt.-Gov.) ; T. De St. Martin (Gov.) ; R. Weston (Gov.) ; Gosselin (Bailiff) ; S. De La Place (Rector) ; De Quetteville (Methodist) ; Le Boutillier (Refounder of Eliz. Coll.).

JOURNALISTS

Alexandre ; J. & P. Dumaresq ; De La Croix ; P.&C. Perrot ; P. Mourant ; J.W. Dupré ; Le Cras ; Romeril.

KNIGHTS

D. & D. De Barentin ; R. De Carteret ; R. Lempriere ; W. Weston (Prior of the Knights-Hospitallers) ; A. Poulet ; Wake ; P. (3) and P. (4) De Carteret ; P. Carteret ; E. & E. De Carteret ; C. De Carteret ; T., C. & C. Le Hardy ; J. Dumaresq ; T. & T. Le Breton ; Philippes De Garroquer ; T.H. Turner ; J. Le Couteur ; R. P. Marett ; R.A. Gosset ; F.H. Jeune ; A.H. Turner ; G.C. Bertram ; Le Bas ; Vernon.

LAUREL PARTY

J.W. Dupré ; F. Godfray ; P. Mourant.

LEGAL PROFESSION (See also Bailiffs, Attorneys-General, Solicitors-General)

Judge in the Star Chamber: R. Weston.
Judge: F. H. Jeune ; W.A. Le Rossignol.
Barristers: P.H. Le Breton ; C. M. Le Breton, K.C.
Jersey Advocates: Le Sueur ; F. Godfray ; P. Baudains ; H. E. Le V. dit Durell.
Notary: M. De Gruchy.

MAGOTS

J. & P. Dumaresq ; Alexandre ; Sivret ; J. Pipon ; Le Geyt ; J. Le Couteur.

MAYORS

D. De Barentin (London) Tehy (Southampton ; Major (Southampton) ; F. Cabot (Southampton) ; J. Dauvergne (Southampton) ; Delagarde (Exeter).

MEDICAL PRACTITIONERS

De La Place ; N. Lempriere ; D. & A. Guerdain ; P. De Carteret (6) ; W. Lempriere ; C. Hue ; Delagarde ; Grandin ; P.J. Marett.

MERCHANTS

D. De Barentin ; P. Pipon ; Langlois ; J. Cabot ; Martel ; Fiott. ; Robin ; A. De Gruchy ; Le Boutillier P. Marett ; J. Bertram ; J.G. Falle ; G.F. De Gruchy.

NAVAL MEN

J. Poulet (Capt.) ; G. Carteret ; J. Lempriere (Capt.) ; P. Carteret (Lt.) ; J. Carteret (Adm.) ; T. Le Hardy (Adm.) ; P. Durell ; T. Durell (Capt.) ; C. Le Hardy (Adm.) ; P. De Carteret, 9, (Adm.) ; Joyce (Mutineer) ; P. Dauvergne (Adm.) ; C.J. Dauvergne (Com.) ; Luce (Com.) ; P. De Carteret, 10, (Capt.) ; P. Pipon (Capt.) ; Le Vesconte (Lt.) ; C. Bertram (Adm.) ; B. Bandinel (Chaplain) ; J.P. Pipon (Capt.).

NEWFOUNDLAND

J.G. Falle.

NEW ZEALAND

W.H. Valpy.

NONCONFORMISTS

Anabaptists: N. Lempriere ; D. Guerdain ; Stocall ; Norman.
Independents: C. & F. Perrot.
Methodists: De Quetteville ; C. Blampied.

Plymouth Brother: De La Haye.
Roman Catholic: M. De Gruchy.
Swedenborgian: Le Cras.

NOIRMONT, SEIGNEURS OF
P. Pipon ; G. De Gruchy.

ORDERS
Order of the Garter
  Chancellor: A. Poulet.
  Knight: J. Carteret.
Order of the Bath
  Knight Grand Cross : Don ; F.
  H. Jeune.
  Knight Commander: R. Weston* ; R.A. Gosset.
  Companions: P. De Carteret
  (10) ; J.P., P.G. & H. Pipon ;
  Le Cornu ; J.W. Godfray ;
  Sinnatt.
Royal Guelphic Order
  Knight Grand Cross: T.H. Turner.
  Knight: Philippes de Garroquer.
Order of St. Michael & St. George
  Knight Grand Cross: Don.
  Companion: H. Pipon.
Royal Victorian Order
  Commander: J.W. Godfray.
Order of the British Empire
  Knight: Vernon ;
  O.B.E.: C.M. Le Breton.
Order of St. John of Jerusalem
  Knight of Grace: Le Bas.

OXFORD UNIVERSITY
D. Le V. dit Durell & F. Jeune
(Vice-Chancellors) ; Wake & J.
Bandinel (Public Orators) ; B.
Bandinel (Librarian).
Balliol
  Graduates: F.H. Jeune ; R.R.
  Marett.
Christ Church
  Graduates: C. Le Couteur ; J.
  Bandinel ; A.H. Turner.
Exeter
  Rector: R.R. Marett.
  Fellows: Poindexter ; T. Le
  Breton ; D. Dumaresq ; F.
  Le Couteur ; J. & M. Dupré ;
  W.C. Le Breton.

  Graduates: P. De Carteret (6) ;
  P. Falle ; I. Gosset ; H.M.
  Godfray.
Hertford
  Principal: D. Le V. dit Durell.
  Fellow: F.H. Jeune.
  Graduate: R.R. Lempriere
Jesus
  Fellows: Brévint ; F. Payn ;
  J. Bandinel ; Hue.
Merton
  Fellow: Wake.
  Graduates: P. De Carteret, 3,
  (St. Alban's Hall) ; De La
  Place (St. Alban's Hall) ; P.
  Maret.
New
  Fellow: B. Bandinel.
  Graduate: F. Le Breton.
Pembroke
  Master: F. Jeune.
  Fellows: E. Dupré ; T. Le Breton ; A.J. Valpy ; Mowat.
  Graduates: E. Dauvergne ; P.
  Morant ; F. Payn ; D. Dumaresq ; J. & E. Dupré ; R.
  Valpy ; M. Dupré ; C. Hue ;
  T. Le Breton ; J. Lemprie-
  re ; Knapp ; P. Filleul ; F.
  Jeune.
Queen's
  Fellow: G.O. Balleine.
St. John's
  Graduates: R. Carteret ; C.
  Lempriere.

PARLIAMENT
House of Lords: W. Weston (Prior) ; J., R. & F. Carteret ; F.
H. Jeune.
House of Commons: J. Poulet
(Somerset) ; Wake (Oxford) ;
A. or D. Guerdain ; G. Carteret
(Portsmouth) ; T. Le Hardy
(Weymouth) ; C. Le Hardy
(Portsmouth) ; Burrard (Lymington) ; W. Gosset (Truro).
French Chamber of Deputies:
Bouillon.

PHILANTHROPISTS
Hue ; Tehy ; Neel ; L. Baudains ;
Bartlet ; Denton ; Gruchy ; P.
Marett ; Westaway ; T.B. Davis.

PRIVATEERS
P. Dumaresq ; Pickstock ; J. Syvret.

PUBLIC LIBRARY
P. Falle ; D. Dumaresq.

PUBLISHERS
A.J. Valpy ; Le Bas.

RECEIVERS-GENERAL
C. Marett ; P. Pipon ; Fall ; J. Pipon ; J. Dumaresq ; T. Le Breton (jnr.) ; J. Pipon.

RECTORS
St. Brelade's: D. Bandinel ; E. Dauvergne ; Filleul.
St. Clement's: J. Dupré.
Grouville: Faleyse ; De Soulemont ; Brévint.
St. Helier's: Walden ; P. D'Assigny ; F. Le Couteur ; E. Dupré ; C. Hue ; F. Jeune ; Hemery ; Filleul ; W.C. Le Breton ; G.O. Balleine ; S. Falle.
St. John's: C. Le Couteur ; T. Syvret ; M. Dupré.
St. Martin's: G. De Carteret ; T. Le Hardy ; Mabon ; J. Poulet ; D. Bandinel ; P. D'Assigny ; P. & F. Le Couteur ; F. Payn ; F. Le Couteur.
St. Mary's: De La Place: D. & J. Bandinel ; P. Le Couteur ; T. Le Breton ; F. Payn.
St. Ouen's: E. La Cloche ; J. Le V. dit Durell.
St. Peter's: E. Messervy ; P. Filleul.
St. Saviour's: J. Hue ; P. Falle ; E. Le V. dit Durell ; P. Filleul ; W.C. Le Breton.
Trinity: P. Falle.

ROSE PARTY
P. & C. Perrot ; Romeril ; A. Mourant ; Le Sueur ; E. Le V. dit Durell.

ROYAL HOUSEHOLD
T. De St. Martin (Gentleman-Usher) ; Neel (Chaplain) ; R. Weston (Knight of the Body) ; De Soulemont (Sec. to the King) ;

P. Maret (Gentleman of the Bedchamber) ; G. Carteret (Treasurer of the Household) ; E. De Carteret (Usher of the Black Rod) ; E. De Carteret (Cup Bearer) ; J. Carteret (Lord of the Bedchamber) ; C. De Carteret (Gentleman of the Privy Chamber) ; T.H. Turner (Groom of the Bedchamber).

ROYAL SOCIETY FELLOWS
P. De Carteret (6) ; P. Carteret ; D. Dumaresq ; I. Gosset ; F. Payn ; P. Dauvergne ; J. Le Couteur ; Sinnatt.

ROZEL, SEIGNEURS OF
D., G., D. & P. De Barentin ; R., R., J. & R.R. Lempriere.

SAINTS
St. Helier ; St. Marculf.

ST. OUEN'S, SEIGNEURS OF
See Carteret, De Carteret & Malet De Carteret.

SAMARES, SEIGNEURS OF
P. De Barentin ; R. Lempriere ; H. & P. Dumaresq.

SARK
H. De Carteret (Colonizer) ; E. De Carteret (Bailiff).

SCHOOLS
Founders: J. Hue ; Tehy ; Neel.
Schoolmasters: M. D'Assigny ; (Basingstoke) ; R. Valpy (Reading) ; J. Dupré (Tring & Berkhampstead) ; J. Lempriere (Abingdon & Exeter) ; E. Valpy (Norwich) ; F. Jeune (King Edward's, Birmingham).
Scholars
  Aberdeen: E. De Faye.
  Abingdon: P. Morant ; D. Dumaresq ; C. Hue.
  Cheltenham: J.W. Godfray.

Christ's Hospital: J.L. Hammond.

Merchant Taylor's : N. & C. Lempriere.

Reading: B. Bandinel ; W.H. & A.J. Valpy ; Le Maistre.

Rugby: W.L. De Gruchy.

St. Mannelier: D. Dumaresq ; P. Valpy ; T. Sivret ; J. Lempriere ; P.G. Pipon ; W.L. De Gruchy.

Victoria College: G.O. Balleine ; Le Gros ; G.C. Bertram ; E. Le V. dit Durell ; A.H. Turner ; Gavey ; C. Messervy ; W.W. Ouless ; J.W. Godfray ; C.M. Le Breton ; J.A. Messervy ; Le Gallais ; H.M. Godfray ; Saunders ; E.T. Nicolle ; C.E. Malet De Carteret ; R.R. Marett ; Joslin ; Barreau.

Wellington: J.P. Pipon ; G.F. B. De Gruchy.

Westminster: J. Carteret ; J. Hemery ; C.E. Malet De Carteret.

Winchester: A. De Carteret ; J. Bandinel ; F. Le Breton ; J. Dumaresq ; J. Lempriere ; T. Le Breton ; P. De Carteret (10) ; B. Bandinel ; W. C. Le Breton ; R.R. Lempriere.

SCIENTISTS
Sinnatt.

SECRET SERVICE
J. Lempriere ; P. Dauvergne ; J. Le Couteur.

SOLDIERS
M. Corbet (Major) ; J. Dauvergne (Gen.) ; C.W. Le Geyt (Capt.) ; P. Fall (Lt.-Col.) ; Don (Gen.) ; Burrard (Gen.) ; J. Le Couteur (Gen.) ; Peirson (Maj.) ; Rullecourt (Col.) ; Turner (Gen.) ; Gosset (Maj.-Gen.) ; Philippes de Garroquer (Col.) ; Anquetil (Gen.) ; J. Le Couteur (Col.) ; P. G. Pipon (Gen.) ; E.C. Malet De Carteret (Lieut.-Col.) ; H. Pipon (Gen.) ; J.W. Godfray (Gen.) ; P.

W.J. Le Gallais (Col.) ; Joslin (Maj.) ; Mesny (Gen. Chinese Army).

SOLICITORS-GENERAL
J. De Carteret ; C. Lempriere ; J. Pipon ; J.W. Dupré ; J. Hammond ; R.P. Marett ; G.C. Bertram ; Vernon ; Turner ; H.E. Le V. dit Durell ; C.E. Malet De Carteret.

TRINITY, SEIGNEURS OF
J., G. & T. De St. Martin ; A. De Carteret ; P. (9) & P. (10) De Carteret.

UNIVERSITIES (See also Oxford & Cambridge)
Aberdeen: E. De Faye.

Caen: N. Lempriere ; P. Le Geyt ; J. Le V. dit Durell ; T. Le Breton (jnr.) ; J. Hammond ; R.P. Marett ; H.E. Le V. dit Durell ; J.A. Messervy ; Vernon.

Leyden: P. De Carteret (6).

Paris: Wace ; Neel ; P. Le Geyt ; F. & H. Godfray.

Rheims: A. Guerdain.

Saumur: M. Lempriere ; Brevint ; P. Le Geyt ; F. Jeune.

Toulouse: Vernon.

VICOMTES
Hamptonne ; Norman ; J. Nicolle ; E. De Carteret ; J. Le Couteur ; R.R. Lempriere ; E.T. Nicolle.

WRITERS
Anthropology ; R.R. Marett.

Botany: Piquet.

Classies: J. Lempriere ; R. & E. Valpy.

Diaries: Chevalier ; D. Messervy.

Divinity: Brévint ; M. D'Assigny ; J. Le V. dit Durell ; E. Valpy ; J. Dupré ; E. De Faye.

Fiction: Manley ; H. Balleine.

Jersey Description: P. Dumaresq ;